# MACRO
# ECONOMICS

10E

## ROGER A. ARNOLD

California State University
San Marcos

SOUTH-WESTERN
CENGAGE Learning™

Australia • Brazil • Canada • Mexico • Singapore • Spain • United Kingdom • United States

**SOUTH-WESTERN**
CENGAGE Learning™

**Macroeconomics 10E**

**Roger A. Arnold**

Vice President of Editorial, Business: Jack W. Calhoun

Publisher: Joe Sabatino

Executive Editor: Mike Worls

Sr. Developmental Editors: Jennifer Thomas and Laura Bofinger Ansara

Sr. Marketing Manager: John Carey

Associate Marketing Manager: Betty Jung

Sr. Marketing Communications Manager: Sarah Greber

Sr. Content Project Manager: Cliff Kallemeyn

Sr. Media Editor: Deepak Kumar

Sr. Frontlist Buyer, Manufacturing: Sandee Milewski

Compositor: MPS Limited, a Macmillan Company

Sr. Art Director: Michelle Kunkler

Sr. Rights Specialist: Mardell Glinski Schultz

Cover and Internal Designer: Diane Gliebe/ Design Matters

For product information and technology assistance, contact us at **Cengage Learning Customer & Sales Support, 1-800-354-9706**

For permission to use material from this text or product, submit all requests online at **www.cengage.com/permissions**

Further permissions questions can be emailed to **permissionrequest@cengage.com**

Library of Congress Control Number: 2010934482
Student Edition ISBN 13: 978-0-538-45287-8
Student Edition ISBN 10: 0-538-45287-0

**South-Western Cengage Learning**
5191 Natorp Boulevard
Mason, OH 45040
USA

Cengage Learning products are represented in Canada by Nelson Education, Ltd.

For your course and learning solutions, visit www.cengage.com
Purchase any of our products at your local college store or at our preferred online store **www.cengagebrain.com**

Printed in the United States of America
1 2 3 4 5 6 7 13 12 11 10

*To*
*Sheila, Daniel,*
*and David*

Dear Student,

If you visit an art museum without knowing much about art, you will usually look at the paintings and simply decide whether you like them or not. "I like that painting by X," you say, "but I don't like that painting by Y."

Your trip to the art museum is different if you know much about art. You look at the paintings and "see" much more. No doubt, you have a richer experience at the art museum than you had when you knew little to nothing about art.

The world is a little like a painting in an art museum. Some people look at what is happening in the world and see very little. Others look at what is happening in the world and see quite a lot.

If I wanted to enjoy art more, I would take a few courses in art. But if I wanted to have a better sense of what is happening in the world, if I wanted to "see" the world more clearly and more accurately, if I wanted to see the shading, subtleties, and secrets hidden in the world, I would take a few courses in economics. With a knowledge of economics, I have a much better chance of understanding what is going on in the world in which I inhabit than I do without a knowledge of economics. Economics has the ability to make visible what was once invisible. It has a way of opening up our eyes to what we couldn't see before.

Now economics isn't unique in this regard. Other subjects – such as physics, mathematics, and biology – are capable of opening up worlds to us. What is special about economics, though, is that so much of the world you live in every day – the world of buying and selling, getting a job, paying your rent, taking out a mortgage, getting an education, earning an income, and the world of economic growth, ups and downs in the economy, and financial crises -- comes in clearer once we know economics. Economics helps us to understand the world we actually inhabit every day of our lives. If there is such a thing as the "real world," then it is the real world to which economics addresses itself.

So, is it worth learning economics? Yes, without a doubt. But don't think that learning economics comes without effort. First, you can't read an economics textbook the way you read a novel. You have to read, think, and study. You have to constantly ask yourself how what you just learned fits in with what you learned before. To aid in this endeavor, we need to tell you how this book is set up.

There are two major parts of the book that you should be aware of before you start to read and study. First, there is the main content of the book. This makes up 80 percent of the book. It consists of most of the words and diagrams in each chapter. It is the "meat and potatoes" of the economics course. You need to read this material more than once. When it comes to learning the economics contained in the diagrams, go slowly. Look at a curve in the diagram and tell yourself what it says. Then look at the various points and tell yourself what they say. Each diagram tells a story – from beginning to end. Learn to tell yourself that story as you go through each diagram.

Second, there are various boxed and stand-alone features in each chapter – such as 24/7, *Thinking Like an Economist*, *Office Hours*, and *Finding Economics*. It is in the features where we step away from the "meat and potatoes" of the text and start applying what we have learned there. Applying what you know is an extremely important part of learning economics. Don't think the boxed and stand-alone features are peripheral to the main material and therefore can be ignored. The features are the material in different form.

Keep in mind that it takes sustained effort – and some dedicated patience – to learn economics. But, as we said before, the effort is well worth it.

The best of luck as you begin your study of economics.

Sincerely,

Roger A. Arnold

Roger A. Arnold

# BRIEF CONTENTS

# CONTENTS

## AN INTRODUCTION TO ECONOMICS

### PART 1 ECONOMICS: THE SCIENCE OF SCARCITY

**OFFICE HOURS**

**OFFICE HOURS**
*"I Thought Price Ceilings Were Good for Consumers"* **97**

**OFFICE HOURS**
*"Doesn't High Demand Mean High Quantity Demanded?"* **114**

# MACROECONOMICS

## PART 2 MACROECONOMIC FUNDAMENTALS

**economics 24/7**
*Economics at the Movies* **121**
*Woodstock, 1969* **122**
*What Was a Penny Worth?* **125**

**OFFICE HOURS**
*"Is There More Than One Reason the Unemployment Rate Will Fall?"* **128**

# PART 3  MACROECONIMIC STABILITY, INSTABILITY, AND FISCAL POLICY

## CHAPTER 9: CLASSICAL MACROECONOMICS AND THE SELF-REGULATING ECONOMY 182

## CHAPTER 10: KEYNESIAN MACROECONOMICS AND ECONOMIC INSTABILITY: A CRITIQUE OF THE SELF-REGULATING ECONOMY 204

# PART 4  MONEY, THE ECONOMY, AND MONETARY POLICY

## APPENDIX C: THE MARKET FOR RESERVES (OR THE FEDERAL FUNDS MARKET) 285

## CHAPTER 14: MONEY AND THE ECONOMY 289

## CHAPTER 15: MONETARY POLICY 314

# PART 5  EXPECTATIONS AND GROWTH

## CHAPTER 16: EXPECTATIONS THEORY AND THE ECONOMY 335

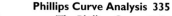
## CHAPTER 17: ECONOMIC GROWTH: RESOURCES, TECHNOLOGY, IDEAS, AND INSTITUTIONS 358

**OFFICE HOURS**
*"What Is the Difference Between Business Cycle Macroeconomics and Economic Growth Macroeconomics?"* **372**

# PART 6  THE FINANCIAL CRISIS OF 2007–2009

## CHAPTER 18: THE FINANCIAL CRISIS OF 2007–2009 375

economics 24/7
*Too Big to Fail* **387**

**OFFICE HOURS**
*"Do Economists and the Public Always Understand the Causes of Financial Crises?"* **392**

# PART 7  GOVERNMENT AND THE ECONOMY

## CHAPTER 19: DEBATES IN MACROECONOMICS OVER THE ROLE AND EFFECTS OF GOVERNMENT 396

economics 24/7
*What Does a Stimulus Bill Look Like?* **402**

**OFFICE HOURS**
*"What Kinds of Debates Do Macroeconomists Have?"* **407**

# PART 8    PUBLIC CHOICE AND SPECIAL-INTEREST-GROUP POLITICS

## CHAPTER 20:  PUBLIC CHOICE AND SPECIAL-INTEREST-GROUP POLITICS 410

economics 24/7

*A Simple Majority Voting Rule: The Case of the Statue in the Public Square* 413

*Economic Illiteracy and Democracy* 416

*Inheritance, Heirs, and Why the Firstborn Became King or Queen* 424

OFFICE HOURS

*"Doesn't Public Choice Paint a Bleak Picture of Politics and Government?"* 426

# THE GLOBAL ECONOMY

# PART 9    INTERNATIONAL ECONOMICS AND GLOBALIZATION

## CHAPTER 21: INTERNATIONAL TRADE 430

economics 24/7

*Dividing the Work* 433

*You're Getting Better Because Others Are Getting Better* 435

*Offshore Outsourcing, or Offshoring* 441

# PRACTICAL ECONOMICS

## PART 10  FINANCIAL MATTERS

### CHAPTER 24: STOCKS, BONDS, FUTURES, AND OPTIONS 504

# WEB CHAPTER

## PART 11  WEB CHAPTER

### CHAPTER 25: AGRICULTURE: PROBLEMS, POLICIES, AND UNINTENDED EFFECTS

**Agricultural Policies**
> Price Supports   Restricting Suppl   Target Prices and Deficiency Payments   Production Flexibility Contract Payments, (Fixed) Direct Payments, and Countercyclical Payments   Nonrecourse Commodity Loans

**Chapter Summary**

**Key Terms and Concepts**

**Questions and Problems**

**Working with Numbers and Graphs**

# Roger Arnold

## THE ECONOMY IS TOUGH—
## ECONOMICS DOESN'T HAVE TO BE!

Ever wonder what economic factors might determine your first job after college or if a tax on soda would reduce obesity? **MACROECONOMICS** answers these questions and many more. Using intriguing pop culture examples, Arnold's tenth edition is revised to include the most comprehensive coverage of the financial and economic crisis available. Self-tests help determine how well you're grasping concepts, a traditional study guide prepares you for tests, and **Economics CourseMate** offers a graphing tutorial, quizzes, videos and more. It's all carefully designed to help you get the best grade possible!

# Features for Student Understanding

### Office Hours

Emulating common questions asked by economics students, just like you, replace the need to wait in line for office hours with your instructor.

### Enhanced "Thinking Like an Economist"

This classic feature now rotates with Finding Economics throughout the text to illustrate that economics is all around us.

### Economics 24/7

Illustrates the practical relevance of key concepts by exploring anything that can be explained through economic analysis.

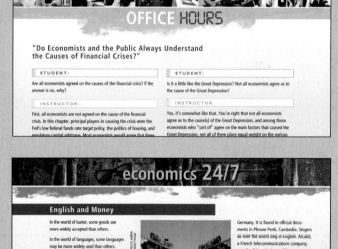

# CourseMate and Video Office Hours

## Make the Grade with Economics CourseMate.

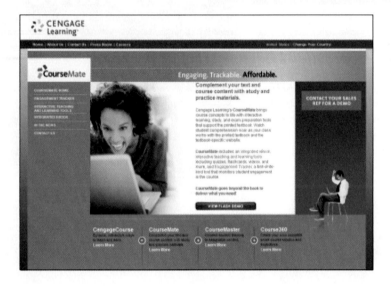

**Complement your text and course content with study and practice materials.**
Economics CourseMate brings course concepts to life with interactive learning, study, and exam preparation tools that support the printed textbook. Use Economics CourseMate to make the grade!

## Economics CourseMate includes:

- an interactive eBook, with highlighting, note taking and search capabilities
- interactive learning tools including:
  - Quizzes
  - Flashcards
  - Videos
  - Graphing Tutorials
  - News, Debates, and Data
  - and more!

Go to login.cengagebrain.com to access these resources.

# Make Learning Economics Easier!

## Video Office Hours with Roger Arnold

**New Video Lectures!** Roger Arnold takes you through key concepts and graphs in each chapter—just like you were in the classroom with him. Using innovative video, he provides both short concept pieces and longer lectures for each chapter, talking through the concepts just as he would in class, while displaying lecture points and demonstrating graphs visually. For your convenience, you can play and replay these video lectures as often as is needed to review concepts.

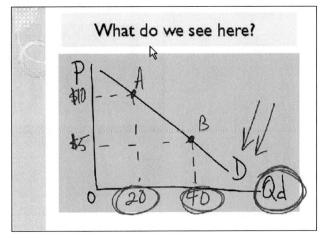

# The Global Economic Watch

**Cengage Learning's Global Economic Watch: Lessons from real life right now!** Cengage Learning's Global Economic Watch adds current events into your studies—through a powerful, continuously updated online suite of content, discussion forums, and more.

The Watch will help you thoroughly understand the global economic downturn. Benefit from these specific features:

- A content-rich blog of breaking news, expert analysis and commentary—updated multiple times each day—plus links to many other blogs.

- A powerful real-time database of hundreds of relevant and vetted journal, newspaper, and periodical articles and videos and podcasts—updated four times every day.

- A thorough overview and timeline of events leading up to the global economic crisis.

- Forums for sharing questions, ideas, and opinions.

**History is happening now.** Benefit from this resource by learning all the details. **Learn more at www.cengage.com/thewatch.**

# IN APPRECIATION

This book could not have been written and published without the generous expert assistance of many people. A deep debt of gratitude is owed to the reviewers of the first through ninth editions and to the reviewers of this edition, the tenth.

## First Edition Reviewers

Jack Adams
*University of Arkansas, Little Rock*

William Askwig
*University of Southern Colorado*

Michael Babcock
*Kansas State University*

Dan Barszcz
*College of DuPage, Illinois*

Robert Berry
*Miami University, Ohio*

George Bohler
*Florida Junior College*

Tom Bonsor
*Eastern Washington University*

Michael D. Brendler
*Louisiana State University*

Baird Brock
*Central Missouri State University*

Kathleen Bromley
*Monroe Community College, New York*

Douglas Brown
*Georgetown University*

Ernest Buchholz
*Santa Monica Community College, California*

Gary Burbridge
*Grand Rapids Junior College, Michigan*

Maureen Burton
*California Polytechnic University, Pomona*

Carol Carnes
*Kansas State University*

Paul Coomes
*University of Louisville, Kentucky*

Eleanor Craig
*University of Delaware*

Wilford Cummings
*Grosmont College, California*

Diane Cunningham
*Glendale Community College, California*

Douglas C. Darran
*University of South Carolina*

Edward Day
*University of Southern Florida*

Johan Deprez
*University of Tennessee*

James Dietz
*California State University, Fullerton*

Stuart Dorsey
*University of West Virginia*

Natalia Drury
*Northern Virginia Community College*

Lu Ann Duffus
*California State University, Hayward*

John Eckalbar
*California State University, Chico*

John Elliot
*University of Southern California*

Charles Fischer
*Pittsburg State University, Kansas*

John Gemello
*San Francisco State University*

Carl Guelzo
*Cantonsville Community College, Maryland*

Jan Hansen
*University of Wisconsin, Eau Claire*

John Henderson
*Georgia State University*

Ken Howard
*East Texas Baptist University*

Mark Karscig
*Central Missouri State University*

Stanley Keil
*Ball State University, Indiana*

Richard Kieffer
*State University of New York, Buffalo*

Gene Kimmett
*William Rainey Harper College, Illinois*

Luther Lawson
*University of North Carolina*

Frank Leori
*College of San Mateo, California*

Kenneth Long
*New River Community College, Virginia*

Michael Magura
*University of Toledo, Ohio*

Bruce McCrea
*Lansing Community College, Michigan*

Gerald McDougall
*Wichita State University, Kansas*

Kevin McGee
*University of Wisconsin, Oshkosh*

Francois Melese
*Auburn University, Alabama*

Herbert Miliken
*American River College, California*

Richard Miller
*Pennsylvania State University*

Ernest Moser
*Northeast Louisiana University*

Farhang Niroomand
*University of Southern Mississippi*

Eliot Orton
*New Mexico State University*

Marty Perline
*Wichita State University, Kansas*

Harold Petersen
*Boston College*

Douglas Poe
*University of Texas, Austin*

Joseph Rezney
*St. Louis Community College, Missouri*

Terry Ridgway
*University of Nevada, Las Vegas*

Thomas Romans
*State University of New York, Buffalo*

Robert Ross
*Bloomsburg State College, Pennsylvania*

Keith A. Rowley
*Baylor University, Texas*

Anandi Sahu
*Oakland University, Michigan*

Richard Scoggins
*California State University, Long Beach*

Paul Seidenstat
*Temple University, Pennsylvania*

Shahram Shafiee
*North Harris County College, Texas*

Alan Sleeman
*Western Washington University*

John Sondey
*University of Idaho*

Robert W. Thomas
*Iowa State University*

Richard L. Tontz
*California State University, Northridge*

Roger Trenary
*Kansas State University*

Bruce Vanderporten
*Loyola University, Illinois*

Thomas Weiss
*University of Kansas*

Richard O. Welch
*University of Texas at San Antonio*

Donald A. Wells
*University of Arizona*

John Wight
*University of Richmond, Virginia*

Thomas Wyrick
*Southwest Missouri State University*

## Second Edition Reviewers

Scott Bloom
*North Dakota State University*

Thomas Carroll
*University of Nevada, Las Vegas*

Larry Cox
*Southwest Missouri State University*

Diane Cunningham
*Los Angeles Valley College*

Emit Deal
*Macon College*

Michael Fabritius
*University of Mary Hardin Baylor*

Frederick Fagal
*Marywood College*

Ralph Fowler
*Diablo Valley College*

Bob Gilette
*Texas A&M University*

Lynn Gillette
*Indiana University, Indianapolis*

Simon Hakim
*Temple University*

Lewis Karstensson
*University of Nevada, Las Vegas*

Abraham Kidane
*California State University, Dominguez Hills*

W. Barbara Killen
*University of Minnesota*

J. David Lages
*Southwest Missouri State University*

Anthony Lee
*Austin Community College*

Marjory Mabery
*Delaware County Community College*

Bernard Malamud
*University of Nevada, Las Vegas*

Michael Marlow
*California Polytechnic State University, San Luis Obispo*

Phil J. McLewin
*Ramapo College of New Jersey*

Tina Quinn
*Arkansas State University*

Terry Ridgway
*University of Nevada, Las Vegas*

Paul Snoonian
*University of Lowell*

Paul Taube
*Pan American University*

Roger Trenary
*Kansas State University*

Charles Van Eaton
*Hillsdale College*

Mark Wheeler
*Bowling Green State University*

Thomas Wyrick
*Southwest Missouri State University*

## Third Edition Reviewers

Carlos Aguilar
*University of Texas, El Paso*

Rebecca Ann Benakis
*New Mexico State University*

Scott Bloom
*North Dakota State University*

Howard Erdman
*Southwest Texas Junior College*

Arthur Friedberg
*Mohawk Valley Community College*

Nancy A. Jianakoplos
*Colorado State University*

Lewis Karstensson
*University of Nevada, Las Vegas*

Rose Kilburn
*Modesto Junior College*

Ruby P. Kishan
*Southeastern Community College*

Duane Kline
*Southeastern Community College*

Charles A. Roberts
*Western Kentucky University*

Bill Robinson
*University of Nevada, Las Vegas*

Susan C. Stephenson
*Drake University*

Charles Van Eaton
*Hillsdale College*

Richard O. Welch
*The University of Texas at San Antonio*

Calla Wiemer
*University of Hawaii at Manoa*

## Fourth Edition Reviewers

Uzo Agulefo
*North Lake College*

Kari Battaglia
*University of North Texas*

Scott Bloom
*North Dakota State University*

Harry Ellis, Jr.
*University of North Texas*

Mary Ann Hendryson
*Western Washington University*

Eugene Jones
*Ohio State University*

Ki Hoon Him
*Central Connecticut State University*

James McBrearty
*University of Arizona*

John A. Panagakis
*Onondaga Community College*

Bill Robinson
*University of Nevada, Las Vegas*

George E. Samuels
*Sam Houston State University*

Ed Scahill
*University of Scranton*

Charles Van Eaton
*Hillsdale College*

Thomas Wyrick
*Southwest Missouri State University*

## Fifth Edition Reviewers

Kari Battaglia
*University of North Texas*

Douglas A. Conway
*Mesa Community College*

Lee A. Craig
*North Carolina State University*

Harry Ellis, Jr.
*University of North Texas*

Joe W. Essuman
*University of Wisconsin, Waukesha*

Dipak Ghosh
*Emporia State University*

Shirley J. Gideon
*The University of Vermont*

Mary Ann Hendryson
*Western Washington University*

Calvin A. Hoerneman
*Delta College*

George H. Jones
*University of Wisconsin, Rock County*

Donald R. Morgan
*Monterey Peninsula College*

John A. Panagakis
*Onondaga Community College*

Bill Robinson
*University of Nevada, Las Vegas*

Steve Robinson
*The University of North Carolina at Wilmington*

David W. Yoskowitz
*Texas Tech University*

## Sixth Edition Reviewers

Hendrikus J.E.M. Brand
*Albion College*

Curtis Clarke
*Dallas County Community College*

Andrea Gorospe
*Kent State University, Trumbull*

Mehrdad Madresehee
*Lycoming College*

L. Wayne Plumly
*Valdosta State University*

Craig Rogers
*Canisius College*

Uri Simonsohn
*Carnegie Mellon University*

Philip Sprunger
*Lycoming College*

Lea Templer
*College of the Canyons*

Soumya Tohamy
*Berry College*

Lee Van Scyoc
*University of Wisconsin, Oshkosh*

## Seventh Edition Reviewers

Pam Coates
*San Diego Mesa College*

Peggy F. Crane
*Southwestern College*

Richard Croxdale
*Austin Community College*

Harry Ellis, Jr.
*University of North Texas*

Craig Gallet
*California State University, Sacramento*

Kelly George
*Embry-Riddle Aeronautical University*

Anne-Marie Gilliam
*Central Piedmont Community College*

Richard C. Schiming
*Minnesota State University, Mankato*

Lea Templer
*College of the Canyons*

Jennifer VanGilder
*California State University, Bakersfield*

William W. Wilkes
*Athens State University*

Janice Yee
*Wartburg College*

## Eighth Edition Reviewers

Dr. Clive R. Belfied
*Queens College, City University of New York*

Barry Bomboy
*J. Sargeant Reynolds Community College*

James Bryan
*North Harris Montgomery Community College*

Peggy F. Crane
*Southwestern College*

Richard Croxdale
*Austin Community College*

Harry Ellis, Jr.
*University of North Texas*

Kelly George
*Embry Riddle Aeronautical University*

Alan Kessler
*Providence College*

Denny Myers
*Oklahoma City Community College*

Charles Newton
*Houston Community College*

Ahmad Saranjam
*Northeastern University*

Jennifer VanGilder, PhD
*California State University
Bakersfield*

Janice Yee
*Wartburg College*

## Ninth Edition Reviewers

Bart Allen
*Northern Oklahoma College*

Nand Arora
*Cleary University*

Fathollah Bagheri
*University of North Dakota*

Mohammad Bajwa
*Northampton Community College*

Atin Basuchoudhary
*Virginia Military Institute*

Susan Bell
*Seminole Community College*

Douglas Campbell
*University of Memphis*

Franny Chan
*Mt. San Antonio College*

Stephen B. Davis
*Southwest Minnesota State University*

William L. Davis
*University of Tennessee, Martin*

James Dulgeroff
*California State University, San Bernandino*

Dr. J. Pat Fuller
*Brevard Community College*

Dr. Robert Garnett
*Texas Christian University*

Lynde Gilliam
*Metropolitan State College of Denver*

Judith A. Grenkowicz
*Kirtland Community College*

Pablo Hernandez
*Hollins University*

Philip L. Hersch
*Wichita State University*

Michael Heslop
*Northern Virginia Community College
(NOVA)*

Chandrea Hopkins
*College of Lake County*

Brian K. Jackson
*Oklahoma Wesleyan University*

Bun Song Lee
*Northwestern State University*

Joanne Leoni
*Johnson & Wales University*

Michael L. Marlow
*California Polytechnic State
University*

Peter Mavrokordatos
*Tarrant County Community
College*

Dominic F. Minadeo
*Troy University*

Dr. Barbara B. Murray
*Baltimore City Community College*

Bernard J. Sharkey, Jr.
*Louisiana State University*

Joe Silverman
*MiraCosta College*

Martha Stuffler
*Irvine Valley College*

Vicky Tucker
*Lewis University*

Mary Louis White
*Albright University*

## Tenth Edition Reviewers

Ercument Aksoy
*Los Angeles Valley College*

Carol Decker
*Tennessee Wesleyan College*

Stephen Elliott
*Northwestern State
University*

Kelly Whealan George
*Embry Riddle Aeronautical
University*

Aubrey P. Haynes
*Southwest Texas Junior College*

Tori Knight
*Carson-Newman College*

Bun Song Lee
*Northwestern State University*

Lucy Malakar
*Lorain County Community
College*

Lea Templer
*College of the Canyons*

Jan Wyatt
*Hesser College*

I would like to thank Peggy Crane of Southwestern College, who revised the Test Bank, and Jane Himarios of the University of Texas at Arlington, who revised the Instructor's Manual. I would also like to thank Paul Schneiderman of Southern New Hampshire University for creating the PowerPoint slides that accompany this text. I owe a dept of gratitude to all the fine and creative people I worked with at South-Western/Cengage Learning. These persons include Jack Calhoun; Michael Worls, Executive Editor for Economics; Jennifer Thomas and Laura Ansara, Senior Developmental Editors; Cliff Kallemeyn, Senior Content Project Manager; John Carey, Senior Marketing Manager; Michelle Kunkler, Senior Art Director; and Sandee Milewski, Senior Frontlist Buyer.

My deepest debt of gratitude goes to my wife, Sheila, and to my two sons, David, twenty years old, and Daniel, twenty-three years old. They continue to make all my days happy ones.

Roger A. Arnold

# MACRO
# ECONOMICS
10E

## CHAPTER 1

# WHAT ECONOMICS IS ABOUT

**Introduction** You are about to begin your study of economics. Before discussing particular topics in economics, we think it best to give you an overview of what economics is and of some of the key concepts. The key concepts can be compared to musical notes: Just as musical notes are repeated in any song (you hear the musical note G over and over again), so are the key concepts in economics repeated. Some of these concepts are scarcity, opportunity cost, efficiency, marginal decision making, incentives, and exchange.

## A DEFINITION OF ECONOMICS

In this section, we discuss a few key economic concepts; then we incorporate knowledge of these concepts into a definition of economics.

### Goods and Bads

Economists talk about *goods* and *bads*. A good is anything that gives a person utility, or satisfaction. Here is a partial list of some goods: a computer, a car, a watch, a television set, friendship, and love. You will notice from our list that a good can be either tangible or intangible. A computer is a tangible good; friendship is an intangible good. Simply put, for something to be a good (whether tangible or intangible), it only has to give someone utility or satisfaction.

A bad is something that gives a person disutility, or dissatisfaction. If the flu gives you disutility or dissatisfaction, then it is a bad. If the constant nagging of an acquaintance is something that gives you disutility or dissatisfaction, then it is a bad.

People want goods, and they do not want bads. In fact, they will pay to get goods ("Here is $1,000 for the computer"), and they will pay to get rid of bads ("I'd be willing to pay you, doctor, if you can prescribe something that will shorten the time I have the flu").

Can something be a *good* for one person and a *bad* for another person? Smoking cigarettes gives some people utility; it gives others disutility. We conclude that smoking cigarettes can be a *good* for some people and a *bad* for others. This must be why the wife tells her husband, "If you want to smoke, you should do it outside." In other words, "Get those *bads* away from me."

**Good**
Anything from which individuals receive utility or satisfaction.

**Utility**
The satisfaction one receives from a good.

**Bad**
Anything from which individuals receive disutility or dissatisfaction.

**Disutility**
The dissatisfaction one receives from a bad.

## Resources

Goods do not just appear before us when we snap our fingers. It takes resources to produce goods. (Sometimes *resources* are referred to as *inputs* or *factors of production*.)

Generally, economists divide resources into four broad categories: *land, labor, capital,* and *entrepreneurship.*

- Land includes natural resources, such as minerals, forests, water, and unimproved land. For example, oil, wood, and animals fall into this category. (Sometimes economists refer to this category simply as *natural resources*.)
- Labor consists of the physical and mental talents that people contribute to the production process. For example, a person building a house is using his or her own labor.
- Capital consists of produced goods that can be used as inputs for further production. Factories, machinery, tools, computers, and buildings are examples of capital. One country might have more capital than another; that is, it has more factories, machinery, tools, and the like.
- Entrepreneurship refers to the talent that some people have for organizing the resources of land, labor, and capital to produce goods, seek new business opportunities, and develop new ways of doing things.

## Scarcity and a Definition of Economics

We are now ready to define a key concept in economics: *scarcity*. Scarcity is the condition in which our wants (for goods) are greater than the limited resources (land, labor, capital, and entrepreneurship) available to satisfy those wants. In other words, we want goods, but not enough resources are available to provide us with all the goods we want.

Look at it this way: Our wants (for goods) are infinite, but our resources (which we need to produce the goods) are finite. Scarcity is the result of our infinite wants hitting up against finite resources.

Many economists say that if scarcity didn't exist, neither would economics. In other words, if our wants weren't greater than the limited resources available to satisfy them, there would be no field of study called economics. This is similar to saying that if matter and motion didn't exist, neither would physics or that if living things didn't exist, neither would biology. For this reason, we define economics in this text as the science of scarcity. More completely, *economics is the science of how individuals and societies deal with the fact that wants are greater than the limited resources available to satisfy those wants.*

## ⓣhinking like AN ECONOMIST

**Scarcity Affects Everyone** Everyone in the world has to face scarcity, even billionaires. Billionaires may be able to satisfy more of their wants for tangible goods (houses, cars) than most people, but they still may not have the resources to satisfy all their wants. Their wants might include more time with their children, more friendship, no disease in the world, peace on earth, and a hundred other things that they don't have the resources to "produce." ▰ ▰ ▰

**THINKING IN TERMS OF SCARCITY'S EFFECTS** Scarcity has effects. Here are three: (1) the need to make choices, (2) the need for a rationing device, and (3) competition.

**Choices** People have to make choices because of scarcity. Because our unlimited wants are greater than our limited resources, some wants must go unsatisfied. We must choose which wants we will satisfy and which we will not. Jeremy asks, "Do I go to

---

**Land**
All natural resources, such as minerals, forests, water, and unimproved land.

**Labor**
The physical and mental talents people contribute to the production process.

**Capital**
Produced goods that can be used as inputs for further production, such as factories, machinery, tools, computers, and buildings.

**Entrepreneurship**
The talent that some people have for organizing the resources of land, labor, and capital to produce goods, seek new business opportunities, and develop new ways of doing things.

**Scarcity**
The condition in which our wants are greater than the limited resources available to satisfy those wants.

**Economics**
The science of scarcity; the science of how individuals and societies deal with the fact that wants are greater than the limited resources available to satisfy those wants.

## Why Did the British Soldiers Wear Red Uniforms?

When George Washington and the colonists fought the British, the colonists were dressed in rags, whereas the British troops were clad in fine bright red uniforms. Commenting on this difference, people often say, "The British were foolish to have worn bright red uniforms. You could see them coming for miles."

Economists would not be so quick to label the British as foolish. Instead, they would ask why the British troops wore bright red. For instance, David Friedman, an economist, thinks it is odd that the British, who at the time were the greatest fighting force in the world, would make such a seemingly obvious mistake. He has an alternative explanation, an economics explanation.

Friedman reasons that the British generals did not want their men to break ranks and desert because winning the war would be hard, if not impossible, if a lot of men deserted. Thus, the generals had to think up a way to make the opportunity cost of desertion high for their soldiers. The generals reasoned that the higher the cost of desertion was, the fewer deserters there would be. The British generals effectively told their soldiers that if they deserted, they would have to forfeit their freedom or their lives.

Of course, the problem is that a stiff penalty is not effective if deserters cannot be found. Therefore, the generals had to make it easy to find deserters, and they did so by dressing them in bright red uniforms. Certainly, a deserter could throw off his uniform and walk through the countryside in his underwear alone, but in the harsh winters of New England, doing so would guarantee death. He had almost no choice but to wear the bright red uniform.

NORTH WIND PICTURES/PHOTOLIBRARY

you summarize your thinking process? What question or questions do you ask yourself to decide whether to study another hour?

Perhaps without knowing it, you think in terms of the costs and benefits of further study. You probably realize that studying an additional hour has certain benefits (you may be able to raise your grade a few points), but it has costs too (you will get less sleep or have less time to watch television or talk on the phone with a friend). That you think in terms of costs and benefits, however, doesn't tell us *how* you think in terms of costs and benefits. For example, when deciding what to do, do you look at the total costs and total benefits of the proposed action, or do you look at something less than the total costs and benefits? According to economists, for most decisions, you think in terms of *additional,* or *marginal,* costs and benefits, not *total* costs and benefits. That's because most decisions deal with making a small, or additional, change.

To illustrate, suppose you just finished eating a hamburger and drinking a soda for lunch. You are still a little hungry and are considering whether to order another hamburger. An economist would say that in deciding whether to order another hamburger, you compare the additional benefits of the second hamburger to its additional costs. In economics, the word *marginal* is a synonym for *additional.* So we say that you compare the marginal benefits ($MB$) of the (next) hamburger to its marginal costs ($MC$). If the marginal benefits are greater than the marginal costs, you obviously expect a net benefit to ordering the next hamburger, and therefore you order another. If, however, the marginal benefits are less than the marginal costs, you obviously expect a net cost to ordering the next hamburger, and therefore you do not order another.

**Marginal Benefits**
Additional benefits; the benefits connected with consuming an additional unit of a good or undertaking one more unit of an activity.

**Marginal Costs**
Additional costs; the costs connected with consuming an additional unit of a good or undertaking one more unit of an activity.

| Condition | Action |
|---|---|
| $MB$ of next hamburger $>$ $MC$ of next hamburger | Buy next hamburger |
| $MB$ of next hamburger $<$ $MC$ of next hamburger | Do not buy next hamburger |

What you don't consider when making this decision are the total benefits and total costs of hamburgers. That's because the benefits and costs connected with the first hamburger (the one you have already eaten) are no longer relevant to the current decision. You are not deciding between eating two hamburgers or eating no hamburgers; your decision is whether to eat a second hamburger after you have already eaten one.

**Decisions at the Margin**
Decision making characterized by weighing the additional (marginal) benefits of a change against the additional (marginal) costs of a change with respect to current conditions.

According to economists, when individuals make decisions by comparing marginal benefits to marginal costs, they are making decisions at the margin. The employee makes a decision at the margin when deciding whether to work two hours overtime; the economics professor makes a decision at the margin when deciding whether to put an additional question on the final exam.

## Efficiency

**Efficiency**
Exists when marginal benefits equal marginal costs.

What is the right amount of time to study for a test? In economics, the *right amount* of anything is the *optimal* or *efficient* amount—the amount for which the marginal benefits equal the marginal costs. Stated differently, you have achieved efficiency when the marginal benefits equal the marginal costs.

Suppose you are studying for an economics test, and for the first hour of studying, the marginal benefits ($MB$) are greater than the marginal costs ($MC$):

$$MB \text{ studying first hour} > MC \text{ studying first hour}$$

Given this condition, you will certainly study for the first hour because it is worth it: The additional benefits are greater than the additional costs; so there is a net benefit to studying.

Suppose for the second hour of studying, the marginal benefits are still greater than the marginal costs:

$$MB \text{ studying second hour} > MC \text{ studying second hour}$$

You will study for the second hour because the additional benefits are still greater than the additional costs. In other words, studying the second hour is worthwhile. In fact, you will continue to study as long as the marginal benefits are greater than the marginal costs. Exhibit 2 graphically illustrates this discussion.

The marginal benefit ($MB$) curve of studying is downward sloping because we have assumed that the benefits of studying for the first hour are greater than the benefits of studying for the second hour and so on. The marginal cost ($MC$) curve of studying is upward sloping because we assume that studying the second hour costs a person more (in terms of goods forfeited) than the first, the third costs more than the second, and so on. (If we assume the additional costs of studying are constant over time, the $MC$ curve is horizontal.)

In the exhibit, the marginal benefits of studying equal the marginal costs at three hours. So three hours is the *efficient* length of time to study in this situation. At fewer than three hours, the marginal benefits of studying are greater than the marginal costs; thus, at all these hours, studying has net benefits. At more than three hours, the marginal costs of studying are greater than the marginal benefits, and so studying beyond three hours is not worthwhile.

MAXIMIZING NET BENEFITS Take another look at Exhibit 2. Suppose you had stopped studying after the first hour (or after the 60th minute). Would you have given up

---

**EXHIBIT 2**

**Efficiency**

$MB$ = marginal benefits and $MC$ = marginal costs. In the exhibit, the $MB$ curve of studying is downward sloping and the $MC$ curve of studying is upward sloping. As long as $MB > MC$, the person will study. The person stops studying when $MB = MC$. This is where efficiency is achieved.

anything? Yes, you would have given up the *net benefits* of studying longer. To illustrate, notice that between the first and the second hour, the marginal benefits (*MB*) curve lies above the marginal costs (*MC*). This means studying the second hour has net benefits. But if you hadn't studied that second hour—if you had stopped after the first hour—then you would have given up the opportunity to collect those net benefits. The same analysis holds for the third hour. We conclude that by studying three hours (but not one minute longer), you have maximized net benefits. In short, efficiency, which is consistent with *MB* = *MC*, is also consistent with maximizing net benefits.

## ⓣhinking like AN ECONOMIST

**No $10 Bills on the Sidewalk** An economist says that people try to maximize their net benefits. You ask for proof. The economist says, "You don't find any $10 bills on the sidewalk." What is the economist getting at by making this statement? Keep in mind that you don't find any $10 bills on the sidewalk because if there were a $10 bill on the sidewalk, the first person to see it would pick it up; when you came along, it wouldn't be there. But why would the first person to find the $10 bill pick it up? The reason is that people don't pass by net benefits, and picking up the $10 bill comes with net benefits. The *benefits* of having an additional $10 are obvious; the *costs* of obtaining the additional $10 bill are simply what you give up during the time you are stooping down to pick it up. In short, the marginal benefits are likely to be greater than the marginal costs (giving us net benefits), and that is why the $10 bill is picked up. Saying there are no $10 bills on the sidewalk is the same as saying no one leaves net benefits on the sidewalk. In other words, people try to maximize net benefits. ▬ ▬ ▬

## Economics Is About Incentives

**Incentive**
Something that encourages or motivates a person to undertake an action.

An incentive is something that encourages or motivates a person to undertake an action.

Often what motivates a person to undertake an action is the belief that by taking that action she can make herself better off. For example, if we say that Jane has an incentive to study for the upcoming exam, we imply that by studying Jane can make herself better off, probably in terms of receiving a higher grade on the exam than if she didn't study.

Incentives are closely related to benefits and costs. Individuals have an incentive to undertake actions for which the benefits are greater than the costs or, stated differently, for which they expect to receive net benefits (benefits greater than costs).

Economists are interested in what motivates behavior. Why does the person buy more of good *X* when its price falls? Why might a person work longer hours when income tax rates decline? Why might a person buy more of a particular good today if he expects the price of that good will go up next week? The general answer to many of these questions is that people do what they have an incentive to do. Economists then hunt for what the incentive is. For example, if a person buys more of good *X* when its price goes down, what specifically is the incentive? How, specifically, does the person make himself better off by buying a good when its price declines. Does he get more utility or satisfaction? Or how does a person make herself better off if she buys a good today that she expects will go up in price next week?

## Unintended Effects

Economists think in terms of unintended effects. For example, Andres, 16 years old, currently works after school at a grocery store. He earns $6.50 an hour.

Suppose the state legislature passes a law specifying that the minimum dollar wage a person can be paid to do a job is $9.50 an hour. The legislators' intention in passing the law is to help people like Andres earn more income.

Will the $9.50 an hour legislation have the intended effect? Perhaps not. The manager of the grocery store may not find it worthwhile to continue employing Andres if she has to pay him $9.50 an hour. In other words, Andres may have a job at $6.50 an hour but not at \$9.50 an hour. If the law specifies that no one may earn less than \$9.50 an hour and the manager of the grocery store decides to fire Andres rather than pay this amount, then an unintended effect of the legislation is Andres' losing his job.

As another example, let's analyze mandatory seatbelt laws to see whether they have any unintended effects. States have laws that require drivers to wear seatbelts. The intended effect is to reduce the number of car fatalities by making it more likely that drivers will survive accidents.

Could these laws have an unintended effect? Some economists think so. They look at accident fatalities in terms of this equation:

Total number of fatalities = Number of accidents × Fatalities per accident

For example, if there are 200,000 accidents and 0.10 fatalities per accident, the total number of fatalities is 20,000.

The objective of a mandatory seatbelt program is to reduce the total number of fatalities by reducing the fatalities per accident. Many studies have found that wearing seatbelts does just this. If you are in an accident, you have a better chance of not being killed if you are wearing a seatbelt.

Let's assume that with seatbelts, there are 0.08 instead of 0.10 fatalities per accident. If there are still 200,000 accidents, the total number of fatalities falls from 20,000 to 16,000. Thus, the total number of fatalities drops if fatalities per accident are reduced and the number of accidents is constant.

| Number of Accidents | Fatalities per Accident | Total Number of Fatalities |
|---|---|---|
| 200,000 | 0.10 | 20,000 |
| 200,000 | 0.08 | 16,000 |

However, some economists wonder whether the number of accidents stays constant. Specifically, they suggest that seatbelts may have an unintended effect: *The number of accidents may increase* because wearing seatbelts may make drivers feel safer. Feeling safer may cause them to take chances that they wouldn't ordinarily take, such as driving faster or more aggressively, or concentrating less on their driving and more on the music on the radio. For example, if the number of accidents rises to 250,000, then the total number of fatalities is 20,000.

| Number of Accidents | Fatalities per Accident | Total Number of Fatalities |
|---|---|---|
| 200,000 | 0.10 | 20,000 |
| 250,000 | 0.08 | 20,000 |

We conclude the following: If a mandatory seatbelt law reduces the number of fatalities per accident (intended effect) but increases the number of accidents (unintended effect), it may not, contrary to popular belief, reduce the total number of fatalities. In fact, some economics studies show just this.

What does all this mean for you? You may be safer if you know that this unintended effect exists and you adjust accordingly. To be specific, when you wear your seatbelt, your chances of getting hurt in a car accident are less than if you don't wear your seatbelt. But if this added sense of protection causes you to drive less carefully than you would otherwise, then you could unintentionally offset the measure of protection your seatbelt provides. To reduce the probability of hurting yourself and others in a car accident, *the best policy is to wear a seatbelt and to drive as carefully as you would if you weren't wearing a seatbelt.* Knowing about the unintended effect of wearing your seatbelt could save your life.

## Exchange

**Exchange (Trade)**
The giving up of one thing for something else.

Exchange, or trade, is the giving up of one thing for something else. Economics is sometimes called the "science of exchange" because so much that is discussed in economics has to do with exchange.

We start with a basic question: Why do people enter into exchanges? The answer is that they do so to make themselves better off. When a person voluntarily trades $100 for a jacket, she is saying, "I prefer to have the jacket instead of the $100." And, of course, when the seller of the jacket voluntarily sells the jacket for $100, he is saying, "I prefer to have the $100 instead of the jacket." In short, through trade or exchange, each person gives up something he values less for something he values more.

You can think of trade in terms of utility or satisfaction. Imagine a utility scale that goes from 1 to 10, with 10 being the highest utility you can achieve. Now suppose you currently have $40 in your wallet and you are at 7 on the utility scale. A few minutes later, you are in a store looking at some new CDs. The price of each is $10, and you end up buying four CDs for $40.

After you traded your $40 for the four CDs, are you still at 7 on the utility scale? The likely answer is no. If you expected to have the same utility after the trade as you did before, you probably would not have traded your $40 for the four CDs. The only reason you entered into the trade is that you *expected* to be better off after the trade than you were before it. In other words, you thought trading your $40 for the four CDs would move you up the utility scale from 7 to, say, 8.

### SELF-TEST

1. Give an example to illustrate how a change in opportunity cost can affect behavior.

2. Studying has both costs and benefits. If you continue to study (say, for a test) as long as the marginal benefits of studying are greater than the marginal costs and stop studying when the two are equal, will your action be consistent with having maximized the net benefits of studying? Explain your answer.

3. You stay up an additional hour to study for a test. The intended effect is to raise your test grade. What might be an unintended effect of staying up another hour to study?

# THE MARKET AND GOVERNMENT

In recent years, major economic problems and issues have plagued the United States, such as:

- Financial problems in the banking sector
- The economic effects of falling real estate prices
- Growing federal budget deficits
- A fall in economic activity, as measured by the total output of goods and services produced in the country
- Rising unemployment
- The looming crisis in Social Security
- Health-care issues
- Issues related to climate change and the environment
- The proper role of monetary policy
- The proper role of government regulatory policy in the economy, and much more

When it comes to economic problems, the national debate usually proceeds along these lines:

- First, the problem is *identified* and *defined* or *described*.
- Second, individuals attempt to identify the *cause* of the problem.
- Third, individuals propose *solutions* to the problem.

This three-step process was evident in recent discussions of the U.S. financial crisis of 2007–2009 and in discussions of health care. After first *identifying* the financial crisis and describing it, individuals turned to identifying its *cause(s)* and proposing *solutions*.

In this process, there is little debate about identifying the problem. Most of the debate focuses on the cause(s) of the problem and the proposed solutions. With respect to both the cause and the solution, we often hear two words mentioned: the "market" and "government." For example:

- *Either:* The *market* (or capitalism) is the *cause* of the problem.
- *Or:* The *government* is the *cause* of the problem.
- *Either:* The *market* (or capitalism) is the solution to the problem.
- *Or:* The *government* is the solution to the problem.

The market-versus-government debate is an important one to know about, but it takes time to learn the particulars. Much of this book will help you learn those particulars, including:

- How a market system works.
- What markets are and are not capable of doing.
- How government operates.
- How government actions and policies can affect the market system.

At this point, you may be wondering why we don't simply tell you the "right" way to think. Your thinking might be, "Well, which is it? Did the market or government *cause* the problem? Is the market or government the *solution*?" If these are your questions, we sympathize with your frustration over not getting straight answers. We resist telling you the "right" answer for two reasons: First, not all economists agree on what the "right" answer is in a given case. Second, knowing the "right" answer without first understanding how markets and how governments work will leave you feeling unsatisfied because you will have little foundation on which to understand the answer. After all, no matter which "right" answer we give you now, you are going to want it explained, and this book is part of that explanation.

# CETERIS PARIBUS AND THEORY

We cover two important topics in this section: (1) *ceteris paribus* and (2) theory.

## Ceteris Paribus Thinking

Wilson has eaten regular ice cream for years, and for years his weight has been 170 pounds. One day Wilson decides he wants to lose weight. With this in mind, he buys a new fat-free ice cream at the grocery store. The fat-free ice cream has half the calories of regular ice cream.

Wilson eats the fat-free ice cream for the next few months. He then weighs himself and finds that he has gained two pounds. Does this mean that fat-free ice cream causes people to gain weight and regular ice cream does not? The answer is no. Why, then, did Wilson gain weight when he substituted fat-free ice cream for regular ice cream? Perhaps Wilson ate three times as much fat-free ice cream as regular ice cream. Or perhaps during the time he was eating fat-free ice cream, he wasn't exercising, and during the time he was eating regular ice cream, he was exercising. In other words, a number of factors—such as eating more ice cream or exercising less—may have offset the weight loss that Wilson would have experienced had these other factors not changed.

Now suppose you want to make the point that Wilson would have lost weight by substituting fat-free ice cream for regular ice cream had these other factors not changed.

**Ceteris Paribus**
A Latin term meaning "all other things constant" or "nothing else changes."

What would you say? A scientist would say, "If Wilson has been eating regular ice cream and his weight has stabilized at 170 pounds, then substituting fat-free ice cream for regular ice cream will lead to a decline in weight, *ceteris paribus.*"

The term *ceteris paribus* means "all other things constant" or "nothing else changes." In our ice cream example, if nothing else changes—such as how much ice cream Wilson eats, how much exercise he gets, and so on—then switching to fat-free ice cream will result in weight loss. This expectation is based on the theory that a reduction in calorie consumption will result in weight loss and an increase in calorie consumption will result in weight gain.

Using the *ceteris paribus* assumption is important because, with it, we can clearly designate what we believe is the correct relationship between two variables. In the ice cream example, we can designate the correct relationship between calorie intake and weight gain.

Economists don't often talk about ice cream, but they will often make use of the *ceteris paribus* assumption. An economist might say, "If the price of a good decreases, the quantity of it consumed increases, *ceteris paribus.*" For example, if the price of Pepsi-Cola decreases, people will buy more of it, assuming that nothing else changes.

But some people ask, "Why would economists want to assume that when the price of Pepsi-Cola falls, nothing else changes? Don't other things change in the real world? Why make assumptions that we know are not true?"

Of course, economists do not specify *ceteris paribus* because they want to say something false about the world. They specify it because they want to clearly define what they believe to be the real-world relationship between two variables. Look at it this way. If you drop a ball off the roof of a house, it will fall to the ground unless someone catches it. This statement is true, and probably everyone would willingly accept it as true. But here is another true statement: If you drop a ball off the roof of a house, it will fall to the ground, *ceteris paribus.* In fact, the two statements are identical in meaning. This is because adding the phrase "unless someone catches it" in the first sentence is the same as saying "*ceteris paribus*" in the second sentence. If one statement is acceptable to us, the other should be too.

## What Is a Theory?

Almost everyone, including you, builds and tests theories or models on a regular basis. (In this text, the words *theory* and *model* are used interchangeably.) Perhaps you thought only scientists and others with high-level mathematics at their fingertips built and tested theories. However, theory building and testing is not the domain of only the highly educated and mathematically proficient. Almost everyone builds and test theories.

People build theories any time they do not know the answer to a question. Someone asks, "Why is the crime rate higher in the United States than in Belgium?" Or, "Why did Aaron's girlfriend break up with him?" Or, "Why does Professor Avalos give easier final exams than Professor Shaw even though they teach the same subject?" If you don't know the answer to a question, you are likely to build a theory so that you can provide an answer.

**Theory**
An abstract representation of the real world designed with the intent to better understand it.

**Abstract**
The process (used in building a theory) of focusing on a limited number of variables to explain or predict an event.

What exactly is a theory? To an economist, a theory is an abstract representation of the world. In this context, abstract means to omit certain variables or factors when trying to explain or understand something. For example, suppose you were to draw a map for a friend, showing him how to get from his house to yours. Would you draw a map that showed every single thing your friend would see on the trip, or would you simply draw the main roads and one or two landmarks? If you'd do the latter, you would be abstracting from reality; you would be omitting certain things.

You would abstract for two reasons. First, to get your friend from his house to yours, you don't need to include everything on your map. Simply noting main roads may be enough. Second, if you did note everything on your map, your friend might get confused. Giving too much detail could be as bad as giving too little.

When economists build a theory or model, they do the same thing you do in drawing a map. They abstract from reality; they leave out certain things. They focus on the

# WORKING WITH DIAGRAMS

A picture is worth a thousand words. With this familiar saying in mind, economists construct their diagrams or graphs. With a few lines and a few points, much can be conveyed.

## TWO-VARIABLE DIAGRAMS

Most of the diagrams in this book represent the relationship between two variables. Economists compare two variables to see how a change in one variable affects the other.

Suppose our two variables of interest are *consumption* and *income.* We want to show how consumption changes as income changes. We collect the data in Table 1. Simply by looking at the data in the first two columns, we can see that as income rises (column 1), consumption rises (column 2). If we wanted to show the relationship between income and consumption on a graph, we could place *income* on the horizontal axis, as in Exhibit 1, and *consumption* on the vertical axis. Point *A* represents income of $0 and consumption of $60, point *B* represents income of $100 and consumption of $120, and so on. If we draw a straight line through the points we have plotted, we have a picture of the relationship between income and consumption, based on the data we collected.

Notice that the line in Exhibit 1 slopes upward from left to right. As income rises, so does consumption. For example, as you move from point *A* to point *B*, income rises from $0 to $100 and consumption rises from $60 to $120. The line in Exhibit 1 also shows that as income falls, so does consumption. For example, as you move from point *C* to point *B*, income falls from $200 to $100 and consumption falls from $180 to $120. When two variables—such as consumption and income—change in the same way, they are said to be directly related.

EXHIBIT 1

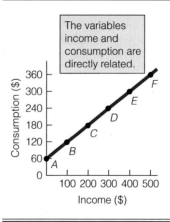

The variables income and consumption are directly related.

**A Two-Variable Diagram Representing a Direct Relationship**

In this exhibit, we have plotted the data in Table 1 and then connected the points with a straight line. The data represent a direct relationship: as one variable (say, income) rises, the other variable (consumption) rises too.

Directly Related
Two variables are directly related if they change in the same way.

| | TABLE 1 | |
| --- | --- | --- |
| **(1)** **When Income Is:** | **(2)** **Consumption Is:** | **(3)** **Point** |
| $ 0 | $ 60 | A |
| 100 | 120 | B |
| 200 | 180 | C |
| 300 | 240 | D |
| 400 | 300 | E |
| 500 | 360 | F |

| | TABLE 2 | |
| --- | --- | --- |
| **(1)**<br>**When Price of CDs Is:** | **(2)**<br>**Quantity Demanded of CDs Is:** | **(3)**<br>**Point** |
| $20 | 100 | A |
| 18 | 120 | B |
| 16 | 140 | C |
| 14 | 160 | D |
| 12 | 180 | E |

**A Two-Variable Diagram Representing an Inverse Relationship**

In this exhibit, we have plotted the data in Table 2 and then connected the points with a straight line. The data represent an inverse relationship: as one variable (price) falls, the other variable (quantity demanded) rises.

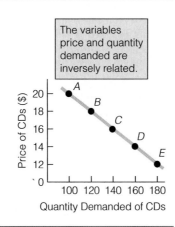

Now let's take a look at the data in Table 2. Our two variables are the *price of compact discs (CDs)* and the quantity demanded of CDs. Just by looking at the data in the first two columns, we see that as price falls (column 1), quantity demanded rises (column 2). Suppose we want to plot these data. We could place *price of CDs* on the vertical axis, as in Exhibit 2, and *quantity demanded of CDs* on the horizontal axis. Point *A* represents a price of $20 and a quantity demanded of 100, point *B* represents a price of $18 and a quantity demanded of 120, and so on. If we draw a straight line through the plotted points, we have a picture of the relationship between price and quantity demanded, based on the data in Table 2.

Notice:

- As price falls, the quantity demanded rises. For example, as price falls from $20 to $18, the quantity demanded rises from 100 to 120.

- As price rises, the quantity demanded falls. For example, when price rises from $12 to $14, quantity demanded falls from 180 to 160.

When two variables—such as price and quantity demanded—change in opposite ways, they are said to be inversely related.

As you have seen so far, variables may be directly related (when one increases, the other also increases) or inversely related (when one increases, the other decreases). Variables can also be independent of each other if, as one variable changes, the other does not.

In Exhibit 3(a), as the *X* variable rises, the *Y* variable remains the same (at 20). Obviously, the *X* and *Y* variables are independent of each other: As one changes, the other does not.

In Exhibit 3(b), as the *Y* variable rises, the *X* variable remains the same (at 30). Again, we conclude that the *X* and *Y* variables are independent of each other: As one changes, the other does not.

**Inversely Related**
Two variables are inversely related if they change in opposite ways.

**Independent**
Two variables are independent if, as one changes, the other does not.

# SLOPE OF A LINE

**Slope**
The ratio of the change in the variable on the vertical axis to the change in the variable on the horizontal axis.

In addition to knowing *how* two variables are related, we also often need to know *how much* one variable changes as the other changes. To find out, we need only calculate the slope of the line. The slope is the ratio of the change in the variable on the vertical axis

**EXHIBIT 3**

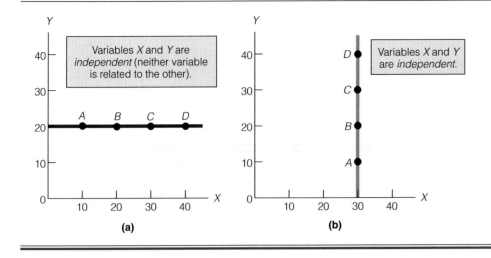

(a)

(b)

**Two Diagrams Representing Independence Between Two Variables**

In (a) and (b), the variables $X$ and $Y$ are independent: as one changes, the other does not.

to the change in the variable on the horizontal axis. For example, if $Y$ is on the vertical axis and $X$ is on the horizontal axis, the slope is equal to $\Delta Y/\Delta X$. (The symbol "$\Delta$" means "change in.")

$$\text{Slope} = \frac{\Delta Y}{\Delta X}$$

Exhibit 4 shows four lines. In each case, the slope is calculated. After studying (a)–(d), see if you understand why the slopes are negative, positive, zero, and infinite.

# SLOPE OF A LINE IS CONSTANT

Look again at the line in Exhibit 4(a). The slope between points $A$ and $B$ is computed to be –1. If we had computed the slope between points $B$ and $C$ or between points $C$ and $D$, would it still be –1? Let's compute the slope between points $B$ and $C$. Moving from point $B$ to point $C$, the change in $Y$ is –10 and the change in $X$ is +10. So the slope is –1, as it was between points $A$ and $B$. Now let's compute the slope between points $A$ and $D$. Moving from point $A$ to point $D$, the change in $Y$ is –30 and the change in $X$ is +30. Again the slope is –1. Our conclusion is that the slope between any two points on a straight line is always the same as the slope between any other two points. To see this for yourself, compute the slope between points $A$ and $B$ and between points $A$ and $C$ using the line in Exhibit 4(b).

# SLOPE OF A CURVE

In addition to straight lines, economics graphs use curves. The slope of a curve is not constant throughout, as it is for a straight line. The slope of a curve varies from one point to another. Calculating the slope of a curve at a given point requires two steps, as illustrated for point $A$ in Exhibit 5. First, draw a line tangent to the curve at the point (a tangent line is one that just touches the curve but does not cross it). Second, pick any two points on the tangent line and determine the slope. In Exhibit 5, the slope of the line between points $B$ and $C$ is 0.67. The slope of the curve at point $A$ (and only at point $A$) is therefore 0.67.

## EXHIBIT 4

### Calculating Slopes

The slope of a line is the ratio of the change in the variable on the vertical axis to the change in the variable on the horizontal axis. In (a)–(d), we have calculated the slope.

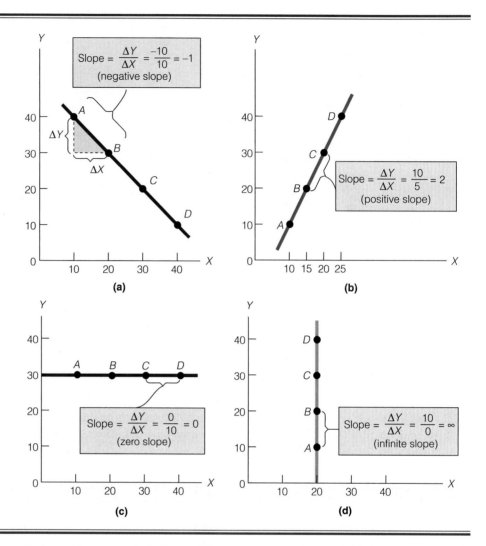

(a)

$$\text{Slope} = \frac{\Delta Y}{\Delta X} = \frac{-10}{10} = -1$$
(negative slope)

(b)

$$\text{Slope} = \frac{\Delta Y}{\Delta X} = \frac{10}{5} = 2$$
(positive slope)

(c)

$$\text{Slope} = \frac{\Delta Y}{\Delta X} = \frac{0}{10} = 0$$
(zero slope)

(d)

$$\text{Slope} = \frac{\Delta Y}{\Delta X} = \frac{10}{0} = \infty$$
(infinite slope)

## EXHIBIT 5

### Calculating the Slope of a Curve at a Particular Point

The slope of the curve at point A is 0.67. This is calculated by drawing a line tangent to the curve at point A and then determining the slope of the line.

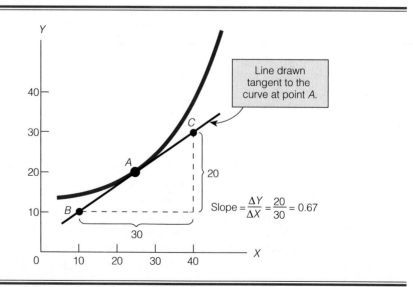

Line drawn tangent to the curve at point A.

$$\text{Slope} = \frac{\Delta Y}{\Delta X} = \frac{20}{30} = 0.67$$

# THE 45-DEGREE LINE

Economists sometimes use a *45-degree line* to represent data. This is a straight line that bisects the right angle formed by the intersection of the vertical and horizontal axes (see Exhibit 6). As a result, the 45-degree line divides the space enclosed by the two axes into *two equal parts*, as shown in the exhibit by the shading in different colors.

The major characteristic of the 45-degree line is that any point on it is equidistant from both the horizontal and vertical axes. For example, point *A* is exactly as far from the horizontal axis as it is from the vertical axis. Thus, point *A* represents as much *X* as it does *Y*. Specifically, in the exhibit, point *A* represents 20 units of *X* and 20 units of *Y*.

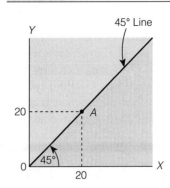

**EXHIBIT 6**

**The 45-Degree Line**

Any point on the 45-degree line is equidistant from each axis. For example, point A is the same distance from the vertical axis as it is from the horizontal axis.

# PIE CHARTS

*Pie charts* appear in numerous places throughout this text. A pie chart is a convenient way to represent the different parts of something that when added together equal the whole. Let's consider a typical 24-hour weekday for Charles Myers. On a typical weekday, Charles spends 8 hours sleeping, 4 hours taking classes at the university, 4 hours working at his part-time job, 2 hours doing homework, 1 hour eating, 2 hours watching television, and 3 hours doing nothing in particular ("hanging around"). Exhibit 7 shows the breakdown of a typical weekday for Charles in pie chart form.

Pie charts send a quick visual message about rough percentage breakdowns and relative relationships. For example, Exhibit 7 clearly shows that Charles spends twice as much time working as doing homework.

**EXHIBIT 7**

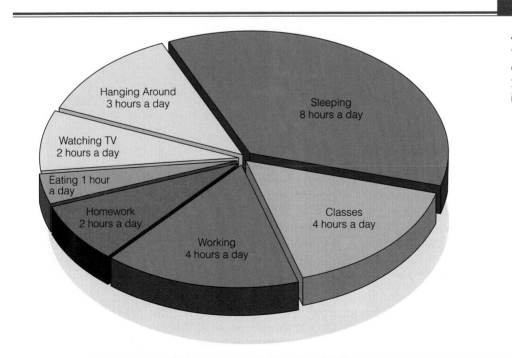

**A Pie Chart**

The breakdown of activities for Charles Myers during a typical 24-hour weekday is represented in pie chart form.

# BAR GRAPHS

**Gross Domestic Product (GDP)**
The value of the entire output produced annually within a country's borders.

The *bar graph* is another visual aid that economists use to convey relative relationships. Suppose we want to represent the gross domestic product for the United States in different years. The gross domestic product (GDP) is the value of the entire output produced annually within a country's borders. The bar graph in Exhibit 8 is a quick picture not only of the actual GDP for each year, but also of the relative relationships between the GDP numbers for different years. For example, the graph makes it easy to see that the GDP in 1990 was more than double what it was in 1980.

# LINE GRAPHS

Sometimes information is best and most easily displayed in a *line graph*, which is particularly useful for illustrating changes in a variable over a time period. Suppose we want to illustrate the variations in average points per game for a college basketball team over a number of years. The line graph in Exhibit 9(a) shows that the basketball team was on a roller coaster during the years 1997–2010. Perhaps the visual message is that the team's performance has not been consistent from one year to the next.

Suppose we plot the same data again, except this time using a different measurement scale on the vertical axis. As you can see in Exhibit 9(b), the variation in the team's

---

**EXHIBIT 8**

**A Bar Graph**

U.S. gross domestic product for different years is illustrated in bar graph form. Source: Bureau of Economic Analysis

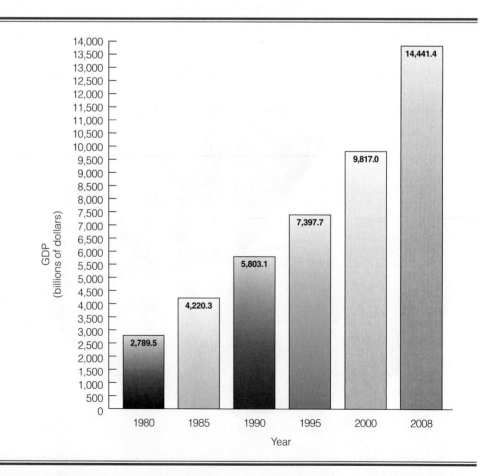

**EXHIBIT 9**

**The Two Line Graphs Plot the Same Data**

In (a) we plotted the average number of points per game for a college basketball team in different years. The variation between the years is pronounced. In (b) we plotted the same data as in (a), but the variation in the performance of the team appears much less pronounced than in (a).

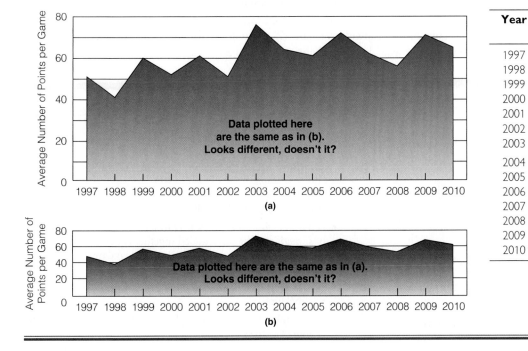

| Year | Average Number of Points per Game |
|------|-----------------------------------|
| 1997 | 50 |
| 1998 | 40 |
| 1999 | 59 |
| 2000 | 51 |
| 2001 | 60 |
| 2002 | 50 |
| 2003 | 75 |
| 2004 | 63 |
| 2005 | 60 |
| 2006 | 71 |
| 2007 | 61 |
| 2008 | 55 |
| 2009 | 70 |
| 2010 | 64 |

**EXHIBIT 10**

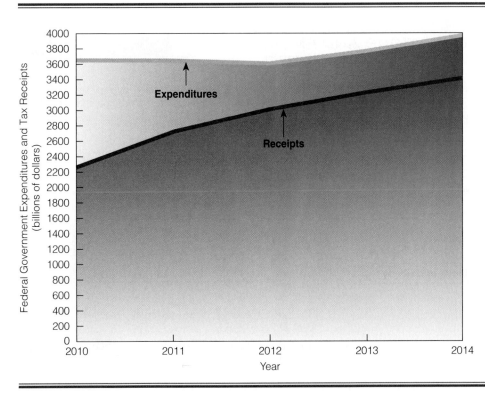

**Projected Federal Government Expenditures and Tax Receipts, 2010–2014**

Projected federal government expenditures and tax receipts are shown in line graph form for the period 2010–2014.

| Year | Expenditures | Receipts |
|------|--------------|----------|
| 2010 | 3,644 | 2,264 |
| 2011 | 3,638 | 2,717 |
| 2012 | 3,600 | 3,010 |
| 2013 | 3,759 | 3,221 |
| 2014 | 3,961 | 3,404 |

*Source:* Congressional Budget Office

performance appears much less pronounced than in part (a). In fact, we could choose a scale that, if we were to plot the data, would give us something close to a straight line. The point is simple: Data plotted in a line graph may convey different messages depending on the measurement scale used.

Sometimes economists show two line graphs on the same axes. Usually, the purpose is to draw attention to either (1) the *relationship* between two variables or (2) the *difference* between them. In Exhibit 10, the line graphs show the variation and trend in (1) projected federal government expenditures and (2) tax receipts for the years 2010–2014, drawing attention to the "gap" between the two over the years.

## APPENDIX SUMMARY

- Two variables are directly related if one variable rises as the other rises.
- An upward-sloping line (left to right) represents two variables that are directly related.
- Two variables are inversely related if one variable rises as the other falls.
- A downward-sloping line (left to right) represents two variables that are inversely related.
- Two variables are independent if one variable rises as the other remains constant.
- The slope of a line is the ratio of the change in the variable on the vertical axis to the change in the variable on the horizontal axis. The slope of a straight line is the same between any two points on the line.

- To determine the slope of a curve at a point, draw a line tangent to the curve at the point and then determine the slope of the tangent line.
- Any point on a 45-degree line is equidistant from the two axes.
- A pie chart is a convenient way to represent the different parts of something that when added together equal the whole. A pie chart visually shows rough percentage breakdowns and relative relationships.
- A bar graph is a convenient way to represent relative relationships.
- Line graphs are particularly useful for illustrating changes in one or more variables over time.

## QUESTIONS AND PROBLEMS

1. What type of relationship would you expect between the following?
   a. Sales of hot dogs and sales of hot dog buns
   b. The price of winter coats and sales of winter coats
   c. The price of personal computers and the production of personal computers
   d. Sales of toothbrushes and sales of cat food
   e. The number of children in a family and the number of toys in a family

2. Represent the following data in bar graph form.

| Year | U.S. Money Supply (billions of dollars) |
|------|------------------------------------------|
| 2005 | 1,374 |
| 2006 | 1,365 |
| 2007 | 1,373 |
| 2008 | 1,595 |
| 2009 | 1,689 |

3. Plot the following data, and specify the type of relationship between the two variables. (Place "Price" on the vertical axis and "Quantity Demanded" on the horizontal axis.)

| Price of Apples ($) | Quantity Demanded of Apples |
|---------------------|------------------------------|
| 0.25 | 1,000 |
| 0.50 | 800 |
| 0.70 | 700 |
| 0.95 | 500 |
| 1.00 | 400 |
| 1.10 | 350 |

4. In Exhibit 4(a), determine the slope between points $C$ and $D$.

5. In Exhibit 4(b), determine the slope between points $A$ and $D$.

6. What is the special characteristic of a 45-degree line?

7. What is the slope of a 45-degree line?

8. When is a pie chart better than a bar graph for illustrating data?

9. Plot the following data, and specify the type of relationship between the two variables. (Place "Price" on the vertical axis and "Quantity Supplied" on the horizontal axis.)

| Price of Apples ($) | Quantity Supplied of Apples |
|---|---|
| 0.25 | 350 |
| 0.50 | 400 |
| 0.70 | 500 |
| 0.95 | 700 |
| 1.00 | 800 |
| 1.10 | 1,000 |

# APPENDIX B

# SHOULD YOU MAJOR IN ECONOMICS?

You are probably reading this textbook as part of your first college course in economics. You may be taking the course to satisfy a requirement in your major. Economics courses are sometimes required for students who plan to major in business, history, liberal studies, social science, or computer science.

Of course, you may also be planning to major in economics. If you are like many college students, you may complain that not enough information is available about the various majors at your college or university. For example, students who major in business sometimes say they are not quite certain what a business major is all about, but then they add that majoring in business is a safe bet. "After all," they assert," you're pretty sure of getting a job if you have a business degree. That's not always the case with other degrees."

Many college students choose their majors based on their high school courses. History majors, for example, might say that they decided to major in history because they "liked history in high school." Similarly, chemistry, biology, and math students say they chose their majors based on their experiences in high school. If a student found both math and economics easy and interesting in high school, then she is likely to major in math or economics. Conversely, if a student had a hard time with chemistry in high school and found it boring, then he doesn't usually want to major in chemistry in college.

Students also often look to the dollars at the end of the college degree. A student may enjoy history and want to learn more of it in college but tell herself that she will earn a higher starting salary after graduation if she majors in computer science or engineering.

Thus, when choosing a major, students often consider (1) how much they enjoy studying a particular subject, (2) what they would like to see themselves doing in the future, and (3) income prospects.

People may weight these three factors differently, but, regardless of the weighting, having more information is better than having, *ceteris paribus*. We note *"ceteris paribus"* because having more information is not necessarily better if you have to pay more for it than it is worth. Who wants to pay $10 for information that only provides $1 in benefits? This appendix is therefore a low-cost way of providing you with more information about an economics major.

We start by dispelling some of the misinformation about an economics major. Stated bluntly, some perceptions about an economics major and about a career in economics are just not true. For example, some people think that economics majors almost never study social relationships, but rather only such things as inflation, interest rates, and unemployment. Not true. Economics majors study some of the same things that sociologists, historians, psychologists, and political scientists study.

In addition to myth busting, the appendix also provides you with information about economics as a major: what courses you study, how many courses you are likely to have to take, and more.

Finally, we tell you something about a career in economics. If you have opted to become an economics major, the day will come when you have your degree in hand. What's next? What is your starting salary likely to be? What will you be doing? Are you going to be happy doing what economists do? (If you never thought economics was about happiness, you already have some misinformation about the field. Contrary to what most laypeople think, economics is not just about money. It is about happiness too.)

# FIVE MYTHS ABOUT ECONOMICS AND BEING AN ECONOMICS MAJOR

**Myth 1: Economics Is All Mathematics and Statistics.** Some students choose not to major in economics because they think economics is all mathematics and statistics. Math and statistics are used in economics, but certainly not overwhelmingly at the undergraduate degree level. Economics majors are usually required to take one statistics course and one math course (usually an introductory calculus course). Even students who say, "Math isn't my subject" are sometimes happy with the amount of math they need in economics. The fact is that at the undergraduate level at many colleges and universities, economics is not a very math-intensive course of study. Economics uses many diagrams, but not a large amount of math.

A proviso: The amount of math in the economics curriculum varies across colleges and universities. Some economics departments do not require their students to learn much math or statistics; others do. The majority of economics departments do not require much math or statistics at the undergraduate level. The graduate level is a different story.

If you are thinking of pursuing economics at the graduate level, you should enroll in numerous mathematics and statistics courses as an undergraduate.

**Myth 2: Economics Is Only About Inflation, Interest Rates, Unemployment, and Other Such Things.** If you study economics at college and then go on to become a practicing economist, no doubt people will ask you certain questions when they learn your chosen profession. Here are some:

- Do you think the economy is going to pick up?
- Do you think the economy is going to slow down?
- What stocks would you recommend?
- Do you think interest rates are going to fall?
- Do you think interest rates are going to rise?
- What do you think about buying bonds right now? Is it a good idea?

People ask these kinds of questions because most believe that economists study only stocks, bonds, interest rates, inflation, unemployment, and so on. Although economists do study these topics, they are only a tiny part of what economists study. It is not hard to find many economists today, both inside and outside academia, who spend most of their time studying anything but inflation, unemployment, stocks, bonds, and the like.

In fact, much of what economists study may surprise you. Some economists use their economic tools and methods to study crime, marriage, divorce, sex, obesity, addiction, sports, voting behavior, bureaucracies, presidential elections, and much more. In short, today's economics is not your grandfather's economics. Many more topics are studied today in economics than were studied in years past.

**Myth 3: People Become Economists Only If They Want to "Make Money."** Awhile back we asked a few well-respected and well-known economists what got them interested in economics. Here is what some of them had to say:[1]

---

1. See various interviews in Roger A. Arnold, *Economics*, 2nd ed. (St. Paul, MN: West Publishing Company, 1992).

Gary Becker, the 1992 winner of the Nobel Prize in Economics, said:

*I got interested in economics when I was an undergraduate in college. I came into college with a strong interest in mathematics, and at the same time with a strong commitment to do something to help society. I learned in the first economics course I took that economics could deal rigorously, àla mathematics, with social problems. That stimulated me because in economics I saw that I could combine both the mathematics and my desire to do something to help society.*

Vernon Smith, the 2002 winner of the Nobel Prize in Economics, said:

*My father's influence started me in science and engineering at Cal Tech, but my mother, who was active in socialist politics, probably accounts for the great interest I found in economics when I took my first introductory course.*

Alice Rivlin, an economist and former member of the Federal Reserve Board, said:

*My interest in economics grew out of concern for improving public policy, both domestic and international. I was a teenager in the tremendously idealistic period after World War II when it seemed terribly important to get nations working together to solve the world's problems peacefully.*

Allan Meltzer said:

*Economics is a social science. At its best it is concerned with ways (1) to improve well-being by allowing individuals the freedom to achieve their personal aims or goals and (2) to harmonize their individual interests. I find working on such issues challenging, and progress is personally rewarding.*

Robert Solow, the 1987 winner of the Nobel Prize in Economics, said:

*I grew up in the 1930s and it was very hard not to be interested in economics. If you were a high school student in the 1930s, you were conscious of the fact that our economy was in deep trouble and no one knew what to do about it.*

Charles Plosser said:

*I was an engineer as an undergraduate with little knowledge of economics. I went to the University of Chicago Graduate School of Business to get an MBA and there became fascinated with economics. I was impressed with the seriousness with which economics was viewed as a way of organizing one's thoughts about the world to address interesting questions and problems.*

Walter Williams said:

*I was a major in sociology in 1963 and I concluded that it was not very rigorous. Over the summer I was reading a book by W.E.B. DuBois,* Black Reconstruction, *and somewhere in the book it said something along the lines that blacks could not melt into the mainstream of American society until they understood economics, and that was something that got me interested in economics.*

Murray Weidenbaum said:

*A specific professor got me interested in economics. He was very prescient: He correctly noted that while lawyers dominated the policy-making process up until the 1940s, in the future economics would be an important tool for developing public policy. And he was right.*

Irma Adelman said:

*"I hesitate to say because it sounds arrogant. My reason [for getting into economics] was that I wanted to benefit humanity. And my perception at the time was that economic problems were the most important problems that humanity has to face. That is what got me into economics and into economic development.*

Lester Thurow said:

*[I got interested in economics because of] the belief, some would see it as naïve belief, that economics was a profession where it would be possible to help make the world better.*

## The PPF and Your Grades

You have your own PPF; you just may not know it. Suppose you are studying for two upcoming exams. You have only a total of six hours before you have to take the first exam, after which you will immediately proceed to take the second exam. Time spent studying for the first exam (in economics) takes away from time that could be spent studying for the second exam (in math), and vice versa. Also, *time studying* is a resource in the production of a good grade: Less time studying for the economics exam and more time spent studying for the math exam means a higher grade in math and a lower grade in economics. For you, the situation may look as it does in Exhibit 7(a). We have identified four points in the exhibit (1–4) corresponding to the four combinations of two grades (one grade in economics and one grade in English).

Also notice that each grade comes with a certain amount of time studying. This time is specified under the grade.

Given the resources you currently have (your labor and time), you can achieve any of the four combinations. For example, you can spend six hours studying for economics and get a *B* (point 1), but this means you study math for zero hours and get an F in that course. Or you can spend four hours studying for economics and get a *C* (point 2), leaving you two hours to study for math, in which you get a *D*.

What do you need to get a higher grade in one course without getting a lower grade in the other course? You need more resources, which in this case is more time. If you have eight hours to study, your PPF shifts rightward, as in Exhibit 7(b). Now point 5 is possible (whereas it was not possible before you got more time). At point 5, you can get a *C* in economics and in math, which was an impossible combination of grades when you had less time (a PPF closer to the origin).

**EXHIBIT 7**

(a)

(b)

# SPECIALIZATION AND TRADE CAN MOVE US BEYOND OUR PPF

In this section we explain how a country that specializes in the production of certain goods, and then trades those goods to countries for other goods, can make itself better off. In terms of its PPF, it can consume at a level *beyond* its PPF.

## A Simple Two-Person PPF Model

Two individuals, Elizabeth and Brian, live near each other, and each engages in two activities: baking bread and growing apples. Let's suppose that within a certain period of time, Elizabeth can produce 20 loaves of bread and no apples, or 10 loaves of bread and 10 apples, or no bread and 20 apples. See Exhibit 8. In other words, three points on Elizabeth's production possibilities frontier correspond to 20 loaves of bread and no apples, 10 loaves of bread and 10 apples, and no bread and 20 apples. As a consumer, Elizabeth likes to eat both bread and apples; so she decides to produce (and consume) 10 loaves of bread and 10 apples. This is represented by point *B* in Exhibit 8(a).

In the same time period, Brian can produce 10 loaves of bread and no apples, or 5 loaves of bread and 15 apples, or no bread and 30 apples. In other words, these three combinations correspond to three points on Brian's production possibilities frontier. Brian, like Elizabeth, likes to eat both bread and apples; so he decides to produce and consume 5 loaves of bread and 15 apples. This is represented by point *F* in Exhibit 8(b).

---

**EXHIBIT 8**

---

**Elizabeth's PPF, Brian's PPF**

In (a) we show the combination of the two goods that Elizabeth can produce, first in terms of a table and next in terms of a PPF. Because Elizabeth wants to consume some of both goods, she chooses to produce the combination of the two goods represented by point B.

In (b) we show the combination of the two goods that Brian can produce, first in terms of a table and next in terms of a PPF. Because Brian wants to consume some of both goods, he chooses to produce the combination of the two goods represented by point F.

| Elizabeth | |
|---|---|
| **Bread** | **Apples** |
| 20 | 0 |
| 10 | 10 |
| 0 | 20 |

| Brian | |
|---|---|
| **Bread** | **Apples** |
| 10 | 0 |
| 5 | 15 |
| 0 | 30 |

Elizabeth produces and consumes this combination of bread and apples.

Brian produces and consumes this combination of bread and apples.

(a)    (b)

Elizabeth thinks that both she and Brian may be better off if each specializes in producing only one of the two goods and trading it for the other. In other words, Elizabeth should produce either bread or apples but not both. Brian thinks this may be a good idea but is not sure which good each person should specialize in producing.

An economist would advise each to produce the good that he or she can produce at a lower cost. In economics, a person who can produce a good at a lower cost than another person is said to have a *comparative advantage* in the production of the good.

Exhibit 8 shows that for every 10 units of bread Elizabeth does not produce, she can produce 10 apples. In other words, the opportunity cost of producing 1 loaf of bread *(B)* is 1 apple *(A)*:

**Comparative Advantage**
The situation where someone can produce a good at lower opportunity cost than someone else can.

Opportunity costs for Elizabeth: $1B = 1A$

$$1A = 1B$$

For every 5 loaves of bread that Brian does not produce, he can produce 15 apples. So, for every 1 loaf of bread he does not produce, he can produce 3 apples. Therefore, for every 1 apple he chooses to produce, he forfeits 1/3 loaf of bread.

Opportunity costs for Brian: $1B = 3A$

$$1A = 1/3B$$

Comparing opportunity costs, we see that Elizabeth can produce bread at a lower opportunity cost than Brian can. (Elizabeth forfeits 1 apple when she produces 1 loaf of bread, whereas Brian forfeits 3 apples for 1 loaf of bread.) On the other hand, Brian can produce apples at a lower opportunity cost than Elizabeth can. We conclude that Elizabeth has a comparative advantage in the production of bread, and Brian has a comparative advantage in the production of apples.

Suppose both specialize in the production of the good in which they have a comparative advantage. Elizabeth produces only bread and makes 20 loaves. Brian produces only apples and grows 30 of them.

Now suppose that Elizabeth and Brian decide to trade 8 loaves of bread for 12 apples. In other words, Elizabeth produces 20 loaves of bread and then trades 8 of them for

**EXHIBIT 9**

**Consumption for Elizabeth and Brian With and Without Specialization and Trade**

A comparison of the consumption of bread and apples before and after specialization and trade shows that both Elizabeth and Brian benefit from producing the good in which each has a comparative advantage and trading for the other good.

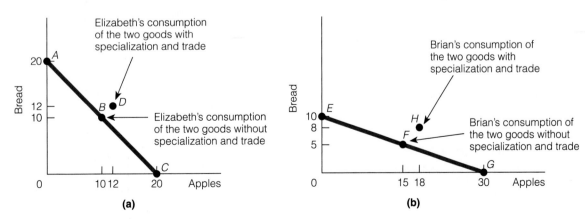

(a)                                        (b)

# economics 24/7

## Political Debates Explained in Terms of the PPF

Strictly speaking, the PPF is simply a curve that represents the combination of two goods that a country can produce under certain conditions (a given amount of resources and a certain technology). But the PPF is not only a curve; it is a framework of analysis. With it, we can often gain insights into what is happening in the real world. Specifically, the PPF, used as a framework of analysis, can give us some idea what is behind political battles.

AP Photo/Al Goldis, file

In Exhibit 10 we show the PPF for a country. We assume that the country is currently located at point A, producing 30 units of good X and 35 units of good Y. Notice also that the country is efficient in its production: It is located at a point *on* its PPF instead of below it.

Now let's suppose that there are two major political parties in this country: the X and Y parties. Party X represents people who would like to move the country in the direction of producing more X. Party X would prefer the country locate at point *B* instead of at point *A* on the PPF.

Party Y, on the other hand, represents people who would like to move the country in the direction of producing more Y. Party Y would prefer the country located at point *C* on the PPF instead of at point *A*.

Will political parties X and Y do battle? Will they be involved in a political tug-of-war, each trying to move the country in a different direction? Probably so.

Now consider what happens when the country falls below its PPF and moves to a point like *D* in the exhibit. Point *D* is representative of a country that has unemployed resources; it is likely to be a representative of an economy in a recession, producing far less than it could be producing. At point *D*, both parties are less content than they were

at point A for the simple reason that less of both goods is being produced at point D than at A. One thing we ought to observe, then, is that both political parties will want to move the country out of the recession. But might the ways they propose to move the country be different? Since political party Y prefers point C to point A, and political party X prefers point B to point A, might each party's proposal for "solving the recession" be geared toward its preferred point on the country's PPF? To illustrate, if each political party is proposing federal monies or tax cuts to stimulate output production, might political party X's specific proposal be geared toward producing more of good X while political party Y's specific proposal is geared toward producing more of good Y?

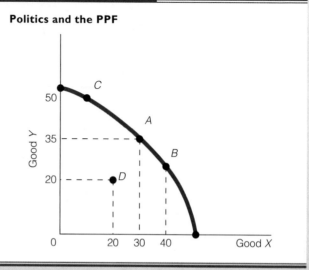

### EXHIBIT 10

**Politics and the PPF**

12 apples. After the trade, Elizabeth consumes 12 loaves of bread and 12 apples. Compare this situation with what she consumed when she didn't specialize and didn't trade. In that situation, she consumed 10 loaves of bread and 10 apples. Clearly, Elizabeth is better off when she specializes and trades than when she does not.

But what about Brian? He produces 30 apples and trades 12 of them to Elizabeth for 8 loaves of bread. In other words, he consumes 8 loaves of bread and 18 apples. Compare this situation with what he consumed when he didn't specialize and didn't trade. In that situation, he consumed 5 loaves of bread and 15 apples. Thus, Brian is also better off when he specializes and trades than when he does not.

## On or Beyond the PPF?

In Exhibit 9(a) we show the PPF for Elizabeth. When she was not specializing and not trading, she consumed the combination of bread and apples represented by point *B* (10 loaves of bread and 10 apples). When she did specialize and trade, her consumption of both goods increased, moving her to point *D* (12 loaves of bread and 12 apples). Lesson learned: Through specialization and trade, Elizabeth's consumption moved beyond her PPF. It is easy to see the benefits of specialization of trade.

In Exhibit 9(b) we show the PPF for Brian. When he was not specializing and not trading, he consumed the combination of bread and apples represented by point *F* (5 loaves of bread and 15 apples). When he did specialize and trade, his consumption of both goods increased, moving him to point *H* (8 loaves of bread and 18 apples). Lesson learned: Through specialization and trade, Brian's consumption moved beyond his PPF.

What holds for Elizabeth and Brian through specialization and trade holds for countries too. For example, if both Americans and Brazilians specialize in producing those goods for which they have a comparative advantage and then trade some of those goods for the others' goods, both Americans and Brazilians can consume more of both goods than if they don't specialize and don't trade.

## 🄵inding ECONOMICS

**At the Airport** You wake up in the morning and drive to the airport. You have your bags checked curbside at the airport. You tip the person who checks your luggage. You then line up to go through security. Once on the plane you hear the pilot telling you the flying time for today's flight. Later in the flight, the flight attendant brings you a soft drink and a snack. What you see at the airport and on board the plane is different people performing different tasks. The pilot is flying the plane and the customer service person at the check-in counter is receiving your luggage, and so on. Can you find the economics? Think about it for a minute before you read on.

What you see at the airport and on board the plane is specialization. The pilot isn't flying the plane and checking your luggage too. He is only flying the plane. The flight attendant isn't serving you food and checking you through security too. He is only serving you food. Why do people specialize? Largely, it's because individuals have found that they are better off specializing than not specializing. And usually what people specialize in is that activity in which they have a comparative advantage. ▲ ▲ ▲

# OFFICE HOURS

## "What Purpose Does the PPF Serve?"

**STUDENT:**

Economists seem to have many uses for the production possibilities frontier (PPF). For example, they can talk about scarcity, choice, opportunity costs, and many other topics in terms of the PPF. Beyond this, what purpose does the PPF serve?

**INSTRUCTOR:**

One purpose is to ground us in reality. For example, the frontier (or boundary) of the PPF represents scarcity, which is a fact of life. In other words, the frontier of the PPF is essentially saying, "Here is scarcity. Work with it." One of the important effects of acknowledging this fact is that we come to understand what *is* and what *is not* possible. For example, if the economy is currently on the frontier of its PPF, producing 100 units of X and 200 units of Y, then getting more of X is possible, but not without getting less of Y. In other words, the frontier of the PPF grounds us in reality: More of one thing means less of something else.

**STUDENT:**

But isn't this something we already knew?

**INSTRUCTOR:**

We understand that more of X means less of Y once someone makes this point, but think of how often we might act as if we don't know it. John thinks he can work more hours at his job and get a good grade on his upcoming chemistry test. Well, he might be able to get a good grade (say, a 90), but this ignores how much higher the grade could have been (say, five points higher) if he hadn't worked more hours at his job. The frontier of the PPF reminds us that there are trade-offs in life. That is an important reality to be aware of. We ignore it at our own peril.

**STUDENT:**

I've also heard that the PPF can show us what is necessary before the so-called average person in a country can become richer? Is this true? And how much richer do we mean here?

**INSTRUCTOR:**

We are talking about becoming richer in terms of having more goods and services. It's possible for the average person to become richer through economic growth. In other words, the average person in society becomes richer if the PPF shifts rightward by more than the population grows. To illustrate, suppose that a 100-person economy

---

## CHAPTER SUMMARY

### AN ECONOMY'S PRODUCTION POSSIBILITIES FRONTIER

- An economy's production possibilities frontier (PPF) represents the possible combinations of two goods that the economy can produce in a certain period of time under the conditions of a given state of technology and fully employed resources.

### INCREASING AND CONSTANT OPPORTUNITY COSTS

- A straight-line PPF represents constant opportunity costs: Increased production of one good comes at a constant opportunity cost.

- A bowed-outward (concave-downward) PPF represents the law of increasing opportunity costs: Increased production of one good comes at an increasing opportunity cost.

### THE PRODUCTION POSSIBILITIES FRONTIER AND VARIOUS ECONOMIC CONCEPTS

- The PPF can be used to illustrate various economic concepts. Scarcity is illustrated by the frontier itself. Choice is illustrated by the fact that we have to find a point either on or below the frontier. In short, of the many attainable positions, one must be chosen. Opportunity cost is illustrated by a movement from one point to another on the PPF. Unemployed resources and productive inefficiency are illustrated by a point below the PPF. Productive efficiency and fully employed resources are is currently producing 100 units of X and 200 units of Y. The average person can then have 1 unit of X and 2 units of Y. Now suppose there is economic growth (shifting the PPF to the right), and the economy can now produce more of both goods, X and Y. It produces 200 units of X and 400 units of Y. If the population has not changed (if it is still 100 people), then the average person can now have 2 units of X and 4 units of Y. The average person is richer in terms of both goods. If we change things, and let the population grow from 100 persons to, say, 125 persons, it is still possible for the average person to have more through economic growth. With a population of 125 people, the average person now has 1.6 units of X and 3.2 units of good Y. In other words, as long as the productive capability of the economy grows by a greater percentage than the population, the average person can become richer (in terms of goods and services).

> ### STUDENT:
>
> Even if the economy is producing more of both goods (X and Y), the average person isn't necessarily better off in terms of goods and services, right? Can't all the extra output end up in the hands of only a few people instead of being evenly distributed across the entire population.

> ### INSTRUCTOR:
>
> That's correct. What we are assuming when we say that the average person can be better off is that if we took the extra output and divided it evenly across the population, then the average person would be better off in terms of having more goods and services. By the way, this is what economists mean when they say that the output (goods and services) per capita in a population has risen.

### POINTS TO REMEMBER

1. The production possibilities frontier (PPF) grounds us in reality. It tells us what *is* and what *is not* possible in terms of producing various combinations of goods and services.
2. The PPF tells us that when we have efficiency (we are at a point on the frontier itself), more of one thing means less of something else. In other words, the PPF tells us life has its trade-offs.
3. If the PPF shifts rightward and the population does not change, then output per capita rises.

illustrated by a point on the PPF. Economic growth is illustrated by a shift outward in the PPF.

## SPECIALIZATION, TRADE, AND THE PPF

- Individuals can make themselves better off by specializing in the production of the good in which they have a comparative advantage and then trading some of that good for other goods.

Someone who can produce the good at a lower opportunity cost than another person can has a comparative advantage in the production of the good.

- By specializing in the production of the good for which they have a comparative advantage and then trading it for other goods, people can move beyond their production possibilities frontier.

## KEY TERMS AND CONCEPTS

Production Possibilities
   Frontier (PPF)

Law of Increasing
   Opportunity Costs

Productive Efficiency
Productive Inefficiency

Technology
Comparative Advantage

## QUESTIONS AND PROBLEMS

1. Describe how each of the following would affect the U.S. production possibilities frontier: (a) an increase in the number of illegal immigrants entering the country, (b) a war that takes place on U.S. soil, (c) the discovery of a new oil field, (d) a decrease in the unemployment rate, and (e) a law that requires individuals to enter lines of work for which they are not suited.

2. Explain how the following can be represented in a PPF framework: (a) the finiteness of resources implicit in the scarcity condition, (b) choice, (c) opportunity cost, (d) productive efficiency, and (e) unemployed resources.

3. What condition must hold for the production possibilities frontier to be bowed outward (concave downward)? To be a straight line?

4. Give an example to illustrate each of the following: (a) constant opportunity costs and (b) increasing opportunity costs.

5. Why are most production possibilities frontiers for goods bowed outward (concave downward)?

6 Within a PPF framework, explain each of the following: (a) a disagreement between a person who favors more domestic welfare spending and one who favors more national defense spending, (b) an increase in the population, and (c) a technological change that makes resources less specialized.

7. Explain how to derive a production possibilities frontier. For instance, how is the extreme point on the vertical axis identified? How is the extreme point on the horizontal axis identified?

8. If the slope of the production possibilities frontier is the same between any two points, what does this imply about costs? Explain your answer.

9. Suppose a nation's PPF shifts inward as its population grows. What happens, on average, to the material standard of living of the people? Explain your answer.

10. Can a technological advancement in sector X of the economy affect the number of people who work in sector Y of the economy? Explain your answer.

11. Use the PPF framework to explain something in your everyday life that was not mentioned in the chapter.

12. What exactly allows individuals to consume more if they specialize and trade than if they don't?

## WORKING WITH NUMBERS AND GRAPHS

1. Illustrate constant opportunity costs in a table similar to the one in Exhibit 1(a). Next, draw a PPF based on the data in the table.

2. Illustrate increasing opportunity costs (for one good) in a table similar to the one in Exhibit 2(a). Next, draw a PPF based on the data in the table.

3. Draw a PPF that represents the production possibilities for goods X and Y if there are constant opportunity costs. Next, represent an advance in technology that makes it possible to produce more of X, but not more of Y. Finally, represent an advance in technology that makes it possible to produce more of Y, but not more of X.

4. In the following figure, which graph depicts a technological breakthrough in the production of good X only?

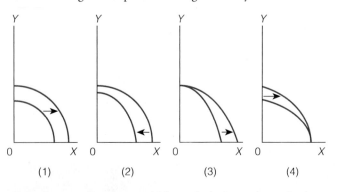

5. In the preceding figure, which graph depicts a change in the PPF that is a likely consequence of war?

6. If $PPF_2$ in the following graph is the relevant production possibilities frontier, then which points are unattainable? Explain your answer.

7. If $PPF_1$ in the preceding figure is the relevant production possibilities frontier, then which point(s) represent productive efficiency? Explain your answer.

8. Tina can produce any of the following combinations of goods X and Y: (a) 100 X and 0 Y, (b) 50 X and 25 Y, (c) 0 X and 50 Y. David can produce any of the following combinations of X and Y: (a) 50 X and 0 Y, (b) 25 X and 40 Y, and (c) 0 X and 80 Y. Who has the comparative advantage in the production of good X ? Of good Y ? Explain your answer.

9. Using the data in problem 8, prove that both Tina and David can be made better off through specialization and trade.

## CHAPTER 3

# SUPPLY AND DEMAND: THEORY

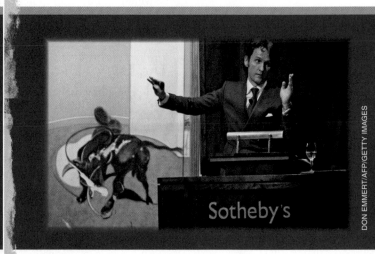

DON EMMERT/AFP/GETTY IMAGES

**Introduction** Psychologists sometimes use a technique called "word association" to learn more about their patients. The psychologist says a word, then the patient says the first word that comes into his or her head: morning, night; boy, girl; sunrise, sunset. If a psychologist ever happened to say "supply" to an economist, the response would undoubtedly be "demand." To economists, supply and demand go together. (Thomas Carlyle, the historian and philosopher, said that "it is easy to train economists. Just teach a parrot to say Supply and Demand."

Not funny, Carlyle.) Supply and demand have been called the "bread and butter" of economics. In this chapter, we discuss them, first separately and then together.

A **market** is any place people come together to trade. Economists often say that every market has *two* sides: a buying side and a selling side. The buying side of the market is usually referred to as the *demand* side; the selling side is usually referred to as the *supply* side. Let's begin with a discussion of *demand*.

## WHAT IS DEMAND?

The word demand has a precise meaning in economics. It refers to:

1. the willingness and ability of buyers to purchase different quantities of a good
2. at different prices
3. during a specific time period (per day, week, etc.).[1]

For example, we can express part of John's demand for magazines by saying that he is willing and able to buy 10 magazines a month at $4 per magazine and that he is willing and able to buy 15 magazines a month at $3 per magazine.

**Market**
Any place people come together to trade.

**Demand**
The willingness and ability of buyers to purchase different quantities of a good at different prices during a specific time period.

---

1. Demand takes into account *services* as well as goods. A few examples of goods are shirts, books, and television sets. A few examples of services are dental care, medical care, and an economics lecture. To simplify the discussion, we refer only to goods.

Remember this important point about demand: Unless both willingness and ability to buy are present, there is no demand, and a person is not a buyer. For example, Josie may be willing to buy a computer but be unable to pay the price; Tanya may be able to buy a computer but be unwilling to do so. Neither Josie nor Tanya demands a computer, and neither is a buyer of a computer.

## The Law of Demand

**Law of Demand**
As the price of a good rises, the quantity demanded of the good falls, and as the price of a good falls, the quantity demanded of the good rises, *ceteris paribus*.

Will people buy more units of a good at lower prices than at higher prices? For example, will people buy more shirts at $10 apiece than at $70 apiece? If your answer is yes, you instinctively understand the law of demand. The law of demand states that as the price of a good rises, the quantity demanded of the good falls and that as the price of a good falls, the quantity demanded of the good rises, *ceteris paribus*. Simply put, the law of demand states that the price of a good and the quantity demanded of it are inversely related, *ceteris paribus*:

$$P \uparrow Q_d \downarrow$$

$$P \downarrow Q_d \uparrow \text{ ceteris paribus}$$

where $P$ = price and $Q_d$ = quantity demanded.

*Quantity demanded* is the number of units of a good that individuals are willing and able to buy at a particular price during a time period. For example, suppose individuals are willing and able to buy 100 TV dinners per week at a price of $4 per dinner. Therefore, 100 units is the quantity demanded of TV dinners at $4.

A warning: We know that the words "demand" and "quantity demanded" sound alike, but keep in mind that they do not describe the same thing. Demand is different from quantity demanded. Keep that in mind as you continue to read this chapter. For now, remind yourself that demand speaks to the willingness and ability of buyers to buy different quantities of a good at different prices. Quantity demanded speaks to the willingness and ability of buyers to buy a specific quantity (say, 100 units of a good) at a specific price (say, $10 per unit).

## Four Ways to Represent the Law of Demand

Here are four ways to represent the law of demand.

- *In Words.* We can represent the law of demand in words; we have done so already. Earlier we said that as the price of a good rises, quantity demanded falls, and as price falls, quantity demanded rises, *ceteris paribus*. That was the statement (in words) of the law of demand.

- *In Symbols.* We can also represent the law of demand in symbols, which we have also already done. In symbols, the law of demand is:

$$P \uparrow Q_d \downarrow$$

$$P \downarrow Q_d \uparrow \text{ ceteris paribus}$$

**Demand Schedule**
The numerical tabulation of the quantity demanded of a good at different prices. A demand schedule is the numerical representation of the law of demand.

**Demand Curve**
The graphical representation of the law of demand.

- *In a Demand Schedule.* A demand schedule is the numerical representation of the law of demand. A demand schedule for good X is illustrated in Exhibit 1(a).

- *As a Demand Curve.* In Exhibit 1(b), the four price–quantity combinations in part (a) are plotted and the points connected, giving us a (downward-sloping) demand curve. A (downward-sloping) demand curve is the graphical representation of the inverse relationship between price and quantity demanded specified by the law of demand. In short, a demand curve is a picture of the law of demand.

**EXHIBIT 1**

**Demand Schedule and Demand Curve**

Part (a) shows a demand schedule for good X. Part (b) shows a demand curve, obtained by plotting the different price-quantity combinations in part (a) and connecting the points. On a demand curve, the price (in dollars) represents price per unit of the good. The quantity demanded, on the horizontal axis, is always relevant for a specific time period (a week, a month, and so on).

**Demand Schedule for Good X**

| Price (dollars) | Quantity Demanded | Point in Part (b) |
| --- | --- | --- |
| 4 | 10 | A |
| 3 | 20 | B |
| 2 | 30 | C |
| 1 | 40 | D |

**(a)**

**(b)**

# ⓕinding ECONOMICS

**In a Visit Home to See Mom** A friend tells you that she flies home to see her mother only once a year. You ask why. She says, "Because the price of the ticket to fly home is $1,100." She then adds, "If the price were, say, $600 instead of $1,100, I'd fly home twice a year instead of once." Can you find any economics in what she is telling you? If you listen closely to what she says, she has identified two points about her demand curve for air travel home: One point corresponds to $1,100 and buying one ticket (home), and the other point corresponds to $600 and buying two tickets home. ▲ ▲ ▲

## Why Does Quantity Demanded Go Down as Price Goes Up?

The law of demand states that price and quantity demanded are inversely related. This much you know. But do you know *why* quantity demanded moves in the opposite direction of price? We identify two reasons:

The first reason is that *people substitute lower priced goods for higher priced goods.* Often, many goods serve the same purpose. Many different goods will satisfy hunger, and many different drinks will satisfy thirst. For example, both orange juice and grapefruit juice will satisfy thirst. On Monday, the price of orange juice equals the price of grapefruit juice, but on Tuesday the price of orange juice rises. As a result, people will choose to buy less of the relatively higher priced orange juice and more of the relatively lower priced grapefruit juice. In other words, a rise in the price of orange juice will lead to a decrease in the quantity demanded of it.

The second reason for the inverse relationship between price and quantity demanded has to do with the law of diminishing marginal utility, which states that for a given time period, the marginal (or additional) utility or satisfaction gained by consuming equal successive units of a good will decline as the amount consumed increases. For example, you may receive more utility, or satisfaction, from eating your first hamburger at lunch than from eating your second and, if you continue, more utility from your second hamburger than from your third.

What does this have to do with the law of demand? Economists state that the more utility you receive from a unit of a good, the higher the price you are willing to pay for it; the less utility you receive from a unit of a good, the lower the price you are willing to pay for it. According to the law of diminishing marginal utility, individuals obtain less utility from additional units of a good. Therefore, they will buy larger quantities of a good only at lower prices, and this is the law of demand.

**Law of Diminishing Marginal Utility**

For a given time period, the marginal (or additional) utility or satisfaction gained by consuming equal successive units of a good will decline as the amount consumed increases.

## Disney World Ticket Prices

The Walt Disney Company operates two major theme parks in the United States: Disneyland in California and Disney World in Florida. Every year, millions of people visit each site. The ticket price for visiting Disneyland or Disney World differs depending on how many days a person visits the theme park. For example, Disney World sells one- to ten-day tickets. Here are the ticket prices for each of 5 days:

| Ticket | Price |
| --- | --- |
| 1-day | $ 79 |
| 2-day | $156 |
| 3-day | $219 |
| 4-day | $225 |
| 5-day | $228 |

GINO SANTA MARIA / DREAMSTIME.COM

Now if we take the price of a one-day ticket and multiply it by 2, we get $158, but oddly enough, the price of a two-day ticket is not $158 but $156. Of course, if we take the price of a one-day ticket and multiply it by 5, we get $395, but Disney World doesn't charge $395 for a five-day ticket;, it charges $228, which is $167 less than $395.

Disney World is effectively telling visitors that if they want to visit the theme park for one day, they have to pay $79. But if they want to visit the theme park for additional days, they don't have to pay $79 for each additional day. They pay less for additional days. But why? Why does Disney World charge less than double the price of a one-day ticket for a two-day ticket, and why does it charge less than 5 times the price of a one-day ticket for a five-day ticket?

An economic concept, the law of diminishing marginal utility, is the reason. The law of diminishing marginal utility states that as a person consumes additional units of a good, eventually the utility from each additional unit of the good decreases. Assuming that the law of

diminishing marginal utility holds for Disney World, individuals will get more utility from the first day at Disney World than from, say, the second, third, or fifth day. The less utility or satisfaction people get from something, the lower the dollar amount they are willing to pay for it. Thus, people would not be willing to pay as much for the second day at Disney World as for the first, and they would not be willing to pay as much for the fifth as for the fourth and so on. Disney World knows this and therefore prices its ticket prices differently depending on how many days one wants to visit Disney World.

## Individual Demand Curve and Market Demand Curve

There is a difference between an individual demand curve and a market demand curve.

An individual demand curve represents the price–quantity combinations of a particular good for a *single buyer.* For example, an individual demand curve could show Jones's demand for CDs. A market demand curve represents the price–quantity combinations of a good for *all buyers.* In this case, the demand curve would show all buyers' demand for CDs.

A market demand curve is derived by "adding up" individual demand curves, as shown in Exhibit 2. The demand schedules for Jones, Smith, and other buyers are shown in part (a). The market demand schedule is obtained by adding the quantities demanded at each price.

For example, at $12, the quantities demanded are 4 units for Jones, 5 units for Smith, and 100 units for other buyers. Thus, a total of 109 units are demanded at $12. In part (b), the data points for the demand schedules are plotted and added to produce a market demand curve. The market demand curve could also be drawn directly from the market demand schedule.

## A Change in Quantity Demanded Versus a Change in Demand

Economists often talk about (1) a change in quantity demanded and (2) a change in demand. As stated earlier, although the phrase "quantity demanded" may sound like "demand," the two are not the same. In short, a change in quantity demanded *is not* the same as a change in demand. (Read the last sentence at least two more times.) We use Exhibit 1 to illustrate the difference between a change in quantity demanded and a change in demand.

**A CHANGE IN QUANTITY DEMANDED** Look at the horizontal axis in Exhibit 1, which is labeled "Quantity Demanded of Good X." Notice that quantity demanded is a *number*—such as 10, 20, 30, 40, and so on. More specifically, it is the number of units of a good that individuals are willing and able to buy at a particular price during some time period. In Exhibit 1, if the price is $4, then quantity demanded is 10 units of good X; if the price is $3, then quantity demanded is 20 units of good X.

Quantity demanded = The *number* of units of a good that individuals are
willing and able to buy at a particular price

---

**EXHIBIT 2**

**Deriving a Market Demand Schedule and a Market Demand Curve**

Part (a) shows four demand schedules combined into one table. The market demand schedule is derived by adding the quantities demanded at each price. In (b), the data points from the demand schedule are plotted to show how a market demand curve is derived. Only two points on the market demand curve are noted.

|  | **Quantity Demanded** | | | |
|---|---|---|---|---|
| **Price** | **Jones** | **Smith** | **Other Buyers** | **All Buyers** |
| $15 | 1 | 2 | 20 | 23 |
| 14 | 2 | 3 | 45 | 50 |
| 13 | 3 | 4 | 70 | 77 |
| 12 | 4 + | 5 + | 100 = | 109 |
| 11 | 5 + | 6 + | 130 = | 141 |
| 10 | 6 | 7 | 160 | 173 |

**(a)**

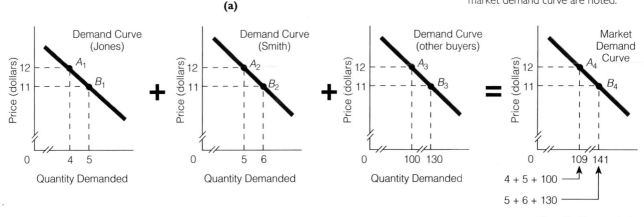

**(b)**

**Own Price**
The price of a good. For example, if the price of oranges is $1, this is its own price.

Now, again looking at Exhibit 1, what can change quantity demanded from 10 (which it is at point *A*) to 20 (which it is at point *B*)? Or what has to change before quantity demanded will change? The answer is on the vertical axis of Exhibit 1. The only thing that can change the quantity demanded of a good is its price, which is called own price.

Change in quantity demanded = A *movement* from one point to another point on the same demand curve *caused* by a change in the price of the good

**A CHANGE IN DEMAND** Look again at Exhibit 1, this time focusing on the demand curve. Demand is represented by the *entire* curve. When talking about a change in demand, an economist is actually talking about a change—or shift—in the entire demand curve.

Change in demand = Shift in demand curve

Demand can change in two ways: Demand can increase, and demand can decrease. Let's look first at an *increase* in demand. Suppose we have the following demand schedule:

| Demand Schedule A | |
| --- | --- |
| Price | Quantity Demanded |
| $20 | 500 |
| $15 | 600 |
| $10 | 700 |
| $ 5 | 800 |

The demand curve for this demand schedule will look like the demand curve labeled $D_A$ in Exhibit 3(a).

---

**EXHIBIT 3**

**Shifts in the Demand Curve**

In part (a), the demand curve shifts rightward from $D_A$ to $D_B$. This shift represents an increase in demand. At each price, the quantity demanded is greater than it was before. For example, the quantity demanded at $20 increases from 500 units to 600 units. In part (b), the demand curve shifts leftward from $D_A$ to $D_C$. This shift represents a decrease in demand. At each price, the quantity demanded is less. For example, the quantity demand at $20 decreases from 500 units to 400 units.

(a)

(b)

What does an increase in demand mean? It means that individuals are willing and able to buy more units of the good at each and every price. In other words, demand schedule $A$ will change as follows:

**Demand Schedule B (increase in demand)**

| Price | Quantity Demanded |
|-------|-------------------|
| $20 | ~~500~~ 600 |
| $15 | ~~600~~ 700 |
| $10 | ~~700~~ 800 |
| $ 5 | ~~800~~ 900 |

Whereas individuals were willing and able to buy 500 units of the good at $20, now they are willing and able to buy 600 units of the good at $20; whereas individuals were willing and able to buy 600 units of the good at $15, now they are willing and able to buy 700 units of the good at $15; and so on.

As shown in Exhibit 3(a), the demand curve that represents demand schedule $B$ $(D_B)$ lies to the right of the demand curve that represents demand schedule $A$ $(D_A)$. We conclude that *an increase in demand is represented by a rightward shift in the demand curve and means that individuals are willing and able to buy more of a good at each and every price.*

Increase in demand = Rightward shift in the demand curve

Now let's look at a decrease in demand. A decrease in demand means that individuals are willing and able to buy less of a good at each and every price. In this case, demand schedule $A$ will change as follows:

**Demand Schedule C (decrease in demand)**

| Price | Quantity Demanded |
|-------|-------------------|
| $20 | ~~500~~ 400 |
| $15 | ~~600~~ 500 |
| $10 | ~~700~~ 600 |
| $ 5 | ~~800~~ 700 |

As shown in Exhibit 3(b), the demand curve that represents demand schedule $C$ $(D_C)$ obviously lies to the left of the demand curve that represents demand schedule $A$ $(D_A)$. We conclude that a *decrease in demand is represented by a leftward shift in the demand curve and means that individuals are willing and able to buy less of a good at each and every price.*

Decrease in demand = Leftward shift in the demand curve

## What Factors Cause the Demand Curve to Shift?

We know what an increase and decrease in demand mean: An increase in demand means consumers are willing and able to buy *more* of a good at every price. A decrease in demand means consumers are willing and able to buy *less* of a good at every price. We also know that an  increase in demand is graphically portrayed as a rightward shift in a demand curve and that a decrease in demand is graphically portrayed as a leftward shift in a demand curve.

## iPods and the Law of Demand

The law of demand holds that the price of a good and the quantity demanded of the good are inversely related. But does the law of demand hold for an individual when it comes to a good like an iPod? Will the individual buy more iPods at $10 than at $200? Perhaps she will, if only to give some iPods to friends.

But suppose we assume that the person doesn't want to give away any iPods as gifts. She wants only an iPod for herself. How many more than one iPod does she need? Probably none, since there is little use in buying two iPods if one iPod holds all the songs she wants. In other words, instead of having a downward-sloping demand curve for iPods, an individual's demand curve might look like the one in Exhibit 4(a). This curve says that the individual will buy one iPod no matter what the price is between zero and $300. But if the price is above $300, she will not buy an iPod because the demand curve doesn't extend that high.

Suppose no person has a downward-sloping demand curve. Is it still possible for the *market demand curve* to be downward sloping? The answer is yes.

AP PHOTO/PAUL SAKUMA

To understand why, suppose another person's demand curve for an iPod is shown in Exhibit 4(b). This demand curve says she is willing and able to buy one iPod if the price is anywhere between zero and $200, but she won't buy an iPod if the price is higher than $200.

If we horizontally sum the two demand curves in parts (a) and (b) to get the market demand curve, we see that at a price of $300, one iPod will be purchased and at $200, two iPods will be purchased. See Exhibit 4(c). Notice that this gives us a downward-sloping demand curve: More iPods are bought at a lower price than at a higher price.

**EXHIBIT 4**

But what factors or variables can increase or decrease demand? What factors or variables can shift demand curves? They are (1) income, (2) preferences, (3) prices of related goods, (4) the number of buyers, and (5) expectations of future prices.

INCOME As a person's income changes (increases or decreases), that individual's demand for a particular good may rise, fall, or remain constant.

For example, suppose Jack's income rises. As a consequence, his demand for CDs rises. For Jack, CDs are a normal good. For a normal good, demand rises as income rises, and demand falls as income falls.

**Normal Good**

A good for which demand rises (falls) as income rises (falls).

X is a normal good: If income ↑ then $D_x$ ↑

If income ↓ then $D_x$ ↓

Now suppose Marie's income rises. As a consequence, her demand for canned baked beans falls. For Marie, canned baked beans are an inferior good. For an inferior good, demand falls as income rises, and demand rises as income falls.

$$\text{Y is an inferior good: If income} \uparrow \text{then } D_Y \downarrow$$

$$\text{If income} \downarrow \text{then } D_Y \uparrow$$

Finally, suppose when George's income rises, his demand for toothpaste neither rises nor falls. For George, toothpaste is neither a normal good nor an inferior good. Instead, it is a neutral good. For a neutral good, demand does not change as income rises or falls.

**PREFERENCES** People's preferences affect the amount of a good they are willing to buy at a particular price. A change in preferences in favor of a good shifts the demand curve rightward. A change in preferences away from the good shifts the demand curve leftward. For example, if people begin to favor Elmore Leonard novels to a greater degree than previously, the demand for his novels increases, and the demand curve shifts rightward.

**PRICES OF RELATED GOODS** There are two types of related goods: substitutes and complements. Two goods are substitutes if they satisfy similar needs or desires. For many people, Coca-Cola and Pepsi-Cola are substitutes. If two goods are substitutes, as the price of one rises (falls), the demand for the other rises (falls). For instance, higher Coca-Cola prices will increase the demand for Pepsi-Cola as people substitute Pepsi for the higher priced Coke [Exhibit 5(a)]. Other examples of substitutes are coffee and tea, corn chips and potato chips, two brands of margarine, and foreign and domestic cars.

$$\text{X and Y are substitutes: If } P_X \uparrow \text{then } D_Y \uparrow$$

$$\text{If } P_X \downarrow \text{then } D_Y \downarrow$$

Two goods are complements if they are consumed jointly. For example, tennis rackets and tennis balls are used together to play tennis. If two goods are complements, as the price of one rises (falls), the demand for the other falls (rises). For example, higher tennis racket prices will decrease the demand for tennis balls, as Exhibit 5(b) shows. Other examples of complements are cars and tires, lightbulbs and lamps, and golf clubs and golf balls.

**NUMBER OF BUYERS** The demand for a good in a particular market area is related to the number of buyers in the area: more buyers, higher demand; fewer buyers, lower demand. The number of buyers may increase owing to a heightened birthrate, increased immigration, the migration of people from one region of the country to another, and so on. The number of buyers may decrease owing to an increased death rate, war, the migration of people from one region of the country to another, and so on.

**EXPECTATIONS OF FUTURE PRICE** Buyers who expect the price of a good to be higher next month may buy it now, thus increasing the current (or present) demand for the good. Buyers who expect the price of a good to be lower next month may wait until next month to buy it, thus decreasing the current (or present) demand for the good.

For example, suppose you are planning to buy a house. One day, you hear that house prices are expected to go down in a few months. Consequently, you decide to delay your purchase for a while. Alternatively, if you hear that prices are expected to rise in a few months, you might go ahead and make your purchase now.

---

**Inferior Good**
A good for which demand falls (rises) as income rises (falls).

**Neutral Good**
A good for which demand does not change as income rises or falls.

**Substitutes**
Two goods that satisfy similar needs or desires. If two goods are substitutes, the demand for one rises as the price of the other rises (or the demand for one falls as the price of the other falls).

**Complements**
Two goods that are used jointly in consumption. If two goods are complements, the demand for one rises as the price of the other falls (or the demand for one falls as the price of the other rises).

### EXHIBIT 5

**Substitutes and Complements**

(a) Coca-Cola and Pepsi-Cola are substitutes: The price of one and the demand for the other are directly related. As the price of Coca-Cola rises, the demand for Pepsi-Cola increases. (b) Tennis rackets and tennis balls are complements: The price of one and the demand for the other are inversely related. As the price of tennis rackets rises, the demand for tennis balls decreases.

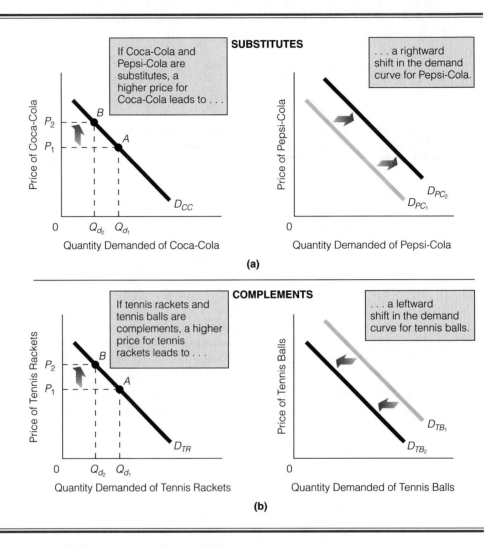

**SUBSTITUTES**

If Coca-Cola and Pepsi-Cola are substitutes, a higher price for Coca-Cola leads to . . .

. . . a rightward shift in the demand curve for Pepsi-Cola.

(a)

**COMPLEMENTS**

If tennis rackets and tennis balls are complements, a higher price for tennis rackets leads to . . .

. . . a leftward shift in the demand curve for tennis balls.

(b)

## Movement Factors and Shift Factors

Economists often distinguish between (1) factors that can bring about movement along curves and (2) factors that can shift curves.

The factors that cause movement along curves are sometimes called *movement* factors. In many economic diagrams, such as the demand curve in Exhibit 1, the movement factor (price) is on the vertical axis.

The factors that actually shift the curves are sometimes called *shift* factors. The shift factors for the demand curve are income, preferences, the price of related goods, and so on. Often, shift factors do not appear in the economic diagrams. For example, although in Exhibit 1 the movement factor—price—is on the vertical axis, the shift factors do not appear anywhere in the diagram. We just know what they are and that they can shift the demand curve.

When you see a curve in this book, first ask which factor will move us along the curve. In other words, what is the movement factor? Second, ask which factors will shift the curve. In other words, what are the shift factors? Exhibit 6 summarizes the shift factors that can change demand and the movement factors that can change quantity demanded.

**EXHIBIT 6**

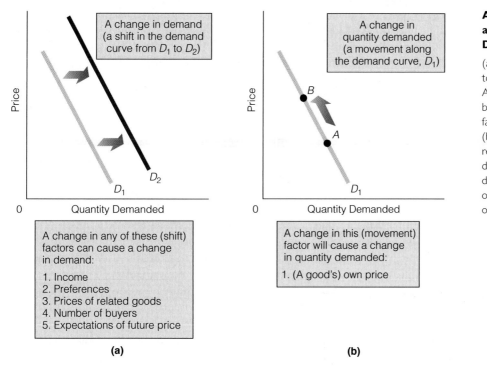

**A Change in Demand Versus a Change in Quantity Demanded**

(a) A change in demand refers to a shift in the demand curve. A change in demand can be brought about by a number of factors (see the exhibit and text). (b) A change in quantity demanded refers to a movement along a given demand curve. A change in quantity demanded is brought about only by a change in (a good's) own price.

## finding ECONOMICS

**Soft Drinks Go on Sale** Karen buys more soft drinks when they go on sale. Two people interpret this action differently. John says that if Karen buys more soft drinks when they go on sale, Karen's demand curve has shifted to the right. Laura says that if Karen buys more soft drinks when they go on sale, Karen is simply moving down on her individual demand curve. "Karen's quantity demanded of soft drinks," says Laura, "has increased." Who is right? Laura is. Saying that soft drinks went on sale is no more than saying that the price of soft drinks declined. As price declines, quantity demanded (not demand) increases. ▲ ▲ ▲

### SELF-TEST

(Answers to Self-Test questions are in Answers to Self-Test Questions at the back of the book.)

1. As Sandi's income rises, her demand for popcorn rises. As Mark's income falls, his demand for prepaid telephone cards rises. What kinds of goods are popcorn and telephone cards for Sandi and Mark?

2. Why are demand curves downward sloping?

3. Give an example that illustrates how to derive a market demand curve.

4. What factors can change demand? What factors can change quantity demanded?

# SUPPLY

Just as the word "demand" has a specific meaning in economics, so does the word "supply." Supply refers to

1. the willingness and ability of sellers to produce and offer to sell different quantities of a good

2. at different prices

3. during a specific time period (per day, week, etc.).

**Supply**
The willingness and ability of sellers to produce and offer to sell different quantities of a good at different prices during a specific time period.

## The Law of Supply

**Law of Supply**
As the price of a good rises, the quantity supplied of the good rises, and as the price of a good falls, the quantity supplied of the good falls, *ceteris paribus*.

**(Upward-Sloping) Supply Curve**
The graphical representation of the law of supply.

The law of supply states that as the price of a good rises, the quantity supplied of the good rises, and as the price of a good falls, the quantity supplied of the good falls, *ceteris paribus*. Simply put, the price of a good and the quantity supplied of the good are directly related, *ceteris paribus*. (The quantity supplied is the number of units that sellers are willing and able to produce and offer to sell at a particular price.) The (upward-sloping) supply curve is the graphical representation of the law of supply (see Exhibit 7). The law of supply can be summarized as follows:

$$P\uparrow Q_s\uparrow$$

$$P\downarrow Q_s\downarrow \textit{ ceteris paribus}$$

where $P$ = price and $Q_s$ = quantity supplied.

The law of supply holds for the production of most goods. It does not hold when there is no time to produce more units of a good. For example, suppose a theater in Atlanta is sold out for tonight's play. Even if ticket prices increased from \$30 to \$40, the theater would have no additional seats and no time to produce more. The supply curve for theater seats is illustrated in Exhibit 8(a). It is fixed at the number of seats in the theater, 500.[2]

The law of supply also does not hold for goods that cannot be produced over any period of time. For example, the violin maker Antonio Stradivari died in 1737. A rise in the price of Stradivarius violins does not affect the number of Stradivarius violins supplied, as Exhibit 8(b) illustrates.

## Why Most Supply Curves Are Upward Sloping

Most supply curves are upward sloping. The fundamental reason for this involves the *law of diminishing marginal returns*, discussed in a later chapter. Here, suffice it to say that an upward-sloping supply curve reflects the fact that, under certain conditions, a higher

**EXHIBIT 7**

**A Supply Curve**

The upward sloping supply curve is the graphical representation of the law of supply, which states that price and quantity supplied are directly related, *ceteris paribus*. On a supply curve, the price (in dollars) represents price per unit of the good. The quantity supplied, on the horizontal axis, is always relevant for a specific time period (a week, a month, and so on).

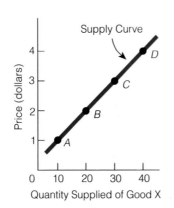

**EXHIBIT 8**

**Supply Curves When There Is No Time to Produce More or No More Can Be Produced**

The supply curve is not upward sloping when there is no time to produce additional units or when additional units cannot be produced. In those cases, the supply curve is vertical.

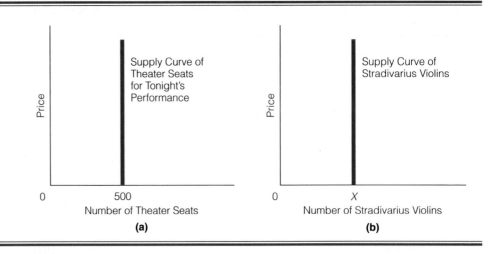

(a)

(b)

2  The vertical supply curve is said to be *perfectly inelastic*.

price is an incentive to producers to produce more of the good. The incentive comes in the form of higher profits. For example, suppose the price of good X rises, and nothing else changes (such as the per-unit costs of producing good X). In that case, the producers of good X will earn higher profits per unit and are thus encouraged to increase the quantity of good X that they supply to the market.

Generally, though, producing more of a good does not come with constant per-unit costs. As we learned in Chapter 2, the law of increasing costs is usually at work. In other words, the increased production of a good comes at increased opportunity costs. An upward-sloping supply curve simply reflects the fact that costs rise when more units of a good are produced.

THE MARKET SUPPLY CURVE An individual supply curve represents the price-quantity combinations for a single seller. The market supply curve represents the price–quantity combinations for all sellers of a particular good. Exhibit 9 shows how a market supply curve can be derived by "adding" individual supply curves. In part (a), a supply schedule, the numerical tabulation of the quantity supplied of a good at different prices, is given for Brown, Alberts, and other suppliers. The market supply schedule is obtained by adding the quantities supplied at each price, *ceteris paribus.* For example, at $11, the quantities supplied are 2 units for Brown, 3 units for Alberts, and 98 units for other suppliers. Thus, a total of 103 units are supplied at $11. In part (b), the data points for the supply schedules are plotted and added to produce a market supply curve (which could also be drawn directly from the market supply schedule).

**Supply Schedule**
The numerical tabulation of the quantity supplied of a good at different prices. A supply schedule is the numerical representation of the law of supply.

**EXHIBIT 9**

**Deriving a Market Supply Schedule and a Market Supply Curve**

Part (a) shows four supply schedules combined into one table. The market supply schedule is derived by adding the quantities supplied at each price. In (b), the data points from the supply schedules are plotted to show how a market supply curve is derived. Only two points on the market supply curve are noted.

| | Quantity Supplied | | | |
| Price | Brown | Alberts | Other Suppliers | All Suppliers |
|---|---|---|---|---|
| $10 | 1 | 2 | 96 | 99 |
| 11 | 2 | 3 | 98 | 103 |
| 12 | 3 | 4 | 102 | 109 |
| 13 | 4 | 5 | 106 | 115 |
| 14 | 5 | 6 | 108 | 119 |
| 15 | 6 | 7 | 110 | 123 |

**(a)**

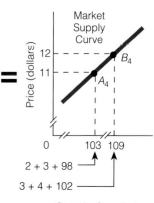

**(b)**

## Changes in Supply Mean Shifts in Supply Curves

Just as demand can change, so can supply. The supply of a good can rise or fall. An increase in the supply of a good means that suppliers are willing and able to produce and offer to sell more of the good at all prices. For example, suppose that in January sellers are willing and able to produce and offer for sale 600 shirts at $25 each and that in February they are willing and able to produce and sell 900 shirts at $25 each. An increase in supply shifts the entire supply curve to the right, as shown in Exhibit 10(a).

The supply of a good decreases if sellers are willing and able to produce and offer to sell less of the good at all prices. For example, suppose that in January sellers are willing and able to produce and offer for sale 600 shirts at $25 each and that in February they are willing and able to produce and sell only 300 shirts at $25 each. A decrease in supply shifts the entire supply curve to the left, as shown in Exhibit 10(b).

## What Factors Cause the Supply Curve to Shift?

We know the supply of any good can change, but what causes supply to change? What causes supply curves to shift? The factors that can change supply include (1) the prices of relevant resources, (2) technology, (3) the prices of other goods, (4) the number of sellers, (5) expectations of future price, (6) taxes and subsidies, and (7) government restrictions.

**PRICES OF RELEVANT RESOURCES** Resources are needed to produce goods. For example, wood is needed to produce doors. If the price of wood falls, producing doors becomes less costly. How will door producers respond? Will they produce more doors, the same number, or fewer? With lower costs and prices unchanged, the profit from producing and selling doors has increased; as a result, the (monetary) incentive to produce doors is increased. Door producers will produce and offer to sell more doors at each and every price. Thus, the supply of doors will increase, and the supply curve of doors will shift rightward. If the price of wood rises, producing doors becomes more costly. Consequently, the supply of doors will decrease, and the supply curve of doors will shift leftward.

**TECHNOLOGY** In Chapter 2, technology was defined as the body of skills and knowledge concerning the use of resources in production. Also, an advance in technology was said to refer to the ability to produce more output with a fixed amount of resources,

---

**EXHIBIT 10**

**Shifts in the Supply Curve**

(a) The supply curve shifts rightward from $S_1$ to $S_2$. This represents an increase in the supply of shirts: At each price the quantity supplied of shirts is greater. For example, the quantity supplied at $25 increases from 600 shirts to 900 shirts. (b) The supply curve shifts leftward from $S_1$ to $S_2$. This represents a decrease in the supply of shirts: At each price the quantity supplied of shirts is less. For example, the quantity supplied at $25 decreases from 600 shirts to 300 shirts.

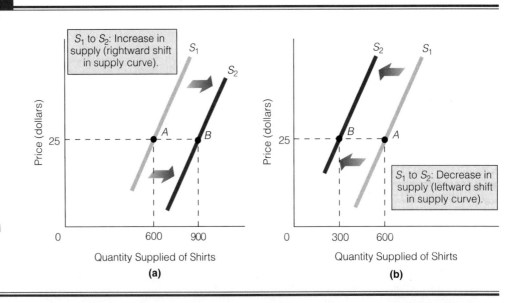

reducing per-unit production costs. To illustrate, suppose it takes $100 to produce 40 units of a good. The per-unit cost is therefore $2.50. If an advance in technology makes it possible to produce 50 units at a cost of $100, then the per-unit cost falls to $2.00.

If the per-unit production costs of a good decline, we expect the quantity supplied of the good at each price to increase. Why? Lower per-unit costs increase profitability and therefore provide producers with an incentive to produce more. For example, if corn growers develop a way to grow more corn using the same amount of water and other resources, then per-unit production costs will fall, profitability will increase, and growers will want to grow and sell more corn at each price. The supply curve of corn will shift rightward.

**PRICES OF OTHER GOODS** Think of a farmer who is producing wheat. Suddenly, the price of something he is not producing (say, corn) rises relative to wheat. The farmer might shift his farming away from wheat to corn. In other words, as the price of corn rises relative to wheat, the farmer switches from wheat to corn production. We conclude that a change in the price of one good can lead to a change in the supply of another good.

**NUMBER OF SELLERS** If more sellers begin producing a good, perhaps because of high profits, the supply curve will shift rightward. If some sellers stop producing a good, perhaps because of losses, the supply curve will shift leftward.

**EXPECTATIONS OF FUTURE PRICE** If the price of a good is expected to be higher in the future, producers may hold back some of the product today (if possible—perishables cannot be held back). Then they will have more to sell at the higher future price. Therefore, the *current* supply curve will shift leftward. For example, if oil producers expect the price of oil to be higher next year, some may hold oil off the market this year to be able to sell it next year. Similarly, if they expect the price of oil to be lower next year, they might pump more oil this year than previously planned.

**TAXES AND SUBSIDIES** Some taxes increase per-unit costs. Suppose a shoe manufacturer must pay a $2 tax per pair of shoes produced. This tax leads to a leftward shift in the supply curve, indicating that the manufacturer wants to produce and offer to sell fewer pairs of shoes at each price. If the tax is eliminated, the supply curve shifts rightward.

Subsidies have the opposite effect. Suppose the government subsidizes the production of corn by paying corn farmers $2 for every bushel of corn they produce. Because of the subsidy, the quantity supplied of corn is greater at each price, and the supply curve of corn shifts rightward. The removal of the subsidy shifts the supply curve of corn leftward. A rough rule of thumb is that we get more of what we subsidize and less of what we tax.

**Subsidy**
A monetary payment by government to a producer of a good or service.

**GOVERNMENT RESTRICTIONS** Sometimes government acts to reduce supply. Consider a U.S. import quota on Japanese television sets. An import quota, or a quantitative restriction on foreign goods, reduces the supply of Japanese television sets in the United States. It shifts the supply curve leftward. The elimination of the import quota allows the supply of Japanese television sets in the United States to shift rightward.

Licensure has a similar effect. With licensure, individuals must meet certain requirements before they can legally carry out a task. For example, owner-operators of day-care centers must meet certain requirements before they are allowed to sell their services. No doubt this requirement reduces the number of day-care centers and shifts the supply curve of day-care centers leftward.

## A Change in Supply Versus a Change in Quantity Supplied

A change in *supply* is not the same as a change in *quantity supplied*. A change in supply refers to a shift in the supply curve, as illustrated in Exhibit 11(a). For example, saying that

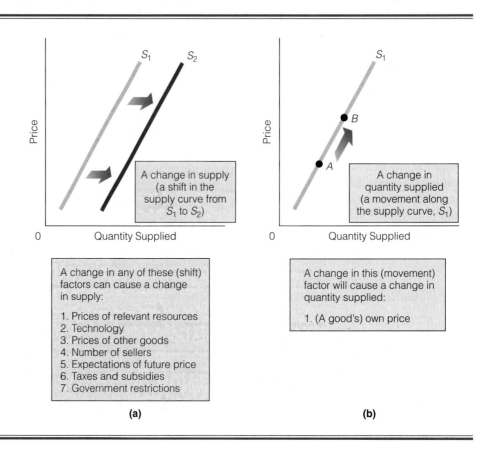

**EXHIBIT 11**

**A Change in Supply Versus a Change in Quantity Supplied**

(a) A change in supply refers to a shift in the supply curve. A change in supply can be brought about by a number of factors (see the exhibit and text). (b) A change in quantity supplied refers to a movement along a given supply curve. A change in quantity supplied is brought about only by a change in (a good's) own price.

A change in supply (a shift in the supply curve from $S_1$ to $S_2$)

A change in quantity supplied (a movement along the supply curve, $S_1$)

A change in any of these (shift) factors can cause a change in supply:

1. Prices of relevant resources
2. Technology
3. Prices of other goods
4. Number of sellers
5. Expectations of future price
6. Taxes and subsidies
7. Government restrictions

A change in this (movement) factor will cause a change in quantity supplied:

1. (A good's) own price

(a)          (b)

the supply of oranges has increased is the same as saying that the supply curve for oranges has shifted rightward. The factors that can change supply (i.e., shift the supply curve) are prices of relevant resources, technology, prices of other goods, the number of sellers, expectations of future prices, taxes and subsidies, and government restrictions.

A change in quantity supplied refers to a movement along a supply curve, as in Exhibit 11(b). The only factor that can directly cause a change in the quantity supplied of a good is a change in the price of the good, or own price.

## SELF-TEST

1. What would the supply curve for houses (in a given city) look like for a time period of (a) the next ten hours and (b) the next three months?

2. What happens to the supply curve if each of the following occurs?

   a. The number of sellers decreases.

   b. A per-unit tax is placed on the production of a good.

   c. The price of a relevant resource falls.

3. "If the price of apples rises, the supply of apples will rise." True or false? Explain your answer.

# THE MARKET: PUTTING SUPPLY AND DEMAND TOGETHER

In this section, we put supply and demand together and discuss the market. The purpose of the discussion is to gain some understanding about how prices are determined.

## Supply and Demand at Work at an Auction

In Exhibit 12, the supply curve of corn is vertical. It intersects the horizontal axis at 40,000 bushels; that is, the quantity supplied is 40,000 bushels. The demand curve for corn is downward sloping.

Now suppose you are at a computerized auction where bushels of corn are bought and sold. At this auction, the auctioneer will adjust the corn price to sell all the corn offered for sale. Each potential buyer of corn is sitting in front of a computer and can immediately input the number of bushels he or she wants to buy. For example, if Nancy wants to buy 5,000 bushels of corn, she simply keys "5,000" into her computer. The total number of bushels that all potential buyers are willing and able to buy appears on the auctioneer's computer screen.

The auction begins. Follow along in Exhibit 12 as it develops. The auctioneer announces the price on the computer screens:

- *$9.00!* The potential buyers think for a second and then register the numbers of bushels they are willing and able to buy at that price. On the auctioneer's screen, the total is 10,000 bushels, which is the quantity demanded of corn at $9.00. The auctioneer, realizing that 30,000 bushels of corn (40,000 − 10,000 = 30,000) will go unsold at this price, decides to lower the price per bushel.

- *$8.00!* The quantity demanded increases to 20,000 bushels, but still the quantity supplied of corn at this price is greater than the quantity demanded. The auctioneer tries again.

- *$7.00!* The quantity demanded increases to 30,000 bushels, but the quantity supplied at $7.00 is still greater than the quantity demanded. The auctioneer drops the price further.

- $4.25! At this price, the quantity demanded jumps to 60,000 bushels, but that is 20,000 bushels more than the quantity supplied. The auctioneer calls out a higher price.

- *$5.25!* The quantity demanded drops to 50,000 bushels, but buyers still want to buy more corn at this price than there is corn to be sold. The auctioneer calls out one more time.

- *$6.10!* At this price, the quantity demanded of corn is 40,000 bushels and the quantity supplied of corn is 40,000 bushels. The auction stops. Sold! The 40,000 bushels of corn are bought and sold at $6.10 per bushel.

## The Language of Supply and Demand: A Few Important Terms

If the quantity supplied is greater than the quantity demanded, a surplus, or excess supply, exists. If the quantity demanded is greater than the quantity supplied, a shortage, or excess demand, exists. In Exhibit 12, a surplus exists at $9.00, $8.00, and $7.00. A shortage exists at $4.25 and $5.25. The price at which the quantity demanded equals the quantity supplied is the equilibrium price, or market-clearing price. In our example, $6.10 is the equilibrium price. The quantity that corresponds to the equilibrium price is the equilibrium quantity.

**EXHIBIT 12**

**Supply and Demand at Work at an Auction**

$Q_d$ = quantity demanded; $Q_s$ = quantity supplied. The auctioneer calls out different prices, and buyers record how much they are willing and able to buy. At prices of $9.00, $8.00, and $7.00, quantity supplied is greater than quantity demanded. At prices of $4.25 and $5.25, quantity demanded is greater than quantity supplied. At a price of $6.10, quantity demanded equals quantity supplied.

**Surplus (Excess Supply)**
A condition in which the quantity supplied is greater than the quantity demanded. Surpluses occur only at prices above equilibrium price.

**Shortage (Excess Demand)**
A condition in which the quantity demanded is greater than the quantity supplied. Shortages occur only at prices below equilibrium price.

**Equilibrium Price (Market-Clearing Price)**
The price at which the quantity demanded of the good equals the quantity supplied.

**Equilibrium Quantity**
The quantity that corresponds to equilibrium price. The quantity at which the amount of the good that buyers are willing and able to buy equals the amount that sellers are willing and able to sell, and both equal the amount actually bought and sold.

**Disequilibrium Price**
A price other than equilibrium price. A price at which the quantity demanded does not equal the quantity supplied.

**Disequilibrium**
A state of either surplus or shortage in a market.

**Equilibrium**
Equilibrium means "at rest." Equilibrium in a market is the price–quantity combination from which buyers or sellers do not tend to move away. Graphically, equilibrium is the intersection point of the supply and demand curves.

In our example, it is 40,000 bushels of corn. Any price at which quantity demanded is not equal to quantity supplied is a disequilibrium price.

A market that exhibits either a surplus $(Q_s > Q_d)$ or a shortage $(Q_d > Q_s)$ is said to be in disequilibrium. A market in which the quantity demanded equals the quantity supplied $(Q_d = Q_s)$ is said to be in equilibrium (point $E$ in Exhibit 12).

## Moving to Equilibrium: What Happens to Price When There Is a Surplus or a Shortage?

What did the auctioneer do when the price was $9.00 and there was a surplus of corn? He lowered the price. What did the auctioneer do when the price was $5.25 and there was a shortage of corn? He raised the price. The behavior of the auctioneer can be summarized this way: If a surplus exists, lower the price; if a shortage exists, raise the price. This is how the auctioneer moved the corn market into equilibrium.

Not all markets have auctioneers. (When was the last time you saw an auctioneer in the grocery store?) But many markets act *as if* an auctioneer were calling out higher and lower prices until equilibrium price is reached. In many real-world auctioneer less markets, prices fall when there is a surplus and rise when there is a shortage. Why?

**WHY DOES PRICE FALL WHEN THERE IS A SURPLUS?** In Exhibit 13, there is a surplus at a price of $15: The quantity supplied (150 units) is greater than the quantity demanded (50 units). Suppliers will not be able to sell all they had hoped to sell at $15. As a result, their inventories will grow beyond the level they hold in preparation for demand changes. Sellers will want to reduce their inventories. Some will lower prices to do so, some will cut back on production, others will do a little of both. As shown in the exhibit, price and output tend to fall until equilibrium is achieved.

**WHY DOES PRICE RISE WHEN THERE IS A SHORTAGE** In Exhibit 13, there is a shortage at a price of $5: The quantity demanded (150 units) is greater than the quantity supplied (50 units). Buyers will not be able to buy all they had hoped to buy at $5. Some buyers will bid up the price to get sellers to sell to them instead of to other buyers.

---

### EXHIBIT 13

**Moving to Equilibrium**

If there is a surplus, sellers' inventories rise above the level they hold in preparation for demand changes. Sellers will want to reduce their inventories. As a result, price and output fall until equilibrium is achieved. If there is a shortage, some buyers will bid up price to get sellers to sell to them instead of to other buyers. Some sellers will realize they can raise the price of the goods they have for sale. Higher prices will call forth added output. Price and output rise until equilibrium is achieved. (Note: Recall that price, on the vertical axis, is price per unit of the good, and quantity, on the horizontal axis, is for a specific time period. In this text, we do not specify this on the axes themselves, but consider it to be understood.)

| Price | $Q_s$ | $Q_d$ | Condition |
|-------|-------|-------|-----------|
| $15 | 150 | 50 | Surplus |
| 10 | 100 | 100 | Equilibrium |
| 5 | 50 | 150 | Shortage |

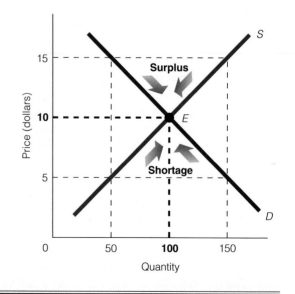

Some sellers, seeing buyers clamor for the goods, will realize that they can raise the price of the goods they have for sale. Higher prices will also call forth added output. Thus, price and output tend to rise until equilibrium is achieved.

Exhibit 14 brings together much of what we have discussed about supply and demand.

## Speed of Moving to Equilibrium

On April 16, 2010, at 10:09 a.m. (Eastern time), the price of a share of IBM stock was $131.50. A few minutes later, the price had risen to $132.00. Obviously, the stock market equilibrates quickly. If demand rises, then initially there is a shortage of the stock at the current equilibrium price. The price is bid up, and there is no longer a shortage. All this happens in seconds.

Now consider a house offered for sale in any city in the United States. The sale price of a house may remain the same even though the house does not sell for months. For example, a person offers to sell her house for $400,000. One month passes, no sale; two months pass, no sale; three months pass, no sale; and so on. Ten months later, the house is still not sold, and the price is still $400,000.

Is $400,000 the equilibrium price of the house? Obviously not. At the equilibrium price, there would be a buyer for the house and a seller of the house: The quantity demanded would equal the quantity supplied. At a price of $400,000, there is a seller but no buyer. The $400,000 price is above the equilibrium price. At $400,000, the housing market has a surplus; equilibrium has not been achieved.

Some people may be tempted to argue that supply and demand are at work in the stock market but not in the housing market. A better explanation, though, is that *not all markets equilibrate at the same speed.* Although the stock market may take only seconds to go from surplus or shortage to equilibrium, the housing market may take months to do so.

## Moving to Equilibrium: Maximum and Minimum Prices

There is another way to demonstrate how a market moves to equilibrium. Exhibit 15 shows the market for good X. Look at the first unit of good X. What is the *maximum*

**EXHIBIT 14**

**A Summary Exhibit of a Market (Supply and Demand)**

This exhibit ties together the topics discussed so far in this chapter. A market is composed of both supply and demand, as shown. Also shown are the factors that affect supply and demand and therefore indirectly affect the equilibrium price and quantity of a good.

## The Dowry and Marriage Market Disequilibrium

Men and women generally accept that monogamy is the ideal marriage practice. In other words, polygyny (the practice of one man being able to have more than one wife) is not the ideal marriage practice and therefore should be illegal. Some anthropologists and evolutionary biologists challenge orthodoxy by arguing that polygyny gives women greater choice. Here is how they structure their argument. Suppose there are 1,000 men and 1,000 women. Suppose each man and each woman is given a ranking of between 1 and 1,000 in terms of a variety of characteristics. The number 1 man is ranked higher than the number 2 man (and so on). Women are also so ranked.

The woman marries the man with whom she shares the same ranking. The number 1 man is matched up with the number 1 woman, the number 2 man with the number 2 woman, and so on. Now suppose the 404th-ranked woman (who is scheduled to marry the 404th-ranked man) prefers to be the second wife of the 40th-ranked man than the only wife of the 404th man. If polygyny is allowed, the 404th-ranked woman could marry the 40th-ranked man and share him with another wife. If polygyny is outlawed, she can't.

Now let's put that argument into economic terms. We know that a shortage exists if the quantity demanded of a good is greater than the quantity supplied. In the event that two women might want to marry the same man, the quantity supplied of the man is one, but the quantity demanded (of him) is two. This sounds like a shortage of the man, unless polygyny is permitted, because in that case the two women can be married to the same man.

But suppose polygyny is not permitted, even though the two women still want to be married to the same man. Now we have the problem of a shortage (of this particular man) that cannot be eliminated through the adoption of polygyny. What other way remains to eliminate the shortage? Normally we think of money as eliminating a shortage, and this is exactly what might be the purpose of the dowry. A dowry is a transfer of assets from the bride's family to the groom's family (usually) before the marriage takes place. If two women want to be married to the same man but only one can be legally married to him, then the dowry may effectively take the place of polygyny in eliminating the shortage of the man. All other things being equal, the prospective bride's family that offers the better dowry to the groom's family ends up with the groom as their son-in-law. This is consistent with the findings of anthropologists Steven J. C. Gaulin and James S. Boster who have shown that the dowry is almost exclusively found in societies where monogamy has been imposed (and polygyny outlawed).

---

### EXHIBIT 15

**Moving to Equilibrium in Terms of Maximum and Minimum Prices**

As long as the maximum buying price is greater than the minimum selling price, an exchange will occur. This condition is met for units 1–4. The market converges on equilibrium through a process of mutually beneficial exchanges.

| Units of Good X | Maximum Buying Price | Minimum Selling Price | Result |
|---|---|---|---|
| 1st | $70 | $10 | Exchange |
| 2nd | 60 | 20 | Exchange |
| 3rd | 50 | 30 | Exchange |
| 4th | 40 | 40 | Exchange |
| 5th | 30 | 50 | No Exchange |

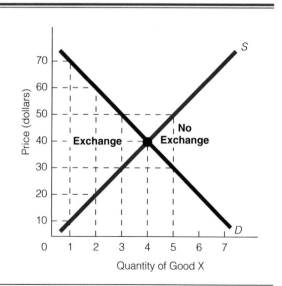

*price buyers are willing to pay* for it? The answer is $70. Just follow the dotted line up from the first unit of the good to the demand curve. What is the *minimum price sellers need to receive before they are willing to sell* this unit of good X? It is $10. Follow the dotted line up from the first unit to the supply curve. Because the maximum buying price is greater than the minimum selling price, the first unit of good X will be exchanged.

What about the second unit? For the second unit, buyers are willing to pay a maximum price of $60, and sellers need to receive a minimum price of $20. The second unit of good X will be exchanged. In fact, exchange will occur as long as the maximum buying price is greater than the minimum selling price. The exhibit shows that a total of four units of good X will be exchanged. The fifth unit will not be exchanged because the maximum buying price ($30) is less than the minimum selling price ($50).

In this process, buyers and sellers trade money for goods as long as both benefit from the trade. The market converges on a quantity of 4 units of good X and a price of $40 per unit. This is equilibrium. In other words, mutually beneficial trade drives the market to equilibrium.

## Equilibrium in Terms of Consumers' and Producers' Surplus

Equilibrium can be viewed in terms of two important economic concepts: consumers' surplus and producers' (or sellers') surplus. Consumers' surplus is the difference between the maximum buying price and the price paid by the buyer.

Consumers' surplus = Maximum buying price − Price paid

For example, if the highest price you would pay to see a movie is $10 and you pay $7 to see it, then you have received a $3 consumers' surplus. Obviously, the more consumers' surplus that consumers receive, the better off they are. Wouldn't you have preferred to pay, say, $4 to see the movie instead of $7? If you had paid only $4, your consumers' surplus would have been $6 instead of $3.

Producers' (or sellers') surplus is the difference between the price received by the producer or seller and the minimum selling price.

Producers' (sellers') surplus = Price received − Minimum selling price

Suppose the minimum price the owner of the movie theater would have accepted for admission is $5. But she sells admission for $7, not $5. Her producers' or sellers' surplus is $2. A seller prefers a large producers' surplus to a small one. The theater owner would have preferred to sell admission to the movie for $8 instead of $7 because then she would have received a $3 producers' surplus.

Total surplus is the sum of the consumers' surplus and producers' surplus.

Total surplus = Consumers' surplus + Producers' surplus

In Exhibit 16(a), consumers' surplus is represented by the shaded triangle. This triangle includes the area under the demand curve and above the equilibrium price. According to the definition, consumers' surplus is the highest price buyers are willing to pay (maximum buying price) minus the price they pay. For example, the window in part (a) shows that buyers are willing to pay as high as $7 for the 50th unit but pay only $5. Thus, the consumers' surplus on the 50th unit of the good is $2. If we add the consumers' surplus on each unit of the good between and including the first and the 100th units (the equilibrium quantity), we obtain the shaded consumers' surplus triangle.

**Consumers' Surplus (CS)**
The difference between the maximum price a buyer is willing and able to pay for a good or service and the price actually paid. CS = Maximum buying price − Price paid

**Producers' (Sellers') Surplus (PS)**
The difference between the price sellers receive for a good and the minimum or lowest price for which they would have sold the good. PS = Price received − Minimum selling price

**Total Surplus (TS)**
The sum of consumers' surplus and producers' surplus. TS = CS + PS

**Consumers' and Producers' Surplus**

(a) Consumers' surplus. As the shaded area indicates, the difference between the maximum or highest amount buyers would be willing to pay and the price they actually pay is consumers' surplus. (b) Producers' surplus. As the shaded area indicates, the difference between the price sellers receive for the good and the minimum or lowest price they would be willing to sell the good for is producers' surplus.

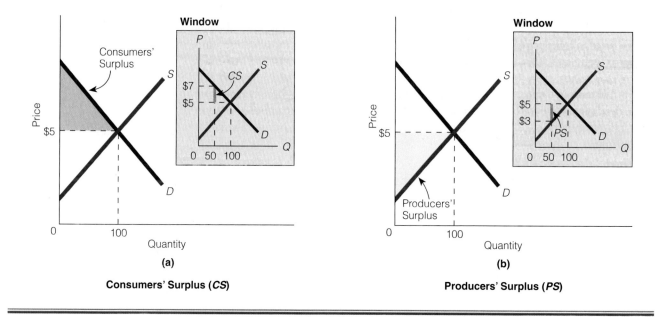

**(a)**

**Consumers' Surplus (CS)**

**(b)**

**Producers' Surplus (PS)**

In Exhibit 16(b), producers' surplus is also represented by a shaded triangle. This triangle includes the area above the supply curve and under the equilibrium price. Keep in mind the definition of producers' surplus: the price received by the seller minus the lowest price the seller would accept for the good. For example, the window in part (b) shows that sellers would have sold the 50th unit for as low as $3 but actually sold it for $5. Thus, the producers' surplus on the 50th unit of the good is $2. If we add the producers' surplus on each unit of the good between and including the first and the 100th, we obtain the shaded producers' surplus triangle.

Now consider consumers' surplus and producers' surplus at the equilibrium quantity. Exhibit 17 shows that the consumers' surplus at equilibrium is equal to areas $A + B + C + D$, and the producers' surplus at equilibrium is equal to areas $E + F + G + H$. At any other exchangeable quantity, such as at 25, 50, or 75 units, both consumers' surplus and producers' surplus are less. For example, at 25 units, consumers' surplus is equal to area $A$, and producers' surplus is equal to area $E$. At 50 units, the consumers' surplus is equal to areas $A + B$, and the producers' surplus is equal to areas $E + F$.

Equilibrium has a special property: At equilibrium, both consumers' surplus and producers' surplus are maximized. In short, total surplus is maximized.

## What Can Change Equilibrium Price and Quantity?

Equilibrium price and quantity are determined by supply and demand. Whenever demand changes, supply changes, or both change, equilibrium price and quantity change. Exhibit 18 illustrates eight different cases where this occurs. Cases (a)−(d) illustrate the four basic changes in supply and demand, where either supply or demand changes. Cases (e)−(h) illustrate changes in both supply and demand.

**EXHIBIT 17**

| Quantity (units) | Consumers' Surplus | Producers' Surplus |
|---|---|---|
| 25 | A | E |
| 50 | A + B | E + F |
| 75 | A + B + C | E + F + G |
| 100 (Equilibrium) | A + B + C + D | E + F + G + H |

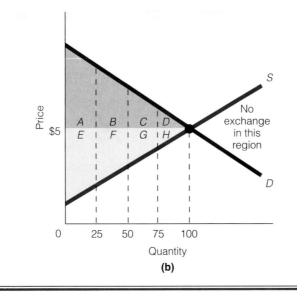

**(b)**

**Equilibrium, Consumers' Surplus, and Producers' Surplus**

Consumers' surplus is greater at equilibrium quantity (100 units) than at any other exchangeable quantity. Producers' surplus is greater at equilibrium quantity than at any other exchangeable quantity. For example, consumers' surplus is areas A + B + C at 75 units, but areas A + B + C + D at 100 units. Producers' surplus is areas E + F + G at 75 units, but areas E + F + G + H at 100 units.

- *Case (a):* Demand rises (the demand curve shifts rightward from $D_1$ to $D_2$), and supply is constant (the supply curve does not move). As a result of demand rising and supply remaining constant, the equilibrium price rises from $P_1$ to $P_2$, and the equilibrium quantity rises from 10 to 12 units. Now let's see if you can identify what has happened to quantity supplied (not supply) as price has risen from $P_1$ to $P_2$. (Remember, quantity supplied changes if *price* changes.) As price rises from $P_1$ to $P_2$, quantity supplied rises from 10 to 12 units. We see this as a movement up the supply curve from point 1 to point 2, which corresponds (on the horizontal axis) as a change from 10 to 12 units.

- *Case (b):* Demand falls (the demand curve shifts leftward from $D_1$ to $D_2$), and supply is constant. As a result, the equilibrium price falls from $P_1$ to $P_2$, and the equilibrium quantity falls from 10 to 8 units . Now ask, has the quantity supplied (not supply) changed? Yes, it has. As a result of price falling from $P_1$ to $P_2$, we move down the supply curve from point 1 to point 2, and the quantity supplied falls from 10 to 8 units.

- *Case (c):* Supply rises (the supply curve shifts rightward from $S_1$ to $S_2$), and demand is constant. As a result, the equilibrium price falls from $P_1$ to $P_2$, and the equilibrium quantity rises from 10 to 12 units. Now ask, has the quantity demanded (not demand) changed? Yes, it has. As a result of price falling from $P_1$ to $P_2$, we move down the demand curve from point 1 to point 2, and the quantity demanded rises from 10 to 12 units.

- *Case (d):* Supply falls (the supply curve shifts leftward from $S_1$ to $S_2$), and demand is constant. As a result, the equilibrium price rises from $P_1$ to $P_2$, and the equilibrium

**EXHIBIT 18**

### Equilibrium Price and Quantity Effects of Supply Curve Shifts and Demand Curve Shifts

The exhibit illustrates the effects on equilibrium price and quantity of a change in demand, a change in supply, or change in both. Below each diagram, the condition leading to the effects is noted, using the following symbols: (1) a bar over a letter means *constant* (thus, $\bar{S}$ means that supply is constant); (2) a downward-pointing arrow ($\downarrow$) indicates a fall; (3) an upward-pointing arrow ($\uparrow$) indicates a rise. A rise (fall) in demand is the same as a rightward (leftward) shift in the demand curve. A rise (fall) in supply is the same as a rightward (leftward) shift in the supply curve.

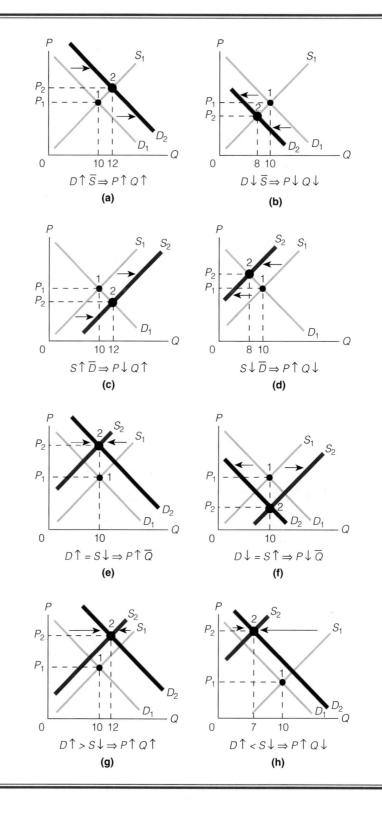

(a) $D\uparrow \bar{S} \Rightarrow P\uparrow Q\uparrow$

(b) $D\downarrow \bar{S} \Rightarrow P\downarrow Q\downarrow$

(c) $S\uparrow \bar{D} \Rightarrow P\downarrow Q\uparrow$

(d) $S\downarrow \bar{D} \Rightarrow P\uparrow Q\downarrow$

(e) $D\uparrow = S\downarrow \Rightarrow P\uparrow \bar{Q}$

(f) $D\downarrow = S\uparrow \Rightarrow P\downarrow \bar{Q}$

(g) $D\uparrow > S\downarrow \Rightarrow P\uparrow Q\uparrow$

(h) $D\uparrow < S\downarrow \Rightarrow P\uparrow Q\downarrow$

1. What is wrong with this statement? Demand refers to the willingness of buyers to purchase different quantities of a good at different prices during a specific time period.

2. What is the difference between *demand* and *quantity demanded*?

3. True or false? As the price of oranges rises, the demand for oranges falls, *ceteris paribus*. Explain your answer.

4. "The price of a bushel of wheat, which was $3.00 last month, is $3.70 today. The demand curve for wheat must have shifted rightward between last month and today." Discuss.

5. Some goods are bought largely because they have 'snob appeal.' For example, the residents of Beverly Hills gain prestige by buying expensive items. In fact, they won't buy some items unless they are expensive. The law of demand, which holds that people buy more at lower prices than higher prices, obviously doesn't hold for the residents of Beverly Hills. The following rules apply in Beverly Hills: high prices, buy; low prices, don't buy. Discuss.

6. "The price of T-shirts keeps rising and rising, and people keep buying more and more. T-shirts must have an upward-sloping demand curve." Identify the error.

7. With respect to each of the following changes, identify whether the demand curve will shift rightward of leftward:

   a. An increase in income (the good under consideration is a normal good)

   b. A rise in the price of a substitute good

   c. A fall in the price of a complementary good

   d. A fall in the number of buyers

8. What does a sale on shirts have to do with the law of demand (as applied to shirts)?

9. What is wrong with this statement: As the price of a good falls, the supply of that good falls, *ceteris paribus*.

10. In the previous chapter you learned about the law of increasing opportunity costs. What does this law have to do with an upward-sloping supply curve?

11. How might the price of corn affect the supply of wheat?

12. What is the difference between supply and quantity supplied?

13. Predict what would happen to the equilibrium price of marijuana if it were legalized.

14. Compare the ratings for television shows with prices for goods. How are ratings like prices? How are ratings different from prices? (Hint: How does rising demand for a particular television manifest itself?)

15. At equilibrium in a market, the maximum price buyers would be willing to pay for the good is equal to the minimum price sellers need to receive before they are willing to sell the good. Do you agree or disagree with this statement? Explain your answer.

16. Must consumers' surplus equal producers' surplus at equilibrium price? Explain your answer.

17. Many movie theaters charge a lower admission price for the first show on weekday afternoons than they do for a weeknight or weekend show. Explain why.

18. A Dell computer is a substitute for a Hewlett-Packard computer. What happens to the demand for Hewlett-Packard computers and the quantity demanded of Dell computers as the price of a Dell falls?

19. Describe how each of the following will affect the demand for personal computers:

   a. A rise in income (assuming computers are a normal good)

   b. A lower expected price for computers

   c. Cheaper software

   d. Simpler-to-operate computers

20. Describe how each of the following will affect the supply of personal computers:

   a. A rise in wage rates

   b. An increase in the number of sellers of computers

   c. A tax placed on the production of computers

   d. A subsidy placed on the production of computers

21. Use the law of diminishing marginal utility to explain why demand curves slope downward.

22. Explain how the market moves to equilibrium in terms of shortages and surpluses and in terms of maximum buying prices and minimum selling prices.

23. Identify what happens to equilibrium price and quantity in each of the following cases:

   a. Demand rises and supply is constant

   b. Demand falls and supply is constant

   c. Supply rises and demand is constant

   d. Supply falls and demand is constant

   e. Demand rises by the same amount that supply falls

   f. Demand falls by the same amount that supply rises

   g. Demand falls less than supply rises

   h. Demand rises more than supply rises

   i. Demand rises less than supply rises

   j. Demand falls more than supply falls

   k. Demand falls less than supply falls

24. Suppose the demand curve for a good is downward sloping and the supply curve is upward sloping. Now suppose demand rises. Will producers' surplus rise or fall? Explain your answers.

25. When speeding tickets were $100, usually 500 speeders were on the roads each month in a given city; when ticket prices were raised to $250, usually 215 speeders were on the roads in the city each month. Can you find any economics in this observation?

26. On most days, more people want to see the taping of *The Tonight Show with Jay Leno* (in Burbank, California) than there are seats in the taping studio. What might explain this shortage?

## WORKING WITH NUMBERS AND GRAPHS

1. Price is $10, the quantity supplied is 50 units, and the quantity demanded is 100 units. For every $1 rise in price, the quantity supplied rises by 5 units and the quantity demanded falls by 5 units. What is the equilibrium price and quantity?

2. Using numbers, explain how a market demand curve is derived from two individual demand curves.

3. Draw a diagram that shows a larger increase in demand than the decrease in supply.

4. Draw a diagram that shows a smaller increase in supply than the increase in demand.

5. At equilibrium in the following figure, what area(s) does the consumers' surplus equal the producers' surplus?

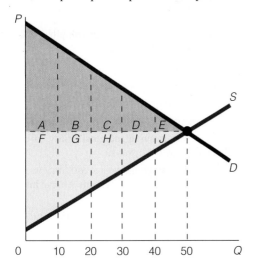

6. At what quantity in the preceding figure is the maximum buying price equal to the minimum selling price?

7. In the following figure, can the movement from point 1 to point 2 be explained by a combination of an increase in the price of a substitute and a decrease in the price of nonlabor resources? Explain your answer.

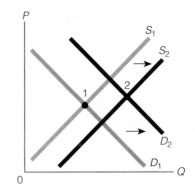

8. The demand curve is downward sloping, the supply curve is upward sloping, and the equilibrium quantity is 50 units. Show on a graph that the difference between the maximum buying price and minimum selling price is greater at 25 units than at 33 units.

## CHAPTER 4

# PRICES: FREE, CONTROLLED, AND RELATIVE

KCPHOTOS / DREAMSTIME.COM

**Introduction** In the last chapter we discussed supply and demand. Mainly, we saw how supply and demand work together to determine prices. In this chapter we discuss prices at greater length. First, we discuss two of the key "jobs" that price performs: (1) rationing resources and goods and (2) transmitting information. Second, we discuss government controls that can be imposed on price. Specifically, we discuss both price ceilings and price floors. Third, we discuss two types of price: absolute (or money) price and relative price.

# PRICE

To most people, price is a number with a dollar sign in front of it, such as $10. But price is much more. Price performs two major jobs: It acts (1) as a rationing device and (2) as a transmitter of information.

## Price as a Rationing Device

In Chapter 1 we said that wants (for goods) are unlimited and resources are limited; so scarcity exists. As a result of scarcity, a rationing device is needed to determine who gets what of the available limited resources and goods. (Because resources are limited, goods are also because the production of goods requires resources.) Price serves as a rationing device. It rations resources to the producers who pay the price for the resources. It rations goods to those buyers who pay the price for the goods. The process is as simple as this: Pay the price, and the resources or goods are yours. Don't pay the price, and they aren't.

Is dollar price a fair rationing device? Doesn't it discriminate against the poor? After all, the poor have fewer dollars than the rich; so the rich can get more of what they want than can the poor. True, dollar price does discriminate against the poor. But then, as economists know, every rationing device discriminates against someone. To illustrate, suppose for some reason that tomorrow dollar price could not be used as a rationing device. Some rationing device would still be necessary because scarcity would still exist. How would we ration gas at the gasoline station, food in the grocery store, or tickets for the Super Bowl? Let's consider some alternatives to dollar price as a rationing device.

Suppose *first-come-first-served* is the rationing device. For example, suppose only 40,000 Super Bowl tickets are available. If you are one of the first 40,000 in line for a Super Bowl ticket, you get a ticket. If you are person number 40,001 in line, you don't. Such a method discriminates against those who can't get in line quickly enough. What about slow walkers or people with disabilities? What about people without cars who can't drive to where the tickets are distributed?

Or suppose *brute force* is the rationing device. For example, of the 40,000 Super Bowl tickets, you get one as long as you can take it away from someone else. Against whom does this rationing method discriminate? Obviously, it discriminates against the weak and nonaggressive.

Or suppose *beauty* is the rationing device. The more beautiful you are, the better your chances are of getting a Super Bowl ticket. Again, the rationing device discriminates against someone.

These and many other alternatives to dollar price could be used as rationing devices. However, each discriminates against someone, and none is clearly superior to dollar price.

In addition, if first-come-first-served, brute force, beauty, or another alternative to dollar price is the rationing device, what incentive would the producer of a good have to produce the good? With dollar price as a rationing device, a person produces computers and sells them for money. He then takes the money and buys what he wants. But if the rationing device were, say, brute force, he would not have an incentive to produce. Why produce anything when someone will end up taking it away from you? In short, in a world where dollar price isn't the rationing device, people are likely to produce much less than in a world where dollar price is the rationing device.

## Price as a Transmitter of Information

*Rationing* isn't the only job that price performs. Price also transmits information. That may sound odd. Consider the following story. On Saturday, Noelle walks into a local grocery store and purchases a half gallon of orange juice for $2.50. On Sunday, unknown to her, a cold spell hits Florida and wipes out half the orange crop. The cold spell ends up shifting the supply curve of oranges leftward, which drives up the price of oranges. Because oranges are a resource in the production of orange juice, the supply curve of orange juice shifts leftward, and the price of orange juice rises.

Noelle returns to the grocery store in a week. She notices the half gallon of orange juice she bought last week for $2.50 has now risen to $3.50. Because Noelle has a downward-sloping demand curve for orange juice, she ends up buying less orange juice. She buys only a quart of orange juice instead of a half gallon.

What role did price play in Noelle's decision to cut back on the consumption of orange juice? It played a major role. If the price hadn't risen, Noelle probably wouldn't have reduced her purchases and consumption of orange juice. Noelle reacted to the price rise, but what the price rise was "saying"—if we had ears to hear it—is this: "The relative scarcity of a good has risen because of a cold spell in Florida. In other words, the gap between people's wants for orange juice and the amount of orange juice available to satisfy those wants has widened."

Now we know that Noelle might not have "heard" price saying this. But if you understand economics, this is what price is saying. In other words, price is a transmitter of information that often relates to the relative scarcity of a good. A market system, oddly enough, is powerful enough to have people respond in appropriate ways to the information that price is transmitting, even if the people do not fully hear or understand it. In the case of Noelle, her cutting back on the consumption of orange juice conserves orange juice in the face of an act of nature that ended up making orange juice relatively scarcer.

Think of how this reaction is similar to what people who tell you to conserve water want. For example, in California in the summer of 2009, advertisements on television asked people to cut back on their consumption of water because water in the state was in short supply. The appropriate behavior to take was to cut back on the consumption of water because it had become relatively scarcer. You were being civic minded if you did so. Well, movements in price can get you to be civic minded too. When the price of orange juice rises due to a cold spell in Florida, you might automatically cut back on your consumption, thus conserving on the consumption of a good that has become relatively more scarce.

## SELF-TEST

(Answers to Self-Test questions are in Answers to Self-Test Questions at the back of the book.)

1. Why is there a need for a rationing device, whether it is price or something else?

2. If price is not the rationing device used, then individuals won't have as sharp an incentive to produce. Explain.

3. What kind of information does price often transmit?

# PRICE CONTROLS

A rationing device—such as dollar price—is needed because scarcity exists. But price is not always allowed to be a rationing device. Sometimes price is controlled. There are two types of price controls: price ceilings and price floors. In the discussion of price controls, the word "price" is used in the generic sense. It refers to the price of an apple, for example, the price of labor (a wage), the price of credit (the interest rate), and so on.

## Price Ceiling

**DEFINITION AND EFFECTS** A price ceiling is a government-mandated maximum price above which legal trades cannot be made. For example, suppose the government mandates that the maximum price at which good X can be bought and sold is $8. Therefore, $8 is a price ceiling. If $8 is below the equilibrium price of good X, as in Exhibit 1, any or all of the following effects may arise:[1] shortages, fewer exchanges, nonprice-rationing devices, buying and selling at prohibited prices, and tie-in sales.

**Shortages** At the $12 equilibrium price in Exhibit 1, the quantity demanded of good X (150) is equal to the quantity supplied (150). At the $8 price ceiling, a shortage exists. The quantity demanded (190) is greater than the quantity supplied (100). When a shortage exists, price and output tend to rise to equilibrium. But when a price ceiling exists, they cannot rise because it is unlawful to trade at the equilibrium price.

**EXHIBIT 1**

**A Price Ceiling**

The price ceiling is $8 and the equilibrium price is $12. At $12, quantity demanded = quantity supplied. At $8 quantity demanded > quantity supplied. (Recall that price, on the vertical axis, always represents price per unit. Quantity, on the horizontal axis, always holds for a specific time period.)

1. If the price ceiling is above the equilibrium price (say, $8 is the price ceiling and $4 is the equilibrium price), it has no effect. Usually, however, a price ceiling is below the equilibrium price.

**Fewer Exchanges** At the equilibrium price of $12 in Exhibit 1, 150 units of good X are bought and sold. At the price ceiling of $8, 100 units of good X are bought and sold. (Buyers would prefer to buy 190 units, but only 100 are supplied.) We conclude that price ceilings cause fewer exchanges to be made.

Notice in Exhibit 1 that the demand curve is above the supply curve for all quantities less than 150 units. (At 150 units, the demand curve and the supply curve intersect and thus share the same point in the two-dimensional space.) Thus the maximum buying price is greater than the minimum selling price for all units less than 150. In particular, the maximum buying price is greater than the minimum selling price for units 101 to 149. For example, buyers might be willing to pay $17 for the 110th unit, and sellers might be willing to sell the 110th unit for $10. But no unit after the 100th unit (not the 110th unit, not the 114th unit, not the 130th unit) will be produced and sold because of the price ceiling. In short, the price ceiling prevents mutually advantageous trades from being realized.

**Nonprice-Rationing Devices** If the equilibrium price $12 fully rations good X before the price ceiling is imposed, then a lower price of $8 only partly rations this good. In short, price ceilings prevent price from rising to the level sufficient to ration goods fully. But if price is responsible for only part of the rationing, what accounts for the rest?

The answer is that some other (nonprice) rationing device, such as first-come-first-served (FCFS). In Exhibit 1, 100 units of good X will be sold at $8, although buyers are willing to buy 190 units at this price. What happens? Possibly, good X will be sold on an FCFS basis for $8 per unit. In other words, to buy good X, a person must not only pay $8 per unit but also be one of the first people in line.

**Buying and Selling at a Prohibited Price** Buyers and sellers may regularly circumvent a price ceiling by making their exchanges under the table. For example, some buyers may offer some sellers more than $8 per unit for good X. No doubt, some sellers will accept the offers. But why would some buyers offer more than $8 per unit when they can buy good X for $8? Because not all buyers can buy the amount of good X they want at $8. As Exhibit 1 shows, there is a shortage. Buyers are willing to buy 190 units at $8, but sellers are willing to sell only 100 units. In short, 90 fewer units will be sold than buyers would like to buy. Some buyers will go unsatisfied. How, then, does any one buyer make it more likely that sellers will sell to him or her instead of to someone else? The answer is by offering to pay a higher price. Because it is illegal to pay a higher price, the transaction must be made under the table.

**Tie-In Sales** In Exhibit 1, the maximum price buyers would be willing and able to pay per unit for 100 units of good X is $18. (This is the price on the demand curve at a quantity of 100 units.) The maximum legal price, however, is $8. This difference between the two prices often prompts a tie-in sale, a sale whereby one good can be purchased only if another good is also purchased. For example, if Ralph's Gas Station sells gasoline to customers only if they buy a car wash, the two goods are linked in a tie-in sale.

Suppose that the sellers of good X in Exhibit 1 also sell good Y. They might offer to sell buyers good X at $8 only if the buyers agree to buy good Y at, say, $10. We choose $10 as the price for good Y because $10 is the difference between the maximum per-unit price buyers are willing and able to pay for 100 units of good X ($18) and the maximum legal price ($8).

In New York City and other communities with rent-control laws, tie-in sales sometimes result from rent ceilings on apartments. Occasionally, to rent an apartment, an individual must agree to buy the furniture in the apartment.

**BUYERS AND HIGHER AND LOWER PRICES** Do buyers prefer lower to higher prices? "Of course," you might say, "buyers prefer lower prices to higher prices. What buyer would want to pay a higher price for anything?" Even though price ceilings

**Tie-in Sale**
A sale whereby one good can be purchased only if another good is also purchased.

**Price Ceiling**
A government-mandated maximum price above which legal trades cannot be made.

are often lower than equilibrium prices, does it follow that buyers prefer price ceilings to equilibrium prices? Not necessarily. Price ceilings have effects that equilibrium prices do not: shortages, use of first-come-first-served as a rationing device, tie-in sales, and so on. A buyer could prefer to pay a higher price (an equilibrium price) than to pay a lower price and have to deal with the effects of a price ceiling. All we can say for certain is that buyers prefer lower prices to higher prices, *ceteris paribus*. As in many cases, the *ceteris paribus* condition makes all the difference.

PRICE CEILINGS AND FALSE INFORMATION   Let's go back to the orange juice example in the first section of this chapter. In that example, a cold spell destroys part of the orange crop, leading to a higher price for oranges and orange juice. The market price of orange juice rose from $2.50 to $3.50 a half gallon.

Now let's change things. Suppose that instead of letting the new, lower supply of orange juice and demand for orange juice determine the market price of orange juice at $3.50 a half gallon, government imposes a price ceiling on orange juice at $2.50 a half gallon. Think about what the price ceiling does to prevent price from transmitting information. Specifically, the price ceiling prevents the correct information about the increased relative scarcity of orange juice (due to the cold spell) from getting through to consumers. It's as if price is a radio signal, and the price ceiling jams the signal. Because of the jammed price signal, consumers mistakenly believe that nothing has changed. As far as they are concerned, they can continue buying orange juice at the same rate of consumption they did earlier. But, of course, they can't: There are fewer oranges and less orange juice in the world. One way or another, some people are going to have to curtail their consumption of orange juice.

The lesson is simple. Price ceilings (that are below the equilibrium price) distort the flow of accurate information to buyers. Buyers get a false view of reality; they then base their buying behavior on incorrect information. Problems follow, and the unintended, unexpected, and undesirable effects of price ceilings soon occur.

## ⓣhinking like AN ECONOMIST

**Look for the Unintended Effects** Economists think in terms of unintended effects. For example, a price ceiling policy intended to lower prices for the poor may cause shortages, the use of nonprice rationing devices, illegal market transactions, and tie-in sales. When we consider both the price ceiling and its effects, whether the poor have been helped is not so clear. The economist knows that wanting to do good (for others) is not sufficient. Knowing how to do good is important too. ● ● ●

## Price Floor: Definition and Effects

A price floor is a government-mandated minimum price below which legal trades cannot be made. For example, suppose the government mandates that the minimum price at which good X can be sold is $20. The $20 minimum is a price floor (see Exhibit 3).

EFFECTS OF A PRICE FLOOR   If the price floor is above the equilibrium price, the following two effects arise:[2] surpluses and fewer exchanges.

**Surpluses**   At the $15 equilibrium price in Exhibit 3, the quantity demanded of good X (130) is equal to the quantity supplied (130). At the $20 price floor, a surplus exists.

The quantity supplied (180) is greater than the quantity demanded (90). Usually, a surplus is temporary. When a surplus exists, price and output tend to fall to equilibrium. But when a price floor exists, they cannot because it is unlawful to trade at the equilibrium price.

**Price Floor**
A government-mandated minimum price below which legal trades cannot be made.

---

2. If the price floor is below the equilibrium price (say, $20 is the price floor and $25 is the equilibrium price), it has no effects. Usually, however, a price floor is above the equilibrium price.

## A Price Ceiling in the Kidney Market

Just as some people want to buy houses, computers, and books, others want to buy kidneys. These people have kidney failure, and they will either die without a new kidney or have to endure years of costly and painful dialysis. This demand for kidneys is shown as $D_K$ in Exhibit 2, and the supply of kidneys is shown as $S_K$.

Notice that at $0 price, the quantity supplied of kidneys is 350. These kidneys are from people who donate their kidneys to others, asking nothing in return. They may donate upon their death, or they may donate one of their two kidneys while living. We have drawn the supply curve as upward sloping because we assume that some people who today are unwilling to donate a kidney for $0 might be willing to do so for some positive dollar amount. Specifically, we assume that as the price of a kidney rises, the quantity supplied of kidneys will rise.

GALINA BARSKAYA, 2009. USED UNDER LICENSE FROM SHUTTERSTOCK.COM

If there were a free market in kidneys, the price of a kidney would be $P_1$ in Exhibit 2. At this price, 1,000 kidneys would be purchased and sold; that is, 1,000 kidney transplants would occur.

Today, there is no free market in kidneys. Buying or selling kidneys is illegal at any dollar amount. In essence, then, there is a price ceiling in the kidney market, and the ceiling is set at $0. What is the effect of the ceiling?

If the demand curve for kidneys and the supply curve of kidneys intersected at $0, there would be neither a surplus nor a shortage of kidneys. But there is evidence that the demand and supply curves do not intersect at $0; they look more like those shown in Exhibit 2. In other words, there is a shortage of kidneys at $0: The quantity supplied of kidneys is 350, and the quantity demanded is 1,500. (Although these are not the actual numbers of kidneys demanded and supplied at $0, they are representative of the current situation in the kidney market.)

This chapter has described the possible effects of a price ceiling set below equilibrium price: shortages, nonprice-rationing devices, fewer exchanges, tie-in sales, and buying and selling at prohibited prices (in other words, illegal trades). Are any of these effects occurring in the kidney market?

First, there is evidence of a shortage. In almost every country in the world, more people on national lists want a kidney than there are kidneys available. Some of these people die waiting for a transplant.

## EXHIBIT 2

### The Market for Kidneys

We have identified the demand for kidneys as $D_K$ and the supply of kidneys as $S_K$. Given the demand for and supply of kidneys, the equilibrium price of a kidney is $P_1$. It does not follow, though, that simply because there is an equilibrium price, people will be allowed to trade at this price. Today, it is unlawful to buy and sell kidneys at any positive price. In short, there is a price ceiling in the kidney market and the ceiling is $0. At the price ceiling, there is a shortage of kidneys, a nonprice rationing device for kidneys (first-come-first-served), fewer kidney transplants (than there would be at $P_1$), and illegal purchases and sales of kidneys.

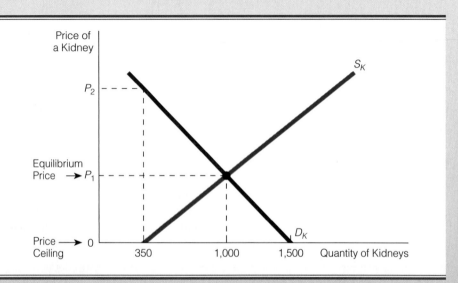

Second, as just indicated, the nonprice rationing device used in the kidney market is (largely) first-come-first-served. A person who wants a kidney registers on a national waiting list. How long people wait is a function of how far down the list their names appear.

Third, there are fewer exchanges; not everyone who needs a kidney gets one. With a price ceiling of $0, only 350 kidneys are supplied. All these kidneys are from people who freely donate their kidneys. If $P_1$ were permitted, some people who are unwilling to supply a kidney (at $0) would be willing to do so. In short, monetary payment would provide the incentive for some people to supply a kidney. At $P_1$, 1,000 kidneys are demanded and supplied; so more people would get kidney transplants when the price of a kidney is $P_1$ (1,000 in all) than when the price of a kidney is $0 (350 in total). More transplants, of course, means fewer people die waiting for a kidney.

Fourth, kidneys are bought and sold at prohibited prices. People buy and sell kidneys today; they just do so illegally. People are reported to have paid between $25,000 and $200,000 for a kidney.

Some people argue that a free market in kidneys would be wrong. Such a system would place the poor at a disadvantage. Think of it: A rich person who needed a kidney could buy one, but a poor person could not. The rich person would get a second chance at life, whereas the poor person would not. No one enjoys contemplating this stark reality.

But consider another stark reality. If it is unlawful to pay someone for a kidney, fewer kidneys will be forthcoming. In other words, the quantity supplied of kidneys is less at $0 than at, say, $20,000. Fewer kidneys supplied means fewer kidney transplants. And fewer kidney transplants means more people will die from kidney failure.

***Fewer Exchanges*** At the equilibrium price in Exhibit 3, 130 units of good X are bought and sold. At the price floor, 90 units are bought and sold. (Sellers want to sell 180 units, but buyers buy only 90.) Thus price floors cause fewer exchanges to be made.

THE MINIMUM WAGE If a price floor is a legislated minimum price below which trades cannot legally be made, then the *minimum wage* is a price floor—a government-mandated minimum price for labor. It affects the market for unskilled labor. In Exhibit 4, we assume the minimum wage is $W_M$ and the equilibrium wage is $W_E$. At the equilibrium wage, $N_1$ workers are employed. At the higher minimum wage, $N_3$ workers want to work, but only $N_2$ actually do work. There is a surplus of workers equal to $N_3 - N_2$ in this unskilled labor market. In addition, fewer workers are working at the minimum wage ($N_2$) than at the equilibrium wage ($N_1$). Overall, the effects of the minimum wage are (1) a surplus of unskilled workers and (2) fewer workers employed.

Suppose two economists decide to test the theory that as the minimum wage rises, some unskilled workers will lose their jobs. They look at the number of unskilled workers before and after the minimum wage is raised, and surprisingly they find that the number of unskilled workers is the same. Is this sufficient evidence to conclude that an increase in the minimum wage does not cause some workers to lose their jobs?

The answer to that question depends on whether the economists

**EXHIBIT 3**

**A Price Floor**

The price floor is $20 and the equilibrium price is $15. At $15, quantity demanded = quantity supplied. At $20, quantity supplied > quantity demanded.

**EXHIBIT 4**

**Effects of the Minimum Wage**

At a minimum wage of $W_M$ an hour, there is a surplus of workers and fewer workers are employed than would be at the equilibrium wage $W_E$.

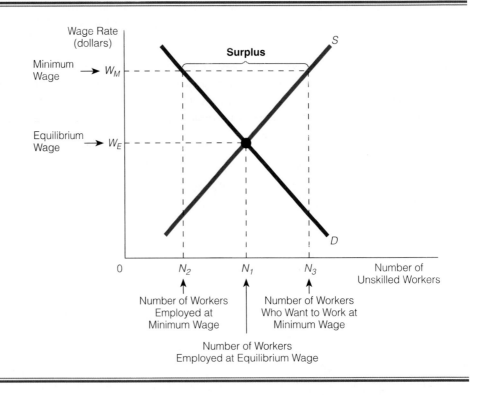

have adequately tested their theory. Instead of focusing on the number of people who lose their jobs, suppose they look at the number of people who keep their jobs but have their hours reduced as a result of the higher minimum wage. Let's look at an example. Suppose a local hardware store currently employs David and Francesca to work after school cleaning up and stocking shelves. The owner of the store pays each of them the minimum wage of, say, $7.25 an hour. Then the minimum wage is raised to $8.75 an hour. Will either David or Francesca lose their jobs as a result? Not necessarily. Instead, the owner of the store could reduce the number of hours he employs the two workers. For example, instead of having each of them work 20 hours a week, he might ask each to work only 14 hours a week.

Now let's reconsider our original question: Has the higher minimum wage eliminated jobs? In a way, no. It has, however, reduced the number of hours a person works in a job. (Of course, if we define a job as including both a particular task and a certain number of hours completing that task, then the minimum wage increase has eliminated "part" of the job.) This discussion argues for changing the label on the horizontal axis in Exhibit 4 from "Number of Unskilled Workers" to "Number of Unskilled Labor Hours."

## ⓣhinking like AN ECONOMIST

**Direction Versus Magnitude** In economics, some questions relate to direction and some to magnitude. For example, suppose someone asks, "If the demand for labor is downward sloping and the labor market is competitive, how will a minimum wage that is above the equilibrium wage affect employment?" This person is asking a question that relates to the direction of the change in employment. Usually, these types of questions can be answered by applying a theory. Applying the theory of demand, an economist might say, "At higher wages, the quantity demanded of labor, or the employment level, will be lower than at lower wages." The word "lower" speaks to the *directional change* in employment.

*(continued)*

# ⓣhinking like **AN ECONOMIST** (continued)

Now suppose someone asks, "How much will employment decline?" This question relates to *magnitude*. Usually, questions that deal with magnitude can be answered only through some kind of empirical (data-collecting and analyzing) work. In other words, we would have to collect employment figures at the equilibrium wage and at the minimum wage and then find the difference. ▪ ▪ ▪

**PRICE FLOORS, CHANGES IN CONSUMERS' AND PRODUCERS' SURPLUS, AND DEADWEIGHT LOSSES** We now turn to a discussion of consumers' surplus, producers' surplus, and price floors in terms of a specific example: a price floor on an agricultural foodstuff.

Exhibit 5 shows the demand for and supply of an agricultural foodstuff (corn, wheat, soybeans, etc.). If the market is allowed to move to equilibrium, the equilibrium price will be $P_1$, and the equilibrium quantity will be $Q_1$. Consumers' surplus will equal the area under the demand curve and above the equilibrium price: areas 1 + 2 + 3. Producers' surplus will equal the area under the equilibrium price and above the supply curve: areas 4 + 5. Total surplus, of course, is the sum of consumers' surplus and producers' surplus: areas 1 + 2 + 3 + 4 + 5.

Now suppose that the suppliers of the foodstuff argue for (and receive) a price floor, $P_F$. At this higher price, consumers do not buy as much as they once did. They now buy $Q_2$, whereas they used to buy $Q_1$. In addition, consumers' surplus is now only area 1, and producers' surplus is areas 2 + 4.

Obviously, consumers have been hurt by the increased (government-mandated) price of $P_F$; specifically, they have lost consumers' surplus equal to areas 2 + 3.

How have suppliers fared? Whereas their producers' surplus was equal to areas 4 + 5 at $P_1$, it is now equal to areas 2 + 4. (Area 2, which used to be part of consumers' surplus, has been transferred to producers and is now part of producers' surplus.) Whether producers are better off depends on whether area 2 (what they gain from $P_F$) is larger than area 5 (what they lose from $P_F$). Visually, we can tell that area 2 is larger than area 5; so producers are better off.

What is the overall effect of the price floor? Have producers gained more than consumers have lost, or have consumers lost more than producers have gained? To answer this question, we note that consumers lose areas 2 + 3 in consumers' surplus; producers gain area 2 in producers' surplus and lose area 5 in producers' surplus. So the gains and losses are:

| | |
|---|---|
| Losses to consumers: | areas 2 + 3 |
| Gains to producers: | area 2 |
| Losses to producers: | area 5 |

Part of the loss to consumers is offset by the gain to producers (area 2); so net losses amount to areas 3 + 5. In other words, the total surplus—the sum of consumers' surplus and producers' surplus—is lower than it was. Whereas it used to be areas 1 + 2 + 3 + 4 + 5, it now is areas 1 + 2 + 4. The total surplus lost is in areas 3 + 5. In short, (1) consumers lose, (2) producers gain, and (3) society (which is the sum of consumers and producers) loses.

You can think of this example in terms of a pie. Initially, the pie was made up of areas 1 + 2 + 3 + 4 + 5.

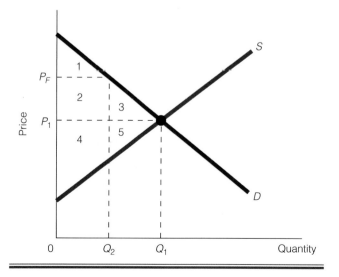

## EXHIBIT 5

**Agricultural Price Floors**

The demand for and supply of an agricultural foodstuff are shown in this exhibit. The equilibrium price is $P_1$; consumers' surplus (CS) is areas 1 + 2 + 3; producers' surplus is areas 4 + 5. A price floor of $P_F$ effectively transfers some of the consumers' surplus to producers in the form of a gain in producers' surplus. Specifically, at $P_F$, consumers' surplus is area 1 and producers' surplus is areas 2 + 4. Consumers are net losers because consumers' surplus has decreased by areas 2 + 3. Producers are net gainers because producers' surplus has increased from areas 4 + 5 to areas 2 + 4 and area 2 is larger than area 5. Overall, the economic pie of CS + PS has decreased from areas 1 + 2 + 3 + 4 + 5 to areas 1 + 2 + 4.

**Deadweight Loss.**
The loss to society of not producing the competitive, or supply-and-demand-determined, level of output.

This rather large pie registered all the gains of consumers and producers. After the price floor of $P_F$ was imposed, the pie shrank to areas $1 + 2 + 4$; in other words, the pie was smaller by areas $3 + 5$.

A loss in total surplus—in our example, areas $3 + 5$—is sometimes called a deadweight loss. This is the loss to society of not producing the competitive, or supply-and-demand-determined, level of output. In terms of Exhibit 5, it is the loss to society of producing $Q_2$ instead of producing $Q_1$.

**WHAT SOME PEOPLE GET WRONG** In closing, some persons argue that a price floor creates a situation in which (1) someone wins and someone loses and (2) the gains for the winner are equal to the losses for the loser (e.g., one person loses $5, and another person wins $5). A quick look at Exhibit 5 tells us that (2) is not true. The losses (for consumers) are not offset by the gains (for producers). A price ceiling ends with a *net loss,* or *deadweight loss,* of areas $3 + 5$. Now think of how hard it would have been to identify this deadweight loss without the tools of supply, demand, consumers' surplus, and producers' surplus. Economic tools often have the ability to make what is invisible visible.

## SELF-TEST

1. Do buyers prefer lower prices to higher prices?

2. "When there are long-lasting shortages, there are long lines of people waiting to buy goods. It follows that the shortages cause the long lines." Do you agree or disagree? Explain your answer.

3. Who might argue for a price ceiling? A price floor?

# TWO PRICES: ABSOLUTE AND RELATIVE

In everyday language, we often use the word "price" without specifying the kind of price. Economists often distinguish the *absolute,* or *money, price* of a good from the *relative price* of a good.

## Absolute (Money) Price and Relative Price

**Absolute (Money) Price**
The price of a good in money terms.

**Relative Price**
The price of a good in terms of another good.

The absolute (money) price is the price of the good in money terms. For example, the absolute price of a car might be $30,000. The relative price is the price of the good *in terms of another good.* To illustrate, suppose the absolute price of a car is $30,000 and the absolute price of a computer is $2,000. The relative price of the car—that is, the price of the car *in terms of computers*—is 15 computers. A person gives up the opportunity to buy 15 computers when buying a car.

$$\text{Relative price of a car (in terms of computers)} = \frac{\text{Absolute price of a car}}{\text{Absolute price of a computer}}$$

$$= \frac{\$30,000}{\$2,000}$$

$$= 15$$

Now let's compute the relative price of a computer—that is, the price of a computer in terms of a car:

$$\text{Relative price of a computer (in terms of cars)} = \frac{\text{Absolute price of a computer}}{\text{Absolute price of a car}}$$

$$= \frac{\$2,000}{\$30,000}$$

$$= \frac{1}{15}$$

# economics 24/7

## Will a Soda Tax Reduce Obesity?

The percentage of the U.S. population that is deemed obese today is higher than it was 20 years ago. Obesity is a health problem; so often we hear proposals directed at trying to reduce the obesity rate in the country. One proposal is to place a tax on high-fat, high-calorie so-called junk food. A similar proposal is to place a tax on soda.

We now know that a tax placed on one good (but not on another) will change the relative prices of the two goods. Placing a tax on good X, but not on good Y, will make good X relatively more expensive and Y relatively cheaper, prompting consumers to purchase relatively less X and relatively more Y.

PAUL BURNS/SHANNON FAGAN/JUPITER IMAGES

Consider a tax placed on soda. We would expect the absolute (money) price of soda to rise. And if the tax is placed only on soda, its relative price will rise too. As soda becomes relatively more expensive, we would expect fewer sodas to be consumed and obesity to decline. Right? Well, fewer sodas might be purchased and consumed, but whether obesity will decline is not so clear. Consider soda and sugared iced tea. Both soda and sugared iced tea are sweet drinks. They might even be substitutes. With this in

mind, suppose the absolute price of a soda is $1 and the absolute price of an iced tea (with sugar) is 50¢. It follows that the relative prices are:

1 soda = 2 sugared iced teas
1 sugared iced tea = ½ soda

Now let's place a tax on soda that drives its price up to $2. The new relative prices for soda and iced tea are:

1 soda = 4 sugared iced teas
1 sugared iced tea = ¼ soda

As a result of the tax on soda, its relative price has risen, but the relative price of sugared iced tea has fallen. We would expect people to consume relatively less soda and relatively more sugared iced tea.

Obesity is lessened by ingesting fewer calories, not the same number or more calories. Simply put, the soda tax might reduce the consumption of sodas, but it doesn't necessarily reduce obesity. The soda tax, although it makes soda relatively more expensive, makes its substitutes (such as sugared iced tea) relatively less expensive and thus makes a rise in the consumption of sugared iced tea likely.

Thus, the relative price of a computer in this example is 1/15 of a car. A person gives up the opportunity to buy 1/15 of a car when buying a computer.

Now consider this question: What happens to the relative price of a good if its absolute price rises and nothing else changes? For example, if the absolute price of a car rises from $30,000 to $40,000, what happens to its relative price? Obviously, the relative price rises from 15 computers to 20 computers. In short, if the absolute price of a good rises and nothing else changes, then its relative price rises too.

## ⓣhinking like AN ECONOMIST

**Higher Absolute Price Can Sometimes Mean Lower Relative Price** Economists know that a good can go up in price at the same time as it becomes relatively cheaper. How can this happen? Suppose the absolute price of a pen is $1, and the absolute price of a pencil is 10¢. The relative price of 1 pen, then, is 10 pencils.

*(continued)*

## ⓣhinking like **AN ECONOMIST** (continued)

Now let the absolute price of a pen rise to $1.20 at the same time that the absolute price of a pencil rises to 20¢. As a result, the relative price of 1 pen falls to 6 pencils. In other words, the absolute price of pens rises (from $1 to $1.20) at the same time as pens become relatively cheaper (in terms of how many pencils you have to give up to buy a pen).

How does this happen? The absolute price of pen went up by 20 percent (from $1 to $1.20) at the same time as the absolute price of pencils doubled (from 10¢ to 20¢). Because the absolute price of a pen went up by *less than* the absolute price increase of a pencil, the relative price of a pen fell. ▲ ▲ ▲

## Taxes on Specific Goods and Relative Price Changes

Suppose that the equilibrium price of good X is $10 and that the equilibrium price of good Y is $20. The relative price of good X is therefore ½ unit of good Y, and the relative price of good Y is 2 units of good X.

$$1X = \tfrac{1}{2}Y$$

$$1Y = 2X$$

Given these relative prices of X and Y, consumers will buy some combination of the two goods. For example, a given consumer might end up buying 10 units of X each week and 12 units of Y.

Now suppose that the government imposes a tax only on the purchase of good X. The tax effectively raises the price the consumer pays for the good from $10 to $15. Because no tax is placed on good Y, its price remains at $20.

The tax thus changes the relative prices of the two goods. The after-tax relative prices are:

$$1X = \tfrac{3}{4}Y$$

$$1Y = 1.33X$$

Comparing the new relative prices with the old relative prices, we recognize that the tax makes X relatively more expensive (going from ½Y to ¾Y) and makes Y relatively cheaper (going from 2X to 1.33X). In other words, a tax placed only on X ends up making X relatively more expensive and Y relatively cheaper. As a result, we would expect consumers to buy relatively less X and relatively more Y. Think in terms of two familiar goods: Coke and Pepsi. A tax placed on Coke, but not on Pepsi, will induce consumers to buy relatively less Coke and relatively more Pepsi.

### SELF-TEST

1. If the absolute (or money) price of good A is $40 and the absolute price of good B is $60, what is the relative price of each good?

2. Someone says, "The price of good X has risen; so good X is more expensive than it used to be." In what sense is this statement correct? In what sense is this statement either incorrect or misleading?

## "I Thought Price Ceilings Were Good for Consumers"

**STUDENT:**

I still don't quite understand how a price ceiling can hurt consumers. After all, a price ceiling is usually set below the equilibrium price of a good, and everyone knows that consumers prefer lower prices to higher prices.

**INSTRUCTOR:**

The problem is that when a price ceiling is imposed on a good, certain things happen that don't benefit consumers. Look at it this way: Consumers like the lower price that goes along with the price ceiling, but what they don't like are some of the effects of the price ceiling.

**STUDENT:**

But it seems to me that if you picked 100 consumers at random and asked them whether they preferred the price of bread to be $1 a loaf as opposed to $2, all 100 consumers would say they prefer the lower price. Because a price ceiling is usually lower than the equilibrium price, doesn't this example prove that consumers benefit from price ceilings? After all, why would they say they prefer paying $1 than $2 for a loaf of bread if they didn't see it benefiting them?

**INSTRUCTOR:**

A couple of things could be going on here. First, consumers might intuitively take the question to mean do they prefer the *$1 supply-and-demand-determined price* to the *$2 supply-and-demand-determined price*. If this is how they understand the question, then it certainly seems reasonable for them to say they prefer the lower price to the higher price. You might not get the same response from consumers, though, if you asked them this question:

Which of the following two options do you prefer?

Option A:
 $2 (equilibrium) price of bread

Option B:
 $1 (price ceiling) price of bread +
 shortages of bread +
 lines of people waiting to buy bread, and so on.

**STUDENT:**

In other words, your point is that consumers prefer lower to higher prices, assuming that nothing else changes but the price of the good. But if lower prices as the result of price ceilings come with shortages and long lines of people waiting to buy bread, then they may not prefer lower to higher prices.

**INSTRUCTOR:**

Yes, that is the point.

**STUDENT:**

A slightly different question: Do you think all consumers know the adverse effects of price ceilings?

**INSTRUCTOR:**

Probably not. In fact, even after government imposes a price ceiling and certain adverse effects set in (shortages, long lines, etc.), consumers may fail to relate the cause to the effects of the price ceiling. In other words, X causes Y, but individuals either don't understand how (so they don't connect the two), or they believe that something else—Z—causes Y.

**POINTS TO REMEMBER**

1. Consumers may prefer a lower to higher price, *ceteris paribus*, but not a lower price with shortages to a higher price without shortages.
2. X may cause Y, but it doesn't necessarily follow that everyone will understand that X causes Y.

## CHAPTER SUMMARY

### PRICE

- As a result of scarcity, a rationing device is needed to determine who gets what of the available limited resources and goods. Price serves as a rationing device.

- Price acts as a transmitter of information relating to the change in the relative scarcity of a good.

### PRICE CEILINGS

- A price ceiling is a government-mandated maximum price. If a price ceiling is below the equilibrium price, some or all of the following effects arise: shortages, fewer exchanges, nonprice-rationing devices, buying and selling at prohibited prices, and tie-in sales.

- Consumers do not necessarily prefer (lower) price ceilings to (higher) equilibrium prices. They may prefer higher prices and

none of the effects of price ceilings to lower prices and some of the effects of price ceilings. All we can say for sure is that consumers prefer lower prices to higher prices, *ceteris paribus.*

### PRICE FLOORS

- A price floor is a government-mandated minimum price. If a price floor is above the equilibrium price, the following effects arise: surpluses and fewer exchanges.

### ABSOLUTE PRICE AND RELATIVE PRICE

- The absolute price of a good is the price of the good in terms of money.

- The relative price of a good is the price of the good in terms of another good.

## KEY TERMS AND CONCEPTS

Price Ceiling                Price Floor              Absolute (Money) Price        Relative Price
Tie-in Sale                  Deadweight Loss

## QUESTIONS AND PROBLEMS

1. "If price were outlawed as the rationing device (used in markets), there would be no need for another rationing device to take its place. We would have reached utopia." Discuss.

2. What kind of information does price transmit?

3. Should grades in an economics class be "rationed" according to dollar price instead of how well a student does on the exams? If they were and prospective employers learned of this, what effect might this have on the value of your college degree?

4. Think of ticket scalpers at a rock concert, a baseball game, and an opera. Might they exist because the tickets to these events were originally sold for less than the equilibrium price? Why or why not? In what way is a ticket scalper like and unlike your retail grocer, who buys food from a wholesaler and then sells it to you?

5. Many of the proponents of price ceilings argue that government-mandated maximum prices simply reduce producers' profits and do not affect the quantity supplied of a good on the market. What must the supply curve look like if the price ceiling does not affect the quantity supplied?

6. James lives in a rent-controlled apartment and has for the past few weeks been trying to get the supervisor to fix his shower. What does waiting to get one's shower fixed have to do with a rent-controlled apartment?

7. Explain why fewer exchanges are made when a disequilibrium price (below equilibrium price) exists than when the equilibrium price exists.

8. Buyers always prefer lower prices to higher prices. Do you agree or disagree with this statement? Explain your answer.

9. What is the difference between a price ceiling and a price floor? What effect is the same for both a price ceiling and a price floor?

10. If the absolute price of good X is $10 and the absolute price of good Y is $14, then what is (a) the relative price of good X in terms of good Y and (b) the relative price of good Y in terms of good X?

11. Give a numerical example that illustrates how a tax placed on the purchase of good X can change the relative price of good X in terms of Y.

## WORKING WITH NUMBERS AND GRAPHS

1. In the diagram, what areas represent the deadweight loss due to the price ceiling ($P_C$)?

2. In the preceding diagram, what areas represent consumers' surplus at the equilibrium price of $P_E$? At $P_C$? (Keep in mind that the equilibrium quantity is not produced and sold at $P_C$.)

# SUPPLY, DEMAND, AND PRICE: APPLICATIONS

**Introduction** In the previous two chapters, we discussed supply, demand, and price. In this chapter, we work with supply, demand, and price. The theory of supply and demand is not very useful to you unless you can use it to explain some of the things you see around you in everyday life. In this chapter, we discuss medical care, changing house prices, college classes at 10 a.m., driving on a freeway, standardized tests (such as the SAT), college athletes, and more—all in the general framework of supply and demand.

## APPLICATION 1: WHY IS IT SO HARD TO GET TICKETS TO THE TAPING OF *THE BIG BANG THEORY*

If you go to tvtickets.com, you can request tickets to view the taping of television shows. There is no charge for the ticket; the ticket price is zero. Now ask yourself whether a zero price is the market equilibrium price. Given some degree of positive demand to see the show, you would think that the market equilibrium price would be positive. You would also expect the market equilibrium ticket price to be higher for some shows than for others.

To illustrate, suppose the supply of seats in a TV studio is 200 seats. Three shows are taped in the studio. Will the market equilibrium price for the three shows be the same—say, $20? It could be, but more probably it is not because the demand for each of the three shows is likely to be different. The equilibrium price might be $100 for one show, $70 for another show, and $20 for the third show.

But the market equilibrium price is not charged for any of the three shows. Instead, the price of a ticket is zero for all of them. What follows, then, is that there will be a shortage of tickets for each show, with the shortage being larger for some shows than for others. See Exhibit 1.

How will the shortage for each show manifest itself? And how will we know whether the shortage is different for each show? The answer has to do with how easy or hard it is to get a ticket to a show. At the tvtickets.com site, the tickets for some shows are sold out and some are not. For example, getting tickets for *The Big Bang Theory* (CBS) is very difficult. When tickets become available for that show, the first people to place their requests for the show get the tickets. In other words, tickets are rationed on a first-come-first-served basis (with the exception of persons who might know someone in the cast of the show). Because of the popularity of *The Big Bang Theory*, tickets go quickly.

Of course, tickets don't go as quickly for all other shows. For instance, the demand for new-show tickets is sometimes less than the supply. When this happens, the market equilibrium price might actually be negative. For example, in Exhibit 2, the demand for seats to a new show and the supply of seats for it intersect at a negative price (–$20), The producers of the show would actually have to pay people to watch a taping, specifically, $20. More often than not, however, producers don't pay people.

How, then, do they deal with the surplus of seats that would exist at the zero price (see Exhibit 2). Often they ask friends and family members to do them a favor and come to the taping of the show. As the show gains real fans, the demand to see the show rises, and there may no longer be any surplus seats at a zero ticket price. Of course, if the problem of surplus seats doesn't go away, you can bet that the TV show will.

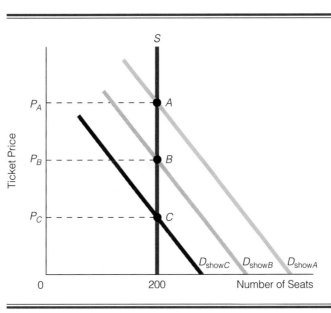

**EXHIBIT 1**

**The Supply and Demand for Viewing the Taping of Different TV Shows**

We show the demand to view the taping of three TV shows: A, B, and C. We also show the supply of seats for each show. If the ticket price for each show is $0, then the shortage will be greater for show A than for B, and greater for B than for C. Also, if an equilibrium price were charged for each show, the equilibrium price for show A would be greater than for show B and greater for B than C.

**EXHIBIT 2**

**A Negative Price: We'll Pay You to View the Taping of the Show**

We have assumed that the demand for seats for the taping of a new TV show is low enough that it intersects the supply of seats at a negative price (–$20). At this point, the producers of the show would have to pay people to view the taping of the show.

**SELF-TEST**

(Answers to Self-Test questions are in Answers to Self-Test Questions at the back of the book.)

1. How can a television network that produces a number of television shows gauge the popularity of each show from ticket requests and the rate at which tickets sell out?

2. Could television networks charge a positive ticket price for the taping of their shows if they wanted to? Explain your answer.

# APPLICATION 2: GOVERNMENT, EASIER LOANS, AND HOUSING PRICES

If the federal government wants to make it easier for people to buy houses, one thing it can do is push for lowered lending standards. For example, suppose lenders require individuals who want a mortgage loan to buy a house to make a down payment of 20 percent of the sale price. The government passes a law stating that no lender can require more than a 5 percent down payment before granting a loan. Will this make it easier for individuals to buy homes? Not necessarily. The interest rate on a mortgage loan that requires only a 5 percent down payment might be higher than the rate on one that requires a 20 percent down payment.

Can government do anything now? It could undertake specific monetary actions that have the effect of lowering interest rates (we will discuss this in detail in a later chapter).

Then what happens? The government seems to have met its objective of making it easier for individuals to buy houses. After all, prospective buyers now have only to come up with a 5 percent down payment (instead of 20 percent), and they end up paying lower interest rates for the loans they receive. So, are home buyers necessarily better off with this kind of government assistance? Not exactly.

By making mortgage loans easier to get, the government has indirectly increased the demand for houses. As the demand for houses rises, so do house prices. In short, making it easier to get home mortgage loans (as described) results in rising home prices, which makes buying a house all the harder.

Lower down payments + Lower interest rates → Easier-to-obtain loans → Higher demand for houses → Higher house prices

The main point is simply this: Government set out to make buying a home easier for more people by passing laws that forced lenders to accept lower down payments and by undertaking actions to put downward pressure on interest rates. But making it easier for individuals to get loans had the effect of raising the demand for and the prices of houses. Higher house prices made it harder for people to buy homes.

Continuing on with the story, suppose government now states that individuals need even more help now to get a home because housing prices have risen. In its attempt to help people to buy a house, it pushes for even lower lending standards (maybe requiring only a 1 percent down payment) and lower interest rates. Will that do the trick? Not likely. The lower lending standards and interest rates are likely to stimulate greater demand for housing, leading to even higher housing prices.

## SELF-TEST

1. If lowering lending standards can indirectly raise housing prices, can increasing lending standards lower housing prices? Explain.

2. Suppose anyone who buys a house in year 1 gets to pay $1,000 less in income taxes (assuming the tax owed is greater than $1,000). Would the tax credit affect house prices? Explain your answer.

# APPLICATION 3: SOUTHWEST AIRLINES AND THE PRICE OF AN AISLE SEAT

Most airlines will reserve an assigned seat for you when you buy a ticket. For example, if you want to buy an airline ticket from U.S. Airways, you can go online, purchase the ticket, and then look at a graphic that shows unreserved seats. If seat 13A is the one you want and no one has chosen it, then it is yours if you click it.

Southwest Airlines does things differently. You do not reserve a seat when you book a flight. You choose a seat when you board the plane. If you are one of the first to board, you have your pick of many seats; if you are one of the last, you have your pick of very few seats.

Keep in mind that aisle seats are more popular than middle seats. Usually, for every aisle seat there is a middle seat (assuming that the row of seats on each side of the plane consists of 3 seats: window, middle, and aisle). So, if the plane has 50 aisle seats, it also has 50 middle seats. In other words, the supply of middle seats equals the supply of aisle seats.

However, the demand for aisle seats is higher than the demand for middle seats. If price were to equilibrate the middle seats market and the aisle seats market, we would expect the price of an aisle seat to be higher than that of a middle seat. See Exhibit 3.

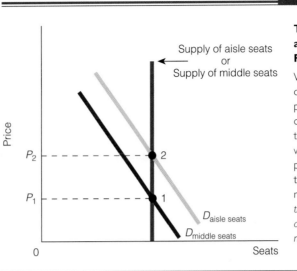

**The Market for Middle and Aisle Seats on Airline Flights**

We have assumed that the supply of aisle seats is equal to the supply of middle seats. Because the demand for aisle seats is higher than the demand for middle seats, we conclude that the equilibrium price for an aisle seat is higher than the equilibrium price for a middle seat. In the diagram, $P_2$ is the equilibrium price for an aisle seat, and $P_1$ is the equilibrium price for a middle seat.

Does Southwest charge more for an aisle seat than a middle seat? Perhaps if you asked the airline this question, its answer would be no. But Southwest does charge more for priority boarding. If you want to board before others, you must choose the Business Select option when purchasing a ticket. If you board before others, you obviously have a larger selection of seats to choose from than later boarders do. Because most people prefer aisle to middle seats, persons who board the plane first will probably choose the aisle seats.

So does Business Select come with an additional charge? Yes. On the day we checked, the added charge was $20. In effect, Southwest was charging $20 more for an aisle seat than a middle seat, as we would expect, because the demand for aisle seats is higher than the demand for middle seats, whereas the supply of each is the same.

**SELF-TEST**

1. If the equilibrium price is $400 for an aisle seat and $350 for a middle seat but an airlines company charges $350 for each seat, we would expect a shortage to appear in the aisle seat market. (More people will want aisle seats than there are aisle seats available.) How will the airlines decide who gets an aisle seat?

2. Suppose the supply of aisle, middle, and window seats is each 100 seats but the demand for aisle seats is greater than the demand for window seats, which, in turn, is greater than the demand for middle seats. If the equilibrium price of an aisle seat is $300, where do the equilibrium prices of middle and window seats stand in relation to this price?

# APPLICATION 4: WHY IS MEDICAL CARE SO EXPENSIVE?

Think of how you buy groceries. You go to the store, place certain products in your basket, and then pay for them at the cash register.

Now think of how you buy medical care. You go to the doctor or hospital, give the doctor's office or hospital your health insurance card, perhaps pay a copayment of $10 or $20, and then receive medical care. Your doctor or the hospital bills your insurance company for the bulk of your expenses.

What is the difference between how you buy groceries and how you buy medical care? In the grocery store, only two parties are involved in the transaction: you (the buyer) and the grocery store (the seller). In the medical care example, three parties are involved: you, the doctor or hospital, and the insurance company. The insurance company is often referred to as the "third party." So no third party is involved in the grocery store transaction, but one is involved in purchasing medical care.

The existence of a third party separates the buying of something from the paying for something. In the grocery store, the person who buys the groceries and the person who pays for them are the same (you). In the medical care example, the person who buys and receives the medical care (you) is different from the person or entity that pays for the medical care (the insurance company).

"Wait a minute," you say. "You indirectly pay for your medical care by paying monthly insurance premiums to the medical insurance company." That is partly true, but what happens is like being at a buffet. You pay a set dollar price for the buffet, and then you can eat all you want. Our guess is that at a buffet you eat more than you would if you had to pay for each plateful.

The same often happens with medical care. You pay a set premium to the insurance company (let's say $250 a month), and then you enter the health-care buffet line. Might you end up buying more health care than you would if each doctor visit and lab test at the health-care buffet were priced separately?

Before we continue, let's consider two objections to this analogy.

First, you might say, "But I don't buy medical care as I buy food in the food buffet line. I like shrimp, steak, salads, and desserts, but who likes being x-rayed, being prodded and poked by doctors, and taking medicine? No one buys MRIs as if they were shrimp cocktails."

That objection is true, of course, but it begs the point: Once you get sick and go to the doctor or hospital, the existence of a third party (who pays for your medical care) makes it easier for your doctor and/or the hospital to opt for more medical examinations/procedures and care than you need. For example, a conversation in your doctor's office may go like this:

**Doctor:** I think you have condition X, but just to be sure let's order some blood tests and get an MRI too.

**You:** Whatever you think is best.

Now ask yourself how you might respond if you had to pay—out of pocket—for the blood test and MRI. The dialogue might change:

**Doctor:** I think you have condition X, but just to be sure let's order some blood tests and get an MRI too.

**You:** How much is this going to cost me, doctor? And is all this really necessary?

The point is simple: Once you have paid your insurance premium, the price you pay for medical care amounts only to your copayment (which is usually minimal). For all practical purposes, the dollar amount you pay for medical care, out of pocket, is close to zero—a fairly low price for health care. We can expect that the quantity demanded of medical care would be greater at zero than at some positive dollar amount.

Second, let's link the *quantity demanded* for medical care in general (which is high if the price of medical care is zero) with the *demand for specific items* that make up medical care. (In our food buffet example, we would link the *quantity demanded* of food with the *demand* for specific food items—shrimp, chocolate ice cream, a Caesar's salad, and the like.)

If the quantity demanded of medical care is higher at a zero price than at some positive price, then we would expect the demand for the *specific items* that make up medical care to be higher than it would be if the quantity demanded of medical care were lower. This is shown diagrammatically in Exhibit 4. In Exhibit 4(a), the demand for medical care is downward sloping. If the price is zero for health care, then the quantity demanded of medical care is 100 units. But if the price is some positive dollar amount (such as $P_1$), then the quantity demanded of medical care is 50 units.

Exhibit 4(b) does not show the demand for medical care in general, just the demand for a specific item of medical care—x-rays. Of the two demand curves in panel (b), the first $(D_1)$ is the demand that exists for x-rays if the *quantity demanded of medical care* is

**EXHIBIT 4**

**The Price of Medical Care and the Demand for X-rays**

(a) If the price of medical care is low (say, zero), the quantity demanded of medical care is 100

units. If the price of medical care for you is $P_1$, the quantity demanded of medical care is 50 units. (b) The lower the price of medical care and the higher the quantity demanded of

medical care in panel (a), then the higher the demand curve for x-rays in (b). (c) The higher the demand for x-rays, the higher the price of x-rays.

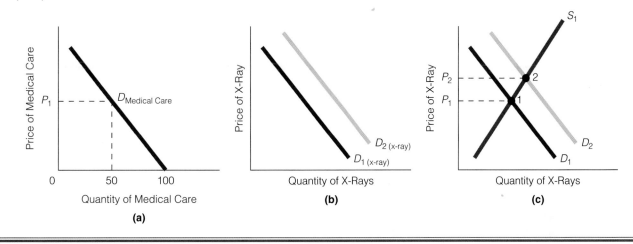

(a)

(b)

(c)

50 units in panel (a); it is the demand for x-rays if the price for medical care (shown in panel a) is $P_1$. The second demand curve $(D_2)$ is the demand curve for x-rays if the *quantity demanded of medical care* is 100 units in panel (a); it is the demand for x-rays if the price for medical care (shown in panel a) is zero.

Here is the point in a nutshell:

- The *lower* the price of medical care, the higher the quantity demanded of medical care and the higher the demand for x-rays.

Price of medical care is low → Quantity demanded of medical care is high → Demand for x-rays is high

- The *higher* the price of medical care, the lower the quantity demanded of medical care and the lower the demand for x-rays.

Price of medical care is high → Quantity demanded of medical care is low → Demand for x-rays is low

Now the question is what does a high demand for x-rays do to the price of an x-ray? Obviously, it pushes the price upward. See Exhibit 4(c).

As a result, the health insurance company finds itself paying more for the x-rays you receive. Can you see what will happen next? The health insurance company makes the argument that with rising medical costs, the premiums for your coverage need to rise too.

Why is health insurance as expensive as it is? You now have a large part of the answer. Think buffet.

**SELF-TEST**

1. Suppose food insurance exists. You pay the food insurance company a certain dollar amount each month and then you purchase all the food you want from your local grocery store. The grocery store sends the bill to your food insurance company. What will happen to

the price of food and to the premium you pay for food insurance?

2. In Exhibit 4(a), suppose that the price a person has to pay for medical care is between $P_1$ and zero. Where would the demand for x-rays in panel (b) be in relationship to $D_1$ and $D_2$?

# APPLICATION 5: WHY DO COLLEGES USE GPAS, ACTS, AND SATS FOR PURPOSES OF ADMISSION?

At many colleges and universities, students pay part of the price of their education (in the form of tuition payments), and taxpayers and private donors pay part (by way of tax payments and charitable donations, respectively). Thus, the tuition that students pay to attend colleges and universities is usually less than the equilibrium tuition. To illustrate, suppose a student pays tuition $T_1$ at a given college or university. As shown in Exhibit 5, $T_1$ is below the equilibrium tuition, $T_E$. At $T_1$, the number of students who want to attend the university ($N_1$) is greater than the number of openings at the university ($N_2$); that is, quantity demanded is greater than quantity supplied. The university receives more applications for admission than there are places available. Something has to be done. But what?

The college or university is likely to ration its available space by a combination of money price and some nonprice-rationing devices. The student must pay the tuition, $T_1$, *and* meet the standards of the nonprice-rationing devices. Colleges and universities typically use such things as GPAs (grade point averages), ACT scores, and SAT scores as rationing devices.

**College and University Admissions**

If the college or university charges $T_1$ in tuition (when $T_E$ is the equilibrium tuition), a shortage will be generated. The college or university will then use some nonprice rationing device, such as GPAs, ACTs, and SATs, as admission criteria.

## ⓣhinking like AN ECONOMIST

**Identifying Rationing Devices**  The layperson sees a GPA of 3.8 and an SAT score of 1,900 or better as requirements for admission. Economists see them as a rationing device. Economists then go on to ask why this particular nonprice-rationing device is used. They reason that a nonprice-rationing device would not be needed if (dollar) price were fully rationing the good or service. ▪ ▪ ▪

### SELF-TEST

1. The demand rises for admission to a university, but both the tuition and the number of openings in the entering class remain the same. Will this change affect the admission standards of the university? Explain your answer.

2. Administrators and faculty at state colleges and universities often say that their standards of admission are independent of whether there is a shortage or surplus of openings at the university. Do you think this is true? Do you think that faculty and administrators ignore surpluses and shortages of openings when setting admission standards? Explain your answer.

# APPLICATION 6 : SUPPLY AND DEMAND ON A FREEWAY

What does a traffic jam on a busy freeway in any large city have to do with supply and demand? Actually, it has quite a bit to do with supply and demand. Look at the question this way: There is a demand for driving on the freeway and a supply of freeway space. The supply of freeway space is fixed (roadways do not expand and contract over a day, week, or month). The demand, however, fluctuates; it is higher at some times than at others. For example, we would expect the demand for driving on the freeway to be higher at 8 a.m. (the rush hour) than at 11 p.m. But even though the demand may vary, the money price for driving on the freeway is always the same: zero. A zero money price means that motorists do not pay tolls to drive on the freeway.

Exhibit 6 shows two demand curves for driving on the freeway: $D_{8 \text{ a.m.}}$ and $D_{11 \text{ p.m.}}$ We have assumed the demand at 8 a.m. to be greater than at 11 p.m. We have also assumed that at $D_{11 \text{ p.m.}}$ and zero money price the freeway market clears: The quantity demanded of freeway space equals the quantity supplied. At the higher demand, $D_{8 \text{ a.m.}}$, this is not the case. At zero money price, a shortage of freeway space exists:

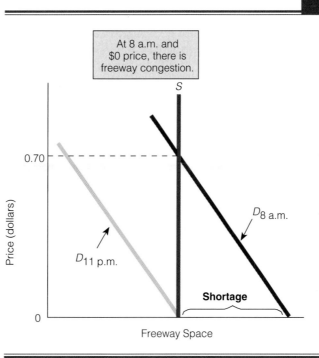

**EXHIBIT 6**

**Freeway Congestion and Supply and Demand**

The demand for driving on the freeway is higher at 8 a.m. than at 11 p.m. At zero money price and $D_{11}$ p.m., the freeway market clears. At zero money price and $D_8$ a.m., there is a shortage of freeway space, which shows up as freeway congestion. At a price (toll) of 70 cents, the shortage is eliminated and freeway congestion disappears.

The quantity demanded of freeway space is greater than the quantity supplied. The shortage appears as freeway congestion and bumper-to-bumper traffic. One way to eliminate the shortage is through an increase in the money price of driving on the freeway at 8 a.m. For example, as Exhibit 6 shows, a toll of 70¢ would clear the freeway market at 8 a.m.

If charging different prices (tolls) depending on the time of day on freeways sounds like an unusual idea, consider how Miami Beach hotels price their rooms. They charge different prices for their rooms depending on time of year. During the winter months, when the demand for vacationing in Miami Beach is high, the hotels charge higher prices than when the demand is (relatively) low. If different prices were charged for freeway space depending on time of day, freeway space would be rationed the same way Miami Beach hotel rooms are rationed.

Finally, consider three alternatives usually proposed to counter freeway congestion:

- *Tolls:* Tolls deal with the congestion problem by adjusting price to its equilibrium level, as shown in Exhibit 6.

- *Building more freeways:* Building more freeways deals with the problem by increasing supply. In Exhibit 6, the supply curve of freeway space would have to be shifted to the right so that there is no longer any shortage of space at 8 a.m.

- *Encouraging carpooling:* More carpooling deals with the problem by decreasing demand. Two people in one car take up less space on a freeway than two people in two cars. In Exhibit 6, if, through carpooling, the demand at 8 a.m. begins to look like the demand at 11 p.m., then there is no longer a shortage of freeway space at 8 a.m.

A final note: A fee to drive in the Central London area was introduced in 2003. Anyone going into or out of the Central London area between 7:00 a.m. and 6:30 p.m., Monday through Friday, must pay a fee of approximately $15. (Not everyone has to pay the fee. For example, taxi drivers, ambulance drivers, police vehicles, motorcycle drivers, and bicyclists are exempt. The residents who live in the area receive a 90 percent discount.) Many people have claimed the fee a success because it has cut down on traffic and travel times and reduced pollution in the area.

Some people have urged New York City to institute a fee program to drive on certain streets in the city. On any given day in New York City, approximately 800,000 cars are on the streets south of 60th Street in Manhattan. According to many, the city is "choking in traffic." We will have to wait to see whether New York City goes the way of London.

## ⓣhinking like AN ECONOMIST

**It's One of Three** The economist knows that when there are buyers and sellers of anything (bread, cars, or freeway space), only three conditions are possible: equilibrium, shortage, or surplus. When the economist sees traffic congestion, the first thing that comes to mind is the shortage of road space. Buy why is there a shortage? The economist knows that shortages occur at prices below equilibrium price. In other words, the price is too low. ▰ ▰ ▰

## SELF-TEST

1. In Exhibit 6, at what price is there a surplus of freeway space at 8 a.m.?

2. If the driving population increases in an area and the supply of freeway space remains constant, what will happen to freeway congestion? Explain your answer.

# APPLICATION 7: ARE RENTERS BETTER OFF?

We begin with an analysis of two laws related to the eviction of a renter.

- Under law 1, a renter has 30 days to vacate an apartment after being served with an eviction notice.

- Under law 2, the renter has 90 days to vacate.

Landlords will find it less expensive to rent apartments under law 1 than under law 2. Under law 1, the most money a landlord can lose after serving an eviction notice is 30 days' rent. Under law 2, a landlord can lose up to 90 days' rent. Obviously, losing 90 days' rent is more costly than losing 30 days' rent.

A different supply curve of apartments exists under each law. The supply curve under law 1 ($S_1$ in Exhibit 7) lies to the right of the supply curve under law 2 ($S_2$). It is less expensive to supply apartments under law 1 than under law 2.

If the supply curve is different under the two laws, the equilibrium rent will be different too. As shown in Exhibit 7, the equilibrium rent will be lower under law 1 ($R_1$) than under law 2 ($R_2$).

So:

- Under law 1, a renter pays lower rent (good) and has fewer days to vacate the apartment (bad).

- Under law 2, a renter pays a higher rent (bad) and has more days to vacate the apartment (good).

## EXHIBIT 7

**Apartment Rent and the Law**

Under law 1, a renter has 30 days to leave an apartment after receiving an eviction notice from his or her landlord. Under law 2, a renter has 90 days to leave an apartment after receiving an eviction notice from his or her landlord. The cost to the landlord of renting an apartment is higher under law 2 than law 1, and so the supply curve of apartments under law 1 lies to the right of the supply curve of apartments under law 2. Different supply curves mean different rents. Apartment rent is higher under law 2 ($R_2$) than under law 1 ($R_1$).

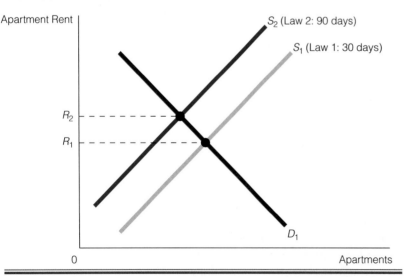

Who pays for the additional days to vacate the apartment under law 2? The renter pays for them by paying a higher rent.

# ⓕinding ECONOMICS

**In an HMO** You may frequently hear people complain about their health maintenance organizations (HMOs). Of the diverse and wide-ranging complaints, a common one is that patients cannot sue their HMOs in state courts for denial of benefits and poor-quality care. Some people argue that patients should have the right to sue their HMOs.

Let's consider two settings: one in which patients cannot sue their HMOs and one in which they can. If patients cannot sue, an HMO's liability cost is lower than if patients can sue. A difference in liability costs is then reflected in different supply curves.

To illustrate, recall that any single point on a supply curve is the minimum price sellers need to receive for them to be willing and able to sell that unit of a good. Suppose that when patients cannot sue, an HMO is willing and able to provide health care to John for $300 a month. If patients can sue, is the HMO still willing and able to provide the service for $300 a month? Not likely. Because of the higher liability cost due to patients' ability to sue, the HMO is still willing and able to provide health care to John, but for, say, $350 month, not $300.

Saying that a seller's minimum price for providing a good or service rises is the same as saying the seller's supply curve has shifted upward and to the left. In other words, the supply curve of HMO-provided health-care will shift upward and to the left if patients have the right to sue. This is how the supply curve of apartments moved in Exhibit 7. So, will a difference in supply curves affect the price patients pay for their HMO-provided health-care coverage? Yes. One effect of moving from a setting where patients do not have the right to sue to one where they do is that patients will have to pay more for their HMO-provided health-care coverage.

Economists don't determine whether a patient having the right to sue is good or bad or right or wrong. Economists use their tools (in this instance, supply and demand) to point out that the things people want, such as the right to sue their HMOs, often come with price tags. Individuals must decide whether the price they pay is worth what they receive in return. ▲ ▲ ▲

## SELF-TEST

1. Economists often say, "There is no such thing as a free lunch." How is this saying related to patients moving from a system where they cannot sue their HMOs to one where they can?

2. A professor tells her students that they can have an extra week to complete their research papers. Under what condition are the students better off with the extra week? Can you think of a case where the students would actually be worse off with the extra week?

# APPLICATION 8: DO YOU PAY FOR GOOD WEATHER?

Some places in the country are considered to have better weather than others. For example, most people would say the weather in San Diego, California, is better than the weather in Fargo, North Dakota. Often, a person in San Diego will say, "You can't beat the weather today. And the good thing about it is that you don't have to pay a thing for it. It's free."

In one sense, the San Diegan is correct: There is no weather market. Specifically, no one comes around each day and asks San Diegans to pay a certain dollar amount for the weather.

But in another sense, the San Diegan is incorrect: San Diegans indirectly do pay for their good weather. How do they pay? To enjoy the weather in San Diego on a regular basis,

**EXHIBIT 8**

**The Price of Weather and Housing Prices**

We show two demand curves, $D_1$ and $D_2$. $D_1$ represents the demand for housing in San Diego if the weather were not so good. The higher demand curve $D_2$ shows the demand for housing in San Diego if the weather is good. Notice that the price of housing in San Diego is higher if the weather is good than not so good. Lesson learned: You pay for good weather (in San Diego) in terms of higher house prices.

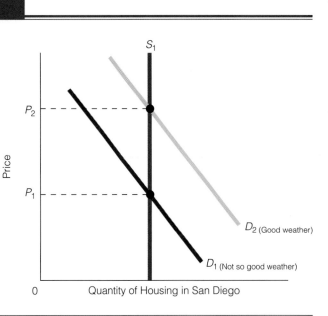

you have to live there; you need to have housing. There is a demand for housing in San Diego just as there is a demand for housing in other places. Is the demand for housing in San Diego higher than it would be if the weather were not so good? Without the good weather, living in San Diego would not be as pleasurable, and therefore the demand to live there would be lower.

See Exhibit 8. In short, the demand for housing in San Diego is higher because the city enjoys good weather. It follows that the price of housing is higher too ($P_2$ as opposed to $P_1$ in Exhibit 8). Thus, San Diegans indirectly pay for their good weather because they pay higher housing prices than they would if area had bad weather.

Was our representative San Diegan right when he said the good weather was free?

## finding ECONOMICS

**Good Schools and House Prices** There are two neighborhoods, A and B. The kids who live in neighborhood A go to school A, and the kids who live in neighborhood B go to school B. Currently, school A has a much better academic reputation than school B. Can you find the economics?

This case is really no more than a disguised version of our good weather example. If school A is better than school B, then the equilibrium price of houses in neighborhood A is likely to be higher than the equilibrium price of similar houses in neighborhood B. Just as we pay for good weather in terms of house prices, we pay for good schools in terms of house prices too. ▲ ▲ ▲

### SELF-TEST

1. Give an example to illustrate that someone may "pay" for clean air in much the same way as she "pays" for good weather.

2. If people pay for good weather, who ultimately receives the "good-weather payment"?

# APPLICATION 9: COLLEGE SUPERATHLETES

A young man, 17 years old, is one of the best high school football players in the country. As a superathlete, the young man will be recruited by many college and university football coaches. Every one of those schools will likely want its coach to be successful at signing up the young athlete; after all, at many universities, athletics is a moneymaker.

Our superathlete decides to attend college A, where he receives a "full ride"—a full scholarship. How should this full scholarship be viewed? One way is to say the superathlete is charged zero tuition to attend the college. (In other words, whereas some students pay a price of $30,000 a year to attend, the superathlete pays nothing.)

Another way to view the full scholarship is as a two-step process. First, the college pays the superathlete a dollar amount equal to the full tuition. Second, it charges the superathlete the full tuition. (In other words, the college gives the athlete $30,000 with one hand and then collects it with the other. )

Either way we view the scholarship, the effect is the same for the athlete. For purposes of our analysis, let's view it the second way: as a payment to the athlete combined with full price being charged. This view leads to two important questions:

1. Can the college pay the athlete more than the full tuition? In other words, if the full tuition is $30,000 a year, can the college pay the athlete, say, $35,000 a year?

2. Is the superathlete being paid what he is worth?

Because of NCAA rules, the answer to the first question is essentially no. The NCAA states that a college or university cannot pay a student to attend, and for all practical purposes the NCAA views payment as anything more than a full scholarship. The NCAA position is that college athletes are amateurs, and amateurs cannot be paid to play their sport.

How does the NCAA rule affect the second question? What if the athlete's worth to the college or university is greater than the dollar amount of the full tuition? For example, suppose the athlete will increase the revenues of the college by $100,000 a year, and the full tuition is $30,000 a year. In this case, the NCAA rule is actually a price ceiling (a below-equilibrium imposed price) on what the college may pay an athlete.

What is the effect of this price ceiling? Let's consider the demand (on the part of various colleges) for a single superathlete and the supply of this single superathlete (see Exhibit 9). We assume that the supply curve for athletic services is vertical at 1. If the representative college charges $30,000 in tuition, because of the NCAA rule, this dollar amount is the effective price ceiling (or wage ceiling). If the single athlete's market equilibrium wage is $35,000 and the NCAA rule did not exist, the athlete's wage would rise to $35,000. This dollar amount is equal to areas $B + C$ in Exhibit 9. The consumers' surplus for the college that buys the athlete's services for $35,000 is obviously equal to area $A$.

However, the NCAA rule stipulates that the college cannot pay the athlete more than $30,000 (full tuition). So the athlete's payment falls from $35,000 to $30,000, or from areas $B + C$ to simply area $C$. The college's consumers' surplus increases to areas $A + B$. Essentially, the NCAA rule transfers part of the athlete's income—area $B$—to the college in the form of greater consumers' surplus.

---

**EXHIBIT 9**

**The College Athlete**

The exhibit shows the demand for and supply of a college athlete. If the market wage for the college athlete is $35,000, then the buyer of the athlete—in this case, the college—receives consumers' surplus equal to area A. If the wage can be held down to the tuition cost of attending the college—$30,000 in this example—then the college receives consumers' surplus of areas A + B.

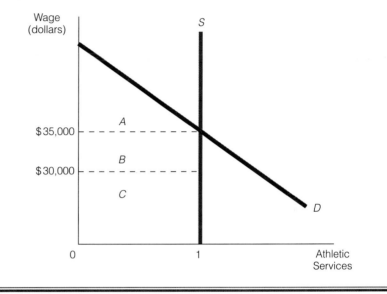

---

1. University X is a large school with a major football team. A new field house and track were just added to the campus. How is this related to the discussion in this application?

2. Sometimes it is argued that if colleges paid student athletes, the demand for college sports would decline. In other words, the demand for college sports is as high as it is because student athletes are not paid (in the same way as professional athletes are paid). How would the analysis in this application change if we assume this argument to be true?

# APPLICATION 10: 10 A.M. CLASSES IN COLLEGE

Suppose an economics class is offered in the same classroom twice in a day: at 10 a.m. in the morning and at 8 p.m. at night. Most students would prefer the 10 a.m. class to the 8 p.m. class. So, in Exhibit 10, the supply of seats in the class is the same at each time, but the demand to occupy those seats is not. Because the demand is greater for the 10 a.m. class than for the 8 p.m. class, the equilibrium price for the morning class is higher than the equilibrium price for the evening class.

But the university or college charges the same tuition no matter what time students choose to take the class. The university doesn't charge students a higher tuition if they enroll in 10 a.m. classes than if they enroll in 8 p.m. classes.

Suppose that tuition $T_1$ is charged for all classes and that $T_1$ is the equilibrium tuition for 8 p.m. classes (see Exhibit 10). $T_1$ is therefore below the equilibrium tuition for 10 a.m. classes. At $T_1$, the quantity demanded of seats for the morning classes will be greater than the quantity supplied; more students will want the earlier class than there is space available.

How will the university allocate the available seats? It may do it in the same way as airlines ration aisle seats: on a first-come-first-served basis. Students who are first to register get the 10 a.m. class; the latecomers have to take the 8 p.m. class. Or the university could ration the high-demand classes by giving their upper-class students (seniors) first priority.

**EXHIBIT 10**

**The Supply and Demand for College Classes at Different Times**

A given class is offered at two times, 10 a.m. and 8 p.m. The supply of seats in the classroom is the same at both times; however, the student demand for the 10 a.m. class is higher than the demand for the 8 p.m. class. The university charges the same tuition, $T_1$, regardless of which class a student takes. At this tuition, there is a shortage of seats for the 10 a.m. class. Seats are likely to be rationed on a first-come-first-served (first to register) basis or on seniority (seniors take precedence over juniors, etc.).

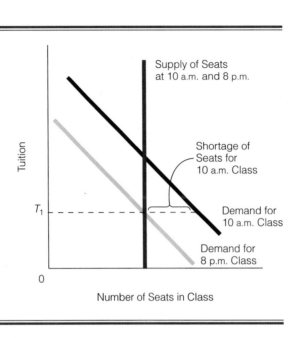

Supply of Seats at 10 a.m. and 8 p.m.

Shortage of Seats for 10 a.m. Class

Demand for 10 a.m. Class

Demand for 8 p.m. Class

Tuition

$T_1$

0

Number of Seats in Class

## ⓣhinking like AN ECONOMIST

**Remembering Price** Laypersons see students clamoring to get 10 a.m. classes and conclude that the demand is high for early classes. They then wonder why the university doesn't schedule more 10 a.m. classes. The economist knows that what laypeople see is as much an effect of price as of demand. The demand for 10 a.m. classes may be high, but the quantity demanded may not be if the price is high enough. In fact, even though the demand for classes at certain times may vary, some set of prices will make the quantity demanded of each class the same. ▪ ▪ ▪

## SELF-TEST

1. Suppose college students are given two options. With option A, the price a student pays for a class is always the equilibrium price. For example, if the equilibrium price to take Economics 101 is $600 at 10 a.m. and $400 at 4 p.m., then students pay more for the early class than they do for the later class. With option B, the price a student pays for a class is the same regardless of the time the class is taken. When given the choice between options A and B, many students would say they prefer option B to option A. Is this the case for you? If so, why would this be your choice?

2. How is the analysis of the 10 a.m. class similar to the analysis of a price ceiling in a market?

# APPLICATION 11: WHAT WILL HAPPEN TO THE PRICE OF MARIJUANA IF THE PURCHASE AND SALE OF MARIJUANA ARE LEGALIZED?

In the United States, the purchase or sale of marijuana is unlawful, but there is still a demand for it and a supply of it. There is also an equilibrium price of marijuana. Let's say that price is $P_1$. If tomorrow the purchase and sale of marijuana become legal, would $P_1$ rise, fall, or remain the same?

The answer, of course, depends on what we think will happen to the demand for and supply of marijuana. If the purchase and sale of marijuana are legal, then some people currently producing corn and wheat will likely choose instead to produce and sell marijuana. So the supply of marijuana will rise. If nothing else changes, its price will fall.

But something else is likely to change. If marijuana consumption is no longer illegal, then the number of people who want to buy and consume it will likely rise. In other words, more people will buy marijuana, thus increasing demand.

So decriminalizing the purchase and sale of marijuana is likely to shift both the marijuana demand and supply curves to the right. What happens to the price of marijuana depends on how much the curves shift. Three possibilities exist:

1. The demand curve shifts to the right by the same amount as the supply curve shifts to the right. In this case, the price of marijuana will not change. (Try to visualize the demand and supply curves shifting.)

2. The demand curve shift to the right is greater than the supply curve shift to the right. In this case, the price of marijuana will rise. (Try to visualize the demand curve shifting to the right more than the supply curve does. Can you see the higher price on the vertical axis?)

3. The supply curve shift to the right is greater than the demand curve shift to the right. In this case, the price of marijuana will fall.

If you can't visualize the shifts of the demand and supply curves for these three possibilities, draw the original demand and supply curves, then draw the shift in each curve, and identify the new equilibrium price.

## SELF-TEST

1. What will happen to the price of marijuana if the supply increases by more than the demand for it?

2. What will happen to the quantity of marijuana (purchased and sold) if the demand for it rises more than its supply falls.

## "Doesn't High Demand Mean High Quantity Demanded?"

**STUDENT:**

The other day in class you said, "The demand for 10 a.m. classes may be high, but the quantity demanded may not be if the price is high enough." In other words, you were saying that high demand doesn't necessarily mean high quantity demanded. But I thought it did. Could you explain?

**INSTRUCTOR:**

Let me explain what's going on by first showing you the demand schedule for two goods, A and B.

| Good A Demand Schedule | | Good B Demand Schedule | |
|---|---|---|---|
| Price | Quantity Demanded | Price | Quantity Demanded |
| $6 | 100 | $6 | 200 |
| 7 | 80 | 7 | 150 |
| 8 | 60 | 8 | 125 |
| 9 | 40 | 9 | 90 |

As you can see from the two demand schedules, the demand for good B is greater than the demand for good A. In other words, if we were to derive a demand curve for each good (based on its demand schedule), the demand curve for good B would lie farther to the right than the demand curve for good A.

Now suppose we look at quantity demanded for each good at the price of $6. The quantity demanded of good A (the low-demand good) is 100 units and the quantity demanded of good B (the high-demand good) is 200 units. What can we conclude? At the same price for each good ($6), the quantity demanded is higher when demand is higher.

But now let's consider quantity demanded for each good when the price of good A is $6 and the price of good B is $9. The quantity demanded of good A (the low-demand good) is 100 units and the quantity demanded of good B (the high-demand good) is 90 units. In other words, if price is high enough for good B (the high-demand good), the quantity demanded of good B may be lower than the quantity demanded of good A (the low-demand good).

Now let's go back and repeat the statement I made in class: "The demand for 10 a.m. classes may be high, but the quantity demanded may not be if the price is high enough." Now do you understand what I was saying?

**STUDENT:**

Yes, I think I do. You were saying that high demand doesn't necessarily mean high quantity demanded if we are dealing with different prices.

**INSTRUCTOR:**

Yes, that's it.

**POINTS TO REMEMBER**

1. High demand means high quantity demanded, but only if the prices for the high-demand good and the low-demand good are the same. From our example, at a price of $6, the quantity demanded for the high-demand good B is greater than quantity demanded for the low-demand good A.

2. The quantity demanded for the low-demand good can be higher than the quantity demanded for the high-demand good if the prices for the two goods are not the same and the price for the high-demand good is high enough. From our example, at a price of $9 for good B (the high-demand good), the quantity demanded is lower than quantity demanded for good A (the low-demand good) at a price of $6.

## CHAPTER SUMMARY

### TICKET PRICES AT THE TAPING OF A TV SHOW

- The ticket price to the taping of a TV show is usually zero, which usually leads to a shortage of tickets. The greater the demand for the show is, the greater the shortage of tickets will be. Because tickets are (mainly) rationed on a first-come-first-served basis, we would expect that tickets for the most popular shows (those with the greatest demand and the largest shortages at a zero ticket price) would sell out faster than tickets for less popular shows.

### GOVERNMENT, LOANS, AND HOUSING PRICES

- Lower lending standards and lower interest rates make it easier to get a mortgage loan. But as the ease of getting a mortgage loan increases, so does the demand for housing rise. As the demand for housing rises, house prices rise.

### THE PRICE OF AN AISLE SEAT

- If the supply of aisle and middle-of-the-row seats is the same, but the demand for aisle seats is greater, then the equilibrium price for aisle seats will be greater than the equilibrium price of middle-of-the-row seats.

### WHY IS MEDICAL CARE SO EXPENSIVE?

- When it comes to medical care, often three parties are involved: the person who sells medical care, the person who buys medical care, and the person who (directly) pays for the medical care (the third party).
- Once a person has paid her medical insurance premium, the price paid thereafter for medical care may amount to no more than a copayment (usually minimal). For all practical purposes, then, the dollar amount she has to pay out of pocket to get medical care is zero. We expect the quantity demanded of medical care to be greater than at some positive dollar amount.

### WHY DO COLLEGES USE GPAs, ACTs, AND SATs FOR PURPOSES OF ADMISSION?

- Colleges and universities charging students less than the equilibrium tuition for admission create a shortage of spaces at their schools. Consequently, colleges and universities have to impose some non-price-rationing device, such as GPAs or ACT or SAT scores.

### SUPPLY AND DEMAND ON A FREEWAY

- The effect of a disequilibrium price (below equilibrium price) for driving on a freeway is a traffic jam. If the price to drive on a freeway is $0 and at this price the quantity demanded of freeway space is greater than the quantity supplied, then a shortage of freeway space will result in the form of freeway congestion.

### ARE WE REALLY MAKING RENTERS BETTER OFF?

- If renters have 90 days instead of 30 days to vacate an apartment, the supply curve of apartments will shift upward and to the left. As a result, renters will pay higher rents when they have 90 days to vacate an apartment.

### DO YOU PAY FOR GOOD WEATHER?

- If good weather gives people utility, then the demand for and the price of housing will be higher in a city with good weather than in a city with bad weather. People who buy houses in good-weather locations indirectly pay for the good weather.

### COLLEGE SUPERATHLETES

- A college superathlete may receive a full scholarship to play a sport at a university, but the full scholarship may be less than the equilibrium wage for the superathlete (because of a mandate that the athlete cannot be paid the difference between his higher equilibrium wage and the dollar amount of his full scholarship). In such a case, the university gains at the expense of the athlete.

### 10 A.M. CLASSES IN COLLEGE

- Colleges usually charge the same tuition for a class no matter when it is taken. The supply of seats in the class may be the same for each time slot, but the demand for the class may be different. At least for some classes, the quantity demanded of seats (in the class) will be greater than the quantity supplied. Thus, some non-price-rationing device will have to be used to achieve equilibrium.

### LEGALIZATION OF MARIJUANA

- If the purchase and sale of marijuana are legalized, the price of marijuana may rise, fall, or remain the same. The price will depend on whether the rise in the demand for marijuana is more than, less than, or equal to the rise in the supply of marijuana.

## QUESTIONS AND PROBLEMS

1. Explain how lower lending standards and lower interest rates can lead to higher house prices.

2. If there were no third parties in medical care, medical care prices would be lower. Do you agree or disagree? Explain your answer.

3. Harvard, Yale, and Princeton all charge relatively high tuition. Still, each uses ACT and SAT scores as admission criteria. Are charging a relatively high tuition and using standardized test scores as admission criteria inconsistent? Explain your answer.

4. Suppose the purchase and sale of marijuana are legalized and the price of marijuana falls. What is the explanation?

5. What do the applications about freeway congestion and 10 a.m.. classes have in common?

6. Economics has been called the "dismal science" because it sometimes "tells us" that things are true when we would prefer they were false. For example, although there are no free lunches, might we prefer that there were? Was there anything in this chapter that you learned was true that you would have preferred to be false? If so, identify it. Then explain why you would have preferred it to be false.

7. In the discussion of health care and the right to sue your HMO, we state, "Saying that a seller's minimum price for providing a good or service rises is the same as saying the seller's supply curve has shifted upward and to the left." Does it follow that if a seller's minimum price falls, the supply curve shifts downward and to the right? Explain your answer.

8. Application 8 explains that even though no one directly and explicitly pays for good weather ("Here is $100 for the good weather"), you may pay for good weather indirectly, such as through housing prices. Identify three other things (besides good weather) that you believe people pay for indirectly.

9. Suppose there exists a costless way to charge drivers on the freeway. Under this costless system, tolls on the freeway would be adjusted according to traffic conditions. For example, when traffic is usually heavy, such as from 6:30 a.m. to 9:00 a.m. on a weekday, the toll to drive on the freeway would be higher than when traffic is light. In other words, freeway tolls would be used to equate the demand for freeway space with its supply. Would you be in favor of such a system to replace our current (largely zero-price) system? Explain your answer.

10. Wilson walks into his economics class ten minutes late because he couldn't find a place to park. Because of his tardiness, he doesn't hear the professor tell the class there will be a quiz at the next session. At the next session, Wilson is unprepared for the quiz and ends up failing it. Might Wilson's failing the quiz have anything to do with the price of parking?

11. University A charges more for a class for which there is high demand than for a class for which there is low demand. University B charges the same for all classes. All other things being equal between the two universities, which university would you prefer to attend? Explain your answer.

12. Suppose the equilibrium wage for a college athlete is $40,000, but, because of NCAA rules, the university can offer him only $22,000 (full tuition). How might the university administrators, coaches, or university alumni lure the college athlete to choose their school over others?

13. Consider the theater in which a Broadway play is performed. If tickets for all seats are the same price (say, $70), what economic effect might arise?

14. What is the relationship between the probability of a person being admitted to the college of his choice and the tuition the college charges?

15. Samantha is flying from San Diego, California, to Arlington, Texas, on a commercial airliner. She asks for an aisle seat, but only middle-of-the-row seats are left. Why aren't any aisle seats left? (*Hint:* The airline charges the same price for an aisle seat as a middle-of-the-row seat.)

## WORKING WITH NUMBERS AND GRAPHS

1. The price to drive on a freeway is $0 at all times of the day. This price establishes equilibrium at 3 a.m. but is too low to establish equilibrium at 5 p.m. There is a shortage of freeway space at 5 p.m.

   a. Graphically show and explain how carpooling may eliminate the shortage.

   b. Graphically show and explain how building more freeways may eliminate the shortage.

2. Diagrammatically show and explain why there is a shortage of classroom space for some college classes and a surplus for others.

3. Smith has been trying to sell his house for six months, but so far he has had no buyers. Draw the market for Smith's house.

## CHAPTER 6

# MACROECONOMIC MEASUREMENTS, PART I: PRICES AND UNEMPLOYMENT

©ROBERT SHAFER/BRAND X PICTURES/JUPITER IMAGES

**Introduction** Government economists often collect and analyze the latest economic data. Their analysis includes computing important economic measurements such as the inflation rate and the unemployment rate. Our elected representatives and certain government officials then use these measurements in formulating economic policy. The structure and timing of that economic policy often affects you in your roles as buyer, seller, taxpayer, and employee.

## MEASURING THE PRICE LEVEL

There is a difference between *price* and the *price level*. The word *price* refers to a single price, such the price of apples or the price of oranges. Price level is a weighted average of the prices of all goods and services. The key phrase in that definition is "a weighted average of all prices." Here is a rough way of thinking about a price level. Suppose an economy consists of three goods: apples, oranges, and pears. The prices of apples, oranges, and pears, respectively, are 50¢, 60¢, and 80¢ cents, respectively. The average price (of these three goods) is 63¢. That is also the price level.

**Price Level**
A weighted average of the prices of all good and services.

### Computing the Price Level Using the CPI

Economists measure the price level by constructing a price index. One major price index is the Consumer Price Index (CPI).[1] The CPI is based on a representative group of goods and services, called the *market basket,* purchased by a typical household. The market basket includes eight major categories of goods and services: (1) food and beverages, (2) housing, (3) apparel, (4) transportation, (5) medical care, (6) recreation, (7) education and communication, and (8) other goods and services.

**Price Index**
A measure of the price level.

**Consumer Price Index (CPI)**
The weighted average of prices of a specific set of goods and services purchased by a typical household; a widely cited index number for the price level.

---

1. Although changes in the CPI are often used to compute the change in the so-called cost of living, one's cost of living usually involves more than what is measured by the CPI. For example, the CPI does not include income taxes, yet income taxes are a part of the cost of living for most people.

To simplify our discussion, we assume the market basket includes only three goods instead of the many goods it actually contains. Our market basket consists of 10 pens, 5 shirts, and 3 pairs of shoes.

To calculate the CPI, first calculate the total dollar expenditure on the market basket in two years: the current year and the base year. The base year is a benchmark year that serves as a basis of comparison for prices in other years.

**Base Year**

The year chosen as a point of reference or basis of comparison for prices in other years; a benchmark year.

In Exhibit 1, we multiply the quantity of each good in the market basket (column 1) by its current-year price (column 2) to compute the current-year expenditure on each good (column 3). By adding the dollar amounts in column 3, we obtain the total dollar expenditure on the market basket in the current year. This amount is $167.

To find the total expenditure on the market basket in the base year, we multiply the quantity of each good in the market basket (column 1A) by its base-year price (column 2A) and then add these products (column 3A). This gives us $67.

To find the CPI, we use the formula:

$$CPI = \left( \frac{\text{Total dollar expenditure on market basket in current year}}{\text{Total dollar expenditure on market basket in base year}} \right) \times 100$$

As shown in Exhibit 1, the CPI for our tiny economy is 249.

The consumer price index for the United States for the years 1959 to 2009 is shown in Exhibit 2.

**MORE ABOUT THE BASE YEAR** Recall that the base year is a benchmark year that serves as a basis of comparison for prices in other years. The CPI in the base year is 100.

---

**EXHIBIT 1**

**Computing the Consumer Price Index**

The exhibit uses hypothetical data to show how the CPI is computed. To find the "total dollar expenditure on market basket in current year," we multiply the quantities of goods in the market basket times their current-year prices and add these products. This gives us $167. To find the "total dollar expenditure on market basket in base year," we multiply the quantities of goods in the market basket times their base-year prices and add these products. This gives us $67. We then divide $167 by $67 and multiply the quotient by 100.

| (1) Market Basket | | (2) Current-Year Prices (per item) | (3) Current-Year Expenditures | (1A) Market Basket | | (2A) Base-Year Prices (per item) | (3A) Base-Year Expenditures |
|---|---|---|---|---|---|---|---|
| 10 pens | × | $ .70 | = $ 7.00 | 10 pens | × | $ .20 | = $ 2.00 |
| 5 shirts | × | 14.00 | = 70.00 | 5 shirts | × | 7.00 | = 35.00 |
| 3 pairs of shoes | × | 30.00 | = 90.00 | 3 pairs of shoes | × | 10.00 | = 30.00 |
| | | | **$167.00** | | | | **$67.00** |

Total dollar expenditure on market basket in current year

Total dollar expenditure on market basket in base year

$$CPI = \left( \frac{\text{Total dollar expenditure on market basket in current year}}{\text{Total dollar expenditure on market basket in base year}} \right) \times 100$$

$$= \left( \frac{\$167}{\$67} \right) \times 100$$

$$= 249$$

How do we know this? Look again at the formula for calculating the CPI: The numerator is the "Total dollar expenditure on market basket in current year," and the denominator is the "Total dollar expenditure on market basket in base year." In the base year, the current year *is* the base year; so the numerator and denominator are the same. The ratio is 1, and $1 \times 100 = 100$.

In Exhibit 2, however, notice that there is no year in which the CPI is 100. This does not mean that there is no base year. The base year has been defined by the government to be the period 1982–1984. Look at the CPI in each of the years 1982, 1983, and 1984. If we add the CPIs for the three years and divide by 3, we get 100: $(96.5 + 99.6 + 103.9) \div 3 = 100$.

**WHEN WE KNOW THE CPI FOR VARIOUS YEARS, WE CAN COMPUTE THE PERCENTAGE CHANGE IN PRICES**
To find the percentage change in prices between any two years, use the following formula:

$$\text{Percentage change in prices} = \left(\frac{\text{CPI}_{\text{later year}} - \text{CPI}_{\text{earlier year}}}{\text{CPI}_{\text{earlier year}}}\right) \times 100$$

For example, Exhibit 2 shows that the CPI in 1990 was 130.7, and the CPI in 2005 was 195.3. The percentage change in prices over this period of time was 49.43 percent:

$$\text{Percentage change} = \left(\frac{195.3 - 130.7}{130.7}\right) \times 100 = 49.43$$

This means that from 1990 to 2005 prices increased 49.43 percent. You can think of the percentage change in prices this way: What cost $1 in 1990 cost approximately $1.49 in 2005.

## Inflation and the CPI

Inflation is an increase in the price level and is usually measured on an annual basis. The *inflation rate* is the positive percentage change in the price level on an annual basis. When you know the inflation rate, you can find out whether your income is (1) keeping up with, (2) not keeping up with, or (3) more than keeping up with inflation. How you are doing depends on whether your income is rising by (1) the same percentage as, (2) a smaller percentage than, or (3) a greater percentage than the inflation rate, respectively. When you make this computation and comparison, you are determining your real income for different years. Real income is a person's nominal income (or current dollar amount of income) adjusted for any change in prices. Real income is computed as follows:

$$\text{Real income} = \left(\frac{\text{Nominal income}}{\text{CPI}}\right) \times 100$$

**CASE 1. KEEPING UP WITH INFLATION: REAL INCOME STAYS CONSTANT**
Jim earns $50,000 in year 1 and $55,000 in year 2. The CPI is 100 in year 1 and 110 in year 2; so the inflation rate is 10 percent: $[(110 - 100)/100] \times 100 = 10$. Jim's income has risen by 10 percent: $[(\$55,000 - \$50,000)/\$50,000] \times 100 = 10$. Jim's income has risen by the same percentage as the inflation rate; so he has kept up with

**EXHIBIT 2**

**CPI, 1959–2009**

*Source: The data were reported at the website for the U.S. Department of Labor, Bureau of Labor Statistics. Site address: http://www.bls.gov/home.htm. Beginning in 2007, the Bureau of Labor Statistics began reporting the CPI to three decimal points.*

| Year | CPI | Year | CPI |
|------|------|------|--------|
| 1959 | 29.1 | 1985 | 107.6 |
| 1960 | 29.6 | 1986 | 109.6 |
| 1961 | 29.9 | 1987 | 113.6 |
| 1962 | 30.2 | 1988 | 118.3 |
| 1963 | 30.6 | 1989 | 124.0 |
| 1964 | 31.0 | 1990 | 130.7 |
| 1965 | 31.5 | 1991 | 136.2 |
| 1966 | 32.4 | 1992 | 140.3 |
| 1967 | 33.4 | 1993 | 144.5 |
| 1968 | 34.8 | 1994 | 148.2 |
| 1969 | 36.7 | 1995 | 152.4 |
| 1970 | 38.8 | 1996 | 156.9 |
| 1971 | 40.5 | 1997 | 160.5 |
| 1972 | 41.8 | 1998 | 163.0 |
| 1973 | 44.4 | 1999 | 166.6 |
| 1974 | 49.3 | 2000 | 172.2 |
| 1975 | 53.8 | 2001 | 177.1 |
| 1976 | 56.9 | 2002 | 179.9 |
| 1977 | 60.6 | 2003 | 184.0 |
| 1978 | 65.2 | 2004 | 188.9 |
| 1979 | 72.6 | 2005 | 195.3 |
| 1980 | 82.4 | 2006 | 201.6 |
| 1981 | 90.9 | 2007 | 207.342 |
| 1982 | 96.5 | 2008 | 215.303 |
| 1983 | 99.6 | 2009 | 214.537 |
| 1984 | 103.9 | | |

**Inflation**
An increase in the price level.

**Real Income**
Nominal income adjusted for price changes.

**Nominal Income**
The current dollar amount of a person's income.

inflation. This is evident when we see that Jim's real income is the same in both years. In year 1 it is $50,000, and in year 2 it is $50,000 too.

$$\text{Real income year 1} = \left(\frac{\$50,000}{100}\right) \times 100 = \$50,000$$

$$\text{Real income year 2} = \left(\frac{\$55,000}{110}\right) \times 100 = \$50,000$$

### CASE 2. NOT KEEPING UP WITH INFLATION: REAL INCOME FALLS

Karen earns $50,000 in year 1 and $52,000 in year 2. The CPI is 100 in year 1 and 110 in year 2. Karen's income has risen by 4 percent, and the inflation rate is 10 percent. Her income has risen by a smaller percentage than the inflation rate; so she has not kept up with inflation. Karen's real income has fallen from $50,000 in year 1 to $47,273 in year 2.

$$\text{Real income year 1} = \left(\frac{\$50,000}{100}\right) \times 100 = \$50,000$$

$$\text{Real income year 2} = \left(\frac{\$52,000}{110}\right) \times 100 = \$47,273$$

### CASE 3. MORE THAN KEEPING UP WITH INFLATION: REAL INCOME RISES

Carl earns $50,000 in year 1 and $60,000 in year 2. The CPI is 100 in year 1 and 110 in year 2. Carl's income has risen by 20 percent, and the inflation rate is 10 percent. His income has risen by a greater percentage than the inflation rate; so he has more than kept up with inflation. Carl's real income has risen from $50,000 in year 1 to $54,545 in year 2.

$$\text{Real income year 1} = \left(\frac{\$50,000}{100}\right) \times 100 = \$50,000$$

$$\text{Real income year 2} = \left(\frac{\$60,000}{110}\right) \times 100 = \$54,545$$

## finding ECONOMICS

**In Your Paycheck** Sharon comments to a friend that she recently received a $5-an-hour raise at work. Her friend congratulates her and then goes on to talk about how prices have been rising lately. Where is the economics?

Obviously, if Sharon's nominal (or money) income has risen, and prices have risen too, then Sharon's real income might have changed. Has her real income risen, fallen, or stayed the same? The answer depends on how much her nominal income has risen relative to how much prices have gone up. Let's say her nominal income has risen by 5 percent and prices have increased by 2 percent. In that case, Sharon's real income has gone up. ▲ ▲ ▲

## thinking like AN ECONOMIST

**Comparing One Thing with Another** Comparing one thing with something else can be extremely useful. For example, in each of the three cases just discussed, we compared the percentage change in a person's nominal income with the inflation rate. Through this comparison, we learned something that we could not have learned by looking at either factor alone: how a person fared under inflation. Making comparisons is part of the economic way of thinking. ▲ ▲ ▲

## GDP Implicit Price Deflator

Besides the CPI, another price index is often cited: the *GDP deflator* or the *GDP implicit price deflator*. Obviously, an economy produces more goods and services than find their

## Economics at the Movies

Some movies do better at the box office than others. For example, *Spider-Man 3*, released in 2007, earned higher gross receipts than *The Bourne Ultimatum*, another movie released in 2007. As of February 2010, the following list ranks the all-time top 10 movies in the United States in terms of domestic gross receipts:

1. Avatar (2009)
2. Titanic (1997)
3. The Dark Knight (2008)
4. Star Wars (1977)
5. Shrek 2 (2004)
6. E.T.: The Extra-Terrestrial (1982)
7. Star Wars: Episode I—The Phantom Menace (1999)
8. Pirates of the Caribbean: Dead Man's Chest (2006)
9. Spider-Man (2002)
10. Transformers: Revenge of the Fallen (2009)

*Avatar,* first on the list, earned gross receipts in the United States of $689 million (as of February 2009), and *Star Wars*, in second place, earned $461 million. Comparing these two dollar amounts, it is easy to conclude that *Avatar* did better at the box office than *Star Wars*.

But *Avatar* was released in 2009, and *Star Wars* was released 32 years earlier in 1977. In other words, the receipts for *Avatar* are in 2009 dollars, and those for *Star Wars* are in 1977 dollars. To accurately compare the receipts of the two movies, we need to put them on an even footing. We need to change each movie's receipts into today's dollars (let today's dollars be 2009 dollars). When we do this, *Star Wars* earned more than *Avatar*. Specifically, *Star Wars* earned $1.6 billion and *Avatar* (as of February 2010) had earned $689 million.

What is the top grossing film of all time in today's dollars? It is *Gone with the Wind*, released in 1939. In today's dollars, it earned approximately $3 billion.

way into the CPI's representative market basket. The GDP implicit price deflator, unlike the CPI, is based on all goods and services produced in an economy.

## Converting Dollars from One Year to Another

Suppose someone says, "Back in 1960, I had an annual salary of $10,000 a year. That sure isn't much these days." Of course, the person is right in one sense: An annual salary of $10,000 doesn't buy much these days, but was it a good salary back in 1960? It certainly could have been, because prices in 1960 weren't as high as they are today. For example, the CPI was 29.6 in 1960 and 214.537 in 2009. In other words, one of the

## Woodstock, 1969

*Actin' funny, but I don't know why*
*'scuse me while I kiss the sky*
—**Purple Haze, Jimi Hendrix**

Officially called the Woodstock Music and Art Fair, it took place at Max Yasgur's 600-acre dairy farm in Bethel, New York (about 43 miles from Woodstock), for a period of three days: August 15, 16, and 17 of 1969. It was advertised as three days of peace and music. To many, it came to represent the counterculture and hippie era of the 1960s. It is simply known as Woodstock.

As for the performers, there were many. Here is a partial list:

Richie Havens
John Sebastian
Sweetwater
Ravi Shankar
Arlo Guthrie
Joan Baez
Santana

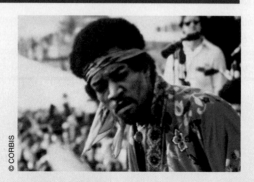
© CORBIS

Canned Heat
Janis Joplin
Sly & the Family Stone
Grateful Dead
Creedence Clearwater Revival
The Who
Jefferson Airplane
Joe Cocker
The Band
Blood, Sweat & Tears
Crosby, Stills, Nash & Young
Jimi Hendrix

The price of a one-day ticket to Woodstock was $8 in 1969. That sounds like a cheap ticket nowadays. But how much is $8 in 1969 comparable to in 2009? We use the following formula:

$$\text{Ticket in 2009 dollars} = \$8 \times \frac{214.537}{36.7}$$
$$= \$46.77$$

Buying a one-day ticket at Woodstock was the same as buying a $46.77 ticket in 2009. Not a bad price at all, especially for all the groups you could see on any given day.

---

### EXHIBIT 3

**C-CPI, 2000–2009**

Here we show the Chained CPI (C-CPI) for the years 2000–2009. The Chained CPI is yet another price index.

| Year | C-CPI |
|------|-------|
| 2000 | 102.0 |
| 2001 | 104.3 |
| 2002 | 105.6 |
| 2003 | 107.8 |
| 2004 | 110.5 |
| 2005 | 113.7 |
| 2006 | 117.0 |
| 2007 | 119.957 |
| 2008 | 124.433 |
| 2009 | 124.353 |

things that make a salary good or not so good is what the salary can buy.

Now suppose someone tells you that a $10,000 salary in 1960 is the same as a $68,000 salary today. Would you then be better able to say whether the 1960 $10,000 salary was good or not so good? Of course you would because you understand what it means to earn $68,000 today. Economists convert a past salary into today's salary by using this formula:

$$\text{Salary in today's (current) dollars} = \text{Salary}_{\text{earlier year}} \times \left( \frac{\text{CPI}_{\text{current year}}}{\text{CPI}_{\text{earlier year}}} \right)$$

Assume the CPI today is the same as the most recent CPI in Exhibit 3 (which is the CPI for 2009). Using the formula, we get:

$$\text{Salary in 2009 dollars} = \$10,000 \times \frac{214.537}{29.6}$$
$$= \$72,479$$

## ⓕinding ECONOMICS

**In What Grandfather Says** Ursula, who is 25, told her grandfather that she just got a job that pays $67,000 a year. Her grandfather said, "That's a lot of money. When I got my first real job I earned only $18,000 a year. You're earning a whole lot more than I did." Where is the economics?

Income earned in one time period cannot always be adequately compared to income earned in another time period. To do so, we need to convert the dollars earned in one period into dollars earned in the other period. Ursula is earning $67,000 today, but her grandfather earned $18,000 (in his first job) many years ago. Obviously, earning $18,000 many years ago is not the same as earning $18,000 today; so Ursula's grandfather's statement that she is earning a whole lot more than he did might not be accurate. ▲ ▲ ▲

### SELF-TEST

(Answers to Self-Test questions are in Answers to Self-Test Questions at the back of the book.)

1. Explain how the CPI is calculated.

2. What is a base year?

3. In year 1, your annual income is $45,000 and the CPI is 143.6; in year 2, your annual income is $51,232 and the CPI is 150.7. Has your real income risen, fallen, or remained constant? Explain your answer.

# MEASURING UNEMPLOYMENT

Every month, the government surveys thousands of households to gather information about labor market activities. It uses the information from the survey to derive the number of Americans unemployed.

## Who Are the Unemployed?

The total population of the United States can be divided into two broad groups (Exhibit 4). One group consists of persons who are (1) under 16 years of age, (2) in the armed forces, or (3) institutionalized (in a prison, mental institution, or home for the aged). The second group, which consists of all others in the total population, is called the *civilian noninstitutional population.*

**EXHIBIT 4**

**Breakdown of the U.S. Population and the Labor Force**

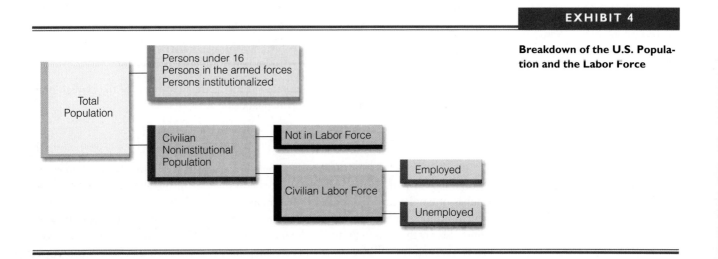

The civilian noninstitutional population, in turn, can be divided into two groups: persons *not in the labor force* and persons in the *civilian labor force.* (Economists often refer to this group as the labor force instead of the civilian labor force.)

Civilian noninstitutional population = Persons not in the labor force + Persons in the labor force

- Persons not in the labor force are neither working nor looking for work. In this category, for example, are people who are retired, who are engaged in own-home housework, or who choose not to work.
- Persons in the civilian labor force fall into one of two categories: *employed* or *unemployed.*

Civilian labor force = Employed persons + Unemployed persons

According to the Bureau of Labor Statistics (BLS), employed persons consist of:

- All persons who did any work for pay or profit during the survey reference week.
- All persons who did at least 15 hours of unpaid work in a family-operated enterprise.
- All persons who were temporarily absent from their regular jobs because of illness, vacation, bad weather, industrial dispute, or various personal reasons.

According to the BLS, unemployed persons consist of:

- All persons who did not have jobs, who made specific active efforts to find a job during the prior four weeks, and who were available for work.
- All persons who were not working and who were waiting to be called back to a job from which they had been temporarily laid off.

## The Unemployment and Employment Rates

The unemployment rate is the percentage of the civilian labor force that is unemployed. It is equal to the number of unemployed persons divided by the civilian labor force.

$$\text{Unemployment rate } (U) = \frac{\text{Number of unemployed persons}}{\text{Civilian labor force}}$$

The employment rate (sometimes referred to as the *employment/population ratio*) is the percentage of the civilian noninstitutional population that is employed. It is equal to the number of employed persons divided by the civilian noninstitutional population:

$$\text{Employment rate } (E) = \frac{\text{Number of employed persons}}{\text{Civilian noninstitutional population}}$$

Finally, the labor force participation rate (LFPR) is the percentage of the civilian noninstitutional population that is in the civilian labor force.

$$\text{Labor force participation rate } (LFPR) = \frac{\text{Civilian labor force}}{\text{Civilian noninstitutional population}}$$

The LFPR may sound like the employment rate, but it is different. Although the denominator in both formulas is the same, the numerator in the employment rate is the number of employed persons, and the numerator in the LFPR is the civilian labor force (which includes both employed persons and unemployed persons). For this reason, some economists say that although the employment rate gives us the percentage of the population that is working, the LFPR gives us the percentage of the population that is *willing to work.*

## What Was a Penny Worth?

You are walking and you look down and see a penny on the sidewalk. Do you stop and pick it up? Many people will say no, explaining that the penny isn't worth their time. After all, a penny is not worth very much, they say.

You buy a magazine at the campus store. The total price (including tax) comes to $6.02. You hand the cashier a $10 bill. Instead of giving you $3.98 in change, she reaches into the cup next to the cash register and pulls out two pennies; she gives you $4 in change. It is easier for her to get the two pennies from the cup than it is to count out $3.98 in change. You say, "Thank you" and go on your way.

The next day, you buy something for $5.99. You hand the cashier $6. When the cashier gives you back one penny in change, you drop it into the cup next to the cash register. One day you take from the cup; another day you give to the cup.

Twenty years ago, there were no penny cups next to cash registers. Why were there no penny cups then, but penny cups now? The reason is that 20 years ago, a penny had more purchasing power than it does today. If a penny today had greater purchasing power than it does, you'd be less likely to drop the penny into the cup; instead, you'd drop it into your pocket.

So what was a penny worth in, say, 1900? A different way of asking the question is, "What coin today is equal to the purchasing power a penny had in 1900?" The answer is a quarter. In other words, having a penny in 1900 was equivalent of having a quarter (25¢) today. So having four pennies in 1900 was the equivalent of having $1 today.

Imagine the year is 1900 and you are walking down the street. You look down and see a penny. Do you stop and pick it up?

## Common Misconceptions About the Unemployment and Employment Rates

Many people mistakenly think that if the unemployment rate is, say, 7 percent, the employment rate must be 93 percent. Their assumption is that the unemployment rate plus the employment rate must equal 100 percent. But the unemployment and employment rates do not add up 100 percent, because the denominator of the unemployment rate is not the same as the denominator of the employment rate. The unemployment rate is a *percentage of the civilian labor force*. The employment rate is a *percentage of the civilian noninstitutional population*, which is a larger number than the civilian labor force.

## Reasons for Unemployment

Usually, we think of an unemployed person as someone who has been fired or laid off from his or her job. Certainly, some unemployed persons fit this description, but not all of them do. According to the BLS, an unemployed person may fall into one of four categories.

1.  *Job loser.* This person was employed in the civilian labor force and was either fired or laid off. Most unemployed persons fall into this category.

2.  *Job leaver.* This person was employed in the civilian labor force and quit the job. For example, if Jim quit his job with company X and is looking for a better job, he is a job leaver.

3.  *Reentrant.* This person was previously employed, hasn't worked for some time, and is currently reentering the labor force.

4.  *New entrant.* This person has never held a full-time job for two weeks or longer and is now in the civilian labor force looking for a job.

Unemployed persons = Job losers + Job leavers + Reentrants + New entrants

## Discouraged Workers

Adam is fired from his job at company A in September, and he looks for a job for about six months. During this time, he is considered an unemployed person and is counted in the unemployment rate. At the end of the sixth month, Adam is very discouraged; he doesn't think he will ever find a job, and he stops looking. A month passes and he still is not looking for a job. Is Adam considered an unemployed person? The answer is no. To be an unemployed person, you have to meet certain conditions, one of which is that you have to be actively looking for work. But Adam isn't actively looking for work, and he isn't waiting to be called back to a job or to report to a job. So Adam isn't unemployed, and for that reason he does not get counted in the unemployment rate.

The BLS considers Adam a *discouraged worker*. You may think that for all practical purposes, a discouraged worker is the same as an unemployed person because neither has a job. But they aren't the same for calculating the unemployment rate. The unemployed person gets counted, but the discouraged worker does not.

Some economists think that because discouraged workers are not considered unemployed, the unemployment rate is biased downward. Consequently, it doesn't really give us a good fix on the "real" unemployment problem in society.

## Types of Unemployment

This section describes a few types of unemployment.

**FRICTIONAL UNEMPLOYMENT**  Every day, demand conditions change in some markets, causing qualified individuals with transferable skills to leave some jobs and move to others. To illustrate, suppose there are two computer firms, A and B. For some reason, the demand falls for firm A's computers and rises for firm B's computers. Consequently, firm A produces fewer computers. With fewer computers being produced, firm A doesn't need as many employees; so it fires some employees. On the other hand, firm B is producing more computers. With more computers being produced, firm B hires additional employees. The employees fired from firm A have skills that they can transfer to firm B; after all, both firms produce computers. However, it takes time for people to make the transfer. During this time, they are said to be frictionally unemployed.

**Frictional Unemployment**

Unemployment that is due to the natural so-called frictions in the economy and that is caused by changing market conditions and represented by qualified individuals with transferable skills who change jobs.

**Frictional unemployment** is unemployment that is due to the natural so-called frictions in the economy and that is caused by changing market conditions and represented by qualified individuals with transferable skills who change jobs. The frictional unemployment rate ($U_F$) is the percentage of the labor force that is frictionally unemployed.

$$U_F = \frac{\text{Number of frictionally unemployed persons}}{\text{Civilian labor force}}$$

A dynamic, changing economy like that of the United States always has frictional unemployment. Many economists believe that the basic cause of frictional unemployment is imperfect or incomplete information, which prevents individuals from leaving one job and finding another instantly. For example, imagine an economy with 1,000 job vacancies and 1,000 persons qualified to fill the jobs. Some unemployment is likely because not every one of the 1,000 job seekers will know where the available job are. Nor will all employers give the job to the first applicant who knocks on the door. Employers don't know whether better applicants are around the corner. Matching qualified workers with the available jobs takes time.

STRUCTURAL UNEMPLOYMENT Structural unemployment is unemployment due to structural changes in the economy that eliminate some jobs and create others for which the unemployed are unqualified. Most economists argue that structural unemployment is largely the consequence of automation (labor-saving devices) and long-lasting shifts in demand. The structurally unemployed differ from the frictionally unemployed mainly in that they do not have transferable skills. Their choice is between prolonged unemployment and retraining. For example, suppose automobile workers are being laid off and the demand for computer analysts is rising. If the automobile workers do not currently have the skills needed to become computer analysts, they are structurally unemployed. The structural unemployment rate $(U_S)$ is the percentage of the labor force that is structurally unemployed.

$$U_S = \frac{\text{Number of structurally unemployed persons}}{\text{Civilian labor force}}$$

**Structural Unemployment**
Unemployment due to structural changes in the economy that eliminate some jobs and create others for which the unemployed are unqualified.

NATURAL UNEMPLOYMENT Adding the frictional unemployment rate and the structural unemployment rate gives the natural unemployment rate (or natural rate of unemployment, $U_N$). Currently, most economists estimate the natural unemployment rate at between 4 and 6.5 percent.

$$\text{Natural unemployment rate } (U_N) = \text{Frictional unemployment rate } (U_F) + \text{Structural unemployment rate } (U_S)$$

**Natural Unemployment**
Unemployment caused by frictional and structural factors in the economy: Natural unemployment rate = Frictional unemployment rate + Structural unemployment rate.

## The Natural Unemployment Rate and Full Employment

What do you think of when you hear the term "full employment"? Most people think *full employment* means that the actual or reported unemployment rate is zero. But a dynamic, changing economy can never have full employment of this type due to the frictional and structural changes that continually occur. In fact, it is natural for some unemployment to exist—some natural unemployment, that is. For this reason, economists *do not* equate full employment with a zero unemployment rate. Instead, full employment exists *when the economy is operating at its natural unemployment rate.* For example, if the natural unemployment rate is 5 percent, then full employment exists when the unemployment rate (in the economy) is 5 percent. In other words, the economy can be operating at full employment, and some people will be unemployed.

**Full Employment**
The condition that exists when the unemployment rate is equal to the natural unemployment rate.

## Cyclical Unemployment

The unemployment rate in the economy is not always the natural rate. The difference between the existing unemployment rate and the natural unemployment rate is the cyclical unemployment rate $(U_C)$.

$$\text{Cyclical unemployment rate } (U_C) = \text{Unemployment rate } (U) - \text{Natural unemployment rate } (U_N)$$

**Cyclical Unemployment Rate**
The difference between the unemployment rate and the natural unemployment rate

When the existing unemployment rate $(U)$ is greater than the natural unemployment rate $(U_N)$, the cyclical unemployment rate $(U_C)$ is positive. For example, if $U = 8$ percent and $U_N = 5$ percent, then $U_C = 3$ percent. When the unemployment rate is less than the natural unemployment rate, the cyclical unemployment rate is negative. For example, if $U = 4$ percent and $U_N = 5$ percent, then $U_C = -1$ percent.

A review of variety of unemployment rates can be seen in Exhibit 5.

**EXHIBIT 5**

**Various Unemployment Rates**

# OFFICE HOURS

## "Is There More Than One Reason the Unemployment Rate Will Fall?"

**STUDENT:**

If the unemployment rate drops, does it follow that some of the people who were once unemployed are now employed?

**INSTRUCTOR:**

Not always. To see why, recall that the unemployment rate is equal to the number of unemployed persons divided by the civilian labor force.

$$\text{Unemployment rate} = \frac{\text{Number of unemployed persons}}{\text{Civilian labor force}}$$

Now let's say there are 100 unemployed persons and the civilian labor force consists of 1,000 persons. The unemployment rate is 10 percent. Suppose the number of unemployed persons rises to 105 (a 5 percent increase) at the same time that the civilian labor force rises to 1,120 (a 12 percent increase). The new unemployment rate is 9.4 percent, even

though the number of unemployed persons has not decreased. In fact, it has increased from 100 to 105.

**STUDENT:**

In other words, if the number of unemployed persons rises by a smaller percentage than the civilian labor force rises, the unemployment rate will decline—even though the number of unemployed persons has risen.

**INSTRUCTOR:**

Yes, that's correct. Now consider something else. Again suppose 100 unemployed persons and a civilian labor force of 1,000 persons. These numbers give us an unemployment rate of 10 percent. Now suppose 10 of the unemployed persons become discouraged workers and stop looking for work. The number of unemployed falls to 90, and

1. What is the major difference between a person who is frictionally unemployed and one who is structurally unemployed?

2. What does a positive cyclical unemployment rate imply?

the civilian labor force (which consists of employed plus unemployed persons) falls to 990. The unemployment rate now is 9.09 percent. The unemployment rate has dropped, but not for the reason most people think. It hasn't dropped because some of the unemployed persons found jobs. It has dropped because some of the unemployed became so discouraged that they stopped looking for jobs.

**STUDENT:**

In other words, we might think that the unemployment rate has dropped because 10 of the 100 unemployed persons found work, but in reality those 10 persons did not find work. They just became so discouraged that they left the civilian labor force.

**INSTRUCTOR:**

Yes, that's correct.

**STUDENT:**

Does the government do anything to take these discouraged workers into account?

**INSTRUCTOR:**

The Bureau of Labor Statistics computes an alternative unemployment rate that includes discouraged workers in the ranks of both the unemployed and the civilian labor force. In short, it computes what it calls "total unemployed plus discouraged workers, as a percent of the civilian labor force plus discouraged workers."

$$\text{Alternative Unemployment rate} = \frac{\text{Number of unemployed persons} + \text{Discouraged workers}}{\text{Civilian labor force} + \text{Discouraged workers}}$$

This alternative unemployment rate tells us what the unemployment rate would look like if we include discouraged workers in our calculation.

**POINTS TO REMEMBER**

1. The unemployment rate can decline even if the number of unemployed persons has not declined. For example, if the number of unemployed persons rises by a smaller percentage than that of the civilian labor force, the unemployment rate will decline (even though more, not fewer, persons are unemployed).

2. The alternative unemployment rate is defined as:

$$\text{Alternative Unemployment rate} = \frac{\text{Number of unemployed persons} + \text{Discouraged workers}}{\text{Civilian labor force} + \text{Discouraged workers}}$$

# CHAPTER SUMMARY

## MEASURING PRICES

- A major price index is the consumer price index (CPI).
- Inflation is an increase in the price level or price index.
- A given dollar amount in an earlier year does not have the same purchasing power in a later year (or current year) if prices are different in the two years. To convert a dollar amount of an earlier year into today's (or current) dollars, we use the formula:

$$\text{Dollar amount in today's (current) dollars} =$$
$$\text{Dollar amount}_{\text{earlier year}} \times \left( \frac{\text{CPI}_{\text{current year}}}{\text{CPI}_{\text{earlier year}}} \right)$$

## UNEMPLOYMENT AND EMPLOYMENT

- An unemployed person may be a job loser, a job leaver, a reentrant, or a new entrant.

- The unemployment rate may be biased downward because discouraged workers are not considered unemployed.
- Frictional unemployment, due to the natural so-called frictions of the economy, is caused by changing market conditions and is represented by qualified individuals with transferable skills who change jobs.
- Structural unemployment is due to structural changes in the economy that eliminate some jobs and create others for which the unemployed are unqualified.
- Natural unemployment is caused by frictional and structural factors in the economy. The natural unemployment rate equals the sum of the frictional unemployment rate and the structural unemployment rate.
- Full employment exists when the unemployment rate is equal to the natural unemployment rate.
- The cyclical unemployment rate is the difference between the existing unemployment rate and the natural unemployment rate.

# KEY TERMS AND CONCEPTS

| | | | |
|---|---|---|---|
| Price Level | Inflation | Employment Rate | Natural Unemployment |
| Price Index | Real Income | Labor Force Participation Rate | Full Employment |
| Consumer Price Index (CPI) | Nominal Income | Frictional Unemployment | Cyclical Unemployment Rate |
| Base Year | Unemployment Rate | Structural Unemployment | |

# QUESTIONS AND PROBLEMS

1. What does the CPI in the base year equal? Explain your answer.
2. Show that if the percentage rise in prices is equal to the percentage rise in nominal income, then one's real income does not change.
3. What does it mean if the expenditure weights of the market basket used to compute the CPI are changed?
4. How does structural unemployment differ from frictional unemployment?
5. What does it mean to say that the country is operating at full employment?
6. What is "natural" about natural unemployment?
7. What is the difference between the employment rate and the labor force participation rate?

8. If the unemployment rate is 4 percent, it does not follow that the employment rate is 96 percent. Explain why.
9. What criteria must be met for a person to be characterized as unemployed?
10. What is the difference between a job leaver and a reentrant?
11. How is a discouraged worker different from an unemployed worker?
12. If the price of, say, oranges has risen, does it follow that the price level has risen too? Explain your answer.
13. What is the relationship between your nominal income and the inflation rate if you are more than keeping up with inflation?
14. Explain how the CPI is computed.

# WORKING WITH NUMBERS AND GRAPHS

1. Suppose 60 million people are employed, 10 million unemployed, and 30 million not in the labor force. What does the civilian noninstitutional population equal?

2. Suppose 100 million people are in the civilian labor force and 90 million people are employed. How many people are unemployed? What is the unemployment rate?

3. Change the current-year prices in Exhibit 1 to $1 for pens, $28 for shirts, and $32 for a pair of shoes. What is the CPI for the current year based on these prices?

4. Jim earned an annual salary of $15,000 in 1965. What is this equivalent to in 2005 dollars? (Use Exhibit 2 to find the CPI in the years mentioned.)

5. A house cost $10,000 in 1976. What is this equivalent to in 2001 dollars? (Use Exhibit 2 to find the CPI in the years mentioned.)

6. Using the following data, compute (a) the unemployment rate, (b) the employment rate, and (c) the labor force participation rate.

| | |
|---|---|
| Civilian noninstitutional population | 200 million |
| Number of employed persons | 126 million |
| Number of unemployed persons | 8 million |

7. Based on the following data, compute (a) the unemployment rate, (b) the structural unemployment rate, and (c) the cyclical unemployment rate.

| | |
|---|---|
| Frictional unemployment rate | 2 percent |
| Natural unemployment rate | 5 percent |
| Civilian labor force | 100 million |
| Number of employed persons | 82 million |

8. Using Exhibit 2, compute the percentage change in prices between (a) 1966 and 1969, (b) 1976 and 1986, and (c) 1990 and 1999.

9. Assume the market basket contains 10X, 20Y, and 45Z. The current-year prices for goods X, Y, and Z are $1, $4, and $6, respectively. The base-year prices are $1, $3, and $5, respectively. What is the CPI in the current year?

10. If the CPI is 150 and nominal income is $100,000, what does real income equal?

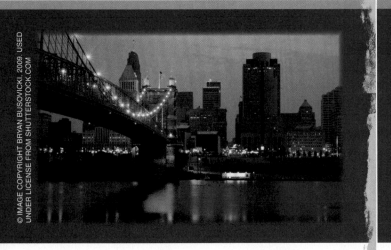

# 7

## MACROECONOMIC MEASUREMENTS, PART II: GDP AND REAL GDP

**Introduction** Each day in the United States, many thousands of goods and services are produced. How do we measure all this economic activity? One of the principal ways is to compute GDP, or gross domestic product. GDP is one of the most important economic measurements used by economists. In this chapter we explain what GDP is and discuss how to compute it. We then turn to a discussion of Real GDP and how to compute it.

## GROSS DOMESTIC PRODUCT

In any given year, people in the United States produce goods and services—television sets, books, pencil sharpeners, DVD players, attorney services, haircuts, and much more. Have you ever wondered what the total dollar value is for all those goods and services? In 2009, it was $14.26 trillion. In other words, in 2009, people living and working in the United States produced $14.26 trillion worth of goods and services. That dollar amount—$14.26 trillion—is what economists call the gross domestic product. Simply put, gross domestic product (GDP) is the *total market value of all final goods and services produced annually within a country's borders.*

**Gross Domestic Product (GDP)**
The total market value of all final goods and services produced annually within a country's borders.

### Calculating GDP

To show how GDP is computed, suppose the following data represent the prices and quantities of three goods produced in a tiny economy this year.

| Goods | Quantities Produced of Each Good | Price of Each Good |
|-------|----------------------------------|--------------------|
| A | 10 | $2 |
| B | 20 | $3 |
| C | 30 | $5 |

What is the GDP in this tiny economy? GDP is the total market value of all final goods and services produced annually within a country's borders. GDP, then, is the sum ($\Sigma$) of the prices ($P$) of all goods times the quantities ($Q$) of those goods produced.

$$GDP = \Sigma PQ$$

In our case:

$$GDP = (\$2 \times 10 \text{ units}) + (\$3 \times 20 \text{ units}) + (\$5 \times 30 \text{ units}) = \$230$$

## Final Goods and Intermediate Goods

In our definition of GDP, reference was made to "final goods and services." If GDP is the total market value of these final goods and services, why do we need to specify them as *final*? There is a difference between a final good and an intermediate good. A final good (or service) is a good in the hands of the final user, the ultimate consumer. It is the orange juice that the consumer buys in the store.

So, then, what are the oranges that go to make the orange juice? The oranges are an *intermediate good*. An intermediate good is an input to the production of a final good. In other words, the oranges were used to produce orange juice (the final good).

Only expenditures on final goods are counted when computing GDP to avoid the *double counting* that would occur if we counted expenditures on both final and intermediate goods. Double counting refers to counting a good more than once when computing GDP. To illustrate, if we count the oranges and the orange juice, then we count the oranges twice because they are in the orange juice.

**Final Good**
A good in the hands of its final user.

**Intermediate Good**
A good that is an input to the production of a final good.

**Double Counting**
Counting a good more than once when computing GDP.

## finding ECONOMICS

**In a Factory, Restaurant, and Law Office** James works in a car factory in Detroit. Where is the economics? Obviously, cars are being produced in the car factory in Detroit. The production of these cars will add to the GDP for the current year.

Marion works as a cook in a coffee house. Bill has just ordered an egg salad sandwich on rye (toasted) with cole slaw and a root beer. Where is the economics? Marion will make the sandwich and cole slaw. These two items plus the root beer are part of the GDP for the current year.

Oliver is in his attorney's office talking about his upcoming court case. Where is the economics? The service the attorney is providing to Oliver is part of the GDP for the current year. ▲ ▲ ▲

## What GDP Omits

Some exchanges that take place in an economy are not included in GDP. These trades range from sales of used cars to illegal drug deals.

CERTAIN NONMARKET GOODS AND SERVICES If a family hires a person through the classified section of the newspaper to cook and clean, the service is counted in GDP. If family members perform the same tasks, however, their services are not counted in GDP. In the first case, a service is bought and sold for a price in a market setting. In the second case, it is not; no transaction takes place.

Some nonmarket goods are included in GDP. For example, the market value of food produced on a farm and consumed by the farm family is estimated, and this imputed value is part of GDP.

UNDERGROUND ACTIVITIES, BOTH LEGAL AND ILLEGAL The underground economy consists of unreported exchanges that take place outside the normal recorded markets. Some underground activities involve illegal goods (e.g., cocaine), and others involve legal goods and tax evasion. Illegal goods and services are not counted in

## Gross Family Product

One of the ways to understand GDP is to think of what it would be comparable to in a family. Instead of talking about what a country produces in a year, let's talk about what a family produces. Let's call the total market value of what the family produces gross family product (GFP).

Just as not every country has the same GDP, not every family has the same GFP. One family can have a higher or lower GFP than another. The difference in GFP might be because more people are producing in one family than in another. For example, family A is composed of five individuals, and family B is composed of eight. More family members (more resources) can produce more output.

The same holds for countries. China might have a higher GDP than, say, France because China has a larger population. The national Chinese "family" is larger than the French "family."

Of course, one family might have a higher GFP than another for other reasons. For example, even with the same number of persons in two families, one family might have a higher GFP. Perhaps the members of,

say, family A work more hours than those of family B. All other things equal, more work can result in more output.

The same holds for countries. The GDP of one country might be higher than the GDP of another because the workers in one country work more hours a week than those in the other country.

Finally, consider that even when the size of two families is the same and when the number of hours worked each week by the two families is the same, one family could still have a higher GFP than another. To understand why, keep in mind that GFP measures the total market value of the family output. Note the phrase "total market value," computed by multiplying the price of each unit of output by the number of units produced. If a family is producing chairs, then its GFP will be equal to the price of each chair multiplied by the number of chairs produced. One hundred dollars ($100) per chair multiplied by, say, 100 chairs equals a GFP of $10,000. If another family produces, say, 100 shirts at a price of $25, its GPF will be lower. Thus one family's GFP might be higher than another's GFP because the per-unit price of what it produces is higher.

GDP because no record exists of the related transactions. There are no written records of illegal drug sales, illegal gambling, and illegal prostitution. Nor are there written records of some legal activities that individuals want to keep from government notice. For example, a gardener might agree to do gardening work only on the condition that he is paid in cash. Obviously, a person may legally buy or sell gardening services, but the transaction might not be recorded if one or both parties do not want it to be. Why might the gardener want to be paid in cash? Perhaps he doesn't want to pay taxes on the income received—an objective more easily accomplished if no written record of the income is generated.

**SALES OF USED GOODS** GDP measures *current production* (i.e., production occurring during the current year). A used car sale, for example, does not enter into the current-year statistics because the car was counted when it was originally produced.

**FINANCIAL TRANSACTIONS** The trading of stocks and bonds is not counted in GDP because it does not represent the production of new assets. It is simply the trading of existing assets (the exchange of stocks or bonds for money).

**Transfer Payment**
A payment to a person that is not made in return for goods and services currently supplied.

**GOVERNMENT TRANSFER PAYMENTS** A transfer payment is a payment to a person that is not made in return for goods and services currently supplied. Government transfer payments, such as Social Security benefits and veterans' benefits, are not counted in GDP because they are not payments to individuals for *current production.*

# economics 24/7

## Happiness and the Economist

In one survey, students at Harvard University were asked whether they would prefer (a) $50,000 a year while others got $25,000 a year or (b) $100,000 a year while others got $200,000 a year. A majority of the students chose (a). In other words, they chose a lower absolute income but a higher relative income. They chose to be poorer in absolute terms, as long as they could be richer in relative terms.

COMSTOCK IMAGES/JUPITER IMAGES

Sometimes, researchers conclude from such a survey that an increase in absolute standard of living (say, as measured by per-capita GDP) does not matter as much to happiness as a rise in one's relative standard of living (say, as measured by moving up from being poor to being middle income or from being middle income to being "rich"). In short, what matters is not so much how we are doing but how we are doing relative to everyone else.

Now the real question is whether survey results—such as the Harvard University student survey—are meaningful. For example, what would we observe if people cared more about their relative standing than their absolute standing? Some economists have suggested that more affluent people would move into poorer neighborhoods so that they could experience higher relative incomes. The economists go on to say that because we don't see this very often, then individuals do not care about their relative income as much as the survey results suggest. Another question is what would we *not* see if people cared about their relative incomes? Poor immigrants would not come to a rich country; after all, when poor immigrants come to a rich country, they know they will be near the bottom of the income scale. Yet they come, perhaps because they enjoy a higher absolute income in the rich country than they would in the country they leave.

What can we learn about economists? A key lesson is that economists don't always trust survey results—or what people say when answering certain questions. For economists, if we want to know something about people's preferences, we should observe how they act instead of noting what they say.

LEISURE The length of the workweek has fallen in the United States since the beginning of the twentieth century, and the leisure time individuals have to consume has increased. Leisure is a good in much the same way that cars, houses, and shoes are goods. But leisure is not counted in GDP because it is too difficult to quantify.

## GDP Is Not Adjusted for Bads Generated in the Production of Goods

Economic growth often comes with certain bads (anything from which individuals receive disutility or dissatisfaction). For example, producing cars, furniture, and steel often generates air and water pollution, which most people consider as bads. GDP counts the goods and services, but it does not deduct the air and water pollution. Thus, some economists argue that GDP overstates our overall economic welfare.

## Per Capita GDP

If we divide a country's GDP by the population in the country, we get *per-capita GDP.* For example, if a country has a GDP of $5 trillion and its population is 200 million, per-capita GDP is $25,000 ($5 trillion ÷ 200 million people). In 2009, the per-capita GDP in the United States was $46,400.

## Is Either GDP or Per-Capita GDP a Measure of Happiness or Well-Being?

Are the people in a country with a higher GDP or higher per-capita GDP better off or happier than the people in a country with a lower GDP or lower per-capita GDP? We cannot answer that question because well-being and happiness are subjective. A person with more goods may be happier than a person with fewer goods, but possibly not. The person with fewer goods but a lot of leisure, little air pollution, and a relaxed way of life may be much happier than the person with many goods, little leisure, and a polluted, stressful environment.

So it is possible to read too much into GDP figures. GDP figures are useful for obtaining an estimate of the productive capabilities of an economy, but they do not necessarily measure happiness or well-being.

### SELF-TEST

(Answers to Self-Test questions are in Answers to Self-Test Questions at the back of the book.)

1. Why aren't stock purchases and sales counted in GDP?

2. Suppose the GDP for a country is $0. Does this mean that there was no productive activity in the country? Explain your answer.

## THE EXPENDITURE APPROACH TO COMPUTING GDP FOR A REAL-WORLD ECONOMY

In a tiny economy, we can compute GDP by simply multiplying the quantity of each good produced by the quantity of the good produced:

$$GDP = \sum PQ$$

The U.S. economy is anything but tiny. Economists cannot simply multiply the price of each good produced by the quantity of it. In a large economy, GDP can be measured in a number of different ways. A principal way is called the *expenditure approach* to measuring GDP. In this approach, economists sum the spending (on final goods and services) in usually four sectors of the economy: (1) household, (2) business, (3) government, and (4) foreign.

In each of these four sectors, economic actors buy goods and services; in other words, they spend. By sector, the expenditures are called, respectively, (1) *consumption;* (2) gross private domestic investment, or simply *investment*; (3) government consumption expenditures and gross investment, or simply *government purchases;* and (4) *net exports.*

| Sectors of the Economy | Spending Called . . . |
| --- | --- |
| Household | Consumption |
| Business | Investment |
| Government | Government purchases |
| Foreign | Net Exports |

Before we see how economists add up the expenditures of these sectors, let's discuss each of the expenditure components.

CONSUMPTION Consumption (C) includes spending on:

- **Durable goods.** Durable goods are goods that are expected to last for more than three years, such as refrigerators, ovens, or cars.

- **Nondurable goods.** Nondurable goods are goods that are not expected to last for more than three years, such as food.

- **Services.** Services are intangible items such as lawn care, car repair, and entertainment.

Consumption expenditures in the United States usually account for 70 percent of GDP. In short, consumption is the largest spending component of GDP.

INVESTMENT Investment (I) is the sum of:

- Purchases of newly produced capital goods.

- Changes in business inventories, sometimes referred to as inventory investment.

- Purchases of new residential housing.[1]

The sum of the purchases of newly produced capital goods and the purchases of new residential housing is often referred to as fixed investment. In other words:

Investment = Fixed investment + Inventory investment.

Fixed investment is the larger of the two components.

GOVERNMENT PURCHASES Government purchases (G) include federal, state, and local government purchases of goods and services and gross investment in highways, bridges, and so on. Not included in government purchases are government transfer payments, which are payments to persons that are not made in return for currently supplied goods and services. Social Security benefits and welfare payments are two examples of transfer payments; neither is a payment for current productive efforts.

NET EXPORTS People, firms, and governments in the United States sometimes purchase foreign-produced goods. These purchases are referred to as imports (IM). Foreign residents, firms, and governments sometimes purchase U.S.-produced goods. These purchases are referred to as exports (EX). If imports are subtracted from exports, we are left with net exports (NX).

$$NX = EX - IM$$

Obviously, net exports (NX) can be positive or negative. If exports are greater than imports, then NX is positive; if imports are greater than exports, then NX is negative.

## Computing GDP Using the Expenditure Approach

So the expenditure approach to measuring or computing GDP calls for the totaling of the purchases of final goods and services made in the four sectors of the economy (see Exhibit 1). This may give you reason to pause because our earlier definition of GDP did not mention *purchases* of final goods and services. Rather, we defined GDP as the total market value of all final goods and services *produced* annually within a nation's borders.

**Consumption**
The sum of spending on durable goods, nondurable goods, and services.

**Investment**
The sum of all purchases of newly produced capital goods, changes in business inventories, and purchases of new residential housing.

**Inventory Investment**
Changes in the stock of unsold goods.

**Fixed Investment**
Business purchases of capital goods, such as machinery and factories, and purchases of new residential housing.

**Government Purchases**
Federal, state, and local government purchases of goods and services and gross investment in highways, bridges, and so on.

**Government Transfer Payments**
Payments to persons that are not made in return for currently supplied goods and services.

**Imports**
Total domestic (U.S.) spending on foreign goods.

**Exports**
Total foreign spending on domestic (U.S.) goods.

**Net Exports**
Exports minus imports.

---

1. For purposes of computing GDP, the purchases of new residential housing (although undertaken by members of the household sector) are considered investment.

**EXHIBIT 1**

**The Expenditure Approach to Computing GDP**

The expenditure components of GDP are consumption, investment, government purchases, and net exports. The exhibit shows what is included in each of these components.

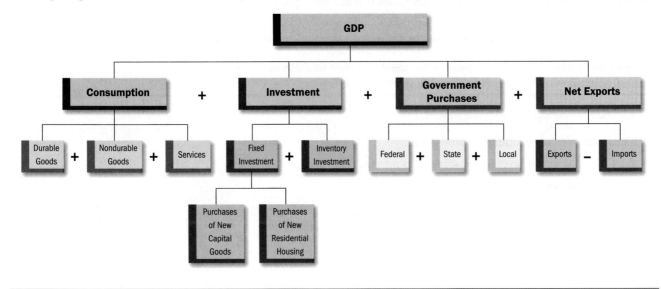

The discrepancy is cleared up quickly when we note that national income accountants (persons who compute GDP for the government) assume that anything produced but not sold to consumers is "bought" by the firm that produced it. In other words, if a car is produced but not sold, it goes into business inventory and is consider "purchased" by the automaker firm that produced it. Thus, we can compute GDP by summing the purchases made by the four sectors of the economy. GDP equals consumption ($C$) plus investment ($I$) plus government purchases ($G$) plus net exports ($EX - IM$).

$$GDP = C + I + G + (EX - IM)$$

**EXHIBIT 2**

**Components of GDP (Expenditure Approach)**

The expenditure approach to computing GDP sums the purchases made by final users of goods and services. The expenditure components include consumption, investment, government purchases, and net exports. The data are for 2009.

Exhibit 2 shows the dollar amounts of the four components of GDP for the United States in 2009.

## Common Misconceptions about Increases in GDP

Are all increases in GDP good for the economy? To answer this question, consider that if investment rises and no other component of GDP declines, GDP will rise. Recall that investment can rise for one of three reasons: (1) Firms may purchase more newly produced capital goods (firms buy more factories and machinery); (2) individuals may purchase new residential housing (someone buys a new home); or (3) firms' inventory investment rises. Further, firms' inventory investment can rise in two ways:

- *Planned inventory investment.* Firms may deliberately produce more units of a good and add them to inventory.

- *Unplanned inventory investment.* Consumers don't buy as many units of output as firms have produced, and unsold units are added to inventory.

Now compare two settings:

- *Setting 1.* Firms purchase more newly produced capital goods (more factories and machinery). As a result, investment rises and so does GDP, all other things remaining constant.

- *Setting 2.* Buyers don't buy as many units of output as firms have produced. The unsold units find their way into (unplanned) inventory investment. As a result, investment rises and so GDP rises too, all other things remaining constant.

Is the higher GDP in settings 1 and 2 equivalent? We think not. As far as the health and strength of the economy are concerned, the increase in GDP in setting 1 is superior to the increase in GDP in setting 2.

## SELF-TEST

1. Describe the expenditure approach to computing GDP in a real-world economy.

2. Will GDP be smaller than the sum of consumption, investment, and government purchases if net exports are negative? Explain your answer.

3. If GDP is $400 billion and the country's population is 100 million, does it follow that each individual in the country has $40,000 worth of goods and services?

# THE INCOME APPROACH TO COMPUTING GDP FOR A REAL-WORLD ECONOMY

A second way to compute GDP, the income approach, and the expenditure approach should give us the same dollar amount of GDP. Let's look at an example. In a given economy, 10 units of good A are produced, and 20 units of good B are produced. Further, the price of good A is $1, and the price of good B is $2. If buyers purchase all the units of each of the two goods, then they will have spent $50 on these two goods: ($1 × 10 units) + ($2 × 20 units) = $50. In other words, the expenditure approach to measuring GDP gives us $50 of GDP in this little economy.

However, money spent by one person is money earned by another. The person who sells 10 units of good A at $1 per unit receives an income of $10. The $10 spent by the buyer is $10 earned by the seller.

Exhibit 3 shows a circular flow diagram of the economy. This diagram illustrates that, in a simple economy, GDP computed by summing the purchases of the four sectors of the economy is equal to GDP computed by summing the income earned by the different resources. In other words, dollar purchases (or dollar expenditures) equal dollar income. More specifically, money spent to buy goods and services ends up flowing to the resources that produce them. (Again, think in terms of a tiny economy in which one person buys 10 oranges for $1 each. His expenditures equal $10. But the $10 also represents income for the person who sold the buyer the oranges. An expenditure for one person is income for another.)

Two steps are involved in computing GDP using the income approach. First, compute national income. Second, adjust national income for certain things. The end result is GDP.

**EXHIBIT 3**

### The Circular Flow: Total Purchases (Expenditures) Equal Total Income in a Simple Economy

The exhibit shows an economy with four sectors: Households, Business Firms, Government, and Foreign Economies. Each sector purchases goods and services. The sum of these purchases is GDP [GDP = C + I + G + (EX − IM)].

The purchases (expenditures) made in product markets flow to business firms. Business firms then use these monies to buy resources in resource markets. In other words, these monies flow to the owners (suppliers) of land, labor, capital, and entrepreneurship. The sum of these resource payments is total income, which flows to households. In this simple economy, where some things have been ignored, total purchases (expenditures) equal total income. Because total purchases (expenditures) equal GDP and total purchases equal total income, it follows that GDP equals total income.

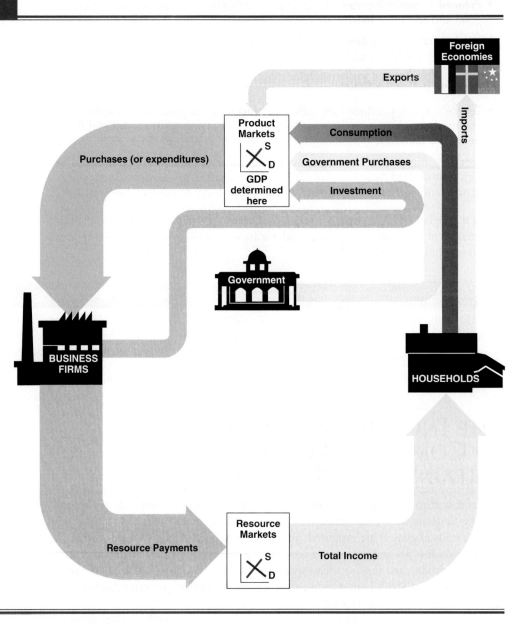

---

### National Income

Total income earned by U.S. citizens and businesses, no matter where they reside or are located. National income is the sum of the payments to resources (land, labor, capital, and entrepreneurship): National income = Compensation of employees + Proprietors' income + Corporate profits + Rental income of persons + Net interest.

## Computing National Income

National income is the sum of five components: (1) compensation of employees, (2) proprietors' income, (3) corporate profits, (4) rental income of persons, and (5) net interest.

**COMPENSATION OF EMPLOYEES** The compensation of employees is equal to the total of (1) wages and salaries paid to employees, (2) employers' contributions to Social Security and employee benefit plans, and (3) the monetary value of fringe benefits, tips, and paid vacations. The compensation of employees is the largest component of national income. In 2009, in the United States it was $7.84 trillion.

**PROPRIETORS' INCOME** Proprietors' income includes all forms of income earned by self-employed individuals and the owners of unincorporated businesses, including

## 1820

Most people are interested in knowing what the per-capita GDP is today in different countries. Also interesting is the per-capita GDP in different countries over the years. For example, what country had the highest per-capita GDP in, say, 1820? The answer is the Netherlands. In 1900, New Zealand was the high country. The following three tables identify the top 10 countries in various years in terms of per-capita GDP.

**EXHIBIT 4**

| | 1820 | | | 1900 | | | 1950 | |
|---|---|---|---|---|---|---|---|---|
| **Rank** | **Country** | **Per-Capita GDP** | **Rank** | **Country** | **Per-Capita GDP** | **Rank** | **Country** | **Per-Capita GDP** |
| 1 | Netherlands | $1,561 | 1 | New Zealand | $4,320 | 1 | United States | $9,573 |
| 2 | Australia | $1,528 | 2 | Australia | $4,299 | 2 | Switzerland | $8,939 |
| 3 | Austria | $1,295 | 3 | United States | $4,096 | 3 | New Zealand | $8,495 |
| 4 | Belgium | $1,291 | 4 | Belgium | $3,652 | 4 | Venezuela | $7,424 |
| 5 | United States | $1,287 | 5 | Netherlands | $3,533 | 5 | Australia | $7,218 |
| 6 | Denmark | $1,225 | 6 | Switzerland | $3,531 | 6 | Canada | $7,047 |
| 7 | France | $1,218 | 7 | Germany | $3,134 | 7 | Sweden | $6,738 |
| 8 | Sweden | $1,198 | 8 | Denmark | $2,902 | 8 | Denmark | $6,683 |
| 9 | Germany | $1,112 | 9 | Austria | $2,901 | 9 | Netherlands | $5,850 |
| 10 | Italy | $1,092 | 10 | France | $2,849 | 10 | Belgium | $5,346 |

unincorporated farmers. Included in farm income is an estimate of the value of the food grown and consumed on farms.

CORPORATE PROFITS  Corporate profits include all the income earned by the stockholders of corporations. Some of the profits are paid to stockholders in the form of dividends, some are kept within the firm to finance investments (these are called *undistributed profits* or *retained earnings*), and some are used to pay corporate profits taxes. (The portion of corporate profits used to pay corporate profits taxes is counted as income "earned" by households even though households do not receive the income.)

RENTAL INCOME (OF PERSONS)  Rental income is the income received by individuals for the use of their nonmonetary assets (land, houses, offices). It also includes returns to individuals who hold copyrights and patents. Finally, it includes an imputed value to owner-occupied houses. For example, someone may own the house she lives in and therefore not pay any rent, but for purposes of national income accounting, a rental value is imputed. In short, home ownership is viewed as a business that produces a service that is sold to the owner of the business.

NET INTEREST  Net interest is the interest income received by U.S. households and government minus the interest they paid out.

**NATIONAL INCOME**  We can summarize national income and its components as follows:

$$
\begin{aligned}
\text{National income} = \ &\text{Compensation of employees} \\
&+ \text{Proprietors' income} \\
&+ \text{Corporate profits} \\
&+ \text{Rental income} \\
&+ \text{Net interest}
\end{aligned}
$$

## From National Income to GDP: Making Some Adjustments

After computing national income, we might think that there is nothing else to do—that national income should equal GDP. We naturally think that every dollar spent is someone's income. But when we check the actual figures for national income and GDP, we find that they are not equal. In other words, not every dollar spent is someone else's income. For example, if Jones spends $10 to buy a book, $9.50 of the $10 might end up in the seller's pocket as income, but remaining 50¢ might go for taxes.

With this in mind, the income approach to computing GDP requires us to add certain things to national income and to subtract certain things from it. The following equation and Exhibit 5 show what must be added to and subtracted from national income to compute GDP. Keep the equation and exhibit in mind as you continue to read.

$$
\begin{aligned}
\text{GDP} = \ &\text{National income} \\
&- \text{Income earned from the rest of the world} \\
&+ \text{Income earned by the rest of the world} \\
&+ \text{Indirect business taxes} \\
&+ \text{Capital consumption allowance} \\
&+ \text{Statistical discrepancy}
\end{aligned}
$$

**INCOME EARNED FROM THE REST OF THE WORLD, INCOME EARNED BY THE REST OF THE WORLD**  In computing national income, we include the income earned by U.S. citizens who work and live in other countries, but we do not include the income earned by foreigners who work and live in the United States. If we want to compute GDP, we have to adjust for both these incomes. We do so by (1) subtracting from

---

**EXHIBIT 5**

**The Income Approach to Computing GDP**

The exhibit identifies the components of national income and the adjustments necessary to compute GDP using the income approach.

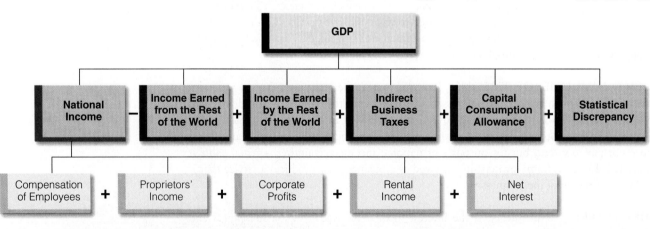

## GDP: Proceed with Caution

Making incorrect comparisons between countries based on GDP figures is easy to do. For example, a person might notice that Austria's GDP ($374 billion) is smaller than Germany's GDP ($2,810 billion) and conclude that Austrians are not as well off as Germans.

First, however, we would expect a country with a smaller population to have a smaller GDP than a country with a larger population. With fewer people, usually less output is produced. Austria has a population of 8.2 million, whereas Germany has a population of 82 million. In other words, Germany has over 10 times the population of Austria; so we would expect it to have a higher GDP.

Also, GDP doesn't matter as much as per-capita GDP. For example, currently Austria has a higher per-capita GDP ($39,400) than Germany ($34,200).

But even per-capita GDP can be deceiving. When an economist states that the per-capita GDP of, say, Austria, is $39,400, this is the dollar amount each person in Austria would have *if* the GDP of the country

© IMAGE COPYRIGHT FEVERPITCH, 2009. USED UNDER LICENSE FROM SHUTTERSTOCK.COM

were divided equally among the entire population—in other words, if everyone in the country had an equal slice of GDP.

In actuality, not everyone in the country gets an equal slice. Some people have a much smaller slice than others. Whereas one person may have a slice equal to $400,000, another person might have a slice equal to $7,000.

Finally, keep in mind that we can witness an increase in GDP in two ways. GDP will rise if the inhabitants of a country actually produce more goods and services and if output remains constant while only prices rise. A rise in GDP due to only rising prices does not mean the same thing as a rise in GDP due to rising output while prices remain constant. Obviously, the overall standard of living of the people in the country is better served when GDP rises because output is higher than when it rises due to increasing prices.

The bottom line is that GDP is a useful economic variable that is readily measured and reported on. But we need to be careful to use it incorrectly when making comparisons, discussing well-being, and drawing conclusions.

---

national income the income earned from the rest of the world (this is income that U.S. citizens living abroad earned by producing and selling goods) and (2) adding to national income the income earned by the rest of the world (this is income that non-U.S. citizens earned by producing and selling goods in the United States).

**INDIRECT BUSINESS TAXES** Indirect business taxes are made up mainly of excise taxes, sales taxes, and property taxes. These taxes are not part of national income because they are not considered a payment to any resource (land, labor, etc.). Think of them as monies collected by government, not payments to land, labor, capital, or entrepreneurship.

Indirect taxes are included in the purchases of goods and services (you pay a sales tax when you buy most goods) and so are included when the expenditure approach is used to compute GDP. Therefore, we must add indirect business taxes to national income.

**CAPITAL CONSUMPTION ALLOWANCE** Some capital goods are used up in the production process through natural wear, obsolescence, or accidental destruction (e.g., the

**Capital Consumption Allowance (Depreciation)**
The estimated amount of capital goods used up in production through natural wear, obsolescence, and accidental destruction.

machinery that breaks down and cannot be repaired). The cost to replace these capital goods is called the capital consumption allowance, or depreciation. It is added to national income because we want a measure of all the income earned in the economy. National income, by itself, doesn't include the income payments implicit in the capital consumption allowance.

**STATISTICAL DISCREPANCY** GDP and national income are computed using different sets of data. Hence, statistical discrepancies or pure computational errors often occur and must be accounted for in the national income accounts.

## Other National Income Accounting Measurements

Besides gross domestic product (GDP) and national income, three other national income accounting measurements are important: net domestic product, personal income, and disposable income. All five measurements—gross domestic product, national income, net domestic product, personal income, and disposable income—are often used interchangeably to measure the output produced and income earned in an economy.

## Net Domestic Product

**Net Domestic Product (NDP)**
GDP minus the capital consumption allowance.

If we use the expenditure approach to compute GDP, we add consumption, investment, government purchases, and net exports. Investment (or more specifically, gross private domestic investment) includes fixed investment and inventory investment. Some of the fixed investment, however, is used to replace worn-out or obsolete capital goods, not to produce new goods. In short, gross private domestic investment contains the capital consumption allowance. If we subtract the capital consumption allowance from GDP, we are left with net domestic product (NDP). NDP measures the total value of new goods available in the economy in a given year after worn-out capital goods have been replaced.

$$\text{Net domestic product (NDP)} = \text{GDP} - \text{Capital consumption allowance}$$

## Personal Income

**Personal Income**
The amount of income that individuals actually receive. It is equal to national income minus undistributed corporate profits, social insurance taxes, and corporate profits taxes, plus transfer payments.

Not all income earned is received, and not all income received is earned. An example of income earned but not received is undistributed profits, which stockholders earn but do not receive. Instead, the corporation usually reinvests the undistributed profits. An example of income received but not earned is Social Security benefits.

Personal income is the amount of income that individuals actually receive. It is equal to national income minus such major earned-but-not-received items as undistributed corporate profits, social insurance taxes (Social Security contributions), and corporate profits taxes, plus transfer payments (which are received but not earned).

$$
\begin{aligned}
\text{Personal income} = {} & \text{National income} \\
& - \text{ Undistributed corporate profits} \\
& - \text{ Social insurance taxes} \\
& - \text{ Corporate profits taxes} \\
& + \text{ Transfer payments}
\end{aligned}
$$

## Disposable Income

**Disposable Income**
The portion of personal income that can be used for consumption or saving. It is equal to personal income minus personal taxes (especially income taxes).

The portion of personal income that can be used for consumption or saving is referred to as disposable personal income, or simply disposable income. It is equal to personal income minus personal taxes (especially income taxes). Sometimes disposable income is referred to as spendable income, take-home pay, or after-tax income.

$$\text{Disposable income} = \text{Personal income} - \text{Personal taxes}$$

# REAL GDP

This section defines Real GDP, shows how to compute it, and then explains how it is used to measure economic growth.

## Why We Need Real GDP

In 2006, the U.S. GDP was about $13.39 trillion. One year later, in 2007, GDP was about $14.07 trillion. Although you know GDP was higher in 2007 than in 2006, do you know *why?*

As you think about your answer, look at GDP in a one-good economy. Suppose 10 units of this good X are produced and each unit is sold for $10; the GDP in the economy is $100.

$$GDP = \$10 \times 10 \text{ units} = \$100$$

The GDP rises from $100 to $250. Why? It could rise because price increased from $10 to $25:

$$GDP = \$25 \times 10 \text{ units} = \$250$$

Or it could rise because the quantity of output produced increased from 10 units to 25 units:

$$GDP = \$10 \times 25 \text{ units} = \$250$$

Or it could rise because price increased to $12.50 and the quantity increased to 20 units:

$$GDP = \$12.50 \times 20 \text{ units} = \$250$$

To gauge the health of the economy, economists want to know why the GDP increased. If GDP increased simply because price increased, then the economy is not growing. For an economy to grow, more output must be produced.

Because an increase in GDP can be due in part simply to an increase in price, a more meaningful measure is Real GDP. Real GDP is GDP adjusted for price changes.

**Real GDP**
The value of the entire output produced annually within a country's borders, adjusted for price changes.

## Computing Real GDP

One way to compute Real GDP is to find the value of the output for the different years in terms of the same prices, that is, the base-year prices. Consider the following data for our one-good economy:

| Year | Price of Good X | Quantity Produced of Good X (units) | GDP |
|------|------|------|------|
| 1 | $10 | 100 | $10 × 100 = **$1,000** |
| 2 | $12 | 120 | $12 × 120 = **$1,440** |
| 3 | $14 | 140 | $14 × 140 = **$1,960** |

The data show why GDP is higher in years 2 and 3: Both price and quantity have increased. However, we want to separate the part of GDP that is higher due to an increase in quantity from the part that is higher due to an increase in price. We want the Real GDP, the part of GDP that is higher because the quantity of output is higher.

To compute Real GDP for any year, multiply the quantity of the good produced in a given year by the price in the base year. If year 1 is the base year, we multiply the quantity of the good produced in year 2 by the price of the good in year 1. To find Real GDP in year 3, we multiply the quantity of the good produced in year 3 by the price of the good in year 1.

| Year | Price of Good X | Quantity Produced of Good X (units) | GDP | Real GDP |
|------|-----------------|-------------------------------------|-----|----------|
| 1 (Base Year) | $10 | 100 | $10 × 100 = **$1,000** | $10 × 100 = **$1,000** |
| 2 | $12 | 120 | $12 × 120 = **$1,440** | $10 × 120 = **$1,200** |
| 3 | $14 | 140 | $14 × 140 = **$1,960** | $10 × 140 = **$1,400** |

## The General Equation for Real GDP

The real world has more than one good and more than one price. The general equation used to compute Real GDP is:

$$\text{Real GDP} = \Sigma(\text{Base-year prices} \times \text{Current-year quantities})$$

$\Sigma$, the Greek capital letter sigma, stands for summation. Thus, Real GDP is the sum of all the current-year quantities times their base-year prices. In 2009, Real GDP in the United States was $12.98 trillion.

## What Does It Mean If Real GDP Is Higher in One Year Than in Another?

If GDP is, say, $9 trillion in year 1 and $9.5 trillion in year 2, we cannot be sure why it has increased from one year to the next. (1) Did prices rise while output remained constant? (2) Did output rise while prices remained constant? (3) Or did prices and output both rise?

However, if Real GDP is, say, $8 trillion in year 1 and $8.3 trillion in year 2, we know why it has increased. Real GDP rises only if output rises. In other words, Real GDP rises only if more goods and services are produced.

## Real GDP, Economic Growth, and Business Cycles

Suppose you have to choose between two countries. In country A, Real GDP grows by 3 percent each year. In country B, Real GDP is the same each year; if Real GDP was $500 billion last year, it is $500 billion in the current year, and it will be $500 billion next year. In which of the two countries would you prefer to live, *ceteris paribus?*

Or make a choice between countries C and D. In country C, Real GDP takes a roller coaster ride, alternating between rising and falling. It rises for some months, then falls, then rises again, then falls, and so on. In country D, Real GDP simply rises year after year. In which of the two countries would you prefer to live, *ceteris paribus?*

If you chose one country over the other in each of these two cases, then you are implicitly saying that Real GDP matters to you. One of the reasons economists study Real GDP is that it matters to you and others. In other words, because Real GDP is important to you, it is important to economists.

Economists study two major macroeconomic topics that have to do with Real GDP: *economic growth* and *business cycles.*

**ECONOMIC GROWTH** Annual economic growth has occurred if Real GDP in one year is higher than Real GDP in the previous year. For example, if Real GDP is $8.1 trillion in one year and $8.3 trillion in the next, the economy has undergone economic growth. The growth rate is equal to the (positive) percentage change in Real GDP and is computed as follows:

$$\text{Percentage change in Real GDP} = \left( \frac{\text{Real GDP}_{\text{later year}} - \text{Real GDP}_{\text{earlier year}}}{\text{Real GDP}_{\text{earlier year}}} \right) \times 100$$

**Economic Growth**
Increases in Real GDP.

**THE UPS AND DOWNS IN THE ECONOMY: THE BUSINESS CYCLE** If Real GDP is on a roller coaster—rising and falling and rising and falling—the economy is said to be going through a business cycle. Economists usually talk about four or five phases of the business cycle. We identify five in the following list and in Exhibit 6.

**Business Cycle**
Recurrent swings (up and down) in Real GDP.

1. **Peak.** At the *peak* of the business cycle, Real GDP is at a temporary high. In Exhibit 6, Real GDP is at a temporary high at $Q_1$.

2. **Contraction.** The *contraction* phase represents a decline in Real GDP. According to the standard definition of *recession*, two consecutive quarter declines in Real GDP constitute a recession.

3. **Trough.** The low point in Real GDP, just before it begins to turn up, is called the *trough* of the business cycle.

4. **Recovery.** The *recovery* is the period when Real GDP is rising. It begins at the trough and ends at the initial peak. The recovery in Exhibit 6 extends from the trough until Real GDP is again at $Q_1$.

5. **Expansion.** The *expansion* phase refers to increases in Real GDP beyond the recovery. In Exhibit 6, it refers to increases in Real GDP above $Q_1$.

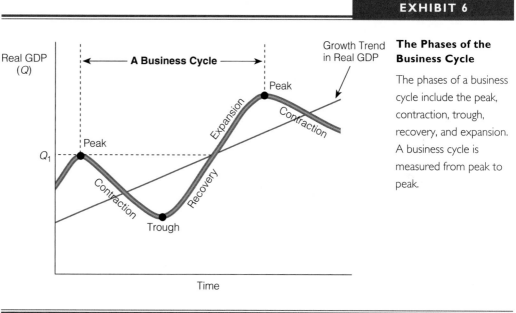

**EXHIBIT 6**

**The Phases of the Business Cycle**

The phases of a business cycle include the peak, contraction, trough, recovery, and expansion. A business cycle is measured from peak to peak.

An entire business cycle is measured from peak to peak. The typical business cycle is approximately four to five years, although a few have been shorter and some have been longer.

# ⓕinding **ECONOMICS**

**After Graduating from College** Yoram has just graduated from college. He has been searching for a job in his chosen field of accounting, but so far he hasn't been offered a job he would like. Where is the economics?

The state (or health) of the economy is closely tied to whether business firms are hiring or firing. When the economy is growing, firms are usually hiring employees; when the economy is in a slump (a recession), firms are often firing employees. As far as one's job prospects go, graduating when the economy is strong and growing is better than when it is weak and declining. ▲ ▲ ▲

**NATIONAL BUREAU OF ECONOMIC RESEARCH (NBER) AND RECESSIONS** The standard definition of a recession is two consecutive quarter declines in Real GDP, but this is not the only definition of a recession. The National Bureau of Economic Research has this to say about a recession.

> *A recession is a period between a peak and a trough . . . During a recession, a significant decline in economic activity spreads across the economy and can last from a few months to more than a year.*

The NBER definition is therefore different from the standard definition of a recession. According to the NBER, "a recession is a significant decline in activity [that] spreads across the economy."

# OFFICE HOURS

## "Why Do We Use the *Expenditure* Approach to Measure *Production?*"

**STUDENT:**

When GDP was first defined, emphasis was placed on goods and services being *produced*. The definition of GDP was "the total market value of all final goods and services *produced* annually with a country's borders."

**INSTRUCTOR:**

Yes, that is correct.

**STUDENT:**

But when we computed GDP, we simply summed the *expenditures* made by each of the four sectors of the economy. In other words, we added consumption, investment, government purchases, and net exports.

Now here is my problem. When we define GDP, we speak about production— final goods and services *produced*. But when we compute GDP, production doesn't seem to come up. Instead we sum *expenditures* made by the four sectors of the economy.

My point is simple: A good can be produced that is not purchased. So if we add up only expenditures (or purchases), aren't we underestimating production?

**INSTRUCTOR:**

I see your point. What you are saying is perhaps 100 chairs, say, are produced in the year, but only 75 of them are purchased. In that case, counting only purchases (or expenditures) underestimates production. And production is what we really want to get at because GDP is defined as the total market value of all final goods and services produced.

**STUDENT:**

Yes, that's right. That's what I am getting at.

**INSTRUCTOR:**

Well, remember one important category of expenditures: investment. Investment consists of the expenditures of the business sector. We know that investment is the sum of fixed investment and inventory investment, but let's focus on inventory investment for a minute. Think of how goods might get into inventory. One way is for the firm to deliberately produce goods and put some into inventory. In other words, a company produces 1,000 chairs, sends 900 of them to different retailers, and then puts 100 into inventory in case there is an unexpected increase in demand for chairs. We'll call these 100 chairs planned inventory.

## SELF-TEST

1. Suppose GDP is $6 trillion in year 1 and $6.2 trillion in year 2. What has caused the rise in GDP?

2. Suppose Real GDP is $5.2 trillion in year 1 and $5.3 trillion in year 2. What has caused the rise in Real GDP?

3. Can an economy be faced with endless business cycles and still see its Real GDP grow over time? Explain your answer.

Now think of another way that chairs can be added to inventory. Suppose that when the firm sends those 900 chairs to different retailers, not all of the chairs sell. Only 700 of them sell. What will retailers do with the remaining 200 chairs? One thing they might do is return them to the producer. So what does the firm do with those 200 returned chairs. For now, they put them into inventory. We'll call these 200 chairs unplanned inventory.

Here is the important point: The 300 chairs in inventory (100 chairs in planned inventory and 200 chairs in unplanned inventory) are part of overall investment. In other words, if investment for the year equals $2.1 trillion (for the economy), the market value of the 300 chairs in inventory are part of that $2.1 trillion.

When computing GDP, we count those 300 chairs the same way we count the 700 that were produced and purchased. In short, everything produced in the economy is purchased by someone. In our example, the 300 chairs were "purchased" by the firm that produced them.

### STUDENT:

Let me see if I have this right. If a firm produces a good and it is bought by, say, a consumer, that good is counted in GDP. But if the good is not bought by a consumer, then it is considered to be purchased by the firm that produced it. In other words, the chair company produces 1,000 chairs, sells 700 to consumers, and "sells" 300 to itself. It "buys" 300 of its own chairs. Is that right?

### INSTRUCTOR:

That's right.

### STUDENT:

But isn't that cheating somehow? After all, the 300 chairs weren't actually sold to anyone? They certainly weren't sold in the way we usually think of something being sold.

### INSTRUCTOR:

That's true. But remember what we are trying to get at with GDP: the total market value of all final goods and services produced. Those 300 chairs were certainly produced. Looking at the 300 chairs as being purchased by the firm that produced them is simply a way of counting them. And counting those 300 chairs is what we want to do when we are trying to measure GDP.

### STUDENT:

Yes, I see that now.

### POINTS TO REMEMBER

1. GDP is the total market value of all final goods and services *produced* annually within a country's borders.

2. We can use the expenditure approach to measure production as long as all goods and services produced but not sold to end consumers are considered to be "purchased" by the firm that produced them.

## CHAPTER SUMMARY

### GROSS DOMESTIC PRODUCT

- Gross domestic product (GDP) is the total market value of all final goods and services produced annually within a country's borders.
- Either the expenditure approach or the income approach can be used to compute GDP.
- To avoid the problem of double counting, only final goods and services are included in GDP.
- GDP omits certain nonmarket goods and services, both legal and illegal underground activities, the sale of used goods, financial transactions, transfer payments, and leisure (even though leisure is a good). Finally, GDP is not adjusted for the bads (e.g., pollution) that sometimes accompany production.

### EXPENDITURES

- The expenditures on U.S. goods and services include consumption, gross private domestic investment (investment), government consumption expenditures and gross investment (government purchases), and net exports (exports–imports).
- Consumption includes spending on durable goods, nondurable goods, and services.
- Investment includes purchases of newly produced capital goods (fixed investment), changes in business inventories (inventory investment), and the purchases of new residential housing (also fixed investment).
- Government purchases include federal, state, and local government purchases of goods and services and gross investment in highways, bridges, and so on. Government purchases do not include transfer payments.
- Net exports equal the total foreign spending on domestic goods (exports) minus the total domestic spending on foreign goods (imports).

### COMPUTING GDP

- Using the expenditure approach, GDP $= C + I + G + (EX - IM)$. In other words, GDP equals consumption plus investment plus government purchases plus net exports.

### MEASUREMENTS OTHER THAN GDP

- Net domestic product (NDP) equals gross domestic product (GDP) minus the capital consumption allowance.

$$NDP = GDP - \text{Capital consumption allowance}$$

- National income equals the sum of resource, or factor, payments.

$$
\begin{aligned}
\text{National income} = \ &\text{Compensation of employees} \\
&+ \text{Proprietors' income} \\
&+ \text{Corporate profits} \\
&+ \text{Rental income} \\
&+ \text{Net interest}
\end{aligned}
$$

- Personal income equals national income minus undistributed corporate profits, social insurance taxes, and corporate profits taxes, plus transfer payments.

$$
\begin{aligned}
\text{Personal Income} = \ &\text{National income} \\
&- \text{Undistributed corporate profits} \\
&- \text{Social insurance taxes} \\
&- \text{Corporate profits taxes} \\
&+ \text{Transfer payments}
\end{aligned}
$$

- Disposable Income $=$ Personal income $-$ Personal taxes

### REAL GDP

- Real GDP is GDP adjusted for price changes. It is GDP in base-year dollars.

### ECONOMIC GROWTH AND BUSINESS CYCLES

- Annual economic growth has occurred if Real GDP in one year is higher than Real GDP in the previous year.
- The business cycle has five phases: peak, contraction, trough, recovery, and expansion. A complete business cycle is measured from peak to peak.

## KEY TERMS AND CONCEPTS

| | | | |
|---|---|---|---|
| Gross Domestic Product (GDP) | Investment | Imports | Net Domestic Product (NDP) |
| Final Good | Inventory Investment | Exports | Personal Income |
| Intermediate Good | Fixed Investment | Net Exports | Disposable Income |
| Double Counting | Government Purchases | National Income | Real GDP |
| Transfer Payment | Government Transfer | Capital Consumption | Economic Growth |
| Consumption |     Payments |     Allowance (Depreciation) | |

## QUESTIONS AND PROBLEMS

1. "I just heard on the news that GDP is higher this year than it was last year. This means that we're better off this year than last year." Comment.

2. Which of the following are included in the calculation of this year's GDP? (a) 12-year-old Johnny mowing his family's lawn; (b) Dave Malone buying a used car; (c) Barbara Wilson buying a bond issued by General Motors; (d) Ed Ferguson's receipt of a Social Security payment; (e) the illegal drug transaction at the corner of Elm and Fifth.

3. Discuss the problems you see in comparing the GDPs of two countries, say, the United States and the People's Republic of China.

4. The manuscript for this book was keyed by the author. Had he hired someone to do the keying, GDP would have been higher than it was. What other activities would increase GDP if they were done differently? What activities would decrease GDP if they were done differently?

5. Why does GDP omit the sales of used goods? Of financial transactions? Of government transfer payments?

6. A business firm produces a good this year that it doesn't sell. As a result, the good is added to the firm's inventory. How does this inventory good find its way into GDP?

7. Economists prefer to compare Real GDP figures for different years instead of comparing GDP figures. Why?

8. What is the difference between a recovery and an expansion?

9. Define each of the following terms:
   a. Contraction
   b. Business cycle
   c. Trough
   d. Disposable income
   e. Net domestic product

10. Does the expenditure approach to computing GDP measure U.S. spending on all goods, U.S. spending on only U.S. goods, or U.S. and foreign spending on only U.S. goods? Explain your answer.

11. In the first quarter of the year, Real GDP was $400 billion; in the second quarter, it was $398 billion; in the third quarter, it was $399 billion; and in the fourth quarter, it was $395 billion. Has there been a recession? Explain your answer.

## WORKING WITH NUMBERS AND GRAPHS

1. Net exports are −$114 billion and exports are $857 billion. What are imports?

2. Consumption spending is $3.708 trillion, spending on nondurable goods is $1.215 trillion, and spending on services is $2.041 trillion. What does spending on durable goods equal?

3. Inventory investment is $62 billion and total investment is $1.122 trillion. What does fixed investment equal?

4. In year 1, the prices of goods X, Y, and Z are $2, $4, and $6 per unit, respectively. In year 2, the prices of goods X, Y, and Z are $3, $4, and $7, respectively. In year 2, twice as many units of each good are produced as in year 1. In year 1, 20 units of X, 40 units of Y, and 60 units of Z are produced. If year 1 is the base year, what does Real GDP equal in year 2?

5. Nondurable goods spending = $400 million, durable goods spending = $300 million, new residential housing spending = $200 million, and spending on services = $500 million. What does consumption equal?

6. According to the circular flow diagram in Exhibit 3, consumption spending flows into U.S. product markets, but import spending does not. But U.S. households buy imported goods in U.S. markets, don't they? Explain.

7. If Real GDP is $487 billion in year 1 and $498 billion in year 2, what is the economic growth rate equal to?

8. The following figure shows a business cycle. Identify each of the following as a phase of the business cycle:
   a. Point A
   b. Between points A and B
   c. Point B
   d. Between points B and C
   e. Point D

## CHAPTER 8

© VASILY SMIRNOV/FOTOLIA.COM

# AGGREGATE DEMAND AND AGGREGATE SUPPLY

**Introduction** Businesses make decisions based on what is happening in the economy today and on what they expect will happen in the economy in the future. For example, their profitability is based in part on the wages they must pay their employees, the prices of their nonlabor inputs, the productivity of their workers, and business taxes. If businesses want to expand in the future, they must consider all these things and try to predict their future sales. If they trade overseas, they must worry about exchange rates and foreign real national income. We discuss all such things and more in this chapter.

## A WAY TO VIEW THE ECONOMY

This chapter begins our theoretical discussion of an economy. We can think of an economy as consisting of two major activities: buying and producing. See Exhibit 1. Specifically, goods and services are produced, and goods and services are bought. When economists speak about aggregate demand ($AD$), they are speaking about the buying side of the economy. When economists speak about aggregate supply, they are speaking about the producing side of the economy.

Buying side of the economy = Aggregate demand

Producing side of the economy = Aggregate supply

With respect to production, two time periods are relevant: production in the short run and production in the long run. When referring to short-run aggregate supply ($SRAS$), economists are speaking about production in the short run. When referring to long-run aggregate supply ($LRAS$), they are speaking about production in the long run.

Production in the short run = Short-run aggregate supply

Production in the long run = Long-run aggregate supply

**EXHIBIT 1**

**An Economy**

There are two sides to an economy: a buying side and a producing side. There are two time periods that relate to the producing side: production in the short run and production in the long run. Buying side = Aggregate demand (AD); Production in the short run = Short-run aggregate supply (SRAS); Production in the long run = Long-run aggregate supply (LRAS).

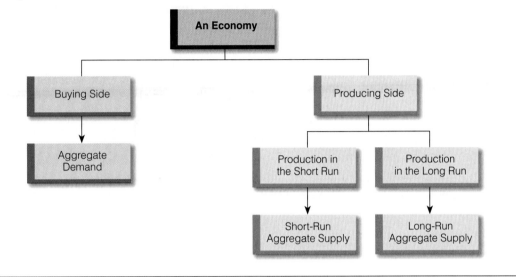

The framework of analysis we use is called aggregate demand–aggregate supply (*AD–AS*). That framework of analysis has three parts:

1. Aggregate demand (*AD*)

2. Short-run aggregate supply (*SRAS*)

3. Long-run aggregate supply (*LRAS*)

# AGGREGATE DEMAND

Recall from the last chapter that people, firms, and governments buy U.S. goods and services. Aggregate demand is the quantity demanded of these U.S. goods and services, or the quantity demanded of U.S. Real GDP, at various price levels, *ceteris paribus*. For example, the following whole set of data represents aggregate demand:

**Aggregate Demand**
The quantity demanded of all goods and services (Real GDP) at different price levels, *ceteris paribus*.

**Aggregate Demand**

| Price Index | Quantity Demanded of Goods and Services (Quantity Demanded of Real GDP) |
|---|---|
| 100 | $1,200 billion worth of goods and services |
| 110 | $1,000 billion worth of goods and services |
| 120 | $800 billion worth of goods and services |

An aggregate demand (*AD*) curve is the graphical representation of aggregate demand. An *AD* curve is shown in Exhibit 2. Notice that it is downward sloping, indicating an inverse relationship between the price level (*P*) and the quantity demanded of Real GDP (*Q*):

**Aggregate Demand (AD) Curve**
A curve that shows the quantity demanded of all goods and services (Real GDP) at different price levels, *ceteris paribus*.

**EXHIBIT 2**

**The Aggregate Demand Curve**

The aggregate demand curve is downward sloping, specifying an inverse relationship between the price level and the quantity demanded of Real GDP.

**Aggregate Demand Curve**
The price level and quantity demanded of Real GDP are inversely related.

As the price level rises, the quantity demanded of Real GDP falls; as the price level falls, the quantity demanded of Real GDP rises, *ceteris paribus*.

## Why Does the Aggregate Demand Curve Slope Downward?

Asking why the *AD* curve slopes downward is the same as asking why the relationship between the price level and the quantity demanded of Real GDP is inverse. This inverse relationship and the resulting downward slope of the *AD* curve are explained by (1) the real balance effect, (2) the interest rate effect, and (3) the international trade effect.

**REAL BALANCE EFFECT (DUE TO A CHANGE IN THE PRICE LEVEL)** The real balance effect states that the inverse relationship between the price level and the quantity demanded of Real GDP is established through changes in the value of monetary wealth, or the value of a person's monetary assets. Changes in monetary wealth usually take the form of increased or decreased purchasing power, that is, the quantity of goods and services that can be purchased with a unit of money.

To illustrate, consider a person who has $50,000 in cash. Suppose the price level falls. As this happens, the purchasing power of the person's $50,000 rises. The $50,000, which once could buy 100 television sets at $500 each, can now buy 125 sets at $400 each. An increase in the purchasing power of the person's $50,000 is identical to saying that his monetary wealth has increased. (Isn't the $50,000 more valuable when it can buy more than when it can buy less?) And, as he becomes wealthier, he buys more goods.

So a fall in the price level causes purchasing power to rise, which increases a person's monetary wealth. As people become wealthier, the quantity demanded of Real GDP rises.

Suppose the price level rises. In this event, the purchasing power of the $50,000 falls. The $50,000, which once could buy 100 television sets at $500 each, can now buy 80 sets at $625 each. A decrease in the purchasing power of the person's $50,000 is identical to saying that his monetary wealth has decreased. And as he becomes less wealthy, he buys fewer goods.

In summary, a rise in the price level causes purchasing power to fall, which decreases a person's monetary wealth. As people become less wealthy, the quantity demanded of Real GDP falls.

**INTEREST RATE EFFECT (DUE TO CHANGE IN THE PRICE LEVEL)** The interest rate effect states that the inverse relationship between the price level and the quantity demanded of Real GDP is established through changes in the part of household and business spending that is sensitive to changes in interest rates.

A person buys a fixed bundle of goods (food, clothing, and shelter) each week. Suppose the price level falls, increasing the purchasing power of the person's money. With more purchasing power (per dollar), she can purchase her fixed bundle of goods with less money. What does she do with part of this increase in her monetary wealth? She saves it. In terms of simple supply-and-demand analysis, the supply of credit increases. Subsequently, the price of credit (the interest rate) drops. As the interest rate drops, households and businesses borrow more; so they end up buying more goods. Thus, the quantity demanded of Real GDP rises.

**Real Balance Effect**
The change in the purchasing power of dollar-denominated assets that results from a change in the price level.

**Monetary Wealth**
The value of a person's monetary assets. Wealth, as distinguished from monetary wealth, refers to the value of all assets owned, both monetary and nonmonetary. In short, a person's wealth equals his or her monetary wealth (e.g., $1,000 cash) plus nonmonetary wealth (e.g., a car or a house).

**Purchasing Power**
The quantity of goods and services that can be purchased with a unit of money. Purchasing power and the price level are inversely related: As the price level goes up (down), purchasing power goes down (up).

**Interest Rate Effect**
The changes in household and business buying as the interest rate changes (in turn, a reflection of a change in the demand for or supply of credit brought on by price level changes).

Now suppose the price level rises, decreasing the purchasing power of the person's money. With less purchasing power (per dollar), she cannot purchase her fixed bundle of goods with the same amount of money. If she wants to continue to buy the goods, she needs to acquire more money. To do that, she goes to a bank and requests a loan. In terms of simple supply-and-demand analysis, the demand for credit increases. Consequently, the interest rate rises. As the interest rate rises, households borrow less to finance, say, automobile purchases, and firms borrow less to finance new capital goods spending. Thus, the quantity demanded of Real GDP falls.

**INTERNATIONAL TRADE EFFECT (DUE TO A CHANGE IN THE PRICE LEVEL)**  The international trade effect is the change in foreign sector spending as the price level changes. The inverse relationship between the price level and the quantity demanded of Real GDP is established through foreign sector spending, which includes U.S. spending on foreign goods (imports) and foreign spending on U.S. goods (exports).

**International Trade Effect**
The change in foreign sector spending as the price level changes.

Suppose the price level in the United States falls. As this happens, U.S. goods become relatively cheaper than foreign goods. As a result, both Americans and foreigners buy more U.S. goods. The quantity demanded of U.S. Real GDP rises.

Suppose the price level in the United States rises. In that event, U.S. goods become relatively more expensive than foreign goods. As a result, both Americans and foreigners buy fewer U.S. goods. The quantity demanded of U.S. Real GDP falls.

For a review of the three effects—real balance, interest rate, and international trade—see Exhibit 3.

## finding ECONOMICS

**In a Store Buying a Watch** Jim is in a store buying a watch imported from Switzerland. What does this purchase have to do with a downward-sloping aggregate demand curve? When we ask Jim why he's buying a Swiss watch, he tells us that the Swiss watch is cheaper than the American watch. The reason could very well be that the U.S. price level has recently risen relative to the Swiss price level. In other words, when Jim buys the Swiss watch instead of the American watch, we could be seeing the international trade effect in action. ▲ ▲ ▲

## An Important Word on the Three Effects

As explained, the aggregate demand curve is downward sloping because of the real balance, interest rate, and international trade effects. However, keep in mind that what caused these three effects is a change in the price level. In other words, when discussing, say, the interest rate effect, we are talking about the interest rate effect of *a change in the price level.*

Price level changes → Interest rate effect

Why is this point important? The interest rate can change due to things *other than the price level changing*, and not everything that changes the interest rate leads to a movement from one point to another point on the *AD* curve. Other things that change the interest rate can lead to a shift in the *AD* curve instead. We will have more to say about this later. For now, though, simply keep in mind the cause of each of the three effects: a change in the price level—the variable on the vertical axis in Exhibit 2.

## A Change in Quantity Demanded of Real GDP Versus a Change in Aggregate Demand

A change in the price level brings about a change in the quantity demanded of Real GDP. As the price level falls, the quantity demanded of Real GDP rises, *ceteris paribus*. In Exhibit 4(a), a change in the quantity demanded of Real GDP is represented as a *movement* from one point (A) on $AD_1$ to another point (B) on $AD_1$.

**EXHIBIT 3**

### Why the Aggregate Demand Curve Is Downward Sloping

This exhibit outlines the three effects that explain why the *AD* curve is downward sloping. Each effect relates to a change in the price level (*P*) leading to a change in the quantity demanded of Real GDP (*Q*).

| Type of Effect | How It Works | Graphical Representation of What Happens |
|---|---|---|
| **Real Balance Effect (due to a change in the price level)** | ***Price level falls*** → purchasing power rises → monetary wealth rises → **buy more goods.** | |
| | ***Price level rises*** → purchasing power falls → monetary wealth falls → **buy fewer goods.** | |
| **Interest Rate Effect (due to a change in the price level)** | ***Price level falls*** → purchasing power rises → less money needed to buy fixed bundle of goods → save more → supply of credit rises → interest rate falls → businesses and households borrow more at lower interest rate → **buy more goods.** | |
| | ***Price level rises*** → purchasing power falls → borrow money in order to continue to buy fixed bundle of goods → demand for credit rises → interest rate rises → businesses and households borrow less at higher interest rate → **buy fewer goods.** | |
| **International Trade Effect (due to a change in the price level)** | ***Price level in U.S. falls*** relative to foreign price levels → U.S. goods relatively less expensive than foreign goods → both Americans and foreigners **buy more U.S. goods.** | |
| | ***Price level in U.S. rises*** relative to foreign price levels → U.S. goods relatively more expensive than foreign goods → both Americans and foreigners **buy fewer U.S. goods.** | |

**EXHIBIT 4**

**A Change in the Quantity Demanded of Real GDP Versus a Change in Aggregate Demand**

(a) A change in the quantity demanded of Real GDP is graphically represented as a *movement* from one point, A, on $AD_1$ to another point, B, on $AD_1$. A change in the quantity demanded of Real GDP is the result of a change in the price level. (b) A change in aggregate demand is graphically represented as a *shift* in the aggregate demand curve from $AD_1$ to $AD_2$.

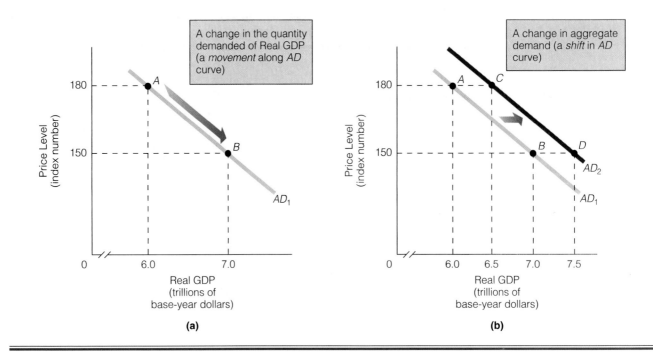

A change in the quantity demanded of Real GDP (a *movement* along *AD* curve)

A change in aggregate demand (a *shift* in *AD* curve)

(a)

(b)

A change in aggregate demand is represented in Exhibit 4(b) as a *shift* in the aggregate demand curve from $AD_1$ to $AD_2$. When the aggregate demand curve shifts, the quantity demanded of Real GDP changes even though the price level remains constant. For example, at a price level (index number) of 180, the quantity demanded of Real GDP on $AD_1$ in Exhibit 4(b) is $6.0 trillion. But at the same price level (180), the quantity demanded of Real GDP on $AD_2$ is $6.5 trillion.

## ⓣhinking like AN ECONOMIST

**Shift Factors Versus Movement Factors, Once Again** To the economist, not all factors are alike. For some factors, the change is from one point to another on the same curve. These are *movement factors*. The price level is a movement factor. Raise it, and we move up on the *AD* curve; lower it, and we move down.

Other factors, if they change, shift curves. These are *shift factors*. We turn now to discuss shift factors with respect to the *AD* curve. ▪▪▪

## Changes in Aggregate Demand: Shifts in the *AD* Curve

What can change aggregate demand? What can cause aggregate demand to rise, and what can cause it to fall?

The simple answer is that aggregate demand changes when spending on U.S. goods and services changes. If spending increases at a given price level, aggregate demand rises; if spending decreases at a given price level, aggregate demand falls.

Spending increases at a given price level → AD rises

Spending decreases at a given price level → AD falls

Suppose the price level in the economy is represented by the consumer price index (CPI) and the index is currently 150. At this price level, U.S. residents, firms, and governments, along with foreigners, foreign firms, and foreign governments, want to buy, say, $7.0 trillion worth of U.S. goods and services. Then something changes, and all of a sudden they all want to buy a total of $7.5 trillion worth of U.S. goods and services. Now, before you conclude that they want to buy more goods and services because the prices of goods and services have fallen, keep in mind that the price level has not changed. The price level—still represented by the CPI—is still 150. In other words, all these people, firms, and governments want to buy more U.S. goods even though the prices of the goods and services have not changed.

When individuals, firms, and governments want to buy more U.S. goods and services even though the prices of the goods have not changed, then we say that aggregate demand has increased. As a result, the *AD* curve *shifts* to the right. Of course, when individuals, firms, and governments want to buy fewer U.S. goods and services at a given price level, then we say that aggregate demand has decreased. As a result, the *AD* curve shifts to the left.

Exhibit 4(b) shows a change in aggregate demand (a shift in the *AD* curve). At point *B*, the price level is 150, and total expenditures on U.S. goods and services are $7.0 trillion. At point *D*, the price level is still 150, but total expenditures on U.S. goods and services have increased to $7.5 trillion. Why has aggregate demand moved from point *B* to point *D*; that is, what has caused the increase in total expenditures? To find out, we have to look at the components of total expenditures.

## How Spending Components Affect Aggregate Demand

The last chapter identified four major spending components: consumption (*C*), investment (*I*), government purchases (*G*), and net exports (*NX*). Let's keep the numbers simple: $C = \$100$, $I = \$100$, $G = \$100$, $EX = \$50$, and $IM = \$15$. If $EX = \$50$ and $IM = \$15$, then net exports = $35.

Using these dollar figures, we calculate that $335 is spent on U.S. goods and services. We get this dollar amount by finding the sum of consumption, investment, government purchases, and net exports.

Total expenditures on U.S. goods and services = C + I + G + NX

Obviously, this dollar amount will go up if (1) *C* rises, (2) *I* rises, (3) *G* rises, and/or (4) *NX* rises. In other words, a rise in consumption, investment, government purchases, or net exports will raise spending on U.S. goods and services:

C↑, I↑, G↑, NX↑ → Total expenditures on U.S. goods and services↑

Now, what will cause spending on U.S. goods to go down? Obviously, it will decline if (1) *C* falls, (2) *I* falls, (3) *G* falls, and/or (4) *NX* falls.

C↓, I↓, G↓, NX↓ → Total expenditures on U.S. goods or services↓

Because we now know what causes total expenditures on U.S. goods and services to change, we can relate the components of spending to (U.S.) aggregate demand. If, *at a given price level*:

- Consumption, investment, government purchases, or net exports *rise*, aggregate demand will rise and the *AD* curve will shift to the right.

- If consumption, investment, government purchases, or net exports *fall*, aggregate demand will fall and the *AD* curve will shift to the left.

We can write these relationships as:

$$\text{If, at a given price level, } C\uparrow, I\uparrow, G\uparrow\ NX\uparrow\ \text{then } AD\uparrow$$

$$\text{If, at a given price level, } C\downarrow, I\downarrow, G\downarrow, NX\downarrow\ \text{then } AD\downarrow$$

The flow charts in Exhibit 5 show how changes in spending components affect aggregate demand.

## Why Is There More Total Spending?

Here is a question that an economics professors might place on an exam:

> *True or false? The price level falls and total spending rises. As a result of total spending rising, aggregate demand in the economy rises and the AD curve shifts rightward.*

You may think the answer is true—perhaps because you are accustomed to thinking that if total spending rises, aggregate demand rises. But aggregate demand rises only if total spending rises at *a given price level*.

To illustrate the difference between (1) total spending rising at a falling price level and (2) total spending rising at a given price level, consider the following two examples.

- *Example 1.* The price level falls, and goods and services become cheaper. As a result of lower prices, individuals start to buy more goods and services. As a result, total spending rises.

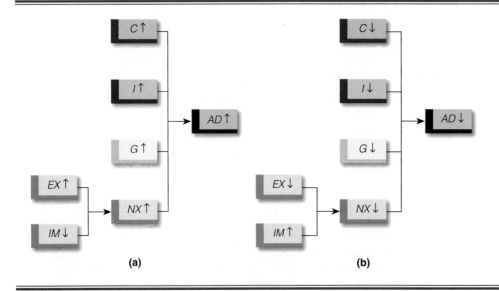

**EXHIBIT 5**

**Changes in Aggregate Demand**

The flow charts show how aggregate demand changes given changes in various spending components. $C$ = consumption, $I$ = investment, $G$ = government purchases, $NX$ = net exports, $EX$ = exports, $IM$ = imports. Keep in mind that $NX = EX - IM$.

- *Example 2.* The price level does not change. Still, something in the economy changes so that people start buying more goods and services. As a result of their buying more goods and services, total spending in the economy rises.

In both cases, total spending rises. But in example 1, total spending rises because prices have fallen. This leads to a *movement* down a given *AD* curve. In example 2, total spending rises even when prices remain unchanged. This leads to a *shift* rightward in the *AD* curve.

Lesson learned: Total spending can rise for one of two reasons. The first deals with a decline in prices and leads to a *movement* along a given *AD* curve. The second deals with a change in some factor other than prices and leads to a *shift* in the *AD* curve.

## Factors That Can Change C, I, G, and NX (EX − IM) and Therefore Can Change AD (Shift the AD Curve)

What can change aggregate demand in the economy? The answer is a change in consumption, investment, government purchases, and/or net exports (exports minus imports). So, for example, if someone asks you why *AD* increased, you might say because consumption increased.

But suppose the person then asks, "What caused consumption to increase?" Your answer to one question simply leads to another. If a change in consumption changes aggregate demand, what changes consumption? The same question can be asked about changes in investment, government purchases, and net exports (i.e., exports and imports). For example, if aggregate demand increased because investment increased, then what caused investment to increase?

This section looks at some of the many factors that can change consumption, investment, and net exports. A later chapter considers the factors that can change government purchases.

CONSUMPTION Four factors can affect consumption: wealth, expectations about future prices and income, the interest rate, and income taxes.

**Wealth**
The value of all assets owned, both monetary and nonmonetary.

1. *Wealth.* Individuals consume not only on the basis of their present income but also on the basis of their wealth. Each of two individuals has an income of $80,000 a year. One has $75,000 in the bank, and the other has no assets at all. We would expect the person with $75,000 in the bank to spend more of her income on consumption goods this year. Greater wealth makes individuals feel financially more secure and thus more willing to spend.

   - Increases in wealth lead to increases in consumption. If consumption increases, aggregate demand rises and the *AD* curve shifts to the right.

   - Decreases in wealth lead to a fall in consumption, which leads to a fall in aggregate demand. Consequently, the *AD* curve shifts to the left.

$$\text{Wealth}\uparrow \rightarrow C\uparrow \rightarrow AD\uparrow$$

$$\text{Wealth}\downarrow \rightarrow C\downarrow \rightarrow AD\downarrow$$

2. *Expectations About Future Prices and Income.* Individuals' expectations of future prices can increase or decrease aggregate demand:

   - If individuals expect *higher* prices in the future, they increase their current consumption expenditures to buy goods at the lower current prices. The increase in consumption leads to an increase in aggregate demand.

- If individuals expect *lower* prices in the future, they decrease current consumption expenditures. The reduction in consumption leads to a decrease in aggregate demand.

$$\text{Expect higher future prices} \rightarrow C\uparrow \rightarrow AD\uparrow$$

$$\text{Expect lower future prices} \rightarrow C\downarrow \rightarrow AD\downarrow$$

Similarly, expectations regarding income can affect aggregate demand:

- Expectations of a *higher* future income increase consumption, leading to an increase in aggregate demand.
- Expectations of a *lower* future income decrease consumption, leading to a decrease in aggregate demand.

$$\text{Expect higher future income} \rightarrow C\uparrow \rightarrow AD\uparrow$$

$$\text{Expect lower future income} \rightarrow C\downarrow \rightarrow AD\downarrow$$

3. *Interest Rate.* Current empirical work shows that spending on consumer durables is sensitive to the interest rate.

- Buyers often pay for these items by borrowing; so an *increase* in the interest rate increases the monthly payment amounts linked to the purchase of durables and thereby reduces their consumption. The reduction in consumption leads to a decline in aggregate demand.
- Alternatively, a *decrease* in the interest rate reduces monthly payment amounts and thereby increases the consumption of durables. The increase in consumption leads to an increase in aggregate demand.

$$\text{Interest rate} \uparrow \rightarrow C\downarrow \rightarrow AD\downarrow$$

$$\text{Interest rate} \downarrow \rightarrow C\uparrow \rightarrow AD\uparrow$$

4. *Income Taxes.* Let's consider personal income taxes, that is, the taxes a person pays on earned income.

- As income taxes *rise*, disposable income decreases. When people have less take-home pay to spend, consumption falls. Consequently, aggregate demand decreases.
- A *decrease* in income taxes has the opposite effect; it raises disposable income. When people have more take-home pay to spend, consumption rises and aggregate demand increases.

$$\text{Income taxes} \uparrow \rightarrow C\downarrow \rightarrow AD\downarrow$$

$$\text{Income taxes} \downarrow \rightarrow C\uparrow \rightarrow AD\uparrow$$

## ⓕinding ECONOMICS

**In a Housing Downturn** A newspaper article reads as follows: "Housing prices have fallen over the past six months, and economists are concerned that this might lead to less overall demand in the economy." Can you find the economics here? Do housing prices have anything to do with aggregate demand? Let's work backward. First, a decline in aggregate demand can be caused by a decline in consumption. Second, a decline in consumption can be caused by a change in any of four factors: wealth, expectations about future prices and income, the interest rate, and income taxes.

*(continued)*

## finding ECONOMICS (continued)

Let's focus on wealth. If housing prices fall, people who own houses will find themselves with less overall wealth. (Think of a person whose house is worth $500,000 one month and $450,000 six months later. She has suffered a decline in wealth.) As a result, these people reduce their consumption, and aggregate demand falls. ▲ ▲ ▲

**INVESTMENT** Three factors can change investment: the interest rate, expectations about future sales, and business taxes.

1. *Interest Rate.* Changes in interest rates affect business decisions.
   - As the interest rate *rises*, the cost of an investment project rises and businesses invest less. As investment decreases, aggregate demand decreases.
   - As the interest rate *falls*, the cost of an investment project falls and businesses invest more. Consequently, aggregate demand increases.

$$\text{Interest rate} \uparrow \rightarrow I\downarrow \rightarrow AD\downarrow$$

$$\text{Interest rate} \downarrow \rightarrow I\uparrow \rightarrow AD\uparrow$$

2. *Expectations About Future Sales.* Businesses invest because they expect to sell the goods they produce.
   - If businesses become *optimistic* about future sales, investment spending grows and aggregate demand increases.
   - If businesses become *pessimistic* about future sales, investment spending contracts and aggregate demand decreases.

$$\text{Businesses become optimistic about future sales} \rightarrow I\uparrow \rightarrow AD\uparrow$$

$$\text{Businesses become pessimistic about future sales} \rightarrow I\downarrow \rightarrow AD\downarrow$$

3. *Business Taxes.* Businesses naturally consider expected after-tax profits when making their investment decisions.
   - An *increase* in business taxes lowers expected profitability. With less profit expected, businesses invest less. As investment spending declines, so does aggregate demand.
   - A *decrease* in business taxes, on the other hand, raises expected profitability and investment spending. This increases aggregate demand.

$$\text{Business taxes} \uparrow \rightarrow I\downarrow \rightarrow AD\downarrow$$

$$\text{Business taxes} \downarrow \rightarrow I\uparrow \rightarrow AD\uparrow$$

**NET EXPORTS** Two factors can change net exports: foreign real national income and the exchange rate.

1. *Foreign Real National Income.* Just as Americans earn a national income, so do people in other countries. That is the foreign national income. By adjusting this foreign national income for price changes, we obtain foreign real national income.
   - As foreign real national income *rises*, foreigners buy more U.S. goods and services. Thus, U.S. exports (*EX*) rise. As exports rise, net exports rise, *ceteris paribus*. As net exports rise, aggregate demand increases.

- This process works in reverse. As foreign real national income *falls*, foreigners buy fewer U.S. goods and exports fall. This lowers net exports, reducing aggregate demand.

  Foreign real national income ↑ → U.S. exports ↑ → U.S. net exports ↑ → AD↑

  Foreign real national income ↓ → U.S. exports ↓ → U.S. net exports ↓ → AD↓

2. *Exchange Rate.* The exchange rate is the price of one currency in terms of another currency; for example, $1.25 may be exchanged for €1. A currency has appreciated in value if more of a foreign currency is needed to buy it. A currency has depreciated in value if more of it is needed to buy a foreign currency. For example, a change in the exchange rate from $1.25 = €1 to $1.50 = €1 means that more dollars are needed to buy 1 euro; the euro has appreciated. And because more dollars are needed to buy €1, the dollar has depreciated.

   - *Depreciation* in a nation's currency makes foreign goods more expensive. Consider an Irish coat that is priced at €200 when the exchange rate is $1.25 = €1. To buy the Irish coat for €200, an American has to pay $250 ($1.25 for each of €200 for a total of $250). Now suppose the dollar depreciates to $1.50 = €1. The American now has to pay $300 for the coat.

   - This process is symmetrical. An *appreciation* in a nation's currency makes foreign goods cheaper. For example, if the exchange rate goes from $1.25 = €1 to $1 = €1, the Irish coat will cost the American only $200.

   The depreciation and appreciation of the U.S. dollar affect net exports.

   - As the dollar *depreciates*, foreign goods become more expensive, Americans cut back on imported goods, and foreigners (whose currency has appreciated) increase their purchases of U.S. exported goods. If exports rise and imports fall, net exports increase and aggregate demand increases.

   - As the dollar *appreciates*, foreign goods become cheaper, Americans increase their purchases of imported goods, and foreigners (whose currency has depreciated) cut back on their purchases of U.S. exported goods. If exports fall and imports rise, net exports decrease, thus lowering aggregate demand.

   Dollar depreciates → U.S. exports ↑ and U.S. imports ↓ → U.S. net exports ↑ → AD↑

   Dollar appreciates → U.S. exports ↓ and U.S. imports ↑ → U.S. net exports ↓ → AD↓

   See Exhibit 6 for a summary of the factors that change aggregate demand.

**Exchange Rate**
The price of one currency in terms of another currency.

**Appreciation**
An increase in the value of one currency relative to other currencies.

**Depreciation**
A decrease in the value of one currency relative to other currencies.

## ⓣhinking like AN ECONOMIST

**The W-X-Y-Z Explanation** In the last discussion, we said, for example, that if the dollar depreciates, U.S. exports will rise and U.S. imports will fall, in turn causing U.S. net exports to rise, in turn causing aggregate demand to rise. A summarization of this type of argument might go like this: A change in W leads to a change in X, which leads to a change in Y, which leads to change in Z. Let's call this kind of explanation the W-X-Y-Z explanation.

Economists often think in terms of one thing changing something else, which in turn changes still something else, and so on. Some people find this kind of thinking curious. They ask, "Why not simply say that W leads to Z instead of saying that W leads to X, which leads to Y, which leads to Z?"

Saying that W leads to Z might make things easier (there would be less to remember), but what the shortcut gains in ease, it loses in completeness. It is best to explain just how one thing eventually leads to something else happening. ▰ ▰ ▰

**EXHIBIT 6**

**Factors That Change Aggregate Demand**

Aggregate demand (AD) changes whenever consumption (C), investment (I), government purchases (G), or net exports (EX − IM) change. The factors that can affect C, I, and EX − IM, thereby indirectly affecting aggregate demand, are listed.

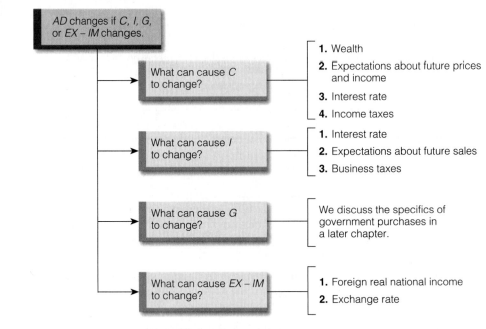

AD changes if C, I, G, or EX − IM changes.

What can cause C to change?
1. Wealth
2. Expectations about future prices and income
3. Interest rate
4. Income taxes

What can cause I to change?
1. Interest rate
2. Expectations about future sales
3. Business taxes

What can cause G to change?
We discuss the specifics of government purchases in a later chapter.

What can cause EX − IM to change?
1. Foreign real national income
2. Exchange rate

## Can a Change in the Money Supply Change Aggregate Demand?

Changes in such factors as interest rates, business taxes, exchange rates, and the like can change aggregate demand (indirectly) by directly changing consumption, investment, and net exports. What about the money supply? Can a change in the money supply lead to a change in aggregate demand?

Let's see. Suppose the money supply rises from, say, $1,400 billion to $1,500 billion. Will this change in the money supply result in an increase in aggregate demand? Most economists would say that it does, but they differ on how. One way to explain the effect (in the context of our discussion) is as follows: (1) A change in the money supply affects interest rates, (2) a change in interest rates changes consumption and investment, and (3) a change in consumption and investment affects aggregate demand. Therefore a change in the money supply is a catalyst in a process that ends with a change in aggregate demand. (We will have much more to say about the money supply and interest rates in later chapters.)

## If Consumption Rises, Does Some Other Spending Component Have to Decline?

Suppose $C = \$100$, $I = \$100$, $G = \$100$, and $NX = \$100$. Total expenditures equal $400. Now suppose C rises by $50 to $150. Must one or more other spending components decline by $50? In other words, if one spending component rises, does another spending component have to decline? To answer that question, we need to talk about two factors: the money supply and velocity.

Let's say that the money supply in the economy is $1 and that $1 is currently in the hands of Joe. Joe takes the $1 and buys good X from Jackie. Later, Jackie takes the $1 (she earlier received from Joe) and buys good Y from John. Still later, John takes the $1 (he earlier received from Jackie) and buys good Z from Jill.

## When Would You Want to Be Paid in a Currency Other Than U.S. Dollars?

Most people who work in the United States are paid in dollars, but when would you not want to be paid in dollars? In thinking about the question, consider the exchange rate between the dollar and the euro. Suppose the exchange rate is $1 = €1 and this exchange rate is expected to stay constant. Your employer owes you $10,000. Does it matter if the employer pays you in dollars or euros? At the current exchange rate, $10,000 is the same as €10,000; so whether you are paid in euros or dollars does not matter.

Now suppose that you expect the exchange rate to change to $2 = €1 and that you expect the dollar to depreciate and the euro to appreciate. Does the currency in which you are paid matter? Yes, it does. Being paid in euros is preferable because the euro is expected to appreciate in value.

To see why, ask yourself what happens if you are paid $10,000 in contrast to €10,000. If the exchange rate changes to $2 = €1 after you are paid $10,000, then the $10,000 dollars is all you have. But if you are paid €10,000, you would have $20,000 because €10,000 can be exchanged for $20,000 dollars at the new rate.

So let's refine the original question: If you are usually paid in dollars, when would you prefer not to be paid in dollars? The answer is when you think the value of the dollar is going to fall relative to other currencies.

Here's the problem, though. Most of us who work for U.S. employers don't have the option of getting paid in the currency of our choice. Most of us cannot go to our employer and say, "This month, could you please pay me in euros instead of dollars?"

However, you can always convert the currency in which we are paid into another currency. Suppose that you are always paid in dollars but think the value of the dollar is going to decline relative to the euro. Your employer pays you $10,000 when the exchange rate is $1 dollar = €1 and you think the dollar is going to depreciate in value relative to the euro. You immediately take the $10,000 your employer paid you and exchange the dollars for €10,000. Then you wait. If the exchange rate actually does change to, say, $2 for €1, you then exchange your €10,000 for $20,000.

So, although we may not be able to get our employers to pay us in the currency of our choice, we can always do something to pay ourselves in the currency of our choice. We can always take the currency in which we are paid (e.g., dollars) and immediately exchange them for a different currency. In short, if you want to be paid in euros or yen or pesos, your employer may not comply with your wishes, but you have the option of acting on your own wishes.

Here is what we know: We started with a money supply of just $1, and that dollar changed hands three times. The number of times a dollar changes hands (or is spent) to buy final goods and services is what economists call velocity. (If we were dealing with a money supply of more than just $1, we would define velocity not as "the number" but as the *average number* of times a dollar is spent to buy final goods and services in a year.) In our simple example, velocity is 3.

The product of our money supply ($1) and velocity (3) is $3, which represents the total amount of spending in the economy. From our example, two things are obvious: First, total spending in the economy can be a greater dollar amount than the money supply. Proof: In our example, the money supply was $1, but total spending equaled $3. Second, total spending depends on the money supply and velocity. Proof: Total spending in our example was the product of the money supply *times* velocity.

Let's return to the original question: If consumption rises, must some other spending component decline? The answer is yes if neither the money supply nor velocity changes. But the answer is no if either the money supply or velocity rises.

To illustrate how the answer can be yes, suppose again that the money supply is $1 and velocity is 3 and that total spending is therefore $3. Let's break up our total of $3 spending this way: $1 goes for consumption, $1 goes for investment, and $1 goes for government

**Velocity**
The average number of times a dollar is spent to buy final goods and services in a year.

purchases. Consumption rises to $2, and the money supply and velocity remain at $1 and 3, respectively. So total spending is still $3, and therefore a $1 increase in consumption necessitates a decline in some other spending component by $1. After all, total spending is locked in at $3; if one spending component rises by a certain amount, another spending component(s) must decline by the same amount.

But total spending isn't locked in if either the money supply or velocity change. Again, suppose that consumption rises from $1 to $2 but that velocity or the money supply increases. Then no other spending component needs to change. To see why, suppose the money supply has risen to $1.40 and velocity is still 3. Total spending now is $4.20 instead of $3; so consumption could have risen to $2 without any decline in investment or government purchases. In other words, $C$ can equal $2 and $I$ can still equal $1, and $G$ can still equal $1 (or even more at $1.20).

The same is true if the money supply remains constant at $1 and velocity increases from 3 to 4. At velocity of 4, total spending is $4. Again, consumption can rise to $2 without requiring any decline in another spending component.

We recap:

- If both the money supply and velocity are constant, a rise in one spending component (such as consumption) necessitates a decline in one or more other spending components.

- If either the money supply or velocity rises, one spending component can rise without requiring other spending components to decline.

## SELF-TEST

(Answers to Self-Test questions are in Answers to Self-Test Questions at the back of the book.)

1. Explain the real balance effect.

2. Explain what happens to the AD curve if the dollar appreciates relative to other currencies.

3. The money supply has risen, but total spending has declined. Is this possible? Explain your answer.

# SHORT-RUN AGGREGATE SUPPLY

**Aggregate Supply**
The quantity supplied of all goods and services (Real GDP) at different price levels, *ceteris paribus*.

Aggregate demand is one side of the economy; aggregate supply is the other. Aggregate supply is the quantity supplied of all goods and services (Real GDP) at various price levels, *ceteris paribus*. Aggregate supply includes both short-run aggregate supply (*SRAS*) and long-run aggregate supply (*LRAS*). Short-run aggregate supply is discussed in this section.

## Short-Run Aggregate Supply Curve: What It Is and Why It Is Upward Sloping

**Short-Run Aggregate Supply (SRAS) Curve**
A curve that shows the quantity supplied of all goods and services (Real GDP) at different price levels, *ceteris paribus*.

A short-run aggregate supply (*SRAS*) curve (see Exhibit 7) shows the quantity supplied of all goods and services (Real GDP or output) at different price levels, *ceteris paribus*. Notice that the *SRAS* curve is upward sloping: As the price level rises, firms increase the quantity supplied of goods and services; as the price level drops, firms decrease the quantity supplied of goods and services. Why is the *SRAS* curve upward sloping? Economists have put forth a few explanations; we discuss two of them.

STICKY WAGES  Some economists believe that wages are sticky, or inflexible. This may be because wages are locked in for a few years due to labor contracts that workers and management enter into. For example, management and labor may agree to lock in wages for the next one to three years. Both labor and management may see this as in their best interest.

Management has some idea of what its labor costs will be during the time of the contract, and workers may have a sense of security knowing that their wages can't be lowered. Wages may also be sticky because of certain social conventions or perceived notions of fairness. Whatever the specific reason for sticky wages, let's see how they provide an explanation of an upward-sloping *SRAS* curve.

Firms pay *nominal wages* (e.g., $30 an hour), but they often decide how many workers to hire based on real wages. *Real wages* are nominal wages divided by the price level.

$$\text{Real wage} = \frac{\text{Nominal wage}}{\text{Price level}}$$

For example, suppose that the nominal wage is $30 an hour and that the price level, as measured by a price index, is 1.50.[1] The real wage is therefore $20.

- The quantity supplied of labor is *directly related* to the real wage: As the real wage rises, the quantity supplied of labor rises; as the real wage falls, the quantity supplied of labor falls. In short, more individuals are willing to work and current workers are willing to work more at higher real wages than at lower real wages.

Real wage ↑ → *Quantity supplied* of labor ↑

Real wage ↓ → *Quantity supplied* of labor ↓

- The quantity demanded of labor is *inversely related* to the real wage: As the real wage rises, the quantity demanded of labor falls; as the real wage falls, the quantity demanded of labor rises. Firms will employ more workers the cheaper it is to hire them.

Real wage ↑ → *Quantity demanded* of labor ↓

Real wage ↓ → *Quantity demanded* of labor ↑

So, suppose that a firm has agreed to pay its workers $30 an hour for the next three years and that it has hired 1,000 workers. When it agreed to this nominal wage, it thought that the price index would remain at 1.50 and that the real wage would stay at $20.

Now suppose the price index *falls* to 1.25. In that event, the real wage rises to $24 ($30 ÷ 1.25), which is higher than the firm expected when it agreed to lock in nominal wages at $30 an hour. If the firm had known that the real wage would turn out to be $24 (and not remain at $20), it would never have hired 1,000 workers. It would have hired, say, 800 workers instead.

So what does the firm do? As we stated, there is an inverse relationship between the real wage and the quantity demanded of labor (the number of workers that firms want to hire). Now that the real wage has risen (from $20 to $24), the firm cuts back on its labor (say, from 1,000 to 800 workers). With fewer workers working, less output is produced.

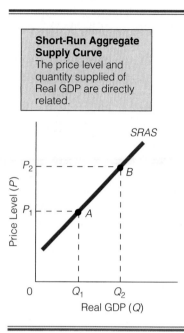

**EXHIBIT 7**

**Short-Run Aggregate Supply Curve**
The price level and quantity supplied of Real GDP are directly related.

**The Short-Run Aggregate Supply Curve**

The short-run aggregate supply curve is upward sloping, specifying a direct relationship between the price level and the quantity supplied of Real GDP.

---

1. Alternatively, you can view the price index as 1.50 times 100, or 150. In this case, the formula for the real wage would change to Real wage = (Nominal wage ÷ Price level) × 100.

So, if wages are sticky, a decrease in the price level (which pushes real wages up) will result in a decrease in output. This is what an upward-sloping *SRAS* curve represents: As the price level falls, the quantity supplied of goods and services declines.

*Decline in price level* and constant nominal wage → Real wage ↑ → Firms hire fewer workers → *Decline in quantity supplied of Real GDP*

**WORKER MISPERCEPTIONS** Another explanation for the upward-sloping *SRAS* curve holds that workers may misperceive real wage changes. To illustrate, if the nominal wage is $30 an hour and the price level, as measured by a price index, is 1.50, then the real wage is $20. Now suppose the nominal wage falls to $25 and the price level falls to 1.25. The real wage is still $20 ($25 ÷ 1.25 = $20), *but workers may not know this*. They know their nominal wage has fallen (i.e., they are earning $25 an hour instead of $30).They also may know that the price level is lower, but they may not know initially *how much* lower the price level is. For example, suppose they mistakenly believe the price level has fallen from 1.50 to 1.39. They will then think that their real wage has actually fallen from $20 ($30 ÷ 1.50) to $17.98 ($25 ÷ 1.39). In response to the misperceived falling real wage, workers may reduce the quantity of labor they are willing to supply. With fewer workers (resources), firms produce less.

So, if workers misperceive real wage changes, then a fall in the price level will bring about a decline in output, which is illustrative of an upward-sloping *SRAS* curve.

Nominal wages and *price level decline* by equal percentage → Real wage remains constant → But workers mistakenly think real wage has fallen → Workers reduce quantity supplied of labor → *Less output is produced*

## What Puts the "Short Run" in the SRAS Curve?

According to most macroeconomists, the *SRAS* curve slopes upward because of sticky wages or worker misperceptions. No matter what the explanation, things are likely to change over time. Wages will not be sticky forever (labor contracts will expire), and workers will figure out that they misperceived real wage changes. Only for a period of time—identified as the short run—are these issues likely to be relevant.

## Changes in Short-Run Aggregate Supply: Shifts in the SRAS Curve

A change in the quantity supplied of Real GDP is brought about by a change in the price level and is shown as a *movement* along the *SRAS* curve. But what can change short-run aggregate supply? What can *shift* the *SRAS* curve? The factors that can shift the *SRAS* curve are wage rates, prices of nonlabor inputs, productivity, and supply shocks.

**WAGE RATES** Changes in wage rates have a major impact on the position of the *SRAS* curve because wage costs are usually a firm's major cost item. The impact of a rise or fall in equilibrium wage rates can be understood in terms of the following equation:

Profit per unit = Price per unit − Cost per unit

Higher wage rates mean higher costs and, at constant prices, translate into lower profits and a reduction in the number of units (of a given good) that firms will want to produce. Lower wage rates mean lower costs and, at constant prices, translate into higher profits and an increase in the number of units (of a given good) firms will decide to produce.

The impact of higher and lower equilibrium wages is shown in Exhibit 8. At the given price level, $P_1$ on $SRAS_1$, the quantity supplied of Real GDP is $Q_1$. When wage rates become higher, a firm's profits at a given price level decrease. Consequently, the firm reduces production. In the diagram, this change corresponds to moving from $Q_1$ to $Q_2$, which at the given price level is point *B* on a new aggregate supply curve ($SRAS_2$). Thus, a rise in equilibrium wage rates leads to a leftward shift in the aggregate supply curve. For a fall in equilibrium wage rates, the steps are simply reversed.

PRICES OF NONLABOR INPUTS There are other inputs to the production process besides labor. Changes in the prices of nonlabor inputs affect the *SRAS* curve in the same way as changes in wage rates do. An increase in the

**EXHIBIT 8**

**Wage Rates and a Shift in the Short-Run Aggregate Supply Curve**

A rise in wage rates shifts the short-run aggregate supply curve leftward. A fall in wage rates shifts the short-run aggregate supply curve rightward.

price of a nonlabor input (e.g., oil) shifts the *SRAS* curve leftward; a decrease in their price shifts the *SRAS* curve rightward.

PRODUCTIVITY *Productivity* is the output produced per unit of input employed over some period of time. Although various inputs can become more productive, let's consider the labor input. An increase in labor productivity means businesses will produce more output with the same amount of labor, causing the *SRAS* curve to shift rightward. A decrease in labor productivity means businesses will produce less output with the same amount of labor, causing the *SRAS* curve to shift leftward. A host of factors lead to increased labor productivity, including a more educated labor force, a larger stock of capital goods, and technological advancements.

SUPPLY SHOCKS Major natural or institutional changes that affect aggregate supply are referred to as *supply shocks*. Supply shocks are of two varieties. *Adverse supply shocks* shift the *SRAS* curve leftward. Bad weather that wipes out a large part of the Midwestern wheat crop would be a supply shock. So would a major cutback in the supply of oil coming to the United States from the Middle East. *Beneficial supply shocks* shift the *SRAS* curve rightward; for example, a major oil discovery or unusually good weather leading to increased production of a food staple. These supply shocks are reflected in resource or input prices.

Exhibit 9 summarizes the factors that affect short-run aggregate supply.

**EXHIBIT 9**

**Changes in Short-Run Aggregate Supply**     The flow charts show how short-run aggregate supply changes given changes in several factors.

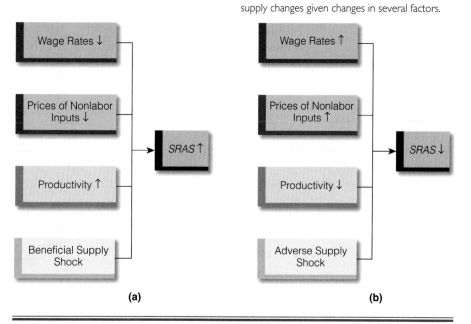

## Subprime Lending, House Price Declines, and Loan Defaults

In 2008–2009, we heard much about subprime lending, especially as it relates to the mortgage loan market. What is a subprime loan, and what is controversial about it? First, a subprime loan is simply a loan made at an elevated credit risk. In contrast, prime loans are made to persons who have a strong credit history and a record of paying back loans. Subprime loans are usually made to persons who usually do not have a good credit history and may have been delinquent on paying back loans in the past.

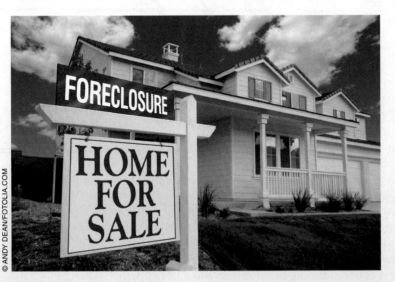

© ANDY DEAN/FOTOLIA.COM

A lender can research a person's credit risk by checking his or her FICO (Fair Isaac Corporation) credit score. These scores usually run between 300 and 850. A score below 620 usually denotes high risk and places a person in the subprime pool of borrowers.

One difference between a prime and a subprime loan is that the latter has a higher loan-to-value ratio. In other words, the subprime loan amount is a greater-than-usual percentage of the value of, say, the property the borrower is buying. To illustrate, suppose the value of the property is $200,000 and the loan is $200,000. In this case, the loan-to-value ratio is 1. If the loan is $100,000 and the value of the property is $200,000, then the loan-to-value ratio is 0.50. The higher loan-to-value ratio for subprime borrowers partly reflects the difficulty they have in making down payments.

In mortgage lending, the percentage of subprime loans grew substantially during the period 1995–2003. For example, in 1994, subprime mortgage loans comprised only 4.5 percent of all mortgage loans. In 1995, this percentage rose to 10.2 percent. It was higher in 1996 at 12.3 percent, and even higher in 1997 at 14.5 percent. As a consequence of the increase in subprime mortgage lending, home ownership increased. Nearly 9 million more people owned their own homes in 2003 than in 1994.

In 2007–2009, subprime lending came under discussion and review, largely because many subprime borrowers were unable to pay off their loans. They were unable to pay off their loans to a large degree because the subprime loans were made at low interest rates that could change if interest rates in general were to rise. To illustrate, you are a subprime borrower paying an initial rate of 5 percent on a $200,000 loan. Your monthly payment is $1,073. Your subprime loan agreement states that your interest rate will rise by the same percentage as some specified interest rate in the economy (such as the Treasury bill rate or some other rate). At some point, this interest rate goes up by 300 basis points (3 percent). Now you pay a new interest rate of 8 percent instead of 5 percent, and your monthly payment is $1,467—$394 more than you were previously paying. You would have been all right if interest rates hadn't risen; you were able to pay $1,073 a month. Now, however, you are having a hard time making your increased monthly mortgage payment. In such a situation, some subprime borrowers defaulted on their loans.

Things might not be so bad if the house (that you bought with the borrowed money) had been rising in value. For example, suppose you took out a $200,000 loan to buy the house priced at $200,000 (no down payment), and now the house is worth $250,000. You could, of course, sell the house for $250,000, pay off the $200,000 loan, and pocket the $50,000. (This solution ignores such things as real estate commissions, taxes, and other transaction costs.)

But in 2007–2009, many subprime mortgage borrowers found themselves in a fix. In many cases, the value of the houses had fallen. Now the $200,000 house was worth, say, $145,000. In this situation, many subprime borrowers could not sell the property and either were delinquent or defaulted on their loans.

## Something More to Come: Peoples' Expectations

So far, in this chapter we have said that several factors are capable of shifting the *SRAS* curve: wage rates, prices of nonlabor inputs, productivity, and supply shocks. In a later chapter (Chapter 16), we will begin to discuss how peoples' expectations (of certain key economic variables) can affect the price level and Real GDP. At that point, we will add another factor that can shift the *SRAS* curve: the *expected price level*.

### SELF-TEST

1. If wage rates decline, explain what happens to the short-run aggregate supply (*SRAS*) curve?

2. Give an example of an increase in labor productivity.

3. Discuss the details of the worker misperceptions explanation for the upward-sloping *SRAS* curve.

# PUTTING *AD* AND *SRAS* TOGETHER: SHORT-RUN EQUILIBRIUM

In this section, we put aggregate demand and short-run aggregate supply together to achieve short-run equilibrium in the economy. Aggregate demand and short-run aggregate supply determine the price level, Real GDP, and the unemployment rate in the short run.

## How Short-Run Equilibrium in the Economy Is Achieved

Exhibit 10 shows an aggregate demand (*AD*) curve and a short-run aggregate supply (*SRAS*) curve. The quantity demanded of Real GDP and the quantity supplied of Real GDP are illustrated at three different price levels: $P_1$, $P_2$, and $P_E$.

At $P_1$, the quantity supplied of Real GDP ($Q_2$) is greater than the quantity demanded ($Q_1$). There is a surplus of goods. As a result, the price level drops, firms decrease output, and consumers increase consumption. Why do consumers increase consumption as the price level drops? (*Hint:* Think of the real balance, interest rate, and international trade effects.)

At $P_2$, the quantity supplied of Real GDP ($Q_1$) is less than the quantity demanded ($Q_2$). There is a shortage of goods. As a result, the price level rises, firms increase output, and consumers decrease consumption.

**EXHIBIT 10**

**Short-Run Equilibrium**

At $P_1$, the quantity supplied of Real GDP is greater than the quantity demanded. As a result, the price level falls and firms decrease output. At $P_2$, the quantity demanded of Real GDP is greater than the quantity supplied. As a result, the price level rises and firms increase output. Short-run equilibrium occurs at point $E$, where the quantity demanded of Real GDP equals the (short-run) quantity supplied. This is at the intersection of the aggregate demand (*AD*) curve and the short-run aggregate supply (*SRAS*) curve. (Note: Although real-world *AD* and *SRAS* curves can, and likely do, have some curvature to them, we have drawn both as straight lines, This does not affect the analysis. Whenever the analysis is not disturbed, we follow suit throughout this text.)

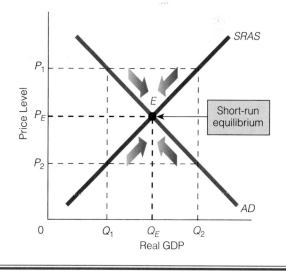

In instances of both surplus and shortage, economic forces are moving the economy toward *E*, where the quantity demanded of Real GDP equals the (short-run) quantity supplied of Real GDP. This is the point of **short-run equilibrium**. $P_E$ is the short-run equilibrium price level; $Q_E$ is the short-run equilibrium Real GDP.

A change in aggregate demand, in short-run aggregate supply, or in both will obviously affect the price level and/or Real GDP. For example, an increase in aggregate demand

**Short-Run Equilibrium**
The condition in the economy when the quantity demanded of Real GDP equals the (short-run) quantity supplied of Real GDP. This condition is met where the aggregate demand curve intersects the short-run aggregate supply curve.

raises the equilibrium price level and, in the short run, Real GDP [Exhibit 11(a)]. An increase in short-run aggregate supply lowers the equilibrium price level and raises Real GDP [Exhibit 11(b)]. A decrease in short-run aggregate supply raises the equilibrium price level and lowers Real GDP [Exhibit 11(c)].

## Thinking in Terms of Short-Run Equilibrium Changes in the Economy

We know that certain factors can lead to a change in aggregate demand or in short-run aggregate supply. We also know that if either aggregate demand or short-run aggregate supply changes, the price level and Real GDP will also change in the short run.

Exhibit 12 shows us how changes in *AD* or *SRAS* can impact the economy and change *P* and *Q*. (Refer to Exhibit 12 as we continue our discussion.) For example, when a factor changes, we ask ourselves a series of questions:

- Does the factor affect the *AD* curve or the *SRAS* curve? If the answer is neither, then there will be no change in either curve.

- If the answer is the *AD* curve, then does it shift to the right or to the left?

- If the answer is the *SRAS* curve, does it shift to the right or to the left?

After the shift in one or more curves, we identify the new equilibrium and what has happened to both the price level and Real GDP in the short run.

To illustrate, suppose there is an adverse supply shock in the economy:

- The shock shifts the *SRAS* curve leftward.

- Nothing has changed on the demand side of the economy, so the *AD* curve remains stable.

- A leftward shift in the *SRAS* curve in the face of an unchanged *AD* curve increases the price level and decreases Real GDP.

**EXHIBIT 11**

**Changes in Short-Run Equilibrium in the Economy**

(a) An increase in aggregate demand increases the price level and Real GDP. (b) An increase in short-run aggregate supply decreases the price level and increases Real GDP. (c) A decrease in short-run aggregate supply increases the price level and decreases Real GDP.

$AD \uparrow \overline{SRAS} \Rightarrow P \uparrow Q \uparrow$

**(a)**

$SRAS \uparrow \overline{AD} \Rightarrow P \downarrow Q \uparrow$

**(b)**

$SRAS \downarrow \overline{AD} \Rightarrow P \uparrow Q \downarrow$

**(c)**

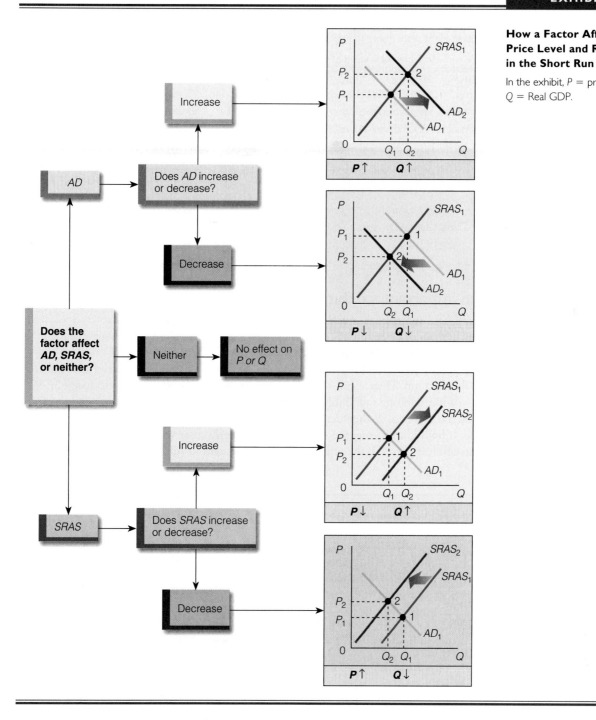

**EXHIBIT** 12

**How a Factor Affects the Price Level and Real GDP in the Short Run**

In the exhibit, $P$ = price level and $Q$ = Real GDP.

# finding ECONOMICS

**In Dollars and in Oil** In November 2007 the barrel price of oil was rising. On November 1, 2007, it had risen to $96 a barrel, and in the same month the value of the dollar was falling in foreign exchange markets. In fact, the value of the dollar had been falling for some time. Although the value of $1 was €0.83 in January 2006, it had fallen to €0.69 by November 1, 2007. In other words, the

(continued)

## ⓕinding ECONOMICS (continued)

dollar had depreciated over that time period. Now what does all this have to do with the predicted change in the price level and Real GDP?

We know that the falling value of the dollar would lead to greater U.S. exports, and this is exactly what was happening at the time. As a result, U.S. net exports were rising, pushing the *AD* curve in the economy to the right. But because oil prices were rising, the *SRAS* curve in the economy was shifting to the left. How would these two changes affect Real GDP? The answer depends on the relative shifts of the *AD* and *SRAS* curves. Picture, in your mind's eye, the three possibilities:

- If the *AD* curve shifted rightward more than the *SRAS* curve shifted leftward, then Real GDP will rise.
- If the *AD* curve shifted rightward by less than the *SRAS* curve shifted leftward, then Real GDP would fall.
- If the *AD* curve shifted rightward by the same amount as the *SRAS* curve shifted leftward, then Real GDP would remain unchanged.

In all three cases, though, the price level would increase. Rising aggregate demand, combined with falling short-run aggregate supply, always results in a rising price level. ▲ ▲ ▲

## An Important Exhibit

Exhibit 13 summarizes much of the material discussed so far in this chapter. Specifically, much of our discussion has been about the economy in the short run, about changes in the price level (*P*) and Real GDP (*Q*) in the short run.

Exhibit 13 tells us that changes in *AD* and *SRAS* will change the price level and Real GDP in the short run. Then it shows which factors actually change *AD* and which change *SRAS*.

While referring to Exhibit 13, consider what a fall in the interest rate will do to *P* and *Q* in the short run. If the interest rate falls, both consumption (*C*) and investment (*I*) will rise. If both *C* and *I* rise, the *AD* will rise or the *AD* curve will shift rightward. If the *AD* curve shifts rightward, the price level (*P*) will rise, and so will Real GDP (*Q*).

---

**EXHIBIT 13**

**A Summary Exhibit of *AD* and *SRAS***

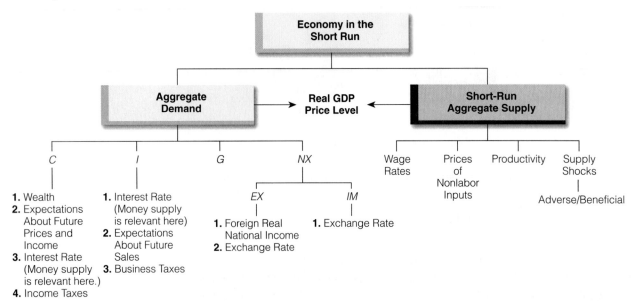

## Your First Job After College May Depend on the *AD* and *SRAS* Curves

There are some things that exist that you can see with your physical eyes. For example, a car exists, and you can see a car with your physical eyes.

There are some things that exist that you can only see with your mind's eye. For example, there actually is an *AD* curve in an economy, but no one has ever seen a real *AD* curve with his physical eyes. No one has walked into his backyard, looked up into the sky, and seen the country's *AD* curve. We can only see *AD* curves with our mind's eye. We then draw those *AD* curves on paper or a board.

Now although we cannot see the real *AD* curve in the economy, we know it exists and we also know that where it is positioned (when transferred to a two-dimensional diagram) affects your job prospects after college. Put it this way: You might have thought that learning what the *AD* curve looks like, and what makes it shift right or left, has nothing to do with you. But that's incorrect. To see why, suppose that you will be graduating from college in, say, two years. In two years, there will be an *AD* curve in the economy just as there is an *AD* curve in the economy right now.

But where will that *AD* curve in two years be positioned relative to the *AD* curve that exists right now? Let's suppose between now and then, something happens in the economy to shift the *AD* curve to the left. Will that matter to you? Well, think of what lower *AD* means in the economy, all other things remaining constant. It means that less Real GDP will be produced. Fewer houses will be built, fewer cars will be produced, fewer attorney services will be demanded. Now again ask: Will that matter to you? It certainly will matter to you if, two years from now when you graduate from college, you are looking for a job. Lower aggregate demand, which translates into less Real GDP, will translate into fewer employers visiting colleges to hire college graduates. It will translate into fewer employers reading your résumé and getting back to you for a job interview.

Our point is a simple one: In a textbook, or on a classroom board, the *AD* curve may look like something that is unrelated to you and your everyday life. But that isn't true at all. That *AD* curve may have much to do with how hard or easy it is for you to get your first job after college.

# LONG-RUN AGGREGATE SUPPLY

In this section, we discuss long-run aggregate supply and draw a long-run aggregate supply (*LRAS*) curve. We also discuss long-run equilibrium and explain how it differs from short-run equilibrium.

## Going from the Short Run to the Long Run

Graphically, short-run equilibrium is at the intersection of the *AD* curve and the (upward-sloping) *SRAS* curve. As explained earlier, economists give different reasons for an upward-sloping *SRAS* curve, which have to do either with sticky wages or with worker misperceptions. So, when either of these two conditions holds, short-run equilibrium

EXHIBIT 14

**Long-Run Aggregate Supply (LRAS) Curve**

The *LRAS* curve is a vertical line at the level of Natural Real GDP. It represents the output the economy produces when all economywide adjustments have taken place and workers do not have any relevant misperceptions.

identifies the Real GDP that the economy produces. In time, though, wages become unstuck, and misperceptions turn into accurate perceptions. In that event, the economy is said to be in the *long run*. In other words, these two conditions do not hold in the long run.

An important macroeconomic question is, "*Will the level of Real GDP that the economy produces in the long run be the same as in the short run?*" Most economists say that it will not. They argue that, in the long run, the economy produces the full-employment Real GDP, or the Natural Real GDP ($Q_N$). The aggregate supply curve that identifies the output the economy produces in the long run, the long-run aggregate supply (*LRAS*) curve, is portrayed as the vertical line in Exhibit 14.

Long-run equilibrium identifies the level of Real GDP the economy produces when wages and prices have adjusted to their final equilibrium levels and when workers have no relevant misperceptions. Graphically, this occurs at the intersection of the *AD* and *LRAS* curves. Further, the level of Real GDP that the economy produces in long-run equilibrium is the Natural Real GDP ($Q_N$).

**Natural Real GDP**

The Real GDP that is produced at the natural unemployment rate. The Real GDP that is produced when the economy is in long-run equilibrium.

**Long-Run Aggregate Supply (LRAS) Curve**

The *LRAS* curve is a vertical line at the level of Natural Real GDP. It represents the output the economy produces when wages and prices have adjusted to their final equilibrium levels and when workers do not have any relevant misperceptions.

## Short-Run Equilibrium, Long-Run Equilibrium, and Disequilibrium

The two equilibrium states in an economy—short-run and long-run—are graphically shown in Exhibit 15. In Exhibit 15(a), the economy is at point 1, producing $Q_1$ amount of Real GDP. At point 1, the quantity supplied of Real GDP (in the short run) is equal to the quantity demanded of Real GDP, and both are $Q_1$. The economy is in short-run equilibrium. In Exhibit 15(b), the economy is at point 1, producing $Q_N$. In other words, it is producing Natural Real GDP. The economy is in long-run equilibrium when it produces $Q_N$.

In both short-run and long-run equilibrium, the quantity supplied of Real GDP equals the quantity demanded. So what is the difference between short-run equilibrium and long-run equilibrium? In long-run equilibrium, the quantities supplied and demanded of Real

EXHIBIT 15

**Equilibrium States of the Economy**

There are two equilibrium states in the economy: short-run equilibrium, shown in part (a), and long-run equilibrium, shown in part (b). During the time an economy moves from one equilibrium to another, it is said to be in disequilibrium.

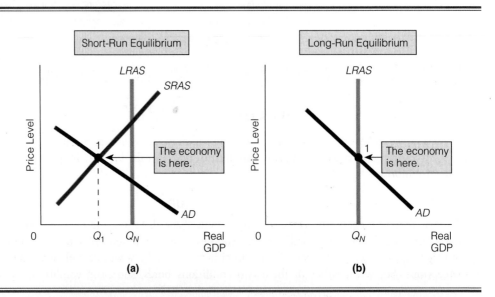

# economics 24/7

## Reality Can Be Messy, and Correct Predictions Can Be Difficult to Make

In a textbook, we can change one factor and then trace its effects through the economy, ultimately to the price level and Real GDP. For instance, a decline in business taxes will lead to a rise in investment, which in turn will lead to a rise in aggregate demand. Now, assuming that SRAS has not changed, a rise in AD will lead to a rise in the price level and a rise in Real GDP. Here are the links:

$$\text{Business taxes} \downarrow \rightarrow C\uparrow \rightarrow AD\uparrow \rightarrow P\uparrow\, Q\uparrow$$

where C = consumption, AD = aggregate demand, P = price level, and Q = Real GDP.

In reality, though, more than one thing can change at a time. Or at a minimum, two or more things could change within a few days or weeks of each other. To illustrate, suppose a factor on the demand side of the economy changes at about the same time as a factor on the supply side. Specifically, wealth rises at the same time as the price of nonlabor inputs rises. What ultimately happens to the price level and Real GDP? Let's break the problem down into small parts and find out.

1. A rise in wealth will raise AD. The AD curve shifts rightward.

2. A rise in nonlabor input prices will lower SRAS. The SRAS curve will shift leftward.

3. Because both the AD and SRAS curves are changing at the same time or at about the same time, the overall change in the price level

and Real GDP will depend on the relative shifts of the AD and SRAS curves.

4. If the AD curve shifts rightward by more than the SRAS curve shifts leftward. the price level and Real GDP will rise. (You may want to draw this.)

5. If, however, the AD curve shifts rightward by less than the SRAS curve shifts leftward, then the price level will rise and Real GDP will fall.

6. Finally, if the AD curve shifts rightward to the same degree that the SRAS curve shifts leftward, Real GDP will not change and the price level will rise.

All this has something to say about economists' predictions. Making correct predictions in economics is easy when only one thing changes and everything else remains constant. Making correct predictions is much harder when more than one thing changes at a time and when the changes pull the economy in opposite directions. We have seen a little of this type of complexity in our example. Specifically, although the increase in AD tends to raise Real GDP, the decrease in SRAS tends to lower it. What will be the final effect on Real GDP? As we have seen, it depends on the relative shifts in AD and SRAS.

The lesson: Reality in economics can be messy.

GDP equal Natural Real GDP [Exhibit 15(b)]. But in short-run equilibrium, the quantities supplied and demanded of Real GDP are either more or less than Natural Real GDP.

Let's illustrate that difference with numbers. Suppose $Q_N$ = $9.0 trillion. In long-run equilibrium, the quantity supplied of Real GDP equals the quantity demanded: $9.0 trillion. In short-run equilibrium, the quantity supplied of Real GDP equals the quantity demanded, but neither equals $9.0 trillion. For example, the quantity supplied of Real GDP could equal the quantity demanded of Real GDP at $8.5 trillion.

When the economy is in neither short-run nor long-run equilibrium, it is said to be in *disequilibrium.* Essentially, disequilibrium is the state of the economy as it moves from one short-run equilibrium to another or from short-run equilibrium to long-run equilibrium. In disequilibrium, the quantity supplied and the quantity demanded of Real GDP are not equal.

**Long-Run Equilibrium**
The condition that exists in the economy when wages and prices have adjusted to their (final) equilibrium levels and when workers do not have any relevant misperceptions. Graphically, long-run equilibrium occurs at the intersection of the AD and LRAS curves.

### SELF-TEST

1. What is the difference between short-run equilibrium and long-run equilibrium?

2. Diagrammatically represent an economy that is in neither short-run nor long-run equilibrium.

# OFFICE HOURS

## "What Purpose Does the *AD–AS* Framework Serve?"

What purpose does the *AD–AS* framework serve?

One purpose is to link some variables to other variables.

How so?

Well, consider a rise in income taxes. We learned in this chapter that a rise in income taxes will lead to a decline in consumption. And we know that a decline in consumption will lead to a decline in aggregate demand. Finally, we know that a decline in aggregate demand will lead to a decline in both the price level and Real GDP. In other words, the *AD–AS* framework helps us to link a rise in *income taxes* to a decline in both the *price level* and *Real GDP*.

Oh, I see. It's sort of like the *AD–AS* framework is a road. We start at one point on the road (where income taxes are being raised), and then we follow the road until we come to the end (where the price level and Real GDP have declined).

That's a good way of putting it. Let's now start at another point along the road. Let's start with a decline in wage rates.

If wage rates decline, short-run aggregate supply increases (the *SRAS* curve shifts to the right). As a result, the price level declines and Real GDP rises.

## CHAPTER SUMMARY

### AGGREGATE DEMAND

- Aggregate demand refers to the quantity demanded of all goods and services (Real GDP) at different price levels, *ceteris paribus.*
- The aggregate demand (*AD*) curve slopes downward, indicating an inverse relationship between the price level and the quantity demanded of Real GDP.
- The *AD* curve slopes downward because of the real balance, interest rate, and international trade effects.
- The real balance effect states that the inverse relationship between the price level and the quantity demanded of Real GDP is established through changes in the value of a person's monetary wealth, or money holdings. Specifically, a fall in the price level causes purchasing power to rise, increasing a person's monetary wealth. As people become wealthier, they buy more goods. A rise in the price level causes purchasing power to fall, reducing a person's monetary wealth. As people become less wealthy, they buy fewer goods.
- The interest rate effect states that the inverse relationship between the price level and the quantity demanded of Real GDP is established through changes in household and business spending that is sensitive to changes in interest rates. If the price level rises, a person needs more money to buy a fixed bundle of goods. In an effort to acquire more money, the demand for credit rises, as does the interest rate. As the interest rate rises, businesses and households borrow less and buy fewer goods. Thus, the quantity demanded of Real GDP falls. If the price level falls, a person needs less money to buy a fixed bundle of goods. Part of the increase in a person's monetary wealth is saved; so the supply of credit rises, and the interest rate falls. As the interest rate falls, businesses and households borrow more and buy more goods. Thus, the quantity demanded of Real GDP rises.

- The international trade effect states that the inverse relationship between the price level and the quantity demanded of Real GDP is established through foreign sector spending. Specifically, as the price level in the United States rises, U.S. goods become relatively more expensive than foreign goods, and both Americans and foreigners buy fewer U.S. goods. The quantity demanded of U.S. Real GDP falls. As the price level in the United States falls, U.S. goods become relatively less expensive than foreign goods, and both Americans and foreigners buy more U.S. goods. The quantity demanded of U.S. Real GDP rises.

- At a given price level, a rise in consumption, investment, government purchases, or net exports will increase aggregate demand

INSTRUCTOR:

That's correct. Now let's go back to your original question: What purpose does the *AD–AS* framework serve? What would your answer be now?

STUDENT:

I think I would say what you said: "It links some variables to other variables." But I'd add that it provides an explanation for changes in the price level and Real GDP too.

INSTRUCTOR:

Explain what you mean by that.

STUDENT:

Well, suppose someone were to ask me what might cause Real GDP to decline. Using the *AD–AS* framework, I would say that either a decline in *AD* or *SRAS* would lead to a decline in Real GDP. Then, if the person wanted more specificity, I could say that such things as an adverse supply shock, a decline in productivity, appreciation in the U.S. dollar, and so on could lead to a decline in Real GDP.

INSTRUCTOR:

You make a good point.

## POINTS TO REMEMBER

1. The *AD–AS* framework serves to link some variables to others. For example, a change in income taxes can ultimately be linked to a change in the price level and Real GDP.
2. The *AD–AS* framework helps us to understand changes in both the price level and Real GDP.

and shift the *AD* curve to the right. At a given price level, a fall in consumption, investment, government purchases, or net exports will decrease aggregate demand and shift the *AD* curve to the left.

## FACTORS THAT CAN CHANGE C, I, AND NX (EX – IM) AND THEREFORE CHANGE AD

- The following factors can change consumption: wealth, expectations about future prices and income, the interest rate, and income taxes. The following factors can change investment: the interest rate, expectations about future sales, and business taxes. The following factors can change net exports (exports less imports): foreign real national income and the exchange rate. A change in the money supply can affect one or more spending components (e.g., consumption) and therefore affect aggregate demand.

## MONEY SUPPLY AND VELOCITY

- Velocity is the average number of times a dollar is spent to buy final goods and services in a year.
- If money supply and velocity are constant, a rise in one spending component (such as consumption) necessitates a decline in one or more other components. If either the money supply or velocity rises, a rise in one component does not necessitate a decline in the others.

## SHORT-RUN AGGREGATE SUPPLY

- Aggregate supply is to the quantity supplied of all goods and services (Real GDP) at different price levels, *ceteris paribus*.
- The short-run aggregate supply (*SRAS*) curve is upward sloping, indicating a direct relationship between the price level and the quantity supplied of Real GDP.
- A decrease in wage rates, a decrease in the price of nonlabor inputs, an increase in productivity, and beneficial supply shocks all shift the *SRAS* curve to the right. An increase in wage rates, an increase in the price of nonlabor inputs, a decrease in productivity, and adverse supply shocks all shift the *SRAS* curve to the left.

## SHORT-RUN EQUILIBRIUM

- Graphically, short-run equilibrium exists at the intersection of the *AD* and *SRAS* curves. A shift in either or both of these curves can change the price level and Real GDP. For example, an increase in aggregate demand increases the price level and Real GDP, *ceteris paribus*.

## LONG-RUN AGGREGATE SUPPLY AND LONG-RUN EQUILIBRIUM

- The long-run aggregate supply (*LRAS*) curve is vertical at the Natural Real GDP level.

- Graphically, long-run equilibrium exists at the intersection of the *AD* and *LRAS* curves. It is the condition that exists in the economy when all economywide adjustments have taken place and workers do not hold any (relevant) misperceptions. In long-run equilibrium, the quantity demanded of Real GDP equals the quantity supplied of Real GDP, which equals Natural Real GDP.

## THREE STATES OF AN ECONOMY

- An economy can be in short-run equilibrium, long-run equilibrium, or disequilibrium.

## KEY TERMS AND CONCEPTS

| | | | |
|---|---|---|---|
| Aggregate Demand | Interest Rate Effect | Depreciation | Short-Run Equilibrium |
| Aggregate Demand (*AD*) Curve | International Trade Effect | Velocity | Natural Real GDP |
| Real Balance Effect | Wealth | Aggregate Supply | Long-Run Aggregate Supply |
| Monetary Wealth | Exchange Rate | Short-Run Aggregate Supply | (*LRAS*) Curve |
| Purchasing Power | Appreciation | (*SRAS*) Curve | Long-Run Equilibrium |

## QUESTIONS AND PROBLEMS

1. Is aggregate demand a specific dollar amount? For example, is it correct to say that aggregate demand is $9 trillion this year?

2. Explain each of the following: (a) real balance effect, (b) interest rate effect, and (c) international trade effect.

3. Graphically portray each of the following: (a) a change in the quantity demanded of Real GDP and (b) a change in aggregate demand.

4. There is a difference between a change in the interest rate that is brought about by a change in the price level and a change in the interest rate that is brought about by a change in some factor other than the price level. The first will change the quantity demanded of Real GDP, and the second will change the *AD* curve. Do you agree or disagree with this statement? Explain your answer.

5. The amount of Real GDP (real output) that households are willing and able to buy may change if there is a change in either (a) the price level or (b) some nonprice factor, such as wealth, interest rates, and the like. Do you agree or disagree? Explain your answer.

6. Explain what happens to aggregate demand in each of the following cases:
   a. The interest rate rises
   b. Wealth falls
   c. The dollar depreciates relative to foreign currencies
   d. Households expect lower prices in the future
   e. Business taxes rise

7. Explain what is likely to happen to U.S. export and import spending as a result of the dollar depreciating in value.

8. Explain how expectations about future prices and income will affect consumption.

9. Explain how expectations about future sales will affect investment.

10. How will an increase in the money supply affect aggregate demand?

11. Under what conditions can consumption rise without some other spending component declining?

12. Can total spending be a greater dollar amount than the money supply? Explain your answer.

13. Will a direct increase in the price of U.S. goods relative to foreign goods lead to a change in the quantity demanded of Real GDP or to a change in aggregate demand? Will a change in the exchange rate that subsequently increases the price of U.S. goods relative to foreign goods lead to a change in the quantity demanded of Real GDP or to a change in aggregate demand? Explain your answers.

14. Explain how each of the following will affect short-run aggregate supply:
   a. An increase in wage rates
   b. A beneficial supply shock
   c. An increase in the productivity of labor
   d. A decrease in the price of a nonlabor resource (e.g., oil)

15. What is the difference between a change in the quantity supplied of Real GDP and a change in short-run aggregate supply?

16. A change in the price level affects which of the following?
   a. The quantity demanded of Real GDP
   b. Aggregate demand
   c. Short-run aggregate supply
   d. The quantity supplied of Real GDP

17. In the short run, what is the impact on the price level and Real GDP of each of the following?
   a. An increase in consumption brought about by a decrease in interest rates
   b. A decrease in exports brought about by an appreciation of the dollar
   c. A rise in wage rates
   d. A beneficial supply shock

e. An adverse supply shock

f. A decline in productivity

18. Identify the details of each of the following explanations for an upward-sloping *SRAS* curve:

a. Sticky-wage explanation

b. Worker-misperception explanation

19. What is the difference between short-run equilibrium and long-run equilibrium?

20. An economist is sitting in the Oval Office of the White House, across the desk from the president of the United States. The president asks, "How does the unemployment rate look for the next quarter?" The economist answers, "It's not good. I don't think Real GDP is going to be as high as we initially thought. The problem seems to be foreign income; it's just not growing at the rate we thought it was going to grow." How can foreign income affect U.S. unemployment?

## WORKING WITH NUMBERS AND GRAPHS

1. Suppose that at a price index of 154, the quantity demanded of U.S. Real GDP is $10.0 trillion worth of goods. Do these data represent aggregate demand or a point on an aggregate demand curve? Explain your answer.

2. Diagrammatically represent the effect on the price level and Real GDP in the short run of each of the following:

a. An increase in wealth

b. An increase in wage rates

c. An increase in labor productivity

3. Diagrammatically represent the following, and identify the effect on Real GDP and the price level in the short run:

a. An increase in *SRAS* that is greater than the increase in *AD*

b. A decrease in *AD* that is greater than the increase in *SRAS*

c. An increase in *SRAS* that is less than the increase in *AD*

4. In the following figure, which part is representative of each of the following?

a. A decrease in wage rates

b. An increase in the price level

c. A beneficial supply shock

d. An increase in the price of nonlabor inputs

(b)

(c)

(a)

# CLASSICAL MACROECONOMICS AND THE SELF-REGULATING ECONOMY

**Introduction** For hundreds of years, scientists have tried to understand humankind and their surroundings. Biologists have observed and conducted experiments to understand human and animal behavior. Ecologists have developed models to try to understand the relationships between the plants and animals in forests and oceans. Astronomers have constructed increasingly powerful telescopes to try to understand phenomena in space. And economists have built and tested theories to try to understand the economy. This chapter presents one view about how the economy works.

## THE CLASSICAL VIEW

The term *classical economics* is often used to refer to an era in the history of economic thought that stretched from about 1750 to the early 1900s. Although classical economists lived and wrote many years ago, their ideas are often employed by some modern-day economists.

### Classical Economists and Say's Law

You know from your study of supply and demand that markets can experience temporary shortages and surpluses, such as a surplus in the apple market. But can the economy have a general surplus, that is, a general glut of goods and services? The classical economists thought not, largely because they believed in Say's law (named after J. B. Say). In its simplest version, Say's law states that supply creates its own demand.

**Say's Law**
Supply creates its own demand. Production creates enough demand to purchase all the goods and services produced.

This law is most easily understood in terms of a barter economy. Consider a person baking bread in a barter economy; the baker is a supplier of bread. According to Say, the baker works at his trade because he plans to demand other goods. As he is baking bread, the baker is thinking of the goods and services he will obtain in exchange for it. Thus, his act of supplying bread is linked to his demand for other goods. Supply creates its own demand.

If supplying some goods leads to a simultaneous demand for other goods, then Say's law implies that there cannot be either (1) a general overproduction of goods (where supply in the economy is greater than demand) or (2) a general underproduction of goods (where demand in the economy is greater than supply).

On the other hand, if the baker is baking bread in a money economy, does Say's law hold? Over a period of time, the baker earns an income as a result of supplying bread, but what does he do with the income? One use of the money is to buy goods and services. However, his demand for goods and services does not necessarily match the income that he generates by supplying bread. The baker may spend less than his full income because he saves. So we might think that Say's law does not hold in a money economy because the act of supplying goods and services—thus earning income—need not create an equal amount of demand.

But the classical economists disagreed. They argued that even in a money economy, where individuals sometimes spend less than their full incomes, Say's law still holds. Their argument was partly based on the assumption of interest rate flexibility.

## Classical Economists and Interest Rate Flexibility

For Say's law to hold in a money economy, the funds saved must give rise to an equal amount of funds invested; that is, what leaves the spending stream through one door must enter it through another door. If not, then some of the income earned from supplying goods may not be used to demand goods (good-bye Say's law). As a result, goods will be overproduced.

The classical economists argued that saving is matched by an equal amount of investment because of interest rate flexibility in the credit market. In Exhibit 1, $I$ represents investment and $S$ represents saving. $I_1$ is downward sloping, indicating an inverse relationship between the amount of funds firms invest and the interest rate ($i$). The reason for the downward slope is straightforward. The interest rate is the cost of borrowing funds. The higher the interest rate is, the fewer funds firms borrow and invest; the lower the interest rate, the more funds firms borrow and invest.

$S_1$ is upward sloping, indicating a direct relationship between the amount of funds that households save and the interest rate. The reason is that the higher the interest rate is, the higher the reward is for saving (or the higher the opportunity cost of consuming). So fewer funds are consumed and more funds are saved. Market-equilibrating forces move the credit market to interest rate $i_1$ and the equilibrium point $E_1$. At $E_1$, the number of dollars households save ($100,000) equals the number of dollars firms invest ($100,000).

Suppose now that saving increases at each interest rate level. In Exhibit 1, the saving increase is represented by a rightward shift in the saving curve from $S_1$ to $S_2$. The classical economists believed that an increase in saving puts downward pressure on the interest rate, moving it to $i_2$, thereby increasing the number of dollars firms invest. Ultimately, the number of dollars households save ($120,000) once again equals the number of dollars firms invest ($120,000). Interest rate

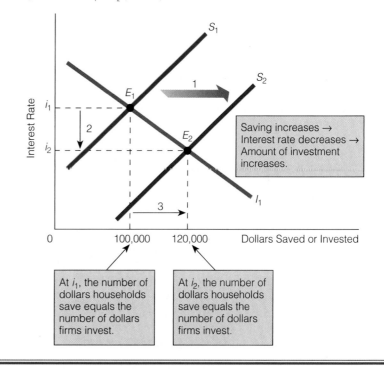

**EXHIBIT 1**

**The Classical View of the Credit Market**

In classical theory, the interest rate is flexible and adjusts so that saving equals investment. Thus, if saving increases and the saving curve shifts rightward from $S_1$ to $S_2$ (arrow 1), the increase in saving eventually puts pressure on the interest rate and moves it downward from $i_1$ to $i_2$ (arrow 2). A new equilibrium is established at $E_2$ (arrow 3), where once again the amount households save equals the amount firms invest.

Saving increases → Interest rate decreases → Amount of investment increases.

At $i_1$, the number of dollars households save equals the number of dollars firms invest.

At $i_2$, the number of dollars households save equals the number of dollars firms invest.

flexibility ensures that saving equals investment. (What goes out one door comes in the other.) In short, changes in the interest rate uphold Say's law in a money economy where there is saving.

Let's use a few numbers to illustrate what classical economists were saying. At a given price level, total expenditures (*TE*) in a very tiny economy are $5,000. Total expenditures (total spending on domestic goods and services) equal the sum of consumption (*C*), investment (*I*), government purchases (*G*), and net exports (*EX − IM*). If *C* = $3,000, *I* = $600, *G* = $1,200, and *EX − IM* = $200, then

$$TE = C + I + G + (EX - IM)$$

$$\$5,000 = \$3,000 + \$600 + \$1,200 + \$200$$

The $5,000 worth of goods and services that the four sectors of the economy want to purchase also happens to be the exact dollar amount of goods and services that suppliers want to sell.

What happens when saving is increased in the economy? Saving (*S*) is equal to the amount of a person's disposable income (*Y_d*) minus consumption (*C*). For example, if Harriet earns a disposable income of $40,000 a year and spends $38,000, she saves $2,000.

$$\text{Saving } (S) = \text{Disposable income } (Y_d) - \text{Consumption } (C)$$

For saving to increase, consumption must decrease. See Exhibit 2. If saving increases by $100, then consumption must fall from $3,000 to $2,900. At first glance, this seems to imply that total expenditures will fall to $4,900. But classical economists disagreed. They said that investment will increase by $100, going from $600 to $700. Total expenditures will remain constant at $5,000 and will be equal to the dollar amount of the goods and services that suppliers want to sell.

$$TE = C + I + G + (EX - IM)$$

$$\$5,000 = \$2,900 + \$700 + \$1,200 + \$200$$

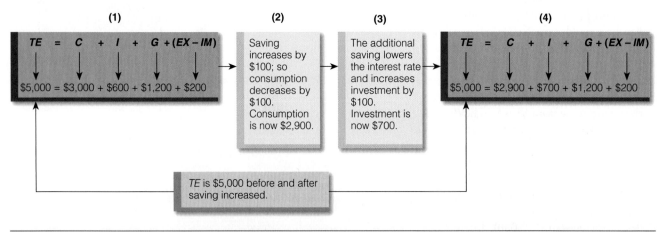

### EXHIBIT 2

**The Classical View of Say's Law in a Money Economy**

According to classical economists, a decrease in consumption and subsequent increase in saving will be matched by an equal increase in investment. Thus, there is no change in total expenditures.

**(1)**

*TE* = *C* + *I* + *G* + (*EX − IM*)

$5,000 = $3,000 + $600 + $1,200 + $200

**(2)** Saving increases by $100; so consumption decreases by $100. Consumption is now $2,900.

**(3)** The additional saving lowers the interest rate and increases investment by $100. Investment is now $700.

**(4)**

*TE* = *C* + *I* + *G* + (*EX − IM*)

$5,000 = $2,900 + $700 + $1,200 + $200

*TE* is $5,000 before and after saving increased.

According to the classical view of the economy, then, Say's law holds both in a barter economy and in a money economy. In a money economy, according to classical economists, interest rates will adjust to equate saving and investment. Therefore, any fall in consumption (and consequent rise in saving) will be matched by an equal rise in investment. In essence, at a given price level, total expenditures will not decrease as a result of an increase in saving.

What does an increase in saving imply for aggregate demand (*AD*)? An earlier chapter explains that aggregate demand changes only if total spending in the economy changes at a given price level. Therefore, because total spending does not change as a result of an increase in saving, aggregate demand does not change.

## Classical Economists on Prices and Wages: Both Are Flexible

Classical economists believed that most, if not all, markets are competitive; that is, supply and demand operate in all markets. If, for example, the labor market has a surplus, the surplus will be temporary. Soon the wage rate will decline, and the quantity supplied of labor will equal the quantity demanded of it. Similarly, given a shortage in the labor market, the wage rate will rise, and the quantity supplied will equal the quantity demanded.

What holds for wages in the labor market holds for prices in the goods and services market. Prices will adjust quickly to any surpluses or shortages, and equilibrium will be quickly reestablished. In short, the classical view is that prices and wages are flexible: They rise and decline in response to shortages and surpluses.

### SELF-TEST

(Answers to Self-Test questions are in Answers to Self-Test Questions at the back of the book.)

1. Explain Say's law in terms of a barter economy.

2. According to classical economists, if saving rises and consumption spending falls, will total spending in the economy decrease? Explain your answer.

3. What is the classical position on prices and wages?

# THREE STATES OF THE ECONOMY

The background information in this section will enable you to understand the views of economists who believe that the economy is self-regulating. Specifically, we discuss three states of the economy, the correspondence between the labor market and the three states of the economy, and more.

## Real GDP and Natural Real GDP: Three Possibilities

In the last chapter, Natural Real GDP was defined as the Real GDP produced at the natural unemployment rate. The Real GDP is produced when the economy is in long-run equilibrium.

Economists often refer to three possible states of an economy when considering the relationship between Real GDP and Natural Real GDP:

- Real GDP is less than Natural Real GDP.
- Real GDP is greater than Natural Real GDP.
- Real GDP is equal to Natural Real GDP.

Let's now graphically portray each of these three possible states of the economy.

**REAL GDP IS LESS THAN NATURAL REAL GDP (RECESSIONARY GAP)** Exhibit 3(a) shows an *AD* curve, an *SRAS* curve, and the *LRAS* curve. It also shows that Natural Real GDP ($Q_N$) is produced in the long run.

Short-run equilibrium is at the intersection of the *AD* and *SRAS* curves; so, in Exhibit 3(a), short-run equilibrium is at point 1. The Real GDP level that the economy is producing at point 1 is designated by $Q_1$.

Compare $Q_1$ with $Q_N$. Obviously, $Q_1$ is less than $Q_N$. In other words, the economy is currently producing a level of Real GDP in the short run that is less than its Natural Real GDP level. When the Real GDP that the economy is producing is less than its Natural Real GDP, the economy is said to be in a **recessionary gap**.

**Recessionary Gap**
The condition in which the Real GDP that the economy is producing is less than the Natural Real GDP and the unemployment rate is greater than the natural unemployment rate.

**REAL GDP IS GREATER THAN NATURAL REAL GDP (INFLATIONARY GAP)** In Exhibit 3(b), the *AD* and *SRAS* curves intersect at point 1; so short-run equilibrium is at point 1. The Real GDP level that the economy is producing at point 1 is designated by $Q_1$. Compare $Q_1$ with $Q_N$. Obviously, $Q_1$ is greater than $Q_N$. In other words, the economy is currently producing a level of Real GDP in the short run that is greater than its Natural Real GDP level or potential output. When the Real GDP that the economy is producing is greater than its Natural Real GDP, the economy is said to be in an inflationary gap.

**Inflationary Gap**
The condition in which the Real GDP that the economy is producing is greater than the Natural Real GDP and the unemployment rate is less than the natural unemployment rate.

**REAL GDP IS EQUAL TO NATURAL REAL GDP (LONG-RUN EQUILIBRIUM)** In Exhibit 3(c), the *AD* and *SRAS* curves indicate that short-run equilibrium is at point 1. The Real GDP level that the economy is producing at point 1 is designated by $Q_1$.

Again compare $Q_1$ and $Q_N$. This time, $Q_1$ is equal to $Q_N$. In other words, the economy is currently producing a level of Real GDP that is equal to its Natural Real GDP or potential output. When the Real GDP that the economy is producing is equal to its Natural Real GDP, the economy is in *long-run equilibrium.*

---

### EXHIBIT 3

**Real GDP and Natural Real GDP: Three Possibilities**

In (a), the economy is currently in short-run equilibrium at a Real GDP level of $Q_1$. $Q_N$ is Natural Real GDP or the potential output of the economy. Notice that $Q_1 < Q_N$. When this condition ($Q_1 < Q_N$) exists, the economy is said to be in a recessionary gap.

In (b), the economy is currently in short-run equilibrium at a Real GDP level of $Q_1$. $Q_N$ is Natural Real GDP or the potential output of the economy. Notice that $Q_1 > Q_N$. When this condition ($Q_1 > Q_N$) exists, the economy is said to be in an inflationary gap.

In (c), the economy is currently operating at a Real GDP level of $Q_1$, which is equal to $Q_N$.

In other words, the economy is producing its Natural Real GDP or potential output. When this condition ($Q_1 = Q_N$) exists, the economy is said to be in long-run equilibrium.

(a)

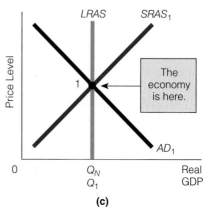

(c)

# ⓣhinking like AN ECONOMIST

**Thinking in Threes** The economist often thinks in threes. For the economist, a market has either (1) a shortage, (2) a surplus, or (3) equilibrium. Similarly, for the economist, an economy is in:

- Either a recessionary gap, producing a level of Real GDP lower than Natural Real GDP.

- Or an inflationary gap, producing a level of Real GDP higher than Natural Real GDP.

- Or long-run equilibrium, producing a level of Real GDP equal to Natural Real GDP. ▰ ▰ ▰

## The Labor Market and the Three States of the Economy

If the economy can be in three possible states, so can the labor market. We identify the three possible states of the labor market and then tie each to a possible state of the economy.

We know that the labor market consists of the demand for and the supply of labor. Like a goods market, the labor market can manifest (1) equilibrium, (2) a shortage, or (3) a surplus. So the three possible states of the labor market are:

- *Equilibrium.* When the labor market is in equilibrium, the same number of jobs are available as the number of people who want to work. The quantity demanded of labor is equal to the quantity supplied.

- *Shortage.* When the labor market has a shortage, more jobs are available than are people who want to work. The quantity demanded of labor is greater than the quantity supplied.

- *Surplus.* When the labor market has a surplus, more people want to work than there are jobs available; the quantity supplied of labor is greater than the quantity demanded.

RECESSIONARY GAP AND THE LABOR MARKET  The unemployment rate that exists when the economy produces Natural Real GDP is, of course, the natural unemployment rate. So if the economy is in a recessionary gap, is the labor market in equilibrium, shortage, or surplus?

In way of an answer, suppose the economy is in a recessionary gap, producing a Real GDP level of $9 trillion (worth of goods and services) when Natural Real GDP, or potential output, is $10 trillion. Is the existing unemployment rate producing $9 trillion worth of goods and services greater or less than the natural unemployment rate that exists when the economy is producing $10 trillion worth of goods and services? In fact, the unemployment rate is greater than the natural unemployment rate because fewer workers are needed to produce a Real GDP of $9 trillion than are needed to produce a Real GDP of $10 trillion. *Ceteris paribus,* the unemployment rate will be higher at a Real GDP level of $9 trillion than it is at a level of $10 trillion.

So, when the economy is in a recessionary gap, the unemployment rate is *higher* than the natural unemployment rate. This conclusion implies a surplus in the labor market: The quantity supplied of labor is greater than the quantity demanded; that is, more people want to work than there are jobs available.

> *If the economy is in a recessionary gap, the unemployment rate is higher than the natural unemployment rate, and a surplus exists in the labor market.*

INFLATIONARY GAP AND THE LABOR MARKET  Now suppose the economy is in an inflationary gap, producing a Real GDP level of $11 trillion (worth of goods and services) when Natural Real GDP, or potential output, is $10 trillion.

Again, the unemployment rate that exists when the economy produces Natural Real GDP is the natural unemployment rate. Is the unemployment rate that exists when the economy is producing $11 trillion worth of goods and services greater or less than the natural unemployment rate when the economy is producing $10 trillion worth? The unemployment rate is less than the natural unemployment rate because more workers are needed to produce a Real GDP of $11 trillion than are needed to produce a Real GDP of $10 trillion. *Ceteris paribus,* the unemployment rate will be lower at a Real GDP level of $11 trillion than it is at $10 trillion.

So, when the economy is in an inflationary gap, the unemployment rate is *lower* than the natural unemployment rate. This conclusion implies a shortage in the labor market: The quantity demanded of labor is greater than the quantity supplied; that is, more jobs are available than there are people who want to work.

*If the economy is in an inflationary gap, the unemployment rate is less than the natural unemployment rate, and a shortage exists in the labor market.*

LONG-RUN EQUILIBRIUM AND THE LABOR MARKET Finally, suppose the economy is in long-run equilibrium. It is producing a Real GDP level equal to Natural Real GDP. In this state, the unemployment rate in the economy is the same as the natural unemployment rate. This conclusion implies that the labor market has neither a shortage nor a surplus but is in equilibrium.

*If the economy is in long-run equilibrium, the unemployment rate equals the natural unemployment rate, and the labor market is in equilibrium.*

The following table summarizes three possible states of the economy and the related states of the labor market.

| State of the Economy | What Do We Call It? | Relationship Between Unemployment Rate and Natural Unemployment Rate | State of the Labor Market |
|---|---|---|---|
| Real GDP < Natural Real GDP | Recessionary gap | Unemployment rate > Natural Unemployment rate | Surplus exists |
| Real GDP > Natural Real GDP | Inflationary gap | Unemployment rate < Natural Unemployment rate | Shortage exists |
| Real GDP = Natural Real GDP | Long-run equilibrium | Unemployment rate = Natural Unemployment rate | Equilibrium exists |

## Common Misconceptions About the Unemployment Rate and the Natural Unemployment Rate

Some people mistakenly think that the economy's unemployment rate *cannot* be lower than the natural unemployment rate (as it is in an inflationary gap). In other words, if the natural unemployment rate is 5 percent, then the unemployment rate can never be 4 percent. But that assumption is a myth.

To explain why, we need to look at two production possibilities frontiers. In Exhibit 4, the two production possibilities frontiers are the physical PPF (purple curve) and the institutional PPF (blue curve). The physical PPF illustrates different combinations of goods that the economy can produce given the physical constraints of (1) finite resources and (2) the current state of technology. The institutional PPF illustrates different combinations of goods that the economy can produce given the two physical constraints of (1) finite resources and (2) the current state of technology, plus (3) any institutional constraints. Broadly defined, an institutional constraint is anything that prevents economic agents from producing the maximum Real GDP that is physically possible.

For example, the minimum wage law, which is an institutional constraint, specifies that workers must be paid at least the legislated minimum wage. One effect of this law is that unskilled persons whose value to employers falls below the legislated minimum wage will not be hired. Having fewer workers means less output, *ceteris paribus.* (This is why the institutional PPF lies closer to the origin than the physical PPF.)

**EXHIBIT 4**

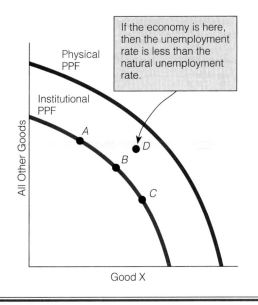

### The Physical and Institutional PPFs

A society has both a physical PPF and an institutional PPF. The physical PPF illustrates different combinations of goods the economy can produce given the physical constraints of (1) finite resources and (2) the current state of technology. The institutional PPF illustrates different combinations of goods the economy can produce given the physical constraints of (1) finite resources, (2) the current state of technology, and (3) any institutional constraints. The economy is at the natural unemployment rate if it is located on its institutional PPF, such as at points A, B, or C. An economy can never operate beyond its physical PPF, but it is possible for it to operate beyond its institutional PPF because institutional constraints are not always equally effective. If the economy does operate beyond its institutional PPF, such as at point D, then the unemployment rate in the economy is lower than the natural unemployment rate.

Within the confines of society's physical and institutional constraints is a natural unemployment rate. This situation is represented by any point on the institutional PPF. In the exhibit, points A, B, and C are all such points.

An economy can never operate beyond its physical PPF, but it can operate beyond its institutional PPF. For example, suppose inflation reduces the purchasing power of the minimum wage, thus reducing or eliminating the constraining influence of the minimum wage law on the unskilled labor market.[1] This change would make one of society's institutional constraints ineffective, allowing the economy to temporarily move beyond the institutional constraint. This is shown as point D in Exhibit 4. At point D, the unemployment rate that exists in the economy is less than the natural unemployment rate.

**THREE STATES OF THE ECONOMY AND TWO PPF CURVES** So an economy can operate beyond its institutional PPF but below its physical PPF. Now, let's tie the three states of an economy to the institutional and physical PPF curves.

Exhibit 5 shows the institutional PPF and the physical PPF, along with three points: A, B, and C. Point A, below the institutional PPF, represents an economy in a recessionary gap, where the economy is producing less than Natural Real GDP, $Q_N$. Point B, on the institutional PPF, represents an economy in long-run equilibrium, producing Natural Real GDP. Finally, point C, beyond the institutional PPF but below the physical PPF, represents an economy in an inflationary gap, where the economy is producing more than Natural Real GDP. Thus, each of the three states of the economy—recessionary gap, inflationary gap, and long-run equilibrium—can be identified as a point in relation to both the institutional PPF and physical PPF.

1. Inflation reduces the real (inflation-adjusted) minimum wage. If the minimum wage rate is $6 and the price level is 1.00, the real minimum wage is $6 ($6 ÷ the price level, 1.00). If the price level rises to 2.00, then the real minimum wage rate falls to $3. The lower the real minimum wage is, the greater the number of unskilled workers whom employers will hire, because the demand curve for unskilled workers is downward sloping.

**EXHIBIT 5**

### Three States of the Economy and Two PPFs

In this exhibit, we show three states of the economy in terms of the institutional PPF and physical PPF. Point A, which is below the institutional PPF, represents an economy in a recessionary gap. Point B, on the institutional PPF, represents an economy in long-run equilibrium. Point C, beyond the institutional PPF but below the physical PPF, represents an economy in an inflationary gap.

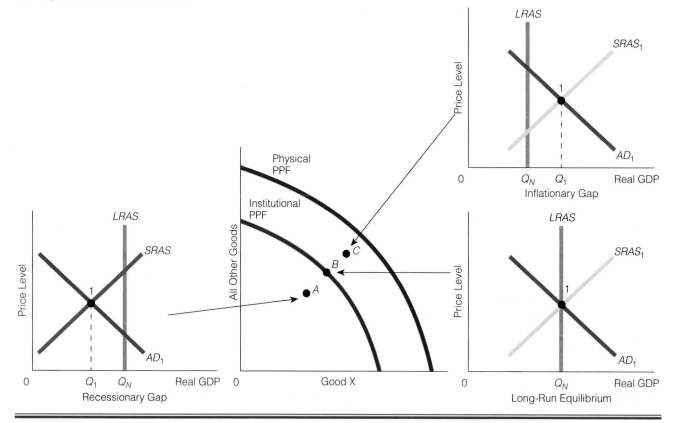

## finding ECONOMICS

**In a Country's Institutional PPF** Assume that in year 1 country A's unemployment rate is equal to its natural unemployment rate at 4.7 percent. In year 2, its unemployment rate is still equal to its natural unemployment rate at 5.4 percent. What was going on in the country over the two years? Where is the economics?

We know that if a country's unemployment rate is equal to its natural unemployment rate, then the country is operating on its institutional PPF. (It is also operating at long-run equilibrium.) Because country A's unemployment rate is equal to its natural unemployment rate in years 1 and 2, the country must be operating on its institutional PPF in both years. But why are both the unemployment and natural unemployment rates higher (each at 5.4 percent) in year 2 than in year 1? What does this difference mean? Obviously the country's institutional PPF has shifted inward between the two years (assuming no change in the country's physical PPF). In other words, some institutional changes came about between years 1 and 2—perhaps changes in the regulatory climate—that made it more difficult to produce goods and services. ▲ ▲ ▲

### SELF-TEST

1. What is a recessionary gap? An inflationary gap?

2. What is the state of the labor market when the economy is in a recessionary gap? In an inflationary gap?

3. If the economy is in an inflationary gap, locate its position in relation to the two PPFs discussed in this section.

# THE SELF-REGULATING ECONOMY

Some economists believe that the economy is self-regulating. In other words, if the economy is not at the natural unemployment rate (or full employment)—that is, it is not producing Natural Real GDP—then it can move on its own to this position. The notion of a self-regulating economy is very classical, but it is also a view held by some modern-day economists. This section describes how a self-regulating economy works.

## What Happens If a Self-Regulating Economy Is in a Recessionary Gap?

If the economy is in a recessionary gap,

1. it is producing a Real GDP level that is less than Natural Real GDP,

2. the unemployment rate is greater than the natural unemployment rate, and

3. a surplus exists in the labor market.

Exhibit 6(a) illustrates this case for a Real GDP of $9 trillion and a Natural Real GDP of $10 trillion. What, if anything, happens in the economy? According to economists who believe the economy is self-regulating, the surplus in the labor market begins to exert downward pressure on wages.[2] In other words, as old wage contracts expire, business firms negotiate contracts that pay workers lower wage rates.

As wage rates fall, the *SRAS* curve begins to shift to the right, ultimately moving from $SRAS_1$ to $SRAS_2$, as in Exhibit 6(b). As a result of the increase in short-run aggregate supply, the price level falls. As the price level falls, the quantity demanded of Real GDP rises due to the real balance, interest rate, and international trade effects (all discussed in the last

---

**EXHIBIT 6**

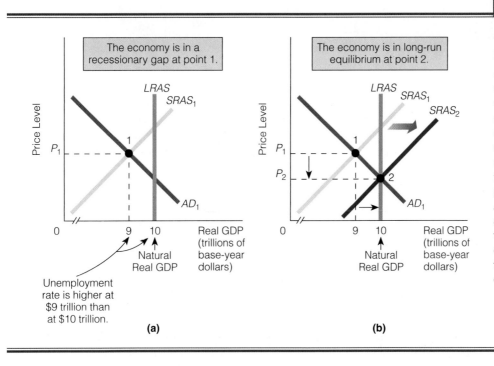

(a)

(b)

**The Self-Regulating Economy: Removing a Recessionary Gap**

(a) The economy is at $P_1$ and Real GDP of $9 trillion. Because Real GDP is less than Natural Real GDP ($10 trillion), the economy is in a recessionary gap and the unemployment rate is higher than the natural unemployment rate. (b) Wage rates fall, and the short-run aggregate supply curve shifts from $SRAS_1$ to $SRAS_2$. As the price level falls, the real balance, interest rate, and international trade effects increase the quantity demanded of Real GDP. Ultimately, the economy moves into long-run equilibrium at point 2.

---

2. In this discussion of how the self-regulating economy eliminates a recessionary gap, we have emphasized wages (in the labor market) adjusting downward. Resource prices other than wages may fall as well.

## Natural Disasters and the Economy

Do natural disasters (such as hurricanes, tornadoes, earthquakes, and some fires) affect the economy? Katrina was a major hurricane that hit the central Gulf Coast on the morning of August 29, 2005. The

rightward are stronger than the leftward forces, like Katrina, the left-shifting forces still have an effect on the final position of the *SRAS* curve.)

AP PHOTO/RIC FELD

storm caused catastrophic damage along the coastlines of Louisiana, Mississippi, and Alabama. The levees that separated Lake Pontchartrain from the city of New Orleans were damaged, ultimately leading to the flooding of about 80 percent of the city.

How does something like Hurricane Katrina affect the economy? Can Katrina (or any natural disaster) be interpreted in terms of our aggregate demand–aggregate supply framework of analysis?

Katrina is an adverse supply shock to the economy, thus shifting the *SRAS* curve to the left. Katrina essentially destroyed lives (labor) and capital (production facilities, oil platforms), and thus it adversely affected the economy's ability to produce goods and services.

Think of what a shift leftward in the *SRAS* curve means in terms of Real GDP. Either Real GDP will experience an absolute decline, or it will not grow as much as it would have had Katrina not hit. (With respect to the latter possibility, think of Katrina as shifting the *SRAS* curve leftward at the same time that other forces in the economy are shifting it rightward. Even if the forces shifting the *SRAS* curve

Soon after Katrina, both private and government economic groups changed their predictions of growth in Real GDP. For example, both Merrill Lynch and Bank of America revised their growth figures for Real GDP downward. The Congressional Budget Office (CBO) reported that the growth rate in Real GDP would decline by 0.5 to 1 percent due to Hurricane Katrina. The CBO also predicted that employment would fall by 400,000 persons due to Katrina.

What about the self-regulating properties of the economy? Could a natural disaster destabilize the economy permanently, so destabilizing an economy that it couldn't find its way back to Natural Real GDP without, say, government intervention? According to economists who believe the economy is self-regulating, the answer is no. Even if a natural disaster moved the economy into a recessionary gap, self-regulating properties would soon exert themselves and move the economy out of the gap. In other words, if a natural disaster happened to move Real GDP below its natural level, in time wages would fall, the *SRAS* curve would shift rightward, and the economy would self-regulate itself toward its Natural Real GDP level.

chapter). As the price level falls, the economy moves from one point on the *AD* curve to a point farther down on the same curve. In Exhibit 6(b), this is a move from point 1 to point 2.

As long as the economy's Real GDP is less than its Natural Real GDP, the price level continues to fall. Ultimately, the economy moves to long-run equilibrium at point 2, corresponding to $P_2$ and a Natural Real GDP of $10 trillion.

> Recessionary gap →
> Unemployment rate > Natural unemployment rate →
> Surplus in labor market → Wages fall → *SRAS* curve shifts to the right →
> Economy moves into long-run equilibrium

## What Happens If the Economy Is in an Inflationary Gap?

If the economy is in an inflationary gap,

1.  it is producing a Real GDP level that is greater than Natural Real GDP,

2.  the unemployment rate is less than the natural unemployment rate, and

3.  a shortage exists in the labor market.

Exhibit 7(a) illustrates this case for a Real GDP of $11 trillion and a Natural Real GDP of $10 trillion. What happens in the economy in this situation? According to economists who believe the economy is self-regulating, the shortage in the labor market begins to exert upward pressure on wages. In other words, as old wage contracts expire, business firms negotiate contracts that pay workers higher wage rates.

**EXHIBIT 7**

**The Self-Regulating Economy: Removing an Inflationary Gap**

(a) The economy is at $P_1$ and Real GDP of $11 trillion. Because Real GDP is greater than Natural Real GDP ($10 trillion), the economy is in an inflationary gap and the unemployment rate is lower than the natural unemployment rate. (b) Wage rates rise, and the short-run aggregate supply curve shifts from $SRAS_1$ to $SRAS_2$. As the price level rises, the real balance, interest rate, and international trade effects decrease the quantity demanded of Real GDP. Ultimately, the economy moves into long-run equilibrium at point 2.

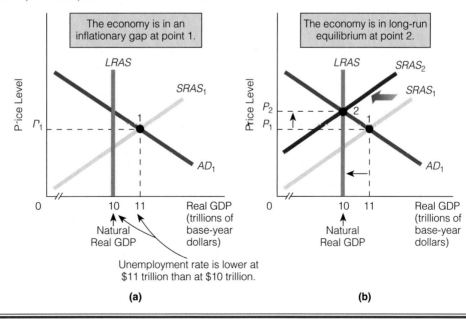

As wage rates rise, the *SRAS* curve begins to shift to the left, ultimately moving from $SRAS_1$ to $SRAS_2$ in Exhibit 7(b). As a result of the decrease in short-run aggregate supply, the price level rises. As the price level rises, the quantity demanded of Real GDP falls due to the real balance, interest rate, and international trade effects. The economy moves from one point on the *AD* curve to a point farther up on the same curve. In Exhibit 7(b), this is a move from point 1 to point 2.

As long as the economy's Real GDP is greater than its Natural Real GDP, the price level will continue to rise. Ultimately, the economy moves to long-run equilibrium at point 2, corresponding to $P_2$, and a Natural Real GDP of $10 trillion.

> Inflationary gap →
> Unemployment rate < Natural unemployment rate →
> Shortage in labor market → Wages rise → *SRAS* curve shifts to the left →
> Economy moves into long-run equilibrium

## The Self-Regulating Economy: A Recap

We have seen that if the economy is in a recessionary gap, wage rates fall (along with other resource prices), and the *SRAS* curve shifts to the right, the price level falls, and the economy moves down the *AD* curve. The economy moves in the direction of long-run equilibrium, ultimately achieving the Natural Real GDP level.

If the economy is in an inflationary gap, wage rates rise (along with other resource prices), and the *SRAS* curve shifts to the left. At the same time, the price level rises and the economy moves up the *AD* curve. The economy moves in the direction of long-run equilibrium, ultimately achieving the Natural Real GDP level.

*Flexible wage rates (and other resource prices) play a critical role in the self-regulating economy.* For example, suppose wage rates are not flexible and do not fall in a recessionary gap. Then the *SRAS* curve does not shift to the right, the price level does not fall, and the economy doesn't move down the *AD* curve toward long-run equilibrium. Similarly, if wage rates are not flexible and do not rise in an inflationary gap, then the economy won't move up the *AD* curve toward long-run equilibrium.

The economists who say the economy is self-regulating believe that wage rates and other resource prices are *flexible* and that they move up and down in response to market conditions. These economists believe that *wage rates will fall* when there is a *surplus of labor* and that *wage rates will rise* when there is a *shortage of labor*. You will see in the next chapter that this flexible wages and prices position has not gone unchallenged.

The following table summarizes how a self-regulating economy works for the three possible states of the economy.

| State of the Economy | What Happens If the Economy Is Self-Regulating? |
| --- | --- |
| Recessionary gap (Real GDP < Natural Real GDP) | Wages fall and *SRAS* curve shifts to the right until Real GDP = Natural Real GDP. |
| Inflationary gap (Real GDP > Natural Real GDP) | Wages rise and *SRAS* curve shifts to the left until Real GDP = Natural Real GDP. |
| Long-run equilibrium (Real GDP = Natural Real GDP) | No change in wages and no change in *SRAS*. |

## Policy Implication of Believing the Economy Is Self-Regulating

For economists who believe in a self-regulating economy, full employment is the norm: *The economy always moves back to Natural Real GDP.* Stated differently, if the economy contracts an "illness"—in the form of a recessionary or an inflationary gap—it is capable of healing itself through changes in wages and prices. This position on how the economy works has led these economists to advocate a macroeconomic policy of laissez-faire, or noninterference. In these economists' view, government does not have an economic management role to play.

**laissez-faire**
A public policy of not interfering with market activities in the economy.

## Changes in a Self-Regulating Economy: Short Run and Long Run

If the economy is self-regulating, how does a change in aggregate demand affect the economy in the short run and the long run? In Exhibit 8(a), the economy is initially in long-run equilibrium at point 1. An increase in aggregate demand is brought about by, say, an increase in government purchases (a possibility discussed in the last chapter). The *AD* curve shifts right from $AD_1$ to $AD_2$, and in the short run the economy moves to point 2, with both Real GDP and the price level higher than at point 1. Now at point 2, the economy is in an inflationary gap. If the economy is self-regulating, wages will soon rise, and the *SRAS* curve will shift to the left—ultimately from $SRAS_1$ to $SRAS_2$. The economy will end up at point 3 in long-run equilibrium.

Let's examine the changes in the short run and the long run. As a result of an increase in aggregate demand, Real GDP rises, and the price level rises in the short run. In addition, because Real GDP rises, the unemployment rate falls. In the long run, when the economy is at point 3, it is producing exactly the same level of Real GDP that it was producing originally ($Q_N$), but at a higher price level.

Conclusion: If the economy is self-regulating, an increase in aggregate demand can raise the price level and Real GDP in the short run, but in the long run the only effect is a

---

**EXHIBIT 8**

**Changes in a Self-Regulating Economy: Short Run and Long Run**

In (a) the economy is initially at point 1 in long-run equilibrium. Aggregate demand rises and the *AD* curve shifts right from $AD_1$ to $AD_2$. The economy is at point 2 in the short run, with a higher Real GDP and a higher price level than at point 1. The economy is also in an inflationary gap at point 2. If the economy is self-regulating, wages will soon rise, the *SRAS* curve will shift left from $SRAS_1$ to $SRAS_2$, and the economy will be in long-run equilibrium at point 3. At point 3, the economy is producing the same Real GDP as it did at point 1. In other words, in the long run, an increase in aggregate demand only raises the price level. In (b) the economy is initially at point 1 in long-run equilibrium. Aggregate demand falls and the *AD* curve shifts left from $AD_1$ to $AD_2$. The economy is at point 2 in the short run, with a lower Real GDP and a lower price level than at point 1. The economy is also in a recessionary gap. If the economy is self-regulating, wages will soon fall, the *SRAS* curve will shift right from $SRAS_1$ to $SRAS_2$, and the economy will be in long-run equilibrium at point 3. At point 3, the economy is producing the same Real GDP as it did at point 1. In other words, in the long run, a decrease in aggregate demand only lowers the price level.

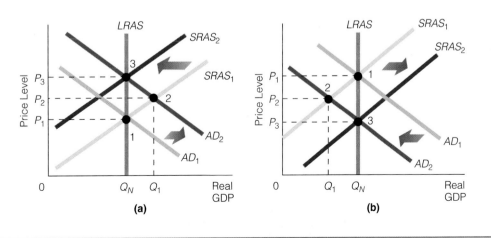

(a)　　　　　　　　(b)

rise in the price level. In other words, in the long run, we have only higher prices to show for an increase in aggregate demand.

Now let's consider what happens if aggregate demand falls. In Exhibit 8(b), the economy is initially in long-run equilibrium at point 1 when aggregate demand decreases. The $AD$ curve shifts left from $AD_1$ to $AD_2$, and in the short run the economy moves to point 2, with both Real GDP and the price level lower than at point 1.

Now at point 2, the economy is in a recessionary gap. If the economy is self-regulating, wages will soon fall and the $SRAS$ curve will shift to the right—ultimately from $SRAS_1$ to $SRAS_2$. The economy winds up at point 3 in long-run equilibrium.

Again, let's examine the changes in the short run and the long run. As a result of a decrease in aggregate demand, Real GDP falls in the short run, as does the price level. In addition, because Real GDP falls, the unemployment rate rises. In the long run, when the economy is at point 3, it is producing exactly the same level of Real GDP that it was producing originally ($Q_N$), but at a lower price level.

Conclusion: If the economy is self-regulating, a decrease in aggregate demand can lower the price level and Real GDP in the short run, but in the long run the only effect is a lower price level.

| Change in **AD** | In the Short Run | In the Long Run |
| --- | --- | --- |
| $AD\uparrow$ | $P\uparrow, Q\uparrow$ | $P\uparrow, Q$ does not change |
| $AD\downarrow$ | $P\downarrow, Q\downarrow$ | $P\downarrow, Q$ does not change |

Let's return to Exhibit 8(a) to clarify a point about long-run equilibrium. In the exhibit, the economy starts at point 1 in long-run equilibrium and then moves to point 2. At point 2, both the price level and Real GDP are higher than they were at point 1. In other words, if $AD$ rises, both the price level and Real GDP rise in the short run. If the economy is self-regulating, it does not remain at point 2 but rather moves to point 3, where it is again in long-run equilibrium. At point 3, the price level is higher than it was at point 2, but Real GDP is lower. Why, then, don't we say that Real GDP is lower in the long run than it is in the short run, instead of saying that Real GDP does not change in the long run? The answer is that the long run is measured from one long-run equilibrium point to another long-run equilibrium point. In terms of Exhibit 8(a), we look at the long run by comparing points 1 and 3. When we make this comparison, we notice two things: The price level is higher at point 3 than at point 1, and Real GDP is the same.

## A Recap of Classical Macroeconomics and a Self-Regulating Economy

1. Say's law holds.

2. Interest rates change such that savings equals investment.

3. The economy is self-regulating, making full employment and an economy producing Natural Real GDP the norm.

4. Prices and wages are flexible. In other words, if the economy is in a recessionary gap, wages fall and the economy soon moves itself toward producing Natural Real GDP (at a lower price level than in the recessionary gap). If the economy is in an inflationary gap, wages rise and the economy soon moves itself toward producing Natural Real GDP (at a higher price level than in the inflationary gap).

5. Because the economy is self-regulating, laissez-faire is the policy prescription.

## Business-Cycle Macroeconomics and Economic-Growth Macroeconomics

In Chapter 8, we introduced the $AD-AS$ model, involving the aggregate demand ($AD$) curve, the short-run aggregate supply ($SRAS$) curve, and the long-run aggregate supply ($LRAS$) curve. In this chapter, working mainly with two of those three curves (the $AD$ and $SRAS$ curves), we did two things: First, we showed what would happen if a self-regulating economy were in either a recessionary or an inflationary gap (see Exhibits 6 and 7). In both cases, the short-run aggregate supply curve would shift so that the economy moved into long-run equilibrium. Second, we started from a point of long-run equilibrium and introduced a change in aggregate demand (see Exhibit 8). We explained what happens in the economy (specifically to the price level and Real GDP) in both the short run and the long run.

You have enough background now to understand the difference between business-cycle macroeconomics and economic-growth macroeconomics. Both can be explained with respect to Real GDP and a few curves. In some upcoming chapters, we will deal with business-cycle macroeconomics, that is, with changes in the $AD$ and $SRAS$ curves around a *fixed LRAS* curve. But in other chapters, we will be dealing with economic-growth macroeconomics, that is, with *rightward-shifting* changes in the $LRAS$ curve. Business-cycle and economic-growth macroeconomics essentially make up two categories of macroeconomics. Keep these two categories in mind as you continue your study of macroeconomics.

BUSINESS-CYCLE MACROECONOMICS In this chapter, we have been looking at the *business cycle*, that is, the recurrent ups and downs in Real GDP. To understand the business cycle, refer to Exhibit 8 (a). The economy starts off in long-run equilibrium at point 1. Next, the aggregate demand shifts to the right. In the short run, Real GDP rises from $Q_N$ to $Q_1$. Eventually, though, the $SRAS$ curve shifts to the left, the economy is back in long-run equilibrium at point 3, and Real GDP returns to its natural level at $Q_N$.

We could describe what happened this way: Real GDP initially rose and then fell with respect to a *fixed LRAS* curve. This is what business-cycle macroeconomics deals with: changes in Real GDP (up and down) around a *fixed LRAS* curve.

In many upcoming chapters, we will delve into business-cycle macroeconomics: What shifts the $AD$ curve? Why might Real GDP initially rise and then fall? Macroeconomists often have to ask and then try to answer such questions relating to business-cycle macroeconomics.

ECONOMIC-GROWTH MACROECONOMICS If business-cycle macroeconomics can be described as changes in Real GDP with respect to a *fixed LRAS* curve, then economic-growth macroeconomics can be described as increases in Real GDP due to a *rightward-shifting LRAS* curve. In Exhibit 9, we start with $AD_1$

**EXHIBIT 9**

**Economic-Growth Macroeconomics**

Economic-growth macroeconomics deals with rightward shifts in the long-run aggregate supply curve ($LRAS$).

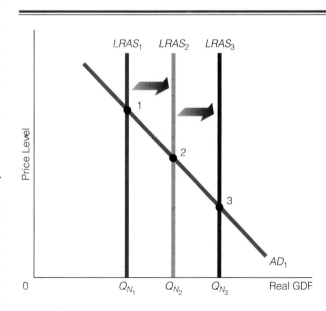

## If the Economy Is Removing Itself from a Recessionary Gap, Where Is the Declining Price Level?

Suppose, in year 1, that the economy is in a recessionary gap, that it is self-regulating, and that it is beginning to remove itself from the recessionary gap. In other words, wages are beginning to fall, and the *SRAS* curve is beginning to shift rightward. As a result, the price level is beginning to decline.

> Recessionary gap → Wages begin to fall → *SRAS* begins to shift rightward → Price level begins to decline

In year 2 , the economy is no longer in a recessionary gap. It is in long-run equilibrium, producing the Natural Real GDP ($Q_N$). But here is the problem: The price level hasn't declined. This development is odd because if the economy were in a recessionary gap and the economy is self-regulating, we would expect the price level to be lower once the economy removes itself from a recessionary gap. For example, look at Exhibit 6(b) to see that the price level is lower at point 2 (once the economy has removed itself from a recessionary gap) than at point 1 (when it was in a recessionary gap).

Does a constant price level mean that the economy is not self-regulating? Not at all. While the economy was self-regulating (and the *SRAS* curve was shifting to the right), aggregate demand in the economy might have risen. Moreover, the rise in aggregate demand could be totally unrelated to the change occurring on the supply side of the economy (as evidenced by the *SRAS* curve's shift to the right).

Think of it this way: The *SRAS* is the right hand, and it is moving. The *AD* curve is the left hand; it is moving too, and its movement is unrelated to what the right hand (*SRAS*) is doing. In the end, both hands (both the *SRAS* and the *AD* curves) determine what happens to the price level.

In Exhibit 10, the economy is initially at point 1, in a recessionary gap. The self-regulating properties of the economy are in force, wages are falling, and the *SRAS* curve is shifting rightward from $SRAS_1$ to $SRAS_2$. At the same time, something has occurred to increase aggregate demand. For example, government purchases or the money supply might have increased, and the *AD* curve shifts rightward from $AD_1$ to $AD_2$. In the end, the two new curves—$SRAS_2$ and $AD_2$—intersect at point 2 in the exhibit. The economy is no longer in a recessionary gap, and the price level has remained constant.

Here's what we should take away from this discussion: Two (or more) things can happen at the same time in an economy, and unless we understand this, we may assume something is false when it is true. If the economy is removing itself from a recessionary gap, we expect the price level to decline, but it doesn't. So is the economy not self-regulating? No. Something else could have been happening at the same time the economy was removing itself from a recessionary gap, and this "something else" (in our example, a rise in aggregate demand) could offset the falling price level.

### EXHIBIT 10

**A Self-Regulating Economy with Aggregate Demand Increasing**

The economy is initially in a recessionary gap at point 1. As the economy is self-regulating and the *SRAS* curve shifts to the right, something unrelated to the self-regulating properties of the economy occurs. Specifically, aggregate demand rises and the *AD* curve shifts rightward. The economy ends up at point 2, out of the recessionary gap but with no change in the price level.

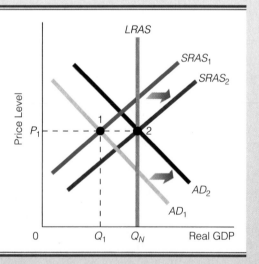

and $LRAS_1$. Long-run equilibrium is at point 1, and Natural Real GDP is $Q_{N1}$. Now suppose the $LRAS$ curve shifts rightward, first to $LRAS_2$ and then to $LRAS_3$. At the same time, Real GDP rises, first to $Q_{N2}$ and then to $Q_{N3}$. These rightward shifts in the long-run aggregate supply ($LRAS$) curve illustrate economic growth. Our study of economic-growth macroeconomics deals with the factors that can lead to a rightward shift in $LRAS$.

## SELF-TEST

1. If the economy is self-regulating, what happens if it is in a recessionary gap?

2. If the economy is self-regulating, what happens if it is in an inflationary gap?

3. If the economy is self-regulating, how do changes in aggregate demand affect the economy in the long run?

## "Do Economists Really Know What the Natural Unemployment Rate Equals?"

**STUDENT:**

Do economists know what the natural unemployment rate equals at any given moment?

**INSTRUCTOR:**

They estimate it but can't be absolutely sure that their estimate of the natural unemployment rate is the same as the actual rate. After all, not all economists get the same estimate for the natural unemployment rate. One economist might estimate it at 4.3 percent, whereas another estimates it at 4.6 percent.

**STUDENT:**

Well, if that's true, then not every economist would agree that the economy is in, say, a recessionary gap if the unemployment rate is, say, 4.5 percent. Am I correct?

**INSTRUCTOR:**

You are correct. For example, the economist who thinks the natural unemployment rate is 4.3 percent will think the economy is in a recessionary gap if the actual unemployment rate is 4.5 percent, but the economist who thinks the natural unemployment rate is 4.6 percent will not. Here's an analogy: Smith thinks that Brown's normal body temperature is 98.9 degrees, and Jones thinks it is only 98.6 degrees. If Brown's body temperature today is 98.9 degrees, Jones will think Brown is running a low-grade fever, but Smith will not.

**STUDENT:**

Does getting a too-high or too-low estimate of the natural unemployment rate matter to the economy? In other words, do the incorrect estimates (that economists sometimes make) matter?

**INSTRUCTOR:**

Actually, the answer is yes and no. The answer is no if the economy is self-regulating and government doesn't plan to try to move the economy out of either a recessionary or inflationary gap by implementing economic policies. As in the example of misestimating Brown's normal body temperature, if no one plans to give Brown any medicine, then misestimating his body temperature probably doesn't matter.

## CHAPTER SUMMARY

### SAY'S LAW

- Say's law states that supply creates its own demand. All economists believe that Say's law holds in a barter economy, where there can be no general overproduction or underproduction of goods. Classical economists believed that Say's law also holds in a money economy. In their view, even if consumption drops and saving rises, economic forces are at work producing an equal increase in investment. According to classical economists, interest rates are flexible, and they move to a level where the amount of saving and the amount of investment in an economy are equal.

### CLASSICAL ECONOMISTS ON MARKETS, WAGES, AND PRICES

- Classical economists believed that most, if not all, markets are competitive and that wages and prices are flexible.

### THREE STATES OF THE ECONOMY

- Natural Real GDP is the level of Real GDP produced when the economy is operating at the natural unemployment rate.

But in later chapters you are going to read about the government implementing economic policies to try to remove the economy from either a recessionary or inflationary gap. Then misestimating the natural unemployment rate does matter.

To illustrate, suppose the natural unemployment rate has fallen from 5.0 percent to 4.7 percent, but economists and government economic policy makers have not figured this out yet. In other words, they still believe that the natural unemployment rate is 5.0 percent. Now if the actual unemployment rate is 4.7 percent, then the economy is in long-run equilibrium. Economists and government economic policy makers, however, mistakenly believe that the economy is in an inflationary gap (with the actual unemployment rate of 4.7 percent lower than their too-high estimate of 5.0 percent). Thinking the economy is in an inflationary gap, economists expect prices to rise in the future. To offset the higher prices in the future, they propose a reduction in the growth rate of the money supply in the hopes of reducing aggregate demand (shifting the *AD* curve to the left). The Federal Reserve [the monetary authority] follows suit and reduces the growth rate of the money supply, and the *AD* curve shifts leftward. But notice the effect of this in terms of our *AD–AS* model. A reduction in aggregate demand throws the economy into a recessionary gap. (Remember, the economy was actually in long-run equilibrium when the monetary policy action was carried out.)

Our conclusion is simple: A misestimate of the natural unemployment rate, if acted on, can move an economy from long-run equilibrium into a recessionary gap.

Back to the original question: Does getting a too-high or too-low estimate of the natural unemployment rate matter to the economy? The answer is yes, it certainly can matter to the economy.

**POINTS TO REMEMBER**

1. Economists can misestimate the natural unemployment rate.
2. Acting on a misestimated natural unemployment rate can affect the economy (sometimes adversely), for example, by influencing economic policy actions.

- The economy can be producing a Real GDP level that (1) is equal to Natural Real GDP, (2) is greater than Natural Real GDP, or (3) is less than Natural Real GDP. In other words, the economy can be in (1) long-run equilibrium, (2) an inflationary gap, or (3) a recessionary gap, respectively.

- In long-run equilibrium, the Real GDP that the economy is producing is equal to the Natural Real GDP. The unemployment rate in the economy is equal to the natural unemployment rate, and the labor market is in equilibrium.

- In a recessionary gap, the Real GDP that the economy is producing is less than the Natural Real GDP. The unemployment rate in the economy is greater than the natural unemployment rate, and a surplus exists in the labor market.

- In an inflationary gap, the Real GDP that the economy is producing is greater than the Natural Real GDP. The unemployment rate in the economy is less than the natural unemployment rate, and a shortage exists in the labor market.

## THE INSTITUTIONAL AND PHYSICAL PRODUCTION POSSIBILITIES FRONTIERS

- The physical PPF illustrates different combinations of goods that the economy can produce given the physical constraints of (1) finite resources and (2) the current state of technology. The institutional PPF illustrates different combinations of goods that the economy can produce given the two physical constraints of (1) finite resources and (2) the current state of technology, plus (3) any institutional constraints.

- If an economy is operating on its institutional PPF, it is operating at the natural unemployment rate. If it is operating at a point beyond the institutional PPF but below the physical PPF, it is operating at an unemployment rate less than the natural unemployment rate.

## THE SELF-REGULATING ECONOMY

- Some economists contend that the economy can eliminate both recessionary and inflationary gaps smoothly and quickly by itself.
- If the economy is self-regulating and in a recessionary gap, then the unemployment rate in the economy is greater than the natural unemployment rate, and a surplus exists in the labor market. As wage contracts expire, wage rates fall. As a result, the SRAS curve shifts to the right, and the price level falls. As the price level falls, the quantity demanded of Real GDP rises.

Ultimately, the economy moves into long-run equilibrium, where it produces Natural Real GDP.

- If the economy is self-regulating and in an inflationary gap, then the unemployment rate in the economy is less than the natural unemployment rate, and a shortage exists in the labor market. As wage contracts expire, wage rates rise. As a result, the SRAS curve shifts to the left, and the price level rises. As the price level rises, the quantity demanded of Real GDP falls. Ultimately, the economy moves into long-run equilibrium, where it produces Natural Real GDP.

## BUSINESS-CYCLE MACROECONOMICS AND ECONOMIC-GROWTH MACROECONOMICS

- This text presents both business-cycle and economic-growth macroeconomics. Business-cycle macroeconomics deals with changes in Real GDP around a fixed LRAS curve. Economic-growth macroeconomics deals with increases in Real GDP due to a rightward-shifting LRAS curve.

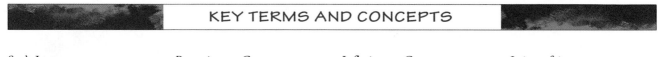

## KEY TERMS AND CONCEPTS

Say's Law          Recessionary Gap          Inflationary Gap          Laissez-faire

## QUESTIONS AND PROBLEMS

1. What is the classical economics position on (a) wages, (b) prices, and (c) interest rates?

2. According to classical economists, does Say's law hold in a money economy? Explain your answer.

3. How do you explain why investment falls as the interest rate rises?

4. Explain why saving rises as the interest rate rises.

5. According to classical economists, does an increase in saving shift the AD curve to the left? Explain your answer.

6. What does it mean to say that the economy is in a recessionary gap? In an inflationary gap? In long-run equilibrium?

7. What is the state of the labor market in (a) a recessionary gap, (b) an inflationary gap, (c) long-run equilibrium?

8. Describe the relationship of the (actual) unemployment rate to the natural unemployment rate in each of the following economic states: (a) a recessionary gap, (b) an inflationary gap, and (c) long-run equilibrium.

9. Diagrammatically represent an economy in (a) an inflationary gap, (b) a recessionary gap, and (c) long-run equilibrium.

10. Explain how an economy can operate beyond its institutional PPF but not beyond its physical PPF.

11. According to economists who believe in a self-regulating economy, what happens—step by step—when the economy is in a recessionary gap? What happens when the economy is in an inflationary gap?

12. If wage rates are not flexible, can the economy be self-regulating? Explain your answer.

13. Explain the importance of the real balance, interest rate, and international trade effects to long-run (equilibrium) adjustment in the economy.

14. Suppose that the economy is self-regulating, that the price level is 132, that the quantity demanded of Real GDP is $4 trillion, that the quantity supplied of Real GDP in the short run is $3.9 trillion, and that the quantity supplied of Real GDP in the long run is $4.3 trillion. Is the economy in short-run equilibrium? Will the price level in long-run equilibrium be greater than, less than, or equal to 132? Explain your answers.

15. Suppose that the economy is self-regulating, that the price level is 110, that the quantity demanded of Real GDP is $4 trillion, that the quantity supplied of Real GDP in the short run is $4.9 trillion, and that the quantity supplied of Real GDP in the long run is $4.1 trillion. Is the economy in short-run equilibrium? Will the price level in long-run equilibrium be greater than, less than, or equal to 110? Explain your answers.

16. Yvonne is telling her friend Wendy that wages are rising but that so is the unemployment rate. She tells Wendy that she may be the next person to be fired at her company and that she may have to move back in with her parents. What does the economy have to do with Yvonne's possibly of having to move back in with her parents?

17. Jim says, "I think it's a little like when you have a cold or the flu. You don't need to see a doctor. In time, your body heals itself. That's sort of the way the economy works too. We don't really need government coming to our rescue every time the economy gets a cold." According to Jim, how does the economy work?

18. Beginning in long-run equilibrium, explain what happens to the price level and Real GDP in the short run and in the long run as a result of (a) a decline in *AD*, (b) a rise in *AD*, (c) a decline in *SRAS*, and (d) a rise in *SRAS*.

## WORKING WITH NUMBERS AND GRAPHS

1. In the following figure, which point is representative of:
   a. The economy on its *LRAS* curve
   b. The economy in a recessionary gap
   c. The economy in an inflationary gap

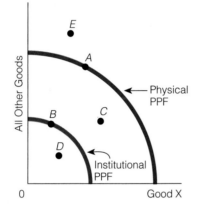

2. In the following figure, which of parts (a)–(c) is consistent with or representative of:
   a. The economy operating at the natural unemployment rate
   b. A surplus in the labor market
   c. A recessionary gap
   d. A cyclical unemployment rate of zero

3. Diagrammatically represent the following:
   a. An economy in which *AD* increases as it is self-regulating out of a recessionary gap
   b. An economy in which *AD* decreases as it is self-regulating out of an inflationary gap

4. Economist Jones believes there is always sufficient (aggregate) demand in the economy to buy all the goods and services supplied at full employment. Diagrammatically represent what the economy looks like for Jones.

5. Diagrammatically show what happens when the institutional constraints in the economy become less effective.

# Keynesian Macroeconomics and Economic Instability: A Critique of the Self-Regulating Economy

**Introduction** In the last chapter we discussed the economy as a self-regulating mechanism. For example, we learned that an economy can remove itself from a recessionary gap. In this chapter we challenge that assertion and discuss the views of economists who believe that the economy may not be able to self-regulate at Natural Real GDP. In other words, the economy may not be able to move itself out of a recessionary gap. The ideas in this chapter are mostly those of one man, John Maynard Keynes, who taught economics at Cambridge University in England.

## QUESTIONING THE CLASSICAL POSITION AND THE SELF-REGULATING ECONOMY

John Maynard Keynes, an English economist, changed how many economists viewed the economy. Keynes's major work, *The General Theory of Employment, Interest and Money*, was published in 1936. Just prior to its publication, the Great Depression had plagued many countries of the world. Looking around at the world during that time, one had to wonder whether the classical view of the economy could be right. Unemployment was sky-high in many countries, and many economies had been contracting. Where was Say's law, with its promise that there would be no general gluts? When was the self-regulating economy going to heal itself of its depression illness? Where was full employment? And, given the depressed state of the economy, could anyone any longer believe that laissez-faire was the right policy? With the Great Depression as recent history, Keynes and the Keynesians thought that although their theory might not be right in every detail, they certainly had enough evidence to say that the classical view of the economy was wrong.

Keynes challenged all four of the following classical position beliefs: (1) Say's law holds, so that insufficient demand in the economy is unlikely. (2) Wages, prices, and interest rates are flexible. (3) The economy is self-regulating. (4) Laissez-faire is the right and sensible economic policy.

## Keynes's Criticism of Say's Law in a Money Economy

According to classical economists and Say's law, if consumption spending falls because saving increases, then total spending will not fall, because the added saving will simply bring about more investment spending. This will happen through changes in the interest rate. The added saving will put downward pressure on the interest rate, and at a lower interest rate businesses will borrow and invest more. Through changes in the interest rate, the amount of saving will always equal the amount invested.

Keynes disagreed. He didn't think that added saving will necessarily stimulate an equal amount of added investment spending. Exhibit 1 illustrates Keynes's point of view. Let consumption equal $3,000, investment equal $600, government purchases equal $1,200, and net exports equal $200. Then saving increases by $100, lowering consumption to $2,900. According to the classical economists, investment will rise by $100 at the same time, going from $600 to $700. Keynes asked, what is the guarantee that an increase in investment will equally match an increase in saving? What if saving rises by $100 (and consumption goes down by $100), but investment rises by, say, only $40 (instead of $100)? Then the original equation $TE = C + I + G + (EX - IM)$ changes from

$$TE = \$3,000 + \$600 + \$1,200 + \$200$$
$$= \$5,000$$

to

$$TE = \$2,900 + \$640 + \$1,200 + \$200$$
$$= \$4,940$$

*not* to

$$TE = \$2,900 + \$700 + \$1,200 + \$200$$
$$= \$5,000$$

**EXHIBIT 1**

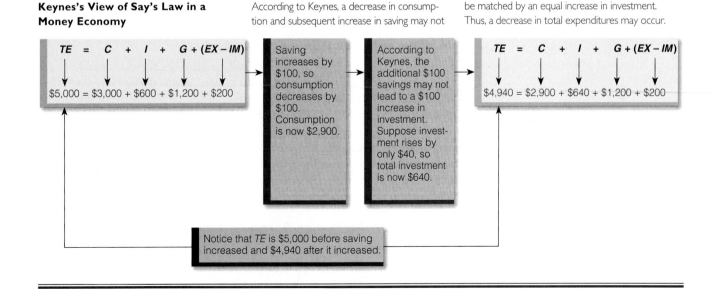

**Keynes's View of Say's Law in a Money Economy**

According to Keynes, a decrease in consumption and subsequent increase in saving may not be matched by an equal increase in investment. Thus, a decrease in total expenditures may occur.

$TE = C + I + G + (EX - IM)$

$\$5,000 = \$3,000 + \$600 + \$1,200 + \$200$

Saving increases by $100, so consumption decreases by $100. Consumption is now $2,900.

According to Keynes, the additional $100 savings may not lead to a $100 increase in investment. Suppose investment rises by only $40, so total investment is now $640.

$TE = C + I + G + (EX - IM)$

$\$4,940 = \$2,900 + \$640 + \$1,200 + \$200$

Notice that *TE* is $5,000 before saving increased and $4,940 after it increased.

Thus, total expenditures decrease from $5,000 to $4,940. And if, at a given price level, total spending falls, so will aggregate demand. In other words, according to Keynes, aggregate demand could fall if saving increases.

Of course, a classical economist would retort that, as a result of a $100 increase in saving, interest rates will fall enough to guarantee that investment will increase by $100. Keynes countered by saying that individuals save and invest for a host of reasons and that no single factor, such as the interest rate, links these activities.

Furthermore, whereas the classical economists believed that saving and investment depend on the interest rate, Keynes believed that both saving and investment depend on a number of factors that may be far more influential than the interest rate. Keynes held that saving is more responsive to changes in income than to changes in the interest rate and that investment is more responsive to technological changes, business expectations, and innovations than to changes in the interest rate.

Consider the difference between Keynes and the classical economists on saving.

- The classical economists held that saving is directly related to the interest rate: As the interest rate goes up, saving rises; as the interest rate goes down, saving falls, *ceteris paribus*.

- Keynes thought this assumption might not always be true. Suppose individuals are saving for a certain goal—say, a retirement fund of $100,000. They might save less per period at an interest rate of 10 percent than at an interest rate of 5 percent because a higher interest rate means that they can save less per period and still meet their goal by retirement. For example, if the interest rate is 5 percent, they need $50,000 in savings to earn $2,500 in interest income per year. If the interest rate is 10 percent, they need only $25,000 in savings to earn $2,500 in interest.

As for investment, Keynes believed that the interest rate is important in determining the level of investment, but not as important as other variables, such as the expected rate of profit on investment. Keynes argued that if business expectations are pessimistic, then much investment is unlikely, regardless of how low the interest rate is.

## Keynes on Wage Rates

As explained in the last chapter, if the unemployment rate in the economy is greater than the natural unemployment rate, a surplus exists in the labor market: The number of job seekers is high relative to the number of jobs available. Consequently, according to classical economists, wage rates will fall.

Keynes didn't see the adjustment as so simple. Instead, he asserted, employees will naturally resist an employer's efforts to cut wages, and labor unions may resist wage cuts. In short, wage rates may be inflexible in a downward direction.

If Keynes is correct and wage rates will not fall, is the economy then unable to get itself out of a recessionary gap? The unequivocal answer is yes. If employee and labor union resistance prevents wage rates from falling, then the *SRAS* curve will not shift to the right. If it does not shift to the right, the price level won't come down. If the price level does not come down, buyers will not purchase more goods and services and move the economy out of a recessionary gap. In terms of Exhibit 2, the economy is stuck at point 1. It cannot get to point 2.

Keynes believed that the economy is inherently unstable and that it may not automatically cure itself of a recessionary gap. *It may not be self-regulating.*

## Different Markets, Different Rates of Adjustment

Keynes's notion that wages may not fall to their equilibrium level brings up the issue of various markets and the adjustment path in each. Let's first look at a market in which prices equilibrate very quickly: the stock market. Consider the market for stock A. There is a demand for this stock and a supply of it. If the demand rises, the price of the stock will rise. If the demand falls, the price of the stock will fall. Stock prices are flexible (upward and downward), and they move quickly to their equilibrium value. For example, the demand for stock A might rise at 10 o'clock in the morning, and one minute later, at 10:01, the new higher equilibrium price of stock A is reached.

Now not all markets adjust to their equilibrium values as quickly as the stock market. Many economists argue that the labor market might be very different from the

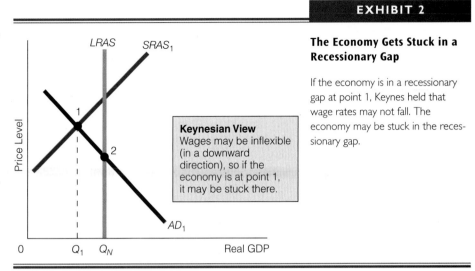

**EXHIBIT 2**

**The Economy Gets Stuck in a Recessionary Gap**

If the economy is in a recessionary gap at point 1, Keynes held that wage rates may not fall. The economy may be stuck in the recessionary gap.

**Keynesian View**
Wages may be inflexible (in a downward direction), so if the economy is at point 1, it may be stuck there.

stock market. Many economists argue that, in the labor market, wages may adjust very slowly to their new equilibrium values. For some period of time, wages may not adjust at all, especially when there is a surplus of labor and we would expect wages to decline.

Exhibit 3 shows the demand for and supply of labor. Currently, the labor market is in equilibrium at $W_1$. At this wage, the quantity demanded of labor equals the quantity supplied of labor, and both are 100 workers. Now let's suppose the demand for goods and services declines in the economy; that is, the aggregate demand (*AD*) curve shifts leftward. As a result of lower *AD* in the economy, firms are producing and selling fewer goods and services. Therefore, their demand for labor decreases; in Exhibit 3, the demand for labor curve shifts leftward from $D_1$ to $D_2$. If the labor market were like the stock market and equilibrated quickly to its new equilibrium wage rate ($W_2$), the labor market would move to point 2. Fewer people would be working at point 2 than at point 1, and the people who were working would be earning less ($W_2$ instead of $W_1$). Also, 25 people would have been fired.

Keynesian economists often argue that the labor market does not adjust the same way or as quickly as the stock market. In other words, wage rates aren't likely to fall simply because the demand for labor has declined (from $D_1$ to $D_2$). The wage rate $W_1$ is likely to be inflexible downward; that is, it isn't likely to *decline*—at least for some time.

Why is the wage rate inflexible downward? One explanation has to do with long-term labor contracts. To illustrate, suppose management and workers enter into a three-year contract that specifies a wage rate of $20 an hour for the duration of the contract. Management might want to enter into such a contract for two reasons: fewer labor negotiations and fewer worker strikes, both of which effectively diminish or disappear while the contract is in force. Workers want to

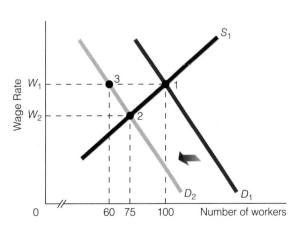

**EXHIBIT 3**

**The Labor Market and Inflexible Wages Downward**

We start with $D_1$ and $S_1$ and the labor market in equilibrium at point 1. The equilibrium wage rate is $W_1$. The demand for labor declines, and the new equilibrium wage rate is $W_2$. Will employers end up paying $W_2$? "Not necessarily," say economists who believe the wage rate (in the labor market) is inflexible downward. The reasons they offer include long-term labor contracts, fear of declining productivity resulting from lower wages, and avoiding having disgruntled workers in the workplace.

enter into such a contract also for two reasons: wage security and fewer strikes (strikes are costly for workers too).

There may also be solid microeconomic reasons for inflexible wages downward. Some economists argue that firms at times find it in their best interest to pay wage rates above equilibrium levels. For example, according to efficiency wage models, labor productivity depends on the wage rate that the firm pays its employees. Specifically, a cut in wages can cause a decline in labor productivity, which, in turn, raises the firm's costs. (Basically, these models say that workers are more productive when they are paid a higher wage than when paid a lower one.) By paying an above-equilibrium wage, firms provide an incentive to workers to be productive and to do less shirking, among other things. If shirking declines, so do the monitoring (management) costs of the firm.

**Efficiency Wage Models**
These models hold that it is sometimes in the best interest of business firms to pay their employees higher-than-equilibrium wage rates.

Refer again to Exhibit 3, and think of how things look from the perspective of the employer, the person hiring workers. The demand for labor has declined, and the new equilibrium wage rate is $W_2$. If the employer decides to go with the new equilibrium wage rate, two things will happen: The employer has to (1) fire 25 workers and (2) pay the 75 remaining workers a lower wage rate than they were previously receiving. This means the employer is likely to have to face 75 disgruntled workers every day. Now, disgruntled workers (who may not understand *why* the employer has decided to pay them less) are not likely to be the same as when they were paid more. They may be less productive, shirk more, perhaps even steal from the employer.

Will things be much different if the employer continues to pay $W_1$ and keeps 60 workers instead of 75 workers (in other words, fire 40 workers instead of 25)? Some economists argue that paying $W_1$ might be better for the employer than paying the lower wage of $W_2$. At $W_2$, the employer has 75 workers who are angry because they are being paid a lower wage—and the employer has to work with these 75 disgruntled workers every day. But if the employer pays $W_1$ instead of $W_2$ and fires 40 workers, they will all be disgruntled, but they won't be disgruntled *at work*. They are disgruntled *at home*, away from the employer. The remaining 60 workers are not disgruntled because they haven't had their wage rate lowered and they haven't been fired. In fact, they may appreciate their employer all the more for not cutting their wage rates and for not firing them.

To recap, Keynesian economists often argue that the labor market is not the same as the stock market. The stock market equilibrates quickly to changes in demand and supply. The labor market may adjust slowly. In particular, a lowered demand for labor may not be met with a declining wage rate. Wage rates might be inflexible downward (at least for some time). If wage rates are inflexible downward, then the self-regulating properties of an economy (discussed in Chapter 9) are in question. Specifically, an economy might get stuck in a recessionary gap, represented by point 1 in Exhibit 2.

## Keynes on Prices

Again, recall what classical economists (among others) believe occurs when a recessionary gap exists: Wage rates fall, the *SRAS* curve shifts to the right, and the price level begins to decrease—stop right there! The phrase "the price level begins to decrease" tells us that classical economists believe that prices in the economy are flexible: They move up and down in response to market forces.

Keynes said that the internal structure of an economy is not always competitive enough to allow prices to fall. Recall from Chapter 3 how the forces of supply and demand operate when price is above equilibrium. A surplus is generated, and price falls until the quantity supplied of the good equals the quantity demanded. Keynes suggested that anticompetitive or monopolistic elements in the economy sometimes prevent price from falling.

## The Financial and Economic Crisis of 2007–2009: Can a Housing Bust Lead to an Imploding Economy?

In the last chapter we discussed a self-regulating economy: When the economy is in a recessionary gap, it regulates itself back to long-run equilibrium. In this chapter, we state that an economy could get stuck in a recessionary gap if wages are inflexible downward. Some economists use the model in this chapter to explain the events of the latest financial and economic crisis.

Suppose an economy in long-run equilibrium undergoes a shock, such as the bursting of the housing bubble, with the prices of houses dropping. In the United States, housing prices started declining in mid-2006. Because the value of a house is a part of a person's overall wealth, a decline in it leads to a decline in a person's wealth. As a result of a decline in wealth, the person is poorer (or less rich) and consequently cuts back on consumption. A decline in consumption leads to a decline in aggregate demand, and so the aggregate demand curve shifts leftward, as in Exhibit 4(a), and the economy is now in a recessionary gap.

If the economy were self-regulating, it could get itself out of the recessionary gap. But if wages are inflexible downward, the economy is stuck in the recessionary gap.

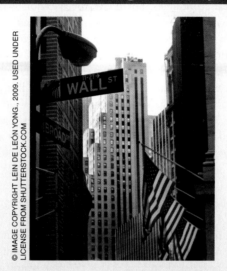

© IMAGE COPYRIGHT LEIN DE LEON YONG., 2009. USED UNDER LICENSE FROM SHUTTERSTOCK.COM

Look at the labor market in Exhibit 4(b). The labor market is initially in equilibrium at point 1. As a result of aggregate demand falling in the economy [see Exhibit 4(a)], firms are selling less output. So they do not need as much labor, and the demand for labor shifts leftward in Exhibit 4(b). Because the wage rate is flexible downward, the number of workers hired in the labor market falls from 10 million to 8 million. Two million workers are fired. As workers are fired, their incomes fall; as a result of lower incomes, individuals cut back on consumption. So aggregate demand shifts leftward again and into a deeper recessionary gap. See Exhibit 4(c).

What does this exposition tell us? A housing bust (declining house prices) can be the catalyst for an economy that falls into a recessionary gap. Further, if the economy is not self-regulating, a cascade of events can cause the economy to "implode" upon itself. A decline in aggregate demand leads to a recessionary gap that, if wages are inflexible downward, leads to some workers being fired, leading in turn to lower incomes and another decline in aggregate demand. Thus the recessionary gap deepens. Graphically, in Exhibit 4, instead of being between $Q_1$ and $Q_2$, the recessionary gap is between $Q_1$ and $Q_3$.

**EXHIBIT 4**

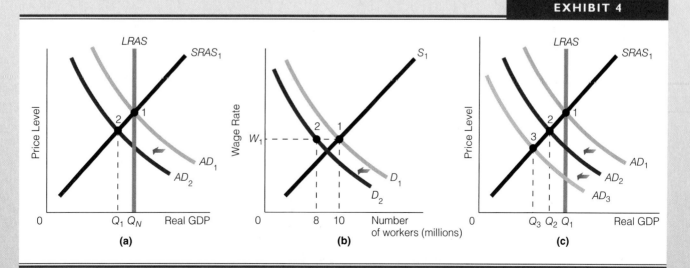

(a)　　　(b)　　　(c)

## Is It a Question of the Time It Takes for Wages and Prices to Adjust?

Classical economists believed that both wages and prices are flexible and adjust downward in a recessionary gap. Keynes, however, suggested that wages and prices are not flexible in a downward direction and may not adjust downward in a recessionary gap.

Many economists today take a position somewhere between Keynes's and that of the classical economists. For them, the question is not whether wages and prices are flexible downward, but *how long it takes for them to adjust downward.*

In Exhibit 5, suppose the economy is currently in a recessionary gap at point 1. The relevant short-run aggregate supply curve is $SRAS_1$, where the wage rate is $10 per hour and the price level is $P_1$. Classical economists expect the wage rate and price level will fall, whereas Keynes said this may not happen. But did Keynes mean that if the economy is in a recessionary gap, *the wage rate will never fall and the price level will never adjust downward?* Most economists think not. The question is *how long* the wage rate and price level will take to fall. Will they fall in a few weeks? In a few months? In five years? The question is relevant because the answer determines how long an economy will be in a recessionary gap and thus how long the economy takes to self-regulate.

Look at the question this way: If it takes only a few weeks or months for wage rates to fall (say, to $8 an hour), for the short-run aggregate supply curve to shift from $SRAS_1$ to $SRAS_2$, and for the price level to fall from $P_1$ to $P_2$, then, for all practical purposes, the economy is almost instantaneously self-regulating. But if all this takes years to happen, the economy can hardly be considered self-regulating over any reasonable amount of time.

The classical position is that the time required for wages and prices to adjust downward is short enough to call the economy self-regulating. The Keynesian position is that the time is long enough to say that the economy is not self-regulating. Instead, the Keynesians believe that the economy is inherently unstable and that it can exist in a recessionary gap for a long time.

### ⓣhinking like AN ECONOMIST

**Different Assumptions, Different Conclusions** The economist knows that assumptions affect conclusions. For example, classical economists assumed that wages are flexible, but Keynes assumed that wages might be inflexible at times. This difference in assumptions affects policy conclusions. For example, classical economists, assuming wages are flexible, will reach different policy conclusions than will Keynes, who is assuming wages are inflexible. ▪▪▪

---

**EXHIBIT 5**

**A Question of How Long It Takes for Wage Rates and Prices to Fall**

Suppose the economy is in a recessionary gap at point 1. Wage rates are $10 per hour, and the price level is $P_1$. The issue may not be whether wage rates and the price level fall, but how long they take to reach long-run levels. If they take a short time, then classical economists are right: The economy is self-regulating. If they take a long time—perhaps years—then Keynes is right: The economy is not self-regulating over any reasonable period of time.

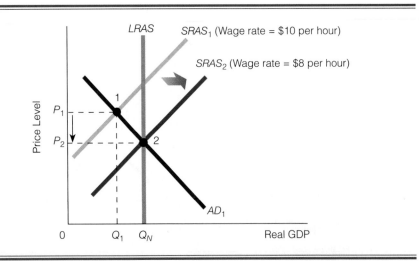

## Was Keynes a Revolutionary in Economics?

John Maynard Keynes was born in Cambridge, England, on June 5, 1883, and died at Tilton (in Sussex) on April 21, 1946. His father was John Neville Keynes, an eminent economist and author of *The Scope and Method of Political Economy*. Keynes's mother was one of the first female students to attend Cambridge University and for a time presided as mayor of the city of Cambridge.

Keynes was educated at Eton and at King's College, Cambridge, where he received a degree in mathematics in 1905. At Cambridge, he studied under the well-known and widely respected economist Alfred Marshall. In 1925, Keynes married Russian ballerina Lydia Lopokova. He was prominent in British social and intellectual circles and enjoyed art, theater, opera, debate, and collecting rare books.

Many economists rank Keynes's *The General Theory of Employment, Interest and Money* (published on February 4, 1936) alongside Adam Smith's *Wealth of Nations* and Karl Marx's *Das Kapital* as the most influential economic treatises ever written.

Before the publication of *The General Theory*, Keynes presented the ideas contained in the work in a series of university lectures that he gave between October 10, 1932, and December 2, 1935. Ten days after his last lecture, he sent off to the publisher the manuscript for what was to become *The General Theory*.

Keynes's lectures were said to be both shocking (he was pointing out the errors of the classical school) and exciting (he was proposing something new). One of the students at these lectures was Lorie Tarshis, who later wrote the first Keynesian introductory textbook, *The Elements of Economics*. In another venue, Tarshis wrote about

TIM GIDAL/PICTURE POST/GETTY IMAGES

the Keynes lectures and specifically about why Keynes's ideas were revolutionary.

*I attended that first lecture, naturally awed but bothered. As the weeks passed, only a stone would not have responded to the growing excitement these lectures generated. So I missed only two over the four years—two out of the thirty lectures. And like others, I would feel the urgency of the task. No wonder! These were the years when everything came loose; when sober dons and excitable students seriously discussed such issues as: Was capitalism not doomed? Should Britain not take the path of Russia or Germany to create jobs? Keynes obviously believed his analysis led to a third means to prosperity far less threatening to the values he prized, but until he had developed the theory and offered it in print, he knew that he could not sway government. So he saw his task as supremely urgent. I was also a bit surprised by his concern over too low a level of output. I had been assured by all I had read that the economy would bob to the surface, like a cork held under water—and output would rise, of its own accord, to an acceptable level. But Keynes proposed something far more shocking: that the economy could reach an equilibrium position with output far below capacity. That was an exciting challenge, sharply at variance with the views of Pigou and Marshall who represented "The Classical [Orthodox] School" in Cambridge, and elsewhere.[1]*

1. L. Tarshis, "Keynesian Revolution," in *The New Palgrave: A Dictionary of Economics*, vol. 3 (London: Macmillan Press, 1987), p. 48.

The following chart is a quick review of some of the differences in the views of the classical economists and Keynes.

| | **Classical Economists** | **Keynes** |
|---|---|---|
| **Say's Law** | Holds in a money economy. In other words, all output produced will be demanded. | May not hold in a money economy. In other words, more output may be produced than will be demanded. |
| **Savings** | Amount saved and interest rate are directly related. Savers save more at higher interest rates and save less at lower interest rates. | Savers may not save more at higher interest rates or save less at lower interest rates. If savers have a savings goal in mind, then a higher interest rate means savers can save less and still reach their goal. |
| **Investment** | Amount invested is inversely related to interest rate. Businesses invest more at lower interest rates and invest less at higher interest rates. | If expectations are pessimistic, a lower interest rate may not stimulate additional investment. |
| **Prices** | Flexible | May be inflexible downward. |
| **Wages** | Flexible | May be inflexible downward. |

## SELF-TEST

(Answers to Self-Test Questions are in Answers to Self-Test Questions at the back of the book.)

1. What do Keynesians mean when they say the economy is inherently unstable?

2. "What matters is not whether the economy is self-regulating, but whether prices and wages are flexible and adjust quickly." Comment.

3. According to Keynes, why might aggregate demand be too low?

# THE SIMPLE KEYNESIAN MODEL

Economists build models and theories to better understand the economic world. Of the many such models, we have already discussed a few: the theory of supply and demand and the classical theory of interest rates. In this section, we identify and discuss a few of the key components and themes of another prominent macroeconomics model: *the simple Keynesian model.*

## Assumptions

In the simple Keynesian model, certain simplifying assumptions hold.

- First, the price level is assumed to be constant until the economy reaches its full-employment or Natural Real GDP level.

- Second, there is no foreign sector: the model represents a *closed economy*, not an *open economy*. So total spending in the economy is the sum of consumption, investment, and government purchases.

- Third, the monetary side of the economy is excluded.

## The Consumption Function

Although Keynes was interested in the level of total spending in general, he was particularly concerned about consumption. Consumption (*C*) was a major concern because it is by far the largest slice of the total spending pie.

Keynes made three basic points about consumption:

1. Consumption depends on disposable income (income minus taxes).

2. Consumption and disposable income move in the same direction.

3. When disposable income changes, consumption changes by less.

These three points make a specific statement about the relationship between consumption and disposable income: the consumption function, which can written as:

$$C = C_0 + (MPC)(Y_d)$$

You know that $C$ is consumption, and we use $Y_d$ to specify disposable income. Let's look at $MPC$ and $C_0$. Think of consumption (as specified by the consumption function) as made up of two parts:

- *Autonomous consumption* $(C_0)$ is independent of disposable income.
- *Induced consumption* $[MPC(Y_d)]$ depends on disposable income.

$MPC$ stands for marginal propensity to consume, which is the ratio of the change in consumption to the change in disposable income:

$$\text{Marginal propensity to consume} = \frac{\text{Change in consumption}}{\text{Change in disposable income}}$$

$$MPC = \frac{\Delta C}{\Delta Y_d}$$

The Greek symbol delta ($\Delta$) stands for "change in." Thus, the $MPC$ is equal to the change in consumption divided by the change in disposable income. To illustrate, suppose consumption rises from $800 to $900 as disposable income rises from $1,000 to $1,200. If we divide the change in consumption ($100) by the change in disposable income ($200), we see that the $MPC$ equals 0.50. (Notice that the $MPC$ is always a positive number between 0 and 1 because of Keynes's points 2 and 3.)

$C_0$ is autonomous consumption, which changes *not* as disposable income changes, but rather due to other factors.

The difference between autonomous and induced consumption can be illustrated with an example. Suppose your taxes are lowered and your disposable income consequently rises. With more disposable income, you buy more goods and services (e.g., entertainment, books, DVDs). The increase in disposable income has *induced* you to consume more; hence the name *induced consumption*. Next, suppose that, even though your disposable income has not changed, for some reason you are consuming more. You might be consuming more medication because you have recently become ill, or you might be consuming more car maintenance services because your car just broke down. Whatever the reason, you are consuming more of various goods and services even though your disposable income has not changed at all. This type of consumption is autonomous (i.e., independent) of disposable income; hence the name *autonomous consumption*.

Look again at the consumption function:

$$\text{Consumption} = \text{Autonomous consumption}$$
$$+ (\text{Marginal propensity to consume} \times \text{Disposable income})$$
$$C = C_0 + (MPC \times Y_d)$$

**Consumption Function**
The relationship between consumption and disposable income. In the consumption function used in this text, consumption is directly related to disposable income and is positive even at zero disposable income: $C = C_0 + (MPC)(Y_d)$.

**Marginal Propensity to Consume (MPC)**
The ratio of the change in consumption to the change in disposable income: $MPC = \Delta C/\Delta Y_d$.

**Autonomous Consumption**
The part of consumption that is independent of disposable income.

Suppose $C_0$ is $800, the $MPC$ is 0.80, and $Y_d$ is $1,500, and we insert these numbers into the consumption function:

$$C = \$800 + (0.80 \times \$1,500) = \$800 + \$1,200 = \$2,000$$

So what will cause an increase in consumption? Consumption, $C$, will increase if any of the variables ($C_0$, $MPC$, or $Y_d$) increases. Thus, $C$ can be increased in three ways:

1. *Raise autonomous consumption.* Suppose in our example that autonomous consumption, $C_0$, goes from $800 to $1,000. This change will raise consumption to $2,200: $C = \$1,000 + (0.80 \times \$1,500) = \$2,200$.

2. *Raise disposable income.* Suppose disposable income, $Y_d$, goes from $1,500 to $1,800. This change will raise consumption to $2,240: $C = \$800 + (0.80 \times \$1,800) = \$2,240$. The increase in consumption from $2,000 to $2,240 is due to an increase of $240 in induced consumption, which the increase in disposable income induced.

3. *Raise the MPC.* Suppose the $MPC$ rises to 0.90. This change will raise consumption to $2,150: $C = \$800 + (0.90 \times \$1,500) = \$2,150$.

In Exhibit 6, $C_0$ is equal to $200 billion and the $MPC$ is equal to 0.80; thus, $C = \$200$ billion $+ (0.8)(Y_d)$. We then calculated different levels of consumption (column 3) for different levels of disposable income (column 1).

## Consumption and Saving

In Exhibit 6, we also calculated the saving levels (column 5) at the different disposable income levels. How did we calculate these levels? We know that $C = C_0 + (MPC)(Y_d)$ and that households can only consume or save. So it follows that saving, $S$, is the difference between disposable income and consumption:

$$\text{Saving} = \text{Disposable income} - \text{Consumption}$$
$$= \text{Disposable income} - [\text{Autonomous consumption}$$
$$+ (\text{Marginal propensity to consume} \times \text{Disposable income})]$$
$$S = Y_d - [C_0 - (MPC \times Y_d)]$$

---

**EXHIBIT 6**

**Consumption and Saving at Different Levels of Disposable Income (in billions)**

Our consumption function is $C = C_0 + (MPC)$ $(Y_d)$, where $C_0$ has been set at $200 billion and $MPC = 0.80$. Saving is the difference between $Y_d$ and $C$: $S = Y_d - [C_0 + (MPC)$ $(Y_d)]$. All dollar amounts are in billions.

| (1) Disposable Income $Y_d$ | (2) Change in Disposable Income $\Delta Y_d$ | (3) Consumption $C = C_0 + (MPC)(Y_d)$ | (4) Change in Consumption | (5) Saving $S = Y_d - [C_0 + (MPC)(Y_d)]$ | (6) Change in Saving |
|---|---|---|---|---|---|
| $ 800 | $___ | $ 840 | $___ | −$40 | $___ |
| 1,000 | 200 | 1,000 | 160 | 0 | 40 |
| 1,200 | 200 | 1,160 | 160 | 40 | 40 |
| 1,400 | 200 | 1,320 | 160 | 80 | 40 |
| 1,600 | 200 | 1,480 | 160 | 120 | 40 |
| 1,800 | 200 | 1,640 | 160 | 160 | 40 |

The marginal propensity to save (MPS) is the ratio of the change in saving to the change in disposable income:

$$\text{Marginal propensity to save} = \frac{\text{Change in saving}}{\text{Change in disposable income}}$$

$$MPS = \frac{\Delta S}{\Delta Y_d}$$

Disposable income can be used only for consumption or saving; that is, $C + S = Y_d$. So any change to disposable income can change only consumption or saving. Therefore, the marginal propensity to consume (MPC) plus the marginal propensity to save (MPS) must equal 1.

$$\text{Marginal propensity to consume} + \text{Marginal propensity to save} = 1$$

$$MPC + MPS = 1$$

In Exhibit 6, the MPC is 0.80; so the MPS is 0.20.

## The Multiplier

We know from the consumption function that a rise in autonomous consumption ($C_0$) will raise consumption ($C$) and, in turn, raise total spending. But *how much* will total spending rise? If $C_0$ rises by $40 billion, will total spending rise by $40 billion? According to Keynes, total spending would not rise by only $40 billion. The rise in $C_0$ will act as a catalyst to additional spending, and total spending will rise, in this case, by *more than* $40 billion.

For example, suppose an economy consists of 10 people, represented by the letters $A-J$. Person $A$ increases his autonomous consumption by buying $40 more additional goods from person $B$. Now person $B$ has witnessed an increase in her income of $40. According to Keynes, person $B$ will spend some fraction of this additional income, and how much she spends depends on her marginal propensity to consume (MPC). If her MPC is 0.80, then she will spend 80 percent of $40, or $32. If she spends this additional $32 on purchasing goods from person $C$, then person $C$'s income rises by $32 and now he will spend some percentage of that additional income. Again, how much he will spend depends on his MPC. If we again assume that the MPC is 0.80, then person $C$ spends $25.60.

Person $A$ increases his *autonomous consumption* by $40 →

This generates $40 *additional income* for person $B$ →

Person $B$ increases her *consumption* by $32 →

This generates $32 *additional income* for person $C$ →

Person $C$ increases his *consumption* by $25.60 →

And so on and so on.

This is the *multiplier process*: An initial rise in autonomous consumption leads to a rise in consumption for one person, generating additional income for another person, and leading to additional consumption spending by that person, and so on and so on.

Suppose we sum the initial rise in autonomous spending ($40) and all the additional spending it generates through the multiplier process. How much additional spending will have been generated? In other words, by how much will total expenditures rise?

**Marginal Propensity to Save (MPS)**
The ratio of the change in saving to the change in disposable income: $MPS = \Delta S/\Delta Y_d$.

**Multiplier**
The number that is multiplied by the change in autonomous spending to obtain the overall change in total spending. The multiplier (*m*) is equal to 1 ÷ (1 − *MPC*). If the economy is operating below Natural Real GDP, then the multiplier is the number that is multiplied by the change in autonomous spending to obtain the change in Real GDP.

The answer depends on the value of the multiplier. The multiplier (*m*) is equal to 1 divided by 1 − *MPC*.

$$\text{Multiplier } (m) = \frac{1}{1 - MPC}$$

For example, if the $MPC = 0.80$ (in each round of spending), then the multiplier equals 5:

$$\begin{aligned} \text{Multiplier } (m) &= \frac{1}{1 - MPC} \\ &= \frac{1}{1 - 0.80} \\ &= \frac{1}{0.20} \\ &= 5 \end{aligned}$$

Our original increase in autonomous consumption ($40), multiplied by the multiplier (5), equals $200. So in our example, a $40 increase in autonomous consumption would increase total spending by $200.

Just as consumption has an autonomous spending component, so do investment and government purchases. The multiplier process holds for these sectors too.

The process also holds for a decrease in autonomous spending by one of these sectors of total spending. So, in general,

Change in total spending = Multiplier × Change in autonomous spending

To illustrate, suppose business owners become optimistic about the future of the economy. They believe that members of the household and government sectors will soon start buying more goods and services. In the expectation of better times, businesses buy more factories and capital goods, and so investment spending rises. In this case, investment spending has risen, even without any change in income or Real GDP; hence, the rise is in autonomous investment spending. According to the multiplier analysis, this additional autonomous investment spending will change total spending by some multiple. For example, if the multiplier is 5, then a $1 increase in autonomous investment will raise total spending by $5.

## The Multiplier and Reality

So, in simple terms, a change in autonomous spending leads to a *greater change* in total spending. Also, in the simple Keynesian model, the change in total spending is *equal to* the change in Real GDP (assuming that the economy is operating below Natural Real GDP). The reason is that, in the model, prices are assumed to be constant until Natural GDP is reached; so any change in nominal total spending is equal to the change in *real* total spending.

However, two reality checks are necessary. First, the multiplier takes time to have an effect. In a textbook, going from an initial increase in autonomous spending to a multiple increase in either total spending or Real GDP takes only seconds. In the real world, this process takes many months.

Second, for the multiplier to increase Real GDP, *idle resources must exist at each spending round.* After all, if Real GDP is increasing (output is increasing) at each spending round, *idle resources must be available to be brought into production.* If they are not available, then increased spending will simply result in higher prices without an increase in Real GDP. Simply put, GDP will increase but not Real GDP.

# economics 24/7

## The Multiplier on Spring Break

During the weeklong spring break, many college students put away their books; pack their shorts, swimsuits, and tanning oil; jump into their cars; and head for the beaches. As they are driving to Fort Lauderdale, Galveston, Myrtle Beach, Daytona Beach, San Diego, and other coastal cities, the multiplier is getting ready to go to work.

Look at it this way. When college students from around the country head for, say, Daytona Beach, they have dollars in their pockets. They will spend many of these dollars in Daytona Beach on food and drink, motel rooms, dance clubs, and so on. As far as Daytona Beach is concerned, the dollars represent autonomous spending. More important, the dollars can raise the total income of Daytona Beach by some multiple. College students buy pizzas, beer, and sodas. The people who sell these items find their incomes rising. They, in turn, spend some fraction of their increase in income, generating additional income for

AP PHOTO/DAYTONA BEACH NEWS-JOURNAL, JIM TILLER

still others, who spend some fraction of their increase in income, and so on and so on.

For example, suppose college students spend $7 million in Daytona Beach during spring break. If the MPC is, say, 0.60 in Daytona Beach and if all the added income generated is spent in Daytona Beach, then college students will increase nominal income in that town by $17.5 million:

$$\frac{1}{1 - MPC} \times \$7 \text{ million}$$
$$= \frac{1}{0.40} \times \$7 \text{ million}$$
$$= 2.5 \times \$7 \text{ million}$$
$$= \$17.5 \text{ million}$$

Do the people who live in Daytona Beach want college students to visit their city during spring break? Many of them do because it means extra dollars in their pockets. College students from out of town, together with the multiplier, often make for robust economic times!

### SELF-TEST

1. How is autonomous consumption different from consumption?

2. If the MPC is 0.70, what does the multiplier equal?

3. What happens to the multiplier as the MPC falls?

# THE SIMPLE KEYNESIAN MODEL IN THE *AD−AS* FRAMEWORK

The first section of this chapter presented a few of Keynes's criticisms of the self-regulating economy, or classical position. The second section identified and discussed some of the key components of the simple Keynesian model, particularly the consumption function and the multiplier. In this section, we analyze the simple Keynesian model in terms of the aggregate demand and aggregate supply (*AD−AS*) framework. In the next section, we discuss the simple Keynesian model in terms of the total expenditures and total production (*TE−TP*) framework.[2]

---

2. Some instructors may choose to assign only one of these two sections. It is clear at the end of the chapter which questions and problems go with which sections.

## Shifts in the Aggregate Demand Curve

Because there is no foreign sector in the simple Keynesian model, total spending consists of consumption ($C$), investment ($I$), and government purchases ($G$). Because the economy has no monetary side, changes in any of these variables ($C, I, G$) can shift the $AD$ curve. For example, a rise in consumption will shift the $AD$ curve to the right; a decrease in investment will shift it to the left.

Let's consider aggregate demand in terms of what we know about the consumption function and the multiplier. A rise in autonomous consumption ($C_0$) will raise consumption ($C$) and therefore shift the $AD$ curve to the right. How much the $AD$ curve will shift depends on the multiplier. In our earlier example, autonomous consumption $C_0$ increases by $40, and the multiplier ($m$) is 5.

$$\text{Change in total spending} = \text{Multiplier} \times \text{Change in autonomous spending}$$
$$= m \times \Delta C_0$$
$$= 5 \times \$40$$
$$= \$200$$

Exhibit 7 illustrates how the $AD$ curve shifts in this situation. The original aggregate demand curve is $AD_1$. Autonomous consumption ($C_0$) rises by $40, shifting the curve to $AD_2$, but the $AD$ curve does not stay here. Because of the multiplier, the initial autonomous consumption spending generates more spending, eventually pushing the $AD$ curve to $AD_3$. In other words, at the end of the process, the $AD$ curve has shifted from $AD_1$ to $AD_3$. Part of this shift ($40) is due to the initial rise in autonomous consumption, and part ($160) is due to the multiplier.

## The Keynesian Aggregate Supply Curve

As noted, in the simple Keynesian model, the price level is assumed to be constant until it reaches its full-employment or Natural Real GDP level. What does this assumption say about the Keynesian aggregate supply curve?

Think back to the discussions of aggregate demand and aggregate supply in the last two chapters and in the first section of this chapter. The $AD$ curve is downward sloping, and the $SRAS$ curve is upward sloping. Therefore, any shift in the $AD$ curve (rightward or leftward) will automatically change (raise or lower) the price level. If the price level is assumed to be constant, then the Keynesian aggregate supply curve must have a horizontal section.

As shown in Exhibit 8, the Keynesian aggregate supply ($AS$) curve has both a horizontal section and a vertical section. The $AS$ curve is horizontal until $Q_N$, or Natural Real GDP, because the simple Keynesian model assumes that the price level is constant until $Q_N$ is reached. Given this $AS$ curve, what happens in the economy when the $AD$ curve shifts? An increase in aggregate demand from $AD_1$ to $AD_2$ raises Real GDP from $Q_1$ to $Q_2$ but does not change the price level. (The price level remains at $P_1$.) On the other hand, once the economy has reached $Q_N$, any increases in aggregate demand change the price level. For example, an increase in aggregate demand from

**EXHIBIT 7**

**The Multiplier and Aggregate Demand**

An initial increase in autonomous consumption raises total spending and shifts the aggregate demand curve from $AD_1$ to $AD_2$. The $AD$ curve does not end here, however. Because of the multiplier, the increase in autonomous spending generates additional income and additional spending, shifting the aggregate demand curve to $AD_3$.

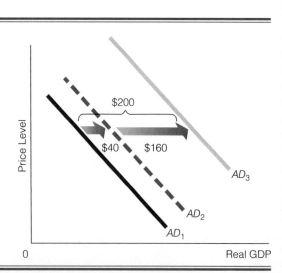

$AD_3$ to $AD_4$ raises the price level from $P_2$ to $P_3$.

According to Keynes, a change in autonomous spending (e.g., a change in autonomous consumption) will stimulate additional spending in the economy. In our example, a rise in autonomous consumption of $40 generated an additional $160 worth of spending so that total spending increased by $200. (The multiplier was 5 because we assumed the *MPC* was 0.80.)

Consider this question: Under what condition will a $200 *increase in total spending* lead to a $200 *increase in Real GDP*? That happens when the

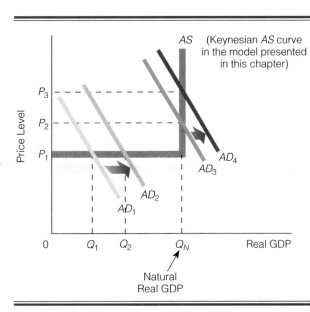

**EXHIBIT 8**

**The *AS* Curve in the Simple Keynesian Model**

The *AS* curve in the simple Keynesian model is horizontal until $Q_N$ (Natural Real GDP) and vertical at $Q_N$. It follows that any changes in aggregate demand in the horizontal section do not change the price level, but any changes in aggregate demand in the vertical section do change the price level.

aggregate supply curve is horizontal, that is (in the simple Keynesian model), when the economy is currently producing less than Natural Real GDP. In other words, the *AD* curve in the economy must be shifting rightward (due to the increased spending) but must be within the *horizontal section* of the Keynesian *AS* curve.

# finding ECONOMICS

**In Unchanging Prices** Suppose you read in the newspaper that the three sectors of a closed economy (household, business, and government) are all spending more but that, so far, there has been little to no change in the price level. Where is the economics?

The picture that should come to mind is the Keynesian aggregate supply curve—in particular, the horizontal section of the curve. Increases in aggregate demand in the horizontal section of the aggregate supply curve do not raise the price level. ▲ ▲ ▲

## The Economy in a Recessionary Gap

If, according to classical economists, the economy is self-regulating, then a recessionary gap or an inflationary gap is only temporary. In time, the economy moves into long-run equilibrium and produces Natural Real GDP ($Q_N$).

Keynes did not accept that the economy always works this way, believing rather that the economy could get stuck in a recessionary gap. As shown in Exhibit 9, the economy could therefore be stuck at $Q_1$ (its equilibrium position) and unable to get to $Q_N$ on its own. In other words, the economy is at point *A*, and it is not able to get to point *B*. Keynes believed that the private sector—consisting of the household and business sectors—may not be able to move the economy from point *A* to point *B*. Stated differently, neither consumption nor investment will rise enough to shift the aggregate demand curve from its current position ($AD_1$).

But suppose the interest rate in the economy falls. Won't this be enough to get businesses to invest more, and thus won't the *AD* curve begin to shift rightward, headed for point *B*? Not necessarily, said Keynes, who didn't believe that investment spending was always responsive to changes in interest rates. For example, suppose businesses are pessimistic about future sales, and the interest rate drops. Are businesses going to invest more just because interest rates have dropped, or might they feel so pessimistic that they choose not to invest, despite the lower interest rate? Keynes believed that the latter scenario could be the case.

**EXHIBIT 9**

**Can the Private Sector Remove the Economy from a Recessionary Gap?**

The economy is at point $A$ producing $Q_1$. $Q_1$ is less than $Q_N$, so the economy is in a recessionary gap. The question is whether the private sector (consisting of consumption and investment spending) can remove the economy from the recessionary gap by increasing spending enough to shift the aggregate demand curve rightward to go through point $B$. Keynes believed that sometimes it could not. No matter how low interest rates fell, investment spending would not rise because of pessimistic business expectations with respect to future sales.

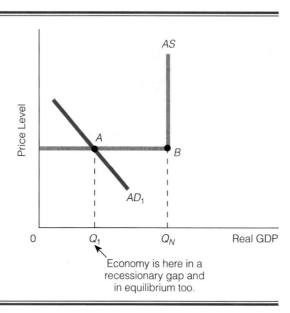

Economy is here in a recessionary gap and in equilibrium too.

## Government's Role in the Economy

In the self-regulating economy of the classical economists, government does not have a management role to play. The private sector (households and businesses) is capable of self-regulating the economy at its Natural Real GDP level. On the other hand, Keynes believed that the economy is not self-regulating and that economic instability is a possibility. In other words, the economy could get stuck in a recessionary gap.

Economic instability opens the door to government's playing a role in the economy. According to Keynes and to many Keynesians, if the private sector cannot self-regulate the economy at its Natural Real GDP level, then maybe the government must help. In terms of Exhibit 9, maybe the government has a role to play in shifting the $AD$ curve rightward so that it goes through point $B$. We discuss the role government might play in the economy in the next chapter.

## ⓣhinking like AN ECONOMIST

**From How the Economy Works to One's Policy Positions** An economist's view of the economy (how the economy works) and policy suggestions are often linked. For example, classical economists and their modern-day counterparts, who view the economy as inherently stable, believe in a laissez-faire policy: Government should keep its hands off the economy. Keynesians, however, who view the economy as inherently unstable, suggest that government has an economic role to play. In short, policy suggestions are sometimes a consequence of how one views the internal, or inherent, workings of an economy. ▪ ▪ ▪

## The Theme of the Simple Keynesian Model

In terms of $AD$ and $AS$, the essence of the simple Keynesian model can be summarized in five statements:

1. The price level is constant until Natural Real GDP is reached.

2. The $AD$ curve shifts if there are changes in $C$, $I$, or $G$.

3. According to Keynes, the economy could be in equilibrium and in a recessionary gap too. In other words, the economy can be at point $A$ in Exhibit 9.

4. The private sector may not be able to get the economy out of a recessionary gap. In other words, the private sector (households and businesses) may not be able to increase $C$ or $I$ enough to get the $AD$ curve in Exhibit 9 to intersect the $AS$ curve at point $B$.

5. The government may have a management role to play in the economy. According to Keynes, government may have to raise aggregate demand enough to stimulate the economy to move it out of the recessionary gap and to its Natural Real GDP level.

6. We show the simple Keynesian model in the $AD$–$AS$ framework in Exhibit 10 in both flowchart form (a) and in diagrammatic form (b).

**EXHIBIT 10**

**The Simple Keynesian Model in the AD−AS Framework**

The purpose of the simple Keynesian model is to explain changes in Real GDP. In (a) the model is presented as a flowchart. Real GDP is determined by aggregate demand and aggregate supply. Aggregate demand depends on C, consumption; I, investment; and G, government purchases. In (b) we show a diagrammatic exposition of the model in the AD−AS framework.

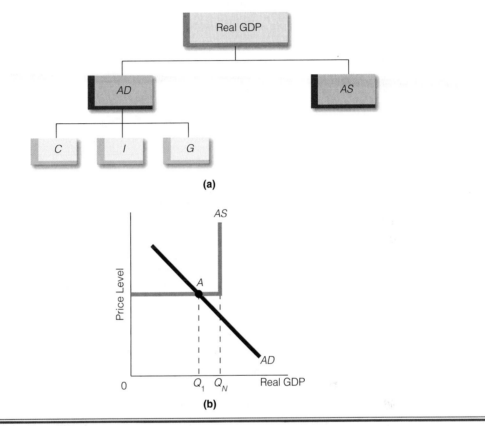

(a)

(b)

1. What was Keynes's position on the self-regulating properties of an economy?

2. What will happen to Real GDP if autonomous spending rises and the economy is operating in the horizontal section of the Keynesian AS curve? Explain your answer.

3. An economist who believes the economy is self-regulating is more likely to advocate laissez-faire than one who believes the economy is inherently unstable. Do you agree or disagree? Explain your answer.

# THE SIMPLE KEYNESIAN MODEL IN THE *TE− TP* FRAMEWORK

Just as a story can be told into different languages, an economic model can be presented in various frameworks. The last section presented the simple Keynesian model in terms of the familiar (diagrammatic) *AD−AS* framework of analysis. But the simple Keynesian model was first presented not in terms of *AD−AS*, but in terms of the *TE− TP* framework. This framework has been known by different names, three of which are the Keynesian cross, income expenditure, and total expenditure–total production. In our discussion, we will refer to it as total expenditure–total production, or simply the *TE− TP* framework.

## Deriving a Total Expenditures (TE) Curve

Just as we derived *AD* and *AS* curves in the *AD–AS* framework, we want to derive a total expenditures (*TE*) curve in the *TE–TP* framework. Total expenditures are the sum of its parts: consumption, investment, and government purchases. To derive a *TE* curve, first derive a diagrammatic representation of consumption, investment, and government purchases, as shown in Exhibit 11.

### EXHIBIT 11

**The Derivation of the Total Expenditures (TE) Curve**

At different levels of Real GDP, we sum consumption (a), investment (b), and government purchases (c) to derive *TE* curve (d).

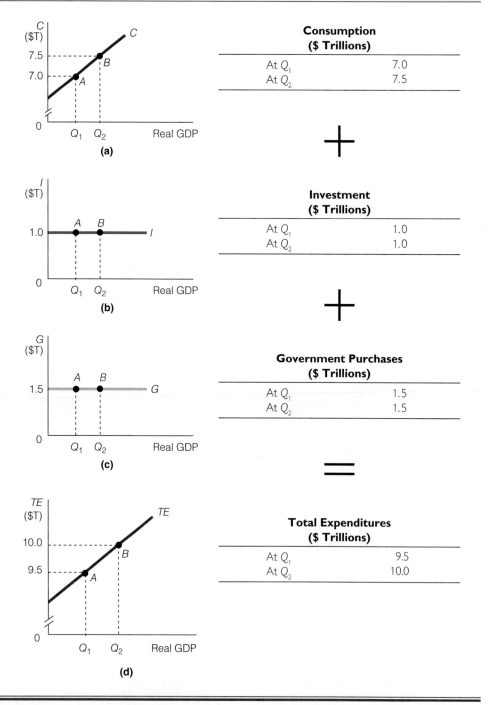

**Consumption ($ Trillions)**

| | |
|---|---|
| At $Q_1$ | 7.0 |
| At $Q_2$ | 7.5 |

**Investment ($ Trillions)**

| | |
|---|---|
| At $Q_1$ | 1.0 |
| At $Q_2$ | 1.0 |

**Government Purchases ($ Trillions)**

| | |
|---|---|
| At $Q_1$ | 1.5 |
| At $Q_2$ | 1.5 |

**Total Expenditures ($ Trillions)**

| | |
|---|---|
| At $Q_1$ | 9.5 |
| At $Q_2$ | 10.0 |

1. *Consumption.* As disposable income rises, so does consumption, as shown arithmetically in columns (1) and (3) of Exhibit 6. Because the *MPC* is less than 1, consumption rises by less than disposable income rises. Consumption also rises as Real GDP rises, but again by a smaller percentage. For example, if Real GDP rises by $100, consumption may rise by $80. Exhibit 11(a) shows consumption as an upward-sloping curve. Notice that as Real GDP rises from $Q_1$ to $Q_2$, consumption rises from $7 trillion to $7.5 trillion.

2. *Investment.* To simplify things in deriving *TE*, the investment curve in Exhibit 11(b) is constant at $1 trillion, whether Real GDP is $Q_1$ or $Q_2$.

3. *Government purchases.* We simplify the government spending curve too. In Exhibit 11(c), government purchases are constant at $1.5 trillion, regardless of the amount of Real GDP.

Exhibit 11(d) shows a *TE* curve. We simply added the components of total expenditures at the two Real GDP levels ($Q_1$ and $Q_2$), plotted the relevant points, and then drew a line through the points. At $Q_1$, total expenditures are $9.5 trillion, and at $Q_2$, they are $10.0 trillion. The *TE* curve is upward-sloping.

## What Will Shift the *TE* Curve?

The *TE* curve in the *TE−TP* framework plays the same role as the *AD* curve in the *AD−AS* framework. Both the *AD* curve and the *TE* curve shift with a change in *C, I,* or *G*. For example, a rise in *C* will shift the *TE* curve upward; a decline in *I* will shift the *TE* curve downward.

## Comparing Total Expenditures (*TE*) and Total Production (*TP*)

Businesses produce the goods and services that are bought in the three sectors of the economy (household, business, and government). Sometimes, though, businesses produce too much or too little in comparison to what the three sectors buy. For example, suppose businesses produce $10 trillion worth of goods and services, but the three sectors buy only $9.5 trillion worth. In this case, businesses have produced too much relative to what the three sectors of the economy buy.

Alternatively, businesses might produce $10 trillion worth of goods and services, but the three sectors of the economy buy $10.5 trillion worth. In this case, businesses have produced too little relative to what the three sectors of the economy buy. (If you are wondering how the three sectors of the economy can possibly buy more than businesses produce, the answer has to do with the goods that businesses hold in inventory. We will soon explain the process.)

Finally, businesses could produce $10 trillion worth of goods and services, and the three sectors of the economy could buy exactly $10 trillion worth. In this case, businesses have produced exactly the right amount of goods and services.

Thus, the economy may be in one of three possible states in the *TE−TP* framework: The total expenditures (*TE*) of the three sectors of the economy can be less than, greater than, or equal to the dollar value of total production (*TP*). In other words:

$$TE < TP$$
$$TE > TP$$
$$TE = TP$$

According to many economists, if the economy is currently operating where $TE < TP$ or $TE > TP$ (both states are described as disequilibrium), it will eventually move to where $TE = TP$ (where the economy is in equilibrium). The next section explains how this happens.

## ⓣhinking like AN ECONOMIST

**Thinking in Threes** The concept of threes first came up when we discussed a single market (in Chapter 3), specifically when we said that a market could be in equilibrium, shortage, or surplus. In other words, a market had three possible states. In Chapter 9, we said the economy could be producing a Real GDP level either greater than, less than, or equal to Natural Real GDP; that is, an economy may have three possible states. Now we are saying that total expenditures (*TE*) can be either less than, greater than, or equal to total production—once again, three possible states. ▪ ▪ ▪

## Moving from Disequilibrium to Equilibrium

Business firms hold an inventory of their goods to guard against unexpected changes in the demand for their product. For example, General Motors may hold an inventory of a certain type of car in case the demand for it unexpectedly and suddenly increases.

Although we know why business firms hold an inventory of their goods, we don't know *how much* inventory they will hold. For example, we do not know whether General Motors will hold an inventory of 1,000 cars, 2,000 cars, or 10,000 cars. (Inventories are usually held in terms of, say, a 45- or 60-day supply, but we have simplified things.) We do know that General Motors and all other business firms have some *optimum inventory*, which is "just the right amount" of inventory—not too much and not too little. With this in mind, consider two cases that illustrate how business inventory levels play an important role in the economy's adjustment from disequilibrium to equilibrium in the *TE–TP* framework.

CASE 1: *TE < TP* Assume that business firms hold an optimum inventory level of $300 billion worth of goods, that the firms produce $11 trillion worth of goods and services, and that the three sectors of the economy buy $10.8 trillion worth of goods and services. In this case, producers produce more than individuals buy (*TE < TP*). The difference is added to inventories, and inventory levels rise unexpectedly to $500 billion, which is $200 billion more than the $300 billion that firms see as optimal.

This unexpected rise in inventories signals to firms that they have *overproduced*. Consequently, they cut back on the quantity of goods they are producing. The cutback in production causes Real GDP to fall, bringing Real GDP closer to the (lower) output level that the three sectors of the economy are willing and able to buy. Ultimately, *TP* will equal *TE*.

CASE 2: *TE > TP* Assume that business firms hold their optimum inventory level ($300 billion worth of goods), that they produce $10.4 trillion worth of goods, and that members of the three sectors buy $10.6 trillion worth of goods. How can individuals buy more than businesses produce? Firms make up the difference out of inventory. In our example, inventory levels fall from $300 billion to $100 billion because individuals purchase $200 billion more of goods than firms produced (to be sold). This is why firms maintain inventories in the first place: to be able to meet an unexpected increase in sales.

The unexpected fall in inventories signals to firms that they have *underproduced*. Consequently, they increase the quantity of goods they produce. The rise in production causes Real GDP to rise, in the process bringing Real GDP closer to the (higher) real output that the three sectors are willing and able to buy. Ultimately, *TP* will equal *TE*.

THE GRAPHICAL REPRESENTATION OF THE THREE STATES OF THE ECONOMY IN THE *TE–TP* FRAMEWORK The three states of the economy are represented in Exhibit 12. The exhibit shows a *TE* curve, which we derived earlier, and a *TP* curve, which is simply a 45-degree line (45 degrees because it bisects the 90-degree angle at the origin). Notice that, at any point on the *TP* curve, total production is equal to Real

**EXHIBIT 12**

**The Three States of the Economy in the *TE − TP* Framework**

At $Q_E$, $TE = TP$ and the economy is in equilibrium. At $Q_1$, $TE < TP$. This results in an unexpected increase in inventories, which signals firms that they have overproduced, which leads firms to cut back production. The cutback in production reduces Real GDP. The economy tends to move from $Q_1$ to $Q_E$. At $Q_2$, $TE > TP$. This results in an unexpected decrease in inventories, which signals firms that they have underproduced, which leads firms to raise production. The increased production raises Real GDP. The economy tends to move from $Q_2$ to $Q_E$.

GDP ($TP$ = Real GDP).[3] This is because $TP$ and Real GDP are different names for the same thing. Real GDP, remember, is simply the total market value of all final goods and services produced annually within a country's borders, adjusted for price changes.

Look at the three Real GDP levels in the exhibit. At $Q_1$, Real GDP is $11 trillion. At this Real GDP level, $TE$ is $10.8 trillion and $TP$ is $11 trillion. This illustrates Case 1, in which producers produce more than individuals buy ($TE < TP$), with the difference added to inventories. This unexpected rise in inventories signals to firms that they have overproduced, and consequently they cut back on the quantity of goods they produce. The cutback in production causes Real GDP to fall, ultimately bringing Real GDP down to $Q_E$ ($10.7 trillion in the exhibit).

Now look at $Q_2$, where Real GDP is $10.4 trillion. At this Real GDP level, $TE$ equals $10.6 trillion and $TP$ equals $10.4 trillion. This illustrates Case 2, in which the three sectors of the economy buy more goods and services than business firms have produced ($TE > TP$). Business firms draw from inventories to make up the difference between what they have produced and what the three sectors of the economy buy. Inventories then fall below optimum levels, and consequently businesses increase the quantity of goods they produce. The rise in production causes Real GDP to rise, ultimately moving Real GDP up to $Q_E$ (again, $10.7 trillion).

When the economy is producing $Q_E$, or $10.7 trillion worth of goods and services, it is in equilibrium. At this Real GDP level, $TP$ and $TE$ are the same at $10.7 trillion. The following table summarizes some key points about the state of the economy in the $TE - TP$ framework.

---

3. Earlier, we said that the $TE$ curve plays the role in the $TE - TP$ framework that the $AD$ curve plays in the $AD - AS$ framework. In other words, roughly speaking, the $AD$ curve is the $TE$ curve. Similarly, the $TP$ curve plays the role in the $TE - TP$ framework that the $AS$ curve plays in the $AD - AS$ framework. In other words, roughly speaking, the $TP$ curve is the $AS$ curve. In the $AD - AS$ framework, equilibrium is at the intersection of the $AD$ and $AS$ curves. As you will soon learn, in the $TE - TP$ framework, equilibrium is at the intersection of the $TE$ and $TP$ curves.

| State of the Economy | What Happens to Inventories? | What Do Firms Do? |
|---|---|---|
| $TE < TP$ Individuals are buying less output than firms produce. | Inventories rise above optimum levels. | Firms cut back production to reduce inventories to their optimum levels. |
| $TE > TP$ Individuals are buying more output than firms produce. | Inventories fall below optimum levels. | Firms increase production to raise inventories to their optimum levels. |
| $TE = TP$ | Inventories are at their optimum levels. | Firms neither increase nor decrease production. |

## The Economy in a Recessionary Gap and the Role of Government

According to Keynes, the economy can be in equilibrium and in a recessionary gap too, as explained in the section on the simple Keynesian model in the $AD-AS$ framework. [To review, look back at Exhibit 10(b).] The same situation can exist in the $TE-TP$ framework. For example, in Exhibit 12, the economy equilibrates at point $E$ and thus produces a Real GDP level of $10.7 trillion worth of goods and services. However, there is no guarantee that the Real GDP level of $10.7 trillion is the Natural Real GDP level. As shown in Exhibit 13, the economy could be in equilibrium at point $A$, producing $Q_E$, when the Natural Real GDP level is $Q_N$. Because the economy is producing at a Real GDP level that is less than Natural Real GDP, it is in a recessionary gap.

How does the economy get out of the recessionary gap? Will the private sector (households and businesses) be capable of pushing the $TE$ curve in Exhibit 13 upward so that it goes through point $B$ so that $Q_N$ is produced? According to Keynes, the economy is not necessarily going to do so. Keynes believed that government may be necessary to get the economy out of a recessionary gap. For example, government may have to raise its purchases (raise $G$) so that the $TE$ curve shifts upward and goes through point $B$.

## Equilibrium in the Economy

Of the many debates in macroeconomics, one concerns equilibrium in the economy: where the economy naturally ends up after all adjustments have been made. As explained in the last chapter, some economists believe that the economy is self-regulating and that an economy naturally ends up in the long run producing Natural Real GDP. In this chapter, we have talked about economists who believe that the economy can be inherently unstable and that it can naturally end up producing a level of Real GDP less than Natural Real GDP. To the first group of economists, equilibrium is a desirable state of affairs; to the second group, equilibrium may not be if Real GDP is less than Natural Real GDP.

---

**EXHIBIT 13**

**The Economy: In Equilibrium, and in a Recessionary Gap Too**

Using the $TE-TP$ framework, the economy is currently in equilibrium at point $A$, producing $Q_E$. Natural Real GDP, however, is greater than $Q_E$, so the economy is in a recessionary gap as well as being in equilibrium.

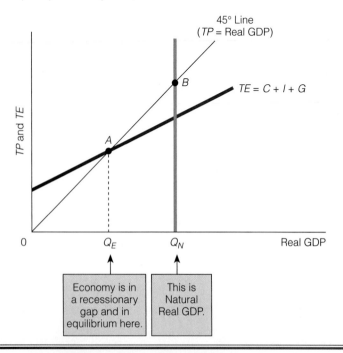

## The Theme of the Simple Keynesian Model

In terms of *TE* and *TP*, the essence of the simple Keynesian model can be summed up in five statements:

1. The price level is constant until Natural Real GDP is reached.

2. The *TE* curve shifts if there are changes in *C, I,* or *G.*

3. According to Keynes, the economy could be in equilibrium and in a recessionary gap too. In other words, the economy can be at point *A* in Exhibit 13.

4. The private sector may not be able to get the economy out of a recessionary gap. In other words, the private sector (households and businesses) may not be able to increase *C* or *I* enough to get the *TE* curve in Exhibit 13 to rise and pass through point *B.*

5. The government may have a management role to play in the economy. According to Keynes, government may have to raise *TE* enough to stimulate the economy to move it out of the recessionary gap and to its Natural Real GDP level.

We show the simple Keynesian model in the *TE−TP* framework in Exhibit 14 in both flowchart form (a) and in diagrammatic form (b).

---

**SELF-TEST**

1. What happens in the economy if total production (*TP*) is greater than total expenditures (*TE*)?

2. What happens in the economy if total expenditures (*TE*) are greater than total production (*TP*)?

---

**EXHIBIT 14**

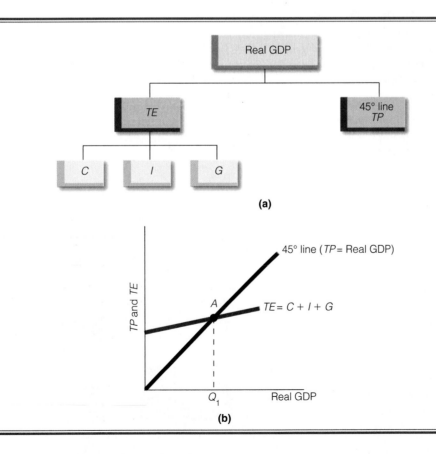

**(a)**

**(b)**

**The Simple Keynesian Model in the *TE–TP* Framework**

The purpose of the simple Keynesian model is to explain changes in Real GDP. In (a) the model is presented as a flowchart. Real GDP is determined by total expenditures (*TE*) and total product (*TP*). Total expenditures (*TE*) depend on *C*, consumption; *I*, investment; and *G*, government purchases. In (b) is a diagrammatic exposition of the model in the *TE−TP* framework.

## "Does a Lot Depend on Whether Wages are Flexible or Inflexible?"

**STUDENT:**

Can what we learned in this chapter be seen as a criticism of what we learned in the last chapter?

**INSTRUCTOR:**

Much of it can be viewed as a criticism. Specifically, in the last chapter you learned the views of economists who believe that the economy *is* self-regulating. In this chapter you learned the views of economists who believe that the economy *is not always* self-regulating.

**STUDENT:**

What is at the heart of the disagreement between these two groups of economists?

**INSTRUCTOR:**

That's a good question. One thing at the heart of the disagreement is whether wages are flexible or inflexible. To illustrate, look back at Exhibit 2. There you see an economy in a recessionary gap. Now if wages are flexible (as stated in the last chapter), then they will soon fall, and the *SRAS* curve in Exhibit 2 will shift to the right. In time, the economy will remove itself from a recessionary gap, to point 2 in the exhibit. However, if wages are inflexible downward (as stated in this chapter), then wages will not fall, the *SRAS* will not shift to the right, and the economy will remain stuck—at point 1 in the exhibit—in a recessionary gap.

**STUDENT:**

Suppose the economists who say the economy can get stuck in a recessionary gap are right. What then? Does the economy just stay stuck forever?

**INSTRUCTOR:**

What these economists usually propose is a government response. Specifically, they advocate fiscal or monetary policy to get the economy unstuck. We haven't discussed either fiscal or monetary policy yet, but we plan to in the next chapter.

**STUDENT:**

It seems to me that a lot depends on whether wages are flexible or inflexible. If wages are flexible, the economy self-regulates, removes itself from a recessionary gap, and thus requires no government

response. On the other hand, if wages are inflexible (downward), the economy can get stuck in a recessionary gap, and a government response may be needed.

**INSTRUCTOR:**

That's right. And because much depends on whether wages are flexible or inflexible, economists research such things as wages in various industries. For example, trying to find out whether wages in industries X and Y are flexible or inflexible may seem abstruse and esoteric to many people—who cares?—but, as you have just pointed out, a lot can depend on having the right answers.

### POINTS TO REMEMBER

1.  Not all economists agree on how the economy works. In the last chapter, you learned the views of economists who believe that the economy is self-regulating. In this chapter, you learned the views of economists who believe that the economy is not always self-regulating.

2.  Often, much depends on what may appear to be a small issue. An economist tells you she is researching the degree of flexibility of wages in industry X. You may think, "What a small issue to research. Who cares about the degree of flexibility of wages? After all, they are what they are." However, as we have shown, sometimes these so-called small issues can make a big difference, such as whether government becomes involved in the economy.

## CHAPTER SUMMARY

### KEYNES ON WAGE RATES AND PRICES

- Keynes believed that wage rates and prices may be inflexible downward. He said that employees and labor unions will resist employer's wage cuts and that, because of anticompetitive or monopolistic elements in the economy, prices will not fall.

### KEYNES ON SAY'S LAW

- Keynes did not agree that Say's law would necessarily hold in a money economy. He thought it was possible for consumption to fall (for saving to increase) by more than investment increased. Consequently, a decrease in consumption (or increase in saving) could lower total expenditures and aggregate demand in the economy.

### CONSUMPTION FUNCTION

- Keynes made three points about consumption and disposable income: (1) Consumption depends on disposable income. (2) Consumption and disposable income move in the same direction. (3) As disposable income changes, consumption changes by less. These three ideas are incorporated into the consumption function, $C = C_0 + (MPC \times Y_d)$, where $C_0$ is autonomous consumption, $MPC$ is the marginal propensity to consume, and $Y_d$ is disposable income.

### THE MULTIPLIER

- A change in autonomous spending will bring about a multiple change in total spending. The overall change in spending is equal to the multiplier $[1/(1 - MPC)]$ times the change in autonomous spending.

### THE SIMPLE KEYNESIAN MODEL IN THE AD–AS FRAMEWORK

- Changes in consumption, investment, and government purchases will change aggregate demand.

- A rise in $C$, $I$, or $G$ will shift the $AD$ curve to the right.
- A decrease in $C$, $I$, or $G$ will shift the $AD$ curve to the left.
- The aggregate supply curve in the simple Keynesian model has both a horizontal section and a vertical section. The kink between the two sections is at the Natural Real GDP level. If aggregate demand changes in the horizontal section of the curve (when the economy is operating below Natural Real GDP), Real GDP changes, but not the price level. If aggregate demand changes in the vertical section of the curve (when the economy is operating at Natural Real GDP), the price level changes but not Real GDP.

### THE SIMPLE KEYNESIAN MODEL IN THE TE–TP FRAMEWORK

- Changes in consumption, investment, and government purchases will change total expenditures.
- A rise in $C$, $I$, or $G$ will shift the $TE$ curve upward.
- A decrease in $C$, $I$, or $G$ will shift the $TE$ curve downward.
- If total expenditures ($TE$) equal total production ($TP$), the economy is in equilibrium. If $TE < TP$, the economy is in disequilibrium and inventories will unexpectedly rise, signaling firms to cut back production. If $TE > TP$, the economy is in disequilibrium and inventories will unexpectedly fall, signaling firms to increase production.
- Equilibrium occurs where $TE = TP$. The equilibrium level of Real GDP may be less than the Natural Real GDP level, and the economy may be stuck at this lower level of Real GDP.

### A KEYNESIAN THEME

- Keynes proposed that the economy could reach its equilibrium position with Real GDP below Natural Real GDP; that is, the economy could be in equilibrium and in a recessionary gap too. Furthermore, he argued that the economy may not be able to get out of a recessionary gap by itself. Government may need to play a management role in the economy.

## KEY TERMS AND CONCEPTS

| | | | |
|---|---|---|---|
| Efficiency Wage Models | Marginal Propensity to | Autonomous Consumption | Multiplier |
| Consumption Function | Consume (*MPC*) | Marginal Propensity to Save (*MPS*) | |

## QUESTIONS AND PROBLEMS

Questions 1–5 are based on the first section of the chapter, questions 6–12 are based on the second section, questions 13–20 are based on the third section, and questions 21–25 are based on the fourth section.

1. How is Keynes's position different from the classical position with respect to wages, prices, and Say's law?

2. Classical economists assumed that wage rates, prices, and interest rates are flexible and will adjust quickly. Consider an

extreme case: Suppose classical economists believed that wage rates, prices, and interest rates will adjust instantaneously. What would the classical aggregate supply (AS) curve look like? Explain your answer.

3. Give two reasons explaining the possibility that wage rates may not fall.

4. How was Keynes's position different from the classical position with respect to saving and investment?

5. According to some economists, why might business firms pay wage rates above market-clearing levels?

6. Given the Keynesian consumption function, how would a cut in income tax rates affect consumption? Explain your answer.

7. Look at the Keynesian consumption function: $C = C_0 + (MPC \times Y_d)$. What part of it relates to autonomous consumption? What part of it relates to induced consumption? Define autonomous consumption and induced consumption.

8. Using the Keynesian consumption function, prove numerically that, as the MPC rises, saving declines.

9. Explain the multiplier process.

10. What is the relationship between the MPC and the multiplier?

11. Explain how a rise in autonomous spending can increase total spending by some multiple.

12. In which factors will a change lead to a change in consumption?

13. According to Keynes, can an increase in saving shift the AD curve to the left? Explain your answer.

14. What factors will shift the AD curve in the simple Keynesian model?

15. According to Keynes, an increase in saving and a decrease in consumption may lower total spending in the economy. But

how could this happen if the increased saving lowers interest rates (as shown in the last chapter)? Wouldn't a decrease in interest rates increase investment spending, thus counteracting the decrease in consumption spending?

16. Can a person believe that wages are inflexible downward for, say, one year and also believe in a self-regulating economy? Explain your answer.

17. According to Keynes, can the private sector always remove the economy from a recessionary gap? Explain your answer.

18. What does the aggregate supply curve look like in the simple Keynesian model?

19. "In the simple Keynesian model, increases in AD that occur below Natural Real GDP will have no effect on the price level." Do you agree or disagree with this statement? Explain your answer.

20. Suppose consumption rises while investment and government purchases remain constant. How will the AD curve shift in the simple Keynesian model? Under what condition will the rise in Real GDP be equal to the rise in total spending?

21. Explain how to derive a total expenditures (TE) curve.

22. What role do inventories play in the equilibrating process in the simple Keynesian model (as described in the TE–TP framework)?

23. Identify the three states of the economy in terms of TE and TP.

24. If Real GDP is $10.4 trillion in Exhibit 12, what is the state of business inventories?

25. How will a rise in government purchases change the TE curve in Exhibit 12?

## WORKING WITH NUMBERS AND GRAPHS

Questions 1–2 are based on the second section of the chapter, questions 3–4 are based on the third section, and questions 5–8 are based on the fourth section.

1. Compute the multiplier in each of the following cases:

   a. $MPC = 0.60$

   b. $MPC = 0.80$

   c. $MPC = 0.50$

2. Write an investment function (equation) that specifies two components:

   a. Autonomous *investment spending*

   b. *Induced inve*stment spending

3. Economist Smith believes that changes in aggregate demand affect only the price level, and economist Jones believes that changes in aggregate demand affect only Real GDP. What do the AD and AS curves look like for each economist?

4. Explain the two statements (that appear at the the top of the next page) using the following figure:

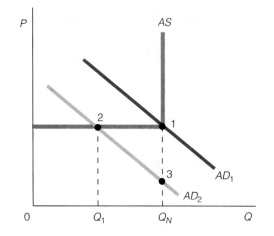

a. According to Keynes, aggregate demand may be insufficient to bring about the full-employment output level (or Natural Real GDP).

b. A decrease in consumption (due to increased saving) is not matched by an increase in investment spending.

5. The *TE* curve in Exhibit 11(d) is upward sloping because the consumption function is upward sloping. Explain.

6. In Exhibit 11(d), what does the vertical distance between the origin and the point at which the *TE* curve cuts the vertical axis represent?

7. In the figure at the right, explain what happens if:

a. The economy is at $Q_1$

b. The economy is at $Q_2$

8. In the figure at the right, if Natural Real GDP is $Q_2$, in what state is the economy at point *A*?

# 11

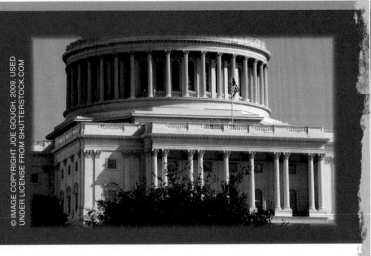

# FISCAL POLICY AND THE FEDERAL BUDGET

**Introduction** This chapter deals with fiscal policy and the federal budget. Fiscal policy consists of changes in government expenditures and/or taxes to achieve economic goals, such as low unemployment, stable prices, and economic growth. In the United States, the Congress and the president, together, fashion fiscal policy. We begin our discussion with some facts and figures about government expenditures and taxation, and we then go on to discuss the effect of fiscal policy on the economy.

## THE FEDERAL BUDGET

The federal budget has two, not necessarily equal, parts: government expenditures and tax revenues. You are familiar with the term *government purchases* from earlier chapters. Government expenditures—sometimes simply called government spending—are not the same as government purchases. Government expenditures are the sum of government purchases and government transfer payments.[1]

### Government Expenditures

In 2009, the federal government spent $3.518 trillion, which was 24.7 percent of GDP for that year. The following table shows government spending as a percentage of GDP in other years:

---

1 Remember from an earlier chapter that government purchases are the purchases of goods and services by government at all levels. Transfer payments are payments to persons, such as Social Security payments, that are not made in return for goods and services currently supplied. In this chapter, the terms *government expenditures, government spending, government purchases,* and *transfer payments* all refer to the *federal* government.

| Year | Government Spending as a Percentage of GDP |
|------|-------------------------------------------|
| 2000 | 18.2 |
| 2001 | 18.2 |
| 2002 | 19.1 |
| 2003 | 19.7 |
| 2004 | 19.6 |
| 2005 | 19.9 |
| 2006 | 20.1 |
| 2007 | 19.6 |
| 2008 | 20.7 |
| 2009 | 24.7 |

The bulk of the $3.518 trillion in government spending in 2009 was spent on four programs: national defense, Social Security, Medicare, and Medicaid. These four programs together accounted for 60 percent of all government spending that year.

## Government Tax Revenues

The federal government imposes taxes and fees that generate revenue. In 2009, government revenues totaled $2.104 trillion. This was 14.8 percent of GDP for the year. The following table shows government tax revenues as a percentage of GDP in other years:

| Year | Government Tax Revenues as a Percentage of GDP |
|------|-----------------------------------------------|
| 2000 | 20.6 |
| 2001 | 19.5 |
| 2002 | 17.6 |
| 2003 | 16.2 |
| 2004 | 16.1 |
| 2005 | 17.3 |
| 2006 | 18.2 |
| 2007 | 18.5 |
| 2008 | 17.5 |
| 2009 | 14.8 |

The bulk of government tax revenues comes from three taxes: the individual income tax, the corporate income tax, and Social Security taxes. In 2009, these three taxes accounted for 92.35 percent of total government tax revenues; the income tax by itself accounted for 43.46 percent of total government revenues.

## Budget Projections

Here are the projections for government spending and tax revenues in various years:

| Year | Government Spending ($ trillions) | Government Tax Revenues ($ trillions) |
|------|-----------------------------------|---------------------------------------|
| 2011 | $3.650 | $2.670 |
| 2012 | 3.613 | 2.964 |
| 2013 | 3.756 | 3.214 |
| 2014 | 3.940 | 3.465 |
| 2015 | 4.105 | 3.625 |

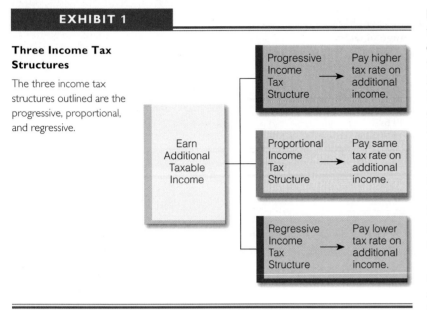

**EXHIBIT 1**

**Three Income Tax Structures**

The three income tax structures outlined are the progressive, proportional, and regressive.

**Progressive Income Tax**

An income tax system in which one's tax rate rises as taxable income rises (up to some point).

**Proportional Income Tax**

An income tax system in which a person's tax rate is the same regardless of taxable income.

**Regressive Income Tax**

An income tax system in which a person's tax rate declines as his or her taxable income rises.

**INCOME TAX STRUCTURES** An income tax structure can be progressive, proportional, or regressive. Under a progressive income tax, the tax rate increases as a person's taxable income level rises. To illustrate, suppose Davidson pays taxes at the rate of 15 percent on a taxable income of $20,000. When his (taxable) income rises to, say, $30,000, he pays at a rate of 28 percent. And when his income rises to, say, $55,000, he pays at a rate of 31 percent. A progressive income tax is usually capped. Currently, the U.S. income tax structure is progressive, with six (marginal) tax rates, ranging (in 2009) from a low of 10 percent to a high of 35 percent.

Under a proportional income tax, the same tax rate is used for all income levels. A proportional income tax is sometimes referred to as a *flat tax.* For example, Kuan's pays taxes at a rate of 10% whether her taxable income is $10,000 or $100,000.

Under a regressive income tax, the tax rate decreases as a person's taxable income level rises. For example, Lowenstein's tax rate is 10 percent when her taxable income is $10,000 and 8 percent when her taxable income rises to $20,000.

See Exhibit 1 for a review of the three income tax structures.

# ⓕinding ECONOMICS

**In How a Presidential Candidate Speaks** A presidential candidate is speaking before a large group in Des Moines, Iowa, and he has just called the current income tax structure unfair. Someone from the crowd asks him what he means by "unfair." The candidate responds that individuals shouldn't pay a higher tax rate just because they earn a higher income. We should all pay the same tax rate, he argues. Where is the economics?

Obviously the candidate favors a proportional income tax (i.e., a flat tax). Under both a progressive and a regressive income tax structure, individuals pay different tax rates at different taxable income levels. Only with a proportional income tax do individuals pay the same tax rate no matter what their taxable income is. ▲ ▲ ▲

**WHO PAYS THE INCOME TAX?** Economists often look at the tax situations of different income groups. For example, in 2007, the top 1 percent of income earners in the United States earned 22.83 percent of the total income earned that year and paid 40.42 percent of the total federal income taxes collected. The following data show the income and taxes for various income groups in 2007. The column labeled "Income Split Point" identifies the dollar amount you would have had to earn in 2007 to be in the income group in that row. For example, to be in the top 1 percent of income earners in 2007, you would have had to earn more than $410,096.

| Income Group | Group's Share of Total Income | Group's Share of Federal Income Taxes | Income Split Point |
|---|---|---|---|
| Top 1% | 22.83 | 40.42 | Greater than $410,096 |
| Top 5% | 37.44 | 60.63 | Greater than $160,041 |
| Top 10% | 48.05 | 71.22 | Greater than $113,018 |
| Top 25% | 68.71 | 85.59 | Greater than $66,532 |
| Top 50% | 87.44 | 97.11 | Greater than $32,879 |
| Bottom 50% | 12.26 | 2.89 | Less than $32,879 |

## Two Plumbers, New Year's Eve, and Progressive Taxation

Many people believe that if two people do the same job, they should be paid the same dollar amount. The question of equal pay for equal work often arises in discussions about the jobs performed by men and women. In other words, if a man and a woman do the same job, many people say that they should be paid the same dollar amount.

Sometimes the question of equal pay for equal work is extended to equal after-tax pay for equal work. That is, if two people do the same job, then they should earn the same after-tax income. However, a progressive income tax structure sometimes makes this impossible.

To illustrate, suppose under a progressive income tax structure, a person who earns between $50,000 and $60,000 pays income tax at a tax rate of 20 percent. For every dollar earned over $60,000 but under $70,000, a person pays at a tax rate of 30 percent.

Consider two plumbers, Smith and Jones. By December 30, Jones has earned $58,000 for the year, and Smith has earned $60,000. Each is asked to do the same kind of plumbing job on December 31, New Year's Eve. Each plumber

© IMAGE COPYRIGHT AUREMAR, 2009. USED UNDER LICENSE FROM SHUTTERSTOCK.COM

charges $1,000 for the job. So Jones and Smith receive equal pay for equal work.

The after-tax income that each receives for the job makes for a different story. On the additional $1,000 that Jones earns, she pays at a tax rate of 20 percent. So she pays $200 in taxes and gets to keep $800 in after-tax income. Smith, on the other hand, now has an annual income of $61,000 and thus falls into a higher marginal tax bracket. He pays at a tax rate of 30 percent on the additional $1,000. So Smith pays $300 in taxes and has $700 in after-tax income. Smith does the same job as Jones but earns only $700 in after-tax pay, whereas Jones earns $800 after taxes.

Our conclusion: The progressive income tax structure can turn equal pay for equal work into unequal after-tax pay for equal work. Stated differently, a person can be in favor of either progressive income taxes or equal after-tax pay for equal work, but not both. Sometimes, you have to decide between one or the other.

## Budget Deficit, Surplus, or Balance

The government budget can be in one of three states:

- If government expenditures are greater than tax revenues, the federal government runs a budget deficit.

- If tax revenues are greater than government expenditures, the federal government runs a budget surplus.

- If government expenditures equal tax revenues, the federal government runs a balanced budget.

In 2009, the budget deficit was $1,414 billion, and budget deficits are projected for ensuing years. Here are the projected deficits in absolute dollars and as percentages of GDP for the years following 2009:

**Budget Deficit**
Government expenditures greater than tax revenues.

**Budget Surplus**
Tax revenues greater than government expenditures.

**Balanced Budget**
Government expenditures equal to tax revenues.

| Year | Deficit ($ billions) | Deficit as a Percentage of GDP (%) |
|------|----------------------|-------------------------------------|
| 2010 | $1,349 | 9.2 |
| 2011 | 980 | 6.5 |
| 2012 | 650 | 4.1 |
| 2013 | 539 | 3.2 |
| 2014 | 475 | 2.7 |
| 2015 | 480 | 2.6 |
| 2016 | 521 | 2.7 |

If the government spends more than its tax revenue and thus runs a budget deficit, where does it get the money to finance the deficit? For example, if the government spends $100 and has $70 only in taxes, where does it get the $30 difference? The federal government—actually the U.S. Treasury—borrows the $30; that is, it finances the budget deficit with borrowed funds.

## Structural and Cyclical Deficits

**Cyclical Deficit**
The part of the budget deficit that is a result of a downturn in economic activity.

**Structural Deficit**
The part of the budget deficit that would exist even if the economy were operating at full employment.

Suppose the budget is currently balanced, and then Real GDP in the economy drops. As Real GDP drops, the tax base of the economy falls, and, if tax rates are held constant, tax revenues will fall. Another result of the decline in Real GDP is that transfer payments (e.g., unemployment compensation) will rise. Thus, government expenditures will rise as tax revenues fall. As a result, a balanced budget turns into a budget deficit—a result of the downturn in economic activity, not from current spending and taxing decisions by the government. Economists use the term cyclical deficit to describe the part of the budget deficit that is a result of a downturn in economic activity. The remainder of the deficit—the part that would exist if the economy were operating at full employment—is called the structural deficit. In other words,

Total budget deficit = Structural deficit + Cyclical deficit

To illustrate, suppose the economy is in a recessionary gap, government expenditures are currently $2.3 trillion, and tax revenues are $2.0 trillion. Thus, the (total) budget deficit is $300 billion. Economists estimate what government expenditures and tax revenues would be if the economy were operating at full employment. Assume they estimate that government expenditures would be only $2.2 trillion and that tax revenues would be $2.1 trillion. The structural deficit—the deficit that would exist at full employment—is therefore $100 billion. The cyclical deficit—the part of the budget deficit that is a result of economic downturn—is $200 billion.

## The Public Debt

**Public Debt**
The total amount that the federal government owes its creditors.

A budget deficit occurs when government expenditures are greater than tax revenues for a *single year*. The public debt, sometimes called the "federal" or "national debt," is the *total* amount the federal government owes its creditors. Some of this debt is held by agencies of the United States government; that is, one entity in the government owes it to another. The remainder of the debt is held by the public and is referred to either as *public debt held by the public* or as *net public debt*. On July 8, 2010, the public debt was $13.19 trillion, and the public debt held by the public was $8.63 trillion. (You can find the current public debt on the Bureau of the Public Debt website at http://www.publicdebt .treas.gov/.) The public debt was at its lowest on January 1, 1835, totaling $33,733.05 on that day. In 2009, the public debt held by the public was 53 percent of GDP. This percentage is expected to rising in upcoming years, reaching 60.3 percent in 2010, 65.3 percent in 2011, 66.6 percent in 2012, and 66.3 percent in 2013.

## Valued-Added Tax

Some persons have proposed higher taxes or new taxes to deal with the enlarged budget deficits and growing public debt. One tax that has been suggested is the value-added tax (VAT). Some have proposed VAT as a supplementary revenue source; others, as a substitute for current taxes.

There are two things to understand about a value-added tax: the value-added part and the tax part.

THE VALUE-ADDED PART  *Value added* is the difference between what a producer sells a (final) good for and what it pays for an (intermediate) good. For example, suppose a farmer finds a seed and plants it. In time, wheat appears. The farmer harvests the wheat and sells it to a baker for $1. The value added is $1.00.

- The farmer sells the wheat to the baker for $1.00.
- The farmer doesn't buy any intermediate goods (so intermediate goods "purchased" = $0.00).
- Value added = $1.00 − $0.00 = $1.00.
- Dollar amount kept by farmer = $1.00.

The baker, who has purchased wheat, turns it into a loaf of bread, which he sells to a (final) consumer for $1.40. The value added is $0.40.

- The baker sells the loaf of bread to a consumer for $1.40.
- The baker bought the wheat (the intermediate good) from the farmer for $1.00.
- Value added = $1.40 − $1.00 = $0.40.
- Dollar amount kept by baker = $0.40.

Notice two things:

- The sum of the values added ($1.00 + $0.40) is equal to the price paid by the final consumer for the loaf of bread ($1.40).

Sum of values added ($1.00 + $0.40 ) = Price of the loaf of bread purchased by consumer ($1.40)

- The value added at each stage of production is equal to the dollar amount kept by the farmer and baker. For instance, the valued added by the farmer was $1.00 and this is the amount he kept.

THE TAX PART  VAT is a *tax* applied to the *value added* at *each stage of production.* Suppose the VAT rate is 10 percent. A VAT rate of 10 percent applied to the $1.00 value added by the farmer is $0.10. A VAT tax rate of 10 percent applied to the $0.40 value added by the baker is $0.04. The total VAT ends up being $0.14.

| | |
|---|---|
| Value added by farmer | $1.00 |
| VAT rate of 10% applied to value added by farmer | $0.10 |
| Value added by baker | $0.40 |
| VAT rate of 10% applied to valued added by baker | $0.04 |
| Total VAT = $0.10 + $0.04 | $0.14 |

To see how the $0.14 ends up with government, we need to revisit our farmer-baker example, but this time with a VAT applied. Initially, the farmer charges the baker $1.00 for wheat. This time, with a VAT tax rate of 10 percent, he charges the baker 10 percent more or $1.10 for the wheat. Here is how things now look for the farmer:

- The farmer sells the wheat to the baker for $1.10.

- The farmer turns over 10¢ to the government (this is the VAT at the farmer's stage of production).

- The farmer keeps $1.00, which is the amount he kept when there was no VAT.

Whereas the baker sold a loaf of bread to the consumer for $1.40, this time, with a VAT rate of 10 percent, he charges 10 percent more, or $1.54 for a loaf of bread. Here is how things now look for baker:

- The baker sells the loaf of bread to the consumer for $1.54.

- The baker paid $1.10 for the wheat.

- The baker turns over $0.04 to government (this is the VAT at the baker's stage of production).

- The baker keeps $1.54 *minus* $1.10 (what he paid to the farmer) *minus* $0.04 (what he turned over to government) or $0.40, which is what he kept when there was no VAT.

Finally, here are how things look for the consumer and government:

- Without VAT, the customer paid $1.40 a loaf of broad. With VAT, she pays $1.54

- Without VAT, government collected no VAT revenues. With VAT, government collects $0.14 in VAT revenue.

So, the VAT (1) generates tax revenue and (2) raises prices.

VAT COMPARED TO A SALES TAX  The VAT is nothing more than a less visible sales tax. To illustrate, in the example of the farmer and baker, this time we impose, instead of VAT, a sales tax of 10 percent at the point of final purchase. In other words, our consumer buys a loaf of bread for a price of $1.40 plus a 10 percent sales tax of $0.14: Price + Tax = $1.54.

Notice two things: (1) The consumer pays $1.54 for the bread when a VAT is applied and when a sales tax is applied. (2) The sales tax of $0.14 is exactly equal to the VAT.

In other words, government has two ways to generate $0.14 in tax revenue: impose VAT or a sales tax. Either way, the customer ends up paying $1.54 for a loaf of bread, and government generates $0.14 in tax revenue.

Finally, in comparing VAT with a sales tax, critics often stress the point that a VAT is less visible than a sales tax. If a sales tax is raised from, say, 5 percent to 6 percent, almost everyone who buys something is aware of the tax increase. The sales receipt plainly identifies the new, higher sales tax. But if the VAT rate is raised by the same amount, not everyone will know that the VAT has been raised. People may simply think that sellers are charging higher prices because the VAT is not itemized separately from what sellers charge other sellers. In the farmer-baker example, with VAT, the farmer simply charged the baker $1.10 for wheat instead of $1.00, and the baker simply charged the consumer $1.54 instead of $1.40 for a loaf of bread. With VAT, consumers find it hard to distinguish between the seller's charging a higher price because the VAT rate has been raised and the seller's charging a higher price even without the VAT rate being raised. The VAT critics add: When a sales tax is raised, people look to government and say, "*Government* raised my taxes." When VAT is raised, people say, "*Sellers* raised the prices I pay."

## SELF-TEST

(Answers to Self-Test questions are in Answers to Self-Test Questions at the back of the book.)

1. Explain the differences among progressive, proportional, and regressive income tax structures.

2. What percentage of all income taxes was paid by the top 5 percent of income earners in 2007? What percentage of total income did this income group receive in 2007?

3. What three taxes account for the bulk of federal tax revenues?

4. What is the cyclical budget deficit?

# FISCAL POLICY

As explained in the last chapter, some economists believe that the economy is inherently unstable. They argue that government should play a role in managing the economy because the economy can get stuck in a recessionary gap. They believe government should try to move the economy out of the recessionary gap and toward Natural Real GDP.

A major way government can influence the economy is through its *fiscal policy*. Fiscal policy consists of changes in government expenditures and/or taxes to achieve economic goals, such as low unemployment, price stability, and economic growth.

## Some Relevant Fiscal Policy Terms

Expansionary fiscal policy consists of increases in government expenditures and/or decreases in taxes to achieve macroeconomic goals. Contractionary fiscal policy is implemented through decreases in government expenditures and/or increases in taxes to achieve these goals.

- *Expansionary fiscal policy.* Government expenditures are up and/or taxes are down.
- *Contractionary fiscal policy.* Government expenditures are down and/or taxes are up.

When deliberate government actions bring about changes in its expenditures and taxes, fiscal policy is said to be *discretionary*. For example, a decision by Congress to increase government spending by, say, $10 billion in an attempt to lower the unemployment rate is an act of discretionary fiscal policy. In contrast, a change in either government expenditures or in taxes that occurs automatically in response to economic events is referred to as automatic fiscal policy. To illustrate, suppose Real GDP in the economy turns down, causing more people to become unemployed and, as a result, automatically receive unemployment benefits. These added unemployment benefits automatically boost government spending.

## Two Important Notes

In your study of this chapter, keep in mind the following two important points:

1. In this chapter, we deal only with *discretionary fiscal policy*, that is, deliberate actions on the part of policy makers to affect the economy through changes in government spending and/or taxes.

2. We assume that any change in government spending is due to a change in government purchases, not to a change in transfer payments. In other words, we assume that transfer payments are constant so that changes in government spending are a reflection only of changes in government purchases.

**Fiscal Policy**
Changes in government expenditures and/or taxes to achieve economic goals, such as low unemployment, stable prices, and economic growth.

**Expansionary Fiscal Policy**
Increases in government expenditures and/or decreases in taxes to achieve particular economic goals.

**Contractionary Fiscal Policy**
Decreases in government expenditures and/or increases in taxes to achieve economic goals.

**Discretionary Fiscal Policy**
Deliberate changes of government expenditures and/or taxes to achieve economic goals.

**Automatic Fiscal Policy**
Changes in government expenditures and/or taxes that occur automatically without (additional) congressional action.

# DEMAND-SIDE FISCAL POLICY

This section focuses on how government spending and taxes—fiscal policy—can affect the demand side of the economy, that is, aggregate demand.

## Shifting the Aggregate Demand Curve

How do changes in government purchases $(G)$ and taxes $(T)$ affect aggregate demand? Recall that a change in consumption, investment, government purchases, or net exports can change aggregate demand and therefore shift the $AD$ curve. For example, an increase in government purchases $(G)$ increases aggregate demand and shifts the $AD$ curve to the right. A decrease in $G$ decreases aggregate demand and shifts the $AD$ curve to the left.[2]

A change in taxes $(T)$ can affect consumption, investment, or both, and they therefore can affect aggregate demand. For example, a decrease in income taxes increases disposable (after-tax) income, permitting individuals to increase their consumption. As consumption rises, the $AD$ curve shifts to the right. An increase in taxes decreases disposable income, lowers consumption , and shifts the AD curve to the left.

## Fiscal Policy: Keynesian Perspective (Economy Is Not Self-Regulating)

The model of the economy in Exhibit 2(a) shows a downward-sloping $AD$ curve and an upward-sloping $SRAS$ curve. As you can see, the economy is initially in a recessionary gap at point 1. Aggregate demand is too low to move the economy to equilibrium at the

---

### EXHIBIT 2

**Fiscal Policy in Keynesian Theory: Ridding the Economy of Recessionary and Inflationary Gaps**

(a) In Keynesian theory, expansionary fiscal policy eliminates a recessionary gap. Increased government purchases, decreased taxes, or both lead to a rightward shift in the aggregate demand curve from $AD_1$ to $AD_2$, restoring the economy to the natural level of Real GDP, $Q_N$. (b) Contractionary fiscal policy is used to eliminate an inflationary gap. Decreased government purchases, increased taxes, or both lead to a leftward shift in the aggregate demand curve from $AD_1$ to $AD_2$, restoring the economy to the natural level of Real GDP, $Q_N$.

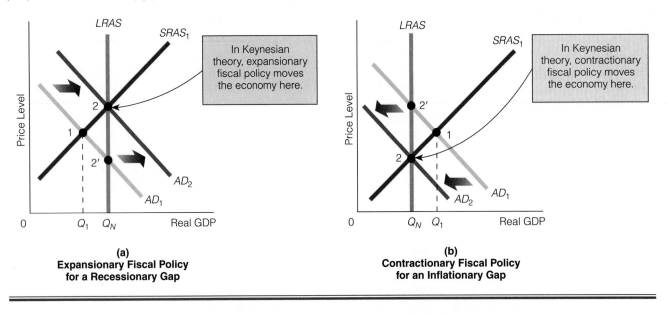

**(a)**
**Expansionary Fiscal Policy for a Recessionary Gap**

**(b)**
**Contractionary Fiscal Policy for an Inflationary Gap**

---

2. Later in this chapter, when we discuss crowding out, we question the effect of an increase in government purchases on aggregate demand.

Natural Real GDP level. The Keynesian *perspective* of the economy is that the economy is not self-regulating. So the Keynesian *prescription* is to enact expansionary fiscal policy measures (an increase in government purchases or a decrease in taxes) to shift the aggregate demand curve rightward from $AD_1$ to $AD_2$ and to move the economy to the Natural Real GDP level at point 2.

Why not simply wait for the short-run aggregate supply curve to shift rightward and intersect the aggregate demand curve at point 2'? Again, the Keynesians usually respond that the economy is not self-regulating, making one of two arguments. (1) The economy is stuck at point 1 and won't move naturally to point 2', perhaps because wage rates won't fall. (2) The short-run aggregate supply curve takes too long to shift rightward, and in the interim we must deal with the high cost of unemployment and a lower level of Real GDP. In Exhibit 2(b), the economy is initially in an inflationary gap at point 1. In this situation, Keynesians are likely to propose a contractionary fiscal measure (a decrease in government purchases or an increase in taxes) to shift the aggregate demand curve leftward from $AD_1$ to $AD_2$ and move the economy to point 2.

In Exhibit 2, fiscal policy has worked as intended. In panel (a), the economy was in a recessionary gap, and expansionary fiscal policy eliminated the gap. In panel (b), the economy was in an inflationary gap, and contractionary fiscal policy eliminated it. In (a) and (b), fiscal policy is at its best and working as intended.

## Crowding Out: Questioning Expansionary Fiscal Policy

Not all economists believe that fiscal policy works as just described. Some economists bring up the subject of *crowding out*. Crowding out is a decrease in private expenditures (consumption, investment, etc.) as a consequence of increased government spending or the financing needs of a budget deficit.

Crowding out can be direct or indirect, as described in these two examples:

1. *Direct effect.* The government spends more on public libraries, and individuals buy fewer books at bookstores.[3]

2. *Indirect effect.* The government spends more on social programs and defense without increasing taxes; as a result, the size of the budget deficit increases. Consequently, the government must borrow more funds to finance the larger deficit. The increase in borrowing causes the demand for credit (i.e., the demand for loanable funds) to rise, which in turn causes the interest rate to rise. As a result, investment drops. More government spending indirectly leads to less investment spending.

**TYPES OF CROWDING OUT** In the first example, the government spends more on public libraries. Let's say that the government spends $2 billion more on public libraries and that consumers choose to spend not $1 less on books at bookstores. Obviously, there is no crowding out, or *zero crowding out*.

Now suppose that, after the government has spent $2 billion more on public libraries, consumers choose to spend $2 billion less at bookstores. Obviously, crowding out exists, and the degree of crowding out is dollar for dollar. When $1 of government spending offsets $1 of private spending, complete crowding out is said to exist.

Finally, suppose that, after the government has spent $2 billion more on public libraries, consumers spend $1.2 billion less on books at bookstores. Again, crowding out occurs, but it is not dollar for dollar, not complete crowding out. Incomplete crowding out occurs when the decrease in one or more components of private spending only partially offsets the increase in government spending.

**Crowding Out**
The decrease in private expenditures that occurs as a consequence of increased government spending or the financing needs of a budget deficit.

**Complete Crowding Out**
A decrease in one or more components of private spending that completely offsets the increase in government spending.

**Incomplete Crowding Out**
The decrease in one or more components of private spending that only partially offsets the increase in government spending.

---

3 We are not saying that, for example, if the government spends more on public libraries, individuals will necessarily buy fewer books at bookstores; rather, if they do, this would be an example of crowding out. The same holds for example 2.

The following table summarizes the different types of crowding out:

| Type of Crowding Out | Example |
|---|---|
| Zero crowding out (sometimes called "no crowding out") | Government spends $2 billion more, and private sector spending stays constant. |
| Complete crowding out | Government spends $2 billion more, and private sector spends $2 billion less. |
| Incomplete crowding out | Government spends $2 billion more, and private sector spends $1.2 billion less. |

**GRAPHICAL REPRESENTATION OF CROWDING OUT**  In the event of *complete* or *incomplete crowding out* occurs, expansionary fiscal policy will have less impact on aggregate demand and Real GDP than Keynesian theory predicts. Let's look at the graphical representation of crowding out. Exhibit 3 illustrates the consequences of complete and incomplete crowding out and, for comparison, includes zero crowding. As shown Exhibit 3, here are the three possibilities for crowding out:

- *Zero crowding out (no crowding out).* In Exhibit 3, the economy is initially at point 1, with Real GDP at $Q_1$. Expansionary fiscal policy shifts the aggregate demand curve to $AD_2$ and moves the economy to point 2. Among other things, the implicit assumption is that there is zero (no) crowding out. Real GDP has increased from $Q_1$ to $Q_N$. Therefore, the unemployment rate will fall from its level at $Q_1$ to a lower level at $Q_N$. So, if there is no crowding out, expansionary fiscal policy increases Real GDP and lowers the unemployment rate.

- *Incomplete crowding out.* The aggregate demand curve shifts (on net) only to $AD'_2$ because a fall in private expenditures *partially offsets* the initial stimulus in aggregate demand due to increased government spending. The economy moves to point 2', and Real GDP increases from $Q_1$ to $Q'_2$. Therefore, the unemployment rate will fall from what it was at $Q_1$ to what it is at $Q'_2$. Also, the changes in both Real GDP and the unemployment rate are smaller with incomplete crowding out than with zero crowding out. So, given incomplete crowding out, expansionary fiscal policy increases Real GDP and lowers the unemployment rate, but not as much as with zero crowding out.

- *Complete crowding out.* A fall in private expenditures *completely offsets* the initial stimulus in aggregate demand due to increased government spending, and the aggregate demand curve does not move (on net) at all. Real GDP does not change, and neither does the unemployment rate. So, with

---

**EXHIBIT 3**

**Zero (No), Incomplete, and Complete Crowding Out**

The exhibit shows the effects of zero, incomplete, and complete crowding out in the AD–AS framework. Starting at point 1, expansionary fiscal policy shifts the aggregate demand curve to $AD_2$ and moves the economy to point 2 and $Q_N$. The Keynesian theory that predicts this outcome assumes zero, or no, crowding out; an increase in, say, government spending does not reduce private expenditures. With incomplete crowding out, an increase in government spending causes private expenditures to decrease by less than the increase in government spending. The net result is a shift in the aggregate demand curve to $AD'_2$. The economy moves to point 2' and $Q'_2$. With complete crowding out, an increase in government spending is completely offset by a decrease in private expenditures, and the net result is that aggregate demand does not increase at all. The economy remains at point 1 and $Q_1$.

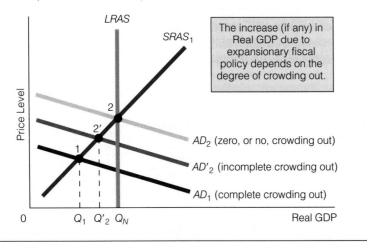

The increase (if any) in Real GDP due to expansionary fiscal policy depends on the degree of crowding out.

complete crowding out, expansionary fiscal policy has no effect on the economy. The economy remains at point 1.

See Exhibit 4 for a summary flowchart of the different types of crowding out.

# ⓣhinking like AN ECONOMIST

**Policy Is Not Necessarily Effective** An ill person goes to the doctor and asks for medicine; the doctor prescribes the medicine, and the person goes home. After a few days, the medicine has not made the person well. The same can be sometimes said about economic policy. Keep in mind what we are and what we are not saying. We are not saying that economic policy is never effective; we are simply saying it is not *necessarily* effective. So far in our discussion, crowding out is only one reason fiscal policy may not be effective. Lags, which we discuss next, are another. ▰ ▰ ▰

## Lags and Fiscal Policy

Even if we prove beyond a shadow of a doubt that there is no (zero) crowding out, should fiscal policy then be used to solve the problems of inflationary and recessionary gaps? Many economists would answer not necessarily, because of *lags*. There are five types of lags:

1. *The data lag.* Policy makers are not aware of changes in the economy as soon as they happen. For example, if the economy turns down in January, the decline may not be apparent for two to three months.

2. *The wait-and-see lag.* After policy makers are aware of a downturn in economic activity, they rarely enact counteractive measures immediately. Instead, they usually adopt a relatively cautious wait-and-see attitude to be sure that the observed events are not just short-run phenomena.

**EXHIBIT 4**

**Expansionary Fiscal Policy (Government Spending Increases), Crowding Out, and Changes in Real GDP and the Unemployment Rate**

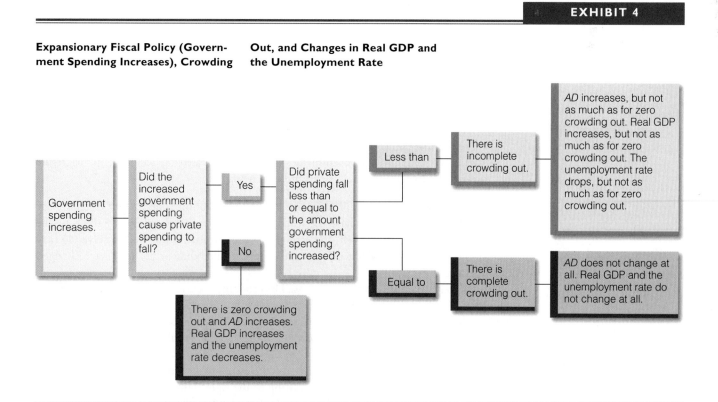

## The Recession and the Stimulus Bill

The U.S. economy moved into a recession at the end of 2007. In terms of the *AD*–AS diagram [Exhibit 2(a)], the economy was in a recessionary gap, producing less than Natural Real GDP, or $Q_N$. From a Keynesian perspective, expansionary fiscal policy is recommended. The objective is to increase spending in the economy so that the *AD* curve shifts rightward, leading to a rise in Real GDP.

On February 17, 2009, President Barack Obama signed the American Recovery and Reinvestment Act of 2009 into law. This act was popularly known as "the stimulus bill." It was an expansionary fiscal policy measure that was made up of some tax cuts and a rise in government purchases. The total dollar amount of stimulus was $787 billion.

The stimulus bill had its proponents and opponents among economists. Some economists argued

AP PHOTO/DAVID ZALUBOWSKI

that the stimulus bill was definitely needed to move the economy out of the recession. They argued that the stimulus bill would work, that is, stimulate spending in the economy, shift the *AD* curve to the right, and remove the economy from the recession. Moreover, they argued that the multiplier (in the economy) was high enough to remove the economy from the recessionary gap given the dollar amount of stimulus. [In the last chapter, we discussed the simple Keynesian multiplier : $1 \div (1 - MPC)$, so that, if $MPC = 0.80$, the multiplier is 5.]

Not all economists agreed, arguing that crowding out would be a problem. In fact, some economists argued that every dollar of government stimulus would lead to one less dollar of private sector spending. In other words, crowding out would be complete.

3. *The legislative lag.* After policy makers decide that some type of fiscal policy measure is required, Congress or the president has to propose the measure, build political support for it, and get it passed. The legislative lag can take many months.

4. *The transmission lag.* Once enacted, a fiscal policy measure takes time to go into effect. For example, a discretionary expansionary fiscal policy measure mandating increased spending for public works projects requires construction companies to submit bids for the work, prepare designs, negotiate contracts, and so on.

5. *The effectiveness lag.* After being actually implemented, a policy measure takes time to affect the economy. If government spending is increased on Monday, the aggregate demand curve does not shift rightward on Tuesday.

Given the cumulative effect of these five lags, some economists argue that discretionary fiscal policy is not likely to have the intended impact on the economy. By the time the full impact of the policy is felt, the economic problem it was designed to solve (1) may no longer exist, (2) may not exist to the degree it once did, or (3) may have changed altogether.

Exhibit 5 illustrates the effect of lags. The economy is currently in a recessionary gap at point 1. The recession is under way before government officials recognize it. After it is recognized, however, Congress and the president consider enacting expansionary fiscal policy in the hope of shifting the *AD* curve from $AD_1$ to $AD_2$ so that it will intersect the *SRAS* curve at point 1′, at Natural Real GDP.

In the interim, unknown to everybody, the economy is said to be healing, or regulating, itself: the *SRAS* curve is already shifting to the right. Government officials don't see this change because collecting and analyzing data about the economy takes time.

Thinking that the economy is not healing itself or not healing itself quickly enough, the government enacts expansionary fiscal policy. In time, the *AD* curve shifts rightward. But by the time the increased demand is felt in the goods and services market, the *AD* curve intersects the *SRAS* curve at point 2. In effect, the government has moved the economy from point 1 to point 2, not, as it had intended, from point 1 to point 1′. The government has moved the economy into an inflationary gap. Instead of stabilizing and moderating the ups and downs in economic activity (the business cycle), the government has intensified the fluctuations.

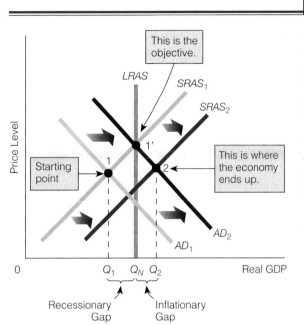

**EXHIBIT 5**

**Fiscal Policy May Destabilize the Economy**

In this scenario, the *SRAS* curve is shifting rightward (healing the economy of its recessionary gap), but this information is unknown to policy makers. Policy makers implement expansionary fiscal policy, and the *AD* curve ends up intersecting $SRAS_2$ at point 2 instead of intersecting $SRAS_1$ at point 1′. Policy makers thereby move the economy into an inflationary gap, thus destabilizing the economy.

## Crowding Out, Lags, and the Effectiveness of Fiscal Policy

Economists who believe that the crowding out is zero and that lags are insignificant conclude that fiscal policy is effective at moving the economy out of a recessionary gap. Economists who believe that crowding out is complete and/or that lags are significant conclude that fiscal policy is ineffective in this respect.

### SELF-TEST

1. How does crowding out create questions about the effectiveness of expansionary demand-side fiscal policy? Give an example.

2. How might lags reduce the effectiveness of fiscal policy?

3. Give an example of the indirect effect of crowding out.

# SUPPLY-SIDE FISCAL POLICY

Fiscal policy effects may be felt on the supply side as well as on the demand side of the economy. For example, a reduction in tax rates may alter an individual's incentive to work and produce, thus altering aggregate supply.

## Marginal Tax Rates and Aggregate Supply

When fiscal policy measures affect tax rates, they may affect both aggregate supply and aggregate demand. Consider a reduction in an individual's marginal tax rate. The marginal (income) tax rate is equal to the change in a person's tax payment divided by the change in the person's taxable income.

$$\text{Marginal tax rate} = \frac{\Delta \text{ Tax payment}}{\Delta \text{ Taxable income}}$$

**Marginal (Income) Tax Rate**
The change in a person's tax payment divided by the change in taxable income: $\Delta$Tax payment ÷ $\Delta$Taxable income.

For example, if Serena's taxable income increases by $1 and her tax payment increases by $0.28, her marginal tax rate is 28 percent. If her taxable income increases by $1 and her tax payment increases by $0.35, then her marginal tax rate is 35 percent.

## EXHIBIT 6

**The Predicted Effect of a Permanent Marginal Tax Rate Cut on Aggregate Supply**

A cut in marginal tax rates increases the attractiveness of productive activity relative to leisure and tax-avoidance activities and shifts resources from the latter to the former, thus shifting rightward both the short-run and the long-run aggregate supply curves.

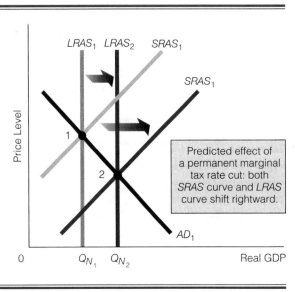

Predicted effect of a permanent marginal tax rate cut: both *SRAS* curve and *LRAS* curve shift rightward.

All other things held constant, lower marginal tax rates increase the incentive to engage in productive activities (work) relative to leisure and tax-avoidance activities.[4] As resources shift from leisure to work, short-run aggregate supply increases. When the lower marginal tax rates are permanent (not a one-shot phenomenon), most economists predict that not only the short-run aggregate supply curve but also the long-run aggregate supply curve will shift rightward. Exhibit 6 illustrates the predicted effect of a permanent marginal tax rate cut on aggregate supply.

## The Laffer Curve: Tax Rates and Tax Revenues

**Laffer Curve**

The curve, named after Arthur Laffer, that shows the relationship between tax rates and tax revenues. According to the Laffer curve, as tax rates rise from zero, tax revenues rise, reach a maximum at some point, and then fall with further increases in tax rates.

*High tax rates are followed by attempts of ingenious men to beat them as surely as snow is followed by little boys on sleds.*

—*Arthur Okun, economist (1928–1980)*

If (marginal) income tax rates are reduced, will income tax revenues increase or decrease? Most people think the answer is obvious: lower tax rates mean lower tax revenues. Economist Arthur Laffer explained why this may not be the case. As the story is told, Laffer, while dining with a journalist at a restaurant in Washington, D.C., drew the curve in Exhibit 7 on a napkin. The curve came to be known as the Laffer curve. Laffer's objective was to explain the possible relationships between tax rates and tax revenues. In the exhibit, tax revenues are on the vertical axis, and tax rates are on the horizontal axis. Laffer made three major points about the curve:

## EXHIBIT 7

**The Laffer Curve**

When the tax rate is either 0 or 100 percent, tax revenues are zero. Starting from a zero tax rate, increases in tax rates first increase (region A to B) and then decrease (region B to C) tax revenues. Starting from a 100 percent tax rate, decreases in tax rates first increase tax revenues (region C to B) and then decrease tax revenues (region B to A). This suggests there is some tax rate that maximizes tax revenues.

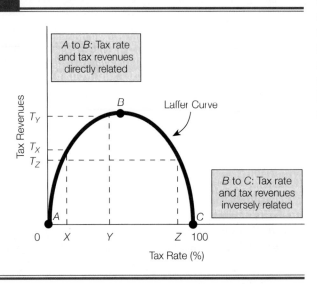

A to B: Tax rate and tax revenues directly related

B to C: Tax rate and tax revenues inversely related

1. Zero tax revenues will be collected at two (marginal) tax rates: 0 percent and 100 percent. Obviously, no tax revenues will be raised if the tax rate is zero, and if the tax rate is 100 percent, no one will work and earn income because the entire amount would be taxed away.

---

4. When marginal tax rates are lowered, two things happen: (1) individuals will have more disposable income, and (2) the amount of money that individuals can earn (and keep) by working increases. As a result of the first effect, individuals will choose to work less. As a result of the second effect, individuals will choose to work more. Whether an individual works less or more on net depends on whether effect 1 is stronger than or weaker than effect 2. We have assumed that effect 2 is stronger than effect 1; so, as marginal tax rates decline, the net effect is that individuals work more.

2. An increase in tax rates could cause tax revenues to increase. For example, an increase in tax rates from $X$ percent to $Y$ percent will increase tax revenues from $T_X$ to $T_Y$.

3. A decrease in tax rates could cause tax revenues to increase. For example, a decrease in tax rates from $Z$ percent to $Y$ percent will increase tax revenues from $T_Z$ to $T_Y$. This point brought public attention to the Laffer curve.

Both an *increase* and a *decrease* in tax rates at different times can increase tax revenues due to the interrelationships among tax rates, the tax base, and tax revenues. Tax revenues equal the tax base times the (average) tax rate:[5]

$$\text{Tax revenues} = \text{Tax base} \times \text{(average) Tax rate}$$

**Tax Base**
In terms of income taxes, the total amount of taxable income. Tax revenue = Tax base × (average) Tax rate.

For example, a tax rate of 20 percent multiplied by a tax base of $100 billion generates $20 billion of tax revenues.

Obviously, tax revenues are a function of two variables: (1) the tax rate and (2) the tax base. Whether tax revenues increase or decrease when the average tax rate is lowered depends on whether the tax base expands by a greater or lesser percentage than the percentage reduction in the tax rate. Exhibit 8 illustrates the point. The tax rate starts at 20 percent, with a tax base of $100 billion and tax revenues of $20 billion. As the tax rate is reduced, the tax base expands: The rationale is that individuals work more, invest more, enter into more trades, and shelter less income from taxes at lower tax rates.

However, the real question is *how much* does the tax base expand following the tax rate reduction? Suppose the tax rate in Exhibit 8 is reduced to 15 percent. In Case 1, the reduction increases the tax base to $120 billion: A 25 percent decrease in the tax rate (from 20 to 15 percent) causes a 20 percent increase in the tax base (from $100 billion to $120 billion). Tax revenues drop to $18 billion. In Case 2, the tax base expands by 50 percent to $150 billion. Because the tax base increases by a greater percentage than the percentage decrease in the tax rate, tax revenues increase (to $22.5 billion).

Of course, either case is possible. In the Laffer curve, tax revenues increase if a tax rate reduction is made on the downward sloping portion of the curve (between points $B$ and $C$ in Exhibit 7); tax revenues decrease following a tax rate reduction on the upward sloping portion of the curve (between points $A$ and $B$).

**EXHIBIT 8**

**Tax Rates, the Tax Base, and Tax Revenues**
Tax revenues equal the tax base times the (average) tax rate. If the percentage reduction in the tax rate is greater than the percentage increase in the tax base, tax revenues decrease (Case 1). If the percentage reduction in the tax rate is less than the percentage increase in the tax base, tax revenues increase (Case 2). All dollar amounts are in billions of dollars.

| | (1) Tax Rate | (2) Tax Base | (3) Tax Revenues (1) × (2) | Summary |
|---|---|---|---|---|
| Start with: | 20% | $100 | $20 | — |
| Case 1: | 15 | 120 | 18 | ↓ Tax rate ↓ Tax revenues |
| Case 2: | 15 | 150 | 22.5 | ↓ Tax rate ↑ Tax revenues |

5. First, the average tax rate is equal to an individual's tax payment divided by taxable income (tax payment ÷ taxable income). Second, a lower average tax rate requires a lower marginal tax rate. This follows from the average-marginal rule, which states that if the marginal magnitude is below the average magnitude, then the average is pulled down; if the marginal is above the average, the average is pulled up. Simply put, if an individual pays less tax on an additional taxable dollar (which is evidence of a marginal tax rate reduction), then his or her average tax naturally falls.

## ⓣhinking Like **AN ECONOMIST**

**Incentives Matter** Contrast how an economist thinks about a tax cut with how the layperson thinks about it. The layperson probably believes that a reduction in tax rates will reduce tax revenues, focusing just on the arithmetic. An economist, however, focuses on the economic incentives, asking a number of questions. What does a lower tax rate imply in terms of a person's incentive to engage in productive activity? How does a lower tax rate affect one's trade-off between work and leisure? The layperson likely sees only the arithmetic effect of a tax cut; the economist sees the incentive effect. ◖ ◖ ◖

## Fiscal Policy and Expectations

Even if, when tax rates are lowered, people do not work more and produce more, it cannot necessarily be said that lower tax rates do not stimulate work and production. Consider two different settings. In setting 1, income tax rates are lowered in year 1 with no further cuts expected in future years. In setting 2, income tax rates are lowered in year 1 with further cuts expected in future years. In setting 1, suppose tax cuts are implemented, and individuals don't respond by working more and producing more. Then we could confidently say, all other things being equal, that lower tax rates do not seem to stimulate work and production. But in setting 2, suppose tax cuts are implemented, and individuals don't

# OFFICE HOURS

## "Is There a Looming Fiscal Crisis?"

**STUDENT:**

I've been reading what some economists have been saying about the future state of the federal budget. They say there is a looming fiscal crisis ahead. What do they mean by "a looming fiscal crisis"?

**INSTRUCTOR:**

They are looking at the changing demographics in the United States, combined with rising health costs. As baby boomers retire and become eligible for Social Security and Medicare (and to a lesser extent, Medicaid), we can expect that Social Security, Medicare, and Medicaid spending will rise.

**STUDENT:**

Will it rise by much? Is this a big spending problem headed our way?

**INSTRUCTOR:**

Well, if our current federal tax burden were to remain constant over the years, it has been estimated that we will be able to pay for only three federal programs and nothing else by the year 2050: Social Security, Medicare, and Medicaid. In short, the so-called looming fiscal crisis is due to the expected growth in Social Security, Medicare, and Medicaid spending in the future. In 2005, spending on these three programs comprised 8.4 percent of GDP. This is projected to be 11 percent in 2020 and 18.1 percent in 2050.

**STUDENT:**

That will mean the public debt will grow, won't it?

**INSTRUCTOR:**

Not only will it grow in absolute terms, but it will grow as a percentage of GDP too.

respond immediately by working more and producing more. We should not conclude that lower tax rates don't stimulate work and production because the tax rates in year 1 are relatively higher than the tax rates expected in future years (such as years 2, 3, and so on). In other words, although the tax cut in year 1 reduced tax rates, the tax rate is still higher in year 1 than it will be in years 2, 3, and 4. People may simply be waiting for tax rates to go down more before they start working more and producing more (and thus earning more income on which to pay taxes).

Now look at the opposite condition: raising tax rates. Raising tax rates should lead to individuals' cutting back on work and production, but this effect isn't necessarily predicted if tax rates are expected to rise more in future years. In fact, raising the tax rate in year 1, with an expected tax rate hike to follow in year 2, could actually get people to work and produce more in year 1. In relative terms, the tax rate is lower in year 1 than it will be in year 2.

## SELF-TEST

1. Give an arithmetic example to illustrate the difference between the marginal and average tax rates.

2. If income tax rates rise, will income tax revenues rise too?

### STUDENT:

Let me see if I have this correct. You're saying (1) that Social Security, Medicare, and Medicaid spending are likely to grow in the future and that these three programs will comprise a larger share of the federal budget than they do today; (2) that if current spending and tax policies continue, both the budget deficit and the public debt will grow as a percentage of GDP. Is this the looming fiscal crisis we hear so much about?

### INSTRUCTOR:

Yes, that's correct.

### STUDENT:

So what does this mean for our future? Are taxes going to have to be raised? Is spending going to have to be cut? Or are we just going to continue on course and end up having to deal with large budget deficits and debt (as a percentage of GDP)?

### INSTRUCTOR:

We're not sure what will happen. What we do know is that some stark fiscal realities are awaiting us. One way of identifying the problem (or the stark reality ahead) is to measure the *fiscal gap*. This is the amount of spending reductions or tax revenue increases needed (say, over the next four decades) if we want to keep our debt-to-GDP ratio at what it is today. It has been estimated (at the low end of estimates) that the fiscal gap requires annual tax revenue increases or spending cuts totaling 5–7 percent of projected GDP for the next four decades. Here's what that means. The Congressional Budget Office forecasts the 2011 GDP at about $15 trillion. If we take 5 percent of this, we get $750 billion. The federal government would need to either (1) cut spending

by this amount in 2011, or (2) raise tax revenues by this amount in 2011, or (3) raise tax revenues by, say, $400 billion and cut spending benefits by $350 billion (for a total of $750 billion), and so on.

### POINTS TO REMEMBER

1. It is likely that in future years the combined spending on Social Security, Medicare, and Medicaid will grow as a percentage of the federal budget.

2. If the nation's current spending and tax policies continue, both the budget deficit and the public debt in the hands of the public will grow as a percentage of GDP.

# CHAPTER SUMMARY

## GOVERNMENT SPENDING

- In 2009, the federal government spent $3.518 trillion. This was 24.7 percent of the country's GDP. About 60 percent of the money went for Social Security, Medicare, Medicaid, and national defense.

- With a proportional income tax, everyone pays taxes at the same rate, regardless of income level. With a progressive income tax, a person pays taxes at a higher rate (up to some top rate) as the income level rises. With a regressive income tax, a person pays taxes at a lower rate as the income level rises.

- The federal income tax is a progressive income tax.

## TAXES

- In 2009, the federal government took in $2.104 trillion in tax revenues. Most of this came from three taxes: the individual income tax, the corporate income tax, and Social Security taxes.

## DEFICITS, SURPLUSES, AND THE PUBLIC DEBT

- If government expenditures are greater than tax revenues, a budget deficit results; if government expenditures are less than tax revenues, a budget surplus results. If government expenditures equal tax revenues, the budget is balanced. Budget deficits are predicted for the near future.

- A cyclical deficit is the part of the budget deficit that is a result of a downturn in economic activity.

- A structural deficit is the part of the deficit that would exist if the economy were operating at full employment.

- Total budget deficit = Structural deficit + Cyclical deficit.

- The public debt is the total amount that the federal government owes its creditors.

## FISCAL POLICY: GENERAL REMARKS

- Fiscal policy consists of changes in government expenditures and/or taxes to achieve economic goals. Expansionary fiscal policy is composed of increases in government expenditures and/or decreases in taxes. Contractionary fiscal policy entails decreases in government expenditures and/or increases in taxes.

## DEMAND-SIDE FISCAL POLICY: A KEYNESIAN PERSPECTIVE

- In Keynesian theory, demand-side fiscal policy can be used to rid the economy of a recessionary gap or an inflationary gap. A recessionary gap calls for expansionary fiscal policy, and an inflationary gap calls for contractionary fiscal policy. Ideally, fiscal policy changes aggregate demand by enough to rid the economy of either a recessionary gap or an inflationary gap.

## CROWDING OUT

- Crowding out is the decrease in private expenditures that occurs as a consequence of increased government spending and/or the greater financing needs of a budget deficit. The crowding-out effect suggests that expansionary fiscal policy does not work to the degree that Keynesian theory predicts.

- Complete (incomplete) crowding out occurs when the decrease in one or more components of private spending completely (partially) offsets the increase in government spending.

## WHY DEMAND-SIDE FISCAL POLICY MAY BE INEFFECTIVE

- Demand-side fiscal policy may be ineffective at achieving certain macroeconomic goals because of (1) crowding out and (2) lags.

## SUPPLY-SIDE FISCAL POLICY

- When fiscal policy measures affect tax rates, they may affect both aggregate supply and aggregate demand. It is generally accepted that a marginal tax rate reduction increases the attractiveness of work relative to leisure and tax-avoidance activities and thus leads to an increase in aggregate supply.

- Tax revenues equal the tax base multiplied by the (average) tax rate. Whether tax revenues decrease or increase as a result of a tax rate reduction depends on whether the percentage increase in the tax base is greater or less than the percentage reduction in the tax rate. If the percentage increase in the tax base is greater than the percentage reduction in the tax rate, then tax revenues will increase. If the percentage increase in the tax base is less than the percentage reduction in the tax rate, then tax revenues will decrease.

# KEY TERMS AND CONCEPTS

| | | | |
|---|---|---|---|
| Progressive Income Tax | Balanced Budget | Expansionary Fiscal Policy | Complete Crowding Out |
| Proportional Income Tax | Cyclical Deficit | Contractionary Fiscal Policy | Incomplete Crowding Out |
| Regressive Income Tax | Structural Deficit | Discretionary Fiscal Policy | Marginal (Income) Tax Rate |
| Budget Deficit | Public Debt | Automatic Fiscal Policy | Laffer Curve |
| Budget Surplus | Fiscal Policy | Crowding Out | Tax Base |

## QUESTIONS AND PROBLEMS

1. What is the difference between government expenditures and government purchases?

2. How much were government expenditures in 2009? How much were government tax revenues in 2009?

3. The bulk of federal government expenditures go for four programs. What are they?

4. What percentage of total income did the top 5 percent of income earners earn in 2007? What percentage of federal income taxes did this group pay in 2007?

5. Is it true that, under a proportional income tax structure, a person who earns a high income will pay more in taxes than a person who earns a low income? Explain your answer.

6. A progressive income tax always raises more revenue than a proportional income tax. Do you agree or disagree? Explain your answer.

7. Jim favors progressive taxation and equal after-tax pay for equal work. Comment.

8. What is the difference between a structural deficit and a cyclical deficit?

9. What is the difference between discretionary fiscal policy and automatic fiscal policy?

10. Explain two ways crowding out may occur.

11. Why is crowding out an important issue in the debate over the use of fiscal policy?

12. Some economists argue for the use of fiscal policy to solve economic problems; others argue against it. What are some of the arguments on both sides?

13. Give a numerical example to illustrate the difference between complete crowding out and incomplete crowding out.

14. The debate over using government spending and taxing powers to stabilize the economy involves more than technical economic issues. Do you agree or disagree? Explain your answer.

15. Is crowding out equally likely under all economic conditions? Explain your answer.

16. Tax cuts will likely affect aggregate demand and aggregate supply. Does it matter which is affected more? Explain in terms of the *AD–AS* framework.

17. Explain how expansionary fiscal policy can, under certain conditions, destabilize the economy.

18. Identify and explain the five lags associated with fiscal policy.

19. The economy is in a recessionary gap, and both Smith and Jones advocate expansionary fiscal policy. Does it follow that both Smith and Jones favor so-called big government?

20. Will tax cuts that the public perceives to be temporary affect the *SRAS* and *LRAS* curves differently than tax cuts that are perceived to be permanent? Explain your answer.

21. What is the difference between a marginal tax rate and an average tax rate?

22. Will tax revenue necessarily rise if tax rates are lowered? Explain your answer.

23. Georgia Dickens is sitting with a friend at a coffee shop, and they are talking about the new tax bill. Georgia thinks that cutting tax rates at this time would be wrong: "Lower tax rates," she says, "will lead to a larger budget deficit, and the budget deficit is already plenty big." Do lower tax rates mean a larger deficit? Why or why not?

## WORKING WITH NUMBERS AND GRAPHS

Use the following table to answer questions 1–4:

| Taxable | Income Taxes |
|---|---|
| $1,000–$5,000 | 10% of taxable income |
| $5,001–$10,000 | $500 + 12% of everything over $5,000 |
| $10,001–$15,000 | $1,100 + 15% of everything over $10,000 |

1. If a person's income is $6,000, how much does he pay in taxes?

2. If a person's income is $14,000, how much does she pay in taxes?

3. What is the marginal tax rate on the 10,001st dollar? What is the marginal tax rate on the 10,000th dollar?

4. What is the average tax rate of someone with a taxable income of $13,766?

5. A hypothetical society has three income earners, and all three must pay income taxes. The taxable income of Smith is $40,000, the taxable income of Jones is $100,000, and the taxable income of Brown is $200,000.

a. How much tax revenue is raised under a proportional income tax when the tax rate is 10 percent? How much is raised if the tax rate is 15 percent?

b. A progressive tax system is installed with a rate of 5 percent on an income of $0–$40,000, a rate of 8 percent on income over $40,000 and under $100,000, and a rate of 15 percent on all income over $100,000. Will this system raise more or less tax revenue than a proportional tax rate of 10 percent? Explain your answer.

6. Graphically show how fiscal policy works in the ideal case.

7. Graphically illustrate how government can use supply-side fiscal policy to get an economy out of a recessionary gap.

8. Graphically illustrate the following:

a. Fiscal policy destabilizes the economy

b. Fiscal policy eliminates an inflationary gap

c. Fiscal policy only partly eliminates a recessionary gap

# CHAPTER 12

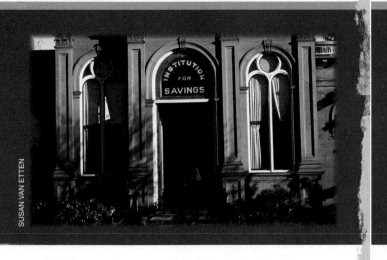

SUSAN VAN ETTEN

# MONEY, BANKING, AND THE FINANCIAL SYSTEM

**Introduction** This chapter is about money: how it emerged out of a barter economy and the functions it serves. It is also about banking: how it came to exist and how it looks today. Finally, it is about the financial system in the United States; specifically, about what it is and what it does.

## MONEY: WHAT IS IT AND HOW DID IT COME TO BE?

The story of money starts with a definition and a history lesson. This section discusses what money is and isn't (the definition) and how money came to be (the history lesson).

### Money: A Definition

To the layperson, the words "income," "credit," and "wealth" are synonyms for "money." In each of the next three sentences, the word "money" is used incorrectly; the word in parentheses is the word an economist would use.

1. How much money (income) did you earn last year?

2. Most of her money (wealth) is tied up in real estate.

3. It sure is difficult to get money (credit) in today's tight mortgage market.

In economics, the words "money," "income," "credit," and "wealth" are not synonyms. The most general definition of money is any good that is widely accepted for purposes of exchange (payment for goods and services) and the repayment of debt.

**Money**
Any good that is widely accepted for purposes of exchange and the repayment of debt.

### Three Functions of Money

Money has three major functions; it is a:

1. medium of exchange.

2. unit of account.

3. store of value.

**MONEY AS A MEDIUM OF EXCHANGE** If money did not exist, goods would have to be exchanged by barter, that is, exchanging goods and services for other goods and services without the use of money. If you wanted a shirt, you would have to trade some good in your possession, say, a jackknife, for it. But first you would have to locate a person who has a shirt and who wants to trade it for a knife. In a money economy, searching for a seller is not necessary. You can either (1) exchange money for a shirt or (2) exchange the knife for money and then the money for the shirt. The buyer of the knife and the seller of the shirt do not have to be the same person. Money is the medium through which the exchange occurs; it acts as a medium of exchange. As such, money reduces the *transaction costs* of exchanges. Exchange is easier and less time-consuming in a money economy than in a barter economy.

**MONEY AS A UNIT OF ACCOUNT** A unit of account is a common measure in which values are expressed. In a barter economy, the value of every good is expressed in terms of all other goods; there is no common unit of measure. For example, 1 horse might equal 100 bushels of wheat, or 200 bushels of apples, or 20 pairs of shoes, or 10 suits, or 55 loaves of bread, and so on. In a money economy, a person doesn't have to know the price of an apple in terms of oranges, pizzas, chickens, or potato chips, as in a barter economy. A person needs only to know the price in terms of money. And because all goods are denominated in money, determining relative prices is easy and quick. For example, if 1 apple is $1 and 1 orange is 50¢, then 1 apple is worth 2 oranges.

**MONEY AS A STORE OF VALUE** The store of value function is related to a good's ability to maintain its value over time. This is the least exclusive function of money because other goods—for example, paintings, houses, and stamps—can store value too. At times, money has not maintained its value well, such as during high-inflationary periods. For the most part, though, money has served as a satisfactory store of value. This function allows us to accept payment in money for our productive efforts and to keep that money until we decide how we want to spend it.

**Barter**
Exchanging goods and services for other goods and services without the use of money.

**Medium of Exchange**
Anything that is generally acceptable in exchange for goods and services; a function of money.

**Unit of Account**
A common measure in which relative values are expressed; a function of money.

**Store of Value**
The ability of an item to hold value over time; a function of money.

## From a Barter to a Money Economy: The Origins of Money

*The thing that differentiates man and animals is money.*

—*Gertrude Stein*

At one time, there was trade but no money. Instead, people bartered. They traded 1 apple for 2 eggs, a banana for a peach.

Today we live in a money economy, but how did we move from a barter to a money economy? Did a king or queen issue an edict: "Let there be money"? Actually, money evolved in a much more natural, market-oriented manner.

Making exchanges takes longer (on average) in a barter economy than in a money economy because the *transaction costs* are higher in a barter economy. In other words, the time and effort incurred to consummate an exchange are greater in a barter economy than in a money economy.

In a barter economy, suppose Smith wants to trade apples for oranges. He locates Jones, who has oranges. Smith offers to trade apples for oranges, but Jones tells Smith that she does not like apples and would rather have peaches. Smith must either (1) find someone who has oranges and who wants to trade oranges for apples or (2) find someone who has peaches and who wants to trade peaches for apples, after which he must return to Jones and trade peaches for oranges. Suppose Smith continues to search and finds Brown, who

**Double Coincidence of Wants**
In a barter economy, a requirement, which must be met before a trade can be made. It specifies that a trader must find another trader who at the same time is willing to trade what the first trader wants and wants what the first trader has.

has oranges and wants to trade oranges for (Smith's) apples. In economics terminology, Smith and Brown are said to have a double coincidence of wants. Two people have a double coincidence of wants if what the first person wants is what the second person has and what the second person wants is what the first person has. A double coincidence of wants is a necessary condition for a trade to take place.

In a barter economy, some goods are more readily accepted than others in exchange. This characteristic may originally be the result of chance, but when traders notice the difference in marketability, their behavior tends to reinforce the effect. Suppose that, of 10 goods A–J, good G is the most marketable (the most acceptable) of the 10. On average, good G is accepted 5 of every 10 times it is offered in an exchange, whereas the remaining goods are accepted, on average, only 2 of every 10 times. Given this difference, some individuals accept good G simply because of its relatively greater acceptability, even though they have no plans to consume it. They accept good G because they know they can easily trade it for most other goods at a later time (unlike the item originally in their possession). Thus the marketability of good G snowballs. The more people accept good G for its relatively greater acceptability, the greater its relative acceptability becomes, in turn causing more people to accept it.

This is how money evolved. When good G's acceptance evolves to the point that it is widely accepted for purposes of exchange, good G is money. Historically, goods that have evolved into money include gold, silver, copper, cattle, salt, cocoa beans, and shells.

## thinking Like AN ECONOMIST

**The Effects of Self-Interest**  The statement that people in a barter economy "accept good G because they know they can easily trade it for most other goods at a later time (unlike the item originally in their possession)" brings up the role of self-interest. At some point in time, people in a barter economy simply wanted to make life easier on themselves; they wanted to cut down on the time and energy required to obtain their preferred bundle of goods. In other words, they began to accept the most marketable or acceptable of all goods out of self-interest—a process that eventually led to the creation of money. ▲ ▲ ▲

## finding ECONOMICS

**In a POW Camp**  You wouldn't think you could find money in a prisoner of war (POW) camp, but you can. During World War II, an American, R. A. Radford, was captured and imprisoned in a POW camp. While in the camp, he made some observations about economic developments, which he later described in the journal *Economica*. He noted that the Red Cross would periodically distribute packages to the prisoners that contained such goods as cigarettes, toiletries, chocolate, cheese, jam, margarine, and tinned beef. Not all the prisoners had the same preferences for the goods. For example, some liked chocolate more than others; some smoked cigarettes, and others did not. Because of their preferences, the prisoners began to trade, say, a chocolate bar for cheese, and a barter system emerged. After a short while, money appeared in the camp, but not U.S. dollars or any other government currency. The good that emerged as money—the good that was widely accepted for purposes of exchange—was cigarettes. As Radford noted, "The cigarette became the standard of value. In the permanent camp people started by wandering through the bungalows calling their offers—'cheese for seven [cigarettes] . . . .'" ▲ ▲ ▲

## Money, Leisure, and Output

Exchanges take less time in a money economy than in a barter economy because a double coincidence of wants is unnecessary: everyone is willing to trade for money. The movement from a barter to a money economy therefore frees up some of the transaction time, which people can use in other ways.

## English and Money

In the world of barter, some goods are more widely accepted than others.

In the world of languages, some languages may be more widely used than others. Today, the most widely used language appears to be English.

English is spoken not only by native English speakers but by many other people around the world. English is the language of computers and the Internet. You can see English on posters everywhere in the world. You can hear it in pop songs sung in Tokyo. English is the working language of the Asian trade group ASEAN (Association of Southeast Asian Nations). It is the language of 98 percent of German research physicists and of 83 percent of German research chemists. It is the official language of the European Central Bank, even though the bank is in Frankfurt,

© IMAGE COPYRIGHT BRUCE AMOS, 2011. USED UNDER LICENSE FROM SHUTTERSTOCK.COM

Germany. It is found in official documents in Phnom Penh, Cambodia. Singers all over the world sing in English. Alcatel, a French telecommunications company, uses English as its internal language. By 2050, half the world's population is expected to be proficient in English.

In a barter economy, if more people accept a good in exchange, then more people will want to accept it. Might the same be true of a language? If more people speak English, then will more non-English-speaking people want to learn English? Just as money lowers the transaction costs of making exchanges, English might lower the transaction costs of communicating.

Is the world evolving toward one universal language, and is that language English?

To illustrate, suppose making trades takes 10 hours a week in a barter economy, but only 1 hour in a money economy. In a money economy, then, each week has 9 hours that don't have to be spent making exchanges and that people can use for other purposes. Some will use them to work, others will use them for leisure, and still others will divide the 9 hours between work and leisure. Thus, a money economy is likely to have both more output (because of the increased production) and more leisure time than a barter economy. In other words, a money economy is likely to be richer in both goods and leisure than a barter economy.

A person's standard of living depends, to a degree, on the number and quality of goods consumed and on the amount of leisure consumed. We would expect the average person's standard of living to be higher in a money economy than in a barter economy.

## finding ECONOMICS

**With William Shakespeare in London (1595)** It is 1595, and William Shakespeare is sitting at a desk writing the Prologue to *Romeo and Juliet.* Where is the economics?

More specifically, what is the connection between Shakespeare's writing a play and the emergence of money out of a barter economy? In a money economy, individuals usually specialize in the production of one good or service because they can do so. In a barter economy, specializing is extremely costly. For Shakespeare, living in a barter economy would mean writing plays all day and then going out and trying to trade what he had written that day for apples, oranges, chickens, and bread. Would the baker trade two loaves of bread for two pages of Romeo and Juliet? Had Shakespeare lived in a barter economy, he would have soon learned that he did not have a double

*(continued)*

## ⓕinding ECONOMICS *(continued)*

coincidence of wants with many people and that if he were going to eat and be housed, he would need to spend time baking bread, raising chickens, and building a shelter instead of thinking about Romeo and Juliet.

In a barter economy, trade is difficult; so people produce for themselves. In a money economy, trade is easy, and so individuals produce one thing, sell it for money, and then buy what they want with the money. A William Shakespeare who lived in a barter economy no doubt spent his days very differently from the William Shakespeare who lived in England in the sixteenth century. Put bluntly: without money, the world might never have enjoyed *Romeo and Juliet.* ▲ ▲ ▲

# DEFINING THE MONEY SUPPLY

If money is any good that is widely accepted for purposes of exchange, is a $10 bill money? Is a dime money? Is a checking account or a savings account money? What constitutes money? In other words, what is included in the money supply? Two frequently used definitions of the money supply are M1 and M2.

## M1

M1 is sometimes referred to as the *narrow definition of the money supply* or as *transactions money.* It is money that can be directly used for everyday transactions—to buy gas for the car, groceries to eat, and clothes to wear. M1 consists of currency held outside banks (by members of the public for use in everyday transactions), checkable deposits, and traveler's checks.

**M1**
Currency held outside banks plus checkable deposits plus traveler's checks.

$$M1 = \text{Currency held outside banks}$$
$$+ \text{ Checkable deposits}$$
$$+ \text{ Traveler's checks}$$

A couple of the components of M1 have specific definitions:

**Currency**
Coins and paper money.

**Federal Reserve Notes**
Paper money issued by the Federal Reserve.

**Checkable Deposits**
Deposits on which checks can be written.

- Currency includes coins minted by the U.S. Treasury and paper money. About 99 percent of the paper money in circulation is in the form of Federal Reserve notes issued by the Federal Reserve District Banks (the Fed).

- Checkable deposits are deposits on which checks can be written. Demand deposits, which are checking accounts that pay no interest, are one kind of checkable deposit. Two others are NOW (negotiated order of withdrawal) and ATS (automatic transfer from savings) accounts, which do pay interest on their balances.

In March 2010 checkable deposits equaled $835 billion, currency held outside banks equaled $871 billion, and traveler's checks were $6 billion. M1, the sum of these figures, was $1,712 billion.

## Money Is More Than Currency

Most laypersons hear the word "money" and think of currency—paper money (dollar bills) and coins. For example, if a thief stops you on a dark street at night and demands, "Your money or your life," you can be sure he wants your currency. People often equate money and currency. To an economist, though, money is more than just currency. According to the M1 definition, money is currency, checkable deposits, and traveler's checks. (However, if robbed by a thief, an economist would be unlikely to hand over her currency and then write a check too.)

## eBay and Match.com

One of the benefits of money's emerging out of a barter economy is that it lowers the transaction costs of making exchanges. In a barter economy, transaction costs are relatively high because no one can be sure that the person who has what you want wants what you have. With the emergence of money, the transaction costs of making exchanges drop because everyone is willing to trade for money.

Just as money has lowered the transaction costs of making exchanges, so has the Internet. Through the Internet, people can find other people they might want to exchange with faster and more easily.

Consider life before the Internet and before both eBay and Match.com. Suppose a person in London has an old Rolling Stones album for sale. He is not sure how to find someone who might want to buy it. Today, the seller simply goes online to eBay and posts the album for sale. In perhaps a matter of hours, people who want to buy the album are bidding

on it. eBay and the Internet lower the transaction costs of bringing buyer and seller together.

Or consider Match.com, an online dating service. When people date each other, an exchange of sorts is going on. Each person is effectively saying to the other, "I demand some of your time, which I hope you will supply to me."

**match.com®**

COURTESY OF MATCH.COM

One of the transaction costs of dating is actually finding a person to date. Match.com and the Internet, however, lower the transaction costs. The dating service is a little like eBay, in that you are offering to "sell" yourself. Instead of describing a Rolling Stones album, you describe yourself. Then, in a sense, people bid on you by getting in touch—and you bid on others.

What do money, eBay, and Match.com tell us about life? People want to trade with each other, and part of being able to trade is lowering the transaction costs. Money, eBay, and Match.com fill the bill.

## M2

M2 is commonly referred to as the *broad definition of the money supply.* M2 is made up of M1 plus savings deposits (including money market deposit accounts), small-denomination time deposits, and money market mutual funds (retail).

M2 = M1
    + Savings deposits (including money market deposit accounts)
    + Small-denomination time deposits
    + Money market mutual funds (retail)

Again, several components of M2 need to be defined:

- A savings deposit, sometimes called a *regular savings deposit,* is an interest-earning account at a commercial bank or thrift institution. (Thrift institutions include savings and loan associations, mutual savings banks, and credit unions.) Normally, checks cannot be written on savings deposits, and the funds in savings deposits can be withdrawn at any time without a penalty payment.

- A time deposit is an interest-earning deposit with a *specified maturity date.* Time deposits are subject to penalties for early withdrawal, that is, withdrawal before the maturity date. Small-denomination time deposits are less than $100,000.

- A money market deposit account (MMDA) is an interest-earning account at a bank or thrift institution, and usually a minimum balance is required. Most MMDAs offer limited check-writing privileges. For example, the owner of an MMDA might be

### M2

M1 plus savings deposits (including money market deposit accounts) plus small-denomination time deposits plus money market mutual funds (retail).

### Savings Deposit

An interest-earning account at a commercial bank or thrift institution. Normally, checks cannot be written on savings deposits, and the funds in a savings deposit can be withdrawn at any time without a penalty payment.

### Time Deposit

An interest-earning deposit with a specified maturity date. Time deposits are subject to penalties for early withdrawal, that is, withdrawal before the maturity date. Small-denomination time deposits are less than $100,000.

### Money Market Deposit Account (MMDA)

An interest-earning account at a bank or thrift institution, for which a minimum balance is usually required and most of which offer limited check-writing privileges.

**Money Market Mutual Fund (MMMF)**
An interest-earning account at a mutual fund company, for which a minimum balance is usually required and most of which offer limited check-writing privileges. Only retail MMMFs are part of M2.

able to write only a certain number of checks each month, and/or each check may have to be above a certain dollar amount (e.g., $500).

- A money market mutual fund (MMMF) is an interest-earning account at a *mutual fund company.* Usually, a minimum balance is required for an MMMF account, and most offer limited check-writing privileges. MMMFs held by large institutions are referred to as institutional MMMFs. MMMFs held by all others (e.g., by individuals) are referred to as retail MMMFs. *Only retail MMMFs are part of M2.*

In March 2010, M2 was $8,512 billion.

## Where Do Credit Cards Fit In?

A credit card is commonly referred to as plastic money, but it is not money. A credit card is an instrument or a document that makes it easier for the holder to obtain a loan. When Tina Ridges hands the department store clerk her MasterCard or Visa, she is, in effect, spending someone else's money (which already existed). The department store submits the claim to the bank, the bank pays the department store, and then the bank bills the holder of its credit card. By using her credit card, Tina spends someone else's money, and she ultimately must repay her credit card debt with money. These transactions shift around the existing quantity of money among individuals and firms, but they do not change the total.

### SELF-TEST

(Answers to Self-Test questions are in Answers to Self-Test Questions at the back of the book.)

1. Why (not how) did money evolve out of a barter economy?

2. If individuals remove funds from their checkable deposits and transfer them to their money market accounts, will M1 fall and M2 rise? Explain your answer.

3. How does money reduce the transaction costs of making trades?

# HOW BANKING DEVELOPED

Just as money evolved, so did banking. This section discusses the origins of banking and sheds some light on and aids in understanding modern banking.

## The Early Bankers

Our money today is easy to carry and transport, but it was not always so portable. For example, when money consisted principally of gold coins, carrying it about was neither easy nor safe. First, gold is heavy. Second, gold was not only inconvenient for customers to carry, but it was also inconvenient for merchants to accept; gold was heavy and unsafe to carry around. Third, a person transporting thousands of gold coins can easily draw the attention of thieves. Yet storing gold at home can also be risky. Most individuals therefore turned to their local goldsmiths for help because they had safe storage facilities. Goldsmiths were thus the first bankers. They took in other people's gold and stored it for them. To acknowledge that they held deposited gold, goldsmiths issued receipts, called *warehouse receipts*, to their customers.

Once people's confidence in the receipts was established, they used the receipts to make payments instead of using the gold itself. In time, the paper warehouse receipts circulated as money. For instance, if Franklin wanted to buy something from Mason that was priced at 10 gold pieces, he could simply give his warehouse receipt to Mason instead of going to the goldsmith, obtaining the gold, and then delivering it to Mason. For both Franklin and Mason, using the receipts was easier than exchanging the actual gold.

At this stage of banking, warehouse receipts were fully backed by gold; they simply represented gold in storage. Goldsmiths later began to recognize that, on an average day, few people redeemed their receipts for gold. Many individuals traded the receipts for goods

# economics 24/7

## Economics on the Yellow Brick Road

*I'll get you, my pretty.*
—**Wicked Witch of the West in**
***The Wizard of Oz***

In 1893, the United States fell into economic depression. The stock market crashed, banks failed, workers were laid off, and many farmers lost their farms. Some people blamed the depression on the gold standard. They proposed that, instead of having only gold backing U.S. currency, the monetary standard should be bimetallic; that is, both gold and silver should back the currency. This change, they said, would lead to an increase in the money supply. Many people thought that, with more money in circulation, economic hard times would soon be a thing of the past.

One of the champions of silver was William Jennings Bryan, the Democratic candidate for the U.S. presidency in 1896. Bryan had established himself as a friend to the many Americans who had been hurt by the economic depression, especially farmers and industrial workers. Bryan's views were shared by L. Frank Baum, the author of *The Wonderful Wizard of Oz*, the book that was the basis for the 1939 movie, *The Wizard of Oz*.

Baum blamed the gold standard for the hardships faced by farmers and workers during the depression. Baum saw the farmer and the worker as the so-called common man, and he saw William Jennings Bryan as the best possible hope for the common man in this country.

Many people believe that Baum's most famous work, *The Wonderful Wizard of Oz*, is an allegory for the presidential election of 1896.[1] Some say that Dorothy, in the book and the movie, represents Bryan. Both Dorothy and Bryan were young (Bryan was a 36-year-old presidential candidate). Like the cyclone in the movie that transported Dorothy to

MGM/THE KOBAL COLLECTION

the Land of Oz, the delegates at the 1896 Democratic convention lifted Bryan into a new political world, the world of presidential politics.

As Dorothy begins her travels to the Emerald City (Washington, D.C.) with Toto (the Democratic party) to meet the Wizard of Oz, she travels down a yellow brick road (the gold standard). On her way, she meets the scarecrow (the farmer), the tin man (the industrial worker), and the cowardly lion, who some believe represents the Populist party of the time. (The Populist party was sometimes depicted as a lion in the political cartoons of the time. It was a cowardly lion in that, as some say, it did not have the courage to fight an independent campaign for the presidency in 1896.) The message is clear: Bryan, with the help of the Democratic and Populist parties and with the votes of the farmers and the industrial workers, will travel to Washington.

But then, when Dorothy and the others reach the Emerald City, they are denied their wishes, just as Bryan is denied the presidency. He loses the election to William McKinley.

But the story is not over. There is still the battle with the Wicked Witch of the West, who wears a golden cap (the gold standard). When the Wicked Witch sees Dorothy's silver shoes—they were changed to ruby in the movie—she desperately wants them for their magical quality. But she is not to get her way. Dorothy kills the Wicked Witch of the West. She then clicks her silver shoes together, and they take her back home, where all is right with the world.

---

1. This interpretation is based on "William Jennings Bryan on the Yellow Brick Road," by John Geer and Thomas Rochon, *Journal of American Culture* (Winter 1993) and "The Wizard of Oz: Parable on Populism," by Henry Littlefield, *American Quarterly* (1964).

and seldom requested the gold itself. In short, the receipts had become money, widely accepted for purposes of exchange.

Sensing opportunity, goldsmiths began to lend some of the stored gold, realizing that they could earn interest on the loans without defaulting on their pledge to redeem the warehouse receipts when presented. In most cases, however, the gold borrowers also preferred warehouse receipts to the actual gold. Thus the warehouse receipts came to represent a greater amount of gold than was actually on deposit. Consequently, the money supply increased, now measured in terms of gold and the paper warehouse receipts issued by the goldsmith-bankers.

**Fractional Reserve Banking**
A banking arrangement that allows banks to hold reserves equal to only a fraction of their deposit liabilities.

Thus fractional reserve banking had begun. In a fractional reserve system, banks create money by holding on reserve only a fraction of the money deposited with them and lending the remainder. Our modern-day banking operates within such a system.

## The Bank's Reserves and More

**Federal Reserve System (the Fed)**
The central bank of the United States.

Many banks have an account with the Federal Reserve System (the Fed), the central bank of the United States. These accounts are very similar to the checking accounts that individuals have with a commercial bank. Economists refer to this account with the Fed as either a *reserve account* or *bank deposits at the Fed*. Banks also have currency or cash in their vaults—called vault cash—on the bank premises. The sum of (1) bank deposits at the Fed and (2) the bank's vault cash is known as reserves.

**Reserves**
The sum of bank deposits at the Fed and vault cash.

$$\text{Reserves} = \text{Bank deposits at the Fed} + \text{Vault cash}$$

For example, if a bank currently has $4 million in deposits at the Fed and $1 million in vault cash, it has $5 million in reserves.

**THE REQUIRED RESERVE RATIO AND REQUIRED RESERVES** The Fed mandates that member commercial banks must hold a certain fraction of their checkable deposits in *reserve form*. In other words, that fraction of checkable deposits must be in the form of bank deposits at the Fed and/or vault cash because the sum of these two accounts equals reserves.

**Required Reserve Ratio (r)**
A percentage of each dollar deposited that must be held in reserve form (specifically, as bank deposits at the Fed or vault cash).

The fraction of checkable deposits that banks must hold in reserve form is called the required reserve ratio (r). The dollar amount of those deposits is called required reserves, and the rule specifying the amount of reserves that a bank must hold to back up deposits is the reserve requirement. To find the required reserves for a given bank, multiply the required reserve ratio by checkable deposits (in the bank):

**Required Reserves**
The minimum dollar amount of reserves a bank must hold against its checkable deposits, as mandated by the Fed.

$$\text{Required reserves} = r \times \text{Checkable deposits}$$

For example, assume that customers have deposited $40 million in a neighborhood bank and that the Fed has set the required reserve ratio at 1/10 or 10 percent. Required reserves for the bank equal $4 million (0.10 × $40 million = $4 million).

**Reserve Requirement**
The Fed rule that specifies the amount of reserves a bank must hold to back up deposits.

**EXCESS RESERVES** The difference between a bank's (total) reserves and its required reserves is its excess reserves:

**Excess Reserves**
Any reserves held beyond the required amount; the difference between (total) reserves and required reserves.

$$\text{Excess reserves} = \text{Reserves} - \text{Required reserves}$$

For example, if the bank's (total) reserves are $5 million and its required reserves are $4 million, then it holds excess reserves of $1 million.

Note: Banks can use excess reserves to make loans. Before late 2008, the Fed did not pay interest on any reserves (required or excess); so banks had a monetary incentive to create loans with their excess reserves. That incentive was lessened when the Fed began paying interest on reserves in late 2008.

## SELF-TEST

1. A bank reduces its deposits at the Fed by $5 million and increases its vault cash by $5 million. What happens to the bank's reserves?

2. If a bank has $87 million in checkable deposits, and it is required to hold $6 million in reserves (required reserves = $6 million), what is the required reserve ratio equal to?

3. If excess reserves are $4 million and (total) reserves are $6 million, what do required reserves and checkable deposits equal? Assume the required reserve ratio is 8 percent.

# The Financial System

A financial system is essentially a means of getting people with surplus funds together with people who have a shortage of funds. Stated differently, it is a means of getting savers and borrowers together.

Why is getting lenders and borrowers together important? The short answer is getting them together is a way to put good ideas into action. Suppose you have saved funds that you want to lend. Elsewhere, someone has a shortage of funds but an idea for a new business venture. That person doesn't have the necessary funds to launch his new business venture. He needs to find people like you—people with funds to lend—who wouldn't mind trading him your funds now in return for his making interest payments to you later.

Thus an economy that can get saved funds to borrowers can not only benefit the lenders but the borrowers too. And it can also benefit others. If the borrower really does have a good idea for a new business venture, future customers will benefit when the business is up and running. Maybe the firm will produce something that many thousands of others want to buy.

## Direct and Indirect Finance

Lenders can get together with borrowers directly or indirectly; that is, there are two types of finance: direct and indirect. In direct finance, the lenders and borrowers come together in a market setting, such as the bond market. In the bond market, people who want to borrow funds issue bonds. For example, company A might issue a bond that promises to pay an interest rate of 10 percent annually for the next 10 years. A person with funds to lend might then buy that bond for a particular price. The buying and selling in a bond market are simply lending and borrowing. The buyer of the bond is the lender, and the seller of the bond is the borrower.

In indirect finance, lenders and borrowers go through a financial intermediary, which takes in funds from people who want to save and then lends the funds to people who want to borrow. For example, a commercial bank is a financial intermediary, doing business with both savers and borrowers. Through one door the savers come in, looking for a place to deposit their funds and earn regular interest payments. Through another door come the borrowers, seeking loans on which they will pay interest. The bank, or the financial intermediary, ends up channeling the saved funds to borrowers.

## Adverse Selection and Moral Hazard Problems

When it comes to lending and borrowing, both adverse selection and moral hazards can arise. Both are the result of asymmetric information. Asymmetric information relates to one side of a transaction having information that the other side does not have. Suppose Ursula is going to sell her house. As the seller of the house, she has more information about the house than potential buyers. Ursula knows whether the house has plumbing problems, cracks in the foundation, and so on. Potential buyers do not.

The effect of asymmetric information can be either an adverse selection problem or a moral hazard problem. The adverse selection problem occurs *before* the loan is made, and the moral hazard problem occurs *afterward*.

**BEFORE THE LOAN IS MADE**   An adverse selection problem occurs when the parties on one side of the market, having information not known to others, self-select in a way that adversely affects the parties on the other side of the market. Think of it this way: Two people want a loan. One person is a good credit risk, and the other is a bad credit risk. The person who is the bad credit risk is the person more likely to ask for the loan.

Suppose two people, Steven and Olivia, want to borrow $10,000, and Jason has $10,000 to lend. Olivia wants to borrow the $10,000 to buy a piece of equipment for her small business. She plans to pay back the loan, and she takes her loan commitments very seriously. Steven wants to borrow the $10,000 so that he can go to Las Vegas and play roulette.

**Direct Finance**
Borrowers and lenders come together in a market setting, such as in the bond market.

**Indirect Finance**
Funds are loaned and borrowed through a financial intermediary.

**Financial Intermediary**
A financial intermediary transfers funds from those who want to lend funds to those who want to borrow them.

**Asymmetric Information**
Relates to an economic agent on one side of a transaction having information that an economic agent on the other side of the transaction does not have.

**Adverse Selection**
A phenomenon that occurs when the parties on one side of the market, who have information not known to others, self-select in a way that adversely affects the parties on the other side of the market.

He will pay back the loan only if he scores big in Las Vegas. He is not the type of person who takes his loan commitments seriously. Who is more likely to ask Jason for the loan, Steven or Olivia? Steven is because he knows that he will pay back the loan only if he wins big in Las Vegas; he sees a loan as essentially "free money." Heads, Steven wins; tails, Jason loses.

Now if Jason gives a little thought to his lending activities, he may realize that there are borrowers like Steven in the world. Ideally, Jason wants to lend only to the Olivias of the world, but Jason can't always tell who is an Olivia and who is a Steven. Olivia will tell Jason the truth about what she wants to do with the loan, and she is likely to pay back the loan. Steven, on the other hand, may lie to Jason about what he plans to do with the loan, and he is not as likely to pay back the loan as Olivia.

If Jason can't tell the Olivias from the Stevens, what can he do? He might just decide not to give a loan to anyone. In other words, his inability to solve the adverse selection problem (that is, to tell the good risks from the bad risks) may be enough for him to decide not to lend to anyone.

At this point, a financial intermediary can help. A financial intermediary, such as a bank, does not require Jason to worry about who will and who will not pay back a loan. Jason needs simply to turn over his saved funds to the bank, in return for the bank's promise to pay him a 5 percent interest rate per year. Then, the bank takes on the responsibility of trying to separate the Olivias from the Stevens. The bank will run a credit check on everyone (the Olivias and Stevens alike); the bank will collect information on who has a job and who doesn't; the bank will ask the borrower to put up some collateral on the loan; and so on. In other words, the bank's job is to solve the adverse selection problem.

**Moral Hazard**
A condition that exists when one party to a transaction changes his or her behavior in a way that is hidden from and costly to the other party.

**AFTER THE LOAN IS MADE**  The moral hazard problem exists when one party to a transaction changes his or her behavior in a way that is hidden from and costly to the other party. Suppose you want to lend some saved funds. You give Tracy a $5,000 loan because she promised you that she was going to use the funds to help her get through college. Instead, once Tracy receives the $5,000, she decides to use the funds to buy some clothes and take a vacation to St. Thomas in the Caribbean.

Because of such potential moral hazard problems, you might decide to cut back on granting loans. You want to protect yourself from borrowers who do things that are costly to you. Again, a financial intermediary has a role to play. A financial intermediary, such as a bank, might try to solve the moral hazard problem by specifying that a loan can only be used for a particular purpose (e.g., paying for college). It might require the borrower to provide regular information on and evidence of how the borrowed funds are being used, giving out the loan in installments ($1,000 this month, $1,000 next month), and so on.

## A Thought Experiment: No Financial Intermediaries

If financial intermediaries did not exist, how would life be different? Would there be as much lending and borrowing activity in a world? Because adverse selection and moral hazard problems reduce the amount of lending (and therefore borrowing), and because financial intermediaries help to solve these two problems, then there would be more lending and borrowing in a world with financial intermediaries than in one without them.

The next question is whether having more lending and borrowing is preferable to having less. To answer this question, recall that lending and borrowing is a process of channeling funds to those who can use those funds to start businesses, to come up with new products, to establish new and better production techniques, and to do other beneficial things. So lending and borrowing are not only beneficial to the lender and the borrower, but to others too. Your current material standard of living would probably not be as high as it is had you not lived in a country with substantial borrowing and lending.

# economics 24/7

## The FDIC and Intended and Unintended Effects

In Chapter 1, we talked about the unintended consequences of actions. For example, a policy maker might undertake policy A because she wants effect X. She gets X, but she also gets the unintended effect Y, which she doesn't want.

As an example, in 1934, the federal government, through the Federal Deposit Insurance Corporation (FDIC), started insuring deposits in banks. Today, the FDIC insures bank depositors up to $250,00. If you have any dollar amount in a bank between $1 and $250,00 and that bank fails (goes out of business), you are guaranteed to get your money back. You will not suffer a loss.

The intended effect of instituting the FDIC and guaranteeing depositors up to $250,000 is to reduce the probability of a run on a bank and a

bank panic. A run on a bank is exactly what it sounds like: individuals "run" to the bank to withdraw their funds because they think the bank might fail. A bank panic occurs when a run on one bank leads to runs on other banks. However, if you know you will get your money back, you have less reason to run to the bank and withdraw your funds. In turn, the bank isn't pushed into a position where it can't pay back its depositors' money.

The unintended effect of the FDIC guarantee is that depositors have less incentive to monitor the bank's activities and the bank has an increased incentive to take on riskier loans than it would if the FDIC did not exist.

---

Second, lending and borrowing allow people to consume earlier in life than they would otherwise be able to. To illustrate, Maria is 26 years old and wants to buy a condominium. Condos in her area sell for about $300,000, but Maria does not have $300,000; she has only $20,000. Without lending and borrowing, Maria would have to do without the condo until she can save $300,000. But with borrowing and lending, Maria can make a $20,000 down payment on the condo and borrow the remaining $280,000. She can begin living in the condo many years earlier than would otherwise be possible.

In conclusion, lending and borrowing not only provide the financing for new businesses and the production of new products, production techniques, and so on, but they also permit individuals to enjoy the benefits of certain goods and services for a greater number of years than would be possible without lending and borrowing. Because someone will lend her $280,000, Maria gets to enjoy the benefits of her condo for many additional years.

## The Bank's Balance Sheet

We can learn a lot about banks by looking at a bank's balance sheet, which lists the bank's assets and liabilities. An asset is anything of value that the bank owns or has claim to. A liability is anything that the bank owes to someone else. A few examples of a bank's assets are the *reserves* the bank holds, any loans the bank has made to borrowers, and any securities the bank might own. A few examples of a bank's liabilities are the checkable deposits it holds for its customers, any nontransaction deposits (such as small-denomination time deposits), and any loans the bank has taken out (for example, a loan the bank might have received from the Fed). Exhibit 1 shows a simplified but typical balance sheet for a bank.

## A Bank's Business: Turning Liabilities into Assets

A bank's business is to turn its liabilities into assets. Suppose you open up a checkable deposit account with bank A and deposit $10,000 into the account. Your checkable deposit is a liability for the bank. The balance in the checkable deposit account is what the bank *owes* you. The bank then turns the bulk of the funds in your checkable deposit account into an asset. Specifically, the bank might use the bulk of those funds to grant a

**Balance Sheet**
A record of the assets and liabilities of a bank.

**Asset**
Anything of value that is owned or that one has claim to.

**Liability**
Anything that is owed to someone else.

# The Financial Crisis, Risky Loans, and Bank Insolvency

At the end of 2008 and throughout 2009, many banks found themselves holding unpaid loans, many of them mortgage loans to home buyers. To understand what was happening at this time, compare two settings.

In setting 1, a person wants to buy a house that is priced at $500,000. The person is asked to make a 20 percent down payment ($100,000) to take out a mortgage loan for the balance ($400,000). Time passes, and the person who took out the loan can't make the monthly payments. What course of action does he have? As long as the house's price hasn't fallen below $400,000, he can sell the property and repay the balance of the loan. In other words, suppose the price of the house has fallen to $425,000. Our house owner and mortgage loan borrower can sell the house for $425,000 and repay the $400,000 loan, leaving him with $25,000. Obviously, the mortgage borrower has ended up losing some of his $100,000 down payment.

In setting 2, a person wants to buy a house that is priced at $500,000. This time, though, the person is not asked for a down payment. The bank gives the buyer a mortgage loan for the entire price of the house: a $500,000 loan. Again, suppose that the person who took out the loan has a hard time making her monthly payments. What now? Can she sell the house and repay the loan? Yes, as long as the price of the house is still $500,000 (ignoring real estate fees and closing costs). But what if

the price of the house has fallen to $425,000. The person who bought the house and took out the $500,000 loan may simply walk away from the house and the loan. The house reverts to the bank, but the bank can't sell the house for a high enough price to recover its loan amount. It sells the house for $425,000 and takes a $75,000 loss on the mortgage loan of $500,000.

Setting 1 describes the state of the mortgage loan business in the 1970s, 1980s, and early 1990s. Setting 2 describes the state of the mortgage loan business in the late 1990s and the early-to-mid 2000s. Why banks moved from one setting to the other is a long story that we will speak about in a later chapter. For now, we are interested in how setting 2 changes things for the bank, especially with respect to the prospects of insolvency.

The peak of the housing boom (rising home prices) in the United States came in mid-2006. Since then, house prices have fallen. The decline in house prices, combined with the percentage of homeowners who can't make their monthly house payments, has the effect of loans going bad for banks. Some of the loans (which, in hindsight, turned out to be risky) were not paid off in full for one reason or another. As a result, the assets of the banks declined, and consequently so did the bank's capital (its net worth). Banks found themselves either falling over, or close to the edge, of the insolvency cliff.

## Exhibit 1

### A Bank's Balance Sheet

Here we show a bank's balance sheet. On the left-hand side are assets (what others owe to the bank): reserves (equal to bank deposits at the Fed plus vault cash), any loans it has made to others (e.g., a car loan the bank gave to someone), and any securities it owns. On the right-hand side are liabilities (what the bank owes to others): checkable deposits (held for its customers), nontransaction deposits (e.g., small-denomination time deposits), and borrowings of the banks (i.e., any loans the banks may have taken out). Also, it is customary to show bank capital (or net worth) -- which is the difference between assets and liabilities -- on the right-hand side of the balance sheet. In this balance sheet, assets are $110 million and liabilities are $100 million; so bank capital (or net worth) is $10 million.

| Assets ($ millions) | | Liabilities ($ millions) | |
| --- | --- | --- | --- |
| Reserves | 10 | Checkable deposits | 50 |
| Loans | 90 | Nontransaction deposits (e.g., small-denomination time deposits) | 50 |
| Securities | 10 | Borrowings | 0 |
| | | Bank Capital (net worth) | 10 |

loan to someone. So, therefore, a bank wants liabilities because liabilities are its sources of funds—the seeds, if you will—for growing its assets.

The difference between a bank's assets and liabilities constitutes the bank's capital, or its net worth:

$$\text{Bank capital (or net worth)} = \text{Assets} - \text{Liabilities}$$

For example, if a bank has $120 million in assets and $112 million in liabilities, its net worth (or the bank's capital) is equal to $8 million. Typically, a bank's capital is recorded on the right-hand side of its balance sheet, as shown in Exhibit 1.

The bank's capital can be viewed as a cushion against insolvency, which exists when a bank's liabilities are greater than its assets. An insolvent bank has failed and can be shut down.

**Insolvency**
A condition in which one's liabilities are greater than one's assets.

$$\text{Insolvency} \rightarrow \text{Liabilities} > \text{Assets}$$

The larger the bank's capital, the bigger the cushion against bank failure or insolvency; the smaller the bank's capital, the smaller the cushion against bank failure or insolvency.

## SELF-TEST

1. Jack promises Samantha that he will pay for any expenses she has on her trip beyond $1,000. Does this create an adverse selection or moral hazard problem? Explain your answer.

2. Bank A finds that many of the loans it extended to individuals are not being paid back. How do the defaults affect bank A's capital or net worth?

3. What do financial intermediaries do?

## "I Thought Money Had to Be Backed by Gold to Have Value"

**STUDENT:**

We know that M1 is equal to currency held outside banks plus checkable deposits plus traveler's checks. None of these components of the money supply are backed by gold. But don't they have to be backed by gold before they can have any value?

**INSTRUCTOR:**

Your question essentially tries to identify that "thing" that gives money value. So let's suppose that paper money were backed by gold. In other words, if you take $100 in paper money, and turn it in to the federal government, it would give you in return $100 worth of gold. At first glance, you might say that paper money has value because it is backed by gold. But then the question becomes what gives gold value? What is gold backed by?

**STUDENT:**

Nothing backs up gold. For example, gold isn't backed by copper or anything else.

**INSTRUCTOR:**

Our point is a simple one: it is a myth that paper money has to be backed by a commodity—such as gold—before it can have value. Our paper money has value because of its *general acceptability*. Specifically, you accept a dollar bill in payment for your goods and services because you know others will accept the dollar bill in payment. To illustrate, suppose our paper money were not generally accepted. Suppose one day that the supermarket clerk would not accept the paper dollars you offered as payment for groceries. Suppose the plumber and the gas station attendant would not take your paper

dollars for fixing your kitchen drain and for servicing your car. In such a case, would you be as likely to accept paper dollars in exchange for what you sell? Probably not. You accept paper dollars because you know that other people will accept them when you spend them. Money has value to people because it is widely accepted in exchange for other valuable goods.

### POINTS TO REMEMBER

1. It is a myth that paper money has to be backed by a commodity (such as gold) before it can have value.
2. General acceptability gives money value.

## CHAPTER SUMMARY

### WHAT MONEY IS

- Money is any good that is widely accepted for purposes of exchange and in the repayment of debts.
- Money serves as a medium of exchange, a unit of account, and a store of value.
- Money evolved out of a barter economy as traders attempted to make exchange easier. A few goods that have been used as money are gold, silver, copper, cattle, rocks, and shells.
- Our money today has value because of its general acceptability.

### THE MONEY SUPPLY

- M1 includes currency held outside banks, checkable deposits, and traveler's checks.
- M2 includes M1, savings deposits (including money market deposit accounts), small-denomination time deposits, and money market mutual funds (retail).
- Credit cards are not money. When a credit card is used to make a purchase, a liability is incurred. This is not the case when money is used to make a purchase.

### RESERVES, REQUIRED AND EXCESS

- Reserves equal bank deposits at the Fed plus vault cash. The dollar amount of reserves a bank must hold is equal to the required reserve ratio times its checkable deposits: Required reserves = $r \times$ Checkable deposits, where $r$ = required reserve ratio. Excess reserves is the difference between total reserves and required reserves: Excess reserves = Reserves − Required reserves.

### THE FINANCIAL SYSTEM

- A financial system is a means of getting people with surplus funds (with funds to lend) together with people who have a shortage of funds (who want to borrow funds).
- Asymmetric information relates to one side of a transaction having information that the other side of the transaction does not. The two types of asymmetric information problems are adverse selection and moral hazard.
- Adverse selection is a phenomenon that occurs when the parties on one side of the market, who have information not known to others, self-select in a way that adversely affects the parties on the other side of the market.
- Moral hazard is the condition that exists when one party to a transaction changes his or her behavior in a way that is hidden from and costly to the other party.

### A BANK'S BALANCE SHEET

- A bank's balance sheet records its assets and liabilities.
- A bank's business is to turn its liabilities into assets.
- Bank capital, or net worth, is the difference between a bank's assets and its liabilities. Bank capital (net worth) = Assets − Liabilities.
- A bank is insolvent if its liabilities are greater than its assets.

## KEY TERMS AND CONCEPTS

| | | | |
|---|---|---|---|
| Money | Checkable Deposits | Federal Reserve System (the Fed) | Financial Intermediary |
| Barter | M2 | Reserves | Asymmetric Information |
| Medium of Exchange | Savings Deposit | Required Reserve Ratio ($r$) | Adverse Selection |
| Unit of Account | Time Deposit | Required Reserves | Moral Hazard |
| Store of Value | Money Market Deposit Account (MMDA) | Reserve Requirement | Balance Sheet |
| Double Coincidence of Wants | Money Market Mutual Fund (MMMF) | Excess Reserves | Asset |
| M1 | Fractional Reserve Banking | Direct Finance | Liability |
| Currency | | Indirect Finance | Insolvency |
| Federal Reserve Notes | | | |

## QUESTIONS AND PROBLEMS

1. "How much money did you make last year?" What is wrong with that statement?

2. Suppose the value of the dollar declines relative to other currencies. How does the decline affect the three functions of money?

3. Does inflation, which is an increase in the price level, affect the three functions of money? If so, how?

4. "People in a barter economy came up with the idea of money because they wanted to do something to make society better

off." Do you agree or disagree with this statement? Explain your answer.

5. "A barter economy would have very few comedians." Do you agree or disagree with this statement? Explain your answer.

6. Money makes trade easier. Would having a money supply twice as large as it is currently make trade twice as easy? Would having a money supply half its current size make trade half as easy?

7. Explain why gold backing is not necessary to give paper money value.

8. "Money is a means of lowering the transaction costs of making exchanges." Do you agree or disagree? Explain your answer.

9. If you were on an island with 10 other people and there were no money, do you think money would emerge on the scene? Why or why not?

10. Can M1 fall as M2 rises? Can M1 rise without M2 rising too? Explain your answers.

11. Why isn't a credit card money?

12. Define the following:

a. Time deposit

b. Money market mutual fund

c. Money market deposit account

d. Fractional reserve banking

e. Reserves

13. Explain the process by which goldsmiths could increase the money supply.

14. What is a financial system, and why would a country with a well-developed and fully functionally financial system be better off than a country without it?

15. Identify each of the following as either an adverse selection or a moral hazard problem:

a. Poor drivers apply for car insurance more than good drivers.

b. The federal government promises to help banks that get into financial problems.

c. The federal government insures checkable deposits (promises to repay the holder of the checkable deposit if the bank fails).

16. Explain how financial intermediaries help to solve adverse selection and moral hazard problems when it comes to lending and borrowing.

17. Explain the difference between a bank's loans and its borrowings.

## WORKING WITH NUMBERS AND GRAPHS

1. Checkable deposits are $50 million, and required reserves are $4 million. What is the required reserve ratio?

2. The required reserve ratio is 9 percent, required reserves are $10 million, and (total) reserves are $50 million. What do excess reserves equal? What do checkable deposits equal?

3. A bank's assets are $90 million, and its liabilities are $71 million. Its assets increase by 10 percent, and its liabilities increase by 6 percent. What is the *percentage change* in the bank's capital, or net worth?

4. A bank currently has $100 million checkable deposits, $4 million in reserves, and $8 million in securities. If the required reserve ratio is 10 percent, is the bank meeting its legal reserve requirements? Explain.

## CHAPTER 13

# THE FEDERAL RESERVE SYSTEM

©LEE SNIDER/PHOTOIMAGES/CORBIS

**Introduction** Tourists in Washington, D.C., usually visit the White House, the Capitol building, and the Supreme Court building, in which major decisions are made that affect peoples' lives. Such decisions affecting peoples' lives are also made in another building in Washington, D.C., but tourists rarely visit it: the Federal Reserve building. In this building, the Board of Governors of the Federal Reserve System and the members of the Federal Open Market Committee determine U.S. monetary policy. We provide you with many of the details of the Federal Reserve System in this chapter.

## THE STRUCTURE AND FUNCTIONS OF THE FEDERAL RESERVE SYSTEM (THE FED)

The Federal Reserve System is the central bank of the United States. Other nations have central banks, such as the Bank of Sweden, the Bank of England, the Banque de France, the Bank of Japan, the Deutsche Bundesbank, and the like.

### The Structure of the Fed

The Federal Reserve System came into existence with the Federal Reserve Act of 1913 and began operations in November 1914. The act divided the country into Federal Reserve Districts. As Exhibit 1 shows, there are 12 districts, each with a Federal Reserve Bank and its own president.

Within the Fed, a seven-member Board of Governors coordinates and controls the activities of the Federal Reserve System. The board members serve 14-year terms and are appointed by the president with U.S. Senate approval. To limit political influence on Fed policy, the terms of the governors are staggered—with one new appointment every other year—so that a president cannot "pack" the board. The president also designates one member as chairman of the board for a four-year term.

The major policy-making group in the Fed is the Federal Open Market Committee (FOMC). Authority to conduct open market operations—the buying and selling of government securities—rests with the FOMC (more on open market operations later in the

**Board of Governors**
The governing body of the Federal Reserve System.

**Federal Open Market Committee (FOMC)**
The 12-member policy-making group in the Fed. The committee has the authority to conduct open market operations.

**Open Market Operations**
The buying and selling of government securities by the Fed.

**EXHIBIT 1**

**Federal Reserve Districts and Federal Reserve Bank Locations**

The boundaries of the Federal Reserve Districts, the cities in which a Federal Reserve Bank is located, and the location of the Board of Governors (Washington, D.C.) are all noted on the map.

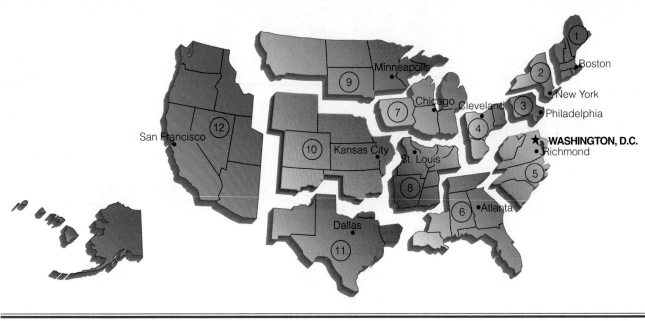

chapter). The FOMC has 12 members: the seven-member Board of Governors and five Federal Reserve District Bank presidents. The president of the Federal Reserve Bank of New York holds a permanent seat on the FOMC because a large amount of financial activity takes place in New York City and because the New York Fed is responsible for executing open market operations. The other four positions are rotated among the Federal Reserve District Bank presidents.

The most important responsibility of the Fed is to conduct monetary policy, or control the money supply. Monetary policy consists of changes in the money supply that are intended to achieve stated macroeconomic goals. More specifically, *expansionary monetary policy* aims to increase the money supply, and *contractionary monetary policy* aims to decrease it. The Fed has tools at its disposal to both increase and decrease the money supply. In a later chapter, we will discuss monetary policy in detail and show how, under certain conditions, it can remove an economy from both recessionary and inflationary gaps.

**Monetary Policy**

Changes in the money supply or in the rate of change of the money supply, intended to achieve stated macroeconomic goals.

## Functions of the Fed

The Fed has eight major responsibilities or functions:

1. *Controlling the money supply.* A full explanation of how the Fed plays this role comes later in the chapter.

2. *Supplying the economy with paper money (Federal Reserve notes).* The Federal Reserve Banks have Federal Reserve notes on hand to meet the demands of the banks and the public. During the Christmas season, for example, more people withdraw larger-than-usual amounts of $1, $5, $20, $50, and $100 notes from banks. Needing to replenish their vault cash, banks turn to their Federal Reserve Banks, which meet cash needs by

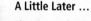

# economics 24/7

## Inside an FOMC Meeting

The major policy-making group in the Federal Reserve System is the Federal Open Market Committee (FOMC), which, to a large degree, makes decisions about monetary policy. The FOMC meets eight times a year, each time on a Tuesday. The meeting is held in the board room of the Federal Reserve Building. The following events occur at a typical FOMC meeting.

©JAY MARTIN/BLOOMBERG NEWS/LANDOV

**8:00 a.m.**

The board room is swept for electronic bugs.

**8:45–9:00 a.m.**

People begin to arrive for the meeting. In addition to the 12 members of the FOMC, about 37 other people will be present.

**8:59 a.m.**

The chairman of the Board of Governors of the Federal Reserve System walks through the door that connects his office to the board room and takes his place at the table.

**9:00 a.m.**

The FOMC meeting commences. The first agenda item is a presentation by the manager of the System Open Market Account at the Federal Reserve Bank of New York. He discusses the financial and foreign exchange markets and provides certain details about open market operations.

**A Little Later …**

The director of research and statistics at the Federal Reserve Board presents the forecast of the U.S. economy. The forecast has previously been circulated to the FOMC members. The latest economic data are reviewed and discussed.

**A Little Later …**

The 12 members of the FOMC present their views of local and national economic conditions.

**A Little Later …**

The director of monetary affairs presents policy options. These policy options have been previously circulated. The chairman of the Board of Governors gives his opinion of the economy and of the policy options.

**A Little Later …**

A general discussion among all the members of the FOMC takes place. At issue is the state of the U.S. economy and current policy options. After the discussion, the chairman summarizes his sense of the policy options. Then the members vote on the options. The chair votes first, the vice chair votes second, and the remaining FOMC members vote in alphabetical order.

**A Little Later …**

The FOMC discusses the wording of the announcement it will make regarding its decision.

**Between 11:30 a.m. and 1:30 p.m.**

The meeting usually adjourns.

**2:15 p.m.**

The decision of the FOMC is released to the public.

---

issuing more paper money (acting as passive suppliers of paper money). The money is actually printed at the Bureau of Engraving and Printing in Washington, D.C., but it is issued to commercial banks by the 12 Federal Reserve Banks.

3. *Providing check-clearing services.* When someone in San Diego writes a check to a person in Los Angeles, what happens to the check? The process by which funds change hands when checks are written is called the *check-clearing process.* That process is summarized in Exhibit 2.

   a. Harry Saito writes a $1,000 check on his San Diego bank account and sends it to Ursula Pevins in Los Angeles.

EXHIBIT 2

**The Check-Clearing Process**

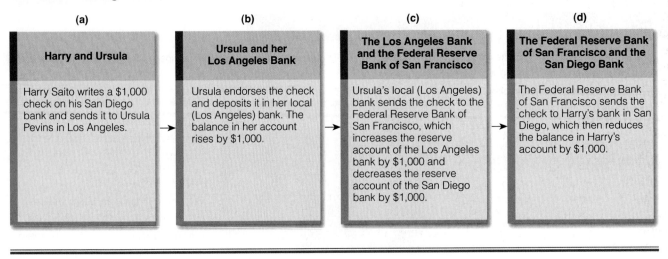

|  (a) | (b) | (c) | (d) |

**Harry and Ursula**

Harry Saito writes a $1,000 check on his San Diego bank and sends it to Ursula Pevins in Los Angeles.

**Ursula and her Los Angeles Bank**

Ursula endorses the check and deposits it in her local (Los Angeles) bank. The balance in her account rises by $1,000.

**The Los Angeles Bank and the Federal Reserve Bank of San Francisco**

Ursula's local (Los Angeles) bank sends the check to the Federal Reserve Bank of San Francisco, which increases the reserve account of the Los Angeles bank by $1,000 and decreases the reserve account of the San Diego bank by $1,000.

**The Federal Reserve Bank of San Francisco and the San Diego Bank**

The Federal Reserve Bank of San Francisco sends the check to Harry's bank in San Diego, which then reduces the balance in Harry's account by $1,000.

 

b. Ursula takes the check to her local bank, endorses it, and deposits it in her checking account. The balance in her account rises by $1,000.

c. Ursula's Los Angeles bank sends the check to its Federal Reserve District Bank, located in San Francisco. The Federal Reserve Bank of San Francisco increases the reserve account of the Los Angeles bank by $1,000 and decreases the reserve account of the San Diego bank by $1,000.

d. The Federal Reserve Bank of San Francisco sends the check to Harry's bank in San Diego, which then reduces the balance in Harry's checking account by $1,000. Harry's bank in San Diego either keeps the check on record or sends it to Harry with his monthly bank statement.

4. *Holding depository institutions' reserves.* As explained in the last chapter, banks are required to keep reserves against customer deposits either in their vaults or in reserve accounts at the Fed. These accounts are maintained by the 12 Federal Reserve Banks for member banks in their respective districts.

5. *Supervising member banks.* Without warning, the Fed can examine the books of member commercial banks to assess the nature of the loans the banks have made, monitor compliance with bank regulations, check the accuracy of bank records, and so on. If the Fed finds that a bank has not been maintaining established banking standards, it can pressure the institution to do so.

6. *Serving as the government's banker.* The federal government collects and spends large sums of money. As a result, it needs a checking account for many of the same reasons an individual does. Its primary checking account is with the Fed, which is the government's banker.

7. *Serving as the lender of last resort.* A traditional function of a central bank is to serve as the lender of last resort for banks suffering cash management, or liquidity, problems.

8. *Handling the sale of U.S. Treasury securities (auctions).* U.S. Treasury securities (bills, notes, and bonds) are sold to raise funds to pay the government's bills. The Federal Reserve District Banks receive the bids for these securities and process them in time for weekly auctions.

**U.S. Treasury Securities**
Bonds and bond-like securities issued by the U.S. Treasury when it borrows.

## Some History of the Fed

Slightly before the passage of the Federal Reserve Act in 1913, there was disagreement about how many districts and banks there should be. Many people thought there should be as few banks as possible—6 to 8—because concentrating activities in only a few cities would enhance efficiency and ease of operation. The Secretary of State at the time, William Jennings Bryan, wanted 50 district banks. He called for a "branch at every major crossroad." It was to be neither 6 nor 50; instead, there was a compromise. Section 2 of the Federal Reserve Act states that "not less than eight nor more than twelve cities" would be designated as Federal Reserve cities.

After the number of cities was determined to be 8 to 12, a commission was set up to identify both the boundaries of the Federal Reserve Districts and the locations of the district banks. The commission was composed of the Comptroller of the Currency, the Secretary of the Treasury, and the Secretary of Agriculture. They had to choose from among the 37 cities that had applied to be locations of a district bank. The commission settled on a 12-bank, 12-city plan. It decided the boundaries of the districts on the basis of trade. In other words, the commission decided the boundaries should include cities or towns that traded the most with each other. If the residents of cities X and Y traded a lot with each other but the residents of city Z did not trade much with the residents of cities X and Y, then cities X and Y should be included in the same district but Z should not. Instead, city Z should be part of the district that included cities with which it traded.

Some commercial banks protested both the number of district banks and the boundaries decided on by the committee. These banks filed petitions for review of the plan with the Federal Reserve Board, thought to be the only group that could alter the plan.[1]

The petitions for review are said to have rekindled the debate about the actual number of district cities. Three members of the Federal Reserve Board wanted to reduce the number of district banks because they thought that one-half of the banks were stronger than the other half were, and they wanted all banks to be of equal strength. Three other members of the Board wanted to stay with the original plan of 12 district banks. This left one member of the Board to break the tie. It looked as though that person's vote was going to be cast for a reduction in the number of district banks. At that point, one of the supporters of the original 12-bank plan went to the Attorney General of the United States and asked for an opinion stating that the Board did not have the authority to alter the original plan. The Attorney General gave that opinion. The Board, afraid of attracting any negative publicity by disagreeing and challenging the opinion, accepted it.

---

1. Before there was a Board of Governors of the Federal Reserve System, there was the Federal Reserve Board. The Banking Act of 1935, approved on August 23, 1935, changed the name of the Federal Reserve Board to the Board of Governors of the Federal Reserve System.

## Common Misconceptions About the U.S. Treasury and the Fed

Some persons confuse the U.S. Treasury with the Fed. They mistakenly believe that the U.S. Treasury does some of the things that the Fed does. However, there are major differences between the Treasury and the Fed.

- The U.S. Treasury is a budgetary agency; the Fed is a monetary agency.

- When the federal government spends funds, the Treasury collects the taxes and borrows the funds needed to pay suppliers and others. In short, the Treasury has an obligation to manage the financial affairs of the federal government. Except for coins, the Treasury does not issue money. It cannot create money out of thin air as the Fed can. (We will soon explain exactly how the Fed does this.)

- The Fed is principally concerned with the availability of money and credit for the entire economy. It does not issue Treasury securities. It does not have an obligation to meet the financial needs of the federal government. Its responsibility is to provide a stable monetary framework for the economy.

(Answers to Self-Test questions are in Answers to Self-Test Questions at the back of the book.)

1. The president of which Federal Reserve District Bank holds a permanent seat on the Federal Open Market Committee (FOMC)?

2. What is the most important responsibility of the Fed?

3. "The Fed acts as lender of last resort." What does that statement mean?

# THE MONEY SUPPLY EXPANSION PROCESS

This section describes the important money supply process, specifically, how the Fed can increase and decrease the money supply. Before we begin, we offer a quick review of reserves, required reserves, and excess reserves.

## A Quick Review of Reserves, Required Reserves, and Excess Reserves

In the last chapter, we made the following points:

1. A bank's reserves equal its bank deposits at the Fed (the balance in its reserve account at the Fed) plus its vault cash.

$$\text{Reserves} = \text{Bank deposits at the Fed} + \text{Vault cash}$$

2. A bank's required reserves are equal to the required reserve ratio ($r$) times its checkable deposits.

$$\text{Required reserves} = r \times \text{Checkable deposits}$$

3. A bank's excess reserves equal its reserves minus its required reserves.

$$\text{Excess reserves} = \text{Reserves} - \text{Required reserves}$$

4. A bank can use its excess reserves to create new loans.

## The Money Supply Expansion Process

We start with the definition of the M1 money supply:

$$M1 = \text{Currency held outside banks} \\ + \text{Checkable deposits} \\ + \text{Traveler's checks}$$

Let's suppose that checkable deposits are $10,000 and that the other two components of the money supply equal $0. It follows that the money supply is $10,000.

$$\text{Money supply} = \$10,000$$

For now we are going to assume that the entire $10,000 in checkable deposits is held in one bank: bank A. We will also assume that the required reserve ratio is 10 percent and that bank A is currently holding $1,000 in required reserves and no excess reserves. Here is the relevant part of the balance sheet for bank A:

| **Bank A** | | | |
|---|---|---|---|
| **Assets** | | **Liabilities** | |
| Reserves | $1,000 | Checkable Deposits | $10,000 |
| Loans | $9,000 | | |

**THE FED CONDUCTS AN OPEN MARKET PURCHASE** The Fed conducts an open market purchase, which is a type of open market operation; specifically, it buys government securities from a bank. In this example it buys $500 worth of government securities from bank A. (Although government securities are assets for banks, we have not shown these assets on Bank A's balance sheet in order that we may focus only on reserves, loans, and checkable deposits.) Bank A turns over the government securities to the Fed, and, in return, the Fed must pay bank A $500.

Where does the Fed get the $500 to pay bank A? The answer is *out of thin air*. Bank A currently has a reserve account (bank deposits at the Fed) of $1,000. The Fed simply changes the balance in that account (with a stroke of a computer key) from $1,000 to $1,500. Here is what the balance sheet now looks like for bank A:

**Open Market Purchase**
The buying of government securities by the Fed.

| **Bank A** | | | |
|---|---|---|---|
| **Assets** | | **Liabilities** | |
| Reserves | $1,500 | Checkable Deposits | $10,000 |
| Loans | $9,000 | | |

**THE SITUATION FOR BANK A** The balance sheet for bank A shows $1,500 in reserves and $10,000 in checkable deposits. If the required reserve ratio is 10 percent, bank A is required to hold only $1,000 in reserves. So bank A has $500 in *excess reserves*.

Suppose bank A takes the entire $500 in excess reserves and creates a loan for Jill. Specifically, it grants Jill a $500 loan in the form of a new checkable deposit with a balance of $500. In other words, instead of giving Jill $500 in currency, bank A simply tells Jill that she now has a checkable deposit (a checking account) with the bank and that the balance in the account is $500.

**WHAT IS THE MONEY SUPPLY NOW?** Checkable deposits started off at $10,000 in bank A but are now $10,500. The extra $500 checkable deposit is the *new deposit* that the bank created for Jill. The money supply is now $10,500.

$$\text{Money Supply} = \$10,500$$

Here is what happened to increase the money supply:

Open market purchase → More reserves for bank A
→ Bank A created more loans in the form of
*new checkable deposits*
→ Money supply increased

**THE PROCESS CONTINUES** Jill now takes the $500 loan from bank A (in the form of a new checkable deposit) and spends it. Specifically, she writes a check for $500 to Joe for the materials she buys from him. Joe then takes the $500 (he received from Jill) and deposits the full amount into his checking account at bank B. The situation for bank B looks like this:

| **Bank B** | | | |
|---|---|---|---|
| **Assets** | | **Liabilities** | |
| Reserves | $500 | Checkable Deposits (Joe's account) | $500 |

Where did $500 in reserves in bank B come from? When the check that Jill wrote to Joe clears, bank A has to turn over $500 to bank B. To make this happen, bank A instructs the Fed to move $500 out of its reserve account and deposit the amount into bank B's reserve account.

Bank B's balance sheet shows $500 in reserves and $500 in checkable deposits. But if the required reserve ratio is 10 percent, bank B is required to hold only $50 in reserves. Bank B has $450 in excess reserves.

Bank B uses the entire $450 in excess reserves to create a loan of $450 for Jamal in the form of a checkable deposit. In other words, bank B creates a new checkable deposit of $450.

**WHAT IS THE MONEY SUPPLY NOW?** The money supply of $10,000 went up to $10,500 because bank A extended a loan (created a new checkable deposit) for Jill. Bank B then extended a loan (created a new checkable deposit) of $450; so the money supply is now $10,950.

$$\text{Money supply} = \$10,950$$

Some people might think that because Jill's checkable deposit balance went from $500 to $0 when her check cleared, the money supply should now be $10,450, not $10,950. But this point ignores the fact that when Jill pays off her $500 loan to bank A, the bank can lend the $500 to someone else. Thus, bank A can create a new checkable deposit of $500 to take the place of Jill's old one of $500.

**THE EFFECTS OF NO CASH LEAKAGE AND ZERO EXCESS RESERVES HELD BY BANKS** Up to this point, we have assumed two things.

First, we assumed that both banks A and B always used *all their excess reserves* to create loans (new checkable deposits); that is, the two banks did not hold any excess reserves. If they had held some positive amount of excess reserves, the money supply would have been affected. Specifically, suppose that when bank A had $500 in excess reserves, it created only a $200 loan (instead of a $500 loan) and held $300 in excess reserves. In that case, the money supply would have increased from $10,000, but only to $10,200, not $10,500. In other words, the more excess reserves banks hold, the smaller the increase will be in the money supply.

Second, when Jill paid $500 to Joe, Joe deposited the entire $500 into bank B, but, of course, Joe didn't have to do that. Instead, he could have deposited only $200 of the $500 into bank B and asked for $300 in currency. In this case, there would have been a cash leakage of $300. Bank B's reserves would have increased by only $200, not $500, and the bank could not have created a new loan (a new checkable deposit) of $450.

Given no cash leakage and zero excess reserves held by banks, how much does the money supply increase? The money supply story is ongoing. As we move from bank B to bank C to bank D and so on, each new bank creates some new loans (new checkable deposits), but each time the amount created is smaller than the amount that the previous bank created. Whereas bank A created $500 and bank B created $450, bank C might create $405, and so on. See Exhibit 3. In total, all the banks (together) create $5,000 in new checkable deposits. Here is the equation we use to calculate this amount:

$$\Delta\text{Checkable deposits (or money supply)} = \frac{1}{r} \times \Delta R$$

where $r$ = the required reserve ratio and $\Delta R$ = the change in reserves resulting from the initial injection of funds. In our example, $r$ = 10 percent and $\Delta R$ = $500. In the equation, the reciprocal of the required reserve ratio $(1/r)$ is known as the simple deposit multiplier. The arithmetic for the example is:

**Cash Leakage**
Occurs when funds are held as currency instead of deposited into a checking account.

**Simple Deposit Multiplier**
The reciprocal of the required reserve ratio, $1/r$.

**EXHIBIT 3**

**The Fed, Banks, and an Increase in Checkable Deposits or the Money Supply**

We assume that $r = 10$ percent, there is no cash leakage, banks hold zero excess reserves, and the Fed ends up increasing the reserves in bank A's reserve account by $500 due to an open market purchase. As a result of the Fed's open market purchase, bank A finds itself with $500 in excess reserves that it uses to create a new loan or new checkable deposit. This starts a process that ends with all relevant banks together creating $5,000 in new checkable deposits (or money).

Creation of New Checkable Deposits, given:

(i) $r = 10\%$
(ii) No cash leakage
(iii) Banks hold zero excess reserves
(iv) $500 increase in reserves for bank A as a result of Fed's open market purchase

| Bank | Increase in Checkable Deposits | New Required Reserves | New Checkable Deposits Created by Extending New Loans |
|------|-------------------------------|-----------------------|------------------------------------------------------|
| A | $ 0 | $ 0 | $ 500 |
| B | 500 | 50 | 450 |
| C | 450 | 45 | 405 |
| D | 405 | 40.50 | 364.50 |
| ⋮ | ⋮ | ⋮ | ⋮ |
| Total | | | $ 5,000 |

$$\Delta\text{Checkable deposits (or money supply)} = \frac{1}{0.10} \times \$500$$
$$= 10 \times \$500$$
$$= \$5,000^3$$

The change in checkable deposits (or the money supply) is $5000; thus, the Fed's open market purchase resulted in the money supply *rising* from $10,000 to $15,000.

## The Money Supply Contraction Process

Let's again start with bank A and its balance sheet:

| Bank A | | | |
|--------|--|--|--|
| **Assets** | | **Liabilities** | |
| Reserves | $1,000 | Checkable Deposits | $10,000 |
| Loans | $9,000 | | |

We will also assume that the initial money supply is $10,000:

Money supply = $10,000

This time the Fed undertakes an open market sale, that is, it sells government securities. Let's say the Fed sells $400 worth of government securities to bank A. The Fed turns the securities over to bank A and then subtracts $400 from bank A's reserve account. Just as

**Open Market Sale**
The selling of government securities by the Fed.

---

3. In the equation, we are looking at the change in checkable deposits or the money supply. Because checkable deposits are the only component of the money supply that is changing (currency and traveler's checks aren't changing), any change in the checkable deposits is equal to the change in the money supply.

the Fed can create money *out of thin* air, it can make it disappear *into thin air*. Here is what bank A's balance sheet (as before, we do not show the securities on the balance sheet so that we can focus on reserves, loans, and checkable deposits) now looks like:

| | **Bank A** | | |
|---|---|---|---|
| **Assets** | | **Liabilities** | |
| Reserves | $600 | Checkable Deposits | $10,000 |
| Loans | $9,000 | | |

**Reserve Deficient**
The situation that exists when a bank holds fewer reserves than specified by the required reserve ratio.

Reserves for bank A have gone from $1,000 to $600. Given that checkable deposits are $10,000, bank A is reserve deficient. If the required reserve ratio is 10 percent, bank A is required to hold $1,000 in reserves ($10,000 × 0.10) . But after the open market sale, bank A is holding only $600 in reserves, and so it is reserve deficient by $400.

When a bank is reserve deficient, it can do a number of things: It can (1) try to get a loan from another bank; (2) try to get a loan from the Fed; or (3) apply some of its loan repayments to the reserve deficiency position. In our example, it chooses option 3. On the day bank A becomes reserve deficient, Harry walks into the bank and pays back the $400 loan he took out months ago.

If bank A weren't reserve deficient, it would probably create a $400 loan (new checkable deposit) for someone else with the $400 it received from Harry. In that case, although Harry's checkable deposit balance would go to zero, someone else's checkable deposit balance would rise by $400. The creation of the loan by the bank would keep the money supply constant.

But because the bank is reserve deficient, it keeps the $400 as reserves. As a result, checkable deposits *decline* by $400; so the money supply declines by $400 to $9,600.

$$\text{Money supply} = \$9,600$$

The contraction of the money supply does not stop with bank A. It moves on to banks B, C, D, and others. To illustrate, suppose the loan repayment that Harry made to bank A was written on a check issued by bank B. When the check clears, the reserves of bank B decline, and it finds itself reserve deficient. Bank B, then, applies loan repayments to its reserve deficiency position. The effect continues with banks C, D, and so on.

To find out how much checkable deposits (the money supply) will decline, apply the equation used earlier:

$$\Delta\text{Checkable deposits (or money supply)} = \frac{1}{r} \times \Delta R$$

where $r$ = the required reserve ratio and $\Delta R$ = the change in reserves resulting from the initial removal of funds. In our example, $r$ = 10 percent and $\Delta R = -\$400$
The arithmetic is:

$$\Delta\text{Checkable deposits (or money supply)} = \frac{1}{0.10} \times -\$400$$
$$= 10 \times -\$400$$
$$= -\$4,000$$

The change in checkable deposits (or the money supply) is $-\$4,000$; thus, the Fed's open market sale resulted in the money supply *falling* from $10,000 to $6,000.

# OTHER FED TOOLS AND RECENT FED ACTIONS

The Fed has other tools to change the money supply. In the last section, we saw how the Fed can use open market operations to change the money supply. In this section, we discuss a few other tools.

## The Required Reserve Ratio

Look again at the equation for computing the change in the money supply:

$$\Delta \text{Checkable deposits (or money supply)} = \frac{1}{r} \times \Delta R$$

Notice the role that the required reserve ratio plays in the equation. If $r = 10$ percent, then the simple deposit multiplier $(1 \div r)$ is 10. For a \$1 change in reserves, the change in checkable deposits (money supply) is \$10. If the Fed lowers the required reserve ratio to, say, 5 percent, then the simple deposit multiplier is 20 $(1 \div 0.05 = 20)$. Now a \$1 rise in reserves will lead to a \$20 increase in the money supply. If instead the required reserve ratio is raised to 20 percent, the simple deposit multiplier $(1 \div r)$ is 5 $(1 \div 0.20 = 5)$. So a \$1 rise in reserves will lead to a \$5 increase in the money supply.

In summary:

- Lowering the required reserve ratio will increase the money supply.
- Raising the required reserve ratio will decrease the money supply.

$$r \downarrow \to \frac{1}{r} \uparrow \to \text{Money supply} \uparrow$$
$$r \uparrow \to \frac{1}{r} \downarrow \to \text{Money supply} \downarrow$$

## The Discount Window and the Federal Funds Market

If bank A wants a \$1 million loan, it can go to the Fed or to another bank (say, bank B) for it. The loan the bank gets from the Fed is called a discount loan, and the interest rate a bank pays for a discount loan is called the discount rate. The discount rate is set by the Fed.

The loan that bank A might get from another bank is usually called an *overnight loan* (because it is typically a loan of short duration, such as overnight). The market in which banks lend reserves to one another, usually for short periods, is called the *market for reserves* or the federal funds market. The interest rate that bank A pays for an overnight loan is called the federal funds rate, which is determined in the federal funds market. Specifically, the demand for and the supply of reserves determine the federal funds rate, in much the same way that the demand for and supply of apples determines the price of apples.

The discount rate is another tool the Fed can use to regulate the money supply. If the Fed wants to increase the money supply, it can drop the discount rate below the federal funds rate. To illustrate, suppose the federal funds rate is 5 percent. All the Fed has to do is set the discount rate at, say, 3 percent. Now bank A has an incentive to go to the Fed instead of to another bank for the \$1 million. The Fed gives the bank the \$1 million discount loan by increasing the balance in the bank's reserve account by \$1 million. With more reserves, the bank can create more loans (more checkable deposits), and, as a result, the money supply rises.

In summary:

Fed sets discount rate below federal funds rate → Banks borrow from Fed →
Banks have more reserves → Banks may make more loans and
checkable deposits → Money supply rises

Alternatively, if the Fed wants to contract  the money supply, it can set the discount rate above the federal funds rate. Now banks will not go to the Fed for loans, and as the banks repay discount loans taken out in the past, reserves in the banking system decline. (When a bank repays a discount loan, the Fed *subtracts* the repayment from the bank's reserve account.)

**Discount Loan**
A loan the Fed makes to a commerical bank.

**Discount Rate**
The interest rate the Fed charges depository institutions that borrow reserves from it; the interest rate charged on a discount loan.

**Federal Funds Rate**
The interest rate in the federal funds market; the interest rate banks charge one another to borrow reserves.

**Federal Funds Market**
A market where banks lend reserves to one another, usually for short periods.

In summary:

Fed sets discount rate above federal funds rate → Banks do not borrow from the
Fed, and as banks repay past discount loans → Banks have fewer reserves →
Money supply declines

## The Fed and the Federal Funds Rate Target

**Federal Funds Rate Target**
The interest rate that the Fed wants
the federal funds market rate to be.

So far, we have identified three tools the Fed has at its disposal to change the money
supply: conducting open market operations, changing the required reserve ratio, and
changing the discount rate relative to the federal funds rate. Normally, however, if the Fed
wants to change the money supply, it takes two measures: (1) It sets a federal funds rate
target and then (2) uses open market operations to change the federal funds rate so as to
"hit" the target.

Suppose the current federal funds rate is 4 percent, and the Fed sets a federal funds rate
target of 3 percent. The Fed then conducts an open market purchase, which, as we know,
has the effect of injecting reserves into the banking system. As a result of the open market
purchase, the supply of reserves in the market for reserves rises. As the supply of reserves
rises, the price of those reserves—the federal funds rate—falls. The Fed continues these
transactions until the federal funds rate falls from 4 percent to 3 percent, the federal funds
rate target.

## Dealing with a Financial Crisis

The actions the Fed takes might differ depending on whether it is simply trying to
change the money supply to meet a macroeconomic objective, such as price stability,
or dealing with a financial crisis. (You will read about the financial crisis of 2007–2009
in Chapter 18.) In way of analogy, your pace is very different if you are taking a
leisurely walk than if you are running a race. The same type of difference exists for
the Fed when it is managing everyday monetary policy compared to dealing with a
financial crisis.

The Fed did three things to deal with the 2007–2009 financial crisis:

- Created the term auction facility (TAF) program
- Extended the lender-of-last-resort function beyond banks
- Bought securities from institutions other than banks

**Term Auction Facility (TAF)
Program**
A program under which the Fed
auctions funds to depository institutions. Each TAF auction is for a
fixed amount, with the TAF rate
determined by the auction process
(subject to a minimum bid rate).

**TERM AUCTION FACILITY (TAF) PROGRAM**  In addition to issuing discount loans
to banks, in late 2007 the Fed created another way banks could get loans from it. Specifically, it created the term auction facility (TAF) program. In this program, instead of banks
asking for a specific dollar loan (as in a discount loan), the Fed first identifies the total
amount of credit it wants to extend (for example, $20 billion). Then it allows banks to bid
on the funds. The bidding process determines the TAF rate (interest rate) for the loans.

If the Fed already offers discount loans to banks, why set up the TAF program? In a
sense, if a bank can already get a loan by knocking on door 1 at the Fed, why add door 2
(TAF)?

One reason is that discount loans often come with a stigma attached. Specifically, if a
bank is in sound financial condition, it customarily borrows from institutions in the private
sector (such as another bank). A discount loan is intended for banks that cannot get loans
elsewhere; thus a bank that requests a discount loan is often viewed as admitting it is in
poor financial health. The bank might not want to make such an admission to either the
Fed or the market.

The Fed dealt with the stigma issue by stating that, as far as it was concerned, no
stigma was attached to borrowing from the term auction facility. It dealt with the issue of

## Flying in with the Money[2]

A banker at a commercial bank located about 200 miles from the Federal Reserve Bank of Minneapolis was frantic. A large crowd was outside his bank, and the people wanted their money now. The banker got on the phone and called the Federal Reserve Bank in Minneapolis. He told the people at the Minneapolis Fed that there was a "mad run" on his bank. If the Fed did not come to his rescue soon, he would be out of currency and unable to give the customers of his bank their money.

Where was their money? Why didn't he have it to give to them? As this chapter explained, banks need to have on hand only a fraction of their customers' deposits.

The Federal Reserve System responded to the call for currency. The Federal Reserve Bank of Minneapolis chartered a small plane, and two Fed officials took it, along with a half million dollars in small-denomination bills, to the nearby town.

Upon approaching the town, the pilot flew the plane over Main Street to dramatize its arrival in the town: the Federal Reserve was flying in to the rescue. The plane landed at a nearby field. From the field, the Fed officials were escorted into town by the police, and the money was stacked in the bank's windows. The sight of all the money calmed the bank's customers, who were now assured they could get their money if they wanted. A banking panic was averted in a very dramatic way.

---

2. This feature is based on "Born of a Panic: Forming the Federal Reserve System," *The Region* (August 1998).

confidentiality in the market by stating that it would not release any information on the participants in the TAF program, except as required by law.

Finally, by determining the TAF rate through a competitive bidding process, banks found that borrowing through the term auction facility was cheaper than with discount loans.

### EXTENDING THE LENDER-OF-LAST-RESORT FUNCTION BEYOND BANKS

As the lender of last resort for banks, the Fed ensures that banks can obtain the funds they need. If a bank has financial problems, it can seek funds from the Fed. During the financial crisis, the Fed extended its lender-of-last-resort function to institutions other than banks.

**BUYING SECURITIES FROM INSTITUTIONS OTHER THAN BANKS** During normal economic times, the Fed buys Treasury securities from banks if it wants to increase reserves in the banking system to raise the money supply. During the financial crisis, the Fed not only bought securities from nonbank institutions, but often bought securities that were not Treasury issues. Often they were mortgage-backed securities that institutions owned that were declining in value.

## SELF-TEST

1. How does the money supply change as a result of (a) an increase in the discount rate, (b) an open market purchase, (c) an increase in the required reserve ratio?

2. What is the difference between the federal funds rate and the discount rate?

3. If bank A borrows $10 million from bank B, what happens to the reserves in bank A? What happens in the banking system?

4. If bank A borrows $10 million from the Fed, what happens to the reserves in bank A? What happens in the banking system?

# "Can Something I Do End Up Changing the Money Supply?"

**STUDENT:**

Let me see if I have this right: if I put $100 in my checking account at a bank, the bank then takes that $100 and adds it to vault cash, so that $100 becomes part of the bank's reserves, right?

**INSTRUCTOR:**

Yes, that's right.

**STUDENT:**

And then the bank holds a percentage of that $100 in reserve form and lends out the rest. So it might hold $10 of the $100 in its vault and lend out the remaining $90.

**INSTRUCTOR:**

That's correct.

**STUDENT:**

Now here's the part I am unsure of. When a bank gives out a loan of $90, does it actually lend out the $90 of currency (let's say nine $10 bills) or simply create a new checkable deposit of $90 for someone?

**INSTRUCTOR:**

It creates a new checkable deposit of $90.

**STUDENT:**

But then that means the full $100 currency is still in the bank's vault, right? When does $90 of the $100 leave the vault?

**INSTRUCTOR:**

Suppose the person who received the $90 loan (or new checkable deposit) writes a check to Marie. Marie then deposits the $90 check in another bank. When the check clears, the $90 is transferred from the first bank (in which you deposited your money) to Marie's bank. And then Marie's bank takes a fraction of that $90 and creates a loan with it, and the process continues.

**STUDENT:**

So, in the end, some portion of that $100 that I deposited into the bank ends up creating loans for a lot of people. Is that correct?

**INSTRUCTOR:**

That is correct.

**STUDENT:**

But this makes it sound like I can change the money supply by simply deciding to put $100 currency into a bank instead of keeping that $100 in my wallet. Is this true?

**INSTRUCTOR:**

Let's put it this way: by putting $100 currency into a bank, you change the composition of the money supply. Specifically, $100 less in currency is held outside banks and $100 more in checkable deposits. Then the banking system can take the $100 and create a multiple of it in terms of new checkable deposits, thereby raising the money supply.

### POINTS TO REMEMBER

1. An individual (any member of the public) can change the composition of the money supply.
2. A change in the composition of the money supply can lead to a dollar change in the money supply

# CHAPTER SUMMARY

## THE FEDERAL RESERVE SYSTEM

- There are 12 Federal Reserve Districts. The Board of Governors controls and coordinates the activities of the Federal Reserve System. The Board is made up of seven members, each appointed to a 14-year term. The major policy-making group in the Fed is the Federal Open Market Committee (FOMC). It is a 12-member group made up of the seven members of the Board of Governors and five Federal Reserve District Bank presidents.
- The major responsibilities of the Fed are to (1) control the money supply, (2) supply the economy with paper money (Federal Reserve notes), (3) provide check-clearing services, (4) hold depository institutions' reserves, (5) supervise member banks, (6) serve as the government's banker, (7) serve as the lender of last resort, and (8) serve as a fiscal agent for the Treasury.

## CONTROLLING THE MONEY SUPPLY

- The following Fed actions increase the money supply: lowering the required reserve ratio, purchasing government securities on the open market, and lowering the discount rate relative to the federal funds rate.
- The following Fed actions decrease the money supply: raising the required reserve ratio, selling government securities on the open market, and raising the discount rate relative to the federal funds rate.

## OPEN MARKET OPERATIONS

- An open market purchase by the Fed increases the money supply.
- An open market sale by the Fed decreases the money supply.

## THE REQUIRED RESERVE RATIO

- An increase in the required reserve ratio leads to a decrease in the money supply.
- A decrease in the required reserve ratio leads to an increase in the money supply.

## DISCOUNT LOANS AND OVERNIGHT LOANS

- A bank obtains discount loans from the Fed and overnight loans from other banks. The interest rate it pays for a discount loan is called the discount rate. The interest rate a bank pays another bank for a loan is called the federal funds rate.
- The discount rate is set by the Fed. The federal funds rate is determined by market forces in the market for reserves (federal funds market).
- If the Fed sets the discount rate below the federal funds rate, banks will borrow from the Fed, and the banks will end up with more reserves. These reserves can be used to create more loans and checkable deposits, thus increasing the money supply.
- If the Fed sets the discount above the federal funds rate, banks will choose not to borrow from the Fed. As the banks repay past discount loans, they have fewer reserves, thus decreasing the money supply.

## THE FEDERAL FUNDS RATE TARGET

- The Fed sets a federal funds rate target. Then it uses open market operations to change the federal funds rate so as to hit the target. For example, if the current federal funds rate is 4 percent, and the target is 3 percent, the Fed can conduct an open market purchase, which results in reserves being injected into the banking system. As the supply of reserves rises, the federal funds rate declines.

# KEY TERMS AND CONCEPTS

| | | | |
|---|---|---|---|
| Board of Governors | U.S. Treasury Securities | Reserve Deficient | Federal Funds Market |
| Federal Open Market Committee (FOMC) | Open Market Purchase | Reserve Requirement | Federal Funds Target Rate |
| Open Market Operations | Cash Leakage | Discount Loan | Term Auction Facility |
| Monetary Policy | Simple Deposit Multiplier | Discount Rate | (TAF) Program |
| | Open Market Sale | Federal Funds Rate | |

# QUESTIONS AND PROBLEMS

1. Identify the major responsibilities of the Federal Reserve System.
2. What are the differences between the Fed and the U.S. Treasury?
3. Explain how an open market purchase increases the money supply.
4. Explain how an open market sale decreases the money supply.

5. Suppose the Fed raises the required reserve ratio, a move that is normally thought to reduce the money supply. However, banks find themselves with a reserve deficiency after the required reserve ratio is increased and are likely to react by requesting a loan from the Fed. Does this action prevent the money supply from contracting as predicted? Explain your answer.

6, Suppose bank A borrows reserves from bank B. Now that bank A has more reserves than previously, will the money supply increase? Explain your answer.

7. Explain how a decrease in the required reserve ratio increases the money supply.

8. Suppose you read in the newspaper that all last week the Fed conducted open market purchases and that on Tuesday of last week it lowered the discount rate. What would you say the Fed is trying to do?

9. Explain how a check is cleared through the Federal Reserve System.

10. The Fed can change the discount rate directly and the federal funds rate indirectly. Explain.

11. What does it mean to say the Fed serves as the lender of last resort?

12. The Fed has announced a new, lower target for the federal funds rate; it wants to lower the federal funds rate from its present level. What does setting a lower target for the federal funds rate have to do with open market operations?

## WORKING WITH NUMBERS AND GRAPHS

1. If reserves increase by $2 million and the required reserve ratio is 8 percent, what is the maximum change in checkable deposits?

2. If reserves increase by $2 million and the required reserves ratio is 10 percent, what is the maximum change in checkable deposits?

3. If the federal funds rate is 6 percent and the discount rate is 5.1 percent, to whom will a bank be more likely to go for a loan: another bank or the Fed? Explain your answer.

4. Complete the following table:

| Federal Reserve Action | Effect on the Money Supply (up or down?) |
| --- | --- |
| Lower the discount rate | A |
| Conduct open market purchase | B |
| Lower required reserve ratio | C |
| Raise the discount rate | D |
| Conduct open market sale | E |
| Raise the required reserve ratio | F |

# THE MARKET FOR RESERVES (OR THE FEDERAL FUNDS MARKET)

Monetary policy can be conducted in various ways. One is to target a specific money supply, such as M1 or M2. Suppose the M1 money supply is currently $1 trillion and the Fed wants to raise it to $1.1 trillion. The $1.1 trillion is the Fed's specific monetary target. The Fed then undertakes to increase the money supply until it hits its monetary target. For example, it might undertake an open market purchase or lower the required reserve ratio, either of which would lead to an increase in the money supply. If, by chance, the Fed overshot its monetary target and the money supply increased to some dollar figure over $1.1 trillion, the Fed then could reverse course. It could undertake an open market sale to bring the money supply back down to $1.1 trillion.

Today, the Fed does not usually have a specific money supply target in its execution of monetary policy. Instead, it tries to target a set federal funds rate. Suppose the federal funds rate is currently 4 percent and the Fed wants to lower it to 3 percent. Three percent is its federal funds rate target. Because the federal funds rate is determined in the market for reserves (or the federal funds market), we need to explain how that market works before we can explain what the Fed can do to reach its federal funds rate target.

## THE DEMAND FOR RESERVES

The demand for reserves originates with banks. A bank may have a demand for reserves for a few reasons. A bank may demand reserves because it has to hold a certain amount of reserves against its checkable deposits. For example, if the required reserve ratio is, say, 10 percent, then for every $1 in checkable deposits a bank holds, it must hold 10¢ in reserves. So if the required reserve ratio is raised (by the Fed), a bank needs to hold more reserves for every $1 of checkable deposits. In Exhibit 1, the demand for reserves is downward-sloping. On the vertical axis is the federal funds rate, and on the horizontal axis is the quantity of reserves. When the bank needs more reserves, the demand curve for reserves (D) shifts to the right; if the required reserve ratio is lowered, a bank needs to hold fewer reserves for every $1 of checkable deposits, and therefore the demand curve for reserves shifts to the left.

Banks demand reserves also because they believe they may face large checkable deposit withdrawals. Suppose a bank believes that its depositors may soon withdraw large amounts of their

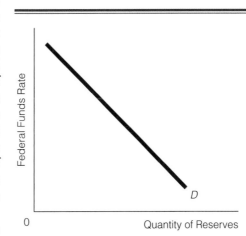

**EXHIBIT 1**

**The Demand for Reserves**

The demand for reserves curve (in the market for reserves or the federal funds market) is downward sloping: the federal funds rate and the quantity demanded of reserves are inversely related. As the federal funds rate moves down, holding reserves becomes cheaper, and therefore banks will buy more "insurance" to guard against checkable deposit withdrawals. As the federal funds rate moves up, holding reserves becomes more expensive, and banks will buy less "insurance" to guard against checkable deposit withdrawals. A change in expected deposit outflows and the required reserve ratio can lead to a shift in the demand for reserves.

money from their checkable deposits. To have the funds to meet the anticipated with-drawals, banks may decide to hold more reserves than they are required to by the required reserve ratio. For example, instead of holding 10¢ in reserves against every $1 in checkable deposits, they might increase that reserve holding to 20¢ or 30¢ or more.

The demand curve for reserves is downward sloping because, as the federal funds rate moves down, it becomes cheaper to hold reserves, and therefore banks will buy more "insurance" to guard against checkable deposit withdrawals. As the federal funds rate moves up, it becomes more expensive to hold reserves, and banks will buy less "insurance" to guard against checkable deposit withdrawals.

# THE SUPPLY OF RESERVES

The supply of reserves comes from essentially two sources. The first source is the Fed. For example, when the Fed undertakes open market operations, it changes the supply of reserves. An open market purchase increases the supply of reserves (in the banking system); an open market sale decreases the supply of reserves.

The second source of reserves comes from banks taking out discount loans from the Fed. If a bank borrows from the Fed, the supply of reserves increases in the banking system. If a bank pays back a discount loan to the Fed, the supply of reserves decreases.

# TWO DIFFERENT SUPPLY CURVES FOR RESERVES

Exhibit 2(a)–(b) shows two supply curves. In (a), we assume that the federal funds rate target [designated by an asterisk (*)] is currently $ffr_1^*$ or 3.0 percent at the intersection of the $D_1$ and $S_1$ curves. We also assume that the Fed has set the discount rate ($dr_1 = 3.5$ percent) slightly above the federal funds rate target. In recent years, the Fed has customarily set the discount rate slightly above its federal funds rate target. To see why, let's suppose the demand curve in (a) shifts to the right from $D_1$ to $D_2$. Will the federal funds rate rise to $ffr_2'$ (3.7 percent)? Under most conditions, the answer is no. Banks would prefer to borrow from the Fed at the discount rate of 3.5 percent instead of borrowing from other banks at the federal funds rate of 3.7 percent. In other words, equilibrium in the market for reserves is likely to occur at point 2 in the exhibit, where the new federal funds rate is 3.5 percent, which is the same as the discount rate. (This is why the supply of reserves curve has a kink in it at the discount rate and does not extend vertically above this point.) The equilibrium amount of reserves in the banking system will rise from $R_1$ to $R_2$, the difference between these two amounts being the dollar amount of discount loans that banks take out at the discount rate of 3.5 percent.

So why does the Fed set its discount rate slightly above the target federal funds rate? The discount rate acts as a ceiling on how high the federal funds rate is likely to go. In other words, if the Fed doesn't want the federal funds rate to go over 3.5 percent, it sets the discount rate at 3.5 percent.

Just as the Fed can set a ceiling above which the federal funds rate is not likely to rise, it can also set a floor. In late 2008, the Fed started to pay an interest rate on reserves that banks held. Until that time, banks did not receive any interest on reserves. To see how the Fed's paying interest on reserves can put a floor on the federal funds rate, look at Exhibit 2(b). The reserves market is initially in equilibrium at point 1. The federal funds rate target is the equilibrium federal funds rate of 3.0 percent, and the equilibrium amount of reserves is $R_1$. Now suppose that the Fed is willing to pay an interest rate on reserves of $ir_1$ ($ir_1 = 2.5$ percent) and that the demand for reserves curve shifts leftward from $D_1$ to $D_2$. Will the

**EXHIBIT 2**

### The Supply of Reserves

Two supply of reserves curves. (a) A kink in the curve at the discount rate. To understand the kink, start with a federal funds rate of 3.0 percent. Next, the demand for reserves curve shifts from $D_1$ to $D_2$. Whether the federal funds rate will rise to 3.7 percent is possible but not likely if banks decide to borrow from the Fed at the lower discount rate of 3.5 percent. In other words, the federal funds rate rises to only 3.5 percent. The discount rate acts as a ceiling on the federal funds rate.

(b) A supply of reserves with two kinds. The uppermost kink, as explained, occurs at the discount rate. The lower one occurs at the interest rate the Fed pays (to banks) on reserves. To understand the lower kink, start with a federal funds rate of 3.0 percent. Next, the demand for reserves curve shifts from $D_1$ to $D_2$. The federal funds rate might fall to 2.3 percent, but it is not likely because banks would rather receive an interest rate of 2.5 percent from the Fed than lend to other banks and receive an interest rate of 2.3 percent. The interest rate the Fed pays on reserves acts as a floor on the federal funds rate.

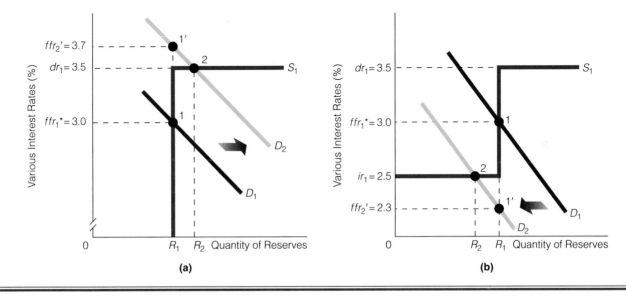

(a)

(b)

federal funds rate fall to $ffr_2$, (2.3 percent)? Not likely, because no bank will prefer to lend reserves to another bank at a federal funds rate of 2.3 percent when it can simply keep the reserves and gain an interest rate on reserves of 2.5 percent. (The difference between $R_1$ and $R_2$ can be seen as a "negative discount loan," in that it is the amount that banks are "lending" to the Fed, for which the Fed pays them interest.) So the federal funds rate is not likely to fall to 2.3 percent. Instead, it is likely to only fall to 2.5 percent. In other words, the interest rate that the Fed pays on reserves acts as a floor below which the federal funds rate will not fall.

## THE CORRIDOR AND CHANGING THE FEDERAL FUNDS RATE

In Exhibit 2(b), the supply curve (of reserves) has two kinks in it: one at the interest rate that the Fed pays on reserves and another at the discount rate. The vertical section between the kinks—or, simply, the vertical section of the supply curve—is called the *corridor*. The federal funds rate moves within this corridor. In other words, the federal funds rate can rise or fall within the corridor, but nowhere else. If the corridor were between a discount rate of 7 percent and an interest rate paid on reserves of 3 percent, the federal funds rate would be somewhere between a high of 7 percent and a low of 3 percent. If the Fed increases the length of the corridor by, say, increasing the discount rate from 7 percent to 8 percent, then the federal funds rate will be somewhere between a high of 8 percent and a low of 3 percent.

**EXHIBIT 3**

**Changing the Federal Funds Rate**

The equilibrium federal funds rate is 3.0 percent. The Fed then decides to lower the federal funds rate to 2.5 percent. To do this, the Fed undertakes an open market purchase, increasing reserves from $R_1$ to $R_2$. At the same time, it lowers the discount rate from 3.5 percent to 3.0 percent and lowers the interest rate it pays on reserves from 2.5 percent to 2.0 percent. The new supply of reserves curve is $S_2$, and the new equilibrium federal funds rate is 2.5 percent.

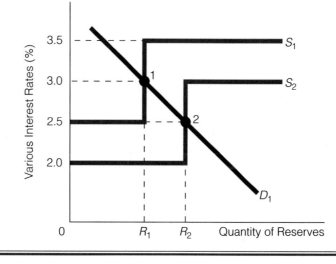

Now look at Exhibit 3. Suppose the federal fund rate is currently at 3.0, the discount rate is 3.5 percent, and the interest rate the Fed pays on reserves is 2.5 percent. The Fed decides that it wants to try to bring the federal funds rate down to its target rate of 2.5 percent. What can it do to achieve its objective of lowering the federal funds rate? It can undertake an open market purchase, thus increasing reserves from $R_1$ to $R_2$. At the same time as it increases reserves, it might then lower its discount rate from 3.5 percent to, say, 3.0 percent, and the interest it pays on reserves from 2.5 percent to, say, 2.0 percent, so that the new supply curve is $S_2$. The demand curve for reserves intersects the supply curve of reserves at point 2 in the exhibit. The equilibrium federal funds rate is now 2.5 percent.

## CHAPTER 14

# MONEY AND THE ECONOMY

**Introduction** Does the money supply matter to the economy? Does a rise or fall in the money supply make a difference? In this chapter we talk about the money supply and its effects on the economy. We discuss changes in the money supply and in the price level, changes in the money supply and in Real GDP, and changes in the money supply and interest rates.

## MONEY AND THE PRICE LEVEL

Classical economists believed that changes in the money supply affect the price level in the economy. Their position was based on the equation of exchange and on the simple quantity theory of money.

### The Equation of Exchange

The equation of exchange is an identity stating that the money supply ($M$) multiplied by velocity ($V$) must be equal to the price level ($P$) times Real GDP ($Q$).

$$MV \equiv PQ$$

where $\equiv$ means "must be equal to." This is an identity, and an identity is valid for all values of the variables.

As we learned in an earlier chapter, *velocity* is the average number of times a dollar is spent to buy final goods and services in a year. For example, assume an economy has only five $1 bills. In January, the first of the $1 bills moves from Smith's hands to Jones's hands to buy good X. Then in June, it goes from Jones's hands to Brown's hands to buy good Y. And in December, it goes from Brown's hands to Peterson's hands to buy good Z. Over the course of the year, this dollar bill has changed hands three times.

The other dollar bills also change hands during the year. The second dollar bill changes hands five times; the third, six times; the fourth, two times; and the fifth, seven times. Given this information, we can calculate the average number of times a dollar changes hands in purchases. In this case, the number is 4.6, which is **velocity**.

**Equation of Exchange**
An identity stating that the money supply ($M$) times velocity ($V$) must be equal to the price level ($P$) times Real GDP ($Q$): $MV \equiv PQ$.

**Velocity**
The average number of times a dollar is spent to buy final goods and services in a year.

In a large economy such as ours, counting how many times each dollar changes hands is impossible; so calculating velocity as we did in our example is impossible. For a large economy, we use a different method.

- First, we calculate GDP.
- Next, we calculate the average money supply ($M$).
- Finally, we divide GDP by the average money supply to obtain velocity ($V$).

$$V \equiv \frac{GDP}{M}$$

For example, if $4,800 billion worth of transactions occur in a year ($GDP$) and the average money supply during the year is $800 billion ($M$), then a dollar must have been used an average of 6 times during the year to purchase goods and services:

$$V \equiv \frac{\$4,800 \text{ billion}}{\$800 \text{ billion}}$$

Because GDP is equal to $P \times Q$, this identity can be written

$$V \equiv \frac{P \times Q}{M}$$

Multiplying both sides by $M$, we get

$$MV \equiv PQ$$

which is the equation of exchange. Thus, the equation of exchange is derived from the definition of velocity.

The equation of exchange can be interpreted in different ways:

1. The money supply multiplied by velocity must equal the price level times Real GDP: $M \times V \equiv P \times Q$.

2. The money supply multiplied by velocity must equal GDP: $M \times V \equiv$ GDP (because $P \times Q \equiv$ GDP).

3. Total spending or expenditures (measured by $MV$) must equal the total sales revenues of business firms (measured by $PQ$): $MV \equiv PQ$.

The third way of interpreting the equation of exchange is perhaps the most intuitively easy to understand: The total expenditures (of buyers) must equal the total sales (of sellers). Consider a simple economy with only one buyer and one seller. If the buyer buys a book for $20, then the seller receives $20. Stated differently, the money supply in the example ($20) times velocity (1) is equal to the price of the book ($20) times the quantity of the book (1).

## From the Equation of Exchange to the Simple Quantity Theory of Money

The equation of exchange is an identity, not an economic theory. To turn it into a theory, we make some assumptions about the variables in the equation. Many eighteenth-century classical economists, as well as American economist Irving Fisher (1867–1947) and English economist Alfred Marshall (1842–1924), made the following assumptions:

1. Changes in velocity are so small that for all practical purposes velocity can be assumed to be constant (especially over short periods of time).

2. Real GDP, or $Q$, is fixed in the short run.

Hence, they turned the equation of exchange, which is simply true by definition, into a theory by assuming that both $V$ and $Q$ are fixed, or constant. With these two assumptions, we have the simple quantity theory of money: If $V$ and $Q$ are constant, then changes in $M$ will bring about *strictly proportional* changes in $P$. In other words, the simple quantity theory of money predicts that changes in the money supply will bring about strictly proportional changes in the price level.

Exhibit 1 shows the assumptions and predictions of the simple quantity theory. On the left side of the exhibit, the key assumptions of the simple quantity theory are noted: $V$ and $Q$ are constant. Also, $M \times \overline{V} = P \times \overline{Q}$ is noted. We use the equals sign $(=)$ instead of the identity sign $(\equiv)$ because we are speaking about the simple quantity theory, not the equation of exchange. (The equals sign can be read as "is predicted to be equal"; that is, given our assumptions, $M \times V$, or $MV$, is predicted to be equal to $P \times Q$, or $PQ$.)

Starting with the first row, the money supply is $500, velocity is 4, the price level, or price index, is $2, and Real GDP ($Q$) is 1,000 units.[1] Therefore, GDP equals $2,000. In the second row, the money supply increases by 100 percent, from $500 to $1,000, and both $V$ and $Q$ are constant, at 4 and 1,000, respectively. The price level moves from $2 to $4. On the right side of the exhibit, we see that a 100 percent increase in $M$ predicts a 100 percent increase in $P$. Changes in $P$ are predicted to be strictly proportional to changes in $M$. In the third row, $M$ increases by 50 percent, and $P$ is predicted to increase by 50 percent. In the fourth row, $M$ decreases by 20 percent, and $P$ is predicted to decrease by 20 percent.

So the simple quantity theory assumes that both $V$ and $Q$ are constant in the short run and therefore predicts that changes in $M$ lead to strictly proportional changes in $P$.

How well does the simple quantity theory of money predict? Do changes in the money supply actually lead to *strictly proportional* changes in the price level? For example, if the money supply goes up by 7 percent, does the price level go up by 7 percent? If the money supply goes down by 4 percent, does the price level go down by 4 percent? The answer is that the strict proportionality between changes in the money supply and changes in the price level does not show up in the data (at least not very often).

Generally, though, the evidence supports the spirit (or essence) of the simple quantity theory of money: the higher the growth rate in the money supply, the greater the growth

**Simple Quantity Theory of Money**

The theory assuming that velocity ($V$) and Real GDP ($Q$) are constant and predicting that changes in the money supply ($M$) lead to strictly proportional changes in the price level ($P$).

---

**EXHIBIT 1**

| Assumptions of Simple Quantity Theory | | | | | | Predictions of Simple Quantity Theory | |
|---|---|---|---|---|---|---|---|
| $M$ | $\times$ | $\overline{V}$ | $=$ | $P$ | $\times$ | $\overline{Q}$ | % Change in $M$ | % Change in $P$ |
| $500 | | 4 | | $2 | | 1,000 | | |
| 1,000 | | 4 | | 4 | | 1,000 | + 100% | + 100% |
| 1,500 | | 4 | | 6 | | 1,000 | + 50 | + 50 |
| 1,200 | | 4 | | 4.80 | | 1,000 | − 20 | − 20 |

**Assumptions and Predictions of the Simple Quantity Theory of Money**

The simple quantity theory of money assumes that both $V$ and $Q$ are constant. (A bar over each indicates this in the exhibit.) The prediction is that changes in $M$ lead to strictly proportional changes in $P$. (Note: For purposes of this example, think of $Q$ as "so many units of goods" and of $P$ as the "average price paid per unit of these goods.")

---

1. You are used to seeing Real GDP expressed as a dollar figure and a price index as a number without a dollar sign in front of it. We have switched things for purposes of this example because it is easier to think of $Q$ as "so many units of goods" and $P$ as "the average price paid per unit of those goods."

## The California Gold Rush, or Really Expensive Apples

*Soon there was too much money in California and too little of everything else.*

—J. S. Holiday, *The World Rushed In*

*The only peacetime rise [in prices] comparable in total magnitude [to the 40 to 50 percent rise in prices from 1897 to 1914] followed the California gold discoveries in the early 1850s. . . .*

—Milton Friedman and Anna Schwartz, *A Monetary History of the United States, 1867–1960*

©BETTMANN/CORBIS

John Sutter was a Swiss immigrant who arrived in California in 1839. On the chilly morning of January 24, 1848, James Marshall, a carpenter, was busy at work building a sawmill for Sutter. Then something glistening caught his eye, and he reached down and picked it up. Marshall said to the workers he had hired, "Boys, by God I believe I have found a gold mine." Marshall later wrote, "I reached my hand down and picked it up; it made my heart thump, for I was certain it was gold. The piece was about half the size and shape of a pea. Then I saw another."

In time, Marshall and his workers came across more gold, and before long people from all across the United States and from many other countries headed to California. The California gold rush had begun.

The California gold rush resulted in an increase in the amount of money in circulation and illustrates how such a fairly dramatic increase

can affect prices. As more gold was mined and the supply of money went up, prices began to rise. Although prices rose generally across the country, the earliest and most dramatic price rises occurred in and near the areas where gold was discovered. Near the gold mines, the prices of food and clothing shot up. For example, whereas a loaf of bread sold for 4¢ in New York (equivalent to 84¢ today), near the mines the price was 75¢ (the equivalent of $15.67 today). Eggs sold for about $2 each ($41 today), apples for $4 ($83.59), a butcher's knife for $30 ($626), and boots went for $100 a pair ($2,089).

In San Francisco, land prices soared dramatically because of the city's relative closeness to the mines. In 18 months, real estate that cost $16 (the equivalent of $334 today) before gold was discovered jumped to $45,000 ($940,000 today).

The sharp rise in prices created by the California gold discoveries followed other gold discoveries too. For example, the gold stock of the world is estimated to have doubled from 1890 to 1914, due both to discoveries (in South Africa, Alaska, and Colorado) and to improved methods of mining and refining gold. During this period, world prices increased too.

---

rate in the price level. To illustrate, we would expect that a growth rate in the money supply of, say, 40 percent would generate a greater increase in the price level than, say, a growth rate in the money supply of 4 percent. Generally, this effect is what we see. For example, countries with more rapid increases in their money supplies often witness more rapid increases in their price levels than do countries that witness less rapid increases in their money supplies.

### The Simple Quantity Theory of Money in an *AD–AS* Framework

In this section, we analyze the simple quantity theory of money in the *AD–AS* framework.

**THE *AD* CURVE IN THE SIMPLE QUANTITY THEORY OF MONEY**  The simple quantity theory of money builds on the equation of exchange. Recall that one way of interpreting the equation of exchange is that the total expenditures of buyers ($MV$) must equal the total sales of sellers ($PQ$). Thus, $MV$ is the total expenditures of buyers, and $PQ$ is the total sales of sellers. Let's take the total expenditures of buyers a few steps further:

$$MV \quad \text{Total expenditures}$$

However, total expenditures ($TE$) is defined as the sum of the expenditures made by the four sectors of the economy (consumption, investment, government purchases, and net exports):

$$TE = C + I + G + (EX - IM)$$

Because $MV = TE$,

$$MV = C + I + G + (EX - IM)$$

At a given price level, anything that changes $C, I, G, EX,$ or $IM$ changes aggregate demand and thus shifts the aggregate demand ($AD$) curve. If $MV$ equals $C + I + G + (EX - IM)$, then *a change in the money supply (M) or a change in velocity (V) will change aggregate demand and therefore lead to a shift in the AD curve.* In other words, aggregate demand depends on *both* the money supply and velocity. Specifically:

- An increase in the money supply will increase aggregate demand and shift the $AD$ curve to the right.
- A decrease in the money supply will decrease aggregate demand and shift the $AD$ curve to the left.
- An increase in velocity will increase aggregate demand and shift the $AD$ curve to the right.
- A decrease in velocity will decrease aggregate demand and shift the $AD$ curve to the left.

But *in the simple quantity theory of money, velocity is assumed to be constant.* Thus, only changes in the money supply can shift the $AD$ curve.

The $AD$ curve for the simple quantity theory of money is shown in Exhibit 2(a). The ($M, V$) next to the curve is a reminder of which factors can shift the $AD$ curve. The bar over $V$ (for velocity) indicates that velocity is assumed to be constant.

**THE AS CURVE IN THE SIMPLE QUANTITY THEORY OF MONEY**  In the simple quantity theory of money, the level of Real GDP is assumed to be constant in the short run. Exhibit 2(b) shows Real GDP fixed at $Q_1$. The $AS$ curve is vertical at this level of Real GDP.

**AD AND AS IN THE SIMPLE QUANTITY THEORY OF MONEY**  Exhibit 2(c) shows both the $AD$ and $AS$ curves in the simple quantity theory of money. Suppose $AD_1$ is initially operational. In the exhibit, $AD_1$ is based on a money supply of $800 billion and a velocity of 2. The price level is $P_1$.

Now suppose we increase the money supply to $820 billion, and velocity remains constant at 2. According to the simple quantity theory of money, the price level will increase, and it does. The increase in the money supply shifts the $AD$ curve from $AD_1$ to $AD_2$ and pushes up the price level from $P_1$ to $P_2$.

Suppose that instead of increasing the money supply, we decrease it to $780 billion, again with velocity remaining constant at 2. According to the simple quantity theory of money, the price level will decrease, and it does. The decrease in the money supply shifts the $AD$ curve from $AD_1$ to $AD_3$ and pushes the price level down from $P_1$ to $P_3$.

**EXHIBIT 2**

**The Simple Quantity Theory of Money in the AD–AS Framework**

(a) In the simple quantity theory of money, the AD curve is downward sloping. Velocity is assumed to be constant, so changes in the money supply will change aggregate demand. (b) In the simple quantity theory of money, Real GDP is fixed in the short run. Thus, the AS curve is vertical. (c) In the simple quantity theory of money, an increase in the money supply will shift the AD curve rightward and increase the price level. A decrease in the money supply will shift the AD curve leftward and decrease the price level.

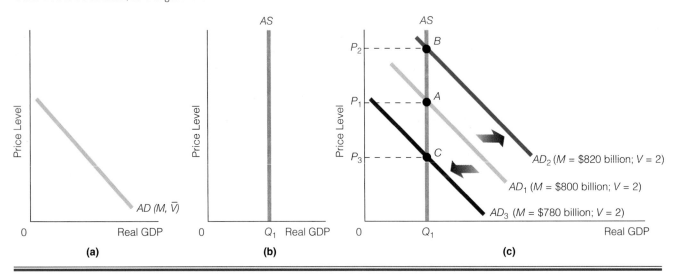

## Dropping the Assumptions that V and Q Are Constant

If we drop the assumptions that velocity ($V$) and Real GDP ($Q$) are constant, we have a more general theory of the factors that cause changes in the price level. In this theory, changes in the price level depend on three variables:

1. Money supply

2. Velocity

3. Real GDP

Let's again start with the equation of exchange.

$$M \times V \equiv P \times Q \tag{1}$$

If the equation of exchange holds, then

$$P \equiv \frac{M \times V}{Q} \tag{2}$$

Equation 2 shows that the money supply, velocity, and Real GDP determine the price level. In other words, the price level depends on the money supply, velocity, and Real GDP.

What kinds of changes in $M$, $V$, and $Q$ will bring about inflation (an increase in the price level), *ceteris paribus*? Obviously, an increase in $M$ or $V$ or a decrease in $Q$ will cause the price level to rise. For example, if velocity rises, the price level will rise; that is, an increase in velocity is inflationary.

Inflationary tendencies: $M\uparrow$, $V\uparrow$, $Q\downarrow$

What will bring about deflation (a decrease in the price level), *ceteris paribus*? Obviously, a decrease in $M$ or $V$ or an increase in $Q$ will cause the price level to fall. For example, if the money supply declines, the price level will drop; that is, a decrease in the money supply is deflationary.

Deflationary tendencies: $M\downarrow$, $V\downarrow$, $Q\uparrow$

## SELF-TEST

(Answers to Self-Test questions are in Answers to Self-Test Questions at the back of the book.)

1. If $M \times V$ increases, why does $P \times Q$ have to rise?

2. What is the difference between the equation of exchange and the simple quantity theory of money?

3. Predict what will happen to the AD curve as a result of each of the following:

   a. The money supply rises.

   b. Velocity falls.

   c. The money supply rises by a greater percentage than velocity falls.

   d. The money supply falls.

# MONETARISM

Economists who call themselves *monetarists* have not been content to rely on the simple quantity theory of money. They do *not* hold that velocity is constant, nor do they hold that output is constant. Monetarist views on the money supply, velocity, aggregate demand, and aggregate supply are discussed in this section.

## The Four Monetarist Positions

We begin with a brief explanation of the four positions held by monetarists. Then we discuss how, based on these positions, monetarists view the economy.

VELOCITY CHANGES IN A PREDICTABLE WAY  In the simple quantity theory of money, velocity is assumed to be constant; therefore, only changes in the money supply bring about changes in aggregate demand. Monetarists do not assume that velocity is constant, but rather that it can and does change. However, they believe that velocity changes in a predictable way, that is, not randomly, but in a way that can be understood and predicted. Monetarists hold that velocity is a function of certain variables—the interest rate, the expected inflation rate, the frequency with which employees receive paychecks, and more—and that changes in it can be predicted.

AGGREGATE DEMAND DEPENDS ON THE MONEY SUPPLY AND ON VELOCITY  Earlier, we showed that total expenditures in the economy ($TE$) equal $MV$. To better understand the economy, some economists—such as Keynesians—focus on the spending components of $TE$ ($C$, $I$, $G$, $EX$, and $IM$). Other economists—such as monetarists—focus on the money supply ($M$) and velocity ($V$). For example, Keynesians often argue that changes in $C$, $I$, $G$, $EX$, or $IM$ can change aggregate demand, whereas monetarists often argue that $M$ and $V$ can change aggregate demand.

THE *SRAS* CURVE IS UPWARD-SLOPING  In the simple quantity theory of money, the level of Real GDP ($Q$) is assumed to be constant in the short run. So the aggregate supply curve is vertical, as shown in Exhibit 3. According to monetarists, Real GDP may change in the short run, and therefore the *SRAS* curve is upward sloping.

**THE ECONOMY IS SELF-REGULATING (PRICES AND WAGES ARE FLEXIBLE)**
Monetarists believe that prices and wages are flexible. Monetarists therefore believe that the economy is self-regulating; it can move itself out of a recessionary or inflationary gap and into long-run equilibrium, producing Natural Real GDP.

## Monetarism and AD–AS

If monetarists tend to stress velocity and the money supply when discussing how the economy works, what effect does this view have in the *AD–AS* framework? Exhibit 3 helps to explain some of the highlights of monetarism. Each of the four parts (a)–(d) is considered separately.

**PART (a)** The economy is initially in long-run equilibrium, producing Natural Real GDP ($Q_N$) at price level $P_1$. Monetarists believe that changes in the money supply will change aggregate demand. For example, suppose the money supply rises from \$800 billion to \$820 billion. If velocity is constant, the *AD* curve shifts to the right, from $AD_1$ to $AD_2$ in the exhibit. As a result, Real GDP rises to $Q_1$, and the price level rises to $P_2$. And, of course, if Real GDP rises, the unemployment rate falls, *ceteris paribus*.

According to monetarists, the economy is in an inflationary gap at $Q_1$. However, given the monetarist belief in a self-regulating economy, soon wages will be bid up because the unemployment rate in an inflationary gap is less than the natural unemployment rate. The increase in wages will cause the *SRAS* curve to shift leftward from $SRAS_1$ to $SRAS_2$. The economy will return to long-run equilibrium, producing the same level of Real GDP as it did originally ($Q_N$), but at a higher price level.

What monetarists predict will happen to the economy in the short run due to an increase in the money supply is slightly different from what they predict will happen in the long run. In the short run, Real GDP will rise and the unemployment rate will fall. In the long run, Real GDP will return to its natural level, as will the unemployment rate, and the price level will be higher.

**PART (b)** The economy is initially in long-run equilibrium, producing Natural Real GDP ($Q_N$) at price level $P_1$. A decrease in the money supply, holding velocity constant, will shift the *AD* curve to the left from $AD_1$ to $AD_2$. This will reduce Real GDP to $Q_1$ and reduce the price level to $P_2$. Because Real GDP has fallen, the unemployment rate will rise.

According to monetarists, the economy in part (b) is in a recessionary gap. Monetarists hold that the economy can get itself out of a recessionary gap because the economy is self-regulating. In time, wages will fall, the *SRAS* curve will shift to the right, and the economy will be back in long-run equilibrium producing $Q_N$, albeit at a lower price level.

Again, the short- and long-run effects of a decrease in the money supply differ, according to monetarists. In the short run, Real GDP will fall and the unemployment rate will rise. In the long run, Real GDP will return to its natural level, as will the unemployment rate, and the price level will be lower.

**PART (c)** Again, we start with the economy in long-run equilibrium. Instead of the money supply, velocity changes. An increase in velocity causes the *AD* curve to shift to the right from $AD_1$ to $AD_2$. As a result, Real GDP rises, as does the price level. The unemployment rate falls as Real GDP rises.

EXHIBIT 3

### Monetarism in an *AD–AS* Framework

According to monetarists, changes in the money supply and velocity can change aggregate demand. In (a), an increase in the money supply shifts the *AD* curve to the right and raises Real GDP and the price level. Monetarists believe the economy is self-regulating; in time it moves back to its Natural Real GDP level at a higher price level. The same self-regulating properties are present in (b)–(d).

(a)

(b)

(c)

(d)

According to monetarists, the economy is in an inflationary gap, but in time it will move back to long-run equilibrium. So in the short run, an increase in velocity raises Real GDP and lowers the unemployment rate. In the long run, Real GDP returns to its natural level, as does the unemployment rate, and the price level is higher.

PART (d) The economy is in long-run equilibrium. A decrease in velocity causes the *AD* curve to shift to the left from $AD_1$ to $AD_2$. As a result, Real GDP falls, as does the price level. The unemployment rate rises as Real GDP falls.

According to monetarists, the economy is in a recessionary gap, but in time it will move back to long-run equilibrium. So in the short run, a decrease in velocity lowers Real GDP and increases the unemployment rate. In the long run, Real GDP returns to its natural level, as does the unemployment rate, and the price level is lower.

## The Monetarist View of the Economy

The diagrammatic exposition of monetarism in Exhibit 3 reveals that monetarists believe that:

- The economy is self-regulating.
- Changes in velocity and the money supply can change aggregate demand.
- Changes in velocity and the money supply will change the price level and Real GDP in the short run but only the price level in the long run.

We need to make one other important point with respect to monetarists. Consider this question: Can a change in velocity offset a change in the money supply? Suppose velocity falls and the money supply rises. By itself, a decrease in velocity will shift the *AD* curve to the left. And, by itself, an increase in the money supply will shift the *AD* curve to the right. The decline in velocity could shift the *AD* curve to the left by the same amount as the increase in the money supply shifts the *AD* curve to the right. If so, then a change in the money supply would have no effect on Real GDP, on the short-run price level, and on the long-run price level. In other words, changes in monetary policy may be ineffective at changing Real GDP and the price level.

Monetarists think that this condition—a change in velocity completely offsetting a change in the money supply—does not occur often. They believe (1) that velocity does not change very much from one period to the next (i.e., it is relatively stable) and (2) that changes in velocity are predictable (as mentioned earlier). In other words, monetarists believe velocity is relatively stable and predictable.

So in the monetarist view of the economy, changes in velocity are not likely to offset changes in the money supply. Therefore, *changes in the money supply will largely determine changes in aggregate demand and thus changes in Real GDP and the price level.* For all practical purposes, an increase in the money supply will raise aggregate demand, increase both Real GDP and the price level in the short run, and increase only the price level in the long run. A decrease in the money supply will lower aggregate demand, decrease both Real GDP and the price level in the short run, and decrease only the price level in the long run.

---

### SELF-TEST

1. What do monetarists predict will happen in the short run and in the long run as a result of each of the following? (In each case, assume the economy is currently in long-run equilibrium.)

   a. Velocity rises.

   b. Velocity falls.

   c. The money supply rises.

   d. The money supply falls.

2. Can a change in velocity offset a change in the money supply (on aggregate demand)? Explain your answer.

## INFLATION

In everyday usage, the word "inflation" refers to any increase in the price level. Economists, though, like to differentiate between two types of increases in the price level: a one-shot increase and a continued increase.

## One-Shot Inflation

One-shot inflation is exactly what it sounds like: a one-shot, or one-time, increase in the price level. Suppose the CPI for years 1 to 5 is as follows:

| Year | CPI |
|------|-----|
| 1 | 100 |
| 2 | 110 |
| 3 | 110 |
| 4 | 110 |
| 5 | 110 |

Notice that the price level is higher in year 2 than in year 1, but after year 2 it does not change. In other words, it takes a one-shot jump in year 2 and then stabilizes. This is an example of one-shot inflation, which can originate on either the demand side or the supply side of the economy.

ONE-SHOT INFLATION: DEMAND-SIDE INDUCED In Exhibit 4(a), the economy is initially in long-run equilibrium at point 1. Suppose the aggregate demand curve shifts rightward from $AD_1$ to $AD_2$. As this happens, the economy moves to point 2, where the price level is $P_2$. At point 2 in Exhibit 4(b), the Real GDP the economy is producing ($Q_2$) is greater than Natural Real GDP; so the unemployment rate in the economy is lower than the natural unemployment rate. Consequently, as old wage contracts expire, workers are paid higher wage rates because unemployment is relatively low. As wage rates rise, the $SRAS$ curve shifts leftward from $SRAS_1$ to $SRAS_2$. The long-run equilibrium position is at point 3. The price level and Real GDP at each of the three points are as follows:

| Point | Price Level | Real GDP |
|-------|-------------|----------|
| 1 (start) | $P_1$ | $Q_1 = Q_N$ |
| 2 | $P_2$ | $Q_2$ |
| 3 (end) | $P_3$ | $Q_1 = Q_N$ |

**EXHIBIT 4**

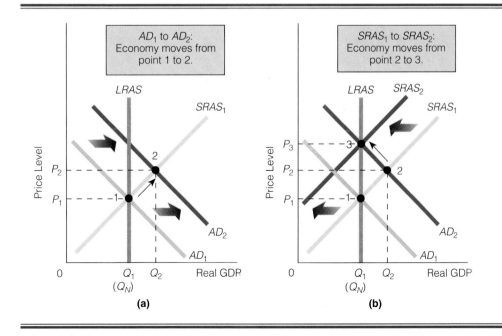

**One-Shot Inflation: Demand-side Induced**

(a) The aggregate demand curve shifts rightward from $AD_1$ to $AD_2$. As a result, the price level increases from $P_1$ to $P_2$; the economy moves from point 1 to point 2. (b) Because the Real GDP the economy produces ($Q_2$) is greater than Natural Real GDP, the unemployment rate that exists is less than the natural unemployment rate. Wage rates rise, and the short-run aggregate supply curve shifts leftward from $SRAS_1$ to $SRAS_2$. Long-run equilibrium is at point 3.

Notice that at point 3 the economy is at a higher price level than at point 1, but at the same Real GDP level.

Price levels that go from $P_1$ to $P_2$ to $P_3$ may seem like more than a one-shot increase. But because the price level stabilizes (at $P_3$), we cannot characterize it as continually rising. So the change in the price level is representative of one-shot inflation.

ONE-SHOT INFLATION: SUPPLY-SIDE INDUCED In Exhibit 5(a), the economy is initially in long-run equilibrium at point 1. Suppose the short-run aggregate supply curve shifts leftward from $SRAS_1$ to $SRAS_2$ because, say, oil prices increase. As the curve shifts, the economy moves to point 2, where the price level is $P_2$.

At point 2 in Exhibit 5(b), the Real GDP that the economy is producing ($Q_2$) is less than Natural Real GDP; so the unemployment rate in the economy is greater than the natural unemployment rate. Consequently, as old wage contracts expire, workers are paid lower wage rates because unemployment is relatively high. As wage rates fall, the short-run aggregate supply curve shifts rightward from $SRAS_2$ to $SRAS_1$. The long-run equilibrium position is at point 1 again. (If wage rates are somewhat inflexible, moving from point 2 back to point 1 may take some time.) The price level and Real GDP at each of the three points are as follows:

| Point | Price Level | Real GDP |
|-------|-------------|----------|
| 1 (start) | $P_1$ | $Q_1 = Q_N$ |
| 2 | $P_2$ | $Q_2$ |
| 3 (end) | $P_1$ | $Q_1 = Q_N$ |

Because the price level initially increased from $P_1$ to $P_2$, this case is descriptive of one-shot inflation.

CONFUSING DEMAND-INDUCED AND SUPPLY-INDUCED ONE-SHOT INFLATION Demand-induced and supply-induced types of one-shot inflation are easy

---

**EXHIBIT 5**

**One-Shot Inflation: Supply-Side Induced**

(a) The short-run aggregate supply curve shifts leftward from $SRAS_1$ to $SRAS_2$. As a result, the price level increases from $P_1$ to $P_2$; the economy moves from point 1 to point 2.
(b) Because the Real GDP the economy produces ($Q_2$) is less than Natural Real GDP, the unemployment rate that exists is greater than the natural unemployment rate. Some economists argue that when this happens, wage rates will fall and the short-run aggregate supply curve will shift rightward from $SRAS_2$ (back to $SRAS_1$). Long-run equilibrium is at point 1.

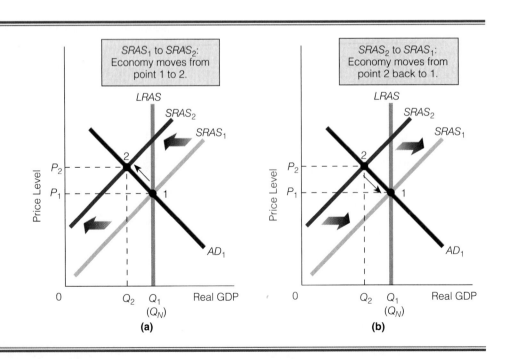

to confuse.[2] To illustrate, suppose the Federal Reserve System increases the money supply. With more money in the economy, there can be greater total spending at any given price level. Consequently, the *AD* curve shifts rightward.

Next, prices begin to rise, and, soon afterward, wage rates begin to rise (because the economy is in an inflationary gap). Many employers, perhaps unaware that the money supply has increased, certainly are aware that they are paying their employees higher wages. Thus, employers may think the higher price level is due to higher wage rates, not to the increased money supply that preceded the higher wage rates. But they would be wrong. What may look like a supply-induced rise in the price level is really demand-induced.

We can tell this same story in terms of the diagrams in Exhibit 4. In (a), the *AD* curve shifts rightward because, as explained, the money supply increases. Employers, however, are unaware of what has happened in part (a). What they see is part (b). They end up paying higher wage rates to their employees, and the *SRAS* curve shifts leftward. Unaware that the *AD* curve shifted rightward in (a) but aware that the *SRAS* curve shifted leftward in (b), employers mistakenly conclude that the rise in the price level originated with a supply-side factor (higher wage rates), not with a demand-side factor (an increase in the money supply).

## ⓣhinking Like **AN ECONOMIST**

**Your Eyes Can Deceive You** People tend to believe that what they see with their own eyes or what they experience directly in their daily lives causes the effects they notice. In our last example, employers mistakenly believed that the stimulus for the rise in the price level was a rise in wage rates (which they had experienced firsthand), not an increase in the money supply (which they probably did not know had occurred). But the economist knows that the cause of a phenomenon may be far removed from our personal orbit. This awareness is part of the economic way of thinking. ▴ ▴ ▴

## ⓕinding **ECONOMICS**

**In a Remodeling Job** Jan is getting her house remodeled. Today her contractor told her that the price he pays for many of his supplies has increased and that the remodeling is going to cost "a little more." That night, Jan says to her husband, Mike, "I guess that's the way life is sometimes. Costs go up; so prices go up." Where is the economics? Could Jan somehow be the real reason that her contractor's costs went up?

What Jan may not see is that she and others who want their houses remodeled are increasing the demand for remodeling. As a result, the demand rises for things such as tile, wood, nails, cement, and related materials. The higher prices for tile, nails, and wood are the higher costs the remodeler is talking about; so when he tells Jan his costs have risen, he is telling the truth. Jan then blames the higher costs for her having to pay more for her remodeling job. Actually, the higher demand stemming from her and others starts the process that ends in higher costs for the remodeler and in higher prices for her.▴ ▴ ▴

## Continued Inflation

Suppose the CPI for years 1 to 5 is as follows:

| Year | CPI |
| --- | --- |
| 1 | 100 |
| 2 | 110 |
| 3 | 120 |
| 4 | 130 |
| 5 | 140 |

2. Sometimes the terms "demand-side inflation" and "supply-side inflation" are used.

# economics 24/7

## Grade Inflation: It's All Relative

Inflation can sometimes be deceptive. Suppose Jones produces and sells motorcycles. The average price for one of his motorcycles is $10,000. Unknown to Jones, the Fed increases the money supply. Months pass, and then one day Jones notices that the demand for his motorcycles has increased. Jones raises the prices of his motorcycles and earns a higher dollar income.

© NAJLAH FEANNY/CORBIS

Jones is excited about earning more income, but soon he realizes that the prices of many of the things he buys have increased too. Food, clothing, and housing prices have all gone up. Jones is earning a higher dollar income, but he is also paying higher prices. In relative terms, Jones's financial position may be the same as it was before the price of motorcycles increased.

Now let's consider grade inflation. Beginning in the 1960s, the average GPA at most colleges and universities across the country began to rise. Whereas professors once gave out the full range of grades—A, B, C, D, and F—today many professors give only As and Bs and a few Cs. The so-called Gentleman's C, once a mainstay on many college campuses, is said to have been replaced by the Gentleperson's B.

Grade inflation can deceive you, just as general price inflation deceived Jones. To illustrate, suppose you get higher grades (without studying more or working harder). Your average grade goes from, say, C+ to B,

and you believe you have an advantage over other college and university students. You reason that with higher grades, you will have a better chance of getting a good job or of getting into graduate school.

But you do only if your grades go up *and no one else's do.* In other words, your relative position must improve. Grade inflation at thousands of colleges and universities across the country prevents you from gaining that advantage. You get higher grades, but so does everyone else. Your GPA increases from, say, 2.90 to 3.60, but other students' GPAs increase similarly.

So, as long as other students are getting higher grades too, better grades for you do not necessarily make it easier for you to compete with others for a job or for admission to graduate school. In essence, grade inflation, like general price inflation, is deceptive. With price inflation, you may initially think your financial position has improved because you are earning more for what you sell, but then you realize that you have to pay more for the things you buy. With grade inflation, you may initially think you have an advantage over other students because you are receiving higher grades, but then you learn that everyone else is getting higher grades too. Your relative position may be the same as it was before grade inflation boosted your GPA.

---

**Continued Inflation**
A continued increase in the price level.

Notice that the CPI goes from 100 to 110, then from 110 to 120, and so on. Each year the CPI is higher than the year before. This continued increase in the price level is an example of continued inflation.

**FROM ONE-SHOT INFLATION TO CONTINUED INFLATION** Continued increases in aggregate demand can turn one-shot inflation into continued inflation. (Later in this chapter we describe what leads to continued increases in aggregate demand.) The process is illustrated in Exhibit 6. (The diagram looks scary, but not when you take it one step at a time.)

Beginning at point 1 in Exhibit 6(a), the aggregate demand curve shifts rightward from $AD_1$ to $AD_2$. The economy moves from point 1 to point 2. At point 2, the unemployment rate in the economy is less than the natural unemployment rate. As a result, wage rates rise and cause the short-run aggregate supply curve to shift leftward from $SRAS_1$ to $SRAS_2$. The economy moves from point 2 to point 3. At point 3, the economy is in long-run equilibrium.

Suppose that at point 3 the economy experiences *another* rightward shift in the aggregate demand curve (to $AD_3$). The process keeps repeating itself, and the economy moves from point 3 to point 4 to point 5. Still *another* rightward shift in the aggregate demand

**EXHIBIT 6**

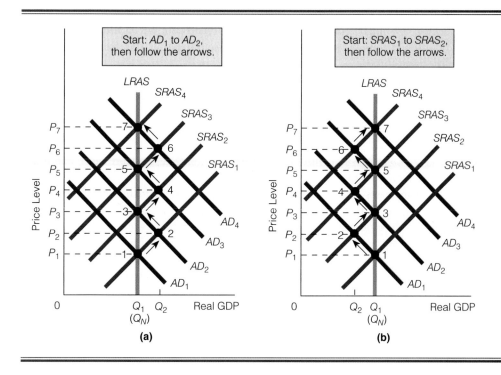

(a)

(b)

**Changing One-Shot Inflation into Continued Inflation**

(a) The aggregate demand curve shifts rightward from $AD_1$ to $AD_2$. The economy initially moves from point 1 to point 2 and finally to point 3. Continued increases in the price level are brought about through continued increases in aggregate demand. (b) The short-run aggregate supply curve shifts leftward from $SRAS_1$ to $SRAS_2$. The economy initially moves from point 1 to point 2. The economy will return to point 1 unless there is an increase in aggregate demand. We see here, as in (a), that continued increases in the price level are brought about through continued increases in aggregate demand.

curve moves the economy from point 5 to point 6 to point 7. The exhibit stops at point 7, but it could have continued. The result of this process is a *continually rising price level*—from $P_1$ to $P_7$ and beyond. Continued increases in aggregate demand cause continued inflation.

Continued inflation from the supply side of the economy is illustrated in Exhibit 6(b). Beginning at point 1, the short-run aggregate supply curve shifts leftward from $SRAS_1$ to $SRAS_2$. The economy moves from point 1 to point 2. At point 2, the unemployment rate in the economy is greater than the natural unemployment rate. According to some economists, the natural tendency is for wage rates to fall and for the $SRAS$ curve to shift rightward, moving the economy back to point 1.

This natural tendency of the economy to return to point 1 will be offset, however, if the aggregate demand curve shifts rightward. Then, instead of moving from point 2 back to point 1, the economy moves from point 2 to point 3. At point 3, the economy is in long-run equilibrium, and the price level is higher than at point 2.

Suppose the economy experiences another leftward shift in the aggregate supply curve (to $SRAS_3$). The economy moves from point 3 to point 4 and would naturally return to point 3 unless the aggregate demand curve shifts rightward. If it does, the economy moves to point 5. The same process moves the economy from point 5 to point 6 to point 7, where the exhibit stops. This process results in a continually rising price level—from $P_1$ to $P_7$ and beyond. Again, *continued increases in aggregate demand cause continued inflation.*

**THE EFFECT OF CONTINUED DECLINES IN** *SRAS* Can continued declines in *SRAS* cause continued inflation? For example, suppose a labor union continually asks for and receives higher wages. As wages continually increase, the *SRAS* curve will continually shift leftward, leading to a continually rising price level. This could happen but isn't likely. Every time workers ask for and receive higher wages—shifting the *SRAS* curve leftward—Real GDP declines. Because not as many workers are needed to produce a lower Real GDP as are needed to produce a higher Real GDP, some of the workers will lose their jobs. Labor unions are not likely to adopt a policy that would put more and more of their members out of work.

There is another argument against declines in *SRAS* causing continued inflation. The CPI and the Real GDP level for, say, 1960 indicate that today both are higher than they were in 1960. The higher price level means that, since 1960, we have experienced continued inflation in the United States but that this continued inflation has accompanied a (generally) rising Real GDP. If the continued inflation of the past few decades had been caused by continued declines in *SRAS*, Real GDP would not have been rising. It would have been falling (as *SRAS* declines, the price level rises and Real GDP falls). In short, the continued inflation in the United States had to be caused by continued increases in *AD*, not by continued decreases in *SRAS*.

**THE BIG QUESTION** If continued increases in aggregate demand cause continued inflation, what causes continued increases in aggregate demand? At a given price level, anything that increases total expenditures increases aggregate demand and shifts the *AD* curve to the right. With this in mind, consider an increase in the money supply. With more money in the economy, total expenditures can be greater at a given price level. Consequently, aggregate demand increases, and the *AD* curve shifts rightward.

Economists widely agree that the only factor that can change *continually* in such a way as to bring about continued increases in aggregate demand is the money supply. Specifically, continued increases in the money supply lead to continued increases in aggregate demand, which generate continued inflation.

Continued increases in the money supply → Continued increases in aggregate demand → Continued inflation

The money supply is the *only* factor that can continually increase without causing a reduction in one of the four components of total expenditures (consumption, investment, government purchases, or net exports). This point is important because someone might ask, "Can't government purchases continually increase and so cause continued inflation?" This is unlikely for two reasons:

- Government purchases cannot go beyond both real and political limits. The real upper limit is 100 percent of GDP. No one knows what the political upper limit is, but it is likely to be less than 100 percent of GDP. In either case, once government purchases reach their limit, they can no longer increase.

- Some economists argue that government purchases that are not financed with new money may crowd out one of the other expenditure components (see Chapter 11.) Thus, increases in government purchases are not guaranteed to raise total expenditures because if government purchases rise, consumption may fall to the degree that government purchases have increased. For example, for every additional dollar government spends on public education, households may spend $1 less on private education.

The emphasis on the money supply as the only factor that can continue to increase and thus cause continued inflation has led most economists to agree with Nobel Laureate Milton Friedman that "inflation is always and everywhere a monetary phenomenon."

## SELF-TEST

1. The prices of houses, cars, and television sets have increased. Has there been inflation?

2. Is continued inflation likely to be supply side induced? Explain your answer.

3. What type of inflation is Milton Friedman referring to when he says that "inflation is always and everywhere a monetary phenomenon"?

# MONEY AND INTEREST RATES

Let's review how changes in the money supply affect different economic variables.

## What Economic Variables Does a Change in the Money Supply Affect?

Money supply can affect interest rates, but to understand how, we need to review how the money supply affects different economic variables. Specifically:

1. *Money and the supply of loans.* The last chapter explained the actions of the Fed that change the money supply. For example, when the Fed undertakes an open market purchase, the money supply increases, as do reserves in the banking system. With greater reserves, banks can extend more loans. In other words, as a result of the Fed's conducting an open market purchase, the supply of loans rises. Similarly, when the Fed conducts an open market sale, the supply of loans decreases.

2. *Money and Real GDP.* This chapter shows how a change in the money supply can change aggregate demand and thereby change the price level and Real GDP in the short run. For example, look back at Exhibit 3(a). The economy starts at point 1, producing $Q_N$. An increase in the money supply shifts the *AD* curve rightward, from $AD_1$ to $AD_2$. In the short run, the economy moves to point 2 and produces a higher level of Real GDP ($Q_1$). Similarly, in the short run, a decrease in the money supply produces a lower level of Real GDP [see Exhibit 3(b)].

3. *Money and the price level.* This chapter also shows how a change in the money supply can change the price level. Again, look back at Exhibit 3(a). Initially, at point 1, the price level is $P_1$. An increase in the money supply shifts the *AD* curve rightward from $AD_1$ to $AD_2$. In the short run, the price level in the economy moves from $P_1$ to $P_2$. In the long run, the economy is at point 3 and the price level is $P_3$. Exhibit 3(b) shows how a decrease in the money supply affects the price level.

So changes in the money supply affect (1) the supply of loans, (2) Real GDP, and (3) the price level.

Can the money supply affect anything else? Many economists say that because the money supply affects the price level, it also affects the *expected inflation rate*, which is the inflation rate that you expect. For example, your expected inflation rate—the inflation rate you expect will be realized over the next year—may be 5 percent, 6 percent, or some other rate. Changes in the money supply affect the expected inflation rate, either directly or indirectly. The equation of exchange indicates that the greater the increase in the money supply is, the greater the rise in the price level will be. And we would expect that the greater the rise in the price level is, the higher the expected inflation rate will be, *ceteris paribus*. For example, we would predict that a money supply growth rate of, say, 10 percent a year generates a greater actual inflation rate and a larger expected inflation rate than a money supply growth rate of 2 percent a year.

So, changes in the money supply (or changes in the rate of growth of the money supply) can affect:

1. the supply of loans.
2. Real GDP.
3. the price level.
4. the expected inflation rate.

## The Money Supply, the Loanable Funds Market, and Interest Rates

Exhibit 7(a) shows the loanable funds market. The demand for loanable funds ($D_{LF}$) is downward sloping, indicating that borrowers will borrow more funds as the interest rate declines. The supply of loanable funds ($S_{LF}$) is upward sloping, indicating that lenders will lend more funds as the interest rate rises. The equilibrium interest rate ($i_1$ percent) is determined through the forces of supply and demand. If there is a surplus of loanable funds, the interest rate falls; if there is a shortage of loanable funds, the interest rate rises.

Anything that affects either the supply of or the demand for loanable funds will obviously affect the interest rate. All four of the factors that are affected by changes in the money supply—the supply of loans, Real GDP, the price level, and the expected inflation rate—affect either the supply of or demand for loanable funds.

**THE SUPPLY OF LOANS** A Fed open market purchase increases reserves in the banking system and therefore increases the supply of loanable funds. As a result, the interest rate declines [see Exhibit 7(b)]. This change in the interest rate due to a change in the supply of loanable funds is called the liquidity effect.

**Liquidity Effect**
The change in the interest rate due to a change in the supply of loanable funds.

**REAL GDP** A change in Real GDP affects both the supply of and the demand for loanable funds.

First, how does Real GDP affect the supply of loanable funds? When Real GDP rises, people's wealth is greater. (Real GDP consists of goods, and goods are a component of wealth.) When people became wealthier, they often demand more bonds (in much the same way that they may demand more houses, cars, and jewelry). Demanding more bonds (buying more bonds), however, is nothing more than lending more money to others. When you buy a bond issued by company A, you are essentially giving the company a loan. The company says. "Do you want to buy this bond for $10,000?" You say yes. When you buy the bond from the company for $10,000, you essentially give the company a $10,000 loan, which it is obligated to repay with interest. When the company pays off the bond to you, it returns the $10,000 plus interest. So, as Real GDP rises, individuals become wealthier, and they tend to buy more bonds, that is, extend more loans. The supply of loanable funds increases.

Second, how does Real GDP affect the demand for loanable funds? When Real GDP rises, profitable business opportunities usually abound, and businesses issue or supply more bonds to take advantage of those opportunities. But, supplying more bonds is nothing more than demanding more loanable funds. So, when Real GDP rises, corporations issue or supply more bonds, thereby demanding more loanable funds.

In summary, when Real GDP increases, both the supply of and the demand for loanable funds increase. The overall effect on the interest rate is that, usually, the demand for loanable funds increases by more than the supply so that the interest rate rises. The change in the interest rate due to a change in Real GDP is called the income effect. See Exhibit 7(c).

**Income Effect**
The change in the interest rate due to a change in Real GDP.

**THE PRICE LEVEL** A downward-sloping *AD* curve is explained by (1) the real balance effect, (2) the interest rate effect, and (3) the international trade effect (see Chapter 8). With respect to the interest rate effect, when the price level rises, the purchasing power of money falls. People may therefore increase their demand for credit or loanable funds to borrow the funds necessary to buy a fixed bundle of goods. This change in the interest rate due to a change in the price level is called the price-level effect. See Exhibit 7(d).

**Price-Level Effect**
The change in the interest rate due to a change in the price level.

**THE EXPECTED INFLATION RATE** A change in the expected inflation rate affects both the supply of and demand for loanable funds. Suppose the expected inflation rate is zero and that when the expected inflation rate is zero, the equilibrium interest rate is 6

**EXHIBIT 7**

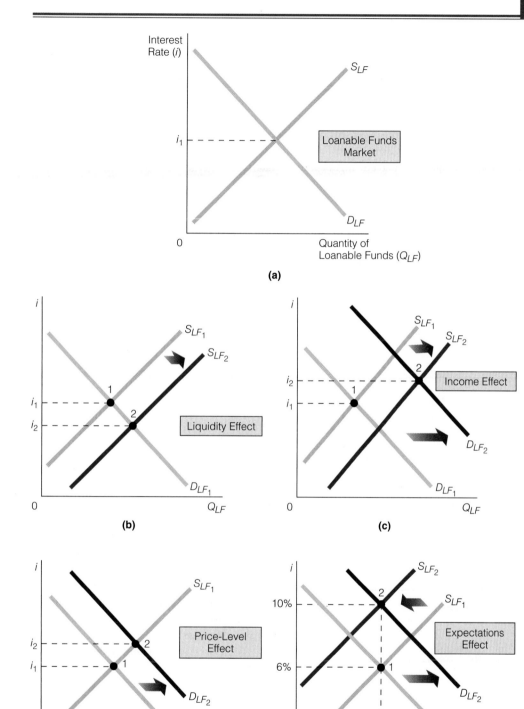

(a)

(b)

(c)

(d)

(e)

**The Interest Rate and the Loanable Funds Market**

The loanable funds market is shown in part (a). The demand for loanable funds is downward sloping; the supply of loanable funds is upward sloping. Part (b) shows the liquidity effect, part (c) shows the income effect, part (d) shows the price-level effect, and part (e) shows the expectations effect.

percent, as in Exhibit 7(e). Now suppose the expected inflation rate rises from 0 percent to 4 percent. What will this rise in the expected inflation rate do to the demand for and supply of loanable funds? Borrowers (demanders of loanable funds) will be willing to pay 4 percent more interest for their loans because they expect to be paying back the loans with dollars that have 4 percent less buying power than the dollars they are borrowing. If they wait to buy goods they want, the prices will have risen by 4 percent. To beat the price rise, consumers are willing to pay up to 4 percent more to borrow money to purchase the goods now. In effect, the demand for loanable funds curve shifts rightward so that at $Q_1$ borrowers are willing to pay a 4 percent higher interest rate.

On the other side of the loanable funds market, the lenders (the suppliers of loanable funds) require a 4 percent higher interest rate to compensate them for the 4 percent less valuable dollars with which the loan will be repaid. In effect, the supply of loanable funds curve shifts leftward, so that at $Q_1$ lenders will receive an interest rate of 10 percent. See Exhibit 7(e).

Thus an expected inflation rate of 4 percent increases the demand for loanable funds and decreases the supply of loanable funds. So the interest rate is 4 percent higher than it was when the expected inflation rate was zero. A change in the interest rate due to a change in the expected inflation rate is referred to as the expectations effect (or *Fisher effect,* after economist Irving Fisher).

Exhibit 8 summarizes how a change in the money supply directly and indirectly affects the interest rate.

**Expectations Effect**

The change in the interest rate due to a change in the expected inflation rate.

### THE DIFFERENCE BETWEEN THE PRICE-LEVEL EFFECT AND THE EXPECTATIONS EFFECT

To many people, the price-level effect sounds the same as the expectations effect. After all, both have something to do with the price level.

But they are different. Consider a one-shot change in the money supply that ultimately moves the price level from a price index of 120 to a price index of 135. The price-level effect refers to the change in the interest rate that is related to the actual rise in price level. The demand for loanable funds creeps up steadily as the price index rises from 120 to 121, to 122, to 123, and so on to 135. Once the price index hits 135, though, there is no further reason for the demand for loanable funds to rise because the price level isn't rising anymore.

As the price level is rising, people's expected inflation rate is rising. They may feel they know where the price level is headed (from 120 to 135) and adjust accordingly. Once the price level hits 135 (and given that the change in the money supply is one-shot), the expected inflation rate falls to zero. Any change in the interest rate due to a rise in the expected inflation rate is now over, and therefore the expected inflation rate no longer has an effect on the interest rate. But certainly the price level still has an effect because the price level is higher than it was originally. In the end, the effect on the interest

---

### EXHIBIT 8

**How the Fed Affects the Interest Rate**

This exhibit summarizes the way the Fed (through its monetary policy) affects the interest rate. For example, an open market operation (OMO) directly affects the supply of loanable funds and affects the interest rate. An OMO also affects Real GDP, the price level, and the expected inflation rate, and therefore indirectly affects either the supply of or demand for loanable funds, which in turn affects the interest rate.

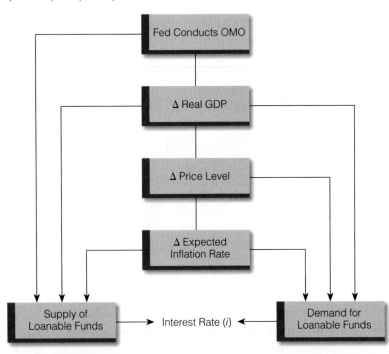

rate due to a rise in the price level remains, and the effect on the interest rate due to a rise in the expected inflation rate disappears.

## What Happens to the Interest Rate as the Money Supply Changes?

Suppose the Fed takes action to raise the rate of growth of the money supply from, say, 3 percent to 5 percent a year. What effect does this action have on the interest rate? Some people will quickly say that it will lower the interest rate, thinking perhaps that only the liquidity effect comes into play. In other words, as the Fed increases the rate of growth of the money supply, more reserves enter the banking system, more loans are extended, and the interest rate falls [Exhibit 7(b)].

That would be the right answer if all an increase in the money supply growth rate did was to affect the supply of loanable funds, but, as explained, this isn't the only effect. Real GDP changes, the price level changes, and the expected inflation rate changes, and all these changes affect the loanable funds market, just as the Fed action did. Figuring out what happens to the interest rate is a matter of trying to figure out when each effect (liquidity, income, price-level, and expectations) occurs and how strong each is.

To illustrate, suppose on December 31 everyone expects the Fed to continue to increase the money supply at a growth rate of 2 percent a year. Then, on January 1, the Fed announces that it will increase the rate of growth in the money supply to 4 percent and will begin open market purchases to effect this outcome immediately. One second after the announcement, people's expected inflation rate may rise. The expectations effect begins to affect interest rates immediately. On January 2, the interest rate is therefore higher than it was one day earlier.

- *Point 1 in time:* Fed says it will increase the growth rate of the money supply.
- *Point 2 in time:* If the expectations effect kicks in immediately, then . . .
- *Point 3 in time:* Interest rates rise.

At point 3 in time, a natural conclusion is that an increase in the rate of growth in the money supply *raises* the interest rate. The problem with this conclusion, though, is that *not all the effects (liquidity, income, etc.) have occurred yet*. In time, the liquidity effect puts downward pressure on the interest rate. Suppose the liquidity effect goes to work on January 15, and the interest rate begins to fall from what it was on January 2. Then, someone on January 15 could say, "Obviously, an increase in the rate of growth of the money supply *lowers* interest rates."

- *Point 4 in time:* Liquidity effect kicks in.
- *Point 5 in time:* As a result of what happened at point 4, the interest rate drops. The interest rate is now lower than it was at point 3.

The point is that a change in the money supply affects the economy in many ways: changing the supply of loanable funds directly, changing Real GDP and therefore changing the demand for and supply of loanable funds, changing the expected inflation rate, and so on. The *timing* and *magnitude* of these effects determine the changes in the interest rate.

## The Nominal and Real Interest Rates

If you were to call a bank and ask what it charges for, say, a car loan, the bank would quote an interest rate. The quoted interest rate is the rate we have been discussing, the interest rate that comes about through the interaction of the demand for and supply of loanable funds. Sometimes, this interest rate is called the nominal interest rate, or market interest rate.

**Nominal Interest Rate**
The interest rate actually charged (or paid) in the market; the market interest rate: Nominal interest rate = Real interest rate + Expected inflation rate.

The nominal interest rate may not be the true cost of borrowing because part of the nominal interest rate is a reflection of the expected inflation rate. Suppose the nominal interest rate is 9 percent, and the expected inflation rate is 2 percent. If you take out a loan for $10,000 at 9 percent, you will have to pay back the loan amount ($10,000) plus $900 in interest at the end of the year. In other words, for a $10,000 loan, you have to repay $10,900.

Now suppose the expected inflation rate turns out to be the actual inflation rate. As an example, people expect the inflation rate to be 2 percent, and it turns out to be 2 percent. In this case, the dollars you pay back will be worth less—by 2 percent—than the dollars you borrowed. In other words, you borrowed dollars that were worth 2 percent more in purchasing power than the dollars you repaid.

**Real Interest Rate**
The nominal interest rate minus the expected inflation rate. When the expected inflation rate is zero, the real interest rate equals the nominal interest rate.

This fact should be taken into account in determining your real cost of borrowing. Economists would say that the real cost of borrowing was not 9 percent, but 7 percent. The real cost of borrowing is sometimes called the real interest rate, which is equal to the nominal interest rate minus the expected inflation rate.[3]

$$\text{Real interest rate} = \text{Nominal interest rate} - \text{Expected inflation rate}$$

Given this equation, the nominal interest rate is therefore equal to the real interest rate plus the expected inflation rate.

$$\text{Nominal interest rate} = \text{Real interest rate} + \text{Expected inflation rate}$$

## SELF-TEST

1. If the expected inflation rate is 4 percent and the nominal interest rate is 7 percent, what is the real interest rate?

2. Is it possible for the nominal interest rate to rise immediately following an increase in the money supply? Explain your answer.

3. The Fed affects only the interest rate via the liquidity effect. Do you agree or disagree? Explain your answer.

---

3. A broader definition is Real interest rate = Nominal interest rate − Expected rate of change in the price level. This definition is useful because we will not always be dealing with an expected inflation rate; we could be dealing with an expected deflation rate.

## "What Is the Current Expected Inflation Rate?"

**STUDENT:**

Is there some way to figure out the expected inflation rate at any given time?

**INSTRUCTOR:**

One way to find out the expected inflation rate is to look at the spread—the difference—between the yield on conventional bonds and the yield on indexed bonds with the same maturity.

**STUDENT:**

What's a a conventional bond? What's an inflation-indexed bond?

**INSTRUCTOR:**

An inflation-indexed bond guarantees the purchaser a certain real rate of return, but a conventional, or nonindexed, bond does not. For example, suppose you purchase an *inflation-indexed*, 10-year, $1,000 bond that pays 4 percent interest. If there is no inflation, the annual interest payment is $40. But if the inflation rate is 3 percent, the bond issuer marks up the value of your security by 3 percent—from $1,000 to $1,030. Your annual interest payment is then 4 percent of this new higher amount, that is, 4 percent of $1,030, or $41.20.

Now investors are willing to accept a lower yield on inflation-indexed bonds because they get something that they don't get with conventional bonds: protection against inflation. So while a conventional bond may yield, say, 6 percent, an inflation-indexed bond may yield 4 percent. The spread is the difference between the two rates.

**STUDENT:**

And how does the spread or difference relate to the expected inflation rate?

**INSTRUCTOR:**

Well, the spread is a measure of the inflation rate that investors expect will exist over the life of the bond. To illustrate with real numbers, let's say that we go to www.bloomberg.com/ and learn that an *inflation-indexed* 10-year Treasury bond has an interest rate of 1.72 percent and that a conventional 10-year Treasury bond has an interest rate

of of 4.02. The difference, or spread, is therefore 2.3 percent. In other words, on this day, investors (or the so-called market) expect that the inflation rate is going to be 2.3 percent.

So, by checking the spread between interest rates on conventional and inflation-indexed bonds of the *same maturity* (that is, both mature in the same number of months or years), you can see what the market expects the inflation rate will be. As the spread widens, the market expects a higher inflation rate; as it narrows, the market expects a lower inflation rate.

### POINTS TO REMEMBER

1. We discussed two types of bonds: inflation-indexed and convential. Each type of bonds pays an interest rate.
2. The spread, or difference, between the interest rates on a convential and an inflation-indexed bond is the market's expected inflation rate. The larger the spread is, the higher is the expected inflation rate (the inflation rate the market expects in the future). The smaller the spread, the lower the expected inflation rate (the lower the inflation rate the market expects in the future).

# CHAPTER SUMMARY

## THE EQUATION OF EXCHANGE

- The equation of exchange is an identity: $MV \equiv PQ$. The equation of exchange can be interpreted in different ways: (1) The money supply multiplied by velocity must equal the price level times Real GDP: $M \times V \equiv P \times Q$. (2) The money supply multiplied by velocity must equal GDP: $M \times V \equiv GDP$. (3) Total expenditures (measured by $MV$) must equal the total sales revenues of business firms (measured by $PQ$): $MV \equiv PQ$.

- The equation of exchange is not a theory of the economy. However, the equation of exchange can be turned into a theory by making assumptions about some of the variables. For example, if we assume that both $V$ and $Q$ are constant, then we have the simple quantity theory of money, which predicts that changes in the money supply cause *strictly proportional* changes in the price level.

- A change in the money supply or a change in velocity will change aggregate demand and therefore lead to a shift in the $AD$ curve. Specifically, either an increase in the money supply or an increase in velocity will increase aggregate demand and therefore shift the $AD$ curve to the right. A decrease in the money supply or a decrease in velocity will decrease aggregate demand and therefore shift the $AD$ curve to the left.

- In the simple quantity theory of money, Real GDP is assumed to be constant in the short run. This means the $AS$ curve is vertical. Also, velocity is assumed to be constant so that only a change in money supply can change aggregate demand. In the face of a vertical $AS$ curve, any change in the money supply shifts the $AD$ curve and changes only the price level, not Real GDP.

## MONETARISM

- According to monetarists, if the economy is initially in long-run equilibrium, (1) an increase in the money supply will raise the price level and Real GDP in the short run and will raise only the price level in the long run; (2) a decrease in the money supply

will lower the price level and Real GDP in the short run and will lower only the price level in the long run; (3) an increase in velocity will raise the price level and Real GDP in the short run and will raise only the price level in the long run; (4) a decrease in velocity will lower the price level and Real GDP in the short run and will lower only the price level in the long run.

## ONE-SHOT INFLATION AND CONTINUED INFLATION

- One-shot inflation can result from an increase in aggregate demand or a decrease in short-run aggregate supply.

- For one-shot inflation to change to continued inflation, a continued increase in aggregate demand is necessary and sufficient. Continued increases in the money supply cause continued increases in aggregate demand and continued inflation.

## THE MONEY SUPPLY AND INTEREST RATES

- Changes in the money supply can affect the interest rate by means of the liquidity, income, price-level, and expectations effects.

- The change in the interest rate due to a change in the supply of loanable funds is called the liquidity effect. The change in the interest rate due to a change in Real GDP is called the income effect. The change in the interest rate due to a change in the price level is called the price-level effect. The change in the interest rate due to a change in the expected inflation rate is called the expectations effect (or Fisher effect).

## NOMINAL AND REAL INTEREST RATES

- Real interest rate = Nominal interest rate − Expected inflation rate.

- Nominal interest rate = Real interest rate + Expected inflation rate.

# KEY TERMS AND CONCEPTS

| | | | |
|---|---|---|---|
| Equation of Exchange | One-Shot Inflation | Income Effect | Nominal Interest Rate |
| Velocity | Continued Inflation | Price-Level Effect | Real Interest Rate |
| Simple Quantity Theory of Money | Liquidity Effect | Expectations Effect | |

# QUESTIONS AND PROBLEMS

1. What are the assumptions and predictions of the simple quantity theory of money? Does the simple quantity theory of money predict well?

2. Can the money supply support a GDP level greater than itself? Explain your answer.

3. In the simple quantity theory of money, the $AS$ curve is vertical. Explain why.

4. In the simple quantity theory of money, what will lead to an increase in aggregate demand? In monetarism, what will lead to an increase in aggregate demand?

5. According to the simple quantity of money, what will happen to Real GDP and the price level as the money supply rises? Explain your answer.

6. In monetarism, how will each of the following affect the price level in the short run?

a. An increase in velocity

b. A decrease in velocity

c. An increase in the money supply

d. A decrease in the money supply

7. According to monetarism, an increase in the money supply will lead to a rise in Real GDP in the long run. Do you agree or disagree with this statement? Explain your answer.

8. Suppose the objective of the Fed is to increase Real GDP. To this end, it increases the money supply. Can anything offset the increase in the money supply so that Real GDP does not rise? Explain your answer.

9. What is the difference in the long run between a one-shot increase in aggregate demand and a one-shot decrease in short-run aggregate supply?

10. "One-shot inflation may be a demand-side (of the economy) or a supply-side phenomenon, but continued inflation is likely to be a demand-side phenomenon." Do you agree or disagree with this statement? Explain your answer.

11. Explain how demand-induced, one-shot inflation may seem like supply-induced, one-shot inflation.

12. In recent years, economists have argued about the true value of the real interest rate at any one time and over time. Given that the Nominal interest rate = Real interest rate + Expected inflation rate, then Real interest rate = Nominal interest rate − Expected inflation rate. Why do you think there is so much disagreement over the true value of the real interest rate?

13. With respect to the interest rate:

a. What is the liquidity effect?

b. What is the price-level effect?

c. What is the expectations effect?

14. The money supply rises. Is the interest rate guaranteed to decline initially? Why or why not?

15. To a potential borrower, which would be more important: the nominal interest rate or the real interest rate? Explain your answer.

16. The money supply rises on Tuesday, and by Thursday the interest rate has risen. Is the rise more likely the result of the income effect or of the expectations effect? Explain your answer.

17. Suppose the money supply increased 30 days ago. Whether the nominal interest rate is higher, lower, or the same today as it was 30 days ago depends on what? Explain your answer.

## WORKING WITH NUMBERS AND GRAPHS

1. How will things change in the *AD–AS* framework if a change in the money supply is completely offset by a change in velocity.

2. Graphically show each of the following:

a. Continued inflation due to supply-side factors

b. One-shot, demand-induced inflation

c. One shot, supply-induced inflation

3. Use the figure to answer questions a and b.

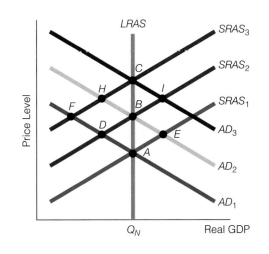

a. The economy is at point *A* when there is a one-shot, demand-induced inflation. Assuming no other changes in the economy, at what point will the economy settle (assuming the economy is self-regulating)?

b. The economy is at point *A* when it is faced with two adverse supply shocks. The Fed tries to counter these shocks by increasing aggregate demand. What path will the economy follow?

4. Starting at a position of long-run equilibrium, use the monetarist model to graphically portray what happens to the price level and Real GDP in the short run and in the long run, as a result of the following: (a) rise in the money supply, (b) decline in velocity.

5. What does the real interest rate equal given the following?

a. Nominal interest rate = 8 percent; expected inflation rate = 2 percent

b. Nominal interest rate = 4 percent; expected inflation rate = −4 percent

c. Nominal interest rate = 4 percent; expected inflation rate = 1 percent?

6. What does the nominal interest rate equal, given the following?

a. Real interest rate = 3 percent; expected inflation rate = 1 percent

b. Real interest rate = 5 percent; expected inflation rate = −3 percent

## CHAPTER 15

# MONETARY POLICY

**Introduction** When it comes to monetary policy, most economists agree that the goals of monetary policy are to stabilize the price level, to achieve low unemployment, and to promote economic growth, among other things. What they sometimes disagree about is the degree to which, and under what conditions, monetary policy achieves these goals. In this chapter we discuss monetary policy, beginning with the details of the money market. Then we discuss how changes in the money market—brought about by changes in the money supply—can affect the economy.

## TRANSMISSION MECHANISMS

**Transmission Mechanism**
The routes, or channels, traveled by the ripple effects that the money market creates and that affect the goods and services market (represented by the aggregate demand and aggregate supply curves in the AD–AS framework).

Changes in one market can often ripple outward to affect other markets. The routes, or channels, that these ripple effects travel are known as the transmission mechanism. In this section we discuss two transmission mechanisms: the Keynesian and the monetarist.

### The Money Market in the Keynesian Transmission Mechanism

**Demand for Money (Balances)**
The inverse relationship between the quantity demanded of money balances and the price of holding money balances.

Like all markets, the money market has two sides: a demand side and a supply side.[1]

THE DEMAND FOR MONEY  In an illustration of the demand for money (balances), the price of holding money balances is on the vertical axis, and the quantity of money is on the horizontal axis. The price of holding money balances—specifically, the opportunity cost of holding money—is the interest rate. By holding money, individuals forfeit the opportunity to hold that portion of their wealth in other forms. For example, the person who holds $1,000 in cash gives up the opportunity to purchase a $1,000 asset that yields interest (e.g., a bond). Thus the interest rate is the opportunity cost of holding money. A person can be described as "paying the price" of forfeited interest by holding money.

Exhibit 1(a) illustrates the demand for money (balances). As the interest rate increases, the opportunity cost of holding money increases, and individuals choose to hold less

---

1. In everyday language, the term "money market" is often used to refer to the market for short-term securities, where there is a demand for and a supply of short-term securities. This is not the money market discussed here. In this money market, there is a demand for and a supply of *money.*

money. As the interest rate decreases, the opportunity cost of holding money decreases, and individuals choose to hold more money.

THE SUPPLY OF MONEY Exhibit 1(b) shows the supply of money as a vertical line at the quantity of money that is largely determined by the Fed. The money supply is largely but not exclusively determined by the Fed because both banks and the public are important players in the money supply process (as explained in earlier chapters). For example, when banks do not lend their entire excess reserves, the money supply is not as large as it is when they do.

EQUILIBRIUM IN THE MONEY MARKET The money market is in equilibrium when the quantity demanded of money equals the quantity supplied. In Exhibit 2, equilibrium exists at the inter-

**EXHIBIT 1**

**The Demand for and Supply of Money**

(a) The demand curve for money is downward sloping. (b) The supply curve of money is a vertical line at the quantity of money that is largely but not exclusively determined by the Fed.

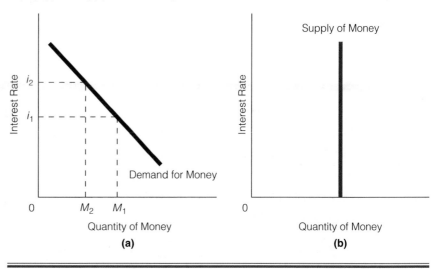

est rate $i_1$. At a higher interest rate, $i_2$, the quantity supplied of money is greater than the quantity demanded, and there is an excess supply of money ("too much" money). At a lower interest rate, $i_3$, the quantity demanded of money is greater than the quantity supplied, and there is an excess demand for money ("too little" money). Only at $i_1$ are the quantity demanded and the quantity supplied of money equal. At $i_1$, there are no shortages or surpluses of money and no excess demands or excess supplies. Individuals are holding the amounts of money they want to hold.

## The Keynesian Transmission Mechanism: Indirect

The Keynesian route between the money market and the goods and services market is an indirect one. Exhibit 3 is a market-by-market depiction of the Keynesian transmission mechanism.

1. *The money market.* Suppose the money market is in equilibrium at interest rate $i_1$ in part (a). Then, the Fed increases the reserves of the banking system through an open market purchase, resulting in an increase in the money supply. The money supply curve shifts rightward from $S_1$ to $S_2$. The reserves of the banking system are increased, resulting in more loans being made. A greater supply of loans puts downward pressure on the interest rate, as reflected in the movement from $i_1$ to $i_2$.

2. *The investment goods market.* A fall in the interest rate stimulates investment. In the investment goods market in part (b), investment rises from $I_1$ to $I_2$.

**EXHIBIT 2**

**Equilibrium in the Money Market**

At an interest rate of $i_1$, the money market is in equilibrium: There is neither an excess supply of money nor an excess demand for money.

**EXHIBIT 3**

**The Keynesian Transmission Mechanism**

The exhibit shows how the Keynesian transmission mechanism operates given an increase in the money supply. (a) An increase in the money supply brings on a lower interest rate. (b) As a result, investment increases. (c) As investment increases, total expenditures rise and the aggregate demand curve shifts rightward. Real GDP rises from $Q_1$ to $Q_2$.

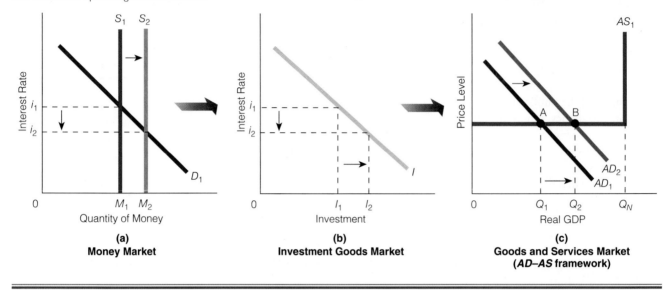

|          | (a)                | (b)                        | (c)                                               |
|----------|--------------------|----------------------------|---------------------------------------------------|
|          | **Money Market**   | **Investment Goods Market**| **Goods and Services Market** (**AD–AS framework**) |

3. *The goods and services market (AD–AS framework).* Recall that the Keynesian model has a horizontal aggregate supply curve in the goods and services market until full employment or Natural Real GDP is reached (see Chapter 10). The decline in the interest rate has brought about an increase in investment, as shown in part (b). Rising investment increases total spending in the economy and shifts the *AD* curve to the right [part (c)]. As a result, Real GDP rises from $Q_1$ to $Q_2$, and the price level does not change.

In summary, when the money supply increases, the Keynesian transmission mechanism works as follows: An increase in the money supply lowers the interest rate, which causes investment to rise and the *AD* curve to shift rightward. As a result, Real GDP increases. The process works in reverse for a decrease in the money supply.

$$\text{Money supply} \uparrow \rightarrow i \downarrow \rightarrow I \uparrow \rightarrow AD \uparrow \rightarrow Q \uparrow, \overline{P}$$
$$\text{Money supply} \downarrow \rightarrow i \uparrow \rightarrow I \downarrow \rightarrow AD \downarrow \rightarrow Q \downarrow, \overline{P}$$

## The Keynesian Mechanism May Get Blocked

The Keynesian transmission mechanism is *indirect*. Changes in the money market *do not directly affect* the goods and services market (and thus Real GDP) because the investment goods market stands between the two markets. Possibly (although not likely), the link between the money market and the goods and services market could be broken in the investment goods market. Here's how.

**INTEREST-INSENSITIVE INVESTMENT** Some Keynesian economists believe that investment is not always responsive to interest rates. For example, when business firms are pessimistic about future economic activity, a decrease in interest rates will do little, if anything, to increase investment. When investment is completely insensitive to changes in interest rates, the investment demand curve is vertical, as in Exhibit 4(a).

**EXHIBIT 4**

**(a)**
**Interest-Insensitive Investment**

**(b)**
**Liquidity Trap**

**Breaking the Link Between the Money Market and the Goods and Services Market: Interest-Insensitive Investment and the Liquidity Trap**

The Keynesian transmission mechanism allows the link between the money market and the goods and services market to be broken in two places. (a) If investment is totally interest sensitive, a change in the interest rate will not change investment; therefore, aggregate demand and Real GDP will not change. (b) If the money market is in the liquidity trap, an increase in the money supply will not lower the interest rate. It follows that there will be no change in investment, aggregate demand, or Real GDP.

This condition has an affect on the Keynesian transmission mechanism described in Exhibit 3. If the investment demand curve is vertical (instead of downward sloping), a fall in interest rates will not increase investment; if investment does not increase, neither will aggregate demand or Real GDP. Thus, the Keynesian transmission mechanism would be short-circuited in the investment goods market, severing the link between the money market in part (a) of Exhibit 3 and the goods and services market in part (c).

$$\text{Money supply} \uparrow \rightarrow i \downarrow$$
$$\text{Investment insensitive to changes in } i \rightarrow I \rightarrow AD \rightarrow Q \quad P$$

**THE LIQUIDITY TRAP** Keynesians have sometimes argued that the demand curve for money could become horizontal at some low interest rate. In Exhibit 4(b), the demand curve for money becomes horizontal at $i_1$. This horizontal section is referred to as the liquidity trap.

If the money supply is increased (e.g., from $S_1$ to $S_2$) when the money market is in the liquidity trap, the money market moves from point 1 to point 2, and individuals are willing to hold all the additional money supply at the given interest rate. Once again, this condition breaks the Keynesian transmission mechanism illustrated in Exhibit 3. Obviously, if an increase in the money supply does not lower the interest rate, then neither investment, aggregate demand, nor Real GDP changes. The liquidity trap can thus break the link between the money market and the goods and services market.

$$\text{Money supply} \uparrow$$
$$\text{Liquidity trap} \rightarrow i \rightarrow I \rightarrow AD \rightarrow Q \quad P$$

Because the Keynesian transmission mechanism is indirect, both *interest-insensitive investment demand* and the *liquidity trap* may occur. Therefore, Keynesians conclude that at times monetary policy will be unable to increase Real GDP and decrease unemployment. Viewing the money supply as a string, some economists have argued that you cannot push on a string. In other words, you cannot always force Real GDP up by increasing (pushing up) the money supply.

See Exhibit 5 for a review of the Keynesian transmission mechanism and how it may get blocked.

**Liquidity Trap**
The horizontal portion of the demand curve for money.

### EXHIBIT 5

**The Keynesian View of Monetary Policy**

According to the Keynesian transmission mechanism, if the Fed increases reserves in the

banking system and therefore raises the money supply, the interest rate will drop, stimulating investment and aggregate demand. Consequently, Real GDP will rise. However,

things may not work out this way if there is a liquidity trap or if investment is insensitive to changes in the interest rate.

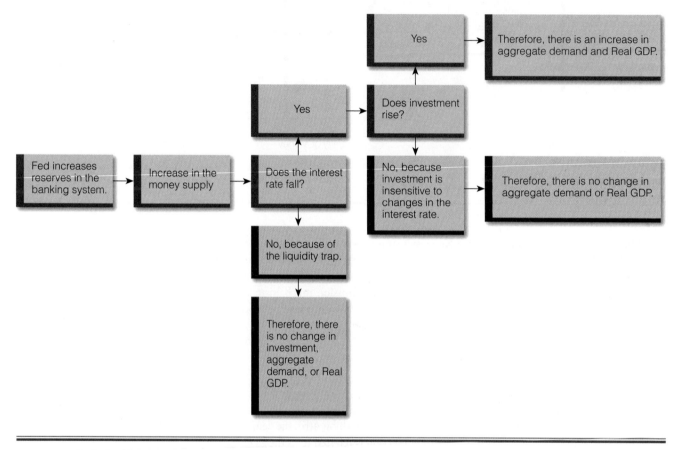

BOND PRICES, INTEREST RATES, AND THE LIQUIDITY TRAP  The liquidity trap, or the horizontal section of the demand curve for money, seems to come out of the clear blue sky. Why might the demand curve for money become horizontal at some low interest rate? To understand the explanation, you must first understand the relationship between bond prices and interest rates.

Consider Jessica Howard, who buys good X for $100 today and sells it one year later for $110. Her actual rate of return is 10 percent; the difference between the selling price and buying price ($10) divided by the buying price ($100) is 10 percent. Now suppose good X is a bond. Jessica buys the bond for $100 and sells it one year later for $110. Her actual interest rate return is the same: 10 percent. If Jessica buys the bond for $90 instead of $100 but still sells it for $110, her interest rate return is 22 percent: $20 ÷ $90 = 22 percent. The point is simple: *As the price of a bond decreases, the actual interest rate return, or the interest rate, increases.*

So bond prices and interest rates are inversely related. For example, last year Rob bought a bond for $1,000 that promises to pay him $100 a year in interest. The annual interest rate return is 10 percent: $100 ÷ $1,000 = 10 percent. Suppose, however, the market, or nominal, interest rate is higher now than last year when Rob bought his bond. Now bond suppliers have to promise to pay $120 a year to someone who buys a $1,000 bond.

The change in rate has an effect on the price Rob can get in the market for the $1,000 bond he bought last year, assuming he wants to sell it. If a purchaser can buy a new $1,000 bond that pays $120 a year, why pay Rob $1,000 for an (old) bond that pays only $100? Rob has to lower the price of his bond below $1,000, but the question is by how much? The price has to be far enough below $1,000 so that the interest rate return on his old bond will be competitive with (i.e., equal to) the interest rate return on new bonds.

Rob's bond will sell for $833. At that price, a buyer of his bond will receive $100 a year and an interest rate of 12 percent—the same interest rate offered by a new $1,000 bond paying $120 a year. In other words, $100 is the same percentage of $833 as $120 is of $1,000: 12 percent. Therefore, *the market interest rate is inversely related to the price of old or existing bonds.*

This relationship can help you understand how a liquidity trap comes to be. At a low interest rate, the money supply increases but does not result in an excess supply of money. Interest rates are very low, and so bond prices are very high. Would-be buyers believe that bond prices are so high that they have no place to go but down. So individuals would rather hold all the additional money supply than use it to buy bonds, .

## finding ECONOMICS

**In Rising Demand for Bonds** Kenneth reads in the newspaper that the demand for bonds is rising. Is there any information here that relates to the interest rate? Yes, if the demand for bonds is rising, then the price of bonds will rise too. Because the price of bonds and the interest rate are inversely related, the interest rate is about to decline. ▲ ▲ ▲

## The Monetarist Transmission Mechanism: Direct

Monetarist theory proposes a direct link between the money market and the goods and services market. The monetarist transmission mechanism is short. Changes in the money market have a direct impact on aggregate demand, as illustrated in Exhibit 6. An increase in the money supply from $S_1$ to $S_2$ in part (a) leaves individuals with an excess supply of money. As a result, they increase their spending on a wide variety of goods. Households buy more refrigerators,

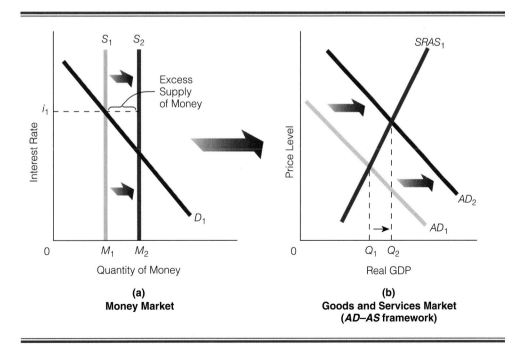

**(a)**
**Money Market**

**(b)**
**Goods and Services Market**
(*AD–AS* framework)

---

**EXHIBIT 6**

**The Monetarist Transmission Mechanism**

The monetarist transmission mechanism is short and direct. Changes in the money market directly affect aggregate demand in the goods and services market. For example, an increase in the money supply leaves individuals with an excess supply of money that they spend on a wide variety of goods.

personal computers, television sets, clothes, and vacations. Businesses purchase additional machinery. The aggregate demand curve in part (b) is directly affected. In the short run, Real GDP rises from $Q_1$ to $Q_2$. The process works in reverse for a decrease in the money supply.

$$\text{Money supply} \uparrow \rightarrow AD\uparrow \rightarrow Q\uparrow, P\uparrow$$
$$\text{Money supply} \downarrow \rightarrow AD\downarrow \rightarrow Q\downarrow, P\downarrow$$

The Keynesian transmission mechanism from the money market to the goods and services market is indirect; the monetarist transmission mechanism is direct.

## SELF-TEST

(Answers to Self-Test questions are in Answers to Self-Test Questions at the back of the book.)

1. Explain the inverse relationship between bond prices and interest rates.

2. "According to the Keynesian transmission mechanism, as the money supply rises, there is a direct impact on the goods and services market." Do you agree or disagree with this statement? Explain your answer.

3. Explain how the monetarist transmission mechanism works when the money supply rises.

# MONETARY POLICY AND THE PROBLEM OF INFLATIONARY AND RECESSIONARY GAPS

In Chapter 11, we explained how expansionary and contractionary fiscal policies might be used to move the economy out of recessionary and inflationary gaps, respectively, and questioned the effectiveness of fiscal policy. In this section, we discuss how monetary policy might be used to eliminate both recessionary and inflationary gaps.

In Exhibit 7(a), the economy is in a recessionary gap at point 1; aggregate demand is too low to bring the economy into equilibrium at Natural Real GDP.

- Economist A argues that, in time, the short-run aggregate supply curve will shift rightward to point 2 [see Exhibit 7(b)]; so it is best to leave things alone.

- Economist B says that the economy will take too long to get to point 2 on its own and that in the interim the economy is suffering the high cost of unemployment and a lower level of output.

- Economist C maintains that the economy is stuck in the recessionary gap.

**Expansionary Monetary Policy**
The policy by which the Fed increases the money supply.

Economists B and C propose expansionary monetary policy to move the economy to its Natural Real GDP level. An appropriate increase in the money supply will shift the aggregate demand curve rightward to $AD_2$, and the economy will be in long-run equilibrium at point 2′ [see Exhibit 7(c)]. The recessionary gap is eliminated through the use of expansionary monetary policy.[2]

In Exhibit 8(a), the economy is in an inflationary gap at point 1.

- Economist A argues that, in time, the economy will move to point 2 [see Exhibit 8(b)]; so it is best to leave things alone.

**Contractionary Monetary Policy**
The policy by which the Fed decreases the money supply.

- Economist B argues that it would be better to decrease the money supply (contractionary monetary policy) so that aggregate demand shifts leftward to $AD_2$ and the economy moves to point 2′ [see Exhibit 8(c)].

2. In a static framework, expansionary monetary policy means an increase in the money supply, and contractionary monetary policy refers to a decrease in the money supply. In a dynamic framework, expansionary monetary policy refers to an increase in the rate of growth of the money supply, and contractionary monetary policy means a decrease in the growth rate of the money supply. In the real world, where things are constantly changing, the growth rate of the money supply is more indicative of the direction of monetary policy.

**EXHIBIT 7**

**Monetary Policy and a Recessionary Gap**

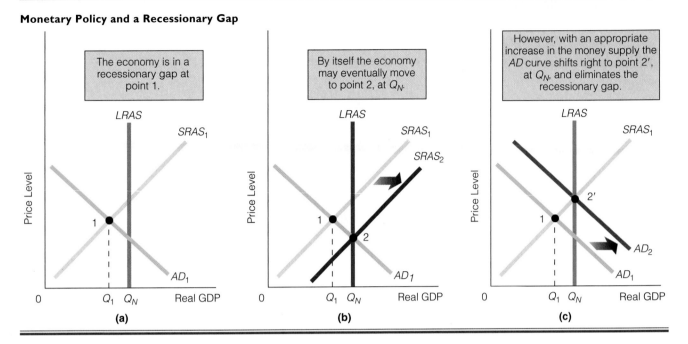

- Economist C agrees with economist B and points out that the price level is lower at point 2′ than at point 2, although Real GDP is the same at both points.

Most Keynesians believe that the natural forces of the market economy work much faster and more assuredly in eliminating an inflationary gap than in eliminating a recessionary gap. In terms of Exhibits 7 and 8, they argue that the short-run aggregate supply curve in Exhibit 8(b) is much more likely to shift leftward to point 2, eliminating the

**EXHIBIT 8**

**Monetary Policy and an Inflationary Gap**

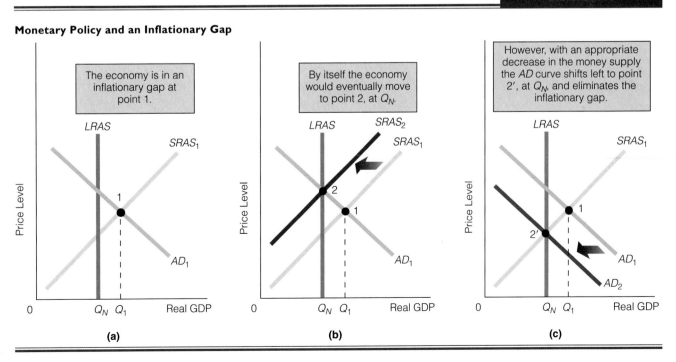

## The Fed Can't Always be Sure Banks Will Lend

One way to stimulate spending is for the Fed to increases reserves in the banking system. Recall the process: The Fed injects reserves into the banking system (say, by undertaking an open market purchase), and then banks use the additional reserves to make loans to individuals and firms. These loans stimulate spending because the people who take out the loans do so in order to increase their spending. In other words, greater reserves in the banking system lead to more loans, which lead to more spending. The AD curve in the economy shifts rightward.

©ISTOCKPHOTO.COM/RICHARD KLOTZ

Reserves increase → More Loans → More Spending → AD curve shifts rightward

However, things do not always work out the way the Fed intends. Something the Fed cannot do is force banks to lend out reserves. At the end of 2008 and into much of 2009, banks were adding to their reserves, but they weren't turning them into loans, largely because of the financial shape they were in. At the time, many banks were either insolvent (their liabilities were greater than their assets) or close to being insolvent. When banks are close to being insolvent, they are particularly wary of making loans, especially in uncertain environments. Even as the Fed was injecting reserves into the banking system, some businesses were failing, and the economic future looked uncertain. Banks couldn't be sure that the loans they created would

be repaid. So, instead of creating loans from the reserves the Fed was injecting into the banking system, the banks took the reserves and bought safe Treasury securities or simply earned the interest rate the Fed paid on reserves.

The banks looked at their plight this way: the interest rate they could earn by creating loans may have been higher than the interest rate they could earn by buying Treasury securities, but if the loans weren't likely to be repaid, what good was the higher rate? In the uncertain economic environment, better to buy low-interest Treasury securities than to create higher-interest loans that wouldn't be repaid.

The ineffectiveness of the Fed at getting the banks to increase their lending caused some economists to wonder whether monetary policy didn't work anymore or, at minimum, didn't work when the economic future looked bleak or uncertain. The so-called textbook model of how monetary policy works (say, in a recessionary gap) is that the Fed undertakes open market purchases, reserves flow into the banking system, banks take the reserves and create loans and new checkable deposits, the money supply rises, and the AD curve shifts to the right. (This is how it works in this textbook.) In 2008 and much of 2009, however, the textbook model was correct most of the time but not always. At times, it seemed, the Fed could try to get the money supply to rise, but the banks just wouldn't go along.

inflationary gap, than that the short-run aggregate supply curve in Exhibit 7(b) will shift rightward to point 2, eliminating the recessionary gap. The reason is that wages and prices rise more quickly than they fall. (Of course, many Keynesians believe wages are inflexible in a downward direction.) Consequently, Keynesians are more likely to advocate expansionary monetary policy to eliminate a stubborn recessionary gap than they are to recommend contractionary monetary policy to eliminate a not-so-stubborn inflationary gap.

# MONETARY POLICY AND THE ACTIVIST-NONACTIVIST DEBATE

Recall that some economists argue that fiscal policy is either ineffective (owing to crowding out) or works in unintended and undesirable ways (owing to lags). Other economists, notably Keynesians, believe that neither is the case and that fiscal policy not only can, but should, be used to smooth out the business cycle. This point of contention is part of the activist–nonactivist debate, which encompasses both fiscal and monetary policy. This section addresses the *monetary policy* component of the activist–nonactivist debate.

Activists argue that monetary policy should be deliberately used to smooth out the business cycle. They are in favor of economic fine-tuning, which is the (usually frequent) use of monetary policy to counteract even small undesirable movements in economic activity. Sometimes, the monetary policy they advocate is called either *activist* or *discretionary monetary policy*.

Nonactivists argue *against* the use of activist or discretionary monetary policy. Instead, they propose a rules-based monetary policy. Sometimes, the monetary policy they propose is called either *nonactivist* or *rules-based monetary policy*. An example of a rules-based monetary policy is one based on a predetermined steady growth rate in the money supply, such as allowing the money supply to grow 3 percent a year, no matter what is happening in the economy.

**Activists**
Persons who argue that monetary and fiscal policies should be deliberately used to smooth out the business cycle.

**Fine-tuning**
The (usually frequent) use of monetary and fiscal policies to counteract even small undesirable movements in economic activity.

**Nonactivists**
Persons who argue against the deliberate use of discretionary fiscal and monetary policies. They believe in a permanent, stable, rule-oriented monetary and fiscal framework.

## The Case for Activist (or Discretionary) Monetary Policy

The case for activist (or discretionary) monetary policy rests on three major claims:

1. *The economy does not always equilibrate quickly enough at Natural Real GDP.* Consider the economy at point 1 in Exhibit 7(a). Some economists maintain that, left on its own, the economy will eventually move to point 2 in part (b). Activists argue that the economy takes too long to move from point 1 to point 2 and that in the interim too much output is lost and too high an unemployment rate must be tolerated. They believe that an activist monetary policy speeds things along so that higher output and a lower unemployment rate can be achieved more quickly.

2. *Activist monetary policy works; it is effective at smoothing out the business cycle.* Activists are quick to point to the undesirable consequences of the constant monetary policy of the mid-1970s. In 1973, 1974, and 1975, the money supply growth rates were 5.5 percent, 4.3 percent, and 4.7 percent, respectively. These percentages represent a nearly constant growth rate in the money supply. The economy, however, went through a recession during this time; Real GDP fell between 1973 and 1974 and between 1974 and 1975. Activists argue that an activist and flexible monetary policy would have reduced the high cost the economy had to pay in terms of lost output and high unemployment.

3. *Activist monetary policy is flexible; nonactivist (rules-based) monetary policy is not.* Activists argue that flexibility is a desirable quality in monetary policy; inflexibility is not. Implicitly, activists maintain that the more closely monetary policy can be designed to meet the particulars of a given economic environment, the better. For example, at certain times the economy requires a sharp increase in the money supply and at other times, a sharp decrease; at still other times, only a slight increase or decrease is needed. Activists argue that activist (discretionary) monetary policy can change as the monetary needs of the economy change; nonactivist, rules-based, or "the-same-for-all-seasons" monetary policy cannot.

## The Case for Nonactivist (or Rules-Based) Monetary Policy

The case for nonactivist (or rules-based) monetary policy also rests on three major claims:

1. *In modern economies, wages and prices are sufficiently flexible to allow the economy to equilibrate at reasonable speed at Natural Real GDP.* For example, nonactivists point to the sharp drop in union wages in 1982 in response to high unemployment. In addition, they argue that government policies largely determine the flexibility of wages and prices. For example, when government decides to cushion people's unemployment (e.g., through unemployment compensation), wages will not fall as quickly as when government does nothing. Nonactivists believe that a laissez-faire, hands-off approach by government promotes speedy wage and price adjustments and thus a quick return to Natural Real GDP.

# economics 24/7

## Monetary Policy and Blue Eyes

Two days before the beginning of the fall semester at a college in the Midwest, Suzanne, a student at the college, was waiting in line to register for classes. As she waited, she looked through the fall schedule. She had to take an economics principles course at 10 a.m., and two sections were listed for that time. Hernandez was the instructor for one section; Jones, for the other. Suzanne, not knowing which section to take, asked the person behind her in line if he had ever taken a course with either instructor. The person said that he had taken a course with Hernandez and that he was very good. That was enough for Suzanne; she signed up for Hernandez's class.

© PHOTODISC GREEN/GETTY IMAGES

While a student in Hernandez's class, Suzanne met the person whom she ended up marrying. His name is Bob. Suzanne often says to Bob, "You know, if that guy behind me in line that day had said that Hernandez wasn't a good teacher or hadn't said anything at all, I might never have taken Professor Hernandez's class. I might have taken Jones's class instead, and I would never have met you. I'd probably be married to someone else right now." This (untrue) story is representative of the many little things that happen every day. Little events can make big differences.

Consider another story (this one about monetary policy) that is also not true but that, if it hasn't happened, certainly can.

A few years ago, Real GDP was below its natural level, and the Fed decided to increase the money supply. As a result, the *AD* curve in the economy shifted to the right. One of the first places to feel the new demand in the economy was Denver, where economic activity increased.

Jake, who lived in Austin at the time, was out of work and looking for a job. He heard about the job prospects in Denver, and so one day he got into his car and headed for Denver. Luckily for him, a few days after arriving in Denver, he got a job and rented an apartment near his workplace. He became a friend of Nick, who lived in the apartment across the hall.

Nick, knowing that Jake was new in town, asked Jake if he wanted a date with his girlfriend's friend, Melanie, and Jake said yes. Jake and Melanie ended up dating for two years, and they've been married now for ten years. They have three children, all of whom have blue eyes.

One day, the youngest child asked her mother why she had blue eyes. Her mother told her it's because both she and her daddy have blue eyes. And that's not an incorrect explanation, as far as it goes. But we can't help wondering if the youngest child has blue eyes because of an event that took place years ago, an event that has to do with the Fed and the money supply. After all, if the Fed hadn't increased the money supply when it did, maybe Denver's job prospects wouldn't have been so attractive, and maybe Jake wouldn't have left Austin. And, if Jake had not left Austin, he wouldn't have married Melanie and had three children, each with blue eyes.

We're just speculating, of course.

2. *Activist monetary policies may not work.* Some economists argue that there are really two types of monetary policy: (1) monetary policy that is anticipated by the public and (2) monetary policy that is not. Anticipated monetary policy may not be effective at changing Real GDP or the unemployment rate. We discuss this subject in detail in the next chapter, but here is a brief explanation. Suppose the public correctly anticipates that the Fed will soon increase the money supply by 10 percent. Consequently, the public reasons that aggregate demand will increase from $AD_1$ to $AD_2$, as shown in Exhibit 9, and prices will rise.

Workers are particularly concerned about the expected higher price level because they know higher prices decrease the buying power of their wages. In an attempt to maintain their real wages, workers bargain for and receive higher money wage rates, thereby shifting the short-run aggregate supply curve from $SRAS_1$ to $SRAS_2$ in Exhibit 9.

Now, if the SRAS curve shifts leftward (owing to higher wage rates) to the same degree as the AD curve shifts rightward (owing to the increased money supply), Real

GDP does not change but stays constant at $Q_1$. Thus, *a correctly anticipated increase in the money supply will be ineffective at raising Real GDP.*

3. *Activist monetary policies are likely to be destabilizing rather than stabilizing; they are likely to make matters worse, not better.* Nonactivists point to *lags* as the main reason that activist (or discretionary) monetary policies are likely to be destabilizing. (The total lag consists of the data, wait-and-see, legislative, transmission, and effectiveness lags discussed in Chapter 11.) Nonactivists argue that a long lag (e.g., 12 to 20 months) makes it almost impossible to conduct effective activist monetary policy. By the time the Fed's monetary stimulus arrives on the scene, the economy may not need any stimulus, and thus the policy measures will likely destabilize the economy. In this instance, the stimulus makes things worse rather than better.

Exhibit 10 illustrates the last point. Suppose the economy is currently in a recessionary gap at point 1. The recession is under way before Fed officials recognize it. Once they become aware of the recession, however, the officials consider expanding the money supply in the hopes of shifting the *AD* curve from $AD_1$ to $AD_2$ so that it will intersect the *SRAS* curve at point 1′, at Natural Real GDP.

In the interim, however, unknown to everybody, the economy is regulating itself: The *SRAS* curve is shifting to the right. Fed officials don't realize that this shift is occurring because collecting and analyzing data about the economy take time. Thinking that the economy is not regulating itself, or not regulating itself quickly enough, Fed officials implement expansionary monetary policy, and the *AD* curve shifts rightward. By the time the increased money supply is felt in the goods and services market, the *AD* curve intersects the *SRAS* curve at point 2. In short, the Fed has moved the economy from point 1 to point 2—not, as it had hoped, from point 1 to point 1′. The Fed has moved the economy into an inflationary gap. Instead of stabilizing and moderating the business cycle, the Fed has intensified it.

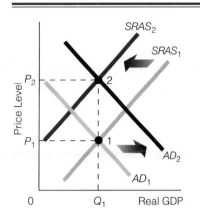

**EXHIBIT 9**

**Expansionary Monetary Policy and No Change in Real GDP**

If expansionary monetary policy is anticipated (thus, a higher price level is anticipated), workers may bargain for and receive higher wage rates. It is possible that the *SRAS* curve will shift leftward to the same degree that expansionary monetary policy shifts the *AD* curve rightward. Result: No change in Real GDP.

**EXHIBIT 10**

**Monetary Policy May Destabilize the Economy**

In this scenario, the *SRAS* curve is shifting rightward (ridding the economy of its recessionary gap), but Fed officials do not realize this is happening. They implement expansionary monetary policy, and the *AD* curve ends up intersecting $SRAS_2$ at point 2 instead of intersecting $SRAS_1$ at point 1′. Fed officials end up moving the economy into an inflationary gap and thus destabilizing the economy.

**SELF-TEST**

1. Why are Keynesians more likely to advocate expansionary monetary policy to eliminate a recessionary gap than they are to advocate contractionary monetary policy to eliminate an inflationary gap?

2. How might monetary policy destabilize the economy?

3. Does an economy stuck in a recessionary gap make the case for activist (expansionary) monetary policy stronger or weaker? Explain your answer.

## Who Gets the Money First, and What Happens to Relative Prices?

Besides expansionary and contractionary monetary policies and their effects on Real GDP and the price level, other effects have to be considered:

- The distribution of the increase in the money supply (in the case of expansionary monetary policy).
- How a change in the money supply might affect relative prices (as opposed to the price level).

Let's look at how these two effects interact. When the money supply expands (say, from $1.41 trillion to $1.42 trillion), not every member of the public gets some of the new money. To illustrate, suppose the Fed undertakes an open market purchase, which results in a rise in reserves in the banking system. Faced with greater (and excess) reserves, banks start to make more loans (new checkable deposits). The first economic actors to get the new money (as a result of the open market purchase) are the banks; the second economic actors are the individuals and firms who take out loans.

Now let's say that one of the second economic actors is Caroline, who spends the money from her new loan to buy good X from Richard. If Caroline would not have purchased good X without the loan, then the demand for good X presumably rises because of the loan (which the bank created as a result of the Fed's open market purchase). Therefore, if the demand for good X rises, so will its absolute (or money) price. If the absolute price of good X rises, so will its relative price, *ceteris paribus*. Conclusion: An increase in the money supply can change not only the price level, but relative prices too.

Of course, an increase in the money supply changes relative prices because not everyone gets the new money at the same time. Caroline gets the new money before the seller of good X (Richard) gets it, and so on. When the money supply is increased, some people get the new money before others, and so the goods and services these people buy rise in price relative to the prices of the goods and services they do not buy. If the Carolines of the world (who get the new money first) buy good X and not good Y, and the non-Carolines of the world (who get the new money later) buy good Y, we can expect that, initially, the price of good X will rise relative to good Y.

# Nonactivist Monetary Proposals

The four nonactivist (or rules-based) monetary proposals are as follows:

1. Constant-money-growth-rate rule
2. Predetermined-money-growth-rate rule
3. The Taylor rule
4. Inflation targeting

## Constant-Money-Growth-Rate Rule

Many nonactivists argue that the sole objective of monetary policy is to stabilize the price level. To this end, they propose a *constant-money-growth-rate rule*. One version of the rule is:

> *The annual money supply growth rate will be constant at the average annual growth rate of Real GDP.*

For example, if the average annual Real GDP growth rate is approximately 3.3 percent, the money supply should be put on automatic pilot and be permitted to grow at an annual rate of 3.3 percent. The money supply will grow at this rate regardless of the state of the economy.

Some economists predict that a constant-money-growth-rate rule will bring about a stable price level over time because of the equation of exchange ($MV \equiv PQ$). If the average annual growth rate in Real GDP ($Q$) is 3.3 percent and the money supply ($M$) grows at 3.3 percent, the price level should remain stable over time. Advocates of this rule argue that in some years the growth rate in Real GDP will be below its average rate, causing an increase in the price level, and that in other years the growth rate in Real GDP will be above its average rate, causing a fall in the price level, but over time, the price level will be stable.

## Predetermined-Money-Growth-Rate Rule

Critics of the constant-money-growth-rate rule point out that it makes two assumptions: (1) Velocity is constant; (2) the money supply is defined correctly. Critics argue that velocity has not been constant in some periods. Also, not yet clear is which definition of the money supply is the proper one and therefore which money supply growth rate should be fixed: M1, M2, or some broader monetary measure.

Largely in response to the charge that velocity is not always constant, some nonactivists prefer the following rule:

*The annual growth rate in the money supply will be equal to the average annual growth rate in Real GDP minus the growth rate in velocity.*

In other words,

$$\%\Delta M = \%\Delta Q - \%\Delta V$$

With this rule, the growth rate of the money supply is not fixed. It can vary from year to year, but it is predetermined in that it is dependent on the growth rates of Real GDP and velocity. For this reason, we call it the *predetermined-money-growth-rate rule.* To illustrate the workings of this rule, consider the following extended version of the equation of exchange:

$$\%\Delta M + \%\Delta V = \%\Delta P + \%\Delta Q$$

Suppose $\%\Delta Q$ is 3 percent and $\%\Delta V$ is 1 percent. The rule specifies that the growth rate in the money supply should be 2 percent. This growth rate would keep the price level stable; there would be a 0 percent change in $P$:

$$\%\Delta M + \%\Delta V = \%\Delta P + \%\Delta Q$$
$$2\% + 1\% = 0\% + 3\%$$

## The Fed and the Taylor Rule

Economist John Taylor has argued for a middle ground, of sorts, between activist and nonactivist monetary policy. He has proposed that monetary authorities use a rule to guide them in making their discretionary decisions.

His rule has come to be known as the *Taylor rule,* which specifies how policy makers should set the federal funds rate target (recall from an earlier chapter that the federal funds rate is the interest rate banks charge one another for reserves). The economic thinking implicit behind the Taylor rule is that there is some federal funds rate target that is consistent with (1) stabilizing inflation around a rather low inflation rate and (2) stabilizing Real GDP around its full-employment level. The aim is to find this target and then to use the Fed's tools to hit it.

Here is how John Taylor, for whom the Taylor Rule is named, defines the particulars of the rule:

*The federal funds rate target "should be one-and-a-half times the inflation rate plus one-half times the GDP gap plus one."*[3]

Algebraically, the Taylor Rule specifies:

Federal funds rate target = 1.5 (inflation rate) + 0.5 (GDP gap) + 1

---

3. See John Taylor, *Getting Office Track* (Hoover Institution Press, 2009), p. 67.

In this equation, the GDP gap measures the percentage deviation of Real GDP from its potential level. Let's use the rule to find the federal funds rate target that Taylor recommends to the Fed. Suppose the inflation rate is 5 percent and the GDP gap is 3 percent. Putting these percentages in our equation, we get:

$$\text{Federal funds rate target} = 1.5 \ (5 \text{ percent}) + 0.5 \ (3 \text{ percent}) + 1$$
$$= 7.5 + 1.5 + 1$$
$$= 10 \text{ percent}$$

## Inflation Targeting

**Inflation Targeting**
Targeting that requires the Fed to keep the inflation rate near a predetermined level.

Many economists recommend inflation targeting, which requires that the Fed try to keep the inflation rate near a predetermined level. Three major issues surround inflation targeting. The first deals with whether the inflation rate target should be a specific percentage rate (e.g., 2.5 percent) or a narrow range (e.g., 1.0–2.5 percent). Second, whether it is a specific percentage rate or range, what should the rate or range be? For example, if it is specific percentage rate, should it be, say, 2.0 percent or 3.5 percent? The last issue deals with whether the inflation rate target should be announced or not. In other words, if the Fed adopts an inflation rate target of, say, 2.5 percent, should the target be disclosed to the public?

# OFFICE HOURS

## "Does Monetary Policy Always Have the Same Effects?"

**STUDENT:**

Does monetary policy always have the same effects?

**INSTRUCTOR:**

Instead of my giving you the answer, think back to the Keynesian transmission mechanism and try to answer your question.

**STUDENT:**

In the transmission mechanism, an increase in the money supply lowers the interest rate. The lower interest rate then increases investment. And the increased investment raises aggregate demand.

**INSTRUCTOR:**

Ask yourself whether the lower interest rate always raises investment.

**STUDENT:**

No, it doesn't always raise investment. If investment is interest insensitive, the lower interest rate will leave investment unchanged.

**INSTRUCTOR:**

There is something else too. Suppose investment is responsive to changes in the interest rate. In other words, if the interest rate falls, investment will rise. But the question is whether investment always rises by the same amount. For example, if in year 1 the interest rate falls from 6 percent to 5 percent and investment rises from $300 billion to $400 billion, does it follow that every time the interest rate falls from 6 percent to 5 percent, investment will rise by $100 billion?

**STUDENT:**

I see your point. You're saying that, although investment might always rise as the interest rate falls, it doesn't necessarily rise by the same

Numerous central banks in the world practice inflation targeting, and they announce their targets. For example, the Bank of Canada has set a target of 2 percent (inflation), and it has been announcing its inflation target since 1991. Other central banks that practice inflation targeting are the Bank of England, the Central Bank of Brazil, the Bank of Israel, and the Reserve Bank of New Zealand.

For an inflation rate target approach, the Fed would undertake monetary policy actions to keep the actual inflation rate near or at its target. For example, if its target rate is 2 percent and the actual inflation rate is, say, 5 percent, it would cut back the growth rate in the money supply (or the absolute money supply) to bring the actual inflation rate nearer to the target.

The proponents of inflation targeting argue that such a policy is more in line with the Fed's objective of maintaining near price stability. The critics of inflation targeting often argue that such a policy would constrain the Fed at times, such as when it might need to overlook the target to deal with a financial crisis.

## SELF-TEST

1. Would a rules-based monetary policy produce price stability?

2. Suppose the inflation rate is 4 percent and the GDP gap is 5 percent. What is the Taylor rule recommendation for the federal funds rate target?

amount every time. If it doesn't rise by the same amount every time, then there is no guarantee that aggregate demand will rise by the same amount every time (because increases in investment lead to increases in aggregate demand).

**INSTRUCTOR:**

That's correct. We'd now have to conclude that expansionary monetary policy won't always increase aggregate demand by the same amount. In other words, a money supply expansion of $30 billion might raise aggregate demand more at one time than at some other time.

**STUDENT:**

So one answer to my question—whether monetary policy always has the same effects—is, no, monetary policy doesn't always change aggregate demand by the same amount.

**INSTRUCTOR:**

That's correct. This discussion also helps us to understand why economists—even those of the same school of thought—might disagree with each other. For example, suppose Smith and Jones both believe that monetary policy affects the economy through the Keynesian transmission mechanism. Just because both accept the Keynesian transmission mechanism, they don't both necessarily think that a given increase in the money supply is going to affect aggregate demand to the same degree. Although both might agree that an expansion in the money supply will increase aggregate demand, they might disagree as to how much aggregate demand will increase. Smith might think aggregate demand will rise only a little because investment will not rise much when the interest rate drops. Jones might think aggregate demand will rise a lot because investment will rise a lot when the interest rate drops.

## POINTS TO REMEMBER

1. Monetary policy doesn't always have the same effects. With reference to the Keynesian transmission mechanism, expansionary monetary policy might lead to a large change in investment at some times (when investment is highly responsive to changes in the interest rate) and only a small change in investment at other times (when investment is somewhat insensitive to changes in the interest rate). Expansionary monetary policy therefore might not always change aggregate demand to the same degree.

2. Even economists of the same school of thought can disagree with each other at times. For example, although two economists might agree that a rise in the money supply will change investment (or aggregate demand), they might disagree as to *how much* investment (or aggregate demand) will change.

# CHAPTER SUMMARY

## THE KEYNESIAN TRANSMISSION MECHANISM

- The Keynesian route between the money market and the goods and services market is indirect. Changes in the money market must affect the investment goods market before the goods and services market is affected. Assuming that no liquidity trap exists and investment is not interest insensitive, the transmission mechanism works as follows for an increase in the money supply: an increase in the money supply lowers the interest rate and increases investment, thereby increasing aggregate demand and thus shifting the *AD* curve rightward. Consequently, Real GDP rises. Under the same assumptions, the transmission mechanism works as follows for a decrease in the money supply: a decrease in the money supply raises the interest rate and decreases investment, thereby decreasing aggregate demand and thus shifting the *AD* curve leftward. As a result, Real GDP falls.

- The Keynesian transmission mechanism may be short-circuited either by the liquidity trap or by interest-insensitive investment. Both are Keynesian notions. If either is present, Keynesians predict that expansionary monetary policy will be unable to change Real GDP.

## THE MONETARIST TRANSMISSION MECHANISM

- The monetarist route between the money market and the goods and services market is direct. Changes in the money supply affect aggregate demand. An increase in the money supply causes individuals to increase their spending on a wide variety of goods.

## BOND PRICES AND INTEREST RATES

- Interest rates and the prices of old or existing bonds are inversely related.

## THE ACTIVIST–NONACTIVIST DEBATE

- Activists argue that monetary policy should be deliberately used to smooth out the business cycle; they favor using activist, or discretionary, monetary policy to fine-tune the economy. Nonactivists argue against the use of discretionary monetary policy; they propose nonactivist, or rules-based, monetary policy.

- The case for discretionary monetary policy rests on three major claims: (1) The economy does not always equilibrate quickly enough at Natural Real GDP. (2) Activist monetary policy works. (3) Activist monetary policy is flexible, and flexibility is a desirable quality in monetary policy.

- The case for nonactivist monetary policy rests on three major claims: (1) There is sufficient flexibility in wages and prices in modern economies to allow them to equilibrate at reasonable speed at Natural Real GDP. (2) Activist monetary policies may not work. (3) Activist monetary policies are likely to make matters worse rather than better.

## NONACTIVIST (OR RULES-BASED) MONETARY PROPOSALS

- The constant-money-growth-rate rule states that the annual money supply growth rate will be constant at the average annual growth rate of Real GDP.

- The predetermined-money-growth-rate rule states that the annual growth rate in the money supply will be equal to the average annual growth rate in Real GDP minus the growth rate in velocity.

- The Taylor rule specifies: Federal funds rate target = 1.5 (inflation rate) + 0.5 (GDP gap) +1.

- Inflation targeting requires the Fed to keep the inflation rate near a predetermined level.

# KEY TERMS AND CONCEPTS

Transmission Mechanism
Demand for Money
  (Balances)

Liquidity Trap
Expansionary Monetary
  Policy

Contractionary Monetary
  Policy
Activists

Fine-tuning
Nonactivists
Inflation Targeting

# QUESTIONS AND PROBLEMS

1. Consider the following: Two researchers, A and B, are trying to determine whether eating fatty foods leads to heart attacks. The researchers proceed differently. Researcher A builds a model in which fatty foods may first affect X in one's body, and if X is affected, then Y may be affected, and if Y is affected, then Z may be affected. Finally, if Z is affected, the heart is affected, and the individual has an increased probability of suffering a heart attack. Researcher B doesn't proceed in this step-by-step fashion. She conducts an experiment to see whether people who eat many fatty foods have more, fewer, or the same number of heart attacks as people who eat few fatty foods. Which researcher's methods have more in common with the research methodology implicit in the Keynesian transmission mechanism? Which researcher's methods have more in common with the research methodology implicit in the monetarist transmission mechanism? Explain your answer.

2. If bond prices fall, will individuals want to hold more or less money? Explain your answer.

3. Why is the demand curve for money downward sloping?

4. Explain how it is possible to have too much money.

5. Explain how the Keynesian transmission mechanism works.

6. Explain how the monetarist transmission mechanism works.

7. It has been suggested that nonactivists are not concerned with the level of Real GDP and unemployment because most (if not all) nonactivist monetary proposals set as their immediate objective the stabilization of the price level. Discuss.

8. Suppose the combination of more accurate data and better forecasting techniques would make it easy for the Fed to predict a recession 10 to 16 months in advance. Would this strengthen the case for activism or nonactivism? Explain your answer.

9. Suppose it were proved that liquidity traps do not occur and that investment is not interest insensitive. Would this be enough to disprove the Keynesian claim that expansionary monetary policy is not always effective at changing Real GDP? Why or why not?

10. Both activists and nonactivists make good points for their respective positions. Do you think activists could say anything to nonactivists to convince them to accept the activist position, and vice versa? If so, what is it? If not, why not?

11. The discussion of supply and demand in Chapter 3 noted that if two goods are substitutes, the price of one and the demand for the other are directly related. For example, if Pepsi-Cola and Coca-Cola are substitutes, an increase in the price of Pepsi-Cola will increase the demand for Coca-Cola. Suppose that bonds and stocks are substitutes. We know that interest rates and bond prices are inversely related. What do you predict is the relationship between stock prices and interest rates? Explain your answer.

12. Argue the case for and against a monetary rule.

13. How does inflation targeting work?

14. Monetary policy can affect relative prices. Do you agree or disagree with this statement? Explain your answer.

## WORKING WITH NUMBERS AND GRAPHS

1. Manuel bought a bond last year for $10,000 that promises to pay him $900 a year. This year, he can buy a bond for $10,000 that promises to pay $1,000 a year. If Manuel wants to sell his old bond, what is its price likely to be?

2. Charu bought a bond last year for $10,000 that promises to pay her $1,000 a year. This year, investors can buy a bond for $10,000 that promises to pay $800 a year. If Charu wants to sell her old bond, what is its price likely to be?

3. The annual average percentage change in Real GDP is 2.3 percent, and the annual average percentage change in velocity is 1.1 percent. Using the monetary rule discussed in the text, what percentage change in the money supply will keep prices stable (on average)?

4. Graphically show that the more interest insensitive the investment demand curve is, the less likely it is that monetary policy will be effective at changing Real GDP.

5. Which panel in the figure best describes the situation in each of parts (a)–(d)?

   a. Expansionary monetary policy that effectively removes the economy from a recessionary gap

   b. Expansionary monetary policy that is destabilizing

   c. Contractionary monetary policy that effectively removes the economy from an inflationary gap

   d. Monetary policy that is ineffective at changing Real GDP

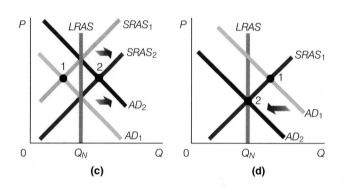

(c)　　　(d)

6. Graphically portray the Keynesian transmission mechanism under the following conditions:

   a. A decrease in the money supply

   b. No liquidity trap

   c. Downward-sloping investment demand

7. Graphically portray the monetarist transmission mechanism when the money supply declines.

8. According to the Taylor rule, if inflation is 8 percent and the GDP gap is 3 percent, what is the recommendation for the federal funds rate target?

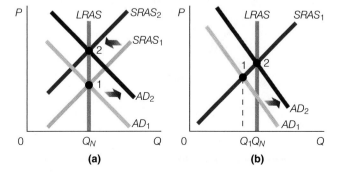

(a)　　　(b)

# APPENDIX D

# BOND PRICES AND THE INTEREST RATE

Bond prices and the interest rate are inversely related: as the price of bonds rises, the interest rate falls; as the price of bonds falls, the interest rate rises. In this appendix, we explain this relationship by looking closely at the money market and the bond market.

The money market is shown in equilibrium in Exhibit 1(a). The equilibrium interest rate is 5 percent. The bond market is shown in equilibrium in Exhibit 1(b). The equilibrium bond price is $P_{B1}$.

Suppose people have only two ways to hold their wealth: in money or in bonds. In other words, a person must always decide, "How much of my wealth do I hold in money and how much do I hold in bonds?" If someone's wealth is currently equal to $100,000, does this person hold $50,000 (of that wealth) in money and $50,000 in bonds, or $25,000 in money and $75,000 in bonds, and so on?

Because wealth can be held only in the form of money and bonds, if someone thinks she is holding *too much* money, she also must be thinking that she is holding too few bonds. In other words, a surplus of money necessarily implies a shortage of bonds. To illustrate, let's say the person is currently holding $25,000 in money and $75,000 in bonds. Then she thinks that she is holding too much money; so she must also think she is holding too little of her wealth in bonds. She might want to take $5,000 of her money and buy $5,000 worth of bonds so that she has $20,000 in money and $80,000 in bonds.

So, if a surplus of money signifies a shortage of bonds, then, in market terms, a surplus in the money market implies a shortage in the bond market.

Suppose our person believes that she is holding *too little* money. Instead of holding $25,000 in money, she would prefer to hold $30,000 in money. But, of course, holding

## EXHIBIT 1

**The Money Market and the Bond Market**

(a) The money market in equilibrium at an interest rate of 5 percent. (b) The bond market is in equilibrium at a bond price of $P_{B1}$. When one of these markets is in equilibrium, the other is too.

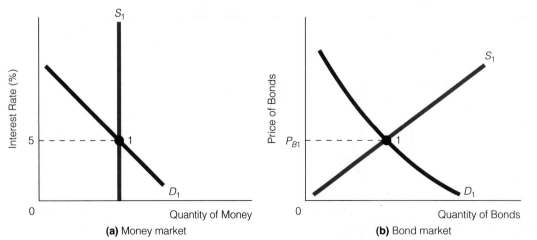

**(a)** Money market

**(b)** Bond market

too little money necessarily implies that our person is holding too much of her wealth in bonds. In other words, a shortage of money implies a surplus of bonds.

So, a shortage in the money market implies a surplus in the bond market. Let's recap:

Holding too much of one's wealth in money → Holding too little of one's wealth in bonds

or

Surplus in the money market → Shortage in the bond market

and

Holding too little of one's wealth in money → holding too much of one's wealth in bonds

or

Shortage in the money market → Surplus in the bond market

Now let's look at Exhibit 2. At point 1 in each market, both the money market and the bond market are in equilibrium. People are holding just the right amount of money and just the right amount of bonds. Suppose the Fed undertakes an action that increases the money supply. The money supply curve in Exhibit 2(a) shifts rightward from $S_1$ to $S_2$. At the initial interest rate of 5 percent, the money market now has a surplus of money.

### EXHIBIT 2

**Changes in the Money Market Affect the Bond Market**

(a) The money market is initially in equilibrium at point 1; the equilibrium interest rate is 5 percent. (b) The bond market is initially in equilibrium at point 1; the equilibrium bond price is $P_{B1}$. The Fed increases the money supply. In the money market [shown in (a)], the supply of money curve shifts rightward from $S_1$ to $S_2$. At the interest rate of 5 percent, there is now a surplus of money. With their surplus of money, individuals start to buy more bonds, so the demand for bonds curve in panel (b) shifts rightward from $D_1$ to $D_2$. The result is a shortage of bonds in the bond market at the price of $P_{B1}$. Both markets are now in disequilibrium. The equilibrating process in the bond market pushes bond prices up. As bond prices rise, the interest rate falls, and that happens in the money market [shown in (a)]. Eventually, both markets are back in equilibrium. The equilibrium interest rate is now 4 percent, and the price of bonds is now $P_{B2}$.

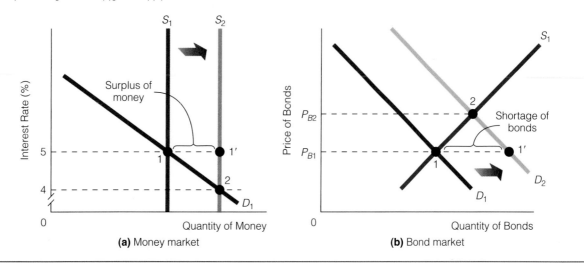

**(a)** Money market

**(b)** Bond market

But, as we recall, a surplus of money in the money market must mean a shortage of bonds in the bond market.

How does this shortage manifest itself? As a result of the surplus in the money market, individuals take their "surplus money" and start to buy bonds. The demand for bonds in the bond market shifts rightward from $D_1$ to $D_2$. So now there is a surplus of money in the money market at 5 percent and a shortage of bonds in the bond market at $P_{B1}$. Both markets are in disequilibrium at the specified interest rate and bond price.

The markets will begin to equilibrate. In the bond market, the price of bonds will begin to rise toward $P_{B2}$. As the price of bonds rises, the interest rate in the money market starts to fall, moving toward its equilibrium level of 4 percent. Finally, both markets are in equilibrium: the money market is at 4 percent and the bond market at $P_{B2}$.

## APPENDIX SUMMARY

- Suppose that an individual can hold his wealth only in terms of money and bonds. So if a person believes he is holding too much of his wealth in money, he also believes that he is holding too little of it in bonds. Similarly, if he believes he is holding too little of his wealth in money, he also believes that he is holding too much of it in bonds.

- A surplus in the money market implies a shortage in the bond market. A shortage in the money market implies a surplus in the bond market.

## QUESTIONS AND PROBLEMS

1. Draw both the money market and bond market in equilibrium. Next, explain and diagrammatically show what happens to the interest rate and the price of bonds as a result of the Fed's increasing the money supply.

2. Draw both the money market and bond market in equilibrium. Next, explain and diagrammatically show what happens to the interest rate and the price of bonds as a result of the Fed's decreasing the money supply.

3. Identify the state of the bond market (equilibrium, shortage, surplus), given each of the following:

   a. Shortage in the money market

   b. Surplus in the money market

   c. Equilibrium in the money market

4. Fed actions affect the money market but not the bond market. Do you agree or disagree with this statement? Explain your answer.

## CHAPTER 16

# EXPECTATIONS THEORY AND THE ECONOMY

© AP PHOTO/PETAR PETROV

**Introduction** In this chapter, we discuss two expectations theories: adaptive and rational. We begin our discussion of expectations theory and the economy with a debate that raged within the economic profession years ago over the shape of the Phillips curve.

## PHILLIPS CURVE ANALYSIS

The Phillips curve is used to analyze the relationship between inflation and unemployment. We begin the discussion of the Phillips curve by focusing on the work of three economists: A. W. Phillips, Paul Samuelson, and Robert Solow.

### The Phillips Curve

In 1958, A. W. Phillips of the London School of Economics published a paper in the economics journal, *Economica*: "The Relation Between Unemployment and the Rate of Change of Money Wages in the United Kingdom, 1861–1957." As the title suggests, Phillips collected data about the rate of change in money wages, sometimes referred to as *wage inflation*, and about *unemployment rates* in the United Kingdom over almost a century. He then plotted the rate of change in money wages against the unemployment rate for each year. Finally, he fit a curve to the data points (Exhibit 1).

**AN INVERSE RELATIONSHIP** The curve, which came to be known as the Phillips curve, is downward sloping, suggesting that the rate of change of money wage rates (wage inflation) and unemployment rates are *inversely related*.[1] This inverse relationship, in turn, suggests a trade-off between wage inflation and unemployment. Higher wage inflation means lower unemployment; lower wage inflation means higher unemployment.

**Phillips Curve**
A curve that originally showed the relationship between wage inflation and unemployment and that now more often shows the relationship between price inflation and unemployment.

---

1. Early explanations *for the* inverse relationship between wage inflation and unemployment focused on the state of the labor market, given changes in aggregate demand. When aggregate demand is increasing, businesses expand production and hire more employees. As the unemployment rate falls, the labor market becomes tighter, and employers find it increasingly difficult to hire workers at old wages. Businesses must offer higher wages to obtain additional workers. Unemployment and money wage rates move in opposite directions.

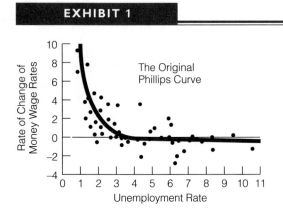

**The Original Phillips Curve**

This curve was constructed by A. W. Phillips, using data for the United Kingdom from 1861 to 1913. (The relationship here is also representative of the experience of the United Kingdom through 1957.) The original Phillips curve suggests an inverse relationship between wage inflation and unemployment; it represents a wage inflation–unemployment trade-off. (Note: Each dot represents a single year.)

Policy makers concluded from the Phillips curve that lowering both wage inflation and unemployment was impossible; they could do only one or the other. So the combination of low wage inflation and low unemployment was unlikely. This was the bad news.

The good news was that rising unemployment and rising wage inflation did not go together either. Thus, the combination of high unemployment and high wage inflation was unlikely.

## Samuelson and Solow: The Americanization of the Phillips Curve

In 1960, two American economists, Paul Samuelson and Robert Solow, published an article in the *American Economic Review* in which they fit a Phillips curve to the U.S. economy from 1935 to 1959. In addition to using American data instead of British data, they measured *price inflation rates* (instead of wage inflation rates) against unemployment rates. They found an inverse relationship between (price) inflation and unemployment (see Exhibit 2).[2]

**Stagflation**

The simultaneous occurrence of high rates of inflation and unemployment.

Economists concluded from the Phillips curve that stagflation, or high inflation together with high unemployment, was extremely unlikely. The economy could register (1) high unemployment and low inflation or (2) low unemployment and high inflation. Also, economists noticed that the Phillips curve presented policy makers with a *menu of choices*. For example, policy makers could choose to move the economy to any of the points on the Phillips curve in Exhibit 2. If they decided that, say, point *A*, with high unemployment and low inflation, was preferable to point *D*, with low unemployment and high inflation, then so be it. Getting the economy to the desired point was simply a matter of reaching the right level of aggregate demand. To Keynesian economists, who were gaining a reputation for advocating fine-tuning the economy (i.e., using small-scale measures to counterbalance undesirable economic trends), this conclusion seemed consistent with their theories and policy proposals.

**The Phillips Curve and a Menu of Choices**

Samuelson and Solow's early work using American data showed that the Phillips curve was downward sloping. Economists reasoned that stagflation was extremely unlikely and that the Phillips curve presented policy makers with a menu of choices—point A, B, C, or D.

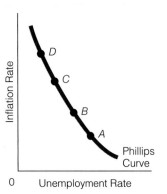

# THE CONTROVERSY BEGINS: ARE THERE REALLY TWO PHILLIPS CURVES?

This section discusses the work of Milton Friedman and the hypothesis that there are two, not one, Phillips curves.

## Things Aren't Always as We Think

In the 1970s and early 1980s, economists began to question many of the conclusions about the Phillips curve—questions

---

2. Today, when economists speak of the Phillips curve, they are usually referring to the relationship between price inflation rates and unemployment rates instead of the relationship between wage inflation rates and unemployment rates.

largely prompted by events after 1969. Exhibit 3 shows U.S. inflation and unemployment rates for the years 1961–2003. The 1961–1969 period, which is shaded, depicts the original Phillips curve trade-off between inflation and unemployment. The remaining period, 1970–2003, as a whole does not, although some subperiods, such as 1976–1979, do.

In the period 1970–2003, note that stagflation—high unemployment and high inflation—is possible. For example, 1975, 1981, and 1982 are definitely years of stagflation. The existence of stagflation implies that a trade-off between inflation and unemployment may not always exist.

## Friedman and the Natural Rate Theory

Milton Friedman, in his presidential address to the American Economic Association in 1967 (published in the *American Economic Review*), attacked the idea of a *permanent* downward-sloping Phillips curve. Friedman's key point was that there are two Phillips curves, not one: a short-run Phillips curve and a long-run Phillips curve. Friedman said, "There is always a temporary tradeoff between inflation and unemployment; there is no permanent tradeoff." Specifically, *there is a trade-off in the short run but not in the long run.*

**EXHIBIT 3**

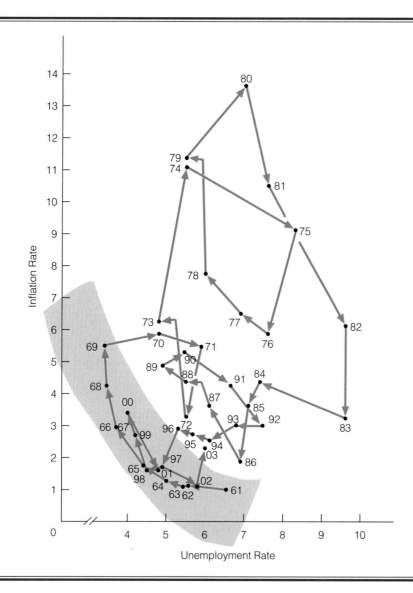

**The Diagram That Raises Questions: Inflation and Unemployment, 1961–2003**

The period 1961–1969 clearly depicts the original Phillips curve trade-off between inflation and unemployment. The later period, 1970–2003, as a whole does not. However, some subperiods do, such as 1976–1979. The diagram presents empirical evidence that stagflation may exist; an inflation–unemployment trade-off may not always hold.

Friedman's discussion not only introduced two types of Phillips curves but also opened the macroeconomics door wide, once and for all, to expectations theory: the idea that people's expectations about economic events affect economic outcomes.

Exhibit 4 illustrates both the short- and long-run Phillips curves. In window 1, the economy is in long-run equilibrium, operating at $Q_1$, which is equal to $Q_N$. In the main diagram, the economy is at point 1 at the natural rate of unemployment, $U_N$. Further and most important, *we assume that the expected inflation rate and the actual inflation rate are the same* at 2 percent.

Now suppose government *unexpectedly* increases aggregate demand from $AD_1$ to $AD_2$, as shown in window 2. As a result, the *actual* inflation rate increases (say, to 4 percent), but in the short run (immediately after the increase in aggregate demand), individual decision makers do not know this. Consequently, the *expected* inflation rate remains at 2 percent. In short, aggregate demand increases at the same time that people's expected inflation rate remains constant.

Because of this combination of events, certain consequences unfold. The higher aggregate demand causes temporary shortages and higher prices. Businesses then respond to higher prices and higher profits by increasing output. Higher output requires more employees, and so businesses start hiring more workers. As hiring increases, many currently unemployed individuals find work. Furthermore, many of the newly employed persons accept the prevailing wage rate because they think the wages will have greater purchasing power (because they expect the inflation rate to be 2 percent) than, in fact, the wages will turn out to have.

---

### EXHIBIT 4

**Short-Run and Long-Run Phillips Curves**

Starting at point 1 in the main diagram, and assuming that the expected inflation rate stays constant as aggregate demand increases, the economy moves to point 2. As the expected inflation rate changes and comes to equal the actual inflation rate, the economy moves to point 3. Points 1 and 2 lie on a short-run Phillips curve. Points 1 and 3 lie on a long-run Phillips curve. (Note: The percentages in parentheses following the *SRAS* curves in the windows refer to the expected inflation rates.)

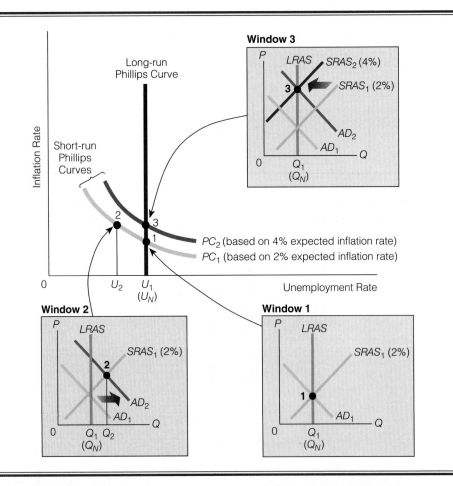

So far, the results of an increase in aggregate demand with no change in the expected inflation rate are (1) an increase in Real GDP from $Q_1$ to $Q_2$ (see window 2) and (2) a corresponding decrease in the unemployment rate from $U_1$ to $U_2$ (see the main diagram). Thus, the economy has moved from point 1 to point 2 in the main diagram.

The question is whether point 2 is a stable equilibrium. Friedman answered that it is not. He argued that, *as long as the expected inflation rate is not equal to the actual inflation rate, the economy is not in long-run equilibrium.*

For Friedman, as for most economists today, the movement from point 1 to point 2 on $PC_1$ is a short-run movement. Economists refer to $PC_1$, along which short-run movements occur, as a *short-run Phillips curve.*

In time, inflation expectations begin to change. As prices continue to climb, wage earners realize that their real (i.e., inflation-adjusted) wages are lower than they thought. In hindsight, they realize that they accepted nominal (money) wages based on an expected inflation rate (2 percent) that was too low. So they revise their inflation expectations upward.

At the same time, some wage earners quit their jobs because they choose not to continue working at such low *real wages.* Eventually, the combination of some workers quitting their jobs and most (if not all) workers revising their inflation expectations upward causes wage rates to move upward.

Higher wage rates shift the short-run aggregate supply curve from $SRAS_1$ to $SRAS_2$ (see window 3), ultimately moving the economy back to Natural Real GDP and to the natural rate of unemployment at point 3 (see the main diagram). The curve that connects point 1, where the economy started, and point 3, where it ended, is called the *long-run Phillips curve.*

Thus, the short-run Phillips curve exhibits a trade-off between inflation and unemployment, whereas the long-run Phillips curve does not. This idea is implicit in what has come to be called the Friedman natural rate theory (or the *Friedman fooling theory*). According to this theory (Exhibit 5), in the long run, the economy returns to its natural rate of unemployment, and it moved away from the natural unemployment rate in the first place only because workers were fooled (in the short run) into thinking the inflation rate was lower than it was.

**Friedman Natural Rate Theory**
Within the Phillips curve framework, the idea that, in the long run, unemployment is at its natural rate and that there is a long-run Phillips curve, which is vertical at the natural rate of unemployment.

**EXHIBIT 5**

**Mechanics of the Friedman Natural Rate Theory**

**The Friedman Natural Rate Theory**
1. Wages and prices are flexible.
2. Expectations are formed adaptively.

AD increases **+** No change in expected inflation rate

Economy moves from point 1 to 2, from $Q_1$ ($Q_N$) to $Q_2$. There is a short-run increase in Real GDP.

In time, workers revise their expected inflation rate upward in response to the higher prices brought on by the increase in aggregate demand. Wage rates begin to rise.

SRAS curve begins to shift left, ultimately intersecting $AD_2$ at point 3. Economy has returned to $Q_1$ ($Q_N$).

How, specifically, do people's expectations relate to the discussion of the short- and long-run Phillips curves? In Exhibit 4, the economy starts out at point 1 in the main diagram, and then something happens: Aggregate demand increases. This increase raises the inflation rate, *but workers don't become aware of the change in the inflation rate for a while.* In the interim, their expected inflation rate is too low, and, as a result, they are willing to work at jobs (and produce output) that they wouldn't work at if they perceived the inflation rate realistically.

In time, workers perceive the inflation rate realistically. Their expected inflation rate is no longer too low; it has risen to equal the actual inflation rate. The response, as predicted, is that the unemployment rate rises and output falls.

So, because workers' expectations (of inflation) are, in the short run, inconsistent with reality, workers produce more output than they would produce if their expectations were consistent with reality. This is how people's expectations can affect such real economic variables as Real GDP and the unemployment rate.

## ⓣhinking Like AN ECONOMIST

**Perceptions of Reality Matter** People say they base their actions on reality. When it rains, the pull out an umbrella; when they have a hard time seeing, they get their eyes checked. People also base their actions on their *perceptions* of reality, as workers do in the Friedman natural rate theory. Although the inflation rate has actually increased, workers don't perceive the change. Thus, in the short run (during the time period in which they misperceive reality), workers base their actions not on reality, but on their perception of it. ▲ ▲ ▲

## How Do People Form Their Expectations?

**Adaptive Expectations**
Expectations that individuals form from past experience and modify slowly as the present and the future become the past (i.e., as time passes).

Implicit in the Friedman natural rate theory is an assumption about how individuals form their expectations. Essentially, the theory holds that individuals form their expected inflation rate by looking at *past inflation rates.* Suppose someone were to ask you your expected inflation rate for the upcoming year. Would your response be closer to 50 percent or to 2 percent? If you arrive at your expected inflation rate using adaptive expectations, the answer is closer to 2 percent than to 50 percent because you haven't seen recent past inflation rates of 50 percent. But you have seen recent past inflation rates near 2 percent.

Notice that, with adaptive expectations, individuals look to the past—they look over their shoulders to see what *has happened*—in formulating their best guess as to what *will happen.* This is what individuals do in the Friedman natural rate theory, which assumes that people have **adaptive expectations**.

Some economists have argued this point. They believe that people form their expected inflation rate not by using adaptive expectations, but by means of *rational expectations.* We discuss this view in the next section.

## ⓕinding ECONOMICS

**At the Bargaining Table** Suppose you read the following report in the newspaper: "Recent wage negotiations between management and labor unions in the city have come to a halt. The two sides in the negotiations are unable so far to come to an agreement on annual wage rate increases for the duration of the four-year contract . . . ." Where is the economics?

First, if the two sides are negotiating an annual wage rate increase, then each is probably basing the increase on an expected inflation rate. Management might be saying, "We believe that the average annual inflation rate over the next four years will be 2 percent; so we are willing to agree to an annual wage rate increase of 2 percent each year for the next four years. The labor unions might be saying, "Because we expect the average annual inflation rate over the next four years to be 3.5 percent, we believe that 3.5 percent is the right annual wage rate increase for us." ▲ ▲ ▲

(Answers to Self-Test questions are in Answers to Self-Test Questions at the back of the book.)

1. What condition must exist for the Phillips curve to present policy makers with a permanent menu of choices (between inflation and unemployment)?

2. Is there a trade-off between inflation and unemployment? Explain your answer.

3. The Friedman natural rate theory is sometimes called the fooling theory. Who is being fooled, and what are they being fooled about?

# RATIONAL EXPECTATIONS AND NEW CLASSICAL THEORY

Rational expectations have played a major role in the Phillips curve controversy. We discuss rational expectations and new classical theory next.

## Rational Expectations

In the early 1970s, a few economists, including Robert Lucas of the University of Chicago (winner of the 1995 Nobel Prize in Economics), began to question the short-run trade-off between inflation and unemployment. Essentially, Lucas combined the natural rate theory with rational expectations.[3]

Rational expectations holds that individuals form the expected inflation rate not only on the basis of their past experience with inflation (looking over their shoulders), but also on their predictions about the effects of present and future policy actions and events (looking around and ahead). In short, the expected inflation rate is formed by looking at the past, present, and future. To illustrate, suppose the inflation rate has been 2 percent for the past seven years. Then, the chairman of the Fed's Board of Governors speaks about "sharply stimulating the economy." Rational expectationists argue that the expected inflation rate might immediately jump upward based on the current announcement by the chairman.

A major difference between adaptive and rational expectations is the *speed* at which the expected inflation rate changes. If the expected inflation rate is formed adaptively, then it is slow to change. Because it is based only on the past, individuals wait until the present becomes the past before changing their expectations. If the expected inflation rate is formed rationally, it changes quickly because it is based on the past, present, and future.

**Rational Expectations**
Expectations that individuals form based on past experience and on their predictions about the effects of present and future policy actions and events.

## Do People Really Anticipate Policy?

One assumption of rational expectations is that people anticipate policy. Suppose you chose people at random on the street and asked them, "What do you think the Fed will do in the next few months?" Do you think you would be more likely to receive an intelligent answer or the response, "What's the Fed?" Most readers of this text would probably expect the second answer. In fact, the general feeling is that the person on the street knows little about economics or economic institutions. So, no, people don't really anticipate policy. But suppose you chose people at random in the Wall Street area of Manhattan and asked

---

3. Rational expectations appeared on the economic scene in 1961, when John Muth published "Rational Expectations and the Theory of Price Movements" in *Econometrica*. For about 10 years, the article received little attention from the economics profession. Then, in the early 1970s, with the work of Robert Lucas, Thomas Sargent, Neil Wallace, Robert Barro, and others, the article began to be noticed.

the same question. In this case, the answer is likely to be well thought out; at least *these* people anticipate policy.

However, not all persons need to anticipate policy. *As long as some do,* the consequences may be the same *as if* all persons do. For example, Juanita Estevez is anticipating policy if she decides to buy 100 shares of SKA because her best friend, Tammy Higgins, heard from her friend Kenny Urich that his broker, Roberta Gunter, told him that SKA's stock is expected to go up. Juanita is anticipating policy because it is likely that Roberta Gunter obtained her information from a researcher in the brokerage firm who makes it his business to watch the Fed and to anticipate its next move.

Of course, anticipating policy is not done just for the purpose of buying and selling securities. Labor unions hire professional forecasters (Fed watchers) to predict future inflation rates, which is important information to have during wage contract negotiations. Banks hire forecasters to predict inflation rates, which they incorporate into the interest rates they charge. Export businesses hire forecasters to predict the future exchange-rate value of the dollar. The average investor may subscribe to a business or investment newsletter for information in order to predict interest rates, the price of gold, or next year's inflation rate more accurately. The person thinking of refinancing a mortgage watches one of the many financial news shows on television to find out about the government's most recent move and how it will affect interest rates in, say, the next three months.

## finding ECONOMICS

**While Playing a Game of Chess** Where is the economics in a game of chess? Chess players often anticipate each others' moves. Player 1 might be thinking that if she moves from e4 to e5, player 2 will move from b5 to c6. But then the first player asks herself, "What comes next? Will my opponent then be likely to move from c3 to d6?"

What people do in a game of chess and what they do when predicting government policy actions might not be all that different. In a game of chess you are playing to win, and whether you win depends on how well you can anticipate your opponent's moves. Anticipating policy actions is not much different, as you will shortly see. How well you do in the economy also has a lot to do with how well you anticipate government policy actions. ▲ ▲ ▲

## Price Level Expectations and the *SRAS* Curve

We know that various factors can shift the *SRAS* curve—wage rates, the price of nonlabor inputs, supply shocks, and so on. In this chapter, we want to show how a change in expectations can lead to a shift in the *SRAS* curve.

REAL WAGE  The real (inflation-adjusted) wage is equal to the nominal wage divided by the price level.

$$\text{Real wage} = \frac{\text{Nominal Wage}}{\text{Price Level}} \times 100$$

Suppose that the nominal wage is $40 and that the price level, as represented by a price index, is 110. The real wage is therefore $36.36: $40 ÷ 110. Obviously, a person's real wage will rise if either the nominal wage rises or the price level declines, or if both occur. For example, suppose the price level falls from 110 to 95. The real wage rises to $42.10. And, under certain conditions, as one's real wage rises, one chooses to work more. Conversely, as one's real wage falls, one chooses to work less.

Price level falls → Real wage rises → Work more

Price level rises → Real wage falls → Work less

**WORKING MORE OR LESS AND SHIFTS IN THE *SRAS* CURVE**  Labor is an input into the production process; so more labor (either in terms of individuals or labor hours) means more output. When people work more, more output is produced; so the *SRAS* curve shifts rightward. When people work less, less output is produced; so the *SRAS* curve shifts leftward.

Now we can connect the expected price level to the *SRAS* curve.

- *Example 1*. Suppose individuals expect the price level to decline. Thus they expect their real wages to rise and will work more. Working more produces more output; so the *SRAS* curve shifts rightward.

  Expect price level to fall → Expect real wage to rise → Work more → Produce more
  output → *SRAS* curve shifts rightward

- *Example 2*. Suppose individuals expect the price level to rise. Thus they expect their real wage to decline and will work less. Working less produces less output; so the *SRAS* curve shifts leftward.

  Expect price level to rise → Expect real wage to fall → Work less → Produce less
  output → *SRAS* curve shifts leftward

Exhibit 6 shows three *SRAS* curves. After each curve is the expected price level in parentheses. The higher the expected price level is, the closer the *SRAS* curve lies to the vertical axis, or the origin. The lower the expected price level is, the farther away from the vertical axis, or origin, the *SRAS* lies. Therefore, a rise in the expected price level will shift the *SRAS* curve to the left; a fall in the expected price level will shift the *SRAS* curve to the right.

## Expected and Actual Price Levels

The difference between an actual price level and an expected price level is fairly clear.

- The *actual price level* is exactly what it sounds like: the price level that actually exists. For example, someone might say that the price level today is 140. This, then, is the actual price level. We will use $P_A$ to represent the actual price level.

**EXHIBIT 6**

**The Expected Price Level and the *SRAS* Curve**

Every *SRAS* curve is based on some expected price level. For example, *SRAS*₁ in the exhibit is based on an *expected price level* of 150. As the expected price level rises, the *SRAS* curve shifts leftward; as the expected price level falls, the *SRAS* curve shifts rightward.

- The *expected price level* is what you expect the price level will be sometime in the future. For example, you might expect that the price level in, say, one year will be 150. This is your expected price level. We will use $P_{EX}$ to represent the expected price level.

Obviously, individuals' expectations ($P_{EX}$) can have one of three relationships with the actual price level ($P_A$):

$$P_{EX} = P_A$$
$$P_{EX} > P_A$$
$$P_{EX} < P_A$$

To illustrate, the Fed increases the money supply, and the *AD* curve shifts rightward. If the *SRAS* curve is upward sloping, then there will be a short-run and a long-run effect on the price level. Suppose that when the economy is back in long-run equilibrium, the actual price level $(P_A)$ will be 155. But when the Fed increases the money supply, you expect that the price level in the future will be 165. In other words, your expected price level is greater than the actual price level: $P_{EX} > P_A$. Obviously you made a mistake; specifically, you overestimated what the price level would be. You "guessed" too high. In the new classical theoretical framework using rational expectations, "guessing" too high, too low, or just right can have an effect on the economy. We show how next.

## New Classical Economics and Four Different Cases

New classical theory holds that individuals have rational expectations and that prices and wages are flexible. With these two points in mind, we apply new classical theory to four different cases (or settings):

- Case 1: Policy Correctly Anticipated
- Case 2: Policy Incorrectly Anticipated (Bias Upward)
- Case 3: Policy Incorrectly Anticipated (Bias Downward)
- Case 4: Policy Unanticipated

Each setting relates to a different perspective individuals have with respect to economic policy. We discuss monetary policy, but everything we say with respect to monetary policy in the upcoming discussion also holds for demand-side fiscal policy.

CASE 1: POLICY CORRECTLY ANTICIPATED An economy is in long-run equilibrium, as shown at point 1 in Exhibit 7. The actual price level is 100, and $SRAS_1$ is based on the expected price level of 100. In other words, in long-run equilibrium the actual price level ($P_A$) and the expected price level ($P_{EX}$) are the same.

Starting point: $P_A = P_{EX}$

The Fed increases the money supply, and this Fed policy action is *correctly anticipated* by the public. What "correctly anticipated" means here is that individuals know not only that the Fed is increasing the money supply, but also know how much the money supply is increasing and what the actual price level will be when the economy reaches its new long-run equilibrium position. The exhibit shows that the actual price level *will be* 110 when the economy reaches its new long-run equilibrium at point 2.

Now how does the fact that individuals are correctly anticipating policy (and the consequences of that policy) affect the *expected price level*? If individuals know where the actual price level is headed (i.e., to 110), they will immediately change their expected price

**EXHIBIT 7**

## Policy Correctly Anticipated

We assume that rational expectations hold, that wages and prices are flexible, that any policy action is anticipated correctly, and that the economy is in long-run equilibrium. The actual price level is 100, and the expected price level (which the $SRAS_1$ curve is based on) is also 100. The Fed increases the money supply, and the $AD$ curve shifts rightward. Because policy is anticipated correctly, individuals know that the new long-run equilibrium price level will be 110. Knowing this, they change their expected price level to 110. As a result, the $SRAS$ curve shifts leftward from $SRAS_1$ to $SRAS_2$. Keep in mind that the $AD$ and $SRAS$ change at the same time. In other words, the $AD$ curve shifts rightward at the same time the $SRAS$ curve shifts leftward. The result is that the Fed action leads to a higher price level but does not change Real GDP. The Fed action is ineffective at changing Real GDP; thus we have the policy ineffectiveness proposition (PIP) holding.

level to 110. Look at it this way: reality is changing in the economy; the price level is going to rise from 100 to 110 because of the Fed action. Correctly anticipating the new price level is like having a crystal ball and knowing exactly what is going to happen. So individuals immediately change their expectations of the future based on their correctly viewed perception of what is really going to happen.

Now if the expected price level changes to 110, the $SRAS$ curve in the exhibit will shift leftward from $SRAS_1$ to $SRAS_2$. However, the $SRAS$ curve shifts leftward at essentially the same time that the $AD$ curve shifts rightward. The economy therefore moves from point 1 (its starting point) to point 2 (or ending point).

Exhibit 7 shows that even though the Fed increases the money supply (and the $AD$ curve shifts rightward), Real GDP does not change. We started at $Q_1$ (or $Q_N$) and ended up at $Q_1$ (or $Q_N$). Therefore, if policy is correctly anticipated and if rational expectations hold, the only thing an increase in the money supply does in the economy is raise the price level. It does not change Real GDP. In other words, the Fed policy action was ineffective at changing Real GDP. This is called the policy ineffectiveness proposition (PIP).

**CASE 2: POLICY INCORRECTLY ANTICIPATED (BIAS UPWARD)** Again, an economy starts at long-run equilibrium, shown as point 1 in Exhibit 8. The two operational curves are $AD_1$ and $SRAS_1$. $SRAS_1$ is based on an expected price level ($P_{EX}$) of 100, which is the same as the actual price level ($P_A$).

Starting point: $P_A = P_{EX}$

**Policy Ineffectiveness Proposition (PIP)**

If (1) a policy change is correctly anticipated, (2) individuals form their expectations rationally, and (3) wages and prices are flexible, then neither fiscal policy nor monetary policy is effective at meeting macroeconomic goals.

**EXHIBIT 8**

**Policy Incorrectly Anticipated—Bias Upward**

(1) The economy starts in long-run equilibrium at point 1 and $P_A = P_{EX}$. (2) The Fed increases the money supply, and the AD curve actually shifts rightward from $AD_1$ to $AD_2$. (3) Individuals have incorrectly anticipated the Fed action. They believe the Fed has increased the money supply more than it actually has, and so they believe the AD curve has shifted from $AD_1$ to

$AD_3$. This is a mistake. (4) Mistakenly assuming that the AD curve has shifted rightward from $AD_1$ to $AD_3$, individuals think the new actual price level will end up being 118, where the $AD_3$ curve intersects the LRAS curve. Accordingly, they change their expected price level to 118, and the SRAS curve shifts leftward from $SRAS_1$ to $SRAS_2$. (5) The short-run equilibrium for the economy turns out to be at point 2. (6) Eventually, individuals figure out that they made

a mistake—that the real AD curve is $AD_2$, not $AD_3$. So the new long-run equilibrium will be 110, not 118 (as earlier believed). As a result, individuals now readjust their expected price level down from 118 to 110. Accordingly, the SRAS curve shifts rightward from $SRAS_2$ to $SRAS_3$. The economy is now in long-run equilibrium at point 3, and the expected price level is equal to the actual price level.

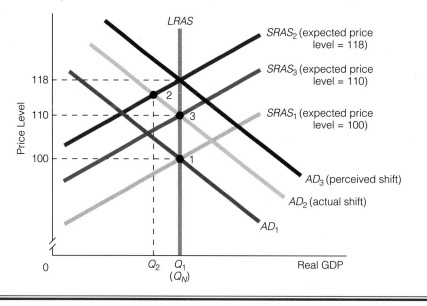

The Fed increases the money supply, and the AD curve shifts rightward from $AD_1$ to $AD_2$. This time, individuals mistakenly believe that the AD curve has shifted to the rightward by more than it has. In other words, they mistakenly think that the AD curve has shifted from $AD_1$ to $AD_3$. Individuals have thus *incorrectly anticipated policy with an upward bias.* In other words, they think that the AD curve has shifted more than it really has.

Obviously individuals have made a mistake, and this mistake is going to have consequences. Specifically, because individuals mistakenly believe the AD curve in the economy is $AD_3$ now, they think the new long-run equilibrium price level (where $AD_3$ intersects LRAS) will be 118; that is, their expected price level is 118. But the actual price level is never going to be 118. The actual price level in the future is going to 110, where the $AD_2$ intersects LRAS. So the expected price level is higher than what the actual price will be.

$$P_{EX} > P_A$$

Now as a result of individuals changing their expected price level from 100 to 118, the SRAS curve shifts leftward from $SRAS_1$ to $SRAS_2$. So far, then, the AD curve has actually shifted from $AD_1$ to $AD_2$, and the SRAS curve has shifted from $SRAS_1$ to $SRAS_2$. So, in the short run, the economy ends up at the intersection of $AD_2$ and $SRAS_2$, at point 2 in the exhibit. This is an odd result because we are accustomed to believing that an increase in the money supply leads to higher, not lower, Real GDP in the short run, but that is not what we see in Exhibit 8. Instead, Real GDP has fallen from $Q_1$ to $Q_2$. In other words, expansionary monetary policy has actually led to a decline in Real GDP. But why? It happened because of the mistake people made; specifically, they anticipated the Fed action incorrectly—with a bias upward.

The time will come when individuals realize that they made a mistake. In time, they will realize that the price level never actually increased to 118 and that $AD_3$ in the exhibit never really existed. They only perceived all that. In time, they will realize that the operational $AD$ curve in the economy *is* $AD_2$ and that the long-run equilibrium price level consistent with this aggregate demand curve is 110. Accordingly, they will adjust their expected price level downward from 118 to 110. As they do, the $SRAS$ curve shifts rightward from $SRAS_2$ to $SRAS_3$, and the economy moves into long-run equilibrium at point 3. The long-run equilibrium condition of $P_A = P_{EX}$ holds at point 3.

Let's recap: (1) The economy starts in long-run equilibrium at point 1, and $P_A = P_{EX}$. (2) The Fed increases the money supply, and the $AD$ curve actually shifts rightward from $AD_1$ to $AD_2$. (3) Individuals have incorrectly anticipated the Fed action. They believe the Fed has increased the money supply more than it actually did, and so they believe the $AD$ curve has shifted from $AD_1$ to $AD_3$. This is a mistake. (4) Mistakenly assuming that the $AD$ curve has shifted rightward from $AD_1$ to $AD_3$, individuals think the new actual price level will end up being 118, which is where the $AD_3$ curve intersects the $LRAS$ curve. Accordingly, they change their expected price level to 118, and the $SRAS$ curve shifts leftward from $SRAS_1$ to $SRAS_2$. (5) The short-run equilibrium for the economy turns out to be at point 2. Interestingly, because individuals have incorrectly anticipated policy with a bias upward, an increase in the money supply actually leads to a decline in Real GDP in the short run. (6) Eventually, individuals figure out that they made a mistake—that the real $AD$ curve is $AD_2$, not $AD_3$. So the new long-run equilibrium will be 110, not 118 (as earlier believed). As a result, individuals now adjust their expected price level down from 118 to 110. Accordingly, the $SRAS$ curve shifts rightward from $SRAS_2$ to $SRAS_3$. The economy is now in long-run equilibrium at point 3, and the expected price level is equal to the actual price level.

**CASE 3: POLICY INCORRECTLY ANTICIPATED (BIAS DOWNWARD)** Just as individuals can incorrectly anticipate policy with a bias upward, they can also incorrectly anticipate policy with a bias downward. In Exhibit 9, an economy starts in long-run equilibrium at point 1. The Fed increases the money supply, and the $AD$ curve shifts from $AD_1$ to $AD_2$. Individuals mistakenly think the $AD$ curve has shifted from $AD_1$ to $AD_3$. In other words, they believe the Fed has increased the money supply by less than it actually has. They have incorrectly anticipated policy with a bias downward.

Because individuals have incorrectly anticipated policy with a bias downward, they mistakenly believe that the new actual long-run equilibrium price level will be 110. So they change their expected price level from 100 to 110, and the $SRAS$ curve shifts leftward from $SRAS_1$ to $SRAS_2$. Short-run equilibrium for the economy comes at the intersection of $AD_2$ and $SRAS_2$, at point 2. In the short run, an increase in the money supply has increased Real GDP from $Q_1$ to $Q_2$.

Eventually, individuals realize they have made a mistake. Eventually, they realize that $AD_3$ does not exist and that $AD_2$ is the only operational $AD$ curve in the economy. So the new long-run equilibrium price level will be 115. Realizing that the long-run equilibrium level will be 115, individuals revise their expected price level from 110 to 115, and the $SRAS$ curve shifts from $SRAS_2$ to $SRAS_3$. The economy is now in long-run equilibrium at point 3, and the expected price level equals the actual price level.

**CASE 4: POLICY UNANTICIPATED** Besides correctly anticipating the new price level, and incorrectly anticipating it with bias upward or downward, the only possibility left is not anticipating it at all.

In Exhibit 10, an economy starts in long-run equilibrium at point 1. Here the actual price level equals the expected price level. The Fed increases the money supply so that the

**EXHIBIT 9**

### Policy Incorrectly Anticipated—Bias Downward

An economy starts in long-run equilibrium at point 1. The expected price level is equal to the actual price level. The Fed increases the money supply, and the AD curve shifts rightward from $AD_1$ to $AD_2$. However, individuals mistakenly believe the AD curve has shifted rightward by less, from $AD_1$ to $AD_3$. As a result of this mistake, individuals mistakenly believe that the new long-run equilibrium price level will be 110. They then change their expected price level to 110, and the SRAS curve shifts leftward from $SRAS_1$ to $SRAS_2$. The short-run equilibrium in the economy comes at point 2. Eventually, individuals realize their mistake. They come to understand that $AD_2$ is the only operational AD curve in the economy and that the long-run equilibrium price level consistent with $AD_2$ is 115. They revise their expected price level from 110 to 115, and the SRAS curve shifts leftward from $SRAS_2$ to $SRAS_3$. The economy moves into long-run equilibrium at point 3.

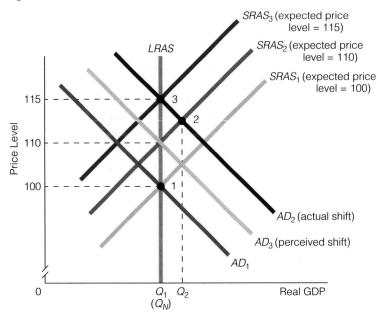

**EXHIBIT 10**

### Policy Unanticipated

An economy starts in long-run equilibrium at point 1. The Fed increases the money supply, and the AD curve shifts rightward from $AD_1$ to $AD_2$. The policy action by the Fed is unanticipated; so individuals mistakenly believe that the AD curve in the economy has not shifted. Thus there is no reason for them to believe that the price level will soon change and therefore no reason for them to revise their expected price level. As a result, the SRAS curve does not shift and in the short run, the economy moves to point 2. In time, individuals revise their expected price level upward, and the SRAS curve shifts leftward. The economy moves back into long-run equilibrium at point 3.

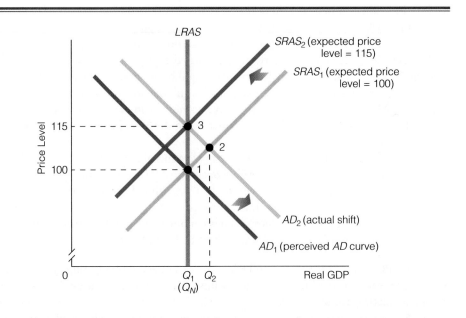

## Deficits, Money, Expectations, and Unintended Effects

Suppose Congress continually takes actions that result in large budget deficits, and every time the deficit increases, the Fed says that it will *not monetize the deficit*. To *monetize the deficits* means to turn the Treasury securities (that have been issued to finance the deficit) into money. Here is an example of moneting the deficit. On Monday the Congress increases government purchases; as a result, the deficit rises by $100 billion. To finance the $100 billion addition to the deficit, the Treasury has to borrow the funds. It does so by issuing (selling) Treasury securites (Treasury debt). Commerical banks buy these newly issued Treasury securities and hold them as assets. Later, the Fed steps in and conducts an open market purchase; specifically, it buys the Treasury securities from the banks. As a result of the purchase, reserves in the banking system rise, and banks can create new loans (checkable deposits). Assuming that the banks choose to do so, the money supply rises. The effect: what started off as an increase in the deficit has ended with an increase in the money supply. The deficit has been monetized.

Suppose that every time the Fed promises not to monetize the deficit, it breaks its promise. In other words, the deficit rises, the Fed promises not to monetize the deficit (the promise), but it ends up monetizing the deficit anyway (the action). The promise is different from the action.

It isn't likely that promises that are not consistent with actions will be believed. More likely, individuals will soon learn to translate promises into expected actions. In other words, the Fed says it will not monetize the deficit, and individuals translate the Fed statement into, "We [the Fed] will probably end up monetizing at least *some* of the deficit."

What does all this mean in terms of expectations and unintended effects on the economy? To answer the question, suppose the economy is in long-run equilibrium, producing Natural Real GDP. Suddenly, members of Congress undertake policy actions that increase the size of the deficit. Soon after, the Fed states that it will not monetize the deficit, but—and here is the point—the Fed has made that statement before and then taken different actions. So this time indviduals *expect* the Fed to end up monetizing some of the deficit. As a result, they expect the *AD* curve in the economy to shift rightward and the price level to rise. Based on what they perceive as a soon-to-be rising price level, they revise their expected price level upward, and then the *SRAS* curve shifts leftward.

Now suppose this time the Fed actually holds to its promise and does not monetize the deficit. All of a sudden the Fed's actions match its promise. What happens now? The *SRAS* curve has shifted leftward, but the *AD* curve remains unchanged. The result is a short-run decline in Real GDP below Natural Real GDP. The economy is now in a recessionary gap.

The economy ended up in a recessionary gap because:

- The Fed had previously made promises that it didn't keep.
- Individuals learned to translate Fed promises into likely actions, even if the actions were inconsistent with the promises.
- Individuals based their behavior on what they thought the Fed would do given its past performance.
- This time, the Fed kept to its promise, and as a result the economy moved into a recessionary gap.

The lesson: If the Fed says one thing and continually does another, then unintended effects may follow when it does what it says it will do. The unintended effect in our example was the economy falling into a recessionary gap.

*AD* curve shifts rightward from $AD_1$ to $AD_2$. In this case, individuals do not anticipate this policy action by the Fed; it is unanticipated. What this means is that individuals do not notice that the *AD* curve in the economy has shifted. They mistakenly believe $AD_1$ (not $AD_2$) is the operational (i.e., the true) *AD* curve in the economy. Because they do not know the *AD* curve has shifted, they do not expect any change in the price level. They expect it to remain at 100. Individuals therefore have no reason to revise their expected price level, and it stays at 100.

In the short run, the economy moves to point 2. So a rising money supply leads to a rise in Real GDP in the short run. In time, individuals will realize that things have changed and that the Fed's action has shifted the *AD* curve in the economy rightward. In short, they will come to realize that the operational *AD* curve in the economy is $AD_2$, not $AD_1$. Individuals will then realize the long-run equilibrium price level consistent with

## Rational Expectations in the College Classroom

If people hold rational expectations, the outcome of a policy will be different if the policy is unanticipated than if it is anticipated. Specifically, unanticipated policy changes can move the economy away from the natural unemployment rate, but correctly anticipated policy changes cannot. Does something similar happen in a college classroom?

Suppose Ana's history class starts at 9:00 a.m., and she "naturally" arrives 1 minute before class starts. In other words, her so-called natural waiting time is 1 minute.

The first day of class, Ana arrives at 8:59, her instructor arrives at 8:59:30, and she starts class promptly at 9:00 a.m.

The second day of class, Ana arrives at 8:59, her instructor arrives at 9:01:30, and she starts class at 9:02 a.m. On this day, Ana has waited 3 minutes, which is more than her natural waiting time of 1 minute.

The timing of the start of class on the third, fourth, and fifth days is the same as on the second. So for the second through fifth days, Ana is operating at more than her natural waiting time.

Rational expectations hold that people will not continue to make the same mistake. In this case, Ana will take her professor's recent arrival time into account and adjust her timing accordingly. On the sixth day

©BANANA STOCK/JUPITER IMAGES

of class, instead of arriving at 8:59, Ana arrives at 9:01. This day, the instructor again arrives at 9:01:30 and begins class at 9:02 a.m., and Ana has moved back to her natural waiting time of 1 minute.

So far, Ana's natural waiting time was met on the first day of class. On the second through fifth days of class, the professor obviously changed her policy as to her arrival time. Ana didn't anticipate this change of policy; so she was fooled into waiting more than her natural waiting time. But Ana did not continue to make the same mistake. She adjusted to her professor's policy change and went back to her 1-minute natural waiting time.

Now let's change the scenario. At the end of the first day of class, the professor announces, "I know I arrived at class at 8:59:30 today, but I won't do this again. From now on, I will arrive at 9:01:30."

In this situation, the professor has announced her policy change. Ana hears the announcement and correctly anticipates the professor's arrival time from now on. With this information, she adjusts her behavior. Instead of arriving at class at 8:59, she arrives at 9:01. Thus, she has correctly anticipated her professor's policy change, and she will remain at her natural waiting time (she will not move from it, even temporarily).

---

$AD_2$ is 115. Accordingly, they will revise their expected price level upward to 115, and the $SRAS$ curve will shift leftward from $SRAS_1$ to $SRAS_2$. The economy will move into long-run equilibrium at point 3, and the expected price level will be equal to the actual price level.

## Comparing Exhibits 9 and 10

The short-run equilibrium positions in Exhibits 9 and 10 led to the same conclusion: that an increase in the money supply could increase Real GDP in the short run. In Exhibit 10, the policy was unanticipated; in Exhibit 9, we assumed that the policy was incorrectly anticipated—bias downward. So how could two very different assumptions lead to the same short-run outcome? The answer is that $Q_2$ in Exhibit 10 represents a higher Real GDP level than $Q_2$ in Exhibit 9. For example, if $Q_2$ in Exhibit 10 is $12 trillion, then $Q_2$ in Exhibit 9 is less—say, $11 trillion. If we assumed that the policy was unanticipated in Exhibit 9, the short-run equilibrium point would not be at point 2, but at the intersection of the $AD_2$ and $SRAS_1$ curves. This point is not identified in Exhibit 9, but it is to the southeast of point 2. If we viewed the Real GDP level that corresponds to this point, it would be greater than $Q_2$ in the exhibit.

## ⓣhinking Like **AN ECONOMIST**

**What People Think Can Matter to Outcomes** Think of how economics might differ from chemistry. In chemistry, if you add two molecules of hydrogen to one molecule of oxygen, you always get water. What is often frustrating to economists is that sometimes the layperson thinks that economics works like chemistry: X plus Y should always give us Z. Sadly, that is not how economics works. If you add expansionary monetary policy to an economy, you don't always get a rise in short-run Real GDP. Sometimes you get a rise (when policy is unanticipated), sometimes no change (when policy is correctly anticipated), and other times a decline (when policy is incorrectly anticipated, bias upward).

The factor affecting economics that is not at work in chemistry is the human factor. What new classical economists teach us about human beings is that their perceptions of things (vis-à-vis reality) have a large part to play in determining outcomes. ▲ ▲ ▲

### SELF-TEST

1. Does the policy ineffectiveness proposition (PIP) always hold?

2. When policy is unanticipated, what difference is there between the natural rate theory built on adaptive expectations and the natural rate theory built on rational expectations?

3. Identify the changes in the price level and Real GDP in both the short run and the long run as a result of the Fed's increasing the money supply. Assume that the Fed action is incorrectly anticipated (bias upward), wages and prices are flexible, and individuals hold rational expectations.

# NEW KEYNESIANS AND RATIONAL EXPECTATIONS

The new classical theory assumes that wages and prices are flexible. In this theory, an increase in the expected price level results in an immediate and equal rise in wages and prices, and the aggregate supply curve immediately shifts to the long-run equilibrium position.

In response to the new classical assumption of flexible wages and prices, a few economists developed what has come to be known as the *new Keynesian rational expectations theory.* This theory assumes that rational expectations are a reasonable characterization of how expectations are formed, but it drops the new classical assumption of complete wage and price flexibility. According to this theory, long-term labor contracts often prevent wages and prices from fully adjusting to changes in the expected price level. (In other words, prices and wages are somewhat sticky, rigid, or inflexible.)

Consider the possible situation at the end of the first year of a three-year wage contract. Workers realize that the actual price level is higher than they expected when they negotiated the contract, but they are unable to do much about it because their wages are locked in for the next two years. Price rigidity might also come into play because firms often engage in fixed-price contracts with their suppliers. As discussed in Chapter 10, Keynesian economists today assert that, for microeconomic-based reasons, long-term labor contracts and above-market wages are sometimes in the best interest of both employers and employees (the efficiency wage theory).

To see what the theory predicts, look at Exhibit 11. The economy is initially in long-run equilibrium at point 1. The public correctly anticipates an increase in aggregate demand from $AD_1$ to $AD_2$, and, as a result, the expected price level changes. Because of some wage and price rigidities, however, the short-run aggregate supply curve does not shift all the way from $SRAS_1$ to $SRAS_2$, and the economy does not move from point 1 to point 2 (as in new classical theory).The short-run aggregate supply curve shifts instead to $SRAS'_2$ because rigidities prevent complete wage and price adjustments. In the short run,

**EXHIBIT 11**

**The Short-Run Response to Aggregate Demand–Increasing Policy (in the New Keynesian Theory)**

Starting at point 1, an increase in aggregate demand is correctly anticipated. As a result, the short-run aggregate supply curve shifts leftward, but not all the way to $SRAS_2$ (as would be the case in the new classical theory). Instead it shifts only to $SRAS'_2$ because of some wage and price rigidities; the economy moves to point 2' (in the short run), and Real GDP increases from $Q_N$ to $Q_A$. If the policy had been unanticipated, Real GDP would have increased from $Q_N$ to $Q_{UA}$.

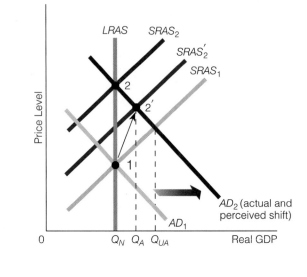

the economy moves from point 1 to point 2', from $Q_N$ to $Q_A$. Had the policy been unanticipated, Real GDP would have increased from $Q_N$ to $Q_{UA}$ in the short run.

# LOOKING AT THINGS FROM THE SUPPLY SIDE: REAL BUSINESS CYCLE THEORISTS

Throughout this chapter, changes in Real GDP have originated on the demand side of the economy. When discussing the Friedman natural rate theory, the new classical theory, and the new Keynesian theory, we began our analysis by shifting the *AD* curve to the right. Then we explained what happens in the economy as a result. The presentation so far in this chapter seems to assume that all changes in Real GDP originate on the demand side of the economy. In fact, some economists believe this to be true.

Other economists do not. One group of such economists, called *real business cycle theorists*, believe that changes on the supply side of the economy can lead to changes in Real GDP and unemployment. Real business cycle theorists argue that a decrease in Real GDP (which refers to the recessionary or contractionary part of a business cycle) can be brought about by a major supply-side change that reduces the capacity of the economy to produce. Moreover, they argue that what looks like a contraction in Real GDP originating on the demand side of the economy can be, in essence, the effect of what has happened on the supply side.

In Exhibit 12, an adverse supply shock reduces the capacity of the economy to produce. This effect is represented by a shift inward in the economy's production possibilities frontier or a leftward shift in the long-run aggregate supply curve from $LRAS_1$ to $LRAS_2$. This moves the economy from point *A* to point *B*. As shown in the exhibit, a leftward shift in the long-run aggregate supply curve means that Natural Real GDP has fallen.

As a result of the leftward shift in the *LRAS* curve and the decline in Real GDP, firms reduce their demand for labor and scale back employment. Due to the lower demand for labor (which puts downward pressure on money wages) and the higher price level, real

**EXHIBIT 12**

**Real Business Cycle Theory**

We start with a supply-side change capable of reducing the capacity of the economy to produce. This is manifested by a leftward shift of the long-run aggregate supply curve from $LRAS_1$ to $LRAS_2$ and a fall in the Natural Real GDP level from $Q_{N1}$ to $Q_{N2}$. A reduction in the productive capacity of the economy filters to the demand side of the economy and, in our example, reduces consumption, investment, and the money supply. The aggregate demand curve shifts leftward from $AD_1$ to $AD_2$.

wages fall. As real wages fall, workers choose to work less, and unemployed persons choose to extend the length of their unemployment. Due to less work and lower real wages, workers have less income. Lower incomes soon lead workers to reduce consumption.

Either because consumption has fallen or because businesses have become pessimistic (prompted by the decline in the productive potential of the economy), or because of both reasons, businesses have less reason to invest. As a result, firms borrow less from banks, the volume of outstanding loans falls, and thus the money supply falls. A decrease in the money supply causes the aggregate demand curve to shift leftward, from $AD_1$ to $AD_2$ in Exhibit 12, and the economy moves to point $C$.

Real business cycle theorists sometimes point out how easily a demand-induced decline in Real GDP can be confused with a supply-induced decline. In our example, both the aggregate supply side and the aggregate demand side of the economy change, but the aggregate supply side changes first. If the change in aggregate supply is overlooked, and only the changes in aggregate demand are observed (or specifically, a change in one of the variables that can change aggregate demand, such as the money supply), then the contraction in Real GDP will appear to be demand induced. In terms of Exhibit 12, the leftward shift in the *LRAS* curve would be overlooked, but the leftward shift in the *AD* curve would be observed, giving the impression that the contraction is demand induced.

If real business cycle theorists are correct, the cause–effect analysis of a contraction in Real GDP would be turned upside down. As just one example, changes in the money supply may be an *effect* of a contraction in Real GDP (which originates on the supply side of the economy), not its *cause*.

1.  *The Wall Street Journal* reports that the money supply has recently declined. Is the decline consistent with a demand-induced business cycle, with a supply-induced business cycle, or with both? Explain your answer.

2.  How are new Keynesians who believe people hold rational expectations different from new classical economists who believe people hold rational expectations?

# OFFICE HOURS

## "Does New Classical Theory Call the Effects of Fiscal and Monetary Policy into Question?"

**STUDENT:**

When I started this course in macroeconomics, I was hoping to learn the unequivocal answers to some simple questions, such as what effect does fiscal policy have on the economy? What effect does monetary policy have on the economy? I don't think I am learning this. For example, fiscal and monetary policy seems to have different effects on Real GDP in the short run depending on whether policy is unanticipated, incorrectly anticipated, or correctly anticipated. Am I right about this?

**INSTRUCTOR:**

You're right. A given policy action (such as expansionary monetary policy) can have different effects on Real GDP (in the short run) depending on whether the policy is unanticipated, correctly anticipated, and so on.

**STUDENT:**

What am I supposed to learn from this?

**INSTRUCTOR:**

The obvious point, which you've identified, is that policy actions have different effects depending on the degree to which individuals correctly anticipate the policy. The not so obvious point is that it might not be wise to use government policy actions to stabilize the economy.

**STUDENT:**

How do you come to that point? What are the details?

**INSTRUCTOR:**

Let's say that the economy is currently in a recessionary gap and Real GDP is $11 trillion. Policy makers want to raise the GDP level to Natural Real GDP at, say, $11.2 trillion. To achieve this goal, either expansionary fiscal or monetary policy is implemented. Are we guaranteed to raise Real GDP from $11 trillion to $11.2 trillion?

**STUDENT:**

No.

---

## CHAPTER SUMMARY

### THE PHILLIPS CURVE

- A. W. Phillips plotted a curve to a set of data points that exhibited an inverse relationship between wage inflation and unemployment. This curve came to be known as the Phillips curve. From the Phillips curve relationship, economists concluded that neither the combination of low inflation and low unemployment nor the combination of high inflation and high unemployment was likely.

- Economists Paul Samuelson and Robert Solow fit a Phillips curve to the U.S. economy. Instead of measuring wage inflation against unemployment rates (as Phillips did), they measured price inflation against unemployment rates. They found an inverse relationship between inflation and unemployment rates.

- Based on the findings of Phillips and Samuelson and Solow, economists concluded the following: (1) Stagflation, or high inflation and high unemployment, is extremely unlikely. (2)

The Phillips curve presents policy makers with a menu of different combinations of inflation and unemployment rates.

### FRIEDMAN NATURAL RATE THEORY

- Milton Friedman pointed out that there are two types of Phillips curves: a short-run and a long-run Phillips curve. The short-run Phillips curve exhibits the inflation–unemployment trade-off; the long-run Phillips curve does not. Consideration of both short- and long-run Phillips curves opened macroeconomics to expectations theory.

- The Friedman natural rate theory holds that, in the short run, a decrease (increase) in inflation is linked to an increase (decrease) in unemployment, but in the long run, the economy returns to its natural rate of unemployment. In other words, there is a trade-off between inflation and unemployment in the short run, but not in the long run.

> **INSTRUCTOR:**

Why is that?

> **STUDENT:**

Well, according to new classical economists, it's because individuals may incorrectly anticipate the policy in such as way as to reduce Real GDP instead of raising it.

> **INSTRUCTOR:**

That's right. Suppose, for example, the Fed plans to raise the money supply by $10 billion, but the public mistakenly believes the Fed will raise the money supply by, say, $18 billion. In the short run, the *AD* curve will shift to the right and the *SRAS* curve will to shift to the left, but the *SRAS* curve will be shifting left *by more than* the *AD* curve will be shifting to the right. (This happened in Exhibit 8.) And the result will be a decline, not an increase, in Real GDP—at least in the short run.

> **STUDENT:**

So the monetary policy action can end up doing the very opposite of what it was intended to do. It was intended to raise Real GDP, but it lowered it instead.

> **INSTRUCTOR:**

That's correct. What the new classical economists are really pointing out is that we can't always be sure of a discretionary policy action's effect on Real GDP. In turn, this should make economists less sure, or

a little more humble, when it comes to advocating certain economic policy actions for government to implement.

**POINTS TO REMEMBER**

1. According to new classical economists, economic policy actions may not always have the intended effect on Real GDP in the short run.
2. Economic policy actions may accomplish the opposite of what they were intended to accomplish.

- The Friedman natural rate theory was expressed in terms of adaptive expectations. Individuals formed their inflation expectations by considering past inflation rates. Later, some economists expressed the theory in terms of rational expectations. Rational expectations theory holds that individuals form their expected inflation rate by considering present and past inflation rates, as well as all other available and relevant information—in particular, the effects of present and future policy actions.

## NEW CLASSICAL THEORY

- Implicit in the new classical theory are two assumptions: (1) Individuals form their expectations rationally. (2) Wages and prices are completely flexible.
- In the new classical theory, policy has different effects (1) when it is unanticipated, (2) when it is incorrectly anticipated—bias upward, (3) when it is incorrectly anticipated—bias downward, and (4) when it is correctly anticipated. To illustrate, consider two cases: (A) when policy is incorrectly anticipated—bias upward and (B) when policy is correctly anticipated. Assume

that in both cases a demand-side policy increases aggregate demand in the economy. In case A, the *AD* curve will shift rightward by less than the *SRAS* initially shifts leftward, bringing about a decline in Real GDP in the short run. In case B, the *AD* curve will shift rightward to the same degree, and at the same time, but in the opposite direction of the *SRAS* curve. In this case, Real GDP does not change.

## NEW KEYNESIAN THEORY

- Implicit in the New Keynesian theory are two assumptions: (1) Individuals form their expectations rationally. (2) Wages and prices are not completely flexible in the short run.
- If policy is correctly anticipated, the economic effects predicted by the new classical theory and the new Keynesian theory are not the same in the short run. Because the new Keynesian theory assumes that wages and prices are not completely flexible in the short run, given an anticipated change in aggregate demand, the short-run aggregate supply curve cannot immediately shift to its long-run equilibrium position. The new Keynesian theory

predicts a short-run trade-off between inflation and unemployment (in the Phillips curve framework).

## REAL BUSINESS CYCLE THEORY

• Real business cycle contractions (in Real GDP) originate on the supply side of the economy. A contraction in Real GDP might follow this pattern: (1) An adverse supply shock reduces the economy's ability to produce. (2) The *LRAS* curve shifts leftward. (3) As a result, Real GDP declines and the price level rises. (4) The number of persons employed falls, as do real wages, owing to a decrease in the demand for labor (which lowers money wages) and a higher price level. (5) Incomes decline. (6) Consumption and investment decline. (7) The volume of outstanding loans declines. (8) The money supply falls. (9) The *AD* curve shifts leftward.

## KEY TERMS AND CONCEPTS

Phillips Curve
Stagflation

Friedman Natural Rate
Theory

Adaptive Expectations
Rational Expectations

Policy Ineffectiveness
Proposition (PIP)

## QUESTIONS AND PROBLEMS

1. What does it mean to say that the Phillips curve presents policy makers with a menu of choices?

2. According to Friedman, how do we know when the economy is in long-run equilibrium?

3. What is a major difference between adaptive and rational expectations? Give an example of each.

4. "The policy ineffectiveness proposition (connected with new classical theory) does not eliminate policy makers' ability to reduce unemployment through aggregate demand–increasing policies because they can always increase aggregate demand by more than the public expects." What might be the weak point in this argument?

5. Why is the new classical theory associated with the word "classical"? Why has it been said that classical theory failed where new classical theory succeeds, because the former could not explain the business cycle (the ups and downs of the economy), but the latter can?

6. Suppose a permanent downward-sloping Phillips curve existed and offered a menu of choices of different combinations of inflation and unemployment rates to policy makers. How do you think society would go about deciding which point on the Phillips curve it wanted to occupy?

7. Assume a current short-run trade-off between inflation and unemployment, as well as a change in technology that permits the wider dispersion of economic policy news. How would the change affect the trade-off? Explain your answer.

8. New Keynesian theory holds that wages are not completely flexible because of such things as long-term labor contracts.

New classical economists often respond that experience teaches labor leaders to develop and bargain for contracts that allow for wage adjustments. Do you think the new classical economists have a good point? Why or why not?

9. What evidence can you point to that suggests individuals form their expectations adaptively? What evidence can you point to that suggests individuals form their expectations rationally?

10. Suppose the government undertakes an expansionary fiscal policy measure that raises aggregate demand, but individuals incorrectly anticipate the policy measure (bias upward). What will the short- and long-run changes be in the price level and Real GDP?

11. Explain both the short- and long-run movements of the Friedman natural rate theory, assuming expectations are formed adaptively.

12. Explain both the short- and long-run movements of the new classical theory, assuming expectations are formed rationally and policy is unanticipated.

13. "Even if some people do not form their expectations rationally, the new classical theory is not necessarily of no value." Discuss this statement.

14. In the real business cycle theory, why can't the change in the money supply prompted by a series of events catalyzed by an adverse supply shock be considered the cause of the business cycle?

15. The expected inflation rate is 5 percent, and the actual inflation rate is 7 percent. According to Friedman, is the economy in long-run equilibrium? Explain your answer.

## WORKING WITH NUMBERS AND GRAPHS

1. Illustrate graphically what would happen in the short run and in the long run if individuals hold rational expectations, prices and wages are flexible, and individuals underestimate the decrease in aggregate demand.

2. In each of the following figures, the starting point is 1. Which part illustrates each of the following?

   a. Friedman natural rate theory (short run)

## WORKING WITH NUMBERS AND GRAPHS

b. New classical theory (unanticipated policy, short run)

c. Real business cycle theory

d. New classical theory (incorrectly anticipated policy, over-estimating increase in aggregate demand, short run)

e. Policy ineffectiveness proposition (PIP)

(a)

(b)

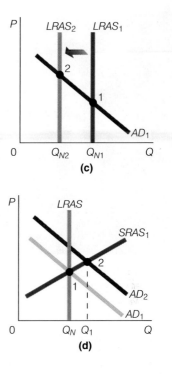
(c)

(d)

3. Illustrate graphically what would happen in the short run and in the long run if individuals hold adaptive expectations, if prices and wages are flexible, and if aggregate demand decreases.

## CHAPTER 17

# ECONOMIC GROWTH: RESOURCES, TECHNOLOGY, IDEAS, AND INSTITUTIONS

**Introduction** Rarely do we think of how we came to have the standard of living we enjoy. Most of us live in comfortable houses, drive nice cars, work on fast computers, enjoy exciting sporting events, attend lively jazz concerts, visit relaxing vacation spots, go to the movies and restaurants, and have many other things to be grateful for. To a large degree, our lives are so enriched because we were born in a country that has experienced a relatively high rate of economic growth. How might your life be different if the U.S. economy had had a lower growth rate over, say, the last century? To answer this question, you need to know the causes of economic growth.

## A FEW BASICS ABOUT ECONOMIC GROWTH

**Absolute Real Economic Growth**
An increase in Real GDP from one period to the next.

**Per-Capita Real Economic Growth**
An increase from one period to the next in per-capita Real GDP, which is Real GDP divided by population.

The term "economic growth" refers either to absolute real economic growth or to per-capita real economic growth. Absolute real economic growth is an increase in Real GDP from one period to the next. Exhibit 1 shows absolute real economic growth (or the percentage change in Real GDP) for the United States for the period 1998–2009.

Per-capita real economic growth is an increase from one period to the next in per-capita Real GDP, which is Real GDP divided by population.

$$\text{Per-capita Real GDP} = \frac{\text{Real GDP}}{\text{Population}}$$

### Do Economic Growth Rates Matter?

Suppose the (absolute) real economic growth rate is 4 percent in one country and 3 percent in another. The difference in growth rates may not seem very significant. But if the growth rates are sustained over a long period of time, the people who live in each country will see a real difference in their standard of living. For example, if a country's economic growth rate

**EXHIBIT 1**

**Absolute Real Economic Growth Rates for the United States, 1998–2009**

This exhibit shows the absolute real economic growth rates (or percentage change in Real GDP) in the United States for the period 1998–2006.

Source: *Economic Report of the President, 2010.*

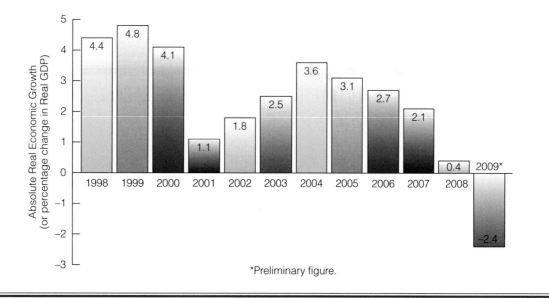

*Preliminary figure.

is 5 percent each year, its Real GDP will double in 14 years. If a country has a 2 percent annual growth rate, its Real GDP will double in 35 years. In other words, a country with a 5 percent growth rate can double its Real GDP in 21 fewer years than a country with a 2 percent growth rate. (To calculate the time required for any variable to double, simply divide its percentage growth rate into 70. This is called the *rule of 70.*)

# finding ECONOMICS

**In a Night Out** It is 6 p.m. and Xavier is driving his new $45,000 car to a restaurant. He and a friend have dinner at the restaurant. The bill comes to $86.75. After dinner, Xavier and his friend attend a play. Later that night, they return to Xavier's 3,500-square-foot house. They sit out by the swimming pool and talk about everything and nothing. Where is the economics? Is economic growth relevant to the evening?

Economic growth is the silent actor of the evening. Because Xavier and his friend live in a country that has experienced economic growth over the years, their night can be as comfortable and satisfying for them as it is.

Or look at it this way. People like Xavier and his friend are all over the world. Not all of them *can* have the same evening. Individuals living in countries that experienced much less economic growth over the years are not as likely to experience the same kind of evening as did Xavier and his friend.

Here is a startling fact: About 24,000 people die every day from hunger or hunger-related causes. Three-fourths of the deaths are children under the age of 5. The vast majority of people who die of hunger live in countries of the world that have experienced relatively little economic growth. ▲ ▲ ▲

## ⓣhinking Like AN ECONOMIST

**Economic Growth Matters** Economic growth has been a major topic of discussion for economists for over two centuries. Adam Smith, the founder of modern economics, wrote a book on the subject that was published in 1776: *An Inquiry into the Nature and Causes of the Wealth of Nations.* In the book, Smith set out to answer the question of why some countries are rich and others are poor. Today, we'd ask, "Why do some countries have a high per-capita Real GDP and others have a low per-capita Real GDP? For economists, getting the right answer to this question is of major importance to the lives of millions—if not billions—of people. ▴ ▴ ▴

# A PRODUCTION FUNCTION AND ECONOMIC GROWTH

**Production Function**
A function that specifies the relation between technology and the quantity of factor inputs to output or Real GDP.

A production function specifies the relation between technology and the quantity of factor inputs to output or Real GDP. For example, look at this production function:

$$\text{Real GDP} = T(L, K)$$

The $L$ stands for labor; the $K$ stands for capital; the $T$ stands for the technology coefficient. Suppose we have 4 units of labor and 2 units of capital. In all, we have 6 units of our two resources, labor and capital.

In an earlier chapter, an advance in technology was defined as being able to produce more output (more Real GDP) with a given level of resources, such as labor and capital. The $T$, or technology coefficient, in our production function captures this idea. Suppose we set our $T$ equal to 0.40. Given that $L$ equals 4 and $K$ equals 2, our production function now reads:

$$\text{Real GDP} = 0.4\,(4 + 2)$$
$$\text{Real GDP} = 0.4\,(6)$$
$$\text{Real GDP} = 2.4 \text{ units of output}$$

In other words, we have taken so much labor and capital, added it together at a certain level of technology—evidenced in a technology coefficient of 0.4—and ended up with 2.4 units of output or Real GDP.

Obviously, given our production function, which focuses on the three factors of $T$, $L$, and $K$, an increase in any one of these factors will lead to a rise in Real GDP. For example, if we increase labor from 4 to 8 units, Real GDP will rise to 4 units of output. Alternatively, if we raise $T$ from 0.4 to 0.5, holding labor at 4 units and capital at 2 units, Real GDP will rise from 2.4 units to 3.0 units.

### The Graphical Representation of the Production Function

Exhibit 2(a) represents the production function graphically. Real GDP ($Q$) is on the vertical axis, and labor ($L$) is on the horizontal axis. The curve in the two-dimensional space is the graphical representation of the production function. At a given level of labor, $L_1$, we get $Q_1$ amount of Real GDP. A change in labor, say from $L_1$ to $L_2$, will give us more Real GDP, as shown in Exhibit 2(b).

Now a change in either $K$ or $T$ will shift the production function up or down. For example, Exhibit 2(c) shows what happens to the production function if $K$ rises. Initially $K = 1$, and this, combined with $L_1$ and a given technology coefficient, produces $Q_1$ Real GDP.

If $K$ rises to 2, and this higher $K$ is combined with the same amount of labor and the same technology coefficient, Real GDP rises to $Q_2$.

Exhibit 2(d) shows what happens if the technology coefficient rises. Initially, $T = 0.4$. Combining this with a given amount of labor and capital produces a Real GDP level of $Q_1$. If $T$ rises to 0.5 and nothing else changes, then Real GDP rises to $Q_2$.

**The Production Function**

(a) The production function is based on labor (L), capital (K), and technology (technology coefficient, T). (b) Changes in L lead to changes in Real GDP (Q). (c) A rise in capital leads to a shift upward in the production function and to more Real GDP (for a given level of L and a given technology coefficient). (d) A rise in the technology coefficient leads to a shift upward in the production function and to more Real GDP (for a given level of L and K).

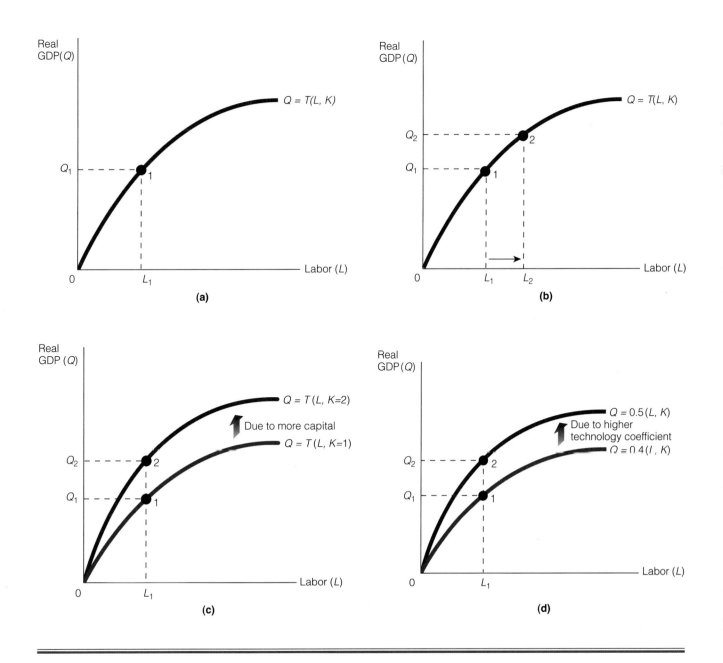

So our production function specifies that output or Real GDP depends on labor, capital, and the technology coefficient (which captures the essence of advances in technology). Specifically, a rise in labor will move us from one point to another on the same production function, ending with more Real GDP. A rise in capital or a rise in the technology coefficient will lead to a shift upward in the production function, ending with more Real GDP.

## From the Production Function to the *LRAS* Curve

The changes in and the movements along the production function can be linked to shifts in the *LRAS* curve. In Exhibit 3(a), we start with $L_1$, which gives us Real GDP of $Q_1$. We then take $Q_1$ from panel (a) and move it to panel (b). This is the Real GDP that the economy is producing when it is at the natural unemployment rate; this is Natural Real GDP. This level of Real GDP is consistent with $LRAS_1$ in the exhibit.

Suppose, in panel (a), we raise labor to $L_2$. This change in labor moves us along our production function, from point 1 to point 2 at a higher Real GDP level, $Q_2$. In panel (b), this new, higher Real GDP is consistent with $LRAS_2$.

Therefore, a rise in labor moves us along the given production function and shifts the *LRAS* curve to the right. If you superimpose an *AD* curve on panel (b), you see that a shift rightward in the *LRAS* curve brings about a lower price level and a higher Real GDP level. With a heightened Real GDP level, we have economic growth.

In panel (c), again we start with $L_1$, which gives us $Q_1$ Real GDP. If the technology coefficient rises from 0.4 to 0.5, the production function shifts upward. At a given level of labor and capital, we have more Real GDP, $Q_2$. Carrying over the changes in Real GDP from panel (c) to panel (d), we see that a rise in the technology coefficient shifts the *LRAS* curve to the right. Again, we have economic growth.

## Emphasis on Labor

Exhibit 3 showed that a rise in labor would lead to a rightward shift in the *LRAS* curve. In other words, a rise in labor would result in economic growth. Then what might lead to a rise in labor? In other words, if *X* and *Y* lead to a rise in labor, then *X* and *Y* are factors that promote economic growth.

One such factor that is often mentioned is taxes. Specifically, some economists propose promoting economic growth by cutting taxes on such activities as working. The idea is that, if the marginal income tax rate is cut, workers will work more, and, as they work more, output will rise. Think of this in terms of the labor market. Exhibit 4(a) shows a labor market that is in equilibrium at point 1. The equilibrium quantity of labor in this market is $L_1$. If $L_1$ is put into our production function, as shown in panel (b), it gives us $Q_1$ amount of Real GDP. Finally, if $Q_1$ from panel (b) is placed in panel (c), $Q_1$ is consistent with the $LRAS_1$ curve.

Now suppose we lower taxes on income. As a result, the labor supply curve in panel (a) shifts rightward. In other words, as the overall return on working increases due to a drop in income taxes, more people decide to go to work, and many of those already working decide to work more. The new equilibrium quantity of labor, $L_2$, is shown in panel (a). If we carry over the greater quantity of labor to panel (b), showing our production function, more labor produces the higher level of Real GDP, $Q_2$. Then, in panel (c), the new higher level of Real GDP corresponds to a new *LRAS* curve, $LRAS_2$.

Therefore, lower income taxes shift the labor supply to the right, raising the equilibrium quantity of labor, which produces more Real GDP or shifts the *LRAS* curve to the right. Again, we have witnessed economic growth.

**EXHIBIT 3**

### The Production Function and the *LRAS* Curve

(a) More labor (*L*) leads to more Real GDP (shown in terms of the production function). (b) More *L* shifts the *LRAS* curve to the right.

(c) A higher technology coefficient shifts the production function up and brings about more Real GDP, *Q*. (d) A heightened technology coefficient leads to a rightward shift in the *LRAS* curve. (Although not shown in this exhibit, a rise

in *K* would do the same thing as a rise in the technology coefficient in terms of shifting up the production function and shifting the *LRAS* curve to the right.)

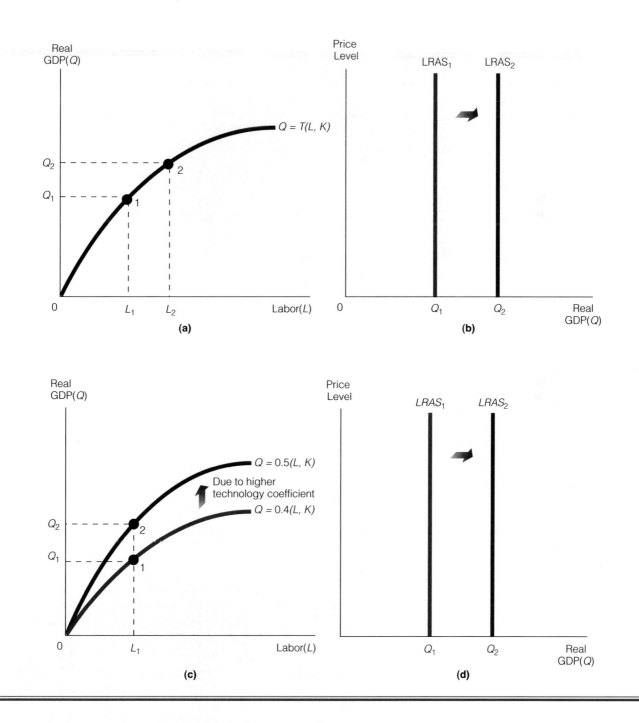

## Growth and Morality[1]

*There is more to life, liberty, and the pursuit of happiness than a faster car and an iPod nano.*
—The Economist (November 10, 2005)

Almost everyone agrees that economic growth, especially sustained economic growth, can produce more, better, and newer goods and services. But what else can it do, if anything? According to economist Benjamin Friedman, it can make people happier, more tolerant, more willing to settle disputes in a peaceful manner, and more inclined to favor an open and democratic society. It can also make people more willing to work toward improving the environment and reducing poverty.

The thought that economic growth can do more than give us more goods and services goes back to Adam Smith. According to Smith, when a nation is acquiring more—when it is getting richer—most of the people are happy and comfortable. When a nation is just maintaining its wealth or declining, its people are not as happy or as comfortable.

What Friedman essentially argues is that economists have looked at the benefits of economic growth too narrowly. They have stressed the rising material standard of living that comes with economic growth. But this perspective, says Friedman, ignores the political, social, and moral aspects of economic growth. In his book, *The Moral Consequences of Economic*

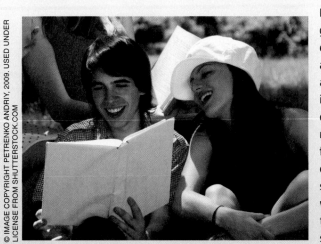

© IMAGE COPYRIGHT PETRENKO ANDRIY, 2009. USED UNDER LICENSE FROM SHUTTERSTOCK.COM

*Growth*, he says that "a rising standard of living lies not just in the concrete improvements it brings to how individuals live but in how it shapes the social, political, and ultimately the moral character of a people."

If Friedman is correct that economic growth affects people not only economically but politically, socially, and morally too, then we need to ask why. Friedman says it has such influence because people's sense of how well off they are is made relative to their (own) past. People feel happiest (and the most tolerant of others) when they believe their standard of living is rising—in other words, if they are better off this year than last year. When they have this sense, people care less about where they stand relative to others. But if they are not witnessing an increase in their standard of living relative to their past, they begin to care more about how they are doing relative to others. This comparison with others usually results in frustration and possibly social friction.

Friedman does not argue that there are absolutely no costs to growth. Instead, he simply makes the point that the benefits emanating from growth may be greater and more far-reaching than we initially thought.

---

1. This feature is based on "Why the Rich Must Get Richer," *The Economist*, November 10, 2005.

## Emphasis on Capital

So more labor can lead to economic growth, but so can more capital. How much capital is available depends on such things as the tax treatment of capital returns and interest rates. Consider two settings. In the first, taxes on the returns to capital are high; in the second, taxes on the returns to capital are low. Which setting offers a stronger incentive to employ capital in the production process? When taxes on the returns to capital are low, we predict the following: as taxes decline on the returns from capital, more capital is utilized in the production process, thus shifting upward the production function and thereby shifting the *LRAS* curve to the right.

The interest rate can also affect the amount of capital employed, because firms often borrow the funds to buy the capital goods used in production. In short, the process can

**EXHIBIT 4**

**The Labor Market, the Production Function, and the _LRAS_ Curve**

(a) Lower taxes on income shifts the labor supply curve rightward from $S_{LF1}$ to $S_{LF2}$. As a result of the lower taxes and the shift rightward in the labor supply curve, the equilibrium amount of labor rises from $L_1$ to $L_2$. (b) More labor leads to more Real GDP in terms of the production function. (c) More Real GDP corresponds to a rightward shift in the _LRAS_ curve.

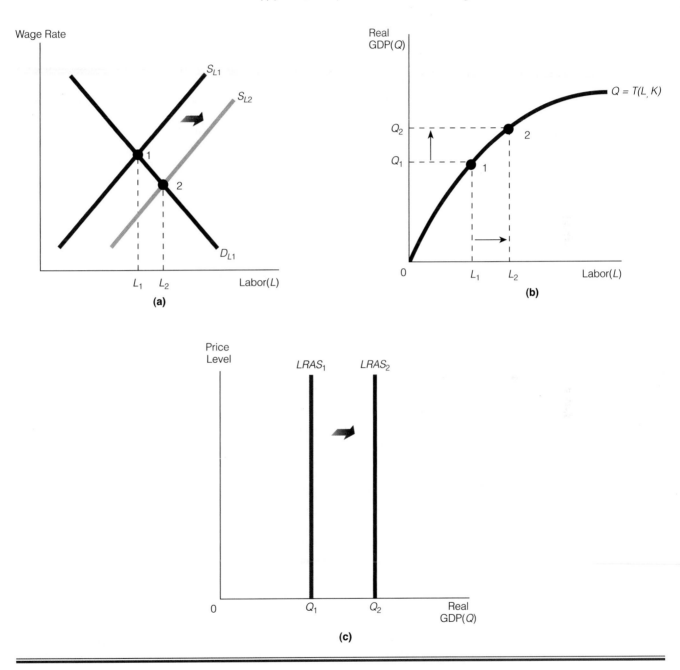

work like this: A decline in interest rates prompts firms to borrow more. The firms use the borrowed funds to purchase capital goods. As they purchase and utilize more capital (in the production process), the production function shifts upward and the _LRAS_ curve shifts rightward.

## Emphasis on Other Resources: Natural Resources and Human Capital

Our production function so far has included only two resources—labor and capital—and technology. When building economic growth models, economists often specify a production function of this sort.

However, for reasons of completeness, a more fully specified production function would also include natural resources ($NR$) and human capital ($H$). For example, producing goods—such as wood to produce chairs, desks, and paper—often takes natural resources. In fact, economists often speak in terms of four resources (Chapter 1): land, labor, capital, and entrepreneurship. The resource of land is simply another name for natural resources.

**Human Capital**
The knowledge and skills a person acquires through education, training, and experience.

Producing many goods also takes human capital, which is different from the kind of capital we represented as $K$. The capital referred to earlier is *physical capital*—such things as machines, computers, and factories. Human capital is what you acquire by attending college and the skills and knowledge you pick up through education, training, and experience. You enroll in a number of courses, learn certain material, and acquire certain thinking skills; these are all components of human capital.

Adding human capital and natural resources to our production function leads us to specify that function this way:

$$\text{Real GDP} = T\,(L, K, NR, H)$$

## Emphasis on the Technology Coefficient and Ideas

Beginning in the 1980s, economists began discussing economic growth differently than they did in previous decades. They placed more attention on technology, ideas, institutions, and education. The discussion often took place under the rubric of *new growth theory*.

The name "new growth theory" implies that a theory of economic growth came before it, and, indeed, neoclassical growth theory preceded new growth theory. Some economists believe that new growth theory came about to answer some of the questions that new neoclassical growth theory could not, in much the same way that a new medical theory may arise to answer questions that an old medical theory cannot answer.

Neoclassical growth theory emphasized two resources: labor and physical capital. Technology was discussed, but only very tangentially. Technology was said to be exogenous; that is, it came from outside the economic system. It fell out of the sky; it was outside our control. We simply accepted this assumption as a given.

New growth theory holds that technology is endogenous; it is a central part of the economic system. More important, the amount and quality of technology that is developed depend on the amount of resources we devote to it: The more resources that go to develop technology, the more and better technology that is developed.

Paul Romer, whose name is synonymous with new growth theory, asks us to think about technology as we would prospecting for gold. For one individual, the chances of finding gold are so small that if someone did find gold, the strike would simply be viewed as good luck. However, if 10,000 individuals are looking for gold across a wide geographical area, the chances of finding it would greatly improve. As with gold prospecting, so it is with technological advances. If one person is trying to advance technology, his or her chances of success are much smaller than if hundreds or thousands of persons are trying.

New growth theory also emphasizes the process of discovering and formulating ideas as they relate to technological advances. The emphasis is on ideas rather than on objects, which are material, tangible things, such as natural resources and capital goods. Some countries are poor because they lack objects (natural resources and capital goods). Yet some countries have had very few objects and have been able to grow economically. For example, in the 1950s, Japan had few natural resources and capital goods, but still it grew economically. Some economists believe that Japan grew because it had access to ideas or knowledge.

## Discovery and Ideas

If discovering ideas is important to technological advances and therefore to economic growth, then we need to figure out ways to promote the discovery process. One way is for business firms not to get locked into doing things one way and one way only. They must let their employees—from the inventor in the lab to the worker on the assembly line—try new ways of getting the job done. Some might carry this further: businesses need to create an environment that is receptive to new ideas. They need to encourage their employees to try new ways of doing things.

Employee flexibility, which is a part of the discovery process, is becoming a larger part of the U.S. economy. To some degree, this process is seen in the amount of time and effort firms devote to discovery in contrast to the amount of time they devote to actually manufacturing goods. Consider the computer software business. Millions of dollars and hundreds of thousands of work hours are devoted to coming up with new and useful software, whereas only a tiny fraction of the work effort and hours go into making, copying, and shipping the disks or CDs that contain the software.

## Expanding Our Horizons

Romer has said that "economic growth occurs whenever people take resources and rearrange them in ways that are more valuable." Let's focus on the word "rearrange." We can think of rearranging as in rearranging the pieces of a puzzle, as in changing the ingredients in a recipe, or as in rearranging the way workers go about their daily work. When we rearrange anything, we do that "thing" differently. Sometimes, differently is better, and sometimes it is worse.

Think of how you study for a test. Perhaps you read the book first, go back and underline, study the book, and then finally study your lecture notes. Would it be better to study differently? You won't know until you try.

As with studying for a test, so it is with producing a car, computer software, or a shopping mall. We do not find better ways of doing things unless we experiment. And with repeated experiments, we often discover new and better ideas, ideas that ultimately lead to economic growth. The research and development of new medicines makes for a good example. Sometimes, what makes a mildly effective medicine into a very effective one is a change in one or two molecules of a certain chemical. A small change—a change perhaps no one would ever think would matter—can make a large difference.

A policy prescription follows from this mind-set: we should think of ways to make the process of discovering ideas, experimenting with different ways of doing things, and developing new technology more likely. Without this kind of effort, we are likely to diminish our growth potential. If we believe ideas are important to economic growth, then we need to have ideas about how to generate more ideas. Paul Romer calls these *meta-ideas*: ideas about how to support the production and transmission of other ideas.

Some ways have been proposed. Perhaps we need to invest more funds in education or research and development. Or perhaps we need to find ways to better protect people's ideas (few people will invest the time, money, and effort to discover better ideas if the ideas can easily be stolen).

In the twenty-first century, countries with the most natural resources and capital goods aren't likely to be the ones that grow the fastest. If new growth theory is correct, the successful ones will be those that have discovered how to encourage and develop the most and best ideas.

## Institutions Matter

Crops don't grow equally well in all soils. Some soils are more conducive to the growing than others. Similarly, many economists argue that some environments are more conducive to economic growth than others.

One of the ways economists differentiate one environment from another is in terms of its institutions. But what are institutions in this context? Douglass North, a well respected economist in this area of research, defines an institution as "the rules of the game in a society or, more formally, the humanly devised constraints that shape human interaction." Specifically, institutions consist of a country's rules and regulations, laws, customs, and business practices. Consider two countries, A and B, each with different institutions. In country A, the rule of law operates (no one is above the law), contracts are enforced, private property rights are protected, and free international trade is permitted. In country B, the rule of law does not hold, contracts are not always enforced, private property is not protected (and is often seized), and high tariffs and quotas are placed on imported goods. In North's terminology, the "rules of the game" are different in these two countries.

Here are a few of the institutions that most economists agree are conducive to economic growth:

- Property rights structure
- The legal system
- Growth-promoting policies versus transfer-promoting policies
- Other institutions

**Institution**

The rules of the game in a society or, more formally, the humanly devised constraints that shape human interaction; the rules and regulations, laws, customs, and business practices of a country.

**PROPERTY RIGHTS STRUCTURE** Think of two property rights structures, X and Y. Under X, a person is allowed to own property (a piece of land, a business, a store, an invention, etc.); that is, private property is permitted. Under Y, a person is not allowed to own property; private property is not permitted. The incentive to produce goods and services is hardly the same in each of the two property rights structures. Undoubtedly, the incentive to produce is greater under property rights structure X than Y. Why produce anything under Y if what you produce does not belong to you? In short, different property rights structures come with different incentives to produce. All other things equal, the property rights structures that permit individuals to own property will be more conducive to production and economic growth than those that do not.

Now consider two other property rights structures, A and B. Under both, individuals are allowed to own property. But in A, a person's private property rights are not as well protected as in B. For example, in A, the government sometimes confiscates a person's private property; in B, this never happens. Again, the incentive to produce is not the same under A and B. The more secure the private property rights are, the greater the incentive is to produce. Why produce if what you produce might be taken away from you?

Therefore, not only do private property rights matter to production and economic growth; so does the security of those private property rights.

**THE LEGAL SYSTEM** In country A, the legal system is dependable, honest, and dedicated to enforcing legitimate contracts and to protecting private property. In country B, the legal system is the polar opposite. In which country, A or B, are individuals more likely to have a greater incentive to start businesses, lend and borrow funds, invest, produce goods, and innovate—all important to the process of economic growth? Most economists would say in country A, where the legal system is dependable, honest, and sound. That conclusion becomes quickly obvious once you think of what is involved with starting a business, lending and borrowing, investing, innovating, and producing: dealing with other people. If you start a business, you will often need to deal with other people to finance the business,

## Economic Freedom and Growth Rates

Does economic freedom matter to a country's economic growth rate? There is some evidence that it does. Consider the time in which there were two Germanys: an East Germany and a West Germany. The two Germanys were much the same in terms of culture, people, climate, language, and so on, except West Germans enjoyed more economic freedom than East Germans. Did this major difference between the two Germanys matter to economic growth? Most economists answer yes. Between 1950 and 1991, the average annual growth rate in East Germany was 1.3 percent; in West Germany it was 4.4 percent.

© BLICKWINKEL / ALAMY

The same sort of difference holds between North Korea and South Korea. South Korea permits much more economic freedom than North Korea. Does this difference affect economic growth rates? During the second half of the twentieth century, the average annual growth rate in South Korea was more than three times higher than in North Korea.

The evidence from the two Koreas and two Germanys tells us that economic freedom does matter to economic growth, especially when other factors (that matter to growth) are much the same between the countries.

But when the other factors are not the same, problems arise. Suppose country A has less economic freedom than country B. Will country A grow less than country B during the next 5 or 10 years? Not necessarily. The economic growth rate in a country could depend on the economic base from which the growth emanates. Suppose that country A has a Real GDP of $10 billion, that country B has a Real GDP of $100 billion, and that Real GDP grows by $2 billion in both countries. The economic growth rate in country A (the country with less economic freedom) is 20 percent, but the economic growth rate in country B (the country with more economic freedom) is only 2 percent. Does it follow that economic freedom is a hindrance to economic growth? Not at all. It may simply look that way because something different between the two countries—namely, the economic base from which growth emanates—isn't being considered.

to hire workers, to buy from suppliers, and so on. In your dealings with other people, you need to be assured that your agreements (or contracts) with them are upheld and enforced and that others cannot steal from you and get away with it. This is why the legal system is important to economic growth. A legal system that is dependable, honest, and dedicated to enforcing legitimate contracts, and protecting private property reduces the transaction costs of dealing with others, thus providing individuals with a greater incentive to engage in activities conducive to economic growth.

### GROWTH-PROMOTING POLICIES VERSUS TRANSFER-PROMOTING POLICIES

Consider two types of economic policies: growth-promoting policies and transfer-promoting policies. A growth-promoting policy increases Real GDP; it enlarges the size of the economic pie. A transfer-promoting policy leaves the size of the economic pie unchanged, but it increases the size of the slice that one group gets relative to another.

## Religious Beliefs and Economic Growth

*For given religious beliefs, increases in church attendance tend to reduce economic growth. In contrast, for given church attendance, increases in some religious beliefs—notably heaven, hell, and an afterlife—tend to increase economic growth.*

*—Robert Barro and Rachel McCleary[2]*

Economists have been studying economic growth for more than 200 years. Some of the questions they have asked and tried to answer are:

- Why are some nations rich and others poor?
- What causes economic growth?
- Why do some nations grow faster than others?

Of the causes of economic growth discussed in this chapter, we do not include cultural determinants. Yet some economic researchers argue that explanations for economic growth should be broadened to include cultural determinants. Culture may influence personal traits, they argue, which may in turn affect economic growth. For example, personal traits such as honesty, thriftiness, the willingness to work hard, and openness to strangers may be related to economic growth.

Two Harvard economists, Robert Barro and Rachel McCleary, have analyzed one such cultural determinant: the role of religion in economic growth. Their work was based partly on the World Values Survey, which looked at a representative sample of people in 66 countries on all six inhabited continents between 1981 and 1997. The survey asked at least 1,000 people in each country about their basic values and beliefs: What is their religious affiliation? How often do they attend a religious service? Were they raised religiously or not?

Barro and McCleary found that economic growth corresponds negatively with church attendance (nations with a high rate of attendance at religious services grow more slowly than those with lower rates of attendance) but positively with religious beliefs in heaven, hell, and an afterlife. Specifically, in countries where the belief in heaven, hell, and an afterlife is strong, the growth of gross domestic product runs about 0.5 percent higher than average. (This result takes into account other factors that influence growth rates, such as education.) Perhaps more telling, the belief in hell matters more to economic growth than the belief in heaven. Barro and McCleary suggest that religious beliefs stimulate growth because they help to sustain aspects of individual behavior that enhance productivity.

2. Robert Barro and Rachel McCleary, "Religion and Economic Growth (NBER Working paper No. 9682).

For example, suppose group A, a special interest group, currently gets 1/1,000 of the economic pie, and the economic pie is $1,000. The group gets a $1 slice. Group A wants to get more than a $1 slice, and it can do so in one of two ways. The first is to lobby for a policy that increases the size of its slice of the economic pie. In other words, group A gets a larger slice (say, a $2 slice) at the expense of someone else's getting a smaller slice. Alternatively, group A can lobby for a policy that increases the size of the pie—say, from $1,000 to $1,500. In this case, group A gets not the full increase of $500, but 1/1,000 of the increase, or 50¢. So group A has to decide whether it is better to lobby for a growth-promoting policy (where it gets 1/1,000 of any increase in Real GDP) or for a transfer-promoting policy (where it gets 100 percent of any transfer).

According to Mancur Olson, in *The Rise and Decline of Nations*, special interest groups are more likely to argue for transfer-promoting policies than growth-promoting policies, and the cost–benefit calculation of each policy is the reason.[3] This behavior affects economic growth in that the more special interest groups there are in a country, the more likely it is that transfer-promoting policies will be lobbied for instead of growth-promoting policies. Individuals will try to get a larger slice of a constant-sized economic pie rather than trying to increase the size of the pie. In short, numerous and politically strong special interest groups are detrimental to economic growth.

3. Mancur Olson, *The Rise and Decline of Nations* (New Haven, CT, and London: Yale University Press, 1982).

**OTHER INSTITUTIONS**   Other institutions are often mentioned as conducive to economic growth: open and competitive markets, free (international) trade, policies that promote economic freedom, a stable monetary system, unburdensome taxes and regulations, and a strong and effective educational system.

## SELF-TEST

(Answers to Self-Test questions are in Answers to Self-Test Questions at the back of the book.)

1. Explain how a decline in taxes that affects the labor market can end up shifting the *LRAS* curve to the right.

2. What is the difference between physical and human capital?

3. What is the difference between neoclassical growth theory and new growth theory with respect to technology?

4. In the production function specified in Exhibit 2(a), what variable(s) are movement factors (will move us along the production function)? What variable(s) are shift factors (will shift the production function)?

# OFFICE HOURS

## "What Is the Difference Between Business Cycle Macroeconomics and Economic Growth Macroeconomics?"

**STUDENT:**

I am searching for a way to put the macroeconomics in this chapter in perspective with the macroeconomics in the other chapters. Can you help?

**INSTRUCTOR:**

In most of the previous chapters, the *LRAS* curve did not move. It was fixed at some Natural Real GDP level. In this chapter, we discussed the factors that can shift the *LRAS* curve; we discussed how the economy can move from one Real GDP level to a higher Real GDP level. This was obvious in all the exhibits.

Let me add some economic terminology to the discussion. In previous chapers we mainly discussed business cycle macroeconomics. In this chapter we discussed economic growth macroeconomics.

**STUDENT:**

Specifically, what does business cycle macroeconomics deal with?

**INSTRUCTOR:**

It deals with two things: (1) differences between Real GDP and Natural Real GDP and (2) ways of moving the economy to its Natural Real GDP level. Suppose Natural Real GDP is $11 trillion and the current Real GDP in the economy is $10 trillion. Obviously, since Real GDP is less than Natural Real GDP, the economy is in a recessionary gap. If the economy is self-regulating, it will eventually move to its Natural Real GDP level. If it is not self-regulating, then perhaps monetary or fiscal policy can be used to move the economy to its Natural Real GDP level.

**STUDENT:**

How does business cycle macroeconomics differ from what was discussed in this chapter?

**INSTRUCTOR:**

In this chapter, we mainly discussed economic growth. This topic deals with the economy moving from one Natural Real GDP level to a higher one—specifically, how the economy might move from a Natural Real GDP level of, say, $11 trillion to a higher Natural Real GDP level of, say, $11.7 trillion.

**STUDENT:**

Does it follow that when we're discussing how the economy moves from one Natural Real GDP level to a higher one, we are simultaneously discussing rightward shifts in the *LRAS* curve?

**INSTRUCTOR:**

Yes, that's correct. In fact, let's define business cycle macroeconomics and economic growth macroeconomics with respect to the *LRAS* curve. Business cycle macroeconomics deals with economic activity occurring around a single *LRAS* curve. Economic growth macroeconomics (starting from an efficient level of production) deals with rightward shifts in the *LRAS* curve.

### POINTS TO REMEMBER

1. Business cycle macroeconomics deals with economic activity occurring around a single *LRAS* curve (or around a specific Natural Real GDP level).
2. Economic growth macroeconomics (starting from an efficient level of production) deals with rightward shifts in the *LRAS* curve (or moving from a lower to a higher level of Natural Real GDP).

## CHAPTER SUMMARY

### ECONOMIC GROWTH

- Absolute real economic growth refers to an increase in Real GDP from one period to the next.
- Per-capita real economic growth refers to an increase from one period to the next in per-capita Real GDP, which is Real GDP divided by population.

### THE PRODUCTION FUNCTION

- A production function specifies the relation between technology and the quantity of factor inputs to output or Real GDP.
- Real GDP = $T(L, K)$. This production function specifies that Real GDP or output is a function of technology—as evidenced in the technology coefficient, $T$—labor ($L$), and (physical) capital ($K$). Another production function is Real GDP = $T(L, K, NR, H)$. This production function specifies that Real GDP or output is a function of technology—as evidenced in the technology coefficient, $T$—labor ($L$), (physical) capital ($K$), natural resources ($NR$), and human capital ($H$).

### THE PRODUCTION FUNCTION AND ECONOMIC GROWTH

- Using the production function Real GDP = $T(L, K)$, we know that increases in $T$, $L$, and $K$ will raise Real GDP and that decreases in $T$, $L$, and $K$ decrease Real GDP. Also, changes in Real GDP, as a result of changes in $T$, $L$, and $K$, will lead to shifts in the *LRAS* curve. For example, a rise in $K$ will raise Real GDP, leading to a rightward shift in the *LRAS* curve.

- A change in taxes affects the supply of labor of supply curve, thus leading to a change in the amount of labor employed in the labor market. In turn, this change in the amount of labor employed leads to a change in Real GDP and to a shift in the *LRAS* curve. See Exhibit 4.
- How much capital is employed in the production process depends on such things as the tax treatment of capital's returns and interest rates.

### NEW GROWTH THEORY

- New growth theory holds that technology is endogenous; neoclassical growth theory holds that technology is exogenous. When something is endogenous, it is part of the economic system, under our control or influence. When something is exogenous, it is not part of the system; it is assumed to be given to us, often mysteriously through a process that we do not understand.
- According to Paul Romer, discovering and implementing new ideas are what causes economic growth.
- Certain institutions can promote the discovery of new ideas and therefore promote economic growth.

### ECONOMIC GROWTH AND SPECIAL INTEREST GROUPS

- According to Mancur Olson, the more special interest groups a country has, the more likely it is that transfer-promoting policies will be lobbied for instead of growth-promoting policies. Individuals will try to get a larger slice of a constant-size economic pie rather than trying to increase the size of the pie.

## KEY TERMS AND CONCEPTS

| | | | |
|---|---|---|---|
| Absolute Real Economic Growth | Per-Capita Real Economic Growth | Production Function Human Capital | Institution |

## QUESTIONS AND PROBLEMS

1. Why might per-capita real economic growth be a more useful measurement than absolute real economic growth?
2. Identify how changes in $L$, $K$, and $T$ can lead to changes in output or Real GDP.
3. What does it mean to say that "a change in labor moves us along a given production function"?
4. What do interest rates and the tax treatment of the returns to capital have to do with economic growth?
5. What is *new* about new growth theory?
6. How does discovering and implementing new ideas cause economic growth?

7. What is the difference between business cycle macroeconomics and economic growth macroeconomics?
8. What is an institution? Why might institutions matter to how much economic growth a country experiences?
9. Some property rights structures provide more and stronger incentives to produce goods and services than other such structures do. Do you agree or disagree with this statement? Explain your answer.
10. Why might special interest groups favor transfer-promoting policies over growth-promoting policies?

## WORKING WITH NUMBERS AND GRAPHS

1. The economy of country $X$ is currently growing at 2 percent a year. How many years will it take to double the Real GDP of country $X$?

2. Explain numerically how an advance in technology can lead to more output or Real GDP.

3. A rise in physical capital can raise Real GDP and lead to a rightward shift in the *LRAS* curve. Show this diagrammatically.

4. A change in the labor market can change the equilibrium amount of labor employed, thus leading to a change in Real GDP and to a shift in the *LRAS* curve. Show this diagrammatically.

## CHAPTER 18

# THE FINANCIAL CRISIS OF 2007–2009

AP PHOTO/SUSAN WALSH, FILE

**Introduction** Every now and then, a major economic event takes center stage in the news. The most recent such event occurred in September and October of 2008, when people throughout the United States first learned of a financial crisis. For weeks, the talk in the country was of banks and other financial institutions, mortgage-backed securities and collateralized debt obligations, leverage, subprime loans, and who did what when. This chapter is about the events leading up to September and October of 2008 and beyond.

## RECENT ECONOMIC EVENTS

To understand recent economic events, first consider an economy as consisting of two sectors: the financial sector and the real sector. The financial sector consists of financial institutions: commercial banks, investment banks, hedge funds, brokerage firms, and others. The real sector consists of firms that produce goods and services, individuals who buy goods and services, and individuals who work for firms, among others.

To a large extent, the financial sector deals with borrowing and lending activities. It takes money that is saved and lends it out. Within the financial sector are financial intermediaries, which are firms that bring borrowers and lenders together. If company X is a financial intermediary, people go to X and deposit their savings. Then X lends out the savings to others. In other words, it grants loans to people using the money other people have saved.

During the period 2007–2009, a financial crisis hit the United States. A financial crisis occurs when financial firms and financial markets undergo a major disruption, making it difficult for persons to obtain loans from banks and other financial institutions. Problems contributing to the financial crisis included people not paying back the loans they took out from the banks, depositors becoming afraid that their deposits were not safe at the banks and en masse trying to withdraw them, banks having a hard time getting loans from other banks, and banks finding themselves with declining asset values, moving them toward insolvency (when their liabilities are greater than their assets).

Problems in the financial sector can bleed over into the real sector, producing problems, such as decreased borrowing and lending, decreased economic activity, a decline in

**Financial Intermediary**
A firm that transfers funds from those who want to lend funds to those who want to borrow funds.

**Insolvency**
The condition when liabilities are greater than assets.

sales, a rise in unemployment, and much more. In other words, if the financial sector gets sick, that sickness can do harm to the real sector. That is what happened in the United States in the crisis of 2007–2009. A crisis in the financial sector adversely affected the real sector of the U.S. economy.

The problems in both the financial and real sectors of the economy have called forth certain government programs. Some have been designed to affect the financial sector, such as the *Troubled Asset Relief Program* (TARP), popularly referred to as part of the financial bailout. Some programs have been designed to affect the real sector, such as the $787 billion fiscal stimulus bill (expansionary fiscal policy). In addition, the Federal Reserve recently played a role in trying to deal with the problems in both the financial and real sectors.

Thus, the financial crisis in this country has affected the real sector of the economy, evoking a response from Congress and the Fed, directed at addressing the problems in both the financial and real sectors of the economy.

The rest of this chapter is about the financial crisis, the real sector crisis, and the actions of the Congress and the Federal Reserve. In short, it is about the 2007–2009 economic events and government actions directed at the economy. Within that general discussion, we will discuss the causes and effects of the financial crisis.

## THE FINANCIAL CRISIS AS A BALANCE SHEET PROBLEM

**Balance Sheet**
A record of the assets and liabilities of a bank.

**Asset**
Anything owned or that one has claim to that has value.

**Liability**
Anything that is owed to someone else.

**Net Worth (or Capital)**
The difference between assets and liabilities. For example, if assets are $100 and liabilities are $80, net worth, or capital, is $20.

Financial institutions have balance sheets consisting of assets, liabilities, and net worth (or capital). For a financial institution, an asset is anything that has value and that generates a flow of income. For example, suppose a commercial bank makes a loan to you for $40,000. You agree to pay $1,200 a month on the loan for so many months. Your loan is an *asset* as far as the bank is concerned. That loan has value to the bank and generates a flow of income for the bank, specifically, $1,200 a month.

A liability (for the bank) is something that it owes. For example, suppose you go to your local bank and open up a checking account. You deposit $5,000 into the account. Your deposit is the bank's *liability*. The bank owes you the $5,000. Another way of looking at that deposit is to say that you are lending the money to the bank. With that $5,000, the bank will make a loan to someone else. It will pay you 3 percent on your deposit, and then lend it to someone else for, say, 4.5 percent.

Let's say the bank has $100 in assets and $80 in liabilities. The difference between its assets and its liabilities is its net worth, or capital: $20. One way to view capital is as a buffer against insolvency. Suppose that the bank initially has assets of $100 and liabilities of $80. Then the value of its assets falls to $85. This might happen if people to whom the bank lent money do not pay it back. The bank can survive this $15 loss in the value of its assets because the capital of $20 cushioned the blow. The value of the bank's assets would have to fall enough to wipe out the entire capital amount before the bank is deemed insolvent. In other words, a $15 decline in asset value wouldn't do it, but a $21 decline would.

The financial crisis can be viewed as a *balance sheet problem*. Many financial firms had assets on their balance sheets that declined in value. As these assets lost value, some financial institutions found themselves insolvent; other financial institutions found themselves coming perilously close to insolvency.

When a financial institution is either insolvent or close to insolvency, the real sector in the economy is affected. If the institution is insolvent, it can go out of the lending business, reducing the amount of lending in the economy. With less lending (and consequently less borrowing), there is less economic activity, which can show up as less buying and less producing. Less buying and producing can, in turn, result in firms going out of business, people getting fired from their jobs, and so on. Even if a bank isn't insolvent but is simply close, it could simply pull back on its lending activities, thereby reducing economic activity in the real sector of the economy.

There are other consequences. As a bank becomes insolvent or close to insolvent, it may find that one of two things happen. First, people may not want to deposit funds in the bank. After all, if a bank is having a problem paying off its liabilities, why put your money there. If you put your money in that bank today, it might not be able to pay you back tomorrow. Also, knowing that a bank is likely to become insolvent, depositors in that bank might make a *run* on it. They might think that if the bank is having a hard time paying off its liabilities, isn't it better for me to be one of the first people the bank pays off? There might not be enough money to pay everyone off.

Part of the run-on-the-bank problem these days is mitigated by the Federal Deposit Insurance Corporation (FDIC). The FDIC insures deposits in banks up to $250,000 per depositor. This insurance cuts down on people running to banks to get their money out if they think the bank is having problems. But it does so at the cost of pushing banks into taking a little more risk than they might take on if deposits weren't insured by the FDIC. To illustrate, if depositors' money is insured by the federal government, the bank knows that it isn't as likely to see a lot of people asking for their money all at once. This environment makes it less likely that the bank will worry about having to pay off all its depositors at once. Consequently, the banks may make riskier loans (riskier loans come with higher expected returns) than it would if its liabilities (specifically, its depositors' deposits) were not insured. But, of course, making riskier loans may raise the probability that the bank will become insolvent. After all, riskier loans do not get paid back as often as less risky loans.

## Thinking Like AN ECONOMIST

**Unintended Effects** Economists know that actions can have both intended and unintended effects. The intended effect of insuring bank deposits is to reduce bank runs. The unintended effect is to push banks into taking on more risk than they would have if bank deposits were not insured. ▰ ● ●

## Which Assets Were Risky?

The assets on the banks' balance sheets that lost value because they turned out to be risky were the *subprime mortgage loans*, other nontraditional mortgage loans, *mortgage-backed securities* (MBS), and *collateralized debt obligations* (CDOs).

Subprime mortgage loans and other nontraditional mortgage loans fall into the same category. They are mortgage loans granted to persons who might have low credit ratings or some other factors that suggest they could default on the debt repayment. Anyone who is not paying for a house with cash has to take out a mortgage loan. Mortgage loans often come with certain restrictions. They might specify that a borrower must make a down payment equal to the a specified percentage (say, 10 percent) of the purchase price of the house, that he needs a certain dollar income, that he has a good credit history, and so on. Generally speaking, mortgage lending practices were stricter in the 1970s and 1980s than they were in the late 1990s and early 2000s. In other words, lending practices loosened up in the latter years. A drastic loosening is reflected in subprime and other nontraditional mortgage loans. With subprime loans, loans were being given out to persons who could not have qualified for traditional loans (with larger down payments, better documentation of income, and so on).

Mortgage-backed securities (MBS) are a type of asset-backed security that is secured by a mortgage or collection of mortgages. Here is how an MBS is created. Bank A has made 5,000 mortgage loans, some of which are subprime and other nontraditional loans. It bundles all 5,000 loans into a package, which consists of the expected future payments that

**Subprime Mortgage Loan**
A nontraditional mortgage loan granted to persons who might have low credit ratings or some other factors that suggest they could default on the debt repayment.

**Mortgage-Backed Securities (MBS)**
A type of asset-backed security that is secured by a mortgage or collection of mortgages.

will be made on the 5,000 loans. For example, one of the 5,000 loans was made to Smith, who pays $2,400 a month on her mortgage loan. The bank cuts up the package of 5,000 loans into slices and sells them; these slices are the mortgage-backed securities themselves. Thus, they are called mortgage-backed securities because they are backed by (or composed of) mortgage loans. For example, if you buy a slice that represents 1/1,000 of the pool of mortgages, then what you will receive is 1/1,000 of the payments made on the 5,000 loans in the pool.

*Collateralized debt obligations* (CDOs) are like mortgage-backed securities, except that the slices are not equal. Some people who hold certain slices get paid before other people with other slices. These are called *tranches*, which are simply slices with different risk.

What is important is that the value of an MBS and a CDO depends on the people who are paying off their mortgage loans. If a lot of people do not pay off their loans, then the MBSs and CDOs lose their value. Look at it this way. You buy a slice of an MBS for $10,000, which entitles you to a payment of $500 a month for *x* number of years. What happens to your payments of $500 a month if the borrowers do not pay off their mortgage loans? All of a sudden, you do not receive the payments you thought you were going to receive, and your MBS is worthless.

In 2006, some people with subprime and other nontraditional loans were not able to make their monthly payments on their mortgage loans. (We explain why later.) As a result, banks and other financial institutions experienced a decline in the value of their assets: the subprime loans, other nontraditional loans, MBSs, and CDOs listed as assets on their balance sheets. As the value declined, some banks and financial institutions slid into insolvency, and others were coming ever closer to insolvency.

## Three Questions

At this point, the story of the financial crisis goes in different directions, which are related to three questions:

- Why were many of the people who had taken out subprime and other nontraditional loans unable to make their monthly payments?

- Why did traditional lending give way to subprime and other nontraditional lending?

- Why didn't the banks and other financial institutions have a bigger capital buffer (against insolvency) when they found themselves with loans that were not being paid off and MBSs and CDOs that were losing their value?

The answer to the first question has to do with the housing market. Related to the housing market is a discussion of the Fed and its monetary policy and a global savings glut.

The answer to the second question relates to Congress, two presidents, Fannie Mae and Freddie Mac, and securitization.

The answer to the third question relates to leverage and regulatory capital arbitrage.

---

### SELF-TEST

(Answers to Self-Test questions are in Answers to Self-Test Questions at the back of the book.)

1. Explain how the net worth, or capital, of a bank can act as a buffer against insolvency.

2. Explain how a decline in a bank's assets values could lead to less lending activity.

3. What is a financial crisis?

# THE FED, INTEREST RATES, AND HOUSING PRICES

We know that the Fed sets a target for the federal funds rate, which is the interest rate banks charge each other for loans. For example, if bank A wants to borrow $4 million from bank B, it would pay bank B the federal funds rate for the loan.

Now the Fed does not set the federal funds rate by edict. Instead it undertakes certain monetary actions so that the market federal funds rate equals its federal funds rate target. To illustrate, if the current market federal funds rate is 5 percent and the Fed's target federal funds rate is 3 percent, the Fed will inject reserves into the banking system so that the federal funds rate falls to 3 percent.

Exhibit 1 shows the federal funds rate for the period from a little before 2001 to 2007. In January of 2001, the federal funds rate was 6 percent, but it was much lower at 1.75 percent in December 2001. During the period 2002–2005, it is in the 1–2 percent range. Then, in June 2006, the federal funds rate rises to 5.25 percent. What is behind the decline in the federal funds rate, some argue, is that, beginning in 2001, the Fed dramatically lowered its federal funds rate target. That target is especially low during the period 2002–2005.

The Fed pursued such a low federal funds rate target because it believed that if the federal funds

**EXHIBIT 1**

**The Federal Funds Rate for Various Years**

The federal funds rate starts out relatively high in early 2001 and then starts to decline. The federal funds rate is in the 1–2 percent category in 2002–2005.

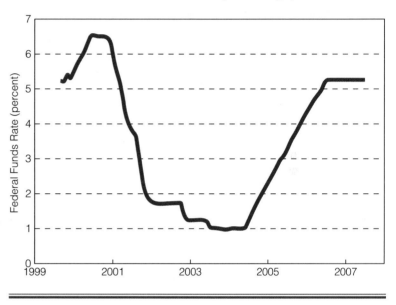

rate decreased, so would other interest rates in the economy (especially short-term rates). And the Fed wanted to lower interest rates in the economy for a number of reasons. It was trying to stimulate economic activity. It was afraid that if it didn't nudge interest rates down, the economy might fall into a recession. And it seemed to be worried about deflation.

The specific reason for the low interest rate policy is not as important as the fact that a low interest rate policy had certain effects. One major effect is that the Fed's low federal fund targets led to a decline in mortgage interest rates. Here is the process. When the Fed lowers its federal funds rate target, it ends up injecting reserves into the banking system to bring the actual federal funds rate down to its new lower target level. As a byproduct of more reserves in the banking system, banks can make more loans—such as mortgage loans. Thus, mortgage rates decline. When mortgage rates decline, more people take out mortgage loans to buy houses; it is cheaper to buy a house when mortgage rates are low than when they are high. Another effect is that people take out bigger loans than they would have taken out at higher interest rates.

So the Fed's low federal funds rate target policy made it possible for more people to take out mortgage loans. But more people with loans—and some people with bigger loans—added demand to the housing market. As demand in the housing market rose, so did housing prices.

## The Global Savings Glut and Low Interest Rates

At this point in our story, some economists mention the "global savings glut" as an alternative explanation for lower interest rates. A *global savings glut* describes an excess of savings over investment. Emerging countries in the world began to save more, and much

**EXHIBIT 2**

**Global Savings and Investment as a Percentage of World GDP**

Global savings is a smaller percentage of World GDP in the period 2002–2004 than it was in the 1970s and 1980s. John Taylor has argued that the data here are more nearly representative of a savings shortage during the period 2002–2004 than a savings glut.

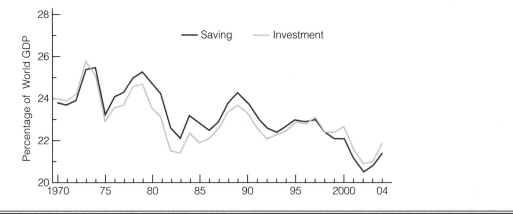

of the extra savings found its way to the United States, where it increased the supply of loanable funds and lowered interest rates. The increased supply of loanable funds played a role in the housing story, in which low mortgage interest rates were already leading to greater borrowing to buy houses and rising house prices.

Some economists have questioned whether there was a global savings glut. One in particular is John Taylor of Stanford University. Taylor makes a major point with the help of Exhibit 2, which is from an International Monetary Fund study that shows global savings and global investment as a share of World GDP for different years. For example, global investment is approximately 22 percent of World GDP in 2004, and savings is slightly over 21 percent of World GDP in the same year. The point that Taylor makes is that global savings as a percentage of World GDP was lower in the period 2002–2004 than it was in 1970s and 1980s. Yet interest rates in the United States were low in the period 2002–2004. In other words, low interest rates in the United States correspond to the time when savings as a percentage of World GDP is low. But one would have thought that low interest rates would have corresponded to a time when savings as percentage of World GDP was high, not low.

If emerging and developing countries supposedly sent their excess savings to the United States, in the process lowering interest rates, what did their savings and investment look like as percentages of GDP? Exhibit 3(a) shows that the savings rate as a percentage of emerging countries' GDP rose during the period from 2002 to 2008. According to the global savings glut story, we would expect that the rising savings rate in emerging countries would lower interest rates in the United States. Yet look at the mortgage rates in the United States [Exhibit 3(b)] on a 30-year mortgage during the period 1998–2009. Specifically, during the period 2000–2008—the period in which savings rates in emerging countries were rising—mortgage rates fell from 2000 to 2003. They stayed low during the period 2003 to 2005, and then they began to rise. In other words, the rising savings rate in emerging countries is consistent with both *falling* and *rising* mortgage interest rates, not simply with lowering interest rates.

## Our Story So Far

So far, we know that the banks had balance sheet problems. When the assets on their balance sheets began to decline in value (especially the subprime loans, MBSs, and CDOs), some banks became insolvent and other banks came critically close to insolvency. As a

| EXHIBIT 3 |
| --- |

**Savings and Investment Rates and 30-Year Conventional Mortgage Rates, Various Years**

(a) Savings and investment in emerging and developing countries as a percentage of the GDP in these countries. (b) The 30-year conventional mortgage rate for various years.

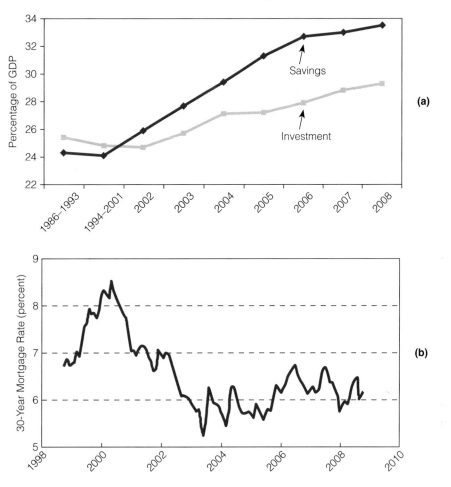

result, banks pulled back their lending, and the reduction in lending adversely affected the real sector of the economy. What we do not yet know is *why* the people who had taken out subprime and other nontraditional loans could not pay back their loans, thus adversely affecting the values of MBSs and CDOs. To explain that part of the story, we need to know more about low interest rates and the housing price boom. This takes us to a discussion of the Taylor rule.

# THE TAYLOR RULE AND INTEREST RATES

As mentioned in earlier chapters, the Taylor rule is a monetary rule of sorts; it is a recommendation of how the Fed should set its federal funds rate target. Essentially, it says that the Fed should raise the federal funds interest rate when inflation increases and lower it when GDP declines. It specifies how much the federal funds rate should change in different circumstances.

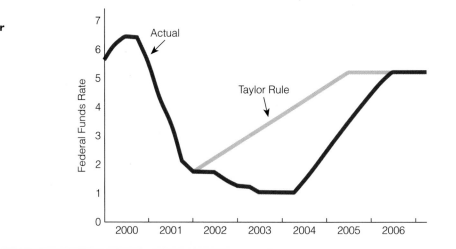

**EXHIBIT 4**

**Federal Funds Rate, Actual and Consistent with the Taylor Rule, Various Years**

The actual federal funds rate and the federal funds rate consistent with the Taylor rule for various years.

According to John Taylor (for whom the Taylor rule is named), during the period 2002–early 2006, the Fed set its federal funds rate target too low. He concludes this by comparing the actual federal funds rate with the rate that would have existed had the Fed set its target according to the Taylor rule. Exhibit 4 shows that the federal funds rate would have been higher during the specified period had the Fed implemented the Taylor rule. Taylor concludes that, when we compare actual Fed monetary policy with the Taylor rule monetary policy, the Fed's policy was "too expansionary" during the period in question. It is this deviation from the Taylor rule that Taylor believes brought about the "too low" interest rates that led to rising house prices in the United States. Is Taylor correct? One piece of evidence in his favor is that there is a strong correlation between a housing boom in different countries (where housing boom is defined in terms of housing investment as a percentage of GDP) and deviations from the Taylor rule. For example, within OECD countries, the countries whose monetary policies deviated most from the Taylor rule had bigger housing booms than those countries whose monetary policies deviated less from the Taylor rule.[1] However, a study by Federal Reserve staff that takes into account more than the OECD countries contradicts that finding, indicating that deviations from the Taylor rule are not correlated with housing prices.

## Alan Greenspan Responds

Alan Greenspan was chair of the Federal Reserve from 1987 to 2006. He has argued in favor of the global savings glut explanation for the decline in interest rates and against the position held by John Taylor. Greenspan argues that the Taylor rule is not really a fail-safe monetary rule for the Fed to follow because it cannot be applied to asset prices (such as house prices). Greenspan's argument is essentially: (1) John Taylor uses the Taylor rule to argue that the Fed held interest rates too low during the early 2000s. In other words, if the Fed had set monetary policy using the Taylor rule during that period, interest rates wouldn't have been too low, and there wouldn't have been a housing boom. (2) But, says Greenspan, the Taylor rule is structured in such a way as to indicate a proper federal funds rate target necessary to balance the trade-off between inflation and unemployment. And the type of inflation that the Taylor rule addresses is *product-price inflation,* not *asset-price*

---

1. OECD stands for Organization for Economic Co-operation and Development, with 30 member countries: Australia, Austria, Belgium, Canada, Czech Republic, Denmark, Finland, France, Germany, Greece, Hungary, Iceland, Ireland, Italy, Japan, Korea, Luxembourg, Mexico, the Netherlands, New Zealand, Norway, Poland, Portugal, Slovak Republic, Spain, Sweden, Switzerland, Turkey, United Kingdom, and the United States.

*inflation* (such as house price inflation). (3) So, unless there is a strong correlation between the consumer price index (CPI) and house prices—and Greenspan says there isn't—then the Taylor rule is *inappropriate* to use when trying to figure out the causes of sharp increases in house prices.

Greenspan has also argued that the boom in housing was caused by low long-term interest rates (such as the 30-year fixed mortgage rate), not short-term interest rates. Moreover, he argues that the Fed has much more control over short-term interest rates (such as the federal funds rate) than over long-term interest rates. Greenspan notes:

> In the United States, the house price bubble was driven by the low level of the 30 year fixed rate mortgage that decline from its mid-2000 peak, six months prior to the FOMC (Federal Open Market Committee) easing of the federal funds rate in January, 2001.[2]

## Rising House Prices, Delinquency Rates, and Foreclosures

During the period 2003–2005, housing prices were rising. But during the same period, delinquency rates (on adjustable rate mortgages, whose interest rate is adjusted periodically depending on various factors) and foreclosure rates were falling. In other words, as house prices were rising, more people were paying off their mortgages loans and fewer people were being foreclosed upon. There is perhaps a good reason for the inverse relationship between housing prices and delinquency and foreclosure rates. When house prices are rising, home owners are gaining equity in their homes. Equity is the difference between the price the house can be sold for and what one owes on the house. To illustrate, if you owe $500,000 on a house and the price of the house is $600,000, you have $100,000 in equity. If the price of the house rises to $650,000, your equity rises to $150,000. When housing prices decline, the benefits of holding on to a house decline. In particular, if the price of the house falls below the value of the mortgage loan (if, for instance, the house can be sold for no more than, say, $480,000 and the mortgage loan is $500,000), some people will not pay off their loans.

Looking at delinquency and foreclosure rates only during a period of rising prices can give a false picture of the risks inherent in giving out mortgage loans. To illustrate, suppose that, during years 1–10, house prices are falling, while delinquency and foreclosure rates are up. During years 11–20, house prices are rising, while delinquency and foreclosure rates are down. Suppose a lender who is considering giving out mortgage loans in year 21 looks only at years 11–20 to get some idea of how risky mortgage loans are. The lender might come away thinking they are not risky at all (because delinquency and foreclosure rates are relatively low). But the picture is very different for years 1–10 and even more different for the period of years 1–20. The point is that, if lenders during the early 2000s were looking only at recent past behavior in delinquency and foreclosure rates when deciding how risky mortgage loans are, then they *underestimated* the risk of mortgage loans. The mortgage loans they were giving out were riskier than they thought they were.

So, if the low interest rate policy of the Fed pushed up home prices, it also led to lower delinquency and foreclosure rates. Lenders, who perhaps were viewing less than the complete time span of delinquency and foreclosure rates, then mistakenly thought that granting mortgage loans was a less risky business than it was. With the benefit of hindsight, we now know that too many risky mortgage loans ended up being made. Hence the subprime loans, the MBSs, and the CDOs, and eventually the declining asset values on banks' balance sheets.

**Adjustable Rate Mortgage**
A mortgage loan where the interest rate on the loan is adjusted periodically depending on various factors.

**Equity (in a House)**
The difference between the price the house can be sold for and what one owes on the house.

---

**SELF-TEST**

1. What is the global-savings-glut explanation of rising housing prices? What is the Fed-low-interest-rate explanation of rising housing prices?

2. According to John Taylor, who or what caused the boom in housing prices in the United States in the early 2000s?

---

2. *The Crisis*, by Alan Greenspan, Second Draft: March 9, 2010.

# THE POLITICS OF HOUSING

Mortgage lending standards in the United States declined in the 1990s and early 2000s. To understand why, we need to compare traditional and nontraditional lending practices. In traditional lending, borrowers must provide proof of income, employment, and assets. In nontraditional lending, borrowers may not be asked to provide proof of income, employment, and assets. Also, in traditional lending, down payments are a larger percentage of the house being purchased than in nontraditional lending. For example, a typical down payment in traditional mortgage lending is 20 percent. In nontraditional mortgage lending it could be 2–5 percent.

In the 1990s and early 2000s, the mortgage market saw a change in the composition of mortgage lending—away from more traditional lending and toward more nontraditional lending. For example, many lenders waived requirements that borrowers document their incomes, assets, and employment information and required down payments of only 2 or 3 percent or, in some cases, 0 percent.

Why lending practices declined makes for an interesting story that tells what was going on in both the private sector and in government. In this section, we talk about what was going on in government, especially as it relates to the politics of housing.

## The Community Reinvestment Act

The Community Reinvestment Act (CRA) was passed in 1977. Its purpose was to encourage financial institutions to meet the needs of borrowers in all segments of their communities, including low- and moderate-income borrowers. In 1995, Congress revised the CRA to give banks a stronger incentive to increase the percentage of mortgage loans (among other loans) going to low- and moderate-income borrowers. Some have argued that Congress was essentially imposing quotas on banks to apply "innovative or flexible" standards to meet the borrowing needs of these borrowers. Some have argued that essentially the CRA forced banks to relax lending standards so that they could make loans that they otherwise would not have made. Some take a different position, arguing that banks did not have to give out loans they didn't want to. However, banks that were not in compliance with CRA could find their applications for new branches, mergers, or acquisitions denied. According to economist Thomas Sowell:

> . . . when legislation was pending in 1999 to permit banks to diversify into selling investment securities, the White House urged "that banks given unsatisfactory ratings under the 1977 Community Reinvestment Act be prohibited from enjoying the new diversification privileges" of this legislation. Accordingly, when Congress passed legislation removing existing prohibitions against banks affiliating with securities or insurance firms, this new scope of banking operations was in fact reserved for those banks that had a "satisfactory record of meeting community credit needs or better, at the most recent examination of each such institution"—that is, banks that met government-imposed quotas.[3]

# FANNIE MAE AND FREDDIE MAC

Fannie Mae (Federal National Mortgage Association, FNMA) came into existence in 1938 to add demand to the housing market. Specifically, Fannie Mae would buy mortgage loans from banks that had originated the loans. For example, bank A might make a mortgage loan to a borrower and then sell the mortgage loan to Fannie Mae, in the process receiving funds from Fannie Mae with which to create more mortgages. In 1970, Freddie Mac (Federal Home Loan Mortgage Corporation, FHLMC) was established to do much the same things as Fannie Mae.

---

3. Thomas Sowell, *The Housing Boom and Bust* (New York: Basic Books, 2010), p. 39.

Fannie Mae and Freddie Mac got the money they used to buy the mortgage loans from banks in a number of ways. One way was to borrow it. Another way was by creating mortgage-backed securities and then selling them. (They also insured them.) Suppose an MBS issued by Fannie Mae includes the loan repayments of 10,000 mortgage loans, and 100 of them are not repaid. Fannie Mae steps in and pays off those loans, but to do so, Fannie Mae has to have enough capital (net worth). In the recent financial crisis, Fannie Mae did not have enough capital to pay off all the loans that were not being repaid. Although Fannie Mae did not have explicit and formal backing from the U.S. government, many of the investors who bought the MBSs that Fannie issued thought the U.S. government would come to Fannie Mae's rescue should she need it. They were proved right. In September 2008, the U.S. government committed $200 billion (as needed on a quarterly basis) to Fannie Mae to correct any deficiencies in its net worth.

Beginning in the early 1990s, government pressure was placed on both Fannie Mae and Freddie Mac to increase their purchases of mortgages made to low- to moderate-income families. In 1996, the Department of Housing and Urban Development (HUD) stipulated that 42 percent of all mortgages purchased by Fannie Mae and Freddie Mac were to be given to individuals with incomes below the median incomes in their areas. In 1999, the quota was raised to 50 percent. In short, HUD placed pressure on Fannie and Freddie to buy nontraditional loans, and that pressure came not only from HUD, but also from key members of Congress. In 2000, Fannie bought $1.2 billion worth of subprime mortgages; in 2001, the amount rose to $9.2 billion; and in 2003, to $15 billion. In 2004, both Fannie and Freddie had spent $175 billion on subprime loans.

The buying of subprime loans by Fannie and Freddie and the emergence of MBSs backed by subprime loans created a market in subprime lending. Specifically, the large-scale expansion of Fannie and Freddie into the subprime loan business made it profitable for other financial institutions to grant subprime loans in order to sell them to Fannie and Freddie.

# THE ROLE OF LEVERAGE AND REGULATORY CAPITAL ARBITRAGE

In this section we discuss the role of leverage and regulatory capital arbitrage in the financial crisis.

## Leverage

Leverage is the use of borrowed funds to increase the returns that can be earned with a given amount of capital. Suppose a bank has $100 in assets (which are primarily outstanding loans), $92 in liabilities, and $8 in capital, or net worth. Its leverage ratio—the ratio of its assets to capital—is 100 to 8, or 12½ to 1.[4] Now suppose the bank's assets increase in value by 10 percent. The bank's assets are now $110, and its liabilities are still $92. The bank now has $18 worth of capital. In other words, the 10 percent increase in the value of the bank's assets has more than doubled the bank's capital (from $8 to $18). This is an increase of 125 percent.

**Leverage**
The use of borrowed funds to increase the returns that can be earned with a given amount of capital.

---

4. One can use different leverage ratios to get an idea of a firm's ability to meet its financial obligations. We have used one particular leverage ratio in our discussion here.

Now change the example. Suppose the bank borrows $5 so that its liabilities rise to $97. Now the bank has only $3 in capital. Its leverage ratio rises from 100 to 8 (12½ to 1) to 100 to 3 (33⅓ to 1). The bank is said to be much more highly leveraged now than it was before. If the assets of the bank rise by 10 percent to $110, the capital rises from $3 to $13, for an increase of 333 percent. The lesson is that borrowing to increase the leverage ratio raises the percentage rise in capital, given a rise in the value of assets. In other words, if the value of assets is rising, a high leverage ratio increases the percentage rise in capital.

There is a downside to a high leverage ratio. A decline in asset values magnifies losses. Suppose that when the bank had a leverage ratio of 12½ to 1, its assets declined in value by 4 percent. The value of its assets fall in value from $100 to $96 as its liabilities remain constant at $92. The bank's capital falls from $8 to $4, for a decline of 50 percent. Of course, the bank is still solvent because its assets are still greater than its liabilities.

However, if the bank has a leverage ratio of 33⅓ to 1 when its assets decline in value by 4 percent to $96, it is now insolvent. Its liabilities are $97. The bank has negative capital (–$1).

So, if a bank is highly leveraged (i.e., has a high leverage ratio), even a small decline in the value of its assets can push it into insolvency. Part of the explanation of the financial crisis of 2007–2009 is that many banks (and other financial institutions) were highly leveraged. So, when the value of their assets (some of which were subprime loans and MBSs backed by subprime loans) declined, they were thrown into insolvency or came very close to insolvency.

When financial institutions are highly leveraged, the availability of credit in the economy can suffer if asset values decline. Suppose a bank, in order to meet its legal capital requirements, must have 5 percent of capital to back every $1 of a loan (an asset) that it grants. If the bank has $100 billion in loans outstanding, it must have $5 billion in capital. If the bank's capital falls to $4 billion as a result of the value of its loans declining, the bank now has to do something to be in compliance with the 5 percent requirement? The owners either to have add more capital to the bank, or the bank has to cut back its loans to $80 billion ($4 billion is 5 percent of $80 billion). So a fall in capital of $1 billion can lead to a $20 billion reduction in bank loans.

A reduction in loans occurring at a number of banks at the same time can dramatically affect the amount of lending and borrowing in the economy. And, as we know, a decline in credit can affect the real sector of the economy, reducing economic activity, leading to a decline in purchases and sales, and raising unemployment.

## Regulatory Capital Arbitrage

**Regulatory Capital**
The amount of capital that a financial institution must hold because of regulatory requirements.

Regulatory capital is the amount of capital that a financial institution must hold because of regulatory requirements. For example, a bank may have to have 5 percent capital for every $1 of a loan it creates. Regulatory capital requirements exist for the sake of bank safety. Supposedly, if a bank is meeting its regulatory capital requirements, it is a safe and sound bank that is unlikely to suffer insolvency due to any losses it may incur.

The important question, though, is *how much* capital is required to keep a bank safe and sound? Is a capital requirement of 10 percent too high or a capital requirement of 2 percent too low? After all, a high capital requirement might make a bank safe and sound (and less likely to become insolvent), but it can also lower a bank's returns. That is the lesson of leverage: A higher leverage ratio increases gains when assets values rise. So there is a *return-safety trade-off* that speaks to how much capital a bank should hold. More capital means more safety, but it also means lower returns when asset values are rising.

Some economists have argued that regulatory capital arbitrage explains why banks (and other financial institutions) were as highly leveraged as they were and why. When asset values began to decline, a cascading effect set in that ended with credit being less available in the economy.

The question of how much capital regulators should require banks to hold is based on the concept of *risk-weighted assets*. The idea is that not all assets are alike; some are

## Too Big to Fail

At one time, the phrase "too big to fail" meant that a company was so large and so diversified in its businesses (conducting business in numerous different areas in different countries) that a downturn in one business area or in one country wouldn't really hurt it; it would still be successful in many other areas. It had its eggs in a lot of different baskets, all over the world; so a broken egg in one or two places didn't mean failure. It was, in a sense, "too big to fail."

Today the term "too big to fail" means something different. It refers to a company or institution that is so big that, if the government were to allow it to fail, there would be negative repercussions for other companies and for the economy as a whole. A more accurate descriptive phrase might be "too big to *let* fail," but still the phrase "too big to fail" is used instead.

Think of the too-big-to-fail (TBTF) company or institution today as occupying the center of a circle, with its many appendages (much like an octopus) extended outward. If the TBTF institution fails, then the repercussions flow outward to adversely affect others. So, to prevent others from being hurt by its failure, government must step in and prevent it from failing, even if it has to use taxpayer funds to do so. In fact, some argue that taxpayer funds are wisely used for such purposes. Better to use $500 billion of taxpayer funds to save the economy than to let the economy contract, resulting in rising unemployment, bankruptcies, and dwindling tax revenues.

In the financial crisis of 2007–2009, both Fannie Mae and Freddie Mac were considered too big to fail, as was General Motors, some investment and commercial banks, and some financial services and insurance companies (such as American International Group, AIG).

Businesses that are TBTF and that are therefore bailed out when they are in trouble have competitive market advantages vis-à-vis

© IMAGE COPYRIGHT LEIN DE LEÓN YONG, 2009. USED UNDER LICENSE FROM SHUTTERSTOCK.COM.

companies that are small enough to let fail. Suppose bank A is considered TBTF but that banks B–Z are not. Many depositors will want to put their money in bank A instead of banks B–Z because they feel safer putting their money there. After all, if their bank—Bank A—has any problems, the government will bail it out.

So banks (and other institutions) that are TBTF are often shielded from risk because they know they will be bailed out if they run into problems. So why not take on the risk in search of the high returns? After all, if the returns materialize, they win; but if they don't, and it looks like failure is around the corner, they will be bailed out. Heads, we win; tails, the taxpayer loses. In other words, being TBTF creates a *moral hazard problem*; a party that is insulated from risk behaves differently than it would behave it if weren't shielded from risk. (Think of how fast you might drive if you knew it were impossible for you to be hurt in a car accident.)

In 2007–2010, with respect to the TBTF issue, some individuals argued that some institutions were truly too big to fail because, if they did fail, not only they, but many others, would feel the consequences. Better to save them today than to let many others suffer tomorrow. Other individuals argued that by not allowing these institutions to fail, the government simply increased the probability that other financial crises would follow. In other words, when government protects institutions from failure, it simply increases the probability that those institutions will fail in the future. Finally, some argued that the least worst course of action was to bail out some TBTF institutions—this time—but then to pass regulatory measures that break up TBTF institutions into a smaller sizes so that TBTF institutions no longer exist. In other words, being "too big to fail" is too big.

riskier than others. To illustrate, if bank A holds assets X and Y, and asset X is very risky and asset Y is not so risky, then the bank should hold more capital for asset X than for asset Y.

Under the 1988 Basel Accord (Basel I), international standards for risk-based capital requirments were introduced. Specifically, banks have to hold capital equivalent to 8 percent of their risk-weighted assets. To understand this, think of a bank with two assets: Treasury bonds and uncollateralized commercial loans. The Treasury bonds are not risky assets. The bank can be sure that the U.S. Treasury is going to redeem those bonds. In comparison, the uncollateralized commercial loans are risky. The bank cannot be sure that all its commercial loans will be paid off. Because Treasury bonds are less risky than uncollateralized commercial loans, the bank would be expected to hold more capital against its commercial loans than its Treasury bonds.

As a concrete example of *regulatory capital arbitrage*, suppose that a bank has three kinds of assets—X, Y, and Z—and that they differ in their degrees of riskiness. In other words, each class of asset has a different *risk weight*. Asset X has zero risk; so zero capital is required. Asset Y has a risk weight of 50 percent; so 50¢ of capital is needed for every $1 of Y asset. Asset Z has a risk weight of 80 percent; so 80¢ of capital is needed for every $1 of Z asset. Further, the total amount of each asset is $100 for a total of $300 in assets. To find the amount of risk-weighted assets, we multiply the amount of each asset by its risk weight and then sum the results:

$$\text{Risk-weighted assets} = (\$100X \times 0 \text{ percent}) + (\$100Y \times 50 \text{ percent}) + (\$100Z \times 80 \text{ percent}) = \$130$$

Now if the requirement is that financial institutions must hold 8 percent capital against their risk-weighted assets, the financial institution with $130 of risk-weighted assets has to hold capital equal to 8 percent of $130, or $10.40:

$$\text{Amount of capital a bank must hold} = \$130 \times 8 \text{ percent}$$
$$= \$10.40$$

**Regulatory Capital Arbitrage**
A means of changing the composition of assets in such a way as to lower the overall amount of capital a financial institution holds for a given level of assets.

Regulatory capital arbitrage is a means of changing the composition of assets in such a way as to lower the overall amount of capital a financial institution holds for a given level of assets. A financial institution might want to practice regulatory capital arbitrage because of what was explained earlier about leverage: hold either less capital for a given amount of assets or more assets for a given amount of capital. In other words, a higher leverage ratio means higher returns as long as asset values are rising. One way of increasing returns, then, is to reduce the amount of capital one needs to hold given the overall capital requirements. Regulatory capital arbitrage offers a means.

**Securitization**
The process by which financial institutions aggregate debt (such as loans) in a pool and then issue securities backed by the pool.

Securitization—the process by which financial institutions aggregate debt (such as loans) in a pool and then issue securities backed by the pool—is one way to accomplish regulatory capital arbitrage. To illustrate, suppose a bank has $100 in mortgages for which it needs to hold $4 in capital. If the bank can create a collateralized debt obligation (CDO) out of these mortgages, it may be able to reduce its capital to *less* than $4. Here's how. The CDO that the bank creates is sold to a special-purpose vehicle (SPV) that issues bonds based on the money that is expected to be forthcoming from the monthly mortgage payments. The bonds are divided up into tranches with different priorities. For example, senior tranches take priority over junior tranches; that is, when the money comes in from the mortgage loans, the people who hold the senior tranches are paid first, then the people who hold the junior tranches are paid. In other words, the people holding the senior tranches are shielded from losses relative to the people holding the junior tranches.

**Special-Purpose Vehicle (SPV)**
A legal entity created to fulfill narrow, specific, or temporary objectives.

So, if most of the mortgage loans are high-quality loans, then most of the risk can be placed in the bottom few tranches, and the higher tranches are safe. The senior tranches get a higher credit rating than the junior tranches. What does all this have to do with the amount of capital a bank holds? By getting high credit ratings for the senior tranches, a bank can lower the risk weight on those assets and, as a result, lower the amount of capital it has to hold for them. Even though the junior tranches require *more* capital, the lower capital requirements on the senior tranches can be organized so that they *outweigh* the requirements on the junior tranches so that overall requirements decline. In other words, securitization is the means by which regulatory capital arbitrage lowers capital requirements.

## Where We Are So Far

The Fed implemented a low interest rate policy in the early 2000s. Low mortgage rates led to increased mortgage borrowing and added demand to the housing market. As a result, house prices increased. At the same time:

- Banks were lowering lending standards to comply with the CRA.

- Fannie and Freddie came under political pressure to buy nontraditional loans (such as subprime loans) and to create a strong secondary market for mortgage-backed securities backed by nontraditional loans.

- Fannie and Freddie securitization and private securitization was going on, the latter of which was the means of achieving regulatory capital arbitrage, a process that increased leverage ratios in financial institutions.

## House Prices Decline

As long as house prices were rising, the dance continued. It took only a small decline in house prices, though, to start things unraveling. And house prices did begin to decline, as shown in Exhibit 5. As house prices came down, some recent home buyers saw the prices they could sell their houses for fall below their loan amounts. (For many new homeowners, even a small price decline brought the value of their homes below the loan amount because they had put down very low—or no—down payments. In other words, their loan amounts were nearly equal to the purchase price of the house.)

Also, some of the mortgage loans that the borrowers had taken out had been adjustable rate mortgages, with a low interest payment in the early years, followed by a reset of the interest rate in later years. What these people found is that their low interest rates

**EXHIBIT 5**

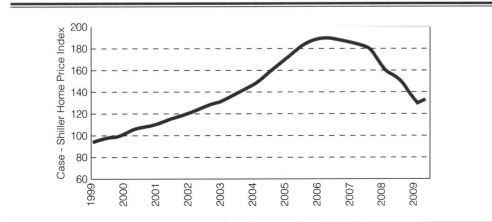

**The Case-Shiller Home Price Index**

House prices begin to decline in mid-2006.

were being reset at higher levels because mortgage rates had risen since they had taken out their loans.

As house prices declined, delinquency rates and foreclosure rates rose for two reasons: (1) Some individuals found their loan amounts greater than the price they could sell their houses for. (2) Other individuals found their mortgage rates resetting at higher rates, making for monthly payments that they could not afford. The banks holding assets in the form of subprime loans and MBSs then started to feel the consequences of the higher delinquency and foreclosure rates. Because of their high leverage ratios, they could not absorb much of a decline in asset values before they were insolvent or nearly so.

## Domino Effects

When one bank finds that it cannot meet its capital requirements, how it responds can adversely affect other banks. For example, if bank A has to hold 5 percent of the value of its loans outstanding in capital, and it has $100 billion in loans outstanding, it must then hold $5 billion in capital. If the bank capital falls to $4 billion because the value of its loans is declining, it must reduce its assets to, say, $80 billion to be in compliance with the 5 percent capital requirement. The reduction in loans outstanding leads to less lending in the economy, which, as we know, can reduce economic activity.

Instead of reducing its outstanding loans to meet its capital requirement, suppose bank A sells some of its assets, including some mortgage-backed securities. Because bank A is in trouble and has to sell some of its MBSs, it might sell the securities at a lower price than it would have liked. Thereafter, bank B, now holding MBSs as assets on its balance sheet, finds the value of its assets declining, thus lowering its capital. As a result, bank B has less than enough capital to meets its capital requirements, and so it sells some of its MBSs to bank C, just as bank A did before. Soon bank C finds itself in the same position as bank B did earlier. And so on.

Thus the banks fall one after another, like dominos. The more dominos that fall, the more likely we are to see a big cutback in lending activity on the part of banks in order to meet their capital requirements. And the bigger the cutback in lending activity is, the more pronounced the effect will be in the real sector of the economy.

At the time, another problem could compound the problems of the banks. As word got out that a bank was near insolvency, the bank might find it harder to borrow money. Suppose bank A's assets have declined and it is approaching insolvency, and bank B hears that bank A is having problems. If bank A happens to ask bank B for a loan, bank B declines because it is afraid that bank A, faced with declining asset values, might not be able to repay the loan. (Banks ultimately must pay off their liabilities out of their assets. If the bank has assets of $100 and liabilities of $80, it could sell off its assets for $100 and pay off all $80 of its liabilities. But if its assets fall in value to, say, $70, then even if it sells off all its assets, it still couldn't pay off all its liabilities.)

## How the Real Sector Affects the Financial Sector

If problems in the financial sector can affect the real sector of the economy, can problems in the real economy, caused by the problems in the financial sector, feed back into the financial sector and cause even bigger financial problems? The answer is yes. Consider the reduced lending that is a consequence of the bank's assets declining and its falling below its capital requirements. The reduced lending leads to problems in the real sector of the economy: less spending, decreased sales, sellers going out of business, unemployment rising, and so on. With sellers going out of business and the ranks of the unemployed swelling, many people and firms will find it increasingly difficult to pay off their debts, many of which are owed to the banks. As a result, even more loans on the bank's balance sheet lose value, pushing the bank ever closer to insolvency.

## The Government Response

The federal government responded to the financial crisis and to the problems in the real sector of the economy in a number of ways. The responses can be categorized as *bailouts*, *fiscal stimulus*, and *easy money*.

- *Bailouts.* The $700 billion Troubled Asset Relief Program (TARP) took several forms: the U.S. Treasury's buying some of the bad assets on the banks' balance sheets, such as MBSs, and the government investing directly in some of the largest banks in the country, thus increasing the capital in banks. Also considered a bailout were the federal loans to General Motors and Chrysler in December 2008 to prevent the bankruptcy of these companies.

- *Fiscal Stimulus.* The Congress passed and President Obama signed a $787 billion fiscal stimulus bill in February 2009 in the hopes of injecting demand into the economy.

- *Easy Money.* In November 2008, the Federal Reserve announced that it would buy $800 billion of private debt. This was its attempt to increase lending and borrowing in the economy.

### SELF-TEST

1. Explain how a high leverage ratio can lead to insolvency if assets decline in value.

2. What happens in the financial sector can affect the real sector, and what happens in the real sector can affect the financial sector. Do you agree or disagree? Explain your answer.

3. What is regulatory capital arbitrage?

# OFFICE HOURS

## "Do Economists and the Public Always Understand the Causes of Financial Crises?"

## CHAPTER SUMMARY

### A VIEW OF THE ECONOMY

- One way to view the economy is as consisting of two sectors: a financial sector and a real sector. The financial sector consists of financial institutions—commercial banks, investment banks, hedge funds, brokerage firms, and more. The real sector consists of firms that produce goods and services, individuals that buy goods and services, individuals that work for firms, and more.

### A FINANCIAL CRISIS

- A financial crisis occurs when financial firms and financial markets undergo a major disruption. In turn, these problems make it difficult for persons to obtain loans from banks and other financial institutions.
- Problems in the financial sector can affect the real sector.

- One way to view a financial crisis is as a balance sheet problem. Specifically, the assets of financial institutions are declining in value, which reduces the net worth (or capital) of the institutions and moves them closer to insolvency. As these institutions approach or reach insolvency, they pull back on lending activities. Pulling back on their lending activities can, in turn, adversely affect the real sector of the economy.

### RISKY ASSETS

- Describing the financial crisis as a balance sheet problem requires us to identify the assets that declined in the mid-2000s, causing asset values for financial institutions to decline and moving them closer to insolvency. These assets include subprime loans, other nontraditional loans, mortgage-backed securities, and collateralized debt obligations.

financial crisis was caused by government, specifically, the Fed and Congress and Fannie and Freddie. Others seem to blame the banks and other financial institutions for taking excessive risks. With respect to the latter, you sometimes hear that the financial community was just out to make a lot of money as fast as possible and so they pushed off these subprime loans to a lot of people. It seems to me that what we think about the cause of the crisis has a lot to do with what we then think is the right preventive medicine for the next crisis.

> **INSTRUCTOR:**

In other words, if the cause of the crisis is that financial institutions weren't regulated enough, then the solution is to regulate banks more. Or if the cause of the crisis was a too lenient Fed combined with a lot of politics in the housing market, then the solution is some sort of monetary rule for the Fed and the depoliticization of the housing market.

> **STUDENT:**

Yes, that is what I am taking about. If you think X caused the crisis, then you want to do something about X. But if you think Y caused the crisis, then, of course, you want to do something about Y.

> **INSTRUCTOR:**

I can only agree with you on that. Whatever one believes about the causes of the financial crisis does seem to influence his or her opinion of what should be done to prevent another such crisis.

**POINTS TO REMEMBER**

1. Not all economists are agreed on the cause(s) of the financial crisis. Not all members of the public are agreed on the cause(s) of the financial crisis.
2. What one identifies as the cause(s) of the financial crisis does influence his opinion of what should be done to prevent another financial crisis.

## THE FED, THE FEDERAL FUNDS RATE TARGET, AND THE GLOBAL SAVINGS GLUT

- Some economists argue that the Fed set its target federal funds rate "too low" in the early 2000s, especially during the period 2002–2005. This had consequences, one of which was that mortgage rates declined, giving individuals an incentive to borrow to buy a house. As a result, the low mortgage interest rates fueled buying in the housing market, driving up house prices.

- Some economists argue that the cause of the low interest rates was the global savings glut. Specifically, emerging countries in the world began to save more, and these extra savings found their way to the United States, where they increased the supply of loanable funds and lowered interest rates (one interest rate in particular was the mortgage interest rate). The low mortgage interest rates fueled buying in the housing market, driving up house prices.

## THE TAYLOR RULES AND INTEREST RATES

- According to economist John Taylor, the Fed set its federal funds rate target "too low" during the early 2000s, as measured

by what it would be if it were set by the Taylor rule. Accordingly, the low interest rates that followed fueled borrowing and the sharp rise in housing prices. One piece of evidence Taylor cited as evidence in favor of his argument is that there is a strong correlation between a housing boom in different countries and deviations from the Taylor Rule.

- Alan Greenspan has argued that low long-term interest rates, not short-term interest rates, were the causing of the housing boom. Moreover, the Fed, he argues, has more control over short-term rates (such as the federal funds rate) than over long-term rates (such as the 30-year fixed mortgage rate).

## THE POLITICS OF HOUSING

- Mortgage lending standards decline in the 1990s and early 2000s in the United States. There was a move away from traditional lending practices to nontraditional lending practices.

- The Community Reinvestment Act (CRA) was passed in 1977 to encourage financial institutions to meet the needs of borrowers in all segments of their communities. In 1995, Congress revised the CRA to give banks a stronger incentive to increase the percentage of mortgage loans (among other loans) going to low- and moderate-income borrowers.

- Beginning in the early 1990s, government pressure was placed on both Fannie Mae and Freddie Mac to increase their purchases of mortgages made to low- to moderate-income families.

- The entrance of Fannie Mae and Freddie Mac into the market of buying subprime loans and creating mortgage-backed securities created a market in subprime lending. Specifically, the large-scale expansion of Fannie and Freddie into the subprime loan business made it profitable for other financial institutions to grant subprime loans in order to sell them to Fannie and Freddie.

## THE ROLE OF LEVERAGE

- Leverage is the use of borrowed funds to increase the returns that can be earned with a given amount of capital.

- Consider a bank with $100 in assets, $92 in liabilities, and $8 net worth or capital. Its leverage ratio—the ratio of its assets to its capital—is 100 to 8, or 12½ to 1.

- A bank with a higher leverage ratio has a higher percentage rise in capital when asset values are rising. Bank A has $100 in assets, $92 in liabilities, and $8 net worth, or capital. Its leverage ratio is 12½ to 1. If asset values rise to $110, its capital is now $18. Going from capital of $8 to $18 is a 125 percent rise in capital. Bank B has $100 in assets, $97 in liabilities, and capital of $3. If assets values rise to $110, its capital is now $13. Going from $3 to $13 capital is a 333 percent rise in capital. Therefore, if asset values are expected to rise, highly leveraged banks will witness a higher percentage rise in their capital than low-leveraged banks will witness. Alternatively, when asset values are expected to decline, highly leveraged banks will witness a higher percentage of decline in their capital than low-leveraged banks will. Finally, a bank with a high leverage ratio is more likely to fall into insolvency when assets decline in value than is a bank with a low leverage ratio.

## REGULATORY CAPITAL, RISK-WEIGHTED ASSETS, AND REGULATORY CAPITAL ARBITRAGE

- Regulatory capital is the amount of capital that a financial institution must hold because of regulatory requirements.

- Regulatory capital arbitrage is a means of changing the composition of assets in such a way as to lower the overall amount of capital a financial institution holds for a given level of assets.

- Financial institutions can increase returns (during a time of rising asset values) by engaging in regulatory capital arbitrage. One way to do this is through securitization. Regulatory capital arbitrage is part of the reason banks and other financial institutions had high leverage ratios when asset values were increasing.

## THINGS BEGIN TO UNRAVEL

- The decline in house prices and the rise in interest rates caused delinquency rates and foreclosure rates to rise, for two reasons: (1) Some individuals found their loan amounts greater than the price they could sell their houses for. (2) Other individuals found their mortgage rates resetting at higher rates.

- Banks that held assets in the form of subprime loans and mortgage-backed securities began to feel the effects of heightened delinquency and foreclosure rates. As a result, asset values for banks began to decline. Because of the high leverage ratios, it didn't take much of a decline in asset values before banks were either insolvent or nearly so.

- As banks became insolvent or approached insolvency, they pulled back on their lending, reducing economic activity in the real sector of the economy.

- Problems in the real sector began to feed back into the financial sector.

## KEY TERMS AND CONCEPTS

Financial Intermediary
Insolvency
Balance Sheet
Asset
Liability

Net Worth (or Capital)
Subprime Mortgage Loans
Mortgage-Backed Securities
  (MBS)
Adjustable Rate Mortgage

Equity (in a Home)
Leverage
Regulatory Capital
Regulatory Capital Arbitrage
Securitization

Special-Purpose Vehicle
  (SPV)

## QUESTIONS AND PROBLEMS

1. What does it mean to say that the financial crisis can be viewed as a balance sheet problem?

2. What is an asset? A liability? Net worth, or capital?

3. Explain how FDIC insurance can cause banks to take on riskier loans than they would if FDIC didn't exist.

4. What are some differences between a subprime loan and a traditional loan? What is the difference between a mortgage-backed security and a collateralized debt obligation?

5. Explain how a low federal funds rate target can influence mortgage interest rates.

6. Some argue that the Fed acted as a catalyst for the boom in housing prices in the early 2000s. What is their argument?

7. Some argue that the global savings glut acted as a catalyst for the boom in housing prices in the early 2000s. What is their argument?

8. What role does Alan Greenspan say that short-term interest rates (such as the federal funds rate) played in the housing boom? What role did long-term interest rates play?

9. Is there any connection between rising housing prices and delinquency and foreclosure rates? Explain your answer.

10. What role, if any, did the CRA play in relaxing lending standards?

11. What role, if any, did Congress, Fannie Mae, and Freddie Mac play in creating a market for subprime lending?

12. What does it mean to say a bank has a leverage ratio of 10 to 1?

13. Illustrate with a numerical example how a high leverage ratio produces a different percentage rise in capital than a lower leverage ratio when asset values are rising.

14. Explain the process of regulatory capital arbitrage.

15. What role does securitization play in regulatory capital arbitrage?

16. It has been said that the decline in house prices precipitated the financial crisis. How so?

17. The financial sector can affect the real sector, and the real sector can affect the financial sector. Do you agree or disagree? Explain your answer.

## WORKING WITH NUMBERS AND GRAPHS

1. A bank has $1 million in assets and $700,000 in liabilities. What is its net worth? What is its leverage ratio?

2. The bank identified in the previous question finds that its assets increase in value by 15 percent. By what percentage does its capital increase?

3. A bank has $1 million in assets and $920,000 in liabilities. What is its net worth? What is its leverage ratio?

4. The bank identified in the previous question finds that its assets decline in value by 4 percent. By what percentage does its capital decrease?

5. A bank has $400 in asset X, $500 in asset Y, and $300 in asset Z. Each asset has a different risk weight. Asset X has a risk weight of 10 percent, Y has a risk weight of 40 percent, and Z has a risk weight of 70 percent. What dollar amount do risk-weighted assets equal? Assuming that the bank has to hold capital equal to 7 percent of its risk-weighted assets, how much capital does the bank have to hold?

## CHAPTER 19

# DEBATES IN MACROECONOMICS OVER THE ROLE AND EFFECTS OF GOVERNMENT

**Introduction** Most of this book has been about economics, with mention of government here and there. This chapter discusses some of the things that economists have to say about government, especially with respect to the role and effects of government in the economy.

## MACROECONOMICS AND GOVERNMENT: THE DEBATE

Macroeconomists are agreed on some things. For example, if you ask 10 economists to identify the tools the Fed has at its disposal to change the money supply, you are likely to get the same answer from all 10 economists. If you ask 10 economists to identify the assumptions in the simple quantity theory of money, again you are likely to get the same answer from all 10.

However, macroeconomists are not agreed on some things. If you ask 10 economists how sensitive investment is likely to be to a change in the interest rate in the current environment, not all 10 are likely to give you the same answer. Some might say that investment is likely to change a lot in response to a change in the interest rate. In other words, the elasticity of investment (the percentage change in investment given a percentage change in the interest rate) is likely to be high. Other economists might disagree and argue that investment will not change much (or at all) if the interest rate changes.

**Elasticity of Investment**
A measure of the responsiveness of investment to changes in the interest rate.

This type of issue—*how much* will investment fall if the interest rate rises—is an *empirical issue*. Although all economists might agree that investment will fall if the interest rate rises, they will not all agree as to *how much* it will fall. Other empirical issues that economists might not agree on are *how much* will aggregate demand rise if government increases its spending or *how flexible or inflexible* wages are in the current economic environment.

Besides disagreements that focus on empirical issues, economists often express disagreement over the role government *should* play in the economy given their understanding of how the economy works. Suppose three economists agree that Real GDP is headed down, that prices are headed up, and that the prospects for economic growth look bleak for the near future. Even though all three economists have the same diagnosis, they will not necessarily recommend the same government policies. The first economist might argue that government should do nothing (no government medicine), the second might argue that medicine X is needed, and the third might recommend medicine Z. The first economist has government doing nothing, the second economist has the government doing X, and the third economist has government doing Z.

Ask most students of macroeconomics (especially those who taking their first course in macroeconomics) what they would like to take away from the course, and they say something like this: "We would like to get explanations for the various macroeconomic phenomena (recessions, inflation, high unemployment) and what is the right approach to deal with a particular macroeconomic phenomenon." Their thinking is like a doctor's: "What is wrong with the patient, and what is the best medicine for the patient to take to get well?" In economic terms, the questions would be, "What is wrong with the economy, and what is the best policy to enact to get the economy well?" But the answers in economics are not so clear-cut. President Harry S. Truman once said, "Give me a one-handed economist. All my economists say 'On the one hand, and then on the other hand.'" No doubt students of macroeconomics experience some of Truman's frustration with economists.

Because this is probably your first college course in macroeconomics, you would probably be content with a "one-handed" answer. But you wouldn't be getting an accurate picture of economics theory and its effects on policy. To present an accurate picture, you need to hear some of the debates in macroeconomics, especially as they relate to the role of government in the economy. Some of what we will discuss here has been discussed in earlier chapters, sometimes with a different emphasis. The outline in this chapter is fairly straightforward. We identify a number of macroeconomic topics. Next, we explain how government comes up in the discussions of various economists with respect to that topic.

# TAX CUTS, TAX REVENUE, AND BUDGET DEFICITS

Suppose the federal government is running a budget deficit; government spending is greater than tax revenues. To reduce the size of the deficit, some economists propose income tax cuts. Other economists argue that income tax cuts will not lead to a smaller deficit. The source of the disagreement between the two sets of economists is the issue of whether tax cuts will or will not raise tax revenue.

One group of economists argues this way: (1) If income tax rates are cut, individuals will choose to work and produce more. (2) As a result, they will generate more income and the tax base will rise. (3) If the tax base rises by more than tax rates are cut, then tax revenue will rise. (4) More tax revenue will end up reducing the size of the budget deficit.

Another group of economists challenges assumption 3. They argue that that the tax base is not likely to rise by more than tax rates are cut, so that result 4 will be less tax revenue and therefore a bigger budget deficit.

The discussion goes back to this equation, first identified in Chapter 11:

$$\text{Tax revenues} = \text{Tax base} \times \text{(average) Tax rate}$$

Almost all economists will agree that if the tax rate is cut, the tax base will rise, but not all economists agree as to *how much* the tax base will rise. In other words, if the tax rate is cut 10 percent, will the tax base rise by more than, less than, or as much as the cut in the tax rate?

What separates economists here is an empirical issue. Specifically, economists sometimes disagree on what is likely to happen given a certain action. In other words, if tax rates are cut, then what? Do tax revenues rise, decline, or remain constant?

To recap in terms of these differing economic perspectives:

- *Economist A:* Tax cuts will raise tax revenue, and increased tax revenue will decrease the size of the budget deficit.

- *Economist B:* Tax cuts will lower tax revenue, and decreased tax revenue will increase the size of the budget deficit.

# THE ECONOMY: SELF-REGULATING OR NOT?

One major debate in macroeconomics focuses on whether the economy is self regulating. Specifically, if an economy is in a recessionary gap, can it move itself into long-run equilibrium? To a degree, the answer depends on whether wages are flexible or inflexible downward. If wages are flexible, then an economy can remove itself from a recessionary gap. Hence, government need not get involved in managing the economy. But if wages are inflexible downward, then an economy cannot remove itself from a recessionary gap; an economy can get stuck in a recessionary gap. The economy can get unstuck only by means of economic policy enacted by either the Congress or the president (in terms of fiscal policy) or by the Fed (in terms of monetary policy).

To recap in terms of these differing economic perspectives:

- *Economist A:* Wages are flexible, so that if the economy is in a recessionary gap, it will soon remove itself from the gap. Government doesn't have to do anything.

- *Economist B:* Wages are inflexible downward, so that if the economy is in a recessionary gap, it may be stuck there. The best course of action is for the federal government to implement expansionary fiscal policy or for the Fed to implement expansionary monetary policy to remove the economy from the recessionary gap.

# MORE GOVERNMENT SPENDING OR A CUT IN TAXES: WHICH GIVES A BIGGER BANG FOR THE BUCK?

The economy is in a recessionary gap, and economists call for a demand-side expansionary fiscal policy measure. As we know, expansionary fiscal policy consists of (1) an increase in government purchases or (2) a cut in taxes or (3) both. Not all economists are likely to agree on the best way to proceed. One economist will argue that a rise in government purchases will give the economy the "biggest bang for the buck." A $1 rise in government purchases will (by changing aggregate demand) raise Real GDP by more than a $1 cut in taxes. In other words, the government spending multiplier [the number that, when multiplied by the change in government spending, gives us the change in total spending (and, if prices are constant, the change in Real GDP)] is larger than the tax multiplier [the number that, when multiplied by the change in taxes, gives us the change in total spending (and if prices are constant, the change in Real GDP]. Another economist argues just the opposite: the tax multiplier is larger than the government spending multiplier, so a $1 cut in taxes will raise Real GDP by more than a $1 rise in government purchases.

Suppose that the government spending multiplier is 1.4 and the tax multiplier is 3. This means that a $1 rise in government spending will increase Real GDP by $1.40, and a $1 tax cut will increase Real GDP by $3. Now the debate and disagreement among economists can focus on the value of the two multipliers.

In the standard textbook Keynesian analysis, there is reason to believe that the government spending multiplier is larger than the tax multiplier. Here is the reasoning: when

**Government Spending Multiplier**
The number that, when multiplied by the change in government spending, gives us the change in total spending (and, if prices are constant, the change in Real GDP).

**Tax Multiplier**
The number that, when multiplied by the change in taxes, gives us the change in total spending (and if prices are constant, the change in Real GDP).

government spends $1, the entire $1 enters the spending stream. However, when government cuts taxes by $1, individuals spend some of the dollar they now get to keep and save some of it. In other words, they might spend 60¢ of the dollar and save 40¢. What separates economists, though, is that not all economists hold to the standard textbook analysis. Some economists argue that the standard textbook analysis does not take into account all the ways that tax cuts can be stimulative.

To recap in terms of these differing economic perspectives:

- *Economist A:* The economy needs expansionary fiscal policy to remove it from a recessionary gap. Government should either raise its spending or cut taxes. I believe the government spending multiplier is larger than the tax multiplier; so I suggest government increase its spending.

- *Economist B:* The economy needs expansionary fiscal policy to remove it from a recessionary gap. Government should either raise its spending or cut taxes. I believe the tax multiplier is larger than the government spending multiplier, so I suggest government cut taxes.

# MORE GOVERNMENT SPENDING OR A CUT IN TAXES: THE SIZE AND SCOPE OF GOVERNMENT

The *size* of government relates to the resources over which government has command. Suppose the economy has 100 units of labor, with 30 of the units allocated through government and 70 units through the private sector. Government grows in size, relative to the private sector, if it begins to allocate more than 30 units of labor and the private sector beings to allocate less than 70 units of labor.

The *scope* of government relates to what government does. Suppose government can provide for the national defense, build roads and bridges, provide schools, institute and operate Social Security. The scope of government relates to how many things government actually does. If it only provides for the national defense and builds roads and bridges, then its scope is more limited than if it provides for the national defense, builds roads and bridges, and implements and operates Social Security.

Both a rise in government purchases and a cut in taxes are expansionary fiscal policy measures, but both don't have the same impact on the size and scope of government. To illustrate, suppose economist A calls specifically for more government spending to get the economy out of a recessionary gap. The argument is standard fare: a rise in government purchases increases aggregate demand and removes the economy from the recessionary gap.

But couldn't a tax cut, instead of greater government spending, do the same thing? For instance, an income tax cut will raise after-tax (or disposable) income. With greater after-tax income, individuals will buy more goods and services, thus increasing consumption in the economy. And a rise in consumption will raise aggregate demand, perhaps by enough to remove the economy out of a recessionary gap.

The decision between government spending and tax cuts depends partly on the effect that each has on the size and scope of government. Economist A favors bigger government (government making more decisions); when it comes to advocating increased government purchases or tax cuts, he argues for increased government purchases. He sees increased government purchases as increasing the size and possibly the scope of government. Economist B favors smaller government (government making fewer decisions); when it comes to advocating increased government purchases or tax cuts, she argues for tax cuts. She sees cutting taxes as decreasing the size and possibly the scope of government.

To recap in terms of these differing economic perspectives:

- *Economist A:* Expansionary fiscal policy is needed to raise aggregate demand and remove the economy from a recessionary gap. The choice of fiscal policy measures is between more government spending or a cut in taxes. Since I am in favor of bigger government, I choose more government spending.

- *Economist B:* Expansionary fiscal policy is needed to raise aggregate demand and remove the economy from a recessionary gap. The choice of fiscal policy measures is between more government spending or a cut in taxes. Since I am in favor of smaller government, I choose a cut in taxes.

# THE DEGREE OF CROWDING OUT

Suppose 10 out of 10 economists agree that the economy is in a recessionary gap. Seven of them argue that an expansionary fiscal policy measure in the form of greater government spending will remove the economy from the recessionary gap. Their argument is that if government purchases increase, aggregate demand in the economy will rise, and the economy will move out of the recessionary gap. Also, any increase in government purchases will not crowd out any private sector spending (i.e., spending by households and businesses).

The other three economists see things a little differently. They argue that a lot of crowding out is likely, thus weakening the impact of the expansionary fiscal policy measure. Their argument is that if government purchases increase, aggregate demand probably will not rise enough to remove the economy from the recessionary gap because for every dollar the government spends, it has to borrow a dollar. In short, to get an additional dollar to spend, government must first borrow it. If the borrowed dollars come from the private sector, then the private sector will have fewer dollars to spend on various goods and services; so more government spending means less private sector spending. The rise in aggregate demand due to more government spending is largely offset by a reduction in aggregate demand because of less private sector spending. In the end, aggregate demand will change little, if at all, so that government will have been ineffective in its attempt to remove the economy from the recessionary gap. In terms of jobs, jobs created or saved because of increased government spending are offset by jobs destroyed by a decline in private sector spending.

To recap in terms of these differing economic perspectives:

- *Economist A:* A rise in government purchases will increase aggregate demand and remove the economy from the recessionary gap because little or no crowding out will occur. A rise in government purchases will end up increasing the number of jobs in the economy.

- *Economist B:* A rise in government purchases will not increase aggregate demand and remove the economy from the recessionary gap because of complete (or nearly complete) crowding out.

# THE POLITICS OF GOVERNMENT SPENDING

Consider two settings. In setting 1, fiscal policy emerges in a political vacuum. In setting 2, it umdergoes a political process. The fiscal policy created in a political vacuum is probably not going to be the same as the fiscal policy that arises from a political process. For example, government spends $100 on good X in setting 1. Will it spend $100 on good X in setting 2? Probably not. In setting 2, it might spend more or less on good X. In fact, in setting 2, it might not spend any money on good X.

As an example, in 2008–2009, the U.S. economy was on a downward slide—Real GDP was declining, the unemployment rate was rising, and some companies were cutting employment, while others were closing down. Many economists argued that an expansionary policy measure was needed to strengthen the economy (specifically, to turn the decline in Real GDP around, to reduce the unemployment rate, etc.). Some economists called for more government spending. However, the government-needs-to-spend-more group contained factions. Some argued that the important objective for the economy is that government spends more; of lesser importance was what government spent the money on. In other words, whether government spent money having people dig ditches and then filling them up or building bridges and roads, a dollar spent is a dollar spent as far as the economy goes.

Other economists disagreed, arguing that how the money was spent would make a difference in the effect on the economy. Money spent on having people dig ditches and then filling them up is not as beneficial to the economy as spending money to build bridges and roads. More importantly, these same economists argued that much of the additional money spent by government would end up motivated by politics instead of economics. In other words, members of Congress might find a large spending bill just the cover they needed to reward their political allies. Of course, from an economic perspective, if a dollar spent here is the same as a dollar spent there, rewarding one's political allies does not come with an economywide cost. But if spending a dollar in some ways is more productive for the economy than spending it in other ways, them how the dollar is spent matters a lot.

To recap in terms of these differing economic perspectives:

- *Economist A:* An expansionary fiscal policy measure is needed to increase Real GDP, lower the unemployment rate, and so on. I propose $100 billion more in government spending. It doesn't really matter what the $100 billion is spent on; the important thing is that the money is spent.

- *Economist B:* An expansionary fiscal policy measure is needed to increase Real GDP, lower the unemployment rate, and so on. Ideally, the economy needs $100 billion more in government spending. But how the money is spent will be determined by Congress, and Congress is likely to be motivated by political interests. Furthermore, not all spending is the same. Some spending is better for the economy than other spending. I think much of the spending that we will get from Congress will be motivated by politics instead of by economics, and sometimes the spending motivated by politics will be of little help in turning the economy around. In the end, I have my doubts as to how effective an increase in government spending will be in aiding the economy.

# MONETARY POLICY: RULES VERSUS DISCRETION

With regard to the creation of monetary policy, some economists argue in favor of a rule-based system, whether it is the Taylor rule or setting the growth of the money supply equal to some fixed percentage rate (such as 3 percent). Other economists argue in favor of discretion for the Fed, saying that the Fed needs to have the flexibility to create the best monetary policy possible given the circumstances.

The debate between these economists centers around two major points. The first has to do with the effects of different types of monetary policy: rule-based versus discretionary. Those who advocate rule-based monetary policy often say that it is more likely than discretionary monetary policy to produce nearly stable prices, low unemployment, low and stable interest rates, and the right overall conditions for sustained economic growth. Economists who advocate discretionary monetary policy argue that it is more likely to achieve the

## What Does a Stimulus Bill Look Like?

In February 2009, the U.S. Congress passed a $787 billion stimulus bill (an expansionary fiscal policy measure). At the time the bill passed, various economists had different things to say about it. Some argued that it was the right thing to do to stimulate the economy. Some argued that it wouldn't stimulate the economy. Some argued that the bill was filled with "political pork," which wasn't always consistent with the kind of spending and tax cuts needed to jump-start the economy. On February 17, 2009, the *Wall Street Journal* published the details of the stimulus bill in terms of (1) classification—such as spending or tax provisions, (2) keyword, (3) description, and (4) cost. The full details of the stimulus can be found at http://online.wsj.com/public/resources/documents/STIMULUS_FINAL_0217.html. Here we show you only a small sample of a few provisions in the stimulus bill.

© IMAGE COPYRIGHT TRAVEL BUG, 2009. USED UNDER LICENSE FROM SHUTTERSTOCK.COM

| Classification | Keyword | Description | Cost ($ millions) |
|---|---|---|---|
| Spending | Farming | Loans to rural homeowners | $ 200 |
| Aid | Food | Adult and child day care meals and snacks | 100 |
| Spending | Commerce | Extra money for Census | 1,000 |
| Spending | Science | NASA climate research | 400 |
| Spending | Energy | Training of electric grid workers | 100 |
| Spending | Government | Oversight of Small Business Administration spending | 10 |
| Spending | Arts | Grants to fund art projects in nonprofit sector | 50 |
| Aid | Education | Increase in Pell grants | 17,114 |
| Spending | Military | Army child development centers | 80 |
| Spending | State | Passport and training funding for State Department | 90 |
| Spending | Transportation | Grants for highway improvements | 29,000 |
| Aid | Aid to States | Aid to states to balance education budgets prevent cutbacks and modernize schools | 40,600 |
| Tax provisions | Business tax cuts | Tax cuts for low-income housing investors | 143 |
| Aid | Other tax cuts | U.S. lumber, steel and other companies can keep money they were given from Canadian and Mexican import duties | 90 |
| Aid | Individual Aid | Extension of jobless benefits up to 33 weeks | 29,960 |
| Tax provision | Individual tax cut | Tax credit up to $2,500 for tuition and college expenses | 13,907 |
| Aid | Healthcare | Federal aid to states for Medicare spending | 90,044 |
| Spending | Transportation | Grants to Amtrak | 1,300 |
| Spending | Housing | Repairs and modernization of public housing projects | 1,000 |
| Tax provisions | Energy tax cuts | Tax credit for plug-in electric vehicle conversion | 2,002 |
| Spending | Outdoors | Priority road, bridge, and trail repairs | 180 |

desired economic results because the monetary authority has the flexibility to shape the best monetary policy to the existing circumstances.

The second major point is that rules-based monetary policy advocates often assert that discretionary monetary policy, all too often, is motivated by political instead of economic interests. A rules-based monetary policy removes monetary policy from politics, they argue, in the end, making for better monetary policy. The money supply is too important an economic variable, with too many far-reaching effects, to have politicians pushing it one way or another to serve their short-run, the next-election-is-around-the-corner interests.

To recap in terms of these differing economic perspectives:

- *Economist A:* A monetary rule is preferred to a discretionary Fed. The former is more likely to bring about stable prices, low unemployment, and so on. In addition, a monetary rule removes monetary policy from politics.

- *Economist B:* A discretionary Fed is preferred to a monetary rule. The Fed needs the flexibility to tailor monetary policy to the existing circumstances.

# BAILOUTS

Not all economists are agreed as to whether government should bail out companies in financial problems. Suppose a large company employs thousands of workers, pays millions of dollars in taxes to the state in which it is located, buys hundreds of parts from its suppliers in assembling its product, and has thousands of bondholders and stockholders. Then the company finds itself in dire financial straits—so dire that the company finds it difficult to repay its debt or to obtain loans. Without some financial assistance, the company will probably go out of business. If it does, its home state will lose millions of dollars in tax revenue, employees will lose their jobs, its suppliers lose sales revenues (perhaps causing them to go out of business), fire workers, and so on, and thousands of investors will see their personal wealth diminished. Does the government have a role to play in bailing out this company?

One way to answer that question is to ask another: "Who loses if the company goes out of business?" Certainly the owners of the business lose, but then there might be others, such as the employees who lose their jobs, the suppliers of the company who lose business, the state that loses the tax revenue, and the investors who lose personal wealth. If the total dollar amount of loss is $50 billion and the federal government bailout of the company comes to $30 billion in taxpayer funds, then, for $30 billion, a $50 billion loss could be averted. Some would argue that bailing out the company (and, one step removed, those who would be adversely affected by the company's failure) would be economically advantageous. In fact, this was the argument when the federal government bailed out several financial institutions and both General Motors and Chrysler during the financial and economic crisis in the mid-to-late 2000s. A little bailing out here and there may be better than letting large businesses fail and in the process drag down others with them.

However, another viewpoint goes like this: (1) The people ultimately doing the bailing out—the taxpayers—incur the cost of the bailout, while others receive the benefits (such as the company owners, the employees, and others). Why should the taxpayers pay the costs while others receive the benefits, especially when many of the taxpayers have less income than the persons who are bailed out? (2) If firms know they will be bailed out, they will take more risks than if they know they won't be. The possibility of a bailout creates an environment in which more and more firms will need bailouts. The owners and managers of firms will want to take ever more risk because if high returns follow, then they are the winners, but if failure comes, the federal government, with taxpayer funds in hand, will bail them out. "Heads, we win; tails, others lose." That will bring on many more business failures than "heads, we win; tails, we lose."

To recap in terms of these differing economic perspectives:

- *Economist A:* Ideally, bailing out companies is not a good idea. But Company X is a large company, and if it goes out of business, that will adversely affect hundreds of thousands of persons. Bailing out the company is better than letting it fail; we lose more by letting the company fail than by saving it. Some companies are simply too big to be allowed to fail. Their failure is like an earthquake, adversely affecting all the people around them. To save the innocent, you sometimes have to save the not-so-innocent.

- *Economist B:* Who is "we" when you say, "We lose more by letting the company fail than by saving it?" Some persons gain by having the company bailed out, and others lose. Furthermore, if we continue to tell companies that the federal government will be there if they fail, we simply create an environment in which we privatize gains (the companies keep the gains if there are any) and socialize the costs (spread the costs among millions of taxpayers if the companies end up in financial problems). In the end, this will lead to more companies that "need" to be bailed out.

# DEMAND-SIDE AND SUPPLY-SIDE VIEWS OF THE ECONOMY AND GOVERNMENT TOOLS TO CHANGE REAL GDP

Much of our discussion of macroeconomics has been in terms of aggregate demand and aggregate supply. Whereas the *AD* curve was always represented as downward sloping, the *AS* curve was shown in different ways according to the macroeconomic model. For example, in the simple quantity theory of money, the *AS* curve is vertical. In many other models we represented, it is upward sloping. Exhibit 1(a)–(b) shows two aggregate supply curves.

Each of these two aggregate supply curves has its own meaning in terms of changes in aggregate demand. If the aggregate supply curve is vertical and aggregate demand rises— the *AD* curve shifts rightward—the price level will rise, but Real GDP will not change. See Exhibit 1(c). But if the aggregate supply curve is upward sloping, a rise in aggregate demand will raise both the price level and Real GDP. See Exhibit 1(d).

Depending on your view of whether the real aggregate supply curve is vertical or upward sloping, how would you respond to this question? "Assuming that the objective is to raise Real GDP, would it be preferable for government to try to increase aggregate demand or aggregate supply?"

The economists who view the *AS* curve as vertical will say that government cannot do anything to raise Real GDP from the demand side of the economy, because changes in *AD* don't change Real GDP if the *AS* curve is vertical. Forget an increase in government purchases, a demand-side tax cut, or expansionary monetary policy. These actions may change *AD*, but a change in *AD*—in the face of a vertical AS curve—will lead only to a change in prices, not in Real GDP. The only way for Real GDP to rise is for the *AS* curve to shift rightward.

Of course, economists who view the *AS* curve as upward sloping will disagree. For them, both a change in *AD* and a change in *AS* will affect Real GDP. Changes in Real GDP may be realized by changes that originate on either the demand side or the supply side of the economy. If the aggregate supply curve is upward sloping, an increase in

**EXHIBIT 1**

### The Aggregate Supply Curve and What Government Can and Cannot Do

Two aggregate supply curves: (a) The curve is vertical; (b) it is upward sloping. In this text, we have often spoken of each of these two differently shaped curves. (c) Changes in aggregate demand will not change Real GDP if the aggregate supply curve is vertical.

(d) Changes in aggregate demand will change Real GDP if the aggregate supply curve is upward sloping. For the vertical-AS economist, changes in Real GDP originate only on the supply-side economy; so government policy that aims to affect the demand side of the economy will change only prices, not Real GDP. For the upward-sloping-AS economist, changes in Real GDP can originate on either

the demand side or the supply side of the economy; so government policy that aims to affect either side of the economy will not only change prices, but Real GDP too. For the vertical-AS economist, government has fewer tools (demand-side fiscal policy and monetary policy won't work) to change Real GDP than the upward-sloping AS economist would say government has.

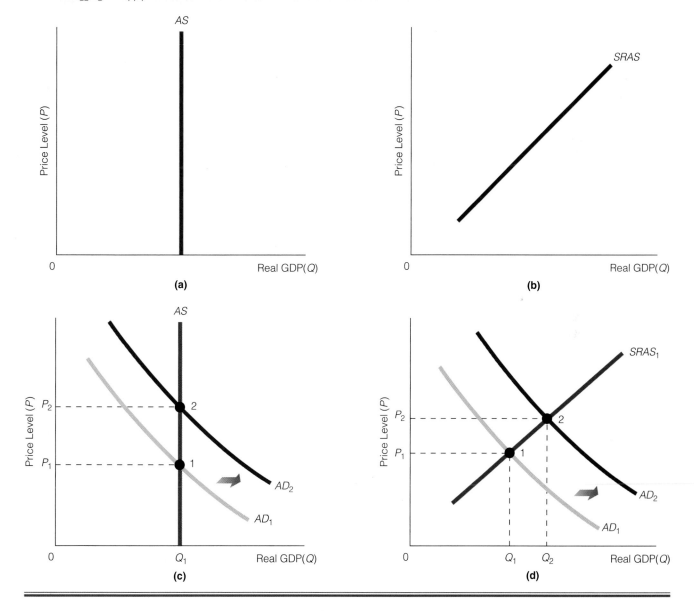

aggregate demand will lead to a rise in Real GDP (at least in the short run), as will an increase in aggregate supply. Viewing things from the demand side of the economy, these economists would argue that a rise in government purchases, a demand-side tax cut, and monetary policy will all be effective at changing Real GDP.

Comparing our two camps of economists, the vertical-*AS* group sees fewer government tools (demand-side fiscal policy and monetary policy won't work) capable of raising Real GDP than do the upward-sloping *AS* economists.

To recap in terms of these differing economic perspectives:

- *Economist A:* The aggregate supply curve is vertical. Therefore, government actions designed to change aggregate demand in the economy will not lead to changes in Real GDP. Changes in Real GDP come from the supply side of the economy, not the demand side. Government has fewer tools (demand-side fiscal policy and monetary policy won't work) capable of raising Real GDP than the upward-sloping *AS* economist believes.

- *Economist B:* The aggregate supply curve is upward sloping (in the short run). Government actions designed to change aggregate demand in the economy will lead to changes in Real GDP (at least in the short run). Changes in Real GDP (in the short run) can come from either the demand side or the supply side of the economy. Government has more tools (demand-side fiscal policy and monetary policy do work) capable of raising Real GDP than the vertical-*AS* economist believes.

## SELF-TEST

(Answers to Self-Test questions are in Answers to Self-Test Questions at the back of the book.)

1. Economist A believes that a reduction in tax rates will lead to increased tax revenue, and economist B believes the opposite. What does each believe with respect to the relationship between the percentage change in tax rates and the percentage change in the tax base?

2. In the standard textbook Keynesian analysis, there is reason to believe that the government spending multiplier is larger than the tax multiplier. Why?

3. Not all economists agree on what constitutes the optimal size and scope of government. Therefore, they won't all agree as to the preferred fiscal policy measure to stimulate the economy—increased government purchases or tax cuts. Do you agree or disagree? Explain your answer.

# OFFICE HOURS

## "What Kinds of Debates Do Macroeconomists Have?"

**STUDENT:**

I'd like some way to categorize the kinds of debates that macroeconomists have. Can you help here?

**INSTRUCTOR:**

Four words: theory, policy, empirics, and government. Here is what we mean by each. Economists sometimes debate theory. For example, think of the economist who builds a theory that assumes wages are inflexible downward and the one who builds a theory that assumes flexible wages.

Economists often debate the kind of policy that will best solve the economic problem at hand. To illustrate, economist A might argue that a supply-side tax cut is better able to solve the problem of lagging economic growth than a demand-side rise in government spending. Economist B might argue the opposite, especially if the increased government spending is directed toward research and development.

Economists often debate empirical results. To illustrate, economist A could say that during period X, the data show that expansionary fiscal policy did raise aggregate demand and did increase Real GDP. Economist B might argue that during period X, many things occurred, only one of which was the implementation of expansionary fiscal policy. Monetary policy was also expansionary during the period, and it, more than expansionary fiscal policy, is the reason why aggregate demand increased and Real GDP increased.

Economists also debate the role government should play in the economy. Often how they argue here is related to their views of how the economy works. For example, as we have stated in this chapter and others, consider an economist who believes that the evidence is consistent with a self-regulating economy—one that regulates itself quickly. He is less likely to advocate government macroeconomic interventions in the economy than an economist who believes that the evidence is consistent with either an unstable economy or with an economy that is unacceptably slow in self-regulating.

**STUDENT:**

One other question about debates in macroeconomics: I've heard about freshwater and saltwater economists. What do these two terms

mean, and what is the essential difference between them when it comes to government's role in the economy?

**INSTRUCTOR:**

Sometimes these macroeconomic differences between economists find a home in two words: freshwater and saltwater, specifically, freshwater economists and saltwater economists. At universities such as Chicago, Minneapolis, and Rochester, which are all located near the Great Lakes, so-called freshwater economists can be found. At universities such as Harvard, MIT, and UC Berkeley—all near oceans—saltwater economists can be found.

Of course, the proximity to freshwater or saltwater isn't what fundamentally separates economists. It is differences in theory, policy, and the role of government. With respect to the latter, freshwater economists see a smaller role for government than do saltwater economists.

### POINTS TO REMEMBER

1. The debates in macroeconomics often focus on theory, policy, empirics, and government.
2. It is not uncommon for an economist's view of how the economy works to influence his or her view on the role government should play in the economy.

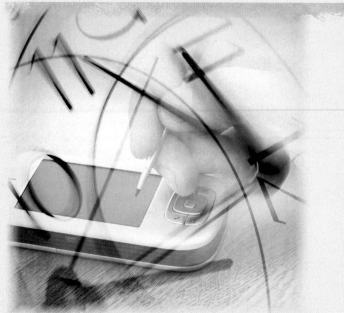

## CHAPTER SUMMARY

In this chapter, the summary is presented in terms of the opposing views of economists on macroeconomic issues.

### TAX CUTS, TAX REVENUE, AND BUDGET DEFICITS

- *Economist A:* Tax cuts will raise tax revenue, and increased tax revenue will decrease the size of the budget deficit.
- *Economist B:* Tax cuts will lower tax revenue, and decreased tax revenue will increase the size of the budget deficit.

### THE ECONOMY: SELF-REGULATING OR NOT?

- *Economist A:* Wages are flexible, so if the economy is in a recessionary gap, it will soon remove itself from the gap. Government need not do anything.
- *Economist B:* Wages are inflexible downward, so if the economy is in a recessionary gap, it may be stuck there. The best course of action is for the federal government to implement expansionary fiscal policy or for the Fed to implement expansionary monetary policy to remove the economy from the recessionary gap.

### MORE GOVERNMENT SPENDING OR A CUT IN TAXES: WHICH GIVES A BIGGER BANG FOR THE BUCK?

- *Economist A:* The economy needs expansionary fiscal policy to remove it from a recessionary gap. Government should either raise its spending or cut taxes. I believe the government spending multiplier is larger than the tax multiplier; so I suggest government increase its spending.
- *Economist B:* The economy needs expansionary fiscal policy to remove it from a recessionary gap. Government should either raise its spending or cut taxes. I believe the tax multiplier is larger than the government spending multiplier; so I suggest government cut taxes.

### MORE GOVERNMENT SPENDING OR A CUT IN TAXES: THE SIZE AND SCOPE OF GOVERNMENT

- *Economist A:* Expansionary fiscal policy is needed to raise aggregate demand and to remove the economy from a recessionary gap. The choice of fiscal policy measures is between either more government spending or a cut in taxes. Since I am in favor of bigger government, I choose more government spending.
- *Economist B:* Expansionary fiscal policy is needed to raise aggregate demand and to remove the economy from a recessionary gap. The choice of fiscal policy measures is between more government spending or a cut in taxes. Since I am in favor of smaller government, I choose a cut in taxes.

### THE DEGREE OF CROWDING OUT

- *Economist A:* A rise in government purchases will increase aggregate demand and remove the economy from the recessionary gap because little or no crowding out will occur. A rise in government purchases will increase the number of jobs in the economy.
- *Economist B:* A rise in government purchases will not increase aggregate demand and remove the economy from the recessionary gap because of complete (or nearly complete) crowding out.

### THE POLITICS OF GOVERNMENT SPENDING

- *Economist A:* An expansionary fiscal policy measure is needed to increase Real GDP, lower the unemployment rate, and so on. I propose $100 billion more in government spending. What the $100 billion is spent on does not matter; the important thing is that the money is spent.
- *Economist B:* An expansionary fiscal policy measure is needed to increase Real GDP, lower the unemployment rate, and so on. Ideally, the economy needs $100 billion more in government spending. But how the money will be spent will be determined by Congress, which is likely to be motivated by political interests when it determines how the money is spent. Furthermore, not all spending is the same. Some spending is better for the economy than other spending. I think much of the spending will be motivated by politics instead of economics, and sometimes the spending motivated by politics will be of little help in turning the economy around. In the end, I have my doubts as to how effective an increase in government spending will be in aiding the economy.

### MONETARY POLICY: RULES OR DISCRETION?

- *Economist A:* A monetary rule is preferred to a discretionary Fed. The former is more likely to bring about stable prices, low unemployment and so on. In addition, a monetary rule removes monetary policy from politics.
- *Economist B:* A discretionary Fed is preferred to a monetary rule. The Fed needs the flexibility to tailor monetary policy to existing circumstances.

### BAILOUTS

- *Economist A:* Ideally, bailing out companies is not a good idea. But Company X is a large company that, if it goes out of business, will adversely affect hundreds of thousands of persons. Bailing out the company is better than letting it fail. We lose more by letting the company fail than by saving it. Some companies are simply too big to be allowed to fail. Their failure is like an earthquake, adversely affecting all the people. To save the innocent, you sometimes have to save the not-so-innocent.
- *Economist B:* Who is "we" when you say, "We lose more by letting the company fail than by saving it?" Some persons gain by having the company bailed out, and others lose. Furthermore, if we continue to tell companies that the federal government will be there if they fail, we simply create an environment in which we privatize gains (the companies keep the gains if there are any) and socialize the costs (spread the costs among millions of taxpayers if

the companies end up in financial problems). In the end, this will lead to more companies that "need" to be bailed out.

## DEMAND-SIDE VERSUS SUPPLY-SIDE VIEW OF THE ECONOMY AND GOVERNMENT TOOLS TO CHANGE REAL GDP

- *Economist A:* The aggregate supply curve is vertical. Therefore, government actions designed to change aggregate demand in the economy will not lead to changes in Real GDP. Changes in Real GDP come from the supply side of the economy, not the demand side. Government has fewer tools (demand-side fiscal policy and monetary policy won't work) capable of raising Real GDP than the upward-sloping *AS* economist believes.

- *Economist B:* The aggregate supply curve is upward sloping (in the short run). Government actions designed to change aggregate demand in the economy will lead to changes in Real GDP (at least in the short run). Changes in Real GDP (in the short run) can come from either the demand side or the supply side of the economy. Government has more tools (demand-side fiscal policy and monetary policy do work) capable of raising Real GDP than the vertical-*AS* economist believes.

## KEY TERMS AND CONCEPTS

Elasticity of Investment        Government Spending Multiplier        Tax Multiplier

## QUESTIONS AND PROBLEMS

1. Can tax revenue rise and the budget deficit decline as a result of an income tax rate cut? Explain your answer.

2. How an economist thinks the economy works—is it self-regulating or not?—influences his opinion of the role government should play in trying to stabilize the economy. Do you agree or disagree? Explain your answer.

3. Whether an economist argues in favor of a rise in government spending or a cut in taxes (as an expansionary fiscal policy measure) could have something to do with whether she views the government spending multiplier as greater or less than the tax multiplier. Do you agree or disagree? Explain your answer.

4. Whether an economist argues in favor of a rise in government spending or a cut in taxes (as an expansionary fiscal policy measure) could have something to do with how he views the current size and scope of government in relationship to his optimal size and scope of government. Do you agree or disagree? Explain your answer.

5. Whether an economist argues in favor of a rise in government spending (as an expansionary fiscal policy measure) could have something to do with the degree of crowding out he expects as a result of the measure. Do you agree or disagree? Explain your answer.

6. Some economists argue that if the economy currently needs to be stimulated to remove it from a recessionary gap, *how* government spends more money (on X or Y) matters less than the fact that it spends more money. Do all economists agree? If not, what do they say in response?

7. Outline the details of the debate between economists who favor a rules-based monetary policy and those who favor a discretionary monetary policy.

8. Something is referred to as a "double-edged sword" if it can have both favorable and unfavorable consequences. In what way might government bailouts of failing companies or financial institutions be a double-edged sword? Explain your answer.

9. The shape of the aggregate supply curve matters to one's view of the ability of government to change Real GDP by way of demand-side fiscal policy and monetary policy. Do you agree or disagree? Explain your answer.

10. What do the values of the government spending and tax multipliers have to do with "getting the biggest bang for the buck"?

11. There is little doubt that if income tax rates are cut, the size of the budget deficit will increase. Do you agree or disagree? Explain your answer.

## WORKING WITH NUMBERS AND GRAPHS

1. A $40 reduction in taxes increases Real GDP by $100, and a $50 increase in government spending increases Real GDP by $120. What does the tax multiplier equal? What does the government spending multiplier equal?

2. A rise in aggregate demand raises Real GDP and the price level. Draw the aggregate supply curve consistent with these results. Next, a rise in aggregate demand raises the price level but leaves Real GDP unchanged. Draw the aggregate supply curve consistent with these results.

## CHAPTER 20

AP PHOTO/PABLO MARTINEZ MONSIVAIS

# PUBLIC CHOICE AND SPECIAL-INTEREST-GROUP POLITICS

**Introduction** Economics is a powerful analytical tool. As you have seen, it can be used to analyze how markets and the economy work. In this chapter we use economics to analyze the behavior of politicians, voters, and members of special interest groups.

Specifically, we analyze public choice, the branch of economics in which economic principles and tools are applied to public sector decision making. Public choice is, in a sense, economics applied to politics.

**Public Choice**
The branch of economics in which economic principles and tools are applied to public sector decision making.

## PUBLIC CHOICE THEORY

Public choice theorists reject the notion that people are like Dr. Jekyll and Mr. Hyde: that is, exhibiting greed and selfishness in their transactions in the private (market) sector and altruism and public spirit in their actions in the public sector. The same people who are the employers, employees, and consumers in the market sector are the politicians, bureaucrats, members of special interest groups, and voters in the public sector. According to public choice theorists, people in the market sector and people in the public sector behave differently not because they have different motives (or are different types of people) but because the two sectors have different institutional arrangements.

As a simple example, Erin Bloom works for a private, profit-seeking firm that makes radio components. Erin is cost conscious, does her work on time, and generally works hard. She knows that she must exhibit this type of work behavior if she wants to keep her job, get a raise, and be promoted. Erin leaves her job at the radio components company and takes a job with the Department of Health and Human Services (HHS) in Washington, D.C. Public choice theorists maintain that Erin is the same person (with different motives) whether working for HHS or for the radio components company.

However, even though Erin is the same person in and out of government, she will not necessarily exhibit the same work behavior. The costs and benefits of certain actions may be substantially different at HHS than at the radio components company. For example, perhaps the cost of being late for work is less in Erin's new job at HHS than it was at her old job. In her former job, she had to work overtime if she came in late; in her new job, her boss doesn't say anything. Erin is therefore more likely to be late in her new job than she was in her old one. She is simply responding to costs and benefits as they exist in her new work environment.

# THE POLITICAL MARKET

Economists who practice positive economics want to understand their world. They want to understand not only the production and pricing of goods, unemployment, inflation, and the firm, but also political outcomes and political behavior. This section is an introduction to the political market.

## Moving Toward the Middle: The Median Voter Model

During political elections, voters often complain that the candidates for office are too much alike. Some find the similarities frustrating, saying they would prefer to have more choice. However, as you will see, two candidates running for the same office often sound alike because they are competing for votes.

In Exhibit 1, parts (a), (b), and (c) all show a distribution of voters in which the political spectrum goes from the Far Left to the Far Right. Relatively few voters hold positions in either of the two extreme wings. Assuming that voters will vote for the candidate who comes closest to matching their ideological or political views, then people whose views are in the Far Left of the political spectrum will vote for the candidate closest to the Far Left, and so on.

Our election process begins with two candidates, a Democrat and a Republican, occupying the positions $D_1$ and $R_1$ in part (a), respectively. If the election were held today, the Republican would receive more votes than his Democrat opponent. The Republican would receive all the votes of the voters who position themselves to the right of $R_1$, the Democrat would receive all the votes of the voters who position themselves to the left of $D_1$, and the voters between $R_1$ and $D_1$ would divide their votes between the two candidates. The Republican would thus receive more votes than the Democrat.

**EXHIBIT 1**

**The Move Toward the Middle**

Political candidates tend to move toward the middle of the political spectrum. Starting with (a), the Republican receives more votes than the Democrat and would win the election if it were held today. To offset this, as shown in (b), the Democrat moves inward toward the middle of the political spectrum. The Republican tries to offset the Democrat's movement inward by also moving inward. As a result, both candidates move toward the political middle, getting closer to each other over time.

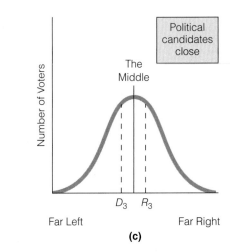

If, however, the election were not held today, the Democrat would likely notice (through polls and other sources) that her opponent was doing better than she was. To offset this, she would move toward the center, or middle, of the political spectrum to pick up some votes. Part (b) in Exhibit 1 illustrates this move by the Democrat. Relative to her position in part (a), the Democrat is closer to the middle of the political spectrum, and as a result she picks up votes. Voters to the left of $D_2$ would vote for the Democrat, voters to the right of $R_2$ would vote for the Republican, and the voters between the two positions would divide their votes between the two candidates. If the election were held now, the Democrat would win.

In part (c), each candidate, in an attempt to get more votes than the opponent, has moved closer to The Middle ($D_3$ and $R_3$). At election time, the two candidates are likely to be positioned side by side at the political center, or middle. In part (c), both candidates have become middle-of-the-roaders in their attempt to pick up votes.

The tendency of political candidates to move toward the center of the voter distribution—captured in the median voter model—is what causes many voters to complain that there is not much difference between candidates.

## What Does the Theory Predict?

Although the median voter model explains why politicians running for the same office often sound alike, what does the model predict? Here are a few of the theory's predictions:

1. *Candidates will label their opponent as being either too far to the right or too far to the left.* The candidates know that whoever is closer to the middle of the political spectrum (in a two-person race) will win more votes and thus the election. To win, they will move toward the political middle, at the same time saying that their opponent is a member of the political fringe (i.e., a person far from the center). A Democrat may argue that his Republican opponent is too conservative; a Republican may argue that her Democrat opponent is too liberal.

2. *Candidates will call themselves middle-of-the-roaders, not right- or left-wingers.* In their move toward the political middle, candidates will try to portray themselves as moderates. In their speeches, they will assert that they represent the majority of voters and that they are practical, not ideological. They will not be likely to refer to themselves as ultraliberal or ultraconservative or as right- or left-wingers because to do so would send a self-defeating message to the voters.

3. *Candidates will take polls, and, if they are not doing well in the polls and their opponents are, they will modify their positions to become more like their opponents.* Polls tell candidates who the likely winner of the election will be. A candidate who finds out that she will lose the election (she is "down in the polls") is not likely to sit back and do nothing. The candidate will change her positions. Often, she will become more like the winner of the poll—that is, more like her political opponent.

4. *Candidates will speak in general, instead of specific, terms.* Voters agree more on ends than on the means of accomplishing those ends. For example, voters of the left, right, and middle believe that a strong economy is better than a weak economy. However, they do not all agree on the best way to make the economy strong. The person on the right might advocate less government intervention as one way, whereas the person on the left might advocate more government intervention. Most political candidates soon learn that addressing the issues specifically requires them to discuss means and that doing so increases the probability of their having an extreme-wing label attached to them. For example, a candidate who advocates more government intervention in the economy is more likely to be labeled "too far left" than a candidate who simply calls for a stronger national economy without discussing any specific means. In the candidate's desire to be perceived as a middle-of-the-roader, he is much more likely to talk about ends, on which voters agree, than about means, on which voters disagree.

**Median Voter Model**
A model suggesting that candidates in a two-person political race will attempt to match the preferences of the median voter (i.e., the person whose preferences are at the center, or in the middle, of the political spectrum).

## A Simple Majority Voting Rule: The Case of the Statue in the Public Square

Public questions are often decided by the simple majority decision rule. Although most people think this is the fair and democratic way to do things, in certain instances a simple majority vote leads to undertaking a project whose costs are greater than its benefits.

Consider a community of 10 people, whose names are listed in column 1 of Exhibit 2. The community is considering whether to purchase a statue to put in the center of the public square. The cost of the statue is $1,000, and the community has previously agreed that if the statue is purchased, the 10 individuals will share the cost equally—that is, each will pay $100 in taxes (see column 3).

Column 2 shows the dollar value of the benefits that each individual will receive from the statue. For example, Applebaum places a dollar value of $150 on the statue, Browning places a dollar value of $140 on the statue, and so on. Column 4 notes the net benefit (+) or net cost (–) of the statue to each individual. A net benefit occurs if the dollar value an individual places on the statue is greater than the tax (cost) incurred. A net cost results if the reverse is true. Finally, column 5 indicates how

each member of the community would vote. An individual who believes the statue has a net benefit will vote for it, and an individual who believes the statue has a net cost will vote against it. Six individuals vote for the statue, and four individuals vote against it. The majority rules, and the statue is purchased and placed in the center of the public square.

However, the total dollar value of benefits to the community ($812) is less than the total tax cost to the community ($1,000). Using the simple majority decision rule has resulted in the purchase of the statue even though the benefits of the statue to the community are less than its costs.

This outcome is not surprising when you understand that the simple majority decision rule does not take into account the intensity of individuals' preferences. No matter how strongly a person feels about an issue, he or she registers only one vote. For example, even though Emerson places a net benefit of $1 on the statue and Isley places a net cost of $90 on the statue, each individual has only one vote. Isley has no way to register that he does not want the statue more than Emerson wants it.

### EXHIBIT 2

**Simple Majority Voting and Inefficiency** — The simple majority decision rule sometimes generates inefficient results. Here the statue is purchased even though the total dollar value of the benefits of the statue is less than the total dollar costs.

| (1)<br>Individuals | (2)<br>Dollar Value of<br>Benefits to Individual | (3)<br>Tax Levied<br>on Individual | (4)<br>Net Benefit (+)<br>or Net Cost (−) | (5)<br>Vote For<br>or Against |
|---|---|---|---|---|
| Applebaum | $150 | $ 100 | +$50 | For |
| Browning | 140 | 100 | + 40 | For |
| Carson | 130 | 100 | + 30 | For |
| Davidson | 110 | 100 | + 10 | For |
| Emerson | 101 | 100 | + 1 | For |
| Finley | 101 | 100 | + 1 | For |
| Gunter | 50 | 100 | − 50 | Against |
| Harris | 10 | 100 | − 90 | Against |
| Isley | 10 | 100 | − 90 | Against |
| Janowitz | 10 | 100 | − 90 | Against |
| Total | $812 | $1,000 | | |

## finding ECONOMICS

**In a Presidential Election Debate** During a presidential election debate, one candidate is asked what his plan is for health care in the country. He says that his plan would make health care more affordable and responsive to peoples' needs. He then goes on to say that health care has been a problem in the United States for a long time and that it is about time for a solution. Where is the economics?

The median voter model predicts that candidates will speak in general, not specific, terms. This is what we have just heard one of the candidates do. He did not get into any specifics about his plan. For example, he probably will not specifically address how much the health care plan will cost, whom it will serve, and so on. ▲ ▲ ▲

## thinking Like AN ECONOMIST

**Testing Theories** An economist thinks about theories and then tests them. She is not content to accept a theory—such as the one that says candidates in a two-person political race will gravitate toward the center of the political distribution—simply because it sounds right. The economist asks, "If the theory is right, what should I expect to see in the real world? If the theory is wrong, what should I expect to see in the real world?" Such questions direct the economist to look at effects to see whether the theory has explanatory and predictive power. If the four predictions of the median voter theory occur in the real world—candidates labeling themselves one way, speaking in general terms, and so on—then the economist can conclude that the evidence supports the theory. But if candidates en masse do not behave as the model predicts, then the economist must reject the theory. ▲ ▲ ▲

# VOTERS AND RATIONAL IGNORANCE

The preceding section explains something about the behavior of politicians, especially near or at election time. We turn now to voters.

## The Costs and Benefits of Voting

Political commentators often remark that the voter turnout for this or that election was low: "Only 54 percent of registered voters actually voted." Are voter turnouts low because Americans are apathetic? Are they uninterested in political issues?

Public choice economists often explain low voter turnouts in terms of the costs and benefits of voting. As an example, Mark Quincy is thinking about voting in a presidential election. Mark may receive many benefits from voting: he may feel more involved in public affairs or think that he has met his civic responsibility. He may see himself as patriotic, or he may believe he has a greater right to criticize government if he takes an active part in it. In short, he may benefit by seeing himself as a doer instead of a talker. Ultimately, however, he will weigh these positive benefits against the costs of voting, which include driving to the polls, standing in line, and so on. If, in the end, Mark perceives the benefits of voting as greater than the costs, he will vote.

But suppose Mark believes he receives only one benefit from voting: determining the election outcome. His benefits-of-voting equation may look like this:

Mark's benefits of voting = Probability of Mark's vote determining the election outcome
× Additional benefits Mark receives if his candidate wins

Suppose two candidates, A and B, are running for office. If Mark votes, he will vote for A because he estimates that he benefits $100 if A is elected but only $40 if B is elected. The difference, $60, represents the additional benefits Mark receives if his candidate wins.

However, the probability of Mark's vote determining the outcome is questionable. With many potential voters, such as in a presidential election, the probability that one person's vote will determine the outcome is close to 0. To recognize this fact on an intuitive level, suppose A and B are the two major candidates in a presidential campaign. If you, as an individual voter, vote for A, the outcome of the election is likely to be the same as if you had voted for B or not voted at all. In other words, whether you vote, vote for A, or vote for B, the outcome is likely to be the same. In short, given many potential voters, the probability of one person's vote changing the outcome of an election is close to zero. In Mark's benefits-of-voting equation, $60 is multiplied by a probability so small that it might as well be 0. So $60 times 0 is 0. In short, Mark receives no benefits from voting.

But Mark may face certain costs. His costs-of-voting equation may look like this:

$$\text{Mark's cost of voting} = \text{Cost of driving to the polls} \\ + \text{Cost of standing in line} \\ + \text{Cost of filling out the ballot}$$

Obviously, Mark faces some positive costs of voting. Because his benefits of voting are 0 and his costs of voting are positive, Mark makes the rational choice if he decides not to vote.

Clearly, not everyone behaves this way, that is, chooses not to vote. Many people do vote in elections. Probably what separates the Marks in the world from the people who vote is that the voters receive some benefits that Mark does not. They might receive benefits simply by being part of the excitement of election day, by doing what they perceive as their civic duty, or for some other reason.

The point that public choice economists make is that if many individual voters will vote only if they perceive their vote as making a difference, then they probably will not vote because their vote is unlikely to make a difference. The low turnouts that appear to be a result of voter apathy may instead be a result of cost-benefit calculations.

## Rational Ignorance

How often have you heard an opinion like this one? "Democracy would be better served if voters would take more of an interest in and become better informed about politics and government. Voters don't know much about the issues."

The problem is not that voters are too stupid to learn about the issues. Many voter-citizens who know little about politics and government are quite capable of learning about both, but they choose not to make the effort. The reason is perhaps predictable: the costs of becoming informed often outweigh the benefits. In short, many persons believe that becoming informed is simply not worth the effort. Hence, on an individual basis, it makes sense to be uninformed about politics and government, that is, to be in a state of rational ignorance.

As an example, Shonia Tyler has many things she can do with her leisure time. She could read a good novel, watch a television program, go out with friends, or become better informed about the candidates and the issues in the upcoming U.S. Senate race. Becoming informed, however, has costs. If Shonia stays home and reads about the issues, she can't go out with her friends. If she stays up late to watch a news program, she might be too tired to work efficiently the next day. These costs have to be weighed against the benefits of becoming better informed about the candidates and the issues. For Shonia, as for many people, the benefits are unlikely to be greater than the costs.

Many people see little personal benefit in becoming more knowledgeable about political candidates and issues. As with voting, the decision to remain uninformed may be linked to the small impact any single individual can have in a large-numbers setting.

**Rational Ignorance**
The state of not acquiring information because the costs of acquiring it are greater than the benefits.

## Economic Illiteracy and Democracy

Citizens can vote even if they have no idea what they are doing. If enough voters fit that description, democratic governments are bound to make foolish decisions.

—**Bryan Caplan,** *Straight Talk About Economic Literacy*

Economist Bryan Caplan argues that a large percentage of the American public is economically illiterate. The result is a lot of foolishness gets turned into national economic policy.[1]

Although determining whether someone is illiterate may be easy, not so easy is ascertaining whether someone is economically illiterate. To determine illiteracy, you can just ask people to read or write something. If they can read and write, they are not illiterate. If they can't read and write, they are illiterate.

Unfortunately, there is no such simple test to determine economically illiteracy. Instead Caplan points to a survey that compared the responses of average Americans (1,510 of them) and professional economists (250 of them) to the same set of questions concerning economics and the economy. Here is one question from the survey: "Which do you think is more responsible for the recent increase in gasoline prices: the normal law of supply and demand, oil companies are trying to increase profits, both, or neither?" Although only 8 percent of economists said recent increases in gas prices were due to oil companies trying to increase profits, 78 percent of the noneconomists polled explained high gas prices this way. The explanation for high gas prices chosen by 83 percent of economists was supply and demand.

Indirectly, Caplan uses the economists' overwhelming response to the question as a benchmark by which to measure the economic illiteracy of the public. The closer the public responses are to the economists' responses, the less economically illiterate the public is; the farther away the public responses are from the economists' responses, the more economically illiterate the public is.

According to Caplan, looking at responses to numerous questions, the American public is largely economically illiterate. Caplan argues that such a great degree of economic illiteracy has to do with the price one pays for it. In fact, the price is rather low, and when the price is low, you would expect a higher degree of economic illiteracy than

when the price is high. In a phrase: False beliefs about economics are cheap. According to Caplan, if you underestimate the costs of excessive drinking, you can ruin your life. But if you underestimate the economic benefits of, say, free international trade, nothing really bad happens to you. Whatever happens to you is what would have happened if you didn't underestimate the economic benefits of free international trade. In other words, when being wrong really has no cost, a lot of people will be wrong—especially if one receives a personal psychological lift from holding an erroneous belief or position. Caplan puts it succinctly: "In a sense, then, there is a method to the average voter's madness. Even when his views are completely wrong, he gets the psychological benefit of emotionally appealing political beliefs at a bargain price. No wonder he buys in bulk."[2] In other words, $x$ might be the wrong answer to the question, but if $x$ is emotionally appealing to the respondent, and if having the wrong answer doesn't adversely affect the respondent, then $x$ it is.

But if many people choose $x$, perhaps at a national level $x$ gets turned into policy. In other words, if the majority of voting Americans believe that placing tariffs on foreign imports is desirable (when economists largely disagree), then, in a political system where politicians compete for votes, the public's erroneous belief is likely to find its way into international trade policy.

If one person's erroneous belief adversely affects only him, that is one thing. But it is quite another thing, Caplan argues, when the erroneous beliefs of many people adversely affect those who do not hold that belief. Yet this is what we often get in a representative democracy. Economically erroneous beliefs, chosen on an individual level because they are cheap to choose, often add up to democracies' choosing bad economic policies.

---

1. See Bryan Caplan's book, *The Myth of the Rational Voter: Why Democracies Choose Bad Policies* (Princeton, NJ: Princeton University Press, 2007).
2. See "The Myth of the Rational Voter," in *Cato Unbound*, November 6, 2006, at http://www.cato-unbound.org/2006/11/06/bryan-caplan/the-myth-of-the-rational-voter/ http://www.cato-unbound.org/2006/11/06/bryan-caplan/the-myth-of-the-rational-voter/

(Answers to Self-Test questions are in Answers to Self-Test Questions at the back of the book.)

1. If a politician running for office does not speak in general terms, does not try to move to the middle of the political spectrum, and does not take polls, is the median voter model therefore wrong?

2. Voters often criticize politicians running for office who do not speak in specific terms (that is, do not specify which spending

programs will be cut, whose taxes will be raised, etc.). If voters want politicians running for office to speak in specific terms, why don't politicians do so?

3. Would bad weather be something that could affect the voter turnout? Explain your answer.

# MORE ABOUT VOTING

Voting is often the method used to make decisions in the public sector. In this section, we discuss two examples to describe some of the effects (some might say problems) of voting as a decision-making method.

## Example 1: Voting for a Nonexcludable Public Good

Suppose a community of 7 persons, A–G, wants to produce or purchase nonexcludable public good X. Each person in the community wants a different number of units of X, as shown in the following table:

| Person | Number of Units of X Desired |
|--------|------------------------------|
| A | 1 |
| B | 2 |
| C | 3 |
| D | 4 |
| E | 5 |
| F | 6 |
| G | 7 |

If the community of 7 persons holds a simple majority vote, then all 7 will vote to produce or purchase at least 1 unit of X. Six people (B–G) will vote for at least 2 units; five people (C–G), for at least 3 units; four people (D–G), for at least 4 units; three people (E–G), for at least 5 units; and two people (F–G), for at least 6 units. Only one person (G) will vote for 7 units.

The largest number of units that receives a simple majority vote (half the total number of voters plus 1, or 4 votes) is 4 units. In other words, the community will vote to produce or purchase 4 units of X. Interestingly, 4 units is the most preferred outcome of only one of the seven members of the community, person D, who is the median voter. Half the voters (A, B, and C) prefer fewer than 4 units, and half the voters (E, F, and G) prefer more. Thus, our voting process has resulted in only the median voter obtaining his most preferred outcome.

The outcome would have been the same even if the numbers had looked as they do in the following table:

| Person | Number of Units of X Desired |
|--------|------------------------------|
| A | 0 |
| B | 0 |
| C | 0 |
| D | 4 |
| E | 7 |
| F | 7 |
| G | 7 |

In this case, four people (D–G) would have voted for at least 4 units, and only three people would have voted for anything less than 4 units. Again, 4 units would have been the outcome of the vote, and only the median voter would have obtained his most preferred outcome.

## Example 2: Voting and Efficiency

Suppose three individuals have the marginal private benefits (*MPB*) shown in the following table for various units of nonexcludable public good Y:

| Person | MPB of First Unit of Y | MPB of Second Unit of Y | MPB of Third Unit of Y |
|--------|-----------------------|------------------------|-----------------------|
| A | $400 | $380 | $190 |
| B | 150 | 110 | 90 |
| C | 100 | 90 | 80 |

If the cost of providing a unit of good Y is $360, what is the socially optimal, or efficient, amount of good Y? To answer this question, recall a few of the relationships from the last chapter:

1. The socially optimal, or efficient, amount of anything is the amount at which the marginal social benefits (*MSB*) equal the marginal social costs (*MSC*).

2. The sum of the marginal private benefits (*MPB*) and the marginal external benefits (*MEB*) equals the marginal social benefits (*MSB*): *MPB* + *MEB* = *MSB*.

3. The sum of the marginal private costs (*MPC*) and the marginal external costs (*MEC*) equals the marginal social costs (*MSC*): *MPC* + *MEC* = *MSC*.

In our example, the *MSC* for each unit is given as $360. We calculate the *MSB* for each unit by summing its *MPB*. For the first unit, the *MSB* is $650 ($400 + $150 + $100); for the second unit, it is $580; and for the third unit, it is $360. The socially optimal, or efficient, amount of good Y is 3 units because at this amount *MSB* = *MSC*.

Whether voting will give us efficiency largely depends on what tax each person, A–C, expects to pay. Suppose each person must pay an equal share of the price of a unit of good Y. In other words, the tax for each person is $120 ($360 per unit ÷ 3 persons = $120 per person per unit).

Person A will vote for 3 units because his *MPB* for each unit is greater than his tax of $120 per unit. Person B will vote for only 1 unit because his *MPB* for the first unit is greater than his tax of $120 per unit, but his *MPB* is not greater for the second or third unit. Person C will not vote for any units because his *MPB* for each unit is less than his tax of $120 per unit. The outcome, using a simple majority vote, is only 1 unit. A process of voting in which each voter pays an equal tax results in an inefficient outcome.

Now suppose, instead of paying an equal tax (of $120), each person pays a tax equal to his *MPB* at the socially optimal, or efficient, outcome. The socially optimal, or efficient, outcome is 3 units of good Y. So person A would pay a tax of $190 (his *MPB* for the third unit is $190). Person B would pay a tax of $90, and person C would pay a tax of $80. (The sum of the taxes paid is equal to the cost of the unit, or $360.)

With this different tax structure, will voting generate efficiency? If each person casts a truthful vote, the answer is yes. Each person will vote for 3 units.[3] In other words, if every-

---

3. Look at the situation for person A: His *MPB* for the first unit is $400 and his tax is $190; so he votes for the first unit. His *MPB* for the second unit is $380 and his tax is $190; so he votes for the second unit. His *MPB* for the third unit is $190 and his tax is $190; so he votes for the third unit. With respect to the last unit for person A, we are assuming that if his *MPB* is equal to the tax, he will vote in favor of the unit. The same holds for the analysis of voting for persons B and C.

one casts a truthful vote and everyone pays a tax equal to his or her *MPB* at the efficient outcome, then voting will generate efficiency.

Comparing the two tax structures—one where each person pays an equal tax and one where each person pays a tax equal to his *MPB*—we see that the tax structure makes the difference. In the case of equal tax shares, voting did not lead to efficiency; in the case of unequal tax shares, it did.

---

## SELF-TEST

1. If the *MSC* in Example 2 had been $580 instead of $360, what would the socially optimal, or efficient, outcome have been?

2. In Example 2 with equal taxes, did the outcome of the vote make anyone worse off? If so, who and by how much?

---

# SPECIAL INTEREST GROUPS

Special interest groups are subsets of the general population that hold (usually) intense preferences for or against a particular government service, activity, or policy. Often, special interest groups gain from public policies that may not be in accord with the interests of the general public. In recent decades, they have played a major role in government.

> **Special Interest Groups**
> Subsets of the general population that hold (usually) intense preferences for or against a particular government service, activity, or policy and that often gain from public policies that may not be in accord with the interests of the general public.

## Information and Lobbying Efforts

Whereas the general voter is usually uninformed about issues, members of a special interest group are very well informed. For example, teachers are likely to know a lot about government education policies, farmers about government agriculture policies, and union members about government union policies. When it comes to their issues of interest, the special interest group members know much more than the general voter. The reason is simple: The more directly and intensely issues affect them, the greater the incentive is for individuals to become informed about them.

Given an electorate composed of uninformed general voters and informed members of special interest groups, the groups are often able to sway politicians in their favor. This effect occurs even when the general public is made worse off by such actions (which, of course, is not always the case).

Suppose special interest group A, composed of 5,000 individuals, favors a policy that will result in the redistribution of $50 million from 100 million general taxpayers to the group. The dollar benefit for each member of the special interest group is $10,000. Given this substantial dollar amount, members of the special interest group are likely to (1) sponsor or propose the legislation and (2) lobby the politicians who will decide the issue.

Further, the politicians will probably not hear from the general voter (i.e., general taxpayer). The general voter/taxpayer will be less informed about the legislation than the members of the special interest group, and, even if adequately informed, each person would have to calculate the benefits and the costs of lobbying against the proposed legislation. If the legislation passes, the average taxpayer will pay approximately 50¢, and the benefits of lobbying against the legislation are probably not greater than 50¢. Therefore, even if informed about the legislation, the general taxpayer would not be likely to argue against it. The benefits just wouldn't be worth the time and effort. Special interest bills therefore have a good chance of being passed in our legislatures.

## Congressional Districts as Special Interest Groups

Most people do not ordinarily think of congressional districts as special interest groups. Special interest groups are commonly thought to include the ranks of public school teachers, steel manufacturers, automobile manufacturers, farmers, environmentalists, bankers, truck drivers, doctors, and the like. For some issues, however, a congressional district may be a special interest group.

Suppose an air force base is located in a Texas congressional district. Then a Pentagon study determines that the base is not needed and that Congress should shut it down. The Pentagon study demonstrates that the cost to the taxpayers of keeping the base open is greater than the benefits to the country of maintaining it. But closing the air force base will hurt the pocketbooks of the people in the congressional district housing the base. Their congressional representative knows not only as much, but also that if she can't keep the base open, she isn't as likely to be reelected to office.

Therefore, she speaks to other members of Congress about the proposed closing. In a way, she acts as a lobbyist for her congressional district. Most members of Congress are probably willing to go along with the Texas representative, even though they know that their constituents will be paying more in taxes than, according to the Pentagon, is necessary to assure the national security of the country. If they don't go along with her, when they need a vote on one of their own special interest projects (sometimes the term "pork barrel" is used), the representative from Texas may not be so cooperative. In short, members of Congress sometimes trade votes: my vote on your air force base for your vote on subsidies to dairy farmers in my district. This type of vote trading—the exchange of votes to gain support for legislation—is commonly referred to as logrolling.

**Logrolling**
The exchange of votes to gain support for legislation.

## Public Interest Talk, Special Interest Legislation

Special interest groups lobbying for special interest legislation usually don't use that phrase, but rather something like "legislation in the best interest of the general public." A couple of examples, both past and present, come to mind.

In the early nineteenth century, the British Parliament passed the Factory Acts, which put restrictions on women and children working. Those who lobbied for the restrictions said they did so for humanitarian reasons, that is, to protect young children and women from difficult and hazardous work in the cotton mills. There is evidence, however, that the men working in the factories were the main lobbyists for the Factory Acts and that a reduced supply of women and children directly benefited them by raising their wages. The male factory workers appealed to individuals' higher sensibilities instead of letting it be known that they would benefit at the expense of others.

Today, people calling for, say, economic protection from foreign competitors or greater federal subsidies rarely explain that they favor the measure because the legislation will make them better off while someone else pays the bill. Instead, they usually voice the public interest argument. Economic protectionism isn't necessary to protect industry X, but it is necessary to protect American jobs and the domestic economy. The special interest message often is, "Help yourself by helping us."

Sometimes this message is sincere, but other times it is not. In either case, it is likely to be as forcefully voiced.

## Rent Seeking

**Rent Seeking**
Actions of individuals and groups who spend resources to influence public policy in the hope of redistributing (transferring) income to themselves from others.

**Rent seeking** consists of the actions of individuals and groups who spend resources to influence public policy in the hope of redistributing (transferring) income to themselves from others. To illustrate, suppose Smith is one of many producers of shoes and that he realizes he would be better off if he were the only one who produces shoes. With less competition from other shoe producers, the supply of shoes would fall, and the price would rise. Smith then would end up selling shoes at $100 a pair instead of $30 a pair.

Smith hires a law firm that specializes in lobbying government for its clients. Members of the law firm go to members of Congress and ask them to pass a law prohibiting all companies other than the Smith Shoe Company from producing shoes. The attorneys representing Smith promise to donate money to the political campaigns of the Congressional members with whom they speak. They also promise that Smith of Smith Shoe Company will try to persuade his workers that their work interests are best served by voting for specific members of Congress.

Smith is using resources to effect a transfer. Smith has spent money to influence Congress to give him a special privilege; specifically, he is asking for the right to be the only producer of shoes. Essentially, Smith is trying to bring about a transfer from shoe consumers to himself. He wants consumers to end up paying more for shoes so that he earns more from producing them. He is spending money to try to bring about this transfer from others to him. Smith is a *rent seeker*. Specifically, he is using resources (the money he spends goes for resources) in order to bring about a transfer from others to him.

Let's say that Smith spends a total of $100,000 to bring about the transfer. This is the cost of his rent seeking. From Smith's perspective, the decision to spend $100,000 to bring about a transfer, of, say $1 million is rational. But from society's perspective, all the resources that Smith uses to effect a transfer are wasted. The $100,000 is wasted because money spent trying to effect a transfer cannot be used to produce goods and services.

To see the negative effects rent-seeking has on society even more clearly, consider an extreme example. Let's say that today 1,000 individuals are all producing goods and services. Together they produce about $2 million worth of output a day. Tomorrow, all 1,000 individuals decide to spend their time and money trying to bring about a transfer. In other words, instead of producing, they spend their time rent seeking. At the end of the day, the cost to society of these 1,000 individuals' rent seeking instead of producing is obviously $2 million worth of output. Society is poorer by $2 million because the 1,000 individuals turned away from producing and toward rent seeking. In short, rent seeking is a socially wasteful activity.

## Bringing About Transfers

In Exhibit 3, the market equilibrium price of the good is $P_1$. At this price, identifying both consumers' surplus and producers' surplus is easy. Consumers' surplus is the area under the demand curve and above the equilibrium price out to the equilibrium quantity, $Q_1$: areas $A + B + C$. Producers' surplus is the area under the equilibrium price and above the supply curve out to the equilibrium quantity, $Q_1$: $D + E$.

Now suppose the producers of the good lobby government for a price floor, $P_2$. If government grants this price floor, then the new price in the market is $P_2$ and consumers' surplus ends up being only area $A$. Consumers lose areas $B + C$ in consumers' surplus. At the new price of $P_2$, producers lose area $E$ in

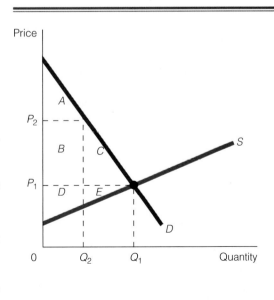

**A Price Floor and a Transfer from Consumers to Producers**

Market equilibrium price of the good is $P_1$. Consumers' surplus is the area $A + B + C$. Producers' surplus is the area $D + E$. If producers of the good lobby for and receive a price floor of $P_2$, then consumers' surplus ends up being only area $A$. Consumers lose areas $B + C$ in consumers' surplus, and producers gain area $B$ in producers' surplus. By obtaining the price floor through government, producers of the good were able to take some consumers' surplus away from consumers and turn it into producers' surplus for themselves.

producers' surplus, and they gain area *B*. As long as area *E* (what they lose) is smaller than area *B* (what they gain), producers are better off selling at price $P_2$ than $P_1$. In Exhibit 3, area *E* is clearly smaller than *B*; so producers are better off.

The price floor has thus created a transfer. Area *B*, which was once consumers' surplus, is now producers' surplus. By getting the price floor, the producers of the good were able to take some consumers' surplus away from consumers and turn it into producers' surplus. If area *B* is equivalent to, say, $1,000, then producers have been able to transfer $1,000 from consumers to themselves. All the resources that the producers expended to get that transfer of $1,000 are referred to as the *rent seeking costs*, that is, the costs of trying to bring about the transfer. Again, from society's perspective, the resources expended to effect the transfer are wasted in that they cannot be used to produce goods and services. Society as a whole is a just a little bit poorer because of the rent seeking behavior of the producers.

## Information, Rational Ignorance, and Seeking Transfers

Will rent seekers tell the truth about their rent seeking efforts (assuming they know the truth). Suppose Smith knows that his rent seeking will lead to greater producers' surplus for him and less consumers' surplus and that the losses to consumers will be greater than his gains. (If you look back at Exhibit 3, you will notice that the losses to consumers from the price floor—areas *B* + *C*—are greater than the gain of area *B* to the producer.) Will he advertise this information? Will he, for instance, lobby government by saying: "I would like a price floor for what I sell. I know that this will end up hurting consumers more than it benefits me, but so be it. As long as I am made better off, I don't really care how much consumers are made worse off. Can I have the transfer?"

He is unlikely to say this. For one thing, making such a barefaced request draws attention to the facts that he gains at consumers' expense and that his gain is smaller than what consumers lose. Smith wouldn't draw attention to this fact. Instead, he might try to argue that what is good for him is good (not bad) for others.

Can such rent-seeking efforts be successful? Won't the politicians turn Smith down because moving from an equilibrium price to a price floor hurts consumers more than it helps producers? (Yet there are price floors in the real world.) Won't the consumers rally against Smith because they know they are being hurt by his actions? And aren't the consumers greater in number than Smith (who is only one), and don't politicians care about votes (which means they must then care about the number of voters)?

First, consumers may not rally against Smith because they may not even know that he is lobbying government for a price floor. Recall the issue of rational ignorance, that is, not acquiring information because the costs of acquiring it are greater than the benefits.

Most individuals are rationally ignorant of many issues. If you know less about French literature than you could possibly know, then you are rationally ignorant of the subject. If you know less about computers than you could possibly know, then you are rationally ignorant of computers.

Similarly, many people are rationally ignorant of politics and government; that is, they know less than they could know largely because the marginal benefits of acquiring this kind of information are so low. And the benefits are low because an individual's one vote matters so little in the determination of an election, as we discussed earlier. In other words, the probability that your one vote will break a tie and decide who wins and who loses in an election—especially when millions of people are eligible to vote—is infinitesimally small.

So, if your vote is not going to determine an election outcome, what does it matter how much or how little information you have about the candidates, the issues, and events?

The answer to that question is perhaps best framed in terms of your options. Let's say two major candidates, A and B, are running for U.S. Senator from your state. You have the following options:

- *Option 1:* Be fully informed (on the Senate election issues) and vote for A.
- *Option 2:* Be fully informed and vote for B.
- *Option 3:* Be rationally ignorant and vote for A.
- *Option 4:* Be rationally ignorant and vote for B.
- *Option 5:* Be fully informed and not vote.
- *Option 6:* Be rationally ignorant and not vote.

No matter which option you choose, the outcome of the election will be what it will be. Your vote will likely not break a tie; your vote will not determine the election outcome. Therefore, the least-cost option is obviously option 6, to be rationally ignorant and not vote.

Of course, not everyone chooses this option. In the last presidential election, approximately 130 million persons voted, although millions of other eligible voters chose not to vote. Of the approximately 130 million who did vote, probably very many were rationally ignorant. Being otherwise would have been just too costly for them, especially given the fact that very few of them were under the delusion that their single vote would determine the election outcome.

Given that fact, if producers seek a transfer that ends up hurting consumers, consumers are not likely to know about it if they are rationally ignorant, and the incentive for them to be rationally ignorant is huge. So, when the producer lobbies the members of Congress for a price floor that helps him and hurts consumers, the consumers may not even know about the rent seeking. And even if they do, do they also know that a price floor leads to a greater loss in consumers' surplus than an increase in producers' surplus, especially when the producer has an incentive not to state the details of the transfer? Instead, the producer will probably wrap his special interest legislation in "public interest talk." Perhaps he will argue that without a price floor for his good, few producers will produce it, and that if few producers produce the good, people will lose their jobs, communities will lose tax revenue, and so forth. None of this has to be true, of course, but trying to figure out whether it might be true may be too costly an effort for most individuals to undertake.

On the other hand, let's say that rational ignorance does not exist. Everyone knows everything about everything. So, when the producer lobbies government for a price floor, the consumers immediately know about his activities; furthermore, they know that the loss of consumers' surplus (as a result of the price floor) will be greater than the gain in producers' surplus. Even so, consumers may still not fight the producers because, simply put, the loss to each individual consumer might be so small that it is not worth fighting to stop the price floor.

As an example, suppose 100 producers will benefit a total of $10 million if the price floor replaces the equilibrium price in the market. That is an average of $100,000 per producer. But suppose consumers will lose $15 million as a result of the price floor. If there are 100 million consumers, the average consumer loses only 15¢. A consumer will probably not spend $1 to fight a policy that costs him or her only 15¢.

The key in seeking transfers is to spread the loss from the transfer over as many people as possible so that on a per-person basis the loss is very small. The loss should be small enough that the individual will have little reason to argue against the policy that inflicts the loss.

## Inheritance, Heirs, and Why the Firstborn Became King or Queen

Some economists have said that rent seeking often goes on within families, especially when an inheritance is involved. We present their argument in the form of a short story.

An elderly widow with three children has an estate worth $10 million, which she will leave to her children upon her death. But, of course, $10 million can be left to three adult children in a number of ways.

- She can split the $10 million into three equal parts, leaving $3.333 million to each.
- She can divide the $10 million unequally, perhaps leaving $9 million to A, $500,000 to B, and $500,000 to C.
- She can either tell each child how much he or she will inherit, or she can keep the dollar amount secret (until after her death).

©YALE CENTER FOR BRITISH ART, PAUL MELLON COLLECTION, USA/THE BRIDGEMAN ART LIBRARY

In other words, the elderly woman has two major decisions to make: how much money she will give each child and whether to tell them what they will receive upon her death.

If the woman is the type of person who craves attention and wants her children to fawn over her, she can use her inheritance to get them to do that. All she has to do is tell her children (1) that she will not divide her estate equally among the three of them and (2) that she hasn't yet decided on the amount each will receive. If she promises unequal inheritances that are yet to be determined, she almost guarantees that her children will engage in a rent-seeking battle for the bulk of her inheritance. The resultant battle is likely to take the form of each child fawning over the mother to curry favor.

The siblings know that the amount of the inheritance is fixed at $10 million and that whatever goes to one sibling will not go to the others. For example, if $3 million goes to sibling B or C, then A gets $3 million less. The widow has effectively put her three children in a situation in which they will invest resources (fawn over her) to effect a pure transfer. This is rent seeking.

The situation is different if the woman tells her children what she plans to leave each and then guarantees that under no circumstances will she change her mind. For example, she tells child A that he will receive $2 million, child B that she will receive $7 million, and child C that he will receive $1 million. The siblings now have no reason to invest resources in rent seeking. The $10 million has already been split up.

Alternatively, the mother can tell her children that she plans to divide her inheritance equally and nothing on earth can get her to do differently. Once again, if the children know how things are guaranteed to turn out and that any resources they use to change the results will be wasted, they will decide against trying to change the outcome. In other words, no child will seek rent.

Rent seeking used to be common in a slightly different context. In the days when kings and queens ruled, the royal firstborn usually inherited the throne. But why the first child? The third child could be a more capable king or queen than the first. Surely not every firstborn was more capable of being king or queen than every second, third, or fourth child.

If the firstborn were not predetermined to inherit the throne, the royal children would have engaged in a rent-seeking battle for it. In and of itself, the queen or king may not have had anything against this outcome, and, in fact, they may have liked it.

But they might not have liked it if their children engaged in such an intense rent-seeking battle that they tried to kill each other. If you were one of the siblings, you could get to the throne in two ways: (1) have the queen or king choose you as heir from among all your brothers and sisters; (2) kill your brothers and sisters so that you were the only one left. One way to cut down on the bloodshed was to simply have a rule stating that the firstborn would become king or queen. This rule didn't eliminate sibling murders completely—the second child might try to kill the first and therefore inherit the throne—but it certainly kept the number of sibling murders lower than what it might have been if any of the children could ascend to the throne.

## SELF-TEST

1. The average farmer is likely to be better informed about federal agricultural policy than the average food consumer is. Why?

2. Consider special interest legislation that will transfer $40 million from group A to group B, where group B includes 10,000 persons. Is this special interest legislation more likely to pass when group A includes (a) 10,000 persons or (b) 10 million persons? Explain your answer.

3. Give an example of public interest talk spoken by a special interest group.

4. Why is rent-seeking activity socially wasteful?

# "Doesn't Public Choice Paint a Bleak Picture of Politics and Government?"

**STUDENT:**

In a way, public choice paints a rather bleak picture of politics and government.

**INSTRUCTOR:**

How so?

**STUDENT:**

Politicians don't seem to care about what is right or wrong. They just move to the middle of the voter distribution. People don't always vote because voting is sometimes too costly. People aren't always well informed on issues because accessing the information is too costly. And to top it off, special interests are engaged in rent seeking. Doesn't all this sound dismal to you?

**INSTRUCTOR:**

It sounds as if you want things to work differently. Unfortunately, we don't always get the results we want.

**STUDENT:**

I have to confess that I do. I want politicians to do the right thing, and I want people to be informed on issues and to cast intelligent votes.

**INSTRUCTOR:**

Probably many people want the same thing. My guess is that public choice economists want the same thing. But we can't let what we want color how we see the world.

**STUDENT:**

But who is to say that public choice economists analyze the world the right way? Maybe they are an overly cynical bunch of economists.

**INSTRUCTOR:**

What they are doesn't matter. What matters is what they say and what they predict. We don't judge an economic theory by how it sounds to us or by how we feel about it; we judge it by how well it explains and predicts what we see in the world.

---

## CHAPTER SUMMARY

### POLITICIANS AND THE MIDDLE: THE MEDIAN VOTER MODEL

- In a two-person race, candidates for the same office will gravitate toward the middle of the political spectrum to pick up votes. If a candidate does not do so and her opponent does, the opponent will win the election.
- Candidates do a number of things during campaigns that indicate they understand where they are headed—toward the middle. For example, candidates attempt to label their opponents as too far either right or left.
- Candidates usually pick labels for themselves that represent the middle of the political spectrum, they speak in general terms, and they take polls and adjust their positions accordingly.

### VOTING AND RATIONAL IGNORANCE

- Voting has both costs and benefits. Many potential voters will not vote because the costs of voting—in terms of time spent going to the polls and so on—outweigh the benefits of voting, measured as the probability of their single vote determining the election outcome.
- Being unable to learn certain information is different from choosing not to learn it. Most voters choose not to be informed about political and government issues because the costs of becoming informed outweigh the benefits of becoming informed. They choose to be rationally ignorant.

If politicians move to the center of the voter distribution, if people are rationally ignorant, and if special interests sometimes engage in rent seeking, then that's the way things are whether we like it or not.

> **STUDENT:**

But aren't economists supposed to be trying to make the world better?

> **INSTRUCTOR:**

Let's assume that they are. Then isn't a good understanding of the world critical to doing this? For example, if the world is X, and I think it is Y, then I might make mistakes when I try to make the world a better place. Basing what I do on how things are has to be better than basing them on how I might want them to be.

> **STUDENT:**

I can see your point. It's sort of like a doctor who wants to know your true condition before she prescribes any therapy. She may not like the fact that you have a particular disease, but it's important that she know about it so that she can prescribe the right medicine.

> **INSTRUCTOR:**

I think that captures the spirit of what I'm talking about.

> **STUDENT:**

Does it follow, then, that everything in public choice theory is right?

> **INSTRUCTOR:**

No, it doesn't follow. Public choice theory—just like any theory in economics—has to be judged on how well it explains and predicts.

**POINTS TO REMEMBER**

1. Theories should be judged on how well they explain and predict (not how how they sound or feel).
2. Good economics seeks to know what exists, no matter how pleasant or unpleasant that is.

## MORE ABOUT VOTING

- In a simple majority vote, given several options to choose from, the voting outcome is the same as the most preferred outcome of the median voter.
- Simple majority voting and equal tax shares can generate a different result from simple majority voting and unequal tax shares.

## SPECIAL INTEREST GROUPS

- Special interest groups are usually well informed about their issues. Individuals have a greater incentive to become informed about issues that directly and intensely affect them.

- Legislation that concentrates the benefits on a few and disperses the costs over many is likely to pass because the beneficiaries will have an incentive to lobby for it, whereas those who pay the bill will not lobby against it because each of them pays such a small part of the bill.
- Special interest groups often engage in rent seeking, which is the expenditure of scarce resources to capture a pure transfer. Rent seeking is a socially wasteful activity because the resources used to effect transfers are not used to produce goods and services.

## KEY TERMS AND CONCEPTS

Public Choice            Rational Ignorance        Logrolling              Rent Seeking
Median Voter Model       Special Interest Groups

## QUESTIONS AND PROBLEMS

1. Some observers maintain that not all politicians move toward the middle of the political spectrum to obtain votes. They often cite Barry Goldwater in the 1964 presidential election and George McGovern in the 1972 presidential election as examples. Goldwater was viewed as occupying the right end of the political spectrum and McGovern the left end. Would this necessarily be evidence that does not support the median voter model? Are the exceptions to the theory explained in this chapter?

2. The economist James Buchanan said, "If men should cease and desist from their talk about and their search for evil men and commence to look instead at the institutions manned by ordinary people, wide avenues for genuine social reform might appear." What did he mean?

3. Would voters have a greater incentive to vote in an election involving only a few registered voters or in one that has many? Why? Why might a Republican label her opponent too far left and a Democrat label his opponent too far right?

4. Many individuals learn more about the car they are thinking of buying than about the candidates running for president of the United States. Explain why.

5. If the model of politics and government presented in this chapter is true, what are some of the things we would expect to see?

6. It has often been said that Democrat candidates are more liberal in Democrat primaries and Republican candidates are more conservative in Republican primaries than either is in the general election, respectively. Explain why.

7. What are some ways of reducing the cost of voting to voters?

8. Provide a numerical example that shows simple majority voting may be consistent with efficiency. Next, provide a numerical example that shows simple majority voting may be inconsistent with efficiency.

9. John chooses not to vote in the presidential election. Does it follow that he is apathetic when it comes to presidential politics? Explain your answer.

10. Some individuals see national defense spending as benefiting special interests—in particular, the defense industry. Others see it as directly benefiting not only the defense industry but the general public as well. Does this same difference between viewpoints apply to issues other than national defense? Name a few.

11. Evaluate each of the following proposals for reform in terms of the material discussed in this chapter:

    a. Linking all spending programs to visible tax hikes

    b. A balanced budget amendment stipulating that Congress cannot spend more than total tax revenues

    c. A budgetary referenda process whereby the voters actually vote on the distribution of federal dollars to the different categories of spending ($x$ percentage to agriculture, $y$ percentage to national defense, etc.) instead of letting elected representatives decide.

12. "Rent seeking may be rational from the individual's perspective, but it is not rational from society's perspective." Do you agree or disagree? Explain your answer.

## WORKING WITH NUMBERS AND GRAPHS

1. Suppose that three major candidates, A, B, and C, are running for president of the United States and that the distribution of voters is the same as shown in Exhibit 1. Two of the candidates, A and B, are currently viewed as right of the median, and C is viewed as left of the median. Is it possible to predict which candidate is the most likely to win?

2. Look back at Exhibit 2. Suppose that the net benefits and net costs for each person are known a week before election day and that it is legal to buy and sell votes. Furthermore, suppose that either buying or selling votes has no conscience cost. Would the outcome of the election be the same? Explain your answer.

3. In part (a) of the following figure, the distribution of voters is skewed to the left; in part (b), the distribution is skewed neither left nor right; and in part (c), it is skewed right. Assuming a two-person race for each distribution, will the candidate who wins the election in (a) hold different positions from the candidates who win the elections in (b) and (c)? Explain your answer.

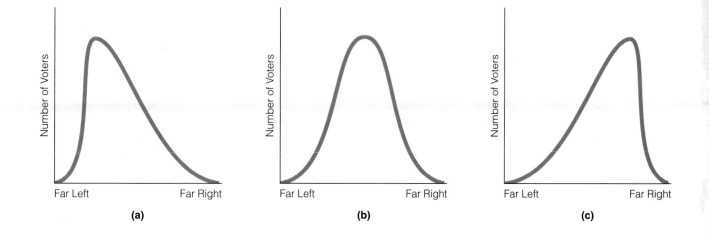

(a)       (b)       (c)

# CHAPTER 21

# INTERNATIONAL TRADE

**Introduction** Economics is about trade, and trade crosses boundaries. People trade not only with people who live in their city, state, or country, but also with people in other countries. Many of the goods you consume are undoubtedly produced in other countries. This chapter examines international trade and the prohibitions sometimes placed on it.

## INTERNATIONAL TRADE THEORY

International trade takes place for the same reasons that trade at any level exists. Individuals trade to make themselves better off. Pat and Zach, both of whom live in Cincinnati, Ohio, trade because they both value something the other has more than they value some of their own possessions. On an international scale, Elaine in the United States trades with Cho in China because Cho has something that Elaine wants and Elaine has something that Cho wants.

Obviously, the countries of the world have different terrains, climates, resources, worker skills, and so on. Therefore, some countries will be able to produce goods that other countries cannot produce or can produce only at extremely high costs. For example, Hong Kong has no oil, and Saudi Arabia has a large supply of it. Bananas do not grow easily in the United States, but they flourish in Honduras. Americans could grow bananas if they used hothouses, but it is cheaper for Americans to buy bananas from Hondurans than to produce bananas themselves.

Major U.S. exports include automobiles, computers, aircraft, corn, wheat, soybeans, scientific instruments, coal, and plastic materials. Major imports include petroleum, automobiles, clothing, iron and steel, office machines, footwear, fish, coffee, and diamonds. Some of the major exporting countries of the world are the United States, Germany, Japan, France, and the United Kingdom. These same countries are also among the major importers in the world.

### How Countries Know What to Trade

Recall the concept of *comparative advantage,* an economic concept first discussed in Chapter 2. In this section, we discuss comparative advantage in terms of countries rather than in terms of individuals.

COMPARATIVE ADVANTAGE  Assume a two-country/two-good world. The countries are the United States and Japan, and the goods are food and clothing. Both countries can produce the two goods in the four different combinations listed in Exhibit 1. For example, the United States can produce 90 units of food and 0 units of clothing, 60 units of food and 10 units of clothing, or other combinations. Japan can produce 15 units of food and 0 units of clothing, 10 units of food and 5 units of clothing, or other combinations.

Suppose the United States is producing and consuming the two goods in the combination represented by point *B* on its production possibilities frontier (PPF), and Japan is producing and consuming the combination of the two goods represented by point *F* on its PPF. In this case, neither of the two countries is specializing in the production of one of the two goods, nor are the two countries trading with each other. We call this the *no-specialization–no-trade (NS–NT) case* (see column 1 in Exhibit 2).

Now suppose the United States and Japan decide to specialize in the production of a specific good and to trade with each other, in what is called the *specialization–trade (S–T) case*. Whether the two countries will be better off through specialization and trade is best explained by means of a numerical example, but first we need to find the answers to two other questions: What good should the United States specialize in producing? What good should Japan specialize in producing? The general answer to both questions is the same: *Countries specialize in the production of the good in which they have a comparative advantage.* A country has a comparative advantage in the production of a good when it can produce the good at lower opportunity cost than another country can.

For example, in the United States, the opportunity cost of producing 1 unit of clothing (*C*) is 3 units of food (*F*); for every 10 units of clothing it produces, it forfeits 30 units of food. So the opportunity cost of producing 1 unit of food is 1/3 unit of clothing. In Japan, the opportunity cost of producing 1 unit of clothing is 1 unit of food (for every 5 units of clothing it produces, it forfeits 5 units of food). So, in the United States, the

**Comparative Advantage**
The advantage a country has when it can produce a good at lower opportunity cost than another country can.

**EXHIBIT 1**

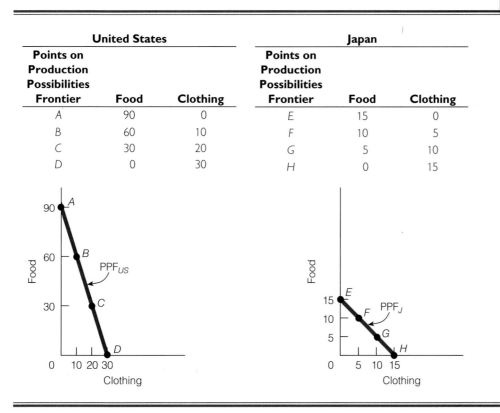

| United States | | | Japan | | |
|---|---|---|---|---|---|
| Points on Production Possibilities Frontier | Food | Clothing | Points on Production Possibilities Frontier | Food | Clothing |
| A | 90 | 0 | E | 15 | 0 |
| B | 60 | 10 | F | 10 | 5 |
| C | 30 | 20 | G | 5 | 10 |
| D | 0 | 30 | H | 0 | 15 |

**Production Possibilities in Two Countries**

The United States and Japan can produce the two goods in the combinations shown. Initially, the United States is at point *B* on its PPF and Japan is at point *F* on its PPF. Both countries can be made better off by specializing in and trading the good in which each has a comparative advantage.

## EXHIBIT 2

**Both Countries Gain from Specialization and Trade**

Column 1: Both the United States and Japan operate independently of each other. The United States produces and consumes 60 units of food and 10 units of clothing. Japan produces and consumes 10 units of food and 5 units of

clothing. Column 2: The United States specializes in the production of food; Japan specializes in the production of clothing. Column 3: The United States and Japan agree to the terms of trade of 2 units of food for 1 unit of clothing. They actually trade 20 units of food for 10 units of clothing. Column 4: Overall, the United

States consumes 70 units of food and 10 units of clothing. Japan consumes 20 units of food and 5 units of clothing. Column 5: Consumption levels are higher for both the United States and Japan in the S–T case than in the NS–NT case.

| | No Specialization-No Trade (NS–NT) Case | | Specialization-Trade (S–T) Case | | | |
| --- | --- | --- | --- | --- | --- | --- |
| Country | **(1)** Production and Consumption in the NS–NT Case | | **(2)** Production in the S–T Case | **(3)** Exports (−) Imports (+) Terms of Trade Are 2F = 1C | **(4)** Consumption in the S–T Case (2) + (3) | **(5)** Gains from Specialization and Trade (4) − (1) |
| **United States** | | | | | | |
| Food | 60 ⎤ Point B in | | 90 ⎤ Point A in | −20 | 70 | 10 |
| Clothing | 10 ⎦ Exhibit 1 | | 0 ⎦ Exhibit 1 | +10 | 10 | 0 |
| **Japan** | | | | | | |
| Food | 10 ⎤ Point F in | | 0 ⎤ Point H in | +20 | 20 | 10 |
| Clothing | 5 ⎦ Exhibit 1 | | 15 ⎦ Exhibit 1 | −10 | 5 | 0 |

situation is $1C = 3F$, or $1F = 1/3C$; in Japan the situation is $1C = 1F$, or $1F = 1C$. The United States can produce food at a lower opportunity cost ($1/3C$, as opposed to $1C$ in Japan), whereas Japan can produce clothing at a lower opportunity cost ($1F$, as opposed to $3F$ in the United States). Thus, the United States has a comparative advantage in food, and Japan has a comparative advantage in clothing.

Suppose the two countries specialize in the production of the goods in which they have a comparative advantage. The United States specializes in the production of food (producing 90 units), and Japan specializes in the production of clothing (producing 15 units). In Exhibit 1, the United States locates at point $A$ on its PPF, and Japan locates at point H on its PPF (see column 2 in Exhibit 2).

SETTLING ON THE TERMS OF TRADE After they have determined the goods to specialize in producing, the two countries must settle on the terms of trade, that is, how much food to trade for how much clothing. The United States faces the following situation: for every 30 units of food it does not produce, it can produce 10 units of clothing, as shown in Exhibit 1.Thus, 3 units of food have an opportunity cost of 1 unit of clothing ($3F = 1C$), or 1 unit of food has a cost of 1/3 unit of clothing ($1F = 1/3C$). Japan faces the following situation: for every 5 units of food it does not produce, it can produce 5 units of clothing. Thus, 1 unit of food has an opportunity cost of 1 unit of clothing ($1F = 1C$). For the United States, $3F = 1C$, and for Japan, $1F = 1C$.

With these cost ratios, both countries should be able to agree on terms of trade that specify $2F = 1C$. The United States would benefit by giving up 2 units of food instead of 3 units for 1 unit of clothing, whereas Japan would benefit by getting 2 units of food instead of only 1 unit for 1 unit of clothing. Suppose the two countries agree to the terms of trade of $2F = 1C$ and trade—in absolute amounts, 20 units of food for 10 units of clothing (see column 3 in Exhibit 2). Will they make themselves better off? We'll soon see that they do.

# economics 24/7

## Dividing the Work

John and Veronica, husband and wife, have divided their household tasks: John usually does all the lawn work, fixes the cars, and does the dinner dishes, and Veronica cleans the house, cooks the meals, and does the laundry. Some sociologists might suggest that John and Veronica divided the household tasks along gender lines: men have for years done the lawn work, fixed the cars, and so on, and women have for years cleaned the house, cooked the meals, and so on. In other words, John is doing man's work, and Veronica is doing woman's work.

© COMSTOCK IMAGES/JUPITER IMAGES

Maybe they have followed gender lines, but the question remains why certain tasks became man's work and others became woman's work. Moreover, their arrangement doesn't explain why John and Veronica don't split every task evenly. In other words, why doesn't John clean half the house and Veronica clean half the house? Why doesn't Veronica mow the lawn on the second and fourth week of every month and John mow the lawn every first and third week of the month?

The law of comparative advantage may be the answer to all these questions. Consider two tasks: cleaning the house and mowing the lawn. The following table shows how long John and Veronica take to complete the two tasks individually.

|  | Time to Clean the House | Time to Mow the Lawn |
|---|---|---|
| **John** | 120 minutes | 50 minutes |
| **Veronica** | 60 minutes | 100 minutes |

Here is the opportunity cost of each task for each person.

|  | Opportunity Cost of Cleaning the House | Opportunity Cost of Mowing the Lawn |
|---|---|---|
| **John** | 2.40 mowed lawns | 0.42 clean houses |
| **Veronica** | 0.60 mowed lawns | 1.67 clean houses |

In other words, John has a comparative advantage in mowing the lawn, and Veronica has a comparative advantage in cleaning the house.

Now let's compare two settings. In setting 1, John and Veronica each do half of each task. In setting 2, John only mows the lawn and Veronica only cleans the house.

In setting 1, John spends 60 minutes cleaning half of the house and 25 minutes mowing half of the lawn, for a total of 85 minutes; Veronica spends 30 minutes cleaning half of the house and 50 minutes mowing half of the lawn, for a total of 80 minutes. The total time spent by Veronica and John cleaning the house and mowing the lawn is 165 minutes.

In setting 2, John spends 50 minutes mowing the lawn, and Veronica spends 60 minutes cleaning the house. The total time spent by Veronica and John cleaning the house and mowing the lawn is 110 minutes.

In which setting are Veronica and John better off? John works 85 minutes in setting 1 and 50 minutes in setting 2; so he is better off in setting 2. Veronica works 80 minutes in setting 1 and 60 minutes in setting 2; so Veronica is also better off in setting 2. Together, John and Veronica spend 55 fewer minutes in setting 2 than in setting 1. Getting the job done in 55 fewer minutes is the benefit of specializing in various duties around the house. Given those numbers, we would expect that John will mow the lawn (and do nothing else) and Veronica will clean the house (and do nothing else).

**RESULTS OF THE SPECIALIZATION–TRADE (S–T) CASE**  Now the United States produces 90 units of food and trades 20 units to Japan, receiving 10 units of clothing in exchange. It consumes 70 units of food and 10 units of clothing. Japan produces 15 units of clothing and trades 10 to the United States, receiving 20 units of food in exchange. It consumes 5 units of clothing and 20 units of food (see column 4 in Exhibit 2).

Comparing the consumption levels in both countries in the two cases, the United States and Japan each consume 10 more units of food and no less clothing in the specialization–trade case than in the no-specialization–no-trade case (column 5 in Exhibit 2). Therefore, a country gains by specializing in producing and trading the good in which it has a comparative advantage.

## Common Misconception About How Much We Can Consume

No country can consume beyond its PPF if it doesn't specialize and trade with other countries. But, as we have just seen, it can do so when there is specialization and trade. Look at the PPF for the United States in Exhibit 1. In the NS–NT case, the United States consumes 60 units of food and 10 units of clothing; that is, the United States consumes at point *B* on its PPF. In the S–T case, however, it consumes 70 units of food and 10 units of clothing. A point that represents this combination of the two goods is beyond the country's PPF.

## How Countries Know When They Have a Comparative Advantage

Government officials of a country do not analyze pages of cost data to determine what their country should specialize in producing and then trade. Bureaucrats do not plot production possibilities frontiers on graph paper or calculate opportunity costs. Instead, the individual's desire to earn a dollar, a peso, or a euro determines the pattern of international trade. The desire to earn a profit determines what a country specializes in and trades.

To illustrate, Henri, an enterprising Frenchman, visits the United States and observes that beef is relatively cheap (compared with the price in France) and that perfume is relatively expensive. Noticing the price differences for beef and perfume between his country and the United States, he decides to buy some perfume in France, bring it to the United States, and sell it for the relatively higher U.S. price. With his profits from the perfume transaction, he buys beef in the United States, ships it to France, and sells it for the relatively higher French price. Obviously, Henri is buying low and selling high. He buys a good in the country where it is cheap and sells it in the country where it is expensive.

Henri's activities have a couple of consequences. First, he is earning a profit. The larger the price differences are between the two countries and the more he shuffles goods between countries, the more profit Henri earns.

Second, Henri's activities are moving each country toward its comparative advantage. The United States ends up exporting beef to France, and France ends up exporting perfume to the United States. Just as the pure theory predicts, individuals in the two countries specialize in and trade the good in which they have a comparative advantage. The outcome is brought about spontaneously through the actions of individuals trying to make themselves better off; they are simply trying to gain through trade.

## ⓣhinking Like **AN ECONOMIST**

**The Benefits of Searching for Profit** Is the desire to earn profit useful to society at large? Henri's desire for profit moved both the United States and France toward specializing in and trading the good in which they had a comparative advantage. And when countries specialize and trade, they are better off than when they do neither. ▬ ▬ ▬

## You're Getting Better Because Others Are Getting Better

Smith can produce X in 30 minutes, and Y in 60 minutes. Jones can produce X in 2 hours and Y in 3 hours. Initially:

- Smith can produce X in 30 minutes and Y in 60 minutes.
- Jones can produce X in 2 hours and Y in 3 hours.

Smith is better at producing X and Y than Jones. Suppose that Smith gets even better at producing X. He can produce X in 15 minutes as opposed to 30 minutes.

- Smith can produce X in 15 minutes and Y in 60 minutes.
- Jones can produce X in 2 hours and Y in 3 hours.

Will Smith's getting better at producing X cause Jones to get better at producing Y? The quick and obvious answer is no. Smith's ability to produce X more quickly doesn't change the time it takes Jones to produce X and Y. It still takes Jones 2 hours to produce X and 3 hours to produce Y.

But look at things in terms of opportunity cost. Initially the opportunity cost for Smith of producing 1X is 1/2Y and the opportunity cost of producing 1Y is 2X. For Jones, the opportunity cost of producing 1X is 2/3Y and the opportunity cost of producing 1Y is 1½X. Given these opportunity costs, Smith has a comparative advantage in producing X, and Jones has a comparative advantage in producing Y.

When Smith gets better at doing X, his opportunity cost of producing 1X now *falls* to 1/4Y and his opportunity cost of doing 1Y *rises* to 4X. In other words, Smith's becoming better at producing X makes him relatively worse at producing Y.

As for Jones, because Smith has become relatively better at producing X, Jones has becoming relatively better at producing Y. We reach this conclusion by comparing Jones's opportunity cost of producing Y *before* and *after* Smith gets better at producing X. Before Smith gets better at producing X, Jones gives up 1½X to get 1Y, whereas Smith has to give up 2X to get 1Y.

- Jones gives up 1½X to get 1Y.
- Smith gives up 2X to get 1Y.

We might say that Jones has only a *slight* comparative advantage over Smith when it comes to producing Y. But after Smith gets better at producing X, Jones gives up 1½X to get 1Y, whereas Smith gives up 4X to get 1Y.

- Jones gives up 1½X to get 1Y.
- Smith gives up 4X to get 1Y.

Jones now has a *substantial* comparative advantage over Smith when it comes to producing Y.

Suppose X is being a lawyer and Y is being a farmer. When Smith becomes better as a lawyer, Jones automatically becomes a better farmer (or a relatively lower low-cost farmer). If we change things and say that X is being an accountant and Y is driving a truck, then as Smith becomes a better accountant, Jones automatically becomes a better trucker.

Looking at things in terms of opportunity cost provides us with an insight into our world. Namely, as some people become better at what they do, they naturally make other people better at what they do. Become a better mathematician, singer, or teacher, and you naturally make others better (a lower low-cost producer) at what they do.

## SELF-TEST

(Answers to Self-Test questions are in Answers to Self-Test Questions at the back of the book.)

1. Suppose the United States can produce 120 units of X at an opportunity cost of 20 units of Y, and Great Britain can produce 40 units of X at an opportunity cost of 80 units of Y. Identify favorable terms of trade for the two countries.

2. If a country can produce more of all of its goods than any other country, would it benefit from specializing and trading? Explain your answer.

3. Do government officials analyze data to determine what their country can produce at a comparative advantage?

# TRADE RESTRICTIONS

International trade theory shows that countries gain from free international trade, that is, from specializing in the production of the goods in which they have a comparative advantage and trading them for other goods. In the real world, however, the numerous types of trade restrictions give rise to the question: If countries gain from international trade, why are there trade restrictions? The answer requires an analysis of costs and benefits; specifically, we need to determine who benefits and who loses when trade is restricted. First, we need to explain some pertinent background information.

## The Distributional Effects of International Trade

The previous section explained that specialization and international trade benefit individuals in different countries, but this is a net benefit. Not every individual person may gain.

To illustrate, Pam Dickson lives and works in the United States making clock radios. She produces and sells 12,000 clock radios per year at a price of $40 each. Currently, clock radios are not traded internationally. Individuals in other countries who make clock radios do not sell them in the United States.

Then one day, the U.S. market is opened to clock radios from China. Chinese manufacturers seem to have a comparative advantage in the production of clock radios because they sell theirs in the United States for $25 each. Pam realizes that she cannot compete at this price. Her sales drop to such a degree that she goes out of business. Thus, the introduction of international trade in this instance has harmed Pam personally.

## Consumers' and Producers' Surpluses

The preceding example raises the issue of the distributional effects of free trade. The benefits of international trade are not equally distributed to all individuals in the population. Therefore, the topics of consumers' and producers' surpluses (Chapter 3) are relevant to our discussion of international trade:

*Consumers' surplus* is the difference between the maximum price a buyer is willing and able to pay for a good or service and the price actually paid.

Consumers' surplus = Maximum buying price – Price paid

Consumers' surplus is a dollar measure of the benefit gained by being able to purchase a unit of a good for less than one is willing to pay for it. For example, if Yakov would have paid $10 to see the movie at the Cinemax but paid only $4, his consumer surplus is $6. Consumers' surplus is the consumers' net gain from trade.

*Producers' surplus* (or sellers' surplus) is the difference between the price sellers receive for a good and the minimum or lowest price for which they would have sold the good.

Producers' surplus = Price received – Minimum selling price

Producers' surplus is a dollar measure of the benefit gained by being able to sell a unit of output for more than one is willing to sell it. For example, if Joan sold her knit sweaters for $24 each but would have sold them for as low as (but no lower than) $14 each, her producer surplus is $10 per sweater. Producers' surplus is the producers' net gain from trade.

Both consumers' and producers' surplus are represented in Exhibit 3. In part (a), the shaded triangle represents consumers' surplus. This triangle includes the area under the demand curve and above the equilibrium price. In part (b), the shaded triangle represents producers' surplus. This triangle includes the area above the supply curve and under the equilibrium price.

**EXHIBIT 3**

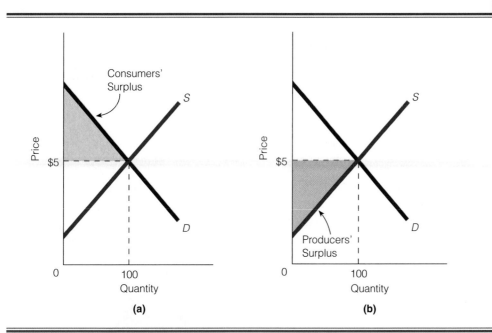

(a)

(b)

**Consumers' and Producers' Surplus**

(a) Consumers' surplus. As the shaded area indicates, the difference between the maximum or highest amount consumers would be willing to pay and the price they actually pay is consumers' surplus. (b) Producers' surplus. As the shaded area indicates, the difference between the price sellers receive for the good and the minimum or lowest price they would be willing to sell the good for is producers' surplus.

## finding ECONOMICS

**While Negotiating the Price of a House** Robin is negotiating the price of the house she wants to buy from Yakov. Her last offer for the house was $478,000, and he countered with $485,000. She is thinking about offering $481,000. Where is the economics?

Obviously, in this negotiation each person is trying to increase his or her surplus at the expense of the other. Specifically, the lower the price Robin pays, the higher her consumers' surplus will be and the lower Yakov's producers' surplus. Alternatively, the higher the price Yakov receives, the higher his producers' surplus will be and the lower Robin's consumers' surplus. ▲ ▲ ▲

## The Benefits and Costs of Trade Restrictions

Of the numerous ways to restrict international trade, tariffs and quotas are two of the more common. We discuss these two methods using the tools of supply and demand, concentrating on two groups: U.S. consumers and U.S. producers.

TARIFFS  A tariff is a tax on imports. The primary effect of a tariff is to raise the price of the imported good for the domestic consumer. Exhibit 4 illustrates the effects of a tariff on cars imported into the United States. The world price for cars is $P_W$, as shown in Exhibit 4(a). At this price in the domestic U.S. market, U.S. consumers buy $Q_2$ cars, as shown in part (b). They buy $Q_1$ from U.S. producers and the difference between $Q_2$ and $Q_1$ ($Q_2 - Q_1$) from foreign producers. In other words, U.S. imports at $P_W$ are $Q_2 - Q_1$.

In this situation, consumers' surplus is the area under the demand curve and above the world price, $P_W$. This is the sum of the areas 1, 2, 3, 4, 5, and 6 [see Exhibit 4(b)]. Producers' surplus is the area above the supply curve and below the world price, $P_W$. This is area 7.

Now suppose a tariff is imposed. The price for imported cars in the U.S. market rises to $P_W + T$ (the world price plus the tariff). At this price, U.S. consumers buy $Q_4$ cars: $Q_3$ from U.S. producers and $Q_4 - Q_3$ from foreign producers. U.S. imports are $Q_4 - Q_3$, which is a smaller number of imports than at the pretariff price. An effect of tariffs, then, is to

**Tariff**
A tax on imports.

**EXHIBIT 4**

**The Effects of a Tariff**

A tariff raises the price of cars from $P_W$ to $P_W + T$, decreases consumers' surplus, increases producers' surplus, and generates tariff revenue. Because consumers lose more than producers and government gain, there is a net loss due to the tariff.

|  | Consumers' Surplus | Producers' Surplus | Government Tariff Revenue |
|---|---|---|---|
| Free trade (No tariff) | $1 + 2 + 3 + 4 + 5 + 6$ | 7 | None |
| Tariff | $1 + 2$ | $3 + 7$ | 5 |
| Loss or Gain | $-(3 + 4 + 5 + 6)$ | $+3$ | $+5$ |

Result of Tariff = Loss to consumers + Gain to producers + Tariff revenue
$$= -(3 + 4 + 5 + 6) \quad\quad +3 \quad\quad\quad\quad +5$$
$$= -(4 + 6)$$

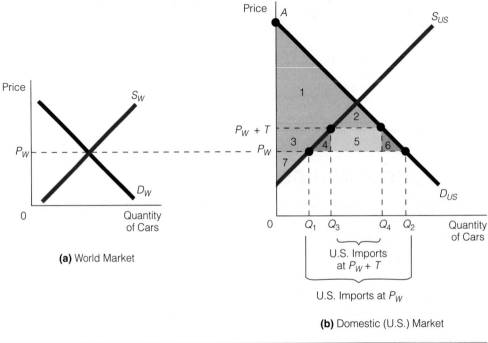

**(a)** World Market

**(b)** Domestic (U.S.) Market

reduce imports. After the tariff has been imposed, at price $P_W + T$, consumers' surplus consists of areas 1 and 2, and producers' surplus consists of areas 3 and 7.

Thus consumers receive more consumers' surplus when tariffs do not exist and less when they do exist. In our example, consumers received areas 1 through 6 in consumers' surplus when the tariff did not exist but only areas 1 and 2 when the tariff did exist. Because of the tariff, consumers' surplus was reduced by an amount equal to areas 3, 4, 5, and 6.

Producers, though, receive less producers' surplus when tariffs do not exist and more when they do exist. In our example, producers received producers' surplus equal to area 7 when the tariff did not exist, but they received producers' surplus equal to areas 3 and 7 with the tariff. Because of the tariff, producers' surplus increased by an amount equal to area 3.

The government collects tariff revenue equal to area 5. This area is obtained by multiplying the number of imports ($Q_4 - Q_3$) by the tariff, which is the difference between $P_W + T$ and $P_W$.[1]

---

1. For example, if the tariff is $100 and the number of imports is 50,000, then the tariff is $5 million.

In conclusion, the effects of the tariff are a decrease in consumers' surplus, an increase in producers' surplus, and tariff revenue for government. Because the loss to consumers (areas 3, 4, 5, 6) is greater than the gain to producers (area 3) plus the gain to government (area 5), *a tariff results in a net loss.* The net loss is areas 4 and 6.

QUOTAS A quota is a legal limit imposed on the amount of a good that may be imported. For example, the government may decide to allow no more than 100,000 foreign cars to be imported, or 10 million barrels of OPEC oil, or 30,000 Japanese television sets. A quota reduces the supply of a good and raises the price of imported goods for domestic consumers (Exhibit 5).

Once again, we consider the situation in the U.S. car market. At a price of $P_W$ (established in the world market for cars), U.S. consumers buy $Q_1$ cars from U.S. producers and $Q_2 - Q_1$ cars from foreign producers. Consumers' surplus is equal to areas 1, 2, 3, 4, 5, and 6. Producers' surplus is equal to area 7.

Suppose now that the U.S. government sets a quota equal to $Q_4 - Q_3$. Because this is the number of foreign cars U.S. consumers imported when the tariff was imposed (see

**Quota**
A legal limit imposed on the amount of a good that may be imported.

**EXHIBIT 5**

**The Effects of a Quota**

A quota that sets the legal limit of imports at $Q_4 - Q_3$ causes the price of cars to increase from $P_W$ to $P_Q$. A quota raises price, decreases consumers' surplus, increases producers' surplus, and increases the total revenue importers earn. Because consumers lose more than producers and importers gain, there is a net loss due to the quota.

|  | Consumers' Surplus | Producers' Surplus | Revenue of Importers |
|---|---|---|---|
| Free trade (No quota) | 1 + 2 + 3 + 4 + 5 + 6 | 7 | 8 |
| Quota | 1 + 2 | 3 + 7 | 5 + 8 |
| Loss or Gain | − (3 + 4 + 5 + 6) | +3 | +5 |

Result of Quota = Loss to consumers + Gain to producers + Gain to importers
= − (3 + 4 + 5 + 6)      +3        +5
= − (4 + 6)

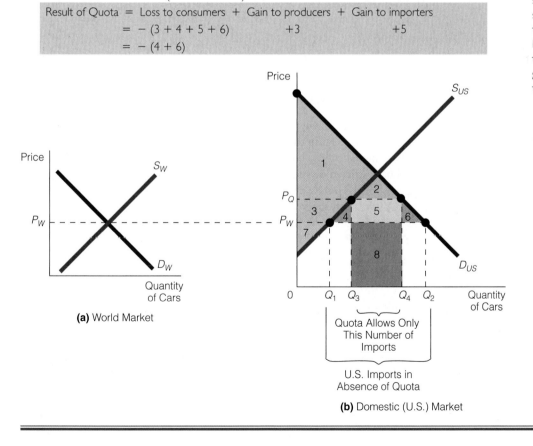

**(a)** World Market

**(b)** Domestic (U.S.) Market

Quota Allows Only This Number of Imports

U.S. Imports in Absence of Quota

Exhibit 4), the price of cars rises to $P_Q$ in Exhibit 5 (which is equal to $P_W + T$ in Exhibit 4). At $P_Q$, consumers' surplus is equal to areas 1 and 2, and producers' surplus consists of areas 3 and 7. The decrease in consumers' surplus due to the quota is equal to areas 3, 4, 5, and 6; the increase in producers' surplus is equal to area 3.

However, area 5 is not transferred to government, as was the case when a tariff was imposed. Rather, it represents the additional revenue earned by the importers (and sellers) of $Q_4 - Q_3$. Before the quota, importers were importing $Q_2 - Q_1$, but only part of this total amount $(Q_4 - Q_3)$ is relevant because this is the amount of imports now that the quota has been established. Before the quota was established, the dollar amount that the importers received for $Q_4 - Q_3$ was $P_W \times (Q_4 - Q_3)$, or area 8. Because of the quota, the price rises to $P_Q$, and they now receive $P_Q \times (Q_4 - Q_3)$, or areas 5 and 8. The difference between the total revenues on $Q_4 - Q_3$ with a quota and without a quota is area 5.

In conclusion, the effects of a quota are a decrease in consumers' surplus, an increase in producers' surplus, and an increase in total revenue for the importers who sell the allowed number of imported units. Because the loss to consumers (areas 3, 4, 5, 6) is greater than the increase in producers' surplus (area 3) plus the gain to importers (area 5), there is a *net loss as a result of the quota.* The net loss is equal to areas 4 and 6.[2]

## finding ECONOMICS

**In a Policy Debate**   There is a debate tonight at the college Irina attends, with four people on either side of the issue: Should the United States practice free trade? Irina attends the debate and comes away thinking that both sides made good points. The no-free-trade side argued that because other countries do not always practice free trade, neither should the United States. The pro-free-trade side argued that free trade leads to lower prices for U.S. consumers. Where is the economics?

Most of the debate, we believe, will fit into our discussion of Exhibits 4 and 5. These two exhibits show what happens to consumers and producers, and to society as a whole, as the result of both free and prohibited trade. The diagrams show (1) the benefits of prohibited free trade to domestic producers, (2) the costs of prohibited trade to domestic consumers, (3) tariff revenue to government, if it exists, and (4) the overall net costs to prohibited trade. ▲ ▲ ▲

## Why Nations Sometimes Restrict Trade

If free trade results in net gain, why do nations sometimes restrict trade? The case for free trade (no tariffs or quotas) so far in this chapter appears to be a strong one. The case for free trade has not gone unchallenged, however. Some persons maintain that at certain times free trade should be restricted or suspended. In almost all cases, they argue that doing so is in the best interest of the public or country as a whole. In a word, they advance a public interest argument. Other persons contend that the public interest argument is only superficial; down deep, they say, it is a special interest argument clothed in pretty words. As you might guess, the debate between the two groups is often heated.

The following sections describe some arguments that have been advanced for trade restrictions.

**THE NATIONAL DEFENSE ARGUMENT**   Certain industries—such as aircraft, petroleum, chemicals, and weapons—are necessary to the national defense. Suppose the United

---

2. It is perhaps incorrect to imply that government receives nothing from a quota. Although it receives nothing directly, it may gain indirectly. Economists generally argue that because government officials are likely to be the persons who decide which importers will get to satisfy the quota, importers will naturally lobby them. Thus, government officials will likely receive something, if only dinner at an expensive restaurant, while the lobbyist makes the pitch. In short, in the course of the lobbying, resources will be spent by lobbyists as they curry favor with government officials or politicians who have the power to decide who gets to sell the limited number of imported goods. In economics, lobbyists' activities geared toward obtaining special privileges are referred to as rent seeking.

## Offshore Outsourcing, or Offshoring

*Outsourcing* is the term used to describe work done for a company by another company or by people other than the originating company's employees. Outsourcing entails purchasing a product or process from an outside supplier rather than producing it in-house. To illustrate, company X has, in the past, hired employees for personnel, accounting, and payroll services, but now a company in another state performs these duties. Company X has outsourced these work activities.

When a company outsources certain work activities to individuals in another country, it is said to be engaged in offshore outsourcing, or offshoring. Consider a few examples. A New York securities firm replaces 800 software engineering employees with a team of software engineers in India. A computer company replaces 200 on-call technicians in its headquarters in Texas with 150 on-call technicians in India.

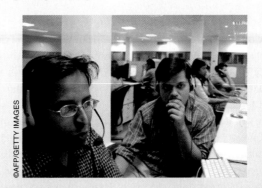

©AFP/GETTY IMAGES

The benefits of offshoring for a U.S. firm are obvious; it pays lower wages to individuals in other countries for the same work that U.S. employees do for higher wages. Benefits also flow to the employees hired in the foreign countries. The costs of offshoring are said to fall on persons who lose their jobs as a result, such as the software engineer in New York or the on-call computer technician in Texas. Some have argued that offshoring will soon become a major political issue and that it could bring with it a wave of protectionism.

Offshoring will undoubtedly have both proponents and opponents. On a net basis, however, are there more benefits than costs or more costs than benefits? Consider a U.S. company that currently employs Jones as a software engineer, paying her $x a year. Then, one day, the company tells Jones that it has to let her go; it is replacing her with a software engineer in India who will work for $z a year (and, yes, $z < x$).

Why doesn't Jones simply agree to work for $z, the same wage as that agreed to by the Indian software engineer? Obviously, Jones can work elsewhere for some wage between $x and $z. Assume this wage is $y. So, even though offshoring has moved Jones from earning $x to earning $y, $y is still more than $z.

In short, the U.S. company is able to lower its costs from $x to $z, and Jones's income falls from $x to $y. The U.S. company lowers its costs more than Jones's income falls because the difference between $x and $z is greater than the difference between $x and $y.

If the U.S. company operates in a competitive environment, its lower costs will shift its supply curve to the right and lower prices. In other words, offshoring can reduce prices for U.S. consumers. The political fallout from offshoring might, in the end, depend on how visible, to the average American, the employment effects of offshoring are relative to the price reduction effect.

States has a comparative advantage in the production of wheat and country X has a comparative advantage in the production of weapons. Many Americans feel that the United States should not specialize in the production of wheat and then trade wheat to country X in exchange for weapons. Leaving weapons production to another country, they maintain, is too dangerous.

The national defense argument may have some validity, but even valid arguments may be abused. Industries that are not really necessary to the national defense may maintain otherwise. In the past, the national defense argument has been used by some firms in the following industries: pens, pottery, peanuts, papers, candles, thumbtacks, tuna fishing, and pencils.

**THE INFANT INDUSTRY ARGUMENT** Alexander Hamilton, the first U.S. secretary of the treasury, argued that so-called infant, or new, industries often need protection from older, established foreign competitors until they are mature enough to compete on an equal basis. Today, some persons voice the same argument. The infant industry argument is clearly an argument for temporary protection. Critics charge, however, that after an industry is protected from foreign competition, removing the protection is almost impossible; the once infant industry will continue to maintain that it isn't old enough to go it alone. Critics of the infant industry argument say that political realities make it unlikely that a benefit, once bestowed, will be removed.

Finally, the infant industry argument, like the national defense argument, may be abused. All new industries, whether they could currently compete successfully with foreign producers or not, would argue for protection on infant industry grounds.

**Dumping**
The sale of goods abroad at a price below their cost and below the price charged in the domestic market.

**THE ANTIDUMPING ARGUMENT** Dumping is the sale of goods abroad at a price below their cost and below the price charged in the domestic market. If a French firm sells wine in the United States for a price below the cost of producing the wine and below the price charged in France, it is dumping wine in the United States. Critics of dumping maintain that it is an unfair trade practice that puts domestic producers of substitute goods at a disadvantage.

In addition, critics charge that dumpers seek only to penetrate a market and drive out domestic competitors, only to raise prices. However, some economists point to the infeasibility of this strategy. After the dumpers have driven out their competition and raised prices, their competition is likely to return. For their efforts, the dumpers, in turn, would have incurred only a string of losses (owing to their selling below cost). Opponents of the antidumping argument also point out that domestic consumers benefit from dumping because they pay lower prices.

**THE FOREIGN EXPORT SUBSIDIES ARGUMENT** Some governments subsidize firms that export goods. If a country offers a below-market (interest rate) loan to a company, it is often argued, the government subsidizes the production of the good the firm produces. If, in turn, the firm exports the good to a foreign country, that country's producers of substitute goods call foul. They complain that the foreign firm has been given an unfair advantage that they should be protected against.[3]

Others say that consumers should not turn their backs on a gift (in the form of lower prices). If foreign governments want to subsidize their exports and thus give a gift to foreign consumers at the expense of their own taxpayers, then the recipients should not complain. Of course, the recipients are usually not the ones who are complaining. Usually, the complainers are the domestic producers who can't sell their goods at as high a price because of the so-called gift domestic consumers are receiving from foreign governments.

**THE LOW FOREIGN WAGES ARGUMENT** Some argue that American producers can't compete with foreign producers because American producers have to pay high wages to their workers and foreign producers pay low wages. The American producers insist that international trade must be restricted, or they will be ruined. However, the argument overlooks why American wages are high and foreign wages are low in the first place: productivity. High productivity and high wages are usually linked, as are low productivity and low wages. If an American worker, who receives $20 per hour, can produce (on average) 100 units of good X per hour, working with numerous capital goods, then the cost per unit may be lower than when a foreign worker, who receives $2 per hour, produces (on average) 5 units of X per hour, working by hand. In short, a country's high-wage disadvantage may be offset by its productivity advantage, and a country's low-wage advantage may be offset by its productivity disadvantage. High wages do not necessarily mean high costs when productivity and the costs of nonlabor resources are included.

---

3. Words are important in this debate. For example, domestic producers who claim that foreign governments have subsidized foreign firms say that they are not asking for economic protectionism, but only retaliation, or reciprocity, or simply tit for tat—words that have less negative connotation than those their opponents use.

**THE SAVING DOMESTIC JOBS ARGUMENT** Sometimes, the argument against completely free trade is made in terms of saving domestic jobs. Actually, this argument has cropped up before in its different guises. For example, the low foreign wages argument is one form of it: if domestic producers cannot compete with foreign producers because foreign producers pay low wages and domestic producers pay high wages, domestic producers will go out of business and domestic jobs will be lost. The foreign export subsidies argument is another version: if foreign government subsidies give a competitive edge to foreign producers, not only will domestic producers fail, but as a result of their failure, domestic jobs will be lost.

Critics of the saving domestic jobs argument (in all its guises) counterargue as follows: if a domestic producer is being outcompeted by foreign producers and if domestic jobs in an industry are being lost as a result, the world market is signaling that those labor resources could be put to better use in an industry in which the country holds a comparative advantage.

## ⓣhinking Like **AN ECONOMIST**

**Economics Versus Politics** International trade often becomes a battleground between economics and politics. The simple tools of supply and demand and of consumers' and producers' surpluses show that free trade leads to net gains. On the whole, tariffs and quotas make living standards lower than they would be if free trade were permitted. On the other side, though, are the realities of business and politics. Domestic producers may advocate quotas and tariffs to make themselves better off, giving little thought to the negative effects on foreign producers or domestic consumers.

Perhaps the battle over international trade comes down to this: policies are largely advocated, argued, and lobbied for based more on their distributional effects than on their aggregate or overall effects. On an aggregate level, free trade produces a net gain for society, whereas restricted trade produces a net loss. But economists understand that even if free trade in the aggregate produces a net gain, not every single person will benefit more from free trade than from restricted trade. An example in this chapter showed how a subset of the population (producers) gains more, in a particular instance, from restricted trade than from free trade. In short, economists realize that the crucial question in determining real-world policies is more often, "How does it affect me?" than "How does it affect us?" ▰ ▰ ▰

### SELF-TEST

1. Who benefits and who loses from tariffs? Explain your answer.

2. Identify the directional change in consumers' surplus and producers' surplus when we move from free trade to tariffs. Is the change in consumers' surplus greater than, less than, or equal to the change in producers' surplus?

3. What is a major difference between the effects of a quota and the effects of a tariff?

4. Outline the details of the infant industry argument for trade restriction.

# OFFICE HOURS

## "Should We Impose Tariffs If They Impose Tariffs?"

**STUDENT:**

Here is a problem I have with our discussion of free and prohibited trade. Essentially, I am in favor of free international trade, but I think the United States should have free trade with countries that practice free trade with us. In other words, if country X practices free trade with the United States, then the United States should practice free trade with it. But if country Y places tariffs on U.S. goods entering the country, then the United States ought to place tariffs on country Y's goods entering this country.

**INSTRUCTOR:**

Many people feel the same way you do, but this opinion overlooks something that we showed in Exhibits 4 and 5: the losses of moving from free trade to prohibited trade (where either tariffs or quotas exist) are greater than the gains. Remember? There is a net loss to society in that move.

**STUDENT:**

I just think it is only fair that other countries get what they give. If they give free trade to us, then we ought to give free trade back to them. If they place tariffs and quotas on our goods, then we ought to do the same to their goods.

**INSTRUCTOR:**

You need to keep in mind the price the United States has to pay for this policy of tit for tat.

**STUDENT:**

What do you mean? What price does the United States have to pay?

**INSTRUCTOR:**

It has to incur the net loss illustrated in Exhibits 4 and 5. If you look back at Exhibit 4, for example, you'll notice that moving from free trade to prohibited trade (1) decreases consumers' surplus, (2) increases producers' surplus, and (3) raises tariff revenue. But when we count up all the gains of prohibited trade and compare them with all the losses, we conclude that the losses are greater than the gains. In other words, prohibited trade leads to a net loss.

**STUDENT:**

But suppose our practicing tit for tat (giving free trade for free trade and prohibited trade for prohibited trade) forces other countries to move away from prohibited trade. In other words, what I am saying is this: we need to look at this issue of free versus prohibited trade

---

## CHAPTER SUMMARY

### SPECIALIZATION AND TRADE

- A country has a comparative advantage in the production of a good if it can produce the good at a lower opportunity cost than another country can.

- Individuals in countries that specialize and trade have a higher standard of living than would be the case if their countries did not specialize and trade.

- Government officials do not analyze cost data to determine what their country should specialize in and trade. Instead, the desire to earn a dollar, peso, or euro guides individuals' actions and produces the unintended consequence that countries specialize in and trade the good(s) in which they have a comparative advantage. However, trade restrictions can change this outcome.

### TARIFFS AND QUOTAS

- A tariff is a tax on imports. A quota is a legal limit on the amount of a good that may be imported.

- Both tariffs and quotas raise the price of imports.

- Tariffs lead to a decrease in consumers' surplus, an increase in producers' surplus, and tariff revenue for the government. Consumers lose more through tariffs than producers and government (together) gain.

444

over time. Maybe the United States has to practice prohibited trade today (with those countries that impose tariffs or quotas on the United States) in order to force those countries to practice free trade tomorrow. Couldn't it work out that way?

> INSTRUCTOR:

It could work out that way. Or, then, things could escalate toward greater prohibited trade. In other words, country A imposes tariffs and quotas on country B, and then country B raises its tariffs and quotas even higher on country A. So country A retaliates and raises its tariffs and quotas on country B, and so on.

> STUDENT:

So what is your point? Is it that free trade is the best policy to practice no matter what other countries do.

> INSTUCTOR:

That is what many economists would say, but that is not really the point I am making here. I am rather making two points with respect to the discussion. First, in response to your position that the United States ought to practice tit for tat (give free trade for free trade, tariffs for tariffs, quotas for quotas), I am simply drawing your attention to the net loss Americans incur if they practice prohibited trade—no matter what other countries are doing. In other words, there is a net loss for Americans even if other countries are practicing free or prohibited trade. Second, with respect to your second point, about prohibited trade leading to free trade tomorrow, I am saying that we can't be sure that prohibited trade today won't lead to greater prohibitions on trade tomorrow. This is not to say you can't be right: it is possible for prohibited trade today to lead to less prohibited trade tomorrow.

**POINTS TO REMEMBER**

1. A country that imposes tariffs or quotas on imported goods incurs a net loss no matter what another country is doing—whether it is practicing free or prohibited trade.

2. We cannot easily predict the outcome of the United States' practicing tit for tat in international trade.

• Quotas lead to a decrease in consumers' surplus, an increase in producers' surplus, and additional revenue for the importers who sell the amount specified by the quota. Consumers lose more through quotas than producers and importers (together) gain.

## ARGUMENTS FOR TRADE RESTRICTIONS

• The national defense argument states that certain goods—such as aircraft, petroleum, chemicals, and weapons—are necessary to the national defense and should be produced domestically whether the country has a comparative advantage in their production or not.

• The infant industry argument states that infant, or new, industries should be protected from free (foreign) trade so that they have time to develop and compete on an equal basis with older, more established foreign industries.

• The antidumping argument states that domestic producers should not have to compete (on an unequal basis) with foreign producers that sell products below cost and below the prices they charge in their domestic markets.

• The foreign export subsidies argument states that domestic producers should not have to compete (on an unequal basis) with foreign producers that have been subsidized by their governments.

• The low foreign wages argument states that domestic producers cannot compete with foreign producers that pay low wages to their employees when domestic producers pay high wages to their employees. For high-paying domestic firms to survive, limits on free trade are proposed.

• The saving domestic jobs argument states that through low foreign wages or government subsidies (or dumping and similar practices), foreign producers will be able to outcompete domestic producers and that therefore domestic jobs will be lost. For domestic firms to survive and domestic jobs not to be lost, limits on free trade are proposed.

- Everyone does not accept the arguments for trade restrictions as valid. Critics often maintain that the arguments can be and are abused and that in most cases they are motivated by self-interest.

## KEY TERMS AND CONCEPTS

Comparative Advantage          Tariff          Quota          Dumping

## QUESTIONS AND PROBLEMS

1. Although a production possibilities frontier is usually drawn for a country, one could be drawn for the world. Picture the world's production possibilities frontier. Is the world positioned at a point on the PPF or below it? Give a reason for your answer.

2. If country A is better than country B at producing all goods, will country A still be made better off by specializing and trading? Explain your answer. (*Hint:* Look at Exhibit 1.)

3. "The desire for profit can end up pushing countries toward producing goods in which they have a comparative advantage." Do you agree or disagree? Explain your answer.

4. "Whatever can be done by a tariff can be done by a quota." Discuss.

5. Neither free trade nor prohibited trade comes with just benefits. Both come with benefits and costs. Therefore, free trade is no better or worse than prohibited trade. Comment.

6. Consider two groups of domestic producers: those that compete with imports and those that export goods. Suppose the domestic producers that compete with imports convince the legislature to impose a high tariff on imports—so high, in fact, that almost all imports are eliminated. Does this policy in any way adversely affect domestic producers that export goods? If so, how?

7. Suppose the U.S. government wants to curtail imports. Would it be likely to favor a tariff or a quota to accomplish its objective? Why?

8. Suppose the landmass known to you as the United States of America had been composed, since the nation's founding, of separate countries instead of separate states. Would you expect the standard of living of the people who inhabit this landmass to be higher, lower, or equal to what it is today? Why?

9. Even though Jeremy is a better gardener and novelist than Bill, Jeremy still hires Bill as his gardener. Why?

10. Suppose that a constitutional convention is called tomorrow and that you are chosen as one of the delegates from your state. You and the other delegates must decide whether it will be constitutional or unconstitutional for the federal government to impose tariffs and quotas or to restrict international trade in any way. What would be your position?

11. Some economists have argued that because domestic consumers gain more from free trade than domestic producers gain from (import) tariffs and quotas, consumers should buy out domestic producers and rid themselves of costly tariffs and quotas. For example, if consumers save $400 million from free trade (through paying lower prices) and producers gain $100 million from tariffs and quotas, consumers can pay producers something more than $100 million but less than $400 million and get producers to favor free trade too. Assuming this scheme were feasible, what do you think of it?

12. If there is a net loss to society from tariffs, why do tariffs exist?

## WORKING WITH NUMBERS AND GRAPHS

1. Using the data in the table, answer the following questions:
   a. For which good does Canada have a comparative advantage?
   b. For which good does Italy have a comparative advantage?
   c. What might be a set of favorable terms of trade for the two countries?
   d. Prove that both countries would be better off in the specialization–trade case than in the no-specialization–no-trade case.

| Points on Production Possibilities Frontier | Canada | | Italy | |
|---|---|---|---|---|
| | **Good X** | **Good Y** | **Good X** | **Good Y** |
| A | 150 | 0 | 90 | 0 |
| B | 100 | 25 | 60 | 60 |
| C | 50 | 50 | 30 | 120 |
| D | 0 | 75 | 0 | 180 |

2. In the following figure, $P_W$ is the world price and $P_W + T$ is the world price plus a tariff. Identify the following:

   a. The level of imports at $P_W$

   b. The level of imports at $P_W + T$

   c. The loss in consumers' surplus as a result of a tariff

   d. The gain in producers' surplus as a result of a tariff

   e. The tariff revenue as the result of a tariff

   f. The net loss to society as a result of a tariff

   g. The net benefit to society of moving from a tariff situation to a no-tariff situation

## CHAPTER 22

PETER MENZEL / PHOTO RESEARCHERS, INC.

# INTERNATIONAL FINANCE

**Introduction** When people travel to a foreign country, they buy goods and services in the country, whose prices are quoted in yen, pounds, euros, pesos, or some other currency. For example, a U.S. tourist in Germany might want to buy a good priced in euros and to know what the good costs in dollars and cents. The answer depends on the current exchange rate between the dollar and the euro, but what determines the exchange rate? This is just one of the many questions answered in this chapter.

## THE BALANCE OF PAYMENTS

Countries keep track of their domestic level of production by calculating their gross domestic product (GDP). Similarly, they keep track of the flow of their international trade (receipts and expenditures) by calculating their balance of payments. The balance of payments is a periodic (usually annual) statement of the money value of all transactions between residents of one country and residents of all other countries. The balance of payments provides information about a nation's imports and exports, domestic residents' earnings on assets located abroad, foreign earnings on domestic assets, gifts to and from foreign countries (including foreign aid), the exchange of assets, and official transactions by governments and central banks.

Balance of payments accounts record both debits and credits. A debit is indicated by a minus (−) sign, and a credit is indicated by a plus (+) sign. *Any transaction that supplies the country's currency in the foreign exchange market is recorded as a* debit. (The foreign exchange market is the market in which currencies of different countries are exchanged.) For example, a U.S. retailer wants to buy Japanese television sets so that he can sell them in his stores in the United States. To buy the TV sets from the Japanese, the retailer first has to supply U.S. dollars (in the foreign exchange market) in return for Japanese yen. Then he will turn over the yen to the Japanese in exchange for the television sets.

*Any transaction that creates a demand for the country's currency in the foreign exchange market is recorded as a* credit. For example, a Russian retailer wants to buy computers from U.S. computer producers. To pay the U.S. producers, who want U.S. dollars,

**Balance of Payments**
A periodic (usually annual) statement of the money value of all transactions between residents of one country and the residents of all other countries.

**Debit**
In the balance of payments, any transaction that supplies the country's currency in the foreign exchange market.

**Foreign Exchange Market**
The market in which currencies of different countries are exchanged.

**Credit**
In the balance of payments, any transaction that creates a demand for the country's currency in the foreign exchange market.

**EXHIBIT 1**

| Item | Definition | Example |
|------|-----------|---------|
| Debit (−) | Any transaction that supplies the country's currency. | Jim, an American, supplies dollars in exchange for yen so that he can use the yen to buy Japanese goods. |
| Credit (+) | Any transaction that creates a demand for the country's currency. | Svetlana, who is Russian and living in Russia, supplies rubles in order to demand dollars so that she can use the dollars to buy U.S. goods. |

**Debits and Credits**

the Russian retailer must supply rubles (in the foreign exchange market) in return for dollars. Then she will turn over the dollars to the U.S. producers in exchange for the computers.

The international transactions that are summarized in the balance of payments can be grouped into three categories, or three accounts—the current account, the capital account, and the official reserve account—and a statistical discrepancy. Exhibit 2 illustrates a U.S. balance of payments account for year Z. The data in the exhibit are hypothetical (to make the calculations simpler), but not unrealistic. In this section, we describe and explain each of the items in the balance of payments using the data in Exhibit 2 for our calculations.

## Current Account

The current account includes all payments related to the purchase and sale of goods and services. The current account has three major components: exports of goods and services, imports of goods and services, and net unilateral transfers abroad.

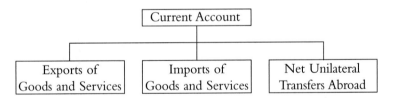

**Current Account**
The account in the balance of payments that includes all payments related to the purchase and sale of goods and services; components of the account include exports, imports, and net unilateral transfers abroad.

**EXPORTS OF GOODS AND SERVICES** Americans export goods (e.g., cars), they export services (e.g., insurance, banking, transportation, and tourism), and they receive income on assets they own abroad. All three activities increase the demand for U.S. dollars while increasing the supply of foreign currencies in the foreign exchange market; thus, they are recorded as credits (+). For example, if a foreigner buys a U.S. computer, payment must ultimately be made in U.S. dollars. Thus, she is required to supply her country's currency when she demands U.S. dollars. (We use "foreigner" in this chapter to refer to a resident of a foreign country.)

**IMPORTS OF GOODS AND SERVICES** Americans import goods and services, and foreigners receive income on assets they own in the United States. These activities increase the demand for foreign currencies while increasing the supply of U.S. dollars to the foreign exchange market; thus, they are recorded as debits (−). For example, if an American buys a Japanese car, payment must ultimately be made in Japanese yen. Thus, he is required to supply U.S. dollars when he demands Japanese yen.

**EXHIBIT 2**

**U.S. Balance of Payments, Year Z**

The data in this exhibit are hypothetical, but not unrealistic. All numbers are in billions of dollars. The plus and minus signs in the exhibit should be viewed as operational signs.

**CURRENT ACCOUNT**

1. EXPORTS OF GOODS AND SERVICES ⟨+340⟩
   a. Merchandise exports (including military sales)    +220
   b. Services    +30
   c. Income from U.S. assets abroad    +90
2. IMPORTS OF GOODS AND SERVICES ⟨−390⟩
   a. Merchandise imports (including military purchases)    −300
   b. Services    −40
   c. Income from foreign assets in U.S.    −50

*Merchandise Trade Balance*
Difference between value of merchandise exports (item 1a) and value of merchandise imports (item 2a): +220 − 300 = −80

3. NET UNILATERAL TRANSFERS ABROAD ⟨−11⟩

*Current Account Balance*
Items 1, 2, 3: +340 − 390 − 11 = ⟶ [−61]

**CAPITAL ACCOUNT**
4. OUTFLOW OF U.S. CAPITAL ⟨−16⟩
5. INFLOW OF FOREIGN CAPITAL ⟨+60⟩

*Capital Account Balance*
Items 4 and 5: −16 + 60 = ⟶ [+44]

**OFFICIAL RESERVE ACCOUNT**
6. INCREASE (−) IN U.S. OFFICIAL RESERVE ASSETS ⟨−4⟩
7. INCREASE (+) IN FOREIGN OFFICIAL ASSETS IN U.S. ⟨+3⟩

*Official Reserve Balance*
Items 6 and 7: −4 + 3 = ⟶ [−1]

**STATISTICAL DISCREPANCY** ⟨+18⟩

TOTAL    $0    $0
(always zero)

**BALANCE OF PAYMENTS =**
Summary statistic of all ⟨⟩ items (items 1–7 and the statistical discrepancy)

+$340 − $390 − $11 − $16 + $60 − $4 + $3 + $18 = $0

or

Summary statistic of all ☐ items (current account balance, capital account balance, official reserve balance, and the statistical discrepancy)

−$61 + $44 − $1 + $18 = $0

Note: The pluses (+) and the minuses (−) in the exhibit serve two purposes. First, they distinguish between credits and debits. A plus is always placed before a credit, and a minus is always placed before a debit. Second, in terms of the calculations, the pluses and minuses are viewed as operational signs. In other words, if a number has a plus in front of it, it is added to the total. If a number has a minus in front of it, it is subtracted from the total.

In Exhibit 2, exports of goods and services total +$340 billion in year Z, and imports of goods and services total −$390 billion.[1] Before discussing the third component of the

---

1. In everyday language, people do not say, "Exports are a positive $x billion and imports are a negative $y billion." Placing a plus sign (+) in front of exports and a minus sign (−) in front of imports simply reinforces the essential point that exports are credits and imports are debits. This will be useful later when we calculate certain account balances.

current account—net unilateral transfers abroad—we define some important relationships between exports and imports.

Look at the difference between the *value of merchandise exports* (item 1a in Exhibit 2) and the *value of merchandise imports* (item 2a in the exhibit). This difference is the merchandise trade balance, or the balance of trade. Specifically, the merchandise trade balance is the difference between the value of merchandise exported and the value of merchandise imported. In year Z, the merchandise trade balance is $220 billion − $300 billion = −$80 billion.

Merchandise trade balance = Value of merchandise exports
− Value of merchandise imports

**Merchandise Trade Balance**
The difference between the value of merchandise exports and the value of merchandise imports.

If the value of a country's merchandise exports is less than the value of its merchandise imports, it is said to have a merchandise trade deficit.

Merchandise trade deficit = Value of merchandise exports
< Value of merchandise imports

**Merchandise Trade Deficit**
The situation when the value of merchandise exports is less than the value of merchandise imports.

If the value of a country's merchandise exports is greater than the value of its merchandise imports, it is said to have a merchandise trade surplus.

Merchandise trade surplus = Value of merchandise exports
> Value of merchandise imports

**Merchandise Trade Surplus**
The situation when the value of merchandise exports is greater than the value of merchandise imports.

Exhibit 3 shows the U.S. merchandise trade balance from 1997 to 2009. Notice that there has been a merchandise trade deficit in each of these years.

**NET UNILATERAL TRANSFERS ABROAD** Unilateral transfers are one-way money payments. They can go from Americans or the U.S. government to foreigners or foreign governments. If an American sends money to a relative in a foreign country, if the U.S. government gives money to a foreign country as a gift or grant, or if an American retires in a foreign country and receives Social Security checks there, all these transactions are referred to as unilateral transfers. If an American or the U.S. government makes a unilateral transfer abroad, this gives rise to a demand for foreign currency and a supply of U.S. dollars; thus, it is entered as a debit item in the U.S. balance of payments accounts.

Unilateral transfers can also go from foreigners or foreign governments to Americans or to the U.S. government. A foreign citizen sending money to a relative living in the United States is a unilateral transfer. A foreigner making a unilateral transfer to an American gives rise to a supply of foreign currency and a demand for U.S. dollars; thus, it is entered as a credit item in the U.S. balance of payments accounts.

Net unilateral transfers abroad include both types of transfers—from the United States to foreign countries and from foreign countries to the United States. The dollar amount of net unilateral transfers is negative if U.S. transfers are greater than foreign transfers. It is positive if foreign transfers are greater than U.S. transfers.

For year Z in Exhibit 2, we have assumed that the unilateral transfers made by Americans to foreign citizens are greater than the unilateral transfers made by foreign citizens to Americans. Thus, there is a *negative* net dollar amount, −$11 billion.

Items 1, 2, and 3 in Exhibit 2—exports of goods and services, imports of goods and services, and net unilateral transfers abroad—comprise the current account. The current account balance is the summary statistic for these three items. In year Z, it is −$61 billion. The news media sometimes call the current account balance the balance of payments. To an economist, this reference is incorrect; the balance of payments includes several more items.

**Current Account Balance**
In the balance of payments, the summary statistic for exports of goods and services, imports of goods and services, and net unilateral transfers abroad.

---

**EXHIBIT 3**

**U.S. Merchandise Trade Balance**

In each of the years shown, 1997–2009, a merchandise trade deficit has existed.

*Source: U.S. Department of Commerce, Bureau of Economic Analysis.*

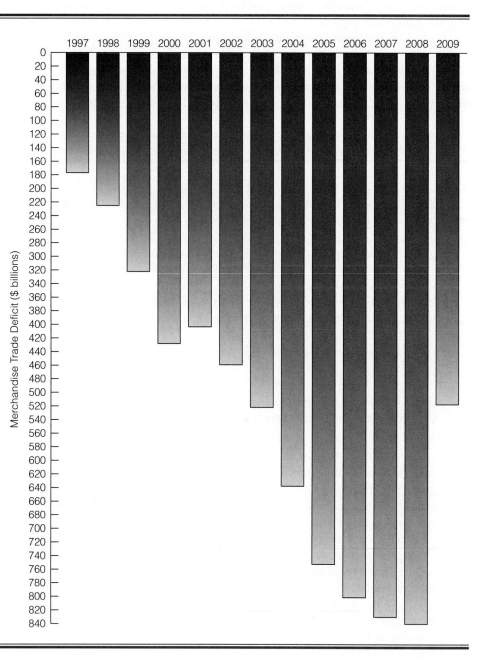

## Capital Account

**Capital Account**

The account in the balance of payments that includes all payments related to the purchase and sale of assets and to borrowing and lending activities. Components include outflow of U.S. capital and inflow of foreign capital.

The capital account includes all payments related to the purchase and sale of assets and to borrowing and lending activities. Its major components are the outflow of U.S. capital and the inflow of foreign capital.

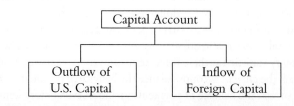

OUTFLOW OF U.S. CAPITAL American purchases of foreign assets and U.S. loans to foreigners are outflows of U.S. capital. As such, they give rise to a demand for foreign currency and a supply of U.S. dollars on the foreign exchange market. Hence, they are considered a debit. For example, if an American wants to buy land in Japan, U.S. dollars must be supplied to purchase (demand) Japanese yen.

INFLOW OF FOREIGN CAPITAL Foreign purchases of U.S. assets and foreign loans to Americans are inflows of foreign capital. As such, they give rise to a demand for U.S. dollars and to a supply of foreign currency on the foreign exchange market. Hence, they are considered a credit. For example, if a Japanese citizen buys a U.S. Treasury bill, Japanese yen must be supplied to purchase (demand) U.S. dollars.

Items 4 and 5 in Exhibit 2—outflow of U.S. capital and inflow of foreign capital—comprise the capital account. The capital account balance is the summary statistic for these two items. It is equal to the difference between the outflow of U.S. capital and the inflow of foreign capital. In year Z, it is $44 billion.

> **Capital Account Balance**
> The summary statistic for the outflow of U.S. capital, equal to the difference between the outflow of U.S. capital and the inflow of foreign capital.

## Official Reserve Account

A government possesses official reserve balances in the form of:

- Foreign currencies.
- Gold.
- Its reserve position in the International Monetary Fund (IMF, an international organization created to oversee the international monetary system).
- Special drawing rights (SDRs, an international money, created by the IMF, in the form of bookkeeping entries, like gold and currencies, which nations can use to settle international accounts).

> **International Monetary Fund (IMF)**
> An international organization created to oversee the international monetary system. The IMF does not control the world's money supply, but it does hold currency reserves for member nations and make loans to central banks.

> **Special Drawing Right (SDR)**
> An international money, created by the IMF, in the form of bookkeeping entries; like gold and currencies, it can be used by nations to settle international accounts.

Countries with a deficit in their combined current and capital accounts can draw on their reserves. For example, if the United States has a deficit in its combined current and capital accounts of $5 billion, it can draw down its official reserves to meet this deficit.

Item 6 in Exhibit 2 shows that the United States increased its reserve assets by $4 billion in year Z. This is a debit item because if the United States acquires official reserves (say, through the purchase of a foreign currency), it has increased the demand for the foreign currency and supplied dollars. Thus, an increase in official reserves is like an outflow of capital in the capital account and appears as a payment with a negative sign. Therefore, an increase in foreign official assets in the United States is a credit item.

## Statistical Discrepancy

If someone buys a U.S. dollar with, say, Japanese yen, someone must sell a U.S. dollar. Thus, dollars purchased equal dollars sold.

In all the transactions discussed so far—exporting goods, importing goods, sending money to relatives in foreign countries, buying land in foreign countries—dollars were bought and sold. The total number of dollars sold must always equal the total number of dollars purchased. However, balance of payments accountants do not have complete information; they can record only the credits and debits they observe. There may be more debits or credits than those observed in a given year.

Suppose in year Z, all debits are observed and recorded, but not all credits, perhaps because of smuggling activities, secret bank accounts, people living in more than one country, and so on. To adjust for this lack of information, balance of payments accountants use the *statistical discrepancy,* which is the part of the balance of payments that adjusts for missing information. In Exhibit 2, the statistical discrepancy is +$18 billion. This means that

## Merchandise Trade Deficit, We Thought We Knew Thee

You read in the newspaper that the United States has a merchandise trade deficit, that is, the value of merchandise exports for the United States is *less than* the value of merchandise imports. In terms of Exhibit 2, item 1a is less than item 2a. For example, Americans exported $600 billion worth of goods and imported $800 billion worth of goods. The merchandise trade deficit is $200 billion.

The word *deficit* has a negative connotation to many people, who think of a trade deficit as something bad. It's bad, some people say, "Because it means Americans owe money to foreigners. Specifically, Americans are 'in debt' to foreigners to the tune of $200 billion." Other people say that because Americans are increasing demand for foreign-produced goods by more [$200 billion more, to be exact] than foreigners are increasing demand for U.S.-produced goods, demand is "leaving the country."

However, neither sentiment is correct. Americans do not owe foreigners anything, and demand is not leaving the country. The reason is obvious: Americans have already paid this $200 billion to foreigners. The $200 billion is part of the overall $800 billion that Americans spent on imported goods.

Still, even if Americans don't owe $200 billion to foreigners, the $200 billion is not gone forever, never to return to the United States. Foreigners may have those dollars now, but they're not going to burn them, they're not going to eat them, and they're not

going to give them away. What they are going to do with those dollars—in fact, the only thing they can do with those dollars—is use them to buy "something American."[2] They could buy real estate in the United States. For example, a Brazilian man with dollars might end up buying an apartment in downtown Manhattan. In other words, the dollars that we thought would leave the country for good are eventually coming back home.

A foreign firm with U.S. dollars could hire a construction company to build a factory in the United States—Tennessee, Virginia, or South Dakota—so that it can produce some of its goods in the United States and thus lower its transportation costs. An American might end up working at that factory and thus be paid with some of the dollars that once were held by foreigners. (And the American worker is likely to spend those dollars to buy U.S. goods and services.)

The main point is simple: the dollars that foreigners initially hold because of the merchandise trade deficit will begin to return to the United States. They are not gone forever.

---

2. If you are thinking that the foreigners who have the $200 billion can trade those dollars for other currencies, you are right. A Frenchman might trade some of his dollars for pesos, euros, or yen, but now someone else has the dollars the Frenchman once had, and we then have to ask what this new person will do with the dollars.

---

$18 billion worth of credits (+) went unobserved in year Z. There may have been some hidden exports and unrecorded capital inflows that year.

## What the Balance of Payments Equals

The balance of payments is the summary statistic for:

- Exports of goods and services (item 1 in Exhibit 2).
- Imports of goods and services (item 2).
- Net unilateral transfers abroad (item 3).
- Outflow of U.S. capital (item 4).
- Inflow of foreign capital (item 5).
- Increase in U.S. official reserve assets (item 6).
- Increase in foreign official assets in the United States (item 7).
- Statistical discrepancy.

Calculating the balance of payments in year Z using these items, we have (in billions of dollars) $+340 - 390 - 11 - 16 + 60 - 4 + 3 + 18 = 0$.

Alternatively, the balance of payments is the summary statistic for the following:

- Current account balance
- Capital account balance
- Official reserve balance
- Statistical discrepancy

Calculating the balance of payments in year Z using these items, we have (in billions of dollars) − 61 + 44 − 1 + 18 = 0. The balance of payments for the United States in year Z equals zero.

## SELF-TEST

(Answers to Self-Test questions are in Answers to Self-Test Questions at the back of the book.)

1. If an American retailer buys cars from a Japanese manufacturer, is this transaction recorded as a debit or a credit? Explain your answer.

2. Exports of goods and services equal $200 billion, and imports of goods and services equal $300 billion. What is the merchandise trade balance?

3. What is the difference between the merchandise trade balance and the current account balance?

# THE FOREIGN EXCHANGE MARKET

If a U.S. buyer wants to purchase a good from a U.S. seller, the buyer simply gives the required number of U.S. dollars to the seller. If, however, a U.S. buyer wants to purchase a good from a seller in Mexico, the U.S. buyer must first exchange her U.S. dollars for Mexican pesos. Then, with the pesos, she buys the good from the Mexican seller. As explained, currencies of different countries are exchanged in the foreign exchange market. In this market, currencies are bought and sold for a price—the exchange rate. For instance, it might take $1.23 to buy a euro, 10¢ to buy a Mexican peso, and 13¢ to buy a Danish krone.

In this section, we explain why currencies are demanded and supplied in the foreign exchange market. Then we discuss how the exchange rate expresses the relationship between the demand for and the supply of currencies.

**Exchange Rate**
The price of one currency in terms of another currency.

## The Demand for Goods

To simplify our analysis, we assume that there are only two countries in the world: the United States and Mexico. Thus there are only two currencies in the world: the U.S. dollar (USD) and the Mexican peso (MXN). We want to answer the following two questions:

1. What creates the demand for and the supply of dollars on the foreign exchange market?

2. What creates the demand for and the supply of pesos on the foreign exchange market?

Suppose an American wants to buy a couch from a Mexican producer. Before he can purchase the couch, the American must buy Mexican pesos; hence, Mexican pesos are demanded. The American buys Mexican pesos with U.S. dollars; that is, he supplies U.S. dollars to the foreign exchange market to demand Mexican pesos. *The U.S. demand for Mexican goods leads to (1) a demand for Mexican pesos and (2) a supply of U.S. dollars on the foreign exchange market* [see Exhibit 4(a)]. Thus, the demand for pesos and the supply of dollars are linked:

Demand for pesos ↔ Supply of dollars

The result is similar for a Mexican who wants to buy a computer from a U.S. producer. Before she can purchase the computer, the Mexican must buy U.S. dollars; hence, U.S. dollars are demanded. The Mexican buys the U.S. dollars with Mexican pesos. *The Mexican demand for U.S. goods leads to (1) a demand for U.S. dollars and (2) a supply of Mexican pesos on the foreign exchange market* [see Exhibit 4(b)]. Thus, the demand for dollars and the supply of pesos are linked:

Demand for dollars ↔ Supply of pesos

## The Demand for and Supply of Currencies

Exhibit 5 shows the markets for pesos and dollars. Part (a) shows the market for Mexican pesos. The quantity of pesos is on the horizontal axis, and the exchange rate—stated in terms of the dollar price per peso—is on the vertical axis. Exhibit 5(b) shows the market for U.S. dollars, which mirrors what is happening in the market for Mexican pesos. Notice that the exchange rates in (a) and (b) are reciprocals of each other. If 0.10 USD = 1 MXN, then 10 MXN = 1 USD.

In Exhibit 5(a), the demand curve for pesos is downward-sloping, indicating that as the dollar price per peso increases, Americans buy fewer pesos and that as the dollar price per peso decreases, Americans buy more pesos.

Dollar price per peso ↑      Americans buy fewer pesos.
Dollar price per peso ↓      Americans buy more pesos.

For example, if it takes $0.10 to buy a peso, Americans will buy more pesos than they would if it takes $0.20 to buy a peso. (It is analogous to buyers purchasing more soft drinks at $3 a six-pack than at $5 a six-pack.) Simply put, the higher the dollar price per peso, the more expensive Mexican goods are for Americans and the fewer Mexican goods Americans will buy. Thus, a smaller quantity of pesos is demanded.

The supply curve for pesos in Exhibit 5(a) is upward sloping. The supply of Mexican pesos is linked to the Mexican demand for U.S. goods and U.S. dollars. Consider a price

---

**EXHIBIT 4**

**The Demand for Goods and the Supply of Currencies**

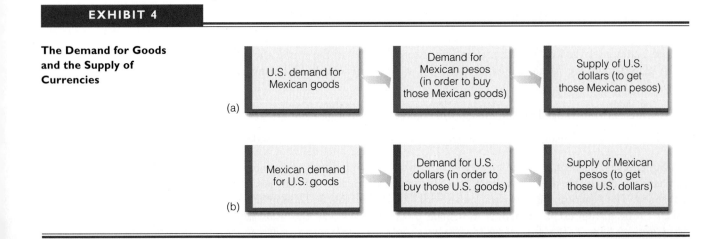

**EXHIBIT 5**

**Translating U.S. Demand for Pesos into U.S. Supply of Dollars and Mexican Demand for Dollars into Mexican Supply of Pesos**

(a) The market for pesos. (b) The market for dollars. The demand for pesos in (a) is linked to the supply of dollars in (b): when Americans demand pesos, they supply dollars. The supply of pesos in (a) is linked to the demand for dollars in (b): when Mexicans demand dollars, they supply pesos. In (a), the exchange rate is 0.10 USD = 1 MXN, which is equal to 10 MXN = 1 USD in (b). Exchange rates are reciprocals of each other.

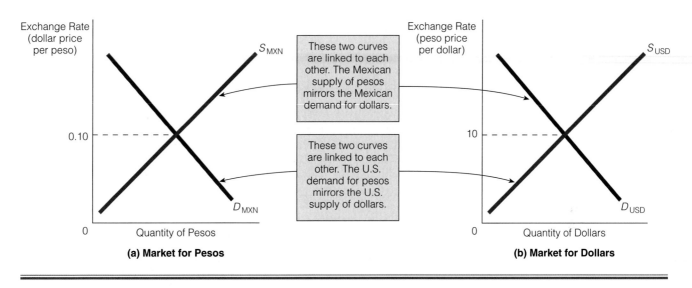

These two curves are linked to each other. The Mexican supply of pesos mirrors the Mexican demand for dollars.

These two curves are linked to each other. The U.S. demand for pesos mirrors the U.S. supply of dollars.

**(a) Market for Pesos**

**(b) Market for Dollars**

of $0.20 for 1 peso compared with a price of $0.10. At 0.10 USD = 1 MXN, a Mexican buyer gives up 1 peso and receives 10¢ in return. But at 0.20 USD = 1 MXN, a Mexican buyer gives up 1 peso and receives 20¢ in return. Thus, U.S. goods are cheaper for Mexicans at the exchange rate of 0.20 USD = 1 MXN.

To illustrate, suppose a U.S. computer has a price tag of $1,000. At an exchange rate of 0.20 USD = 1 MXN, a Mexican will have to pay 5,000 pesos to buy the American computer; but at an exchange rate of 0.10 USD = 1 MXN, a Mexican will have to pay 10,000 pesos for the computer:

$$0.20 \text{ USD} = 1 \text{ MXN}$$
$$1 \text{ USD} = (1 \div 0.20) \text{ MXN}$$
$$1,000 \text{ USD} = (1,000 \div 0.20) \text{ MXN}$$
$$= 5,000 \text{ MXN}$$

$$0.10 \text{ USD} = 1 \text{ MXN}$$
$$1 \text{ USD} = (1 \div 0.10) \text{ MXN}$$
$$1,000 \text{ USD} = (1,000 \div 0.10) \text{ MXN}$$
$$= 10,000 \text{ MXN}$$

To a Mexican buyer, the American computer is cheaper at the exchange rate of $0.20 per peso than at $0.10 per peso.

| Exchange Rate | Dollar Price | Peso Price |
| --- | --- | --- |
| 0.20 USD = 1 MXN | 1,000 USD | 5,000 MXN [(1,000 ÷ 0.20) MXN] |
| 0.10 USD = 1 MXN | 1,000 USD | 10,000 MXN [(1,000 ÷ 0.10) MXN] |

Therefore, the higher the dollar price is per peso, the greater will be the quantity demanded of dollars by Mexicans (because U.S. goods will be cheaper) and hence the greater the quantity supplied of pesos to the foreign exchange market. The upward-sloping supply curve for pesos illustrates this relationship.

## ⓣhinking Like AN ECONOMIST

**Linkages** The demand for dollars is linked to the supply of pesos, and the demand for pesos is linked to the supply of dollars. Economists often think in terms of one activity being linked to another because economics, after all, is about exchange. In an exchange, one gives (supply) and gets (demand): John supplies $25 to demand the new book from the shopkeeper; the shopkeeper supplies the new book so that he may demand the $25. The diagram for such a transaction usually represents the demand for and supply of the new book, but it could also represent the demand for and supply of the money. Of course, in international exchange, where monies are bought and sold before goods are bought and sold, the diagrams reflect both. ▰ ▰ ▰

# FLEXIBLE EXCHANGE RATES

In this section, we discuss how exchange rates are determined in the foreign exchange market when the forces of supply and demand are allowed to rule. Economists refer to this as a flexible exchange rate system. In the next section, we discuss how exchange rates are determined under a fixed exchange rate system.

**Flexible Exchange Rate System**
The system whereby exchange rates are determined by the forces of supply and demand for a currency.

## The Equilibrium Exchange Rate

In a completely flexible exchange rate system, the forces of supply and demand determine the exchange rate. In our two-country–two-currency world, suppose the equilibrium exchange rate (dollar price per peso) is 0.10 USD = 1 MXN, as shown in Exhibit 6. At this dollar price per peso, the quantity demanded of pesos equals the quantity supplied. There are no shortages or surpluses of pesos. At any other exchange rate, however, either an excess demand for pesos or an excess supply of pesos exists.

At the exchange rate of 0.12 USD = 1 MXN, a surplus of pesos exists. As a result, downward pressure will be placed on the dollar price of a peso (just as downward pressure will be placed on the dollar price of an apple if there is a surplus of apples). At the exchange rate of 0.08 USD = 1 MXN, there is a shortage of pesos, and upward pressure will be placed on the dollar price of a peso.

---

### EXHIBIT 6

**A Flexible Exchange Rate System**

The demand curve for pesos is downward sloping. The higher the dollar price for pesos, the fewer pesos will be demanded; the lower the dollar price for pesos, the more pesos will be demanded. At 0.12 USD = 1 MXN, there is a surplus of pesos, placing downward pressure on the exchange rate. At 0.08 USD = 1 MXN, there is a shortage of pesos, placing upward pressure on the exchange rate. At the equilibrium exchange rate, 0.10 USD = 1 MXN, the quantity demanded of pesos equals the quantity supplied of pesos.

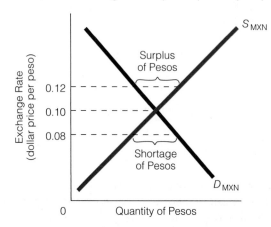

## Changes in the Equilibrium Exchange Rate

Chapter 3 explains that a change in the demand for a good, in the supply of a good, or in both will change the good's equilibrium price. The same holds true for the price of currencies. A change in the demand for pesos, in the supply of pesos, or in both will change the equilibrium dollar price per peso. If the dollar price per peso rises—say, from 0.10 USD − 1 MXN to 0.12 USD = 1 MXN—the peso is said to have appreciated and the dollar to have depreciated. A currency has appreciated in value if it takes more of a foreign currency to buy it. A currency has depreciated in value if it takes more of it to buy a foreign currency.

For example, a movement in the exchange rate from 0.10 USD = 1 MXN to 0.12 USD = 1 MXN means that it now takes 12¢ instead of 10¢ to buy a peso, so the dollar has depreciated. The other side of the coin, so to speak, is that it takes fewer pesos to buy a dollar; so the peso has appreciated. That is, at an exchange rate of 0.10 USD = 1 MXN, it takes 10 pesos to buy $1, but at an exchange rate of 0.12 USD = 1 MXN, it takes only 8.33 pesos to buy $1.

**Appreciation**

An increase in the value of one currency relative to other currencies.

**Depreciation**

A decrease in the value of one currency relative to other currencies.

## Factors That Affect the Equilibrium Exchange Rate

If the equilibrium exchange rate can change owing to a change in the demand for and supply of a currency, then understanding what factors can change demand and supply is important. This section presents three.

**A DIFFERENCE IN INCOME GROWTH RATES** An increase in a nation's income will usually cause the nation's residents to buy more of both domestic and foreign goods. The increased demand for imports will result in an increased demand for foreign currency.

Suppose U.S. residents experience an increase in income, but Mexican residents do not. As a result, the demand curve for pesos shifts rightward, as illustrated in Exhibit 7. This causes the equilibrium exchange rate to rise from 0.10 USD = 1 MXN to 0.12 USD = 1 MXN. *Ceteris paribus,* if one nation's income grows and another's lags behind, the currency of the higher-growth-rate country *depreciates,* and the currency of the lower-growth-rate country *appreciates.* To many persons, this effect seems paradoxical; nevertheless, it is true.

**DIFFERENCES IN RELATIVE INFLATION RATES** Suppose the U.S. price level rises 10 percent at a time when Mexico experiences stable prices. An increase in the U.S. price level will make Mexican goods relatively less expensive for Americans and U.S. goods relatively more expensive for Mexicans. As a result, the U.S. demand for Mexican goods will increase, and the Mexican demand for U.S. goods will decrease.

In turn, the demand for and the supply of Mexican pesos are affected. As shown in Exhibit 8, the demand for Mexican pesos will

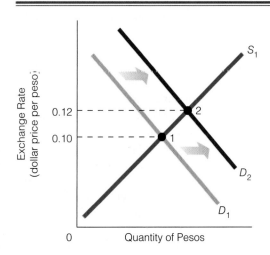

**EXHIBIT 7**

**The Growth Rate of Income and the Exchange Rate**

If U.S. residents experience a growth in income but Mexican residents do not, U.S. demand for Mexican goods will increase, and with it, the demand for pesos. As a result, the exchange rate will change; the dollar price of pesos will rise. The dollar depreciates, the peso appreciates.

# economics 24/7

## Back to the Futures

Bill Whatley is the (fictional) owner of a Toyota dealership in Tulsa, Oklahoma. It is May, and Bill is thinking about a shipment of Toyotas he plans to buy in August. He knows that he must buy the Toyotas from Japan with yen, but he has a problem. The current price of ¥1 is $0.008. Bill wonders what the dollar price of a yen will be in August when he plans to make his purchase. If the price of ¥1 rises to $0.010, then, instead of paying $20,000 for a Toyota priced at ¥2.5 million, he will have to pay $25,000.[3] This difference of $5,000 may be enough to erase his profit on the sale of the cars.

Bill can, however, purchase a futures contract today for the needed quantity of yen in August. A futures contract is a contract in which the seller agrees to provide a good (in this example, a currency) to the buyer on a specified future date at an agreed-on price. In short, Bill can buy yen today at a specified dollar price and take delivery of the yen at a later date (in August). Problem solved.

But if the price of ¥1 falls to $0.007 in August, Bill would have to pay only $17,500 (instead of $20,000) for a Toyota priced at ¥2.5 million. Although he could increase his profit in this case, Bill, like other car dealers, might not be interested in assuming the risk associated with changes in exchange rates. He may prefer to lock in a sure thing.

Who would sell yen to Bill? The answer is someone who is willing to assume the risk of changes in the value of currencies. For example, Julie Jackson thinks that the dollar price of a yen will go down between now and August. Therefore, she'll enter into a contract with Bill requiring her to give him ¥2.5 million in August for $20,000—the exchange rate specified in the contract being 1 JPY = 0.008 USD. If she's right and the actual exchange rate in August is 1 JPY = 0.007 USD, then she can purchase the ¥2.5 million for $17,500 and fulfill the contract with Bill by turning the yen over to him for $20,000. She walks away with $2,500 in profit.

Many economists argue that futures contracts offer people a way of dealing with the risk associated with a flexible exchange rate system. If a person doesn't know what next month's exchange rate will be and doesn't want to take the risk of waiting to see, then he can enter into a futures contract and effectively shift the risk to someone who voluntarily assumes it.

---

3. If ¥1 equals $0.008, then a Toyota with a price of ¥2.5 million costs $20,000 because ¥2.5 million × $0.008 = $20,000. If ¥1 equals $0.010, then a Toyota with a price of ¥2.5 million costs $25,000 dollars because ¥2.5 million × $0.010 equals $25,000.

increase; Mexican goods are relatively cheaper than they were before the U.S. price level rose. The supply of Mexican pesos will decrease; American goods are relatively more expensive, and so Mexicans will buy fewer American goods; thus, they demand fewer U.S. dollars and supply fewer Mexican pesos.

As Exhibit 8 shows, the result of an increase in the demand for Mexican pesos and a decrease in their supply constitutes an *appreciation* in the peso and a *depreciation* in the dollar. It takes 11¢ instead of 10¢ to buy 1 peso (dollar depreciation); it takes 9.09 pesos instead of 10 pesos to buy $1 (peso appreciation).

An important question is how much will the U.S. dollar depreciate as a result of the rise in the U.S. price level? (Mexico's price level does not change.) The purchasing power parity (PPP) theory predicts that the U.S. dollar will depreciate by 10 percent as a result of the 10 percent rise in the U.S. price level. This requires the dollar price of a peso to rise to 11¢ (0.10 × 10¢ = 1¢, 10¢ + 1¢ = 11¢). A 10 percent depreciation in the dollar restores the *original relative prices of American goods to Mexican customers.*

Consider a U.S. car with a price tag of $20,000. If the exchange rate is 0.10 USD = 1 MXN, a Mexican buyer of the car will pay 200,000 pesos. If the car price increases by 10 percent to $22,000 and the dollar depreciates 10 percent (to 0.11 USD = 1 MXN), the Mexican buyer of the car will still pay only 200,000 pesos.

**Purchasing Power Parity (PPP) Theory**
Theory stating that exchange rates between any two currencies will adjust to reflect changes in the relative price levels of the two countries.

**EXHIBIT 8**

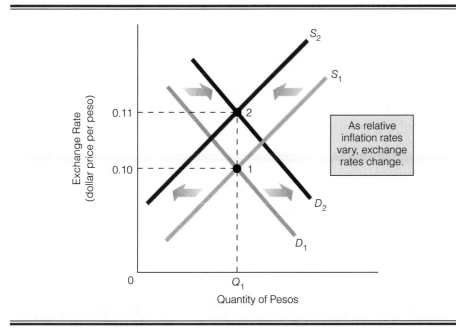

As relative inflation rates vary, exchange rates change.

**Inflation, Exchange Rates, and Purchasing Power Parity (PPP)**

If the price level in the United States increases by 10 percent while the price level in Mexico remains constant, then the U.S. demand for Mexican goods (and therefore pesos) will increase and the supply of pesos will decrease. As a result, the exchange rate will change; the dollar price of pesos will rise. The dollar depreciates, and the peso appreciates. PPP theory predicts that the dollar will depreciate in the foreign exchange market until the original price (in pesos) of American goods to Mexican customers is restored. In this example, this requires the dollar to depreciate 10 percent.

| Exchange Rate | Dollar Price | Peso Price |
|---|---|---|
| 0.10 USD = 1 MXN | 20,000 USD | 200,000 MXN [(20,000 ÷ 0.10) MXN] |
| 0.11 USD = 1 MXN | 22,000 USD | 200,000 MXN [(22,000 ÷ 0.11) MXN] |

In short, the PPP theory predicts that *changes in the relative price levels of two countries will affect the exchange rate in such a way that 1 unit of a country's currency will continue to buy the same amount of foreign goods* as it did before the change in the relative price levels. In our example, the higher U.S. inflation rate causes a change in the equilibrium exchange rate and leads to a depreciated dollar, but 1 peso continues to have the same purchasing power it previously did.

On some occasions, the PPP theory of exchange rates has predicted accurately, but not on others. Many economists suggest that the theory does not always predict accurately because the demand for and the supply of a currency are affected *by more than the difference in inflation rates between countries.* For example, as noted, different income growth rates affect the demand for a currency and therefore the exchange rate. In the *long run,* however, and particularly when the *difference in inflation rates across countries is large,* the PPP theory does predict exchange rates accurately.

**CHANGES IN REAL INTEREST RATES** As shown in the U.S. balance of payments in Exhibit 2, more than goods flow between countries. Financial capital also moves between countries. The flow of financial capital depends on different countries' *real interest rates—* interest rates adjusted for inflation.

To illustrate, suppose initially that the real interest rate is 3 percent in both the United States and Mexico. Then the real interest rate in the United States increases to 4.5 percent. As a result, Mexicans will want to purchase financial assets in the United States that pay a higher real interest rate than do financial assets in Mexico. The Mexican demand for dollars will increase, and therefore Mexicans will supply more pesos. As the supply of pesos increases on the foreign exchange market, the exchange rate (the dollar price per peso) will change; fewer dollars will be needed to buy pesos. In short, the dollar will appreciate, and the peso will depreciate.

## finding ECONOMICS

**In the President Speaking to an Economic Advisor** The president of the United States is speaking to an economic advisor. The president asks, "What are the effects of the rather large budget deficits?" In response, the advisor might say that large budget deficits can affect interest rates, the value of the dollar, exports and imports, and the merchandise trade balance. "How so?" the president asks. Big deficits, the advisor answers, mean that the federal government will have to borrow funds, which will increase the demand for credit. This will push up the interest rate. As the U.S. interest rate rises relative to interest rates in other countries, foreigners will want to purchase financial assets in the United States that pay a higher return. This will increase the demand for dollars, the dollar will appreciate, and foreign currencies will depreciate. In turn, this will affect both import and export spending, and thus it will affect the merchandise trade balance. ▲ ▲ ▲

### SELF-TEST

1. In the foreign exchange market, how is the demand for dollars linked to the supply of pesos?

2. What could cause the U.S. dollar to appreciate against the Mexican peso on the foreign exchange market?

3. Suppose that the U.S. economy grows and that the Swiss economy does not. How will this affect the exchange rate between the dollar and the Swiss franc? Why?

4. What does the purchasing power parity theory say? Give an example to illustrate your answer.

# FIXED EXCHANGE RATES

**Fixed Exchange Rate System**
The system whereby a nation's currency is set at a fixed rate relative to all other currencies, and central banks intervene in the foreign exchange market to maintain the fixed rate.

The major alternative to the flexible exchange rate system is the fixed exchange rate system, which works the way it sounds. Exchange rates are fixed; they are not allowed to fluctuate freely in response to the forces of supply and demand. Central banks buy and sell currencies to maintain agreed-on exchange rates. The workings of the fixed exchange rate system are described in this section.

## Fixed Exchange Rates and Overvalued/Undervalued Currency

Once again, we assume a two-country–two-currency world, but this time the United States and Mexico agree to fix the exchange rate of their currencies. Instead of letting the dollar depreciate or appreciate relative to the peso, the two countries agree to set the price of 1 peso at $0.12; that is, they agree to the exchange rate of 0.12 USD = 1 MXN. Generally, we call this the fixed exchange rate or the *official price* of a peso.[4] Since we will include more than one official price in our discussion, 0.12 USD = 1 MXN is official price 1 (Exhibit 9).

**Overvalued**
A currency is overvalued if its price in terms of other currencies is above the equilibrium price.

If the dollar price of pesos is above its equilibrium level (which is the case at official price 1), a surplus of pesos exists, and the peso is said to be overvalued. In other words, the peso is fetching more dollars than it would at equilibrium. For example, if in equilibrium, 1 peso trades for $0.10, but at the official exchange rate 1 peso trades for $0.12, then the peso is said to be overvalued.

---

4. If the price of 1 peso is $0.12, the price of $1 is approximately 8.33 pesos. Thus, setting the official price of a peso in terms of dollars automatically sets the official price of a dollar in terms of pesos.

**EXHIBIT 9**

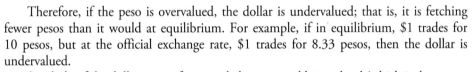

At this exchange rate, the peso is overvalued, the dollar is undervalued, and a surplus of pesos exists.

$S_{MXN}$

Official Price 1:
(0.12 USD = 1 MXN)

Official Price 2:
(0.08 USD = 1 MXN)

$D_{MXN}$

0.12

0.10

0.08

0

Exchange Rate
(dollar price per peso)

Quantity of Pesos

At this exchange rate, the peso is undervalued, the dollar is overvalued, and a shortage of pesos exists.

**A Fixed Exchange Rate System**

In a fixed exchange rate system, the exchange rate is fixed—and it may not be fixed at the equilibrium exchange rate. The exhibit shows two cases. (1) If the exchange rate is fixed at official price **1**, the peso is overvalued, the dollar is undervalued, and a surplus of pesos exists. (2) If the exchange rate is fixed at official price **2**, the peso is undervalued, the dollar is overvalued, and a shortage of pesos exists.

Therefore, if the peso is overvalued, the dollar is undervalued; that is, it is fetching fewer pesos than it would at equilibrium. For example, if in equilibrium, $1 trades for 10 pesos, but at the official exchange rate, $1 trades for 8.33 pesos, then the dollar is undervalued.

Similarly, if the dollar price of pesos is below its equilibrium level (which is the case at official price 2 in Exhibit 9), a shortage of pesos exists, and the peso is undervalued; the peso is not fetching as many dollars as it would at equilibrium. Therefore, if the peso is undervalued, the dollar must be overvalued.

**Undervalued**

A currency is undervalued if its price in terms of other currencies is below the equilibrium price.

Overvalued peso ↔ Undervalued dollar
Undervalued peso ↔ Overvalued dollar

## What Is So Bad About an Overvalued Dollar?

You read in the newspaper that the dollar is overvalued and that economists are concerned about the overvalued dollar. They are concerned because the exchange rate and hence the value of the dollar in terms of other currencies affects the amount of U.S. exports and imports. Because it affects exports and imports, it naturally affects the merchandise trade balance.

To illustrate, suppose the demand for and supply of pesos are represented by $D_1$ and $S_1$ in Exhibit 10. With this demand curve and supply curve, the equilibrium exchange rate is 0.10 USD = 1 MXN. Let's also suppose the exchange rate is fixed at this exchange rate. In other words, the equilibrium exchange rate and the fixed exchange rate are initially the same.

**EXHIBIT 10**

### Fixed Exchange Rates and an Overvalued Dollar

Initially, the demand for and supply of pesos are represented by $D_1$ and $S_1$, respectively. The equilibrium exchange rate is 0.10 USD = 1 MXN, which also happens to be the official (fixed) exchange rate. In time, the demand for pesos rises to $D_2$, and the equilibrium exchange rate rises to 0.12 USD = 1 MXN. The official exchange rate is fixed, however, so the dollar will be overvalued. As explained in the text, this can lead to a trade deficit.

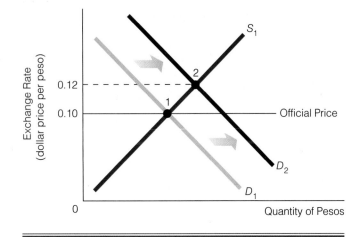

Time passes and eventually the demand curve for pesos shifts to the right, from $D_1$ to $D_2$. Under a flexible exchange rate system, the exchange rate would rise to 0.12 USD = 1 MXN. But a fixed exchange rate is in effect, not a flexible one. The exchange rate stays fixed at 0.10 USD = 1 MXN. So the fixed exchange rate (0.10 USD = 1 MXN) is below the new equilibrium exchange rate (0.12 USD = 1 MXN).

Recall that when the dollar price per peso is below its equilibrium level (which is the case), the peso is undervalued and the dollar is overvalued. At equilibrium (point 2 in Exhibit 10), 1 peso would trade for 0.12 dollars, but at its fixed rate (point 1), it trades for only 0.10 dollars; so the peso is undervalued. At equilibrium (point 2), $1 would trade for 8.33 pesos, but at its fixed rate (point 1), it trades for 10 pesos; so the dollar is overvalued.

What is bad about an overvalued dollar is that it makes U.S. goods more expensive for foreigners to buy, possibly affecting the U.S. merchandise trade balance. For example, suppose a U.S. good costs $100. At the equilibrium exchange rate (0.12 USD = 1 MXN), a Mexican would pay 833 pesos for the good, but at the fixed exchange rate (0.10 USD = 1 MXN), he will pay 1,000 pesos.

| Exchange Rate | Dollar Price | Peso Price |
|---|---|---|
| 0.12 USD = 1 MXN (equilibrium) | 100 USD | 833 MXN [(100 ÷ 0.12) MXN] |
| 0.10 USD = 1 MXN (fixed) | 100 USD | 1,000 MXN [(100 ÷ 0.10) MXN] |

The higher the prices are of U.S. goods (exports), the fewer of those goods Mexicans will buy, and, as just shown, an overvalued dollar makes U.S. export goods higher in price.

Ultimately, an overvalued dollar can affect the U.S. merchandise trade balance. As U.S. exports become more expensive for Mexicans, they buy fewer U.S. exports. If exports fall below imports, the result is a U.S. trade deficit.[5]

## Government Involvement in a Fixed Exchange Rate System

In Exhibit 9, suppose the governments of Mexico and the United States agree to fix the exchange rate at 0.12 USD = 1 MXN. At this exchange rate, a surplus of pesos exists. To maintain the exchange rate at 0.12 USD = 1 MXN, the Federal Reserve System (the Fed) could buy the surplus of pesos with dollars. Consequently, the demand for pesos will increase, and the demand curve will shift to the right, ideally, by enough to raise the equilibrium rate to the current fixed exchange rate.

Alternatively, instead of the Fed's buying pesos (to mop up the excess supply of pesos), the Banco de Mexico (the central bank of Mexico) could buy pesos with some of its reserve dollars. (It doesn't buy pesos with pesos because using pesos would not reduce the surplus of pesos on the market.) This action by the Banco de Mexico will also increase the demand for pesos and raise the equilibrium rate.

5. The other side of the coin, so to speak, is that if the dollar is overvalued, the peso must be undervalued. An undervalued peso makes Mexican goods cheaper for Americans. So while the overvalued dollar is causing Mexicans to buy fewer U.S. exports, the undervalued peso is causing Americans to import more goods from Mexico. In conclusion, U.S. exports fall, U.S. imports rise, and we move closer to a trade deficit, or, if one already exists, it becomes larger.

## Big Mac Economics

In an earlier chapter we explained why goods that can be easily transported from one location to another usually sell for the same price in all locations. For example, if a candy bar can be moved from Atlanta to Seattle, we would expect the candy bar to sell for the same price in both locations. The reason is that if the candy bar is priced higher in Seattle than Atlanta, people will move candy bars from Atlanta (where the price is relatively low) to Seattle to fetch the higher price. In other words, the supply of candy bars will rise in Seattle and fall in Atlanta. These changes in supply in the two locations affect the prices of the candy bars in the two locations. In Seattle the price will fall, and in Atlanta the price will rise. This price movement will stop when the prices of a candy bar are the same in the two locations.

© CHARLES PERTWEE/BLOOMBERG NEWS/ LANDOV

Now consider a good that is sold all over the world: McDonald's Big Mac. Suppose the exchange rate between the dollar and the yen is $1 = ¥100 and the price of a Big Mac in New York City is $3 and ¥400 in Tokyo. Given the exchange rate, a Big Mac is not selling for the same price in the two cities. In New York, it is $3, but in Tokyo it is $4 (the price in Tokyo is ¥400, and $1 = ¥100). Stated differently, in New York, $1 buys one-third of a Big Mac, but in Tokyo, $1 buys only one-fourth of a Big Mac. However, Big Macs won't be shipped from New York to Tokyo to fetch the higher price. Instead, the exchange rate is likely to adjust in such a way that the prices of a Big Mac are the same in both cities.

Now ask yourself what the exchange rate has to be between the dollar and yen before the Big Mac is the same dollar price in New York and Tokyo. Of the following three exchange rates, pick the correct one:

1. $1 = ¥133.33
2. $1 = ¥150.00
3. $1 = ¥89.00

The answer is the first one: $1 = ¥133.33. At this exchange rate, a Big Mac in New York is $3, and a Big Mac in Tokyo that is ¥400 is $3 (once we have computed its price in dollars). At the exchange rate of $1 = ¥133.33, then ¥1 = $0.0075, and

$$\$0.0075 \times ¥400 = \$3.$$

The *purchasing power parity theory* in economics predicts that the exchange rate between two currencies will adjust so that, in the end, $1 buys the same amount of a given good in all places around the world. Thus, if the exchange rate is initially $1 = ¥100 when a Big Mac is $3 in New York and ¥400 in Tokyo, it will change to become $1 = ¥133.33. That is, the dollar will soon appreciate relative to the yen.

*The Economist,* a well-known economics magazine, publishes what it calls the Big Mac index each year. It shows current exchange rates and the cost of a Big Mac in different countries (just as we did here). Then it predicts which currencies will appreciate and depreciate based on this information. *The Economist* does not always predict accurately, but it does do so in many cases.

If you want to predict whether the euro, pound, or peso is going to appreciate or depreciate in the next few months, looking at exchange rates in terms of the price of Big Mac is a useful approach.

Finally, the two actions could be combined; that is, both the Fed and the Banco de Mexico could buy pesos.

## Options Under a Fixed Exchange Rate System

Suppose there is a surplus of pesos in the foreign exchange market, indicating that the peso is overvalued and the dollar is undervalued. Suppose also that although the Fed and the Banco de Mexico each attempt to rectify this situation by buying pesos, this combined action is not successful. The surplus of pesos persists for weeks, along with an overvalued peso and an undervalued dollar. A few options are available.

**DEVALUATION AND REVALUATION** Mexico and the United States could agree to reset the official price of the dollar and the peso. Doing so entails *devaluation* and *revaluation*. A devaluation occurs when the official price of a currency is lowered. A revaluation occurs when the official price of a currency is raised.

For example, suppose the first official price of a peso is 0.10 USD = 1 MXN, and the first official price of $1 is 10 pesos. Mexico and the United States agree to change the official price of their currencies. The second official price is 0.12 USD = 1 MXN, and the second official price of $1 is 8.33 pesos.

Moving from the first official price to the second, the peso has been revalued because it takes *more dollars to buy a peso* (12¢ instead of 10¢). Of course, moving from the first official price to the second means the dollar has been devalued because it takes *fewer pesos to buy a dollar* (8.33 pesos instead of 10).

One country might want to devalue its currency, but another country might not want to revalue its currency. For example, if Mexico wants to devalue its currency relative to the U.S. dollar, U.S. authorities might not always willingly comply because, if they do, the United States will not sell as many goods to Mexico. As explained earlier, revaluing the dollar means Mexicans have to pay more for it; instead of paying, say, 8.33 pesos for $1, Mexicans might have to pay 10 pesos. At a revalued dollar (a higher peso price for a dollar), Mexicans will find U.S. goods more expensive and not want to buy as many. Americans who produce goods to sell to Mexico may see that a revalued dollar will hurt their pocketbooks, and so they will argue against it.

**PROTECTIONIST TRADE POLICY (QUOTAS AND TARIFFS)** Recall that an overvalued dollar can bring on or widen a trade deficit. To deal with both the trade deficit and the overvalued dollar at the same time, some say a country can impose quotas and tariffs to reduce domestic consumption of foreign goods. (An earlier chapter explains how both tariffs and quotas meet this objective.) A drop in the domestic consumption of foreign goods goes hand in hand with a decrease in the demand for foreign currencies. In turn, this decrease can affect the value of the country's currency on the foreign exchange market. In this case, it can get rid of an overvalued dollar.

Economists are quick to point out, though, that trade deficits and overvalued currencies are sometimes used as an excuse to promote trade restrictions, many of which simply benefit special interests (e.g., U.S. producers that compete for sales with foreign producers in the U.S. market).

**CHANGES IN MONETARY POLICY** Sometimes, a nation can use monetary policy to support the exchange rate or the official price of its currency. Suppose the United States is continually running a merchandise trade deficit; year after year, imports are outstripping exports. To remedy this, the United States might enact a tight monetary policy to retard inflation and drive up interest rates (at least in the short run). The tight monetary policy will reduce the U.S. rate of inflation and thereby lower U.S. prices relative to prices in other nations. This effect will make U.S. goods relatively cheaper than they were before (assuming other nations don't also enact a tight monetary policy) promoting U.S. exports and discouraging foreign imports. It will also generate a flow of investment funds into the United States in search of higher real interest rates.

Some economists argue against fixed exchange rates because they think it unwise for a nation to adopt a particular monetary policy simply to maintain an international exchange rate. Instead, they believe domestic monetary policies should be used to meet domestic economic goals, such as price stability, low unemployment, low and stable interest rates, and so forth.

## The Gold Standard

If nations adopt the gold standard, they *automatically fix* their exchange rates. Suppose the United States defines a dollar as equal to 1/10 of an ounce of gold and Mexico defines a peso as equal to 1/100 of an ounce of gold. Therefore, 1 ounce of gold could be bought

---

**Devaluation**
A government action that changes the exchange rate by lowering the official price of a currency.

**Revaluation**
A government act that changes the exchange rate by raising the official price of a currency.

with either $10 or 100 pesos. The fixed exchange rate between dollars and pesos is 10 MXN = 1 USD or 0.10 USD = 1 MXN.

To have an international gold standard, countries must do the following:

1.  Define their currencies in terms of gold.

2.  Stand ready and willing to convert gold into paper money and paper money into gold at the rate specified.

3.  Link their money supplies to their holdings of gold.

With this last point in mind, consider how a gold standard would work. Initially assume that the gold standard (fixed) exchange rate of 0.10 USD = 1 MXN is the equilibrium exchange rate. Then, a change occurs: inflation in Mexico raises prices there by 100 percent. A Mexican table that was priced at 2,000 pesos before the inflation is now priced at 4,000 pesos. At the gold standard (fixed) exchange rate, Americans now have to pay $400 (4,000 pesos ÷ 10 pesos per dollar) to buy the table, whereas before the inflation Americans had to pay only $200 (2,000 pesos ÷ 10 pesos per dollar) for the table. As a result, Americans buy fewer Mexican tables; Americans import less from Mexico.

At the same time, Mexicans import more from the United States because American prices are now relatively lower than before inflation hit Mexico. As a quick example, suppose that before the inflation, an American pair of shoes cost $200 and that, as before, a Mexican table cost 2,000 pesos. At 0.10 USD = 1 MXN, the $200 American shoes cost 2,000 pesos and the 2,000-peso Mexican table cost $200. In other words, 1 pair of American shoes traded for (or equaled) 1 Mexican table.

Then inflation raised the price of the Mexican table to 4,000 pesos, or $400. Because the American shoes are still $200 (there has been no inflation in the United States) and the exchange rate is still fixed at 0.10 USD = 1 MXN, 1 pair of American shoes no longer equals 1 Mexican table; instead, it equals 1/2 of a Mexican table. In short, the inflation in Mexico has made U.S. goods *relatively cheaper* for Mexicans. As a result, Mexicans buy more U.S. goods; they import more from the United States.

To summarize, the inflation in Mexico causes Americans to buy fewer goods from Mexico and Mexicans to buy more goods from the United States. In terms of the merchandise trade balance for each country, in the United States, imports decline (Americans are buying less from Mexico) and exports rise (Mexicans are buying more from the United States); so the U.S. trade balance is likely to move into surplus. Contrarily, in Mexico, exports decline (Americans are buying less from Mexico) and imports rise (Mexicans are buying more from the United States); so Mexico's trade balance is likely to move into deficit.

On a gold standard, Mexicans have to pay for the difference between their imports and exports with gold. Gold is therefore shipped to the United States. An increase in the supply of gold in the United States expands the U.S. money supply. A decrease in the supply of gold in Mexico contracts the Mexican money supply. Prices are affected in both countries. In the United States, prices begin to rise; in Mexico, they begin to fall.

As U.S. prices go up and Mexican prices go down, the earlier situation begins to reverse itself. American goods look more expensive to Mexicans, and they begin to buy less, whereas Mexican goods look cheaper to Americans, and they begin to buy more. Consequently, American imports begin to rise and exports begin to fall; Mexican imports begin to fall and exports begin to rise. Thus, by changing domestic money supplies and price levels, the gold standard begins to correct the initial trade balance disequilibrium.

The change in the money supply that the gold standard sometimes requires has prompted some economists to voice the same charge against the gold standard that is often heard against the fixed exchange rate system: it subjects domestic monetary policy to international instead of domestic considerations. In fact, many economists cite this as part of the reason many nations abandoned the gold standard in the 1930s. At a time when unemployment was unusually high, many nations with trade deficits felt that matters would only get worse if they contracted their money supplies to live by the edicts of the gold standard.

---

### SELF-TEST

1. Under a fixed exchange rate system, if one currency is overvalued, then another currency must be undervalued. Explain why this statement is true.

2. How does an overvalued dollar affect U.S. exports and imports?

3. In each of the following cases, identify whether the U.S. dollar is overvalued or undervalued:

   a. The fixed exchange rate is $2 = £1, and the equilibrium exchange rate is $3 = £1.

   b. The fixed exchange rate is $1.25 = €1, and the equilibrium exchange rate is $1.10 = €1.

   c. The fixed exchange rate is $1 = 10 pesos, and the equilibrium exchange rate is $1 = 14 pesos.

4. Under a fixed exchange rate system, why might the United States want to devalue its currency?

---

# FIXED EXCHANGE RATES VERSUS FLEXIBLE EXCHANGE RATES

As in many economic situations, any exchange rate system has both its costs and its benefits. This section discusses some of the arguments and issues surrounding fixed exchange rates and flexible exchange rates.

## Promoting International Trade

Which are better at promoting international trade: fixed or flexible exchange rates? This section presents the case for each.

THE CASE FOR FIXED EXCHANGE RATES Proponents of a fixed exchange rate system often argue that fixed exchange rates promote international trade, whereas flexible exchange rates stifle it. A major advantage of fixed exchange rates is certainty. Individuals in different countries know from day to day the value of their nation's currency. With flexible exchange rates, individuals are less likely to engage in international trade because of the added risk of not knowing from one day to the next how many dollars, euros, or yen they will have to trade for other currencies. Certainty is a necessary ingredient in international trade; flexible exchange rates promote uncertainty, which hampers international trade.

Economist Charles Kindleberger, a proponent of fixed exchange rates, believes that having fixed exchange rates is analogous to having a single currency for the entire United States instead of having a different currency for each of the 50 states. One currency in the United States promotes trade, whereas 50 different currencies would hamper it. In Kindleberger's view:

> The main case against flexible exchange rates is that they break up the world market.... Imagine trying to conduct interstate trade in the USA if there were fifty different state monies, none of which was dominant. This is akin to barter, the inefficiency of which is explained time and again by textbooks.[6]

THE CASE FOR FLEXIBLE EXCHANGE RATES Advocates of flexible exchange rates, as noted, maintain that it is better for a nation to adopt policies to meet domestic economic goals than to sacrifice domestic economic goals to maintain an exchange rate. Also, the chance is too great that the fixed exchange rate will diverge greatly from the equilibrium exchange rate, creating persistent balance of trade problems leading deficit nations to impose trade restrictions (tariffs and quotas) that hinder international trade.

---

6. Charles Kindleberger, *International Money* (London: Allen and Unwin, 1981), p. 174.

## Optimal Currency Areas

As of 2010, the European Union (EU) consisted of 27 member states. According to the European Union, its ultimate goal is "an ever closer union among the peoples of Europe, in which decisions are taken as closely as possible to the citizen." As part of meeting this goal, the EU established its own currency—the euro—on January 1, 1999.[7] Although euro notes and coins were not issued until January 1, 2002, certain business transactions were made in euros beginning January 1, 1999.

The European Union and the euro are relevant to a discussion of an *optimal currency area*. An optimal currency area is a geographic area in which exchange rates can be fixed or a *common currency* used without sacrificing domestic economic goals, such as low unemployment. The concept of an optimal currency area originated in the debate over whether fixed or flexible exchange rates are better. Most of the pioneering work on optimal currency areas was done by Robert Mundell, the winner of the 1999 Nobel Prize in Economics.

Before discussing an optimal currency area, we need to look at the relationships among labor mobility, trade, and exchange rates. *Labor mobility* means that the residents of one country can move easily to another country.

**Optimal Currency Area**
A geographic area in which exchange rates can be fixed or a common currency used without sacrificing domestic economic goals, such as low unemployment.

**TRADE AND LABOR MOBILITY** Suppose there are only two countries: the United States and Canada. The United States produces calculators and soft drinks, and Canada produces bread and muffins. Currently, the two countries trade with each other, and there is complete labor mobility between them.

One day, the residents of both countries reduce their demand for bread and muffins and increase their demand for calculators and soft drinks. In other words, relative demand changes. Demand increases for U.S. goods and falls for Canadian goods. Business firms in Canada lay off employees because their sales have plummeted. Incomes in Canada begin to fall, and the unemployment rate begins to rise. In the United States, prices initially rise because of the increased demand for calculators and soft drinks. In response to the higher demand for their products, U.S. business firms begin to hire more workers and increase their production. Their efforts to hire more workers drive wages up and reduce the unemployment rate.

Because labor is mobile, some of the newly unemployed Canadian workers move to the United States to find work, easing the economic situation in both countries. The movement of labor will reduce some of the unemployment problems in Canada, and, with more workers in the United States, more output will be produced, thus dampening upward price pressures on calculators and soft drinks. Thus, changes in relative demand pose no major economic problems for either country if labor is mobile.

**TRADE AND LABOR IMMOBILITY** Now let's suppose that relative demand has changed but that labor is *not* mobile between the United States and Canada, perhaps due to either political or cultural barriers. If people cannot move, what happens in the economies of the two countries depends largely on whether exchange rates are fixed or flexible.

If exchange rates are flexible, the value of the U.S. currency changes vis-à-vis the Canadian currency. If Canadians want to buy more U.S. goods, they will have to exchange their domestic currency for U.S. currency. The demand for U.S. currency on the foreign exchange market increases at the same time that the supply of Canadian currency increases. Consequently, U.S. currency appreciates, and Canadian currency depreciates. Because Canadian currency depreciates, U.S. goods become relatively more expensive for Canadians; so they buy fewer. And because U.S. currency appreciates, Canadian goods become relatively cheaper for Americans; so they buy more. Canadian business firms begin to sell more goods; so they hire more workers, the unemployment rate drops, and the bad economic times in Canada begin to disappear.

7. As of 2010, 16 of the 27 member states have adopted the euro as their official currency.

If exchange rates are fixed, however, U.S. goods will not become relatively more expensive for Canadians, and Canadian goods will not become relatively cheaper for Americans. Consequently, the bad economic times in Canada (high unemployment) might last for a long time indeed instead of beginning to reverse. Thus, if labor is immobile, changes in relative demand may pose major economic problems when exchange rates are fixed but not when they are flexible.

COSTS, BENEFITS, AND OPTIMAL CURRENCY AREAS In addition to benefits, flexible exchange rates have costs. Exchanging one currency for another (say, U.S. dollars for Canadian dollars or U.S. dollars for Japanese yen) incurs a charge, and the risk is greater of not knowing what the value of one's currency will be on the foreign exchange market on any given day. For many countries, the benefits outweigh the costs, and so they have flexible exchange rate systems.

Suppose some of the costs of flexible exchange rates could be eliminated, while maintaining the benefits. When labor is mobile between the two countries, they could have a fixed exchange rate or adopt a common currency and retain the benefits of flexible exchange rates. Then they do not have to have separate currencies that float against each other because resources (labor) can move easily and quickly in response to changes in relative demand. The two countries can either fix exchange rates or adopt the same currency.

When labor in countries within a geographic area is mobile enough to move easily and quickly in response to changes in relative demand, the countries are said to constitute an *optimal currency area*. Countries in such an area can either fix their currencies or adopt the same currency and thus keep all the benefits of flexible exchange rates without incurring any of the costs.

The states within the United States are commonly said to constitute an optimal currency area. Labor can move easily and quickly between, say, North Carolina and South Carolina in response to relative demand changes. Some economists argue that the countries that compose the European Union make up an optimal currency area and that adopting a common currency—the euro—will benefit these countries. Other economists disagree. They argue that, although labor is somewhat more mobile in Europe today than in the past, certain language and cultural differences make labor mobility less than sufficient to constitute a true optimal currency area.

# THE CURRENT INTERNATIONAL MONETARY SYSTEM

**Managed Float**
A managed flexible exchange rate system, under which nations now and then intervene to adjust their official reserve holdings to moderate major swings in exchange rates.

Today's international monetary system is best described as a managed flexible exchange rate system, sometimes referred to more casually as a managed float. In a way, this system is a rough compromise between the fixed and flexible exchange rate systems. The current system operates under flexible exchange rates, but not completely. Nations now and then intervene to adjust their official reserve holdings to moderate major swings in exchange rates.

Proponents of the managed float system stress the following advantages:

1. *It allows nations to pursue independent monetary policies.* Under a (strictly) fixed exchange rate system, fixed either by agreement or by gold, a nation with a merchandise trade deficit might have to enact a tight monetary policy to retard inflation and to promote its exports. This type of action is not needed with the managed float, whose proponents argue that solving trade imbalances by adjusting one price—the exchange rate—is better than adjusting the price level.

2. *It solves trade problems without trade restrictions.* As stated earlier, under a fixed exchange rate system, nations sometimes impose tariffs and quotas to solve trade imbalances. For example, a deficit nation might impose import quotas so that exports and imports of goods will be more in line. Under the current system, trade imbalances are usually solved through changes in exchange rates.

3. *It is flexible and therefore can easily adjust to shocks.* In 1973–1974, the OPEC nations dramatically raised the price of oil, resulting in trade deficits for many oil-importing

nations. A fixed exchange rate system would have had a hard time accommodating such a major change in oil prices, but the current system had little trouble. Exchange rates took much of the shock (with large changes in exchange rates), thus allowing most nations' economies to weather the storm with a minimum of difficulty.

Opponents of the current international monetary system stress the following disadvantages:

1. *It promotes exchange rate volatility and uncertainty and results in less international trade than would be the case under fixed exchange rates.* Under a flexible exchange rate system, volatile exchange rates make conducting business riskier for importers and exporters. As a result, there is less international trade than there would be under a fixed exchange rate system. Proponents respond that the futures market in currencies allows importers and exporters to shift the risk of fluctuations in exchange rates to others. For example, if an American company wants to buy a quantity of a good from a Japanese company three months from today, it can contract today for the desired quantity of yen that it will need at a specified price. It will not have to worry about a change in the dollar price of yen during the next three months. Purchasing a futures contract has a cost, but it is usually modest.

2. *It promotes inflation.* As we have seen, the monetary policies of different nations are not independent of one another under a fixed exchange rate system. For example, a nation with a merchandise trade deficit is somewhat restrained from inflating its currency because this will worsen the deficit problem. The deficit will make the nation's goods more expensive relative to foreign goods and promote the purchase of imports. In its attempt to maintain the exchange rate, a nation with a merchandise trade deficit would have to enact a tight monetary policy. Under the current system, a nation with a merchandise trade deficit does not have to maintain exchange rates or try to solve its deficit problem through changes in its money supply. Opponents of the current system argue that this frees nations to inflate, predicting that more inflation will result than would occur under a fixed exchange rate system.

3. *Changes in exchange rates alter trade balances in the desired direction only after a long time; in the short run, a depreciation in a currency can make the situation worse instead of better.* Soon after a depreciation in a trade-deficit nation's currency, the trade deficit, it is often argued, will increase (not decrease, as hoped) because import demand is inelastic in the short run: imports are not very responsive to a change in price. For example, suppose Mexico is running a trade deficit with the United States at the present exchange rate of 0.12 USD = 1 MXN. At this exchange rate, the peso is overvalued. Mexico buys 2,000 television sets from the United States, each with a price tag of $500. Assume Mexico therefore spends 8.33 million pesos on imports of American television sets. Now suppose that the overvalued peso begins to depreciate, say, to 0.11 USD = 1 MXN and that, in the short run, Mexican customers buy only 100 fewer American television sets (1,900). At a price of $500 each and an exchange rate of 0.11 USD = 1 MXN, Mexicans now spend 8.63 million pesos on imports of American television sets. In the short run, then, a depreciation in the peso has widened the trade deficit because the number of American television sets imported by Mexicans fell by less than the price of these television sets (in terms of pesos) increased. As time passes, imports will fall off more (it takes time for Mexican buyers to shift from higher-priced American goods to lower-priced Mexican goods), and the deficit will shrink.

---

## SELF-TEST

1. What is an optimal currency area?

2. Country 1 produces good X, and country 2 produces good Y. People in both countries begin to demand more of good X and less of good Y. Assume that there is no labor mobility between the two countries and that a flexible exchange rate system exists. What will happen to the unemployment rate in country 2? Explain your answer.

3. How important is labor mobility in determining whether an area is an optimal currency area?

# OFFICE HOURS

## "Why Is the Depreciation of One Currency Tied to the Appreciation of Another Currency?"

**STUDENT:**

I know that when the dollar depreciates, some other currency appreciates. Is this just the way it is? For example, if $1 dollar equals €1 euro, and then $1.25 equals €1, the arithmetic of exchange rates tells me that now $1 will only fetch €0.8. Is that all there is to it?

**INSTRUCTOR:**

Not exactly. You're focusing on the arithmetic (of exchange rates) to the exclusion of the economics. There is an economic reason why dollar appreciation is linked to euro appreciation.

**STUDENT:**

What is that economic reason?

**INSTRUCTOR:**

Think of what can lead to the dollar's depreciating. Suppose you want to travel to Germany, where the euro is used. You take your dollars and buy euros with them. In other words, you do two things: You (1) buy euros by (2) supplying dollars.

Now think of how you are affecting the market for euros and the market for dollars. You are increasing the *demand for euros* in the market for euros, and you are increasing the *supply of dollars* in the market for dollars. Remember in Exhibit 5 how we linked the demand for one currency with the supply of another? That is happening here: Your demand for euros is linked to your supply of dollars. So, if you increase the demand for euros, you are automatically increasing the supply of dollars.

**STUDENT:**

I'm used to thinking that my buying something affects only one market. For instance, when I buy more books, the purchase affects only the market for books. You seem to be telling me that this is not the case when I buy a currency, such as the euro. To buy euros is to supply dollars.

**INSTRUCTOR:**

That's right. So when you increase the demand for euros, you automatically increase the supply of dollars. And then we have to ask ourselves what happens in each of the two markets: the market for euros and the market for dollars.

## CHAPTER SUMMARY

### BALANCE OF PAYMENTS

- The balance of payments provides information about a nation's imports and exports, domestic residents' earnings on assets located abroad, foreign earnings on domestic assets, gifts to and from foreign countries, and official transactions by governments and central banks.

- In a nation's balance of payments, any transaction that supplies the country's currency in the foreign exchange market is recorded as a debit ($-$). Any transaction that creates a demand for the country's currency is recorded as a credit ($+$).

- The three main accounts of the balance of payments are the current account, the capital account, and the official reserve account.

- The current account includes all payments related to the purchase and sale of goods and services. The three major components of the account are exports of goods and services, imports of goods and services, and net unilateral transfers abroad.

- The capital account includes all payments related to the purchase and sale of assets and to borrowing and lending activities. The major components are outflow of U.S. capital and inflow of foreign capital.

- The official reserve account includes transactions by the central banks of various countries.

- The merchandise trade balance is the difference between the value of merchandise exports and the value of merchandise

---

> **STUDENT:**
>
> Well, if I increase the demand for euros, the price of a euro in terms of dollars will rise. Also, if I increase the supply of dollars, the price of a dollar in terms of euros will fall.

> **INSTRUCTOR:**
>
> And what do you call it when the price of a euro has risen in terms of dollars?

> **STUDENT:**
>
> We say the dollar has depreciated because it now takes more dollars and cents to buy a euro.

> **INSTRUCTOR:**
>
> And what do you call it when the price of a dollar has fallen in terms of euros?

> **STUDENT:**
>
> We say the euro has appreciated because it now takes fewer euros to buy a dollar.

> **INSTRUCTOR:**
>
> So let's go back to your original query. You wondered whether the dollar's depreciating and the euro's appreciating were just matters of arithmetic. Now we know that they aren't. They are a matter of curves shifting in different markets.

## POINTS TO REMEMBER

1. To buy a currency is to affect two markets, not just one. If you buy euros, you affect the euro market. But by selling dollars to buy euros, you also affect the dollar market.

2. The fact that when one currency depreciates another appreciates is a matter of curves shifting in two currency markets.

---

imports. If exports are greater than imports, a nation has a trade surplus; if imports are greater than exports, a nation has a trade deficit.

- The balance of payments equals Current account balance + Capital account balance + Official reserve balance + Statistical discrepancy.

## THE FOREIGN EXCHANGE MARKET

- The market in which currencies of different countries are exchanged is called the foreign exchange market. In this market, currencies are bought and sold for a price: the exchange rate.

- When the residents of a nation demand a foreign currency, they must supply their own currency. For example, if Americans demand Mexican goods, they also demand Mexican pesos and supply U.S. dollars. If Mexicans demand American goods, they also demand U.S. dollars and supply Mexican pesos.

## FLEXIBLE EXCHANGE RATES

- Under flexible exchange rates, the foreign exchange market will equilibrate at the exchange rate where the quantity demanded of a currency equals the quantity supplied of the currency; for example, the quantity demanded of U.S. dollars equals the quantity supplied of U.S. dollars.

- If the price of a nation's currency increases relative to a foreign currency, the nation's currency is said to have appreciated. For example, if the price of a peso rises from 0.10 USD = 1 MXN to 0.15 USD = 1 MXN, the peso has appreciated. If the price of a nation's currency decreases relative to a foreign currency, the nation's currency is said to have depreciated. For example, if the price of a dollar falls from 10 MXN = 1 USD to 8 MXN = 1 USD, the dollar has depreciated.

- Under a flexible exchange rate system, the equilibrium exchange rate is affected by a difference in income growth rates between countries, a difference in inflation rates between countries, and a change in (real) interest rates between countries.

## FIXED EXCHANGE RATES

• Under a fixed exchange rate system, countries agree to fix the price of their currencies. The central banks of the countries must then buy and sell currencies to maintain the agreed-on exchange rate.

• If a persistent deficit or surplus in a nation's combined current and capital account exists at a fixed exchange rate, the nation has a few options to deal with the problem: devalue or revalue its currency, enact protectionist trade policies (in the case of a deficit), or change its monetary policy.

• A gold standard automatically fixes exchange rates. To have an international gold standard, nations must do the following: (1) define their currencies in terms of gold; (2) stand ready and willing to convert gold into paper money and paper money into gold at a specified rate; and (3) link their money supplies to their holdings of gold. The change in the money supply that the gold standard sometimes requires has prompted some economists to voice the same charge against the gold standard that is often heard against the fixed exchange rate system: it subjects domestic monetary policy to international instead of domestic considerations.

## THE CURRENT INTERNATIONAL MONETARY SYSTEM

• Today's international monetary system is described as a managed flexible exchange rate system, or managed float. For the most part, the exchange rate system is flexible, although nations periodically intervene in the foreign exchange market to adjust rates. Because it is a managed float system, it is difficult to tell whether nations will emphasize the float part or the managed part in the future.

• Proponents of the managed flexible exchange rate system believe it offers several advantages: (1) It allows nations to pursue independent monetary policies. (2) It solves trade problems without trade restrictions. (3) It is flexible and therefore can easily adjust to shocks.

• Opponents of the managed flexible exchange rate system believe it has several disadvantages: (1) It promotes exchange rate volatility and uncertainty and results in less international trade than would be the case under fixed exchange rates. (2) It promotes inflation. (3) It corrects trade deficits only a long time after a depreciation in the currency; in the interim, it can make matters worse.

## KEY TERMS AND CONCEPTS

Balance of Payments
Debit
Foreign Exchange Market
Credit
Current Account
Merchandise Trade Balance
Merchandise Trade Deficit

Merchandise Trade Surplus
Current Account Balance
Capital Account
Capital Account Balance
International Monetary
Fund (IMF)
Special Drawing Right (SDR)

Exchange Rate
Flexible Exchange Rate
System
Appreciation
Depreciation
Purchasing Power Parity
(PPP) Theory

Fixed Exchange Rate System
Overvalued
Undervalued
Devaluation
Revaluation
Optimal Currency Area
Managed Float

## QUESTIONS AND PROBLEMS

1. Suppose the United States and Japan have a flexible exchange rate system. Explain whether each of the following events will lead to an appreciation or depreciation in the U.S. dollar and Japanese yen.

   a. U.S. real interest rates rise above Japanese real interest rates.

   b. The Japanese inflation rate rises relative to the U.S. inflation rate.

   c. Japan imposes a quota on imports of American radios.

2. Give an example that illustrates how a change in the exchange rate changes the relative price of domestic goods in terms of foreign goods.

3. Suppose the media report that the United States has a deficit in its current account. What does this imply about the U.S. capital account balance and official reserve account balance?

4. Suppose Canada has a merchandise trade deficit and Mexico has a merchandise trade surplus. The two countries have a flexible exchange rate system; so the Mexican peso appreciates and the Canadian dollar depreciates. However, soon after the depreciation of the Canadian dollar, Canada's trade deficit grows instead of shrinks. Why might this occur?

5. What are the strong and weak points of the flexible exchange rate system? What are the strong and weak points of the fixed exchange rate system?

6. Individuals do not keep a written account of their balance of trade with other individuals. For example, John doesn't keep an account of how much he sells to Alice and how much he buys from her. In addition, neither cities nor any of the

50 states calculate their balance of trade with all other cities and states. However, nations do calculate their merchandise trade balance with other nations. If nations do so, should individuals, cities, and states do so? Why or why not?

7. Every nation's balance of payments equals zero. Therefore, is each nation on an equal footing in international trade and finance with every other nation? Explain your answer.

8. Suppose your objective is to predict whether the euro (the currency of the European Union) and the U.S. dollar will appreciate or depreciate on the foreign exchange market in the next two months. What information would you need to help make your prediction? Specifically, how would this information help you predict the direction of the foreign exchange value of the euro and dollar? Next, explain how a person who could accurately predict exchange rates could become extremely rich in a short time.

9. Suppose the price of a Big Mac always rises by the percentage rise in the price level of the country in which it is sold. According to the purchasing power parity (PPP) theory, we would expect the price of a Big Mac to be the same everywhere in the world. Why?

10. If everyone in the world spoke the same language, would the world be closer to or further from being an optimal currency area? Explain your answer.

## WORKING WITH NUMBERS AND GRAPHS

1. Use the following information to answer questions.

| | U.S. Dollar Equivalent | | Currency per U.S. Dollar | |
|---|---|---|---|---|
| | **Thurs.** | **Fri.** | **Thurs.** | **Fri.** |
| Russia (ruble) | 0.0318 | 0.0317 | 31.4190 | 31.5290 |
| Brazil (real) | 0.3569 | 0.3623 | 2.8020 | 2.7601 |
| India (rupee) | 0.0204 | 0.0208 | 48.9100 | 47.8521 |

a. Between Thursday and Friday, did the U.S. dollar appreciate or depreciate against the Russian ruble?

b. Between Thursday and Friday, did the U.S. dollar appreciate or depreciate against the Brazilian real?

c. Between Thursday and Friday, did the U.S. dollar appreciate or depreciate against the Indian rupee?

2. If $1 equals ¥0.0093, what does ¥1 equal?

3. If $1 equals 7.7 krone (Danish), what does 1 krone equal?

4. If $1 equals 31 rubles, what does 1 ruble equal?

5. If the current account is −$45 billion, the capital account is +$55 billion, and the official reserve balance is −$1 billion, what does the statistical discrepancy equal?

6. Why does the balance of payments always equal zero?

## CHAPTER 23

# GLOBALIZATION AND INTERNATIONAL IMPACTS ON THE ECONOMY

**Introduction** In the world in which we live, we hear much of *globalization*. In this chapter we discuss what globalization is, the causes of it, the costs and benefits of it, and its future. We then return to a framework of analysis we first used in the macroeconomics part of this text—aggregate demand and aggregate supply (*AD–AS*)—and we use *AD–AS* to discuss some of the effects of globalization on a national economy.

# WHAT IS GLOBALIZATION?

Many economists define globalization as one of two things:

1. A phenomenon by which individuals and businesses in any part of the world are much more affected by events elsewhere in the world than before.

2. The growing integration of the national economies of the world to the degree that we may be witnessing the emergence and operation of a single worldwide economy.

These factors—people and businesses across the world having a greater impact on each other, creating a smaller world, and the movement toward a worldwide economy—are repeated in the many different definitions of globalization. Let's take a closer look at these key features.

> **Globalization**
> A phenomenon by which economic agents in any given part of the world are more affected by events elsewhere in the world than before; the growing integration of the national economies of the world to the degree that we may be witnessing the emergence and operation of a single worldwide economy.

## A Smaller World

The first definition emphasizes that economic agents in any given part of the world are affected by events elsewhere in the world. If you live in the United States, you are affected not only by what happens in the United States but also by what happens in Brazil, Russia, and China. For example, in recent years, the Chinese government was using much of the money it earned in trade with the United States to buy bonds issued by the U.S. government. As a result of these Chinese purchases, interest rates in the United States ended up being lower than they would have been. Because of lowered interest rates, some people were able to take out mortgage loans to buy houses that they would not be eligible for otherwise. Some people took out car loans to buy cars that they otherwise would not have been able to buy.

So, in a sense, globalization makes the world smaller. China has not moved physically; it is no closer to the United States (in terms of distance) than it was 100 years ago. Still, because of globalization, what happens in distant China today has an effect on you, just as, in the past, what happened in locations only 10 miles or 100 miles away would affect you. For all practical purposes, we live in a smaller world today than people did 100 years ago.

## finding ECONOMICS

**In a Clothing Store** Brandon is at a clothing store buying a number of items—shirts, sweaters, trousers, etc. He doesn't check to see in which country each of these items was produced. Instead, he just checks out the item and its price, and he decides whether to buy it. Where is the economics?

Many of the items Brandon buys were very likely produced in other countries. To Brandon, buying an item of clothing produced in China, Brazil, or India is really no different from buying an item of clothing in a factory 10 miles away. For Brandon, China, Brazil, or India might as well be down the street. In some ways, the world Brandon lives in is a small world, one in which distance doesn't matter as much as it used to; it is one in which trades between people living in different countries are becoming increasingly more common. ▲ ▲ ▲

## A World Economy

Globalization is closely aligned with a movement toward more free enterprise, freer markets, and more freedom of movement for people and goods. Thomas Friedman, author of several books on globalization, states that "globalization means the spread of free-market capitalism in the world." Economic globalization is essentially a free enterprise activity, and, to the degree that many countries are globalizing, they are moving toward greater free enterprise practices. Much of this globalization and much of the movement toward freer markets are occurring in the world today.

With globalization, the world is moving from hundreds of national economies toward *one large world economy.* In this world economy, speaking about *different* economic systems does not make as much sense as it once did. Speaking about *the* economic system for that one world economy does make sense. And, as explained, the economic system that best describes what is happening in the world economy is free enterprise, or capitalism.

## finding ECONOMICS

**In *The Economist*** "Mr. Bhattacharjee is not the first leader to preach socialism while practising capitalism." Mr. Bhattacharjee is the chief minister of the Indian state, West Bengal. The statement about him was made in *The Economist* (a news magazine that covers economic issues in particular) in November 2007. Where is the economics?

The statement gives us a glimpse into what is happening in the world today with respect to the adoption of economic systems—specifically, the movement toward capitalism. ▲ ▲ ▲

# TWO WAYS TO SEE GLOBALIZATION

Sometimes, a definition is not as good a description or explanation as a picture. Let's create two mental pictures that should give you a good idea of what globalization is about. The first picture is of a world without any barriers to trade, where the cost of dealing with anyone in the world is essentially the same.

## Should You Leave a Tip?

In the United States, tipping in restaurants is common, amounting to $16 billion a year. Yet 24 percent of the individuals in one study said that they thought tipping was unfair to customers. In the past, some states prohibited tipping. For example, in the early 1900s, Arkansas, Mississippi, Iowa, South Carolina, Tennessee, and Washington passed laws to prohibit tipping.

Of all the people in the rest of the world, some have the same tipping practices as Americans, but certainly not all. For example, adding an automatic service charge to a restaurant bill is increasingly customary in European restaurants, rather than tipping the server. Little tipping of any sort goes on in Argentina and Vietnam. Much less tipping occurs (i.e., fewer service providers expect tips) in Australia, New Zealand, and Italy than in the United States, and more tipping goes on in Mexico and Egypt than in the United States.

In several studies, researchers looked at the number of different service providers (out of a total of 33) for which tipping is customary in a given country: the more service providers it was customary to tip in a country, the higher the country's so-called prevalence of tipping. For example, if it was customary to tip 31 different service providers in country A but only 15 in country B, then country A would have a higher prevalence of tipping than country B.

© MOODBOARD/ALAMY

The conclusion of these studies is that countries where success and materialism were highly valued had a higher prevalence to tip than countries where caring and personal relationships were highly valued. In addition, the prevalence of tipping increased as the national need for achievement and recognition rose. In one study, tipping was more prevalent in countries with lower taxes than in countries with higher taxes.

If speaking in terms of a world economy instead of hundreds of national economies is becoming increasingly relevant, will tipping practices around the world become more uniform? If they do, toward what degree of tipping will they gravitate? Even if we do not know the answers, these questions get us to do two things: first, they get us to think about what changes we are likely to see in our everyday lives as globalization continues, whether the changes will be only in the economic realm (e.g., we can buy more clothes from China), or whether they will disperse outward into the social and cultural realms. Second, the questions force us to separate into categories things that are so deeply embedded in the character of a people (and therefore unlikely to change) from things that are somewhat superficial (and therefore more likely to change). Which is a rock (incapable of absorbing), and which is a sponge (capable of absorbing)?

## No Barriers

Suppose land were not divided into nation states—no United States, no China, no Russia. Also suppose physical, economic, or political barriers to trade did not exist. Essentially, then, you could trade with anyone, no matter where in the world this person lived. You could trade with a person living 5,000 miles away as easily as you could trade with your next-door neighbor.

In this pretend world, businesses could hire workers and set up factories anywhere in the world. People could open savings accounts in banks 7,000 miles away or buy stock in companies located on the other side of the globe.

In a sense, our world—the world that we live in today—is moving in this direction. As it does, a nation's economy (e.g., the U.S. economy) becomes more and more a part of the world economy. Consequently, speaking about a world or global economy, rather than about the Russian, U.S., or Chinese economy, becomes increasingly relevant.

## A Union of States

The second way to see globalization is familiar to people who reside in the United States, made up as it is of 50 states. Today, moving goods and services among these states is easy. A person can produce goods in, say, North Carolina and then transport them (with only a few exceptions) for sale to every state in the country. In addition, a person living anywhere in the United States can move to any state and work, save, purchase, sell, and so on. In other words, within the United States, the free movement of people and goods is possible.

Some people will argue today that economic globalization is, in a way, similar to changing countries (of the world) into states of one country. It is similar to making independent countries such as the United States, Russia, China, Brazil, and Japan into the United States of the World.

# GLOBALIZATION FACTS

You know globalization is occurring, when you see certain things happening in the world:

- Countries in the world opening up to more trade with each other
- People in one country investing some of their money in other countries
- Companies in one country hiring people in other countries

Essentially, you need to see people in the world acting more as they once acted only within their individual countries. Some evidence suggests that all these things are happening.

## International Trade

**Tariff**
A tax on imports.

The average tariff rate in the United States was 40 percent in 1946. The average tariff today is about 1.6 percent. Also, the federal government's revenue from tariffs in the early 1900s accounted for half of all its revenues, whereas today tariffs account for less than 2 percent. Exhibit 1 presents average tariff rates in the United States during the period 1930–2010.

The decline in tariff rates in the United States mirrors similar declines in countries such as India, China, Brazil, and many others. For example, in 2000, the average tariff rate in China was 18.7 percent; one year later, it was 12.8 percent. In 2000, the average tariff rate in India was 30.2 percent; one year later, it was 21 percent. Furthermore, both India and China are trading more with other countries. For example, 15 years ago, China did not

---

**EXHIBIT 1**

**Average U.S. Tariff Rates, 1930–2010**

trade much with the countries of Europe. Today, for most European countries, China is one of their top five trading partners.

As further evidence of globalization, between 1973 and 2010, countries exported and imported more goods. Exports became a larger percentage of a country's total output. On an individual level, suppose you produce computers. Last year, all the computers you produced were purchased by residents of the country in which you live. This year, residents of your country purchase half of your computers, and persons who live in foreign countries purchased the other half. In 2010, U.S. exports and imports were more like the second scenario; in 1973, things were closer to the first scenario.

## Foreign Exchange Trading

When people of one country want to trade with people of another country or invest in a foreign company, they have to buy the currency used in the other country. So if globalization is occurring, we would expect a lot more currency exchanges to take place. In economics, *foreign exchange trading* is the buying and selling of foreign currencies. In 1995, daily foreign exchange trading was 60 times higher than it was in 1977. In 1992, daily foreign exchange trading amounted to $820 billion. In 1998, this amount had risen to $1.5 trillion, close to doubling in just six years. In 2007, foreign exchange trading had risen to over $3 trillion.

## Foreign Direct Investment

If a U.S. company wants to invest in a company in, say, Russia, it undertakes what is called *foreign direct investment.* The more foreign direct investment there is, the more likely it is that the process of globalization is at work. In 1975, foreign direct investment amounted to $23 billion. In 1997, it had risen to $644 billion, a 30-fold increase. In 1980, 6.2 percent of the U.S. population was foreign born; in 2005, it was 12 percent. Between 1984 and 2003, U.S. investment holdings in foreign companies tripled, and foreign investment in the United States increased six-fold.

## Personal Investments

Many people in the United States own stocks, and if you own a number of stocks, you are said to have a stock portfolio. In 1980, these stock portfolios were comprised of no more than 2 percent of foreign stocks. Today, it is 14 percent. Thus, Americans are increasingly buying stock in foreign companies.

## **ⓕinding ECONOMICS**

**In a Foreign Stock Transaction** Two years ago Jake bought a few foreign stocks. Specifically, he bought 1,000 shares of an Irish firm's stock and 400 shares of a French firm's stock. In both Ireland and France the currency used is the euro. In recent months, the value of the dollar in relationship to the euro has been falling. In other words, it now takes more dollars and cents to buy a euro than it did when Jake bought the stock. Where is the economics?

The economics appears in two places. First, buying foreign stocks is part of the overall globalization picture. Second, Jake's return for buying the foreign stocks is rising as the dollar falls. When Jake sells the foreign stock, he will be paid in euros, and euros are rising in value relative to the dollar. So, when he exchanges the euros for dollars, he will get more dollars now than he would have before the dollar fell in value (in relation to the euro). ▲ ▲ ▲

## The World Trade Organization

The World Trade Organization (WTO) is an international organization whose mission is to promote international free trade (trade between countries). In 1948, only 23 countries of the world chose to be members of the precursor to the WTO, GATT (General Agreement on Tariffs and Trade); in mid-2010, that number had risen to 153 countries.

## Business Practices

More and more, Americans are working for foreign companies with offices in the United States. For example, the number of Americans working for foreign companies (with offices in the United States) grew from 4.9 million in 1991 to 6.5 million in 2001, an increase of 1.6 million.

# THE MOVEMENT TOWARD GLOBALIZATION

How did we come to live in a global economy? How and when did the process start? Globalization has been on the world stage for over two decades. In fact, the world has gone through different globalization periods. For example, globalization was occurring during the period from the mid-1800s to the late 1920s, and some people today refer to it as the First Era of Globalization. In some ways, when it came to the movement of people, the world then was freer than the world today, as evidenced by the fact that many people moved from country to country without a passport, which was not required.

The First Era of Globalization was largely ended by World Wars I and II and by the Great Depression. Even though the Great Depression and the world wars were over by 1945, globalization did not start anew right away. The Cold War essentially divided the world into different camps (free versus unfree, capitalist versus communist), which led to relatively high political and economic barriers. The visible symbol of these barriers—the Berlin Wall—separated not only East from West Germany but one group of countries living under one political and economic system from another group of countries living under a different political and economic system.

Today's more recent period of globalization has several causal factors. Not everyone agrees on all of them, and not everyone agrees on the weight one assigns to each. For example, some people will argue that one factor means more to globalization than another. Still, you should be aware of the causal factors of globalization most often mentioned.

## The End of the Cold War

The Cold War intensified after World War II and, most agree, ended with the visible fall of the Berlin Wall in 1989. This event, although historic in and of itself, occurred at the time when the Soviet empire was beginning to crumble, and many of the communist East European countries were breaking away from the Soviet Union. As some explain the event, the end of the Cold War resulted in turning two different worlds (the capitalist and communist worlds) into one. It resulted in a thawing of not only political but economic relations between former enemies. You might not trade with your enemy, but once that person or country is no longer your enemy, you don't feel the same need to exclude him or it from your political and economic life.

At the beginning of this section, we asked you to imagine a world where no barriers affected your trading with anyone in the world. The barriers might be distance, culture, politics, or anything else. The Cold War acted as a political barrier between certain groups of countries; once it ended, one barrier standing in the way of trade disappeared. In fact, if United States and the Soviet Union were still engaged in the Cold War, the current period of economic liberalization (freer markets, lower tariffs) and globalization might not be taking place. Even though the end of the Cold War might not be the full and only cause for the current period of globalization, if it had not ended, globalization would probably not be accelerating at the pace it is today.

# economics 24/7

## Proper Business Etiquette Around the World

Customs and traditions differ among countries, sometimes when it comes to conducting business. Not knowing how business is done in a country can act as a stumbling block to getting it done. What follows is a list of countries and certain rules of business etiquette in the different countries.[1]

**Beijing, China**

- If someone offers you his or her business card, accept with both hands, read it immediately, and then present your business card to the person.
- In business, men normally wear a suit and tie.

**Berlin, Germany**

- When out with German business associates, try not to talk about sports. Many businesspeople believe that sports talk is the domain of the uneducated.
- Drinking before all have raised their glasses together is considered impolite.

**Dubai, United Arab Emirates**

- Do not arrange appointments on Friday because it is Dubai's day of prayer and rest.
- Business slows down during the month of Ramadan (when Muslims fast). Foreign businesspeople are expected to observe the slower pace.

**Hong Kong**

- Running out of business cards is considered impolite.

**Mexico City**

- Having business cards printed in English on one side and in Spanish on the other is considered good form.
- Business clothing is fairly formal.

**Sydney, Australia**

- Knowing about the latest sports matches is important.
- Don't take yourself too seriously.

**Tokyo, Japan**

- Remove your shoes when entering a Japanese home.

**Zurich, Switzerland**

- People often greet each other when entering an office or shop. Try to do the same, even if your greeting is in your own language.
- Talking about money or personal wealth is frowned upon.

1. The reference guide is *The Economist*'s City Guide.

## Advancing Technology

In the past, innovations such as the internal combustion engine, steamship, telephone, and telegraph led to increased trade between people in different countries. All of these inventions led to lower transportation or communication costs, and lower costs mean fewer barriers to trade. What technology often does is lower the hindrances (of physical distance) that act as stumbling blocks to trade. For example, the cost of a 3-minute telephone call from New York to London in 1930 was $250. In 1960, it was $60.42; in 1980, it was $6.32; and in 2000, it was 40¢. Today, the cost is even less. As the costs of communicating continue to fall, in some sense, the hindrance to trade imposed by physical distance is overcome. Businesspeople in the United States, for example, can more cheaply talk with businesspeople in China.

Also consider the price of a computer over the years. In 1960, the cost of a computer—one comparable to the desktop computer that many people today have on their desks at home—was $1.8 million. That computer was $199,983 in 1970, $27,938 in 1980, $7,275 in 1990, $1,000 in 2000, and $500 in 2010. People today not only use computers for their work, but they communicate with others via the Internet. The personal computer and Internet technology enable people to communicate with others over long distances, thus increasing the probability that they will trade with one other.

Today, even farmers in poor developing countries can have access to people and to information that they didn't have access to only a few years ago. A farmer in the Ivory Coast can check agricultural prices in the world with a cell phone—something that was unheard of a decade ago. Or consider such innovations as online banking. Years ago, it was common to have your bank just down the road from you. Today, you can open up an account with an online bank, many of which are located nowhere near you.

## Policy Changes

Governments have the power to slow down the process of globalization if they want. Suppose two countries, A and B, have free economic relations with each other. Neither country imposes tariffs on the goods of the other. Neither country prevents its citizens from going to the other country to live and work. Neither country hampers its citizens from investing in the other country. Then, one day, for whatever reason, the government of country A decides to impose tariffs on the goods of country B and to limit its citizens from traveling to and investing in country B. In other words, the government of country A decides to close its political and economic doors.

Just as a government of one country can close the door on another, it can open the door too, and it can do so a little, more than a little, or a lot. In recent decades, governments of many countries have been opening their doors to other countries. China has opened its door, India has opened its door, and Russia has opened its door.

The driving forces of this most recent period of globalization have been (1) the end of the Cold War, (2) technological changes that lower the costs of transporting goods and communicating with people, and (3) government policy changes that express an openness toward freer markets and long-distance trade.

### SELF-TEST

(Answers to Self-Test questions are in Answers to Self-Test Questions at the back of the book.)

1. Some have said that the end of the Cold War has led to greater globalization. Explain the reasoning.

2. What is globalization?

3. How might advancing technology lead to increased globalization?

# BENEFITS AND COSTS OF GLOBALIZATION

Some people believe that globalization is, in general, a good thing and that its benefits outweigh its costs. Other people take the opposite view that the costs of globalization are greater than the benefits. Let's look at what supporters say are its benefits and what opponents say are its costs. As you read, you will probably begin to form your own opinion.

## The Benefits

TRADE To say that the world is undergoing globalization is really no more than saying that people are trading with more people, at greater distances, than they once did. They are trading different things: money for goods, their labor services for money, their savings for expected returns, and so on. Expanding trade—which is what globalization is about—is no more than extending the benefits of trading to people you might not have traded with earlier.

Economist David Friedman compared free international trade to a technology. He says that you can produce, say, cars in two ways. You can set up factories in Detroit,

Michigan, and produce them. Or you can harvest wheat in the Midwest, load it on ships and send it to Japan, and then wait for the ships to return with cars. Looking at things the second way sometimes brings out the magic of trade. After all, with free trade across countries, wheat gets turned into cars, an accomplishment that really is magical. The lesson Friedman is trying to communicate is that we all think a technological improvement is a good thing because it often leads to a higher standard of living. So, trading with people across the world really is nothing more than a technology of sorts; it is a way to turn wheat into cars. The more we trade with others, the more magic we witness.

INCOME PER PERSON The benefits of globalization can be seen in a slightly more concrete way. As both India and China opened up their economies to globalization in recent decades, they experienced increases in income per person. For example, between 1980 and 2000, income per person doubled in India. Between 1940 and 2000, income per person increased by 400 percent in China, with much of the increase coming in recent years. According to the International Monetary Fund, these dramatic increases in income per person accompanied the expansion of free international trade (a key component of globalization).

PRICES Numerous studies have established a link between lower prices and the degree of international trade and globalization. Simply put, free international trade lowers prices. For example, Exhibit 2 shows the CPI (consumer price index) and an import price index for the period 1990–2004. The CPI (which contains domestic goods and imported goods) rose faster than the import price index (which contains only imported goods). Also, between 1977 and 2004, the inflation-adjusted prices for an array of goods traded between countries fell, whereas the inflation-adjusted prices for an array of goods not traded between countries actually increased. Some of the traded goods whose prices fell are audio equipment (26 percent), TV sets (51 percent), toys (34 percent), and clothing (9 percent); some of the nontraded goods whose prices increased are whole milk (28 percent), butter (23 percent), ice cream (18 percent), and peanut butter (9 percent).

PRODUCTIVITY AND INNOVATION Firms that face global competition are often pushed to increase their productivity and to innovate more. According to the 2006 *Economic Report of the President,* "Studies show that firms exposed to the world's best practices demonstrate higher productivity through many channels, such as learning from these best practices, and also creating new products and processes in response to this exposure." For example, one study from the United Kingdom showed that the number of firms

**EXHIBIT 2**

**CPI and Import Price Index, 1990–2004** The CPI increased at a faster rate during the period 1990–2004 than the import price index (which both increased and decreased during the period).

*Source: Bureau of Labor Statistics.*

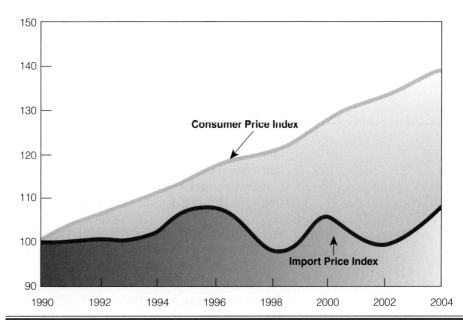

that faced global competition and reported product or process innovations was almost three times the number of firms that did not face global competition.

Or consider the extreme case of North and South Korea. The two countries share a people and a culture, but North Korea avoided the process of globalization during the period in which South Korea embraced it. South Koreans currently enjoy a much higher standard of living than North Koreans.

## The Costs

**INCREASED INCOME INEQUALITY** Globalization's critics often point out that globalization seems to go hand in hand with increased income inequality between rich and poor countries in the world. In fact, income inequality has increased. For example, 100 years ago, people in rich countries had about 10 times more income than people in poor countries. Today, they have about 75 times more income. Without a doubt, globalization and income inequality are strongly correlated. The question, though, is whether globalization causes the inequality. The critics of globalization say it does, whereas the supporters say it does not.

The supporters of globalization liken it to a train. Economic systems that get on the train will benefit and reach their economic destinies faster, but those that do not will get left farther and farther behind. In other words, globalization does not increase income inequality; rather, some other combination of circumstances—of some countries globalizing while others are not—is the cause. In simple terms, if everyone is walking, some faster than others, then some will always be in front. If the fast walkers start to run while the others continue their slow walking pace, the gap between the ones in front and the ones in back will grow.

Of course, getting on the globalization train is not always a matter of choice. The conductor does not always let some people on. Some rich countries work against certain poor countries to counter their globalization efforts. For example, tariffs on goods imported from the poor, developing world are 30 percent above the global average for all tariffs.

**LOSING AMERICAN JOBS** Many critics of globalization argue that it can result in Americans losing certain jobs. Suppose a U.S. company hires engineers in India to do jobs once done by Americans. This practice of hiring people in other countries is often called offshoring.

Some Americans may lose their jobs to workers in other countries due to globalization. It has already happened. In 2003, a major New York securities firm replaced its team of 800 American software engineers, who earned about $150,000 per year each, with an equally competent team in India earning an average of about $20,000 a year per person. Additionally, the number of radiologists in the United States is expected to fall significantly because radiological data can now be sent over the Internet to Asian radiologists, who can analyze it at a fraction of the cost here.

Keep in mind, though, that offshoring is a two-way street: the United States might offshore certain jobs to, say, India or China, but foreign countries around the world offshore jobs to the United States too. Although some Americans lose jobs due to globalization efforts, jobs are always being lost and found in a dynamic economy that is responding to market changes. Even if the degree of offshoring in the United States were zero, people would still be losing old jobs and getting new ones every day.

**MORE POWER TO BIG CORPORATIONS** Many critics of globalization argue that the process will simply hand over the world (and especially the developing countries) to large Western corporations (headquartered in the United States, the United Kingdom, Canada, and other powerful nations). In fact, in the minds of many people, globalization is the process of *corporatizing* the world. Instead of governments deciding what will and will not be done, large corporations will assume the responsibility.

**Offshoring**
Work done for a company by persons other than the original company's employees in a country other than the company's home country.

# economics 24/7

## Will Globalization Change the Sound of Music?

Suppose you had only 100 people to whom you could sell a good. Given this small number, you had better sell something that at least some of the 100 people want to buy. For example, if the 100 people don't like fruit salad, then you better not produce and offer to sell fruit salad; if some of them like bread, then perhaps you should produce and offer to sell bread.

Now increase the number of people from 100 to 1 million. A group of 1 million is much more likely than a group of 100 to contain people who like fruit salad. In other words, as the size of the potential customer base increases, the number of things you can sell increases too. In a world of 100 people, you can sell only bread, but in a world of 1 million people, you can sell fruit salad or bread.

So the larger the size is of the potential customer base (the more people you can possibly sell to), the greater the variety of goods for sale is likely to be. Globalization is, to a large degree, expanding everyone's ability to potentially sell to more people. American companies aren't limited to selling only to Americans; they can sell to others in the world too. Chinese firms aren't limited to selling only to Chinese; they can sell to others around the world.

As a musician, you can play different styles of music: jazz, pop, classical, hard rock, metal, hip-hop, and so on. If you are limited to selling your music to the people of a single state in the United States, you can offer to sell fewer styles of music than if you could sell your music to the people who reside throughout the United States.

More specifically, consider the musician in the United States who is experimenting with a new style of music. With a population of only the United States (310 million) as a potential customer base, the musician might not yet have enough actual customers to make it worth producing and offering to sell this particular, unique, and narrowly defined music. However, if the musician can draw on the population of the world (6.8 billion), then she might be able to find enough people who are willing to buy her new type of music.

As we move toward a world economy, we see a greater variety within almost every category of goods: a greater variety of music to listen to, books to read, types of television shows to watch, and so on. Today, the greater variety of goods you see in your world is an effect of globalization.

The proponents of globalization often point out a major difference between a corporation and a government. First, a government can force people to do certain things (such as pay taxes or join the military). No corporation can coerce people; instead, corporations can simply produce goods that they hope customers will buy. Additionally, the proponents of globalization often argue that the critics overestimate the influence and reach of large transnational companies. For example, in 2000, the top 100 transnational companies produced only 4.3 percent of the entire world's output, which is about as much as what one country, the United Kingdom, produced in 2000.

# THE CONTINUING GLOBALIZATION DEBATE

Many (but certainly not all) economists argue that the worldwide benefits of globalization are likely to be greater than the worldwide costs. Of course, not everyone is going to see the beneficial side of globalization. To a large degree, whether people support or criticize globalization seems to depend on where they are sitting. Globalization does not affect everyone in the same way, and often *how* it affects *you* determines how you feel about it. For example, suppose Sanders, an American worker residing in New York, loses his job to an Indian worker in New Delhi, India, who will do Sanders' job for less pay. In this case, Sanders incurs real costs, but for Sanders' company, the change means lower costs and higher profits. For the company's customers, the change might mean lower prices. So in this case, Sanders is probably a strong opponent of offshoring, but his company and its customers are probably supporters.

Seeing the benefits of globalization is often much more difficult than seeing its costs. For example, the supporters of globalization argue that it brings greater economic wealth, lower prices, more innovation, less poverty, and so on. Yet seeing all these benefits is sometimes difficult. When you buy cheaper or different goods because of globalization, you probably never say, "Wow, I can't believe all the benefits I get from globalization!" In fact, you might not even connect the lower-priced goods with globalization at all. The benefits of globalization tend to be difficult to perceive, partly because they are so widely dispersed.

The costs of globalization, in contrast, are more visible, often because they are so concentrated. A person who loses a job because of freer international trade in the world knows exactly what is to blame for his predicament. He surely could receive some benefits from globalization (as a consumer), but he also could, for a time, incur some rather high costs (as an unemployed worker). This person is likely to know of the costs but be unaware of the benefits.

In the end, the people who receive only benefits from globalization might not be able to see them or to connect them with globalization. The people who receive benefits and costs from globalization may be aware only of the costs. This one-sided view could create strong antiglobalization sentiment in a country.

# MORE OR LESS GLOBALIZATION: A TUG OF WAR?

Is increased globalization inevitable? Will the day come when all countries in the world are like the 50 states in the United States—part of one global economy with easy movement of people, resources, financial capital, goods, and services among the countries? Or will the conditions that prevented globalization reappear and reverse the trend?

This struggle is like a tug of war. The forces of globalization pull in one direction, and the forces of antiglobalization pull in the other. As of today, the forces of globalization are moving things in their direction, but the trend may not continue uninterrupted. Surely, at any time, the forces of antiglobalization could put on a burst of energy and give an extra strong tug on the rope.

To help answer the question about the future of globalization, recall what we said about the driving forces of the most recent era of globalization: the end of the Cold War, changes in technology (which lowered the costs of transportation and communication), and policy changes that opened up countries' economies to each other.

## Less Globalization

**INCREASED POLITICAL TENSION** The end of the Cold War is a historical fact that we cannot undo, but we could enter a period when political tensions among countries or among groups of countries emerge. We are not suggesting that such a period of tension will happen, only that it could. If it did, it could slow down globalization or, depending on the severity of the tension, even reverse it.

**TERRORISM** Another inhibiting factor to globalization is global terrorism. Global terrorism tends to motivate certain countries into closing borders and into being much more careful about the people and goods crossing their borders.

**TECHNOLOGY** We cannot undo our technology. We cannot go from a world with the Internet to one without it. So it is unlikely that anything technological will slow down or reverse globalization.

GOVERNMENT POLICIES Policy changes can slow down or reverse globalization. Governments of countries that opened up their economies to others could reverse their course; doors that opened to other nations can be closed. Whether this sort of isolationism will happen in the future is an unknown.

## More Globalization

Some still argue that even with the forces of antiglobalization looming on the horizon, the forces of globalization are stronger. In the end, these individuals say, the forces of globalization will win the tug of war. They believe that, in the long run, economics influences politics, not the other way around. As some proof of that assertion, they often point to the former Soviet Union and to China, both entrenched communist countries. Both countries saw, in the end, that they were worse off by holding themselves outside the orbit of free market forces. You might say that they found themselves outside the theater where economic forces were playing major roles on the world stage.

Many economists argue that globalization is not just a passing trend. They argue that the basic globalization force that will probably not be overcome—no matter how strong the political forces may be against it—is the human inclination that the founder of modern economics, Adam Smith, noticed more than 200 years ago: human beings want to trade with each other. In fact, the desire to trade separates us from all other species, Smith said. In his words, "Man is an animal that makes bargains: no other animal does this—no dog exchanges bones with another."

We want to trade with people: our next-door neighbor, the person down the street, the person on the other side of town, the person in the next state, the person on the other side of the country, and ultimately the person on the other side of the world. Some economists go on to suggest that our trading inclination is a good thing in that when we trade with people, we not only tolerate them but we have much less reason to fight with them. Robert Wright, a journalist and scholar, argues that it is not a coincidence that religious toleration is high in the United States, a country that is open to trade and globalization. We often see, he argues, that people who live in countries that trade with other people—people who live in countries that are open to other people—are people who tolerate others.

In a similar vein, Thomas Friedman advanced his "Golden Arches theory of conflict prevention," which states that "no two countries that both had McDonald's had fought a war against each other since each got its McDonald's." The United States will not fight Germany because both countries have McDonald's. France won't fight Mexico because both countries have McDonald's. Certainly, the mere presence of a McDonald's does not prevent people from fighting with other people. McDonald's is symbolic of certain forces at work in the country. For Friedman, the franchise is a symbol of a certain degree of economic globalization and a level of economic development sufficient enough to support a large middle class.

### SELF-TEST

1. Identify some of the benefits of globalization.

2. Identify some of the costs of globalization.

# INTERNATIONAL FACTORS AND AGGREGATE DEMAND

Preceding chapters have described domestic factors that can change aggregate demand and thus affect the U.S. economy. Changes that occur in other countries can also influence the U.S. economy. This section discusses two key international factors that can affect the U.S. economy by first affecting U.S. aggregate demand: net exports and the J-curve.

## Net Exports

In an earlier chapter, net exports are defined as the difference between exports (*EX*) and imports (*IM*). For example, if exports are $80 billion and imports are $60 billion, then net exports are $20 billion. Also, recall that if net exports rise, the *AD* curve shifts to the right; if net exports fall, the *AD* curve shifts to the left.

Two factors can change net exports: (1) foreign Real GDP and (2) the exchange rate. To simplify matters, we assume there are only two countries in the world: the United States and Japan.

**FOREIGN REAL GDP (OR FOREIGN REAL NATIONAL INCOME)** As Japan's Real GDP (or real national income) rises, the Japanese buy more U.S. goods. As a result, U.S. net exports rise, and the *AD* curve shifts to the right. As Japan's Real GDP falls, the Japanese buy fewer U.S. goods. As a result, U.S. net exports fall, and the *AD* curve shifts to the left.

Thus economic expansions and contractions in other countries are felt in the United States. Given a contraction in Japan, with a lower Real GDP in Japan, the Japanese buy fewer U.S. goods. U.S. exports fall, and so do net exports. As a result, the *AD* curve in the United States shifts to the left. Because the *AD* curve shifts to the left, Real GDP in the United States falls.

**EXCHANGE RATE** Recall that the exchange rate is the price of one country's currency expressed in terms of another country's currency. If a country's currency *appreciates*, it takes less of that country's currency to buy the other. On the other hand, if a country's currency *depreciates*, it takes more of that country's country to buy the other.

Appreciation and depreciation affect the prices of a country's goods. If, say, the U.S. dollar depreciates relative to the Japanese yen, U.S. residents have to pay more dollars to buy Japanese goods. To illustrate, suppose the dollar price of a yen is $0.012 and that a Toyota is priced at ¥2 million. At this exchange rate, a U.S. resident pays $24,000 for a Toyota ($0.012 × ¥2 million = $24,000). If the dollar depreciates to $0.018 for ¥1, then the U.S. resident will have to pay $36,000 for a Toyota.

As the dollar depreciates, Japanese goods become more expensive for U.S. residents. So they buy fewer Japanese goods, and U.S. imports decline.[2] The other side of the coin is that as the dollar depreciates relative to the yen, the yen appreciates relative to the dollar. Thus U.S. goods become less expensive for the Japanese, and they buy more U.S. goods. So U.S. exports rise.

In summary, a depreciation in the dollar and an appreciation in the yen will raise U.S. exports, lower U.S. imports, and therefore raise U.S. net exports. This shifts the U.S. *AD* curve to the right, leading to a rise in the U.S. Real GDP level.

The series of events are symmetrical if the U.S. dollar appreciates relative to the Japanese yen. In this case, U.S. goods become more expensive for the Japanese, causing them to buy fewer U.S. goods; so U.S. exports fall. And Japanese goods become cheaper for U.S. residents, causing them to buy more Japanese goods; so U.S. imports rise. A decline in U.S. exports, along with a rise in U.S. imports, will cause U.S. net exports to fall. The U.S. *AD* curve shifts to the left, leading to a decline in U.S. Real GDP.

For a quick review of the international factors that can shift the U.S. *AD* curve, see Exhibit 3.

---

2. Throughout this chapter, unless otherwise explicitly stated, we assume that if the physical quantity of exports rises (falls), the total spending on exports rises (falls). Also, if the physical quantity of imports rises (falls), the total spending on imports rises (falls). Because of this assumption, it is not necessary to differentiate constantly between the physical quantity of imports and the total spending on imports. Given our assumption, they go up and down together. One place we explicitly drop this assumption is in the discussion of the J-curve.

**EXHIBIT 3**

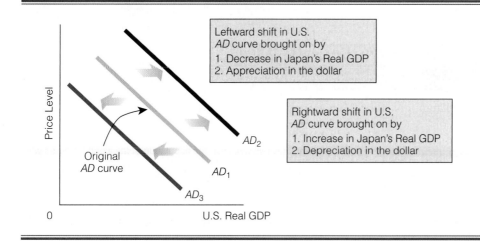

Leftward shift in U.S.
*AD* curve brought on by
1. Decrease in Japan's Real GDP
2. Appreciation in the dollar

Rightward shift in U.S.
*AD* curve brought on by
1. Increase in Japan's Real GDP
2. Depreciation in the dollar

Original
*AD* curve

$AD_2$

$AD_1$

$AD_3$

Price Level

U.S. Real GDP

0

**International Impacts on the U.S. *AD* Curve**

Anything that increases U.S. net exports shifts the U.S. *AD* curve to the right. This includes an increase in Japan's Real GDP (in a two-country world, where the two countries are Japan and the United States) and a depreciation in the dollar. Anything that decreases U.S. net exports shifts the U.S. *AD* curve to the left. This includes a decrease in Japan's Real GDP and an appreciation in the dollar.

## The J-Curve

So far, we have assumed that if the dollar depreciates relative to the Japanese yen, U.S. residents and the Japanese will buy more U.S. goods and fewer Japanese goods. Thus, U.S. exports rise, U.S. imports fall, and U.S. net exports rise.

But this scenario may not happen initially. There may be a difference between what *initially* happens and what *ultimately* happens. To illustrate, suppose U.S. residents are currently buying 100,000 cars from the Japanese, the average Japanese car sells for ¥2 million, and the exchange rate is currently $0.012 per yen. This means U.S. residents are spending an average of $24,000 a car for 100,000 cars. Thus, a total of $2.4 billion is spent on imported Japanese cars.

Then the exchange rate changes, and the dollar depreciates to $0.018 per yen, causing the average price of a Japanese car to jump to $36,000. At this higher price, U.S. residents buy fewer Japanese cars, but they don't buy that many fewer right away. Instead of buying 100,000 cars, they initially buy 90,000 cars. Now a total of $3.24 billion is spent on imported Japanese cars. Instead of declining after a depreciation in the dollar, U.S. spending on imports initially rises. If we assume U.S. exports have not changed yet, a rise in U.S. imports will lead to a fall in U.S. net exports and cause the U.S. *AD* curve to shift to the left.

But this situation is not likely to last. In time, U.S. residents will switch from the higher-priced Japanese goods to lower-priced U.S. goods. For example, after a while, U.S. residents purchase only 60,000 Japanese cars. At this number, with the exchange rate of $0.018 per yen, U.S. spending on imported Japanese cars is $2.16 billion. In time, too, U.S. exports will rise, and the combination of rising exports and falling imports will lead to an increase in net exports. The U.S. *AD* curve will shift to the right.

This phenomenon, in which import spending initially rises after a depreciation and then later falls, is summarized in the J-curve, so-called because the curve showing the change in net exports due to a currency depreciation has the shape of a J. In Exhibit 4, the United States initially has negative net exports of –$40 billion (its imports of $130 billion are greater than its exports of $90 billion). This position is represented by point *A* in the exhibit.

Next, the dollar depreciates relative to the yen. Total spending on imports rises to, say, $150 billion; so net exports rise to –$60 billion, as represented by point *B*.

In time, though, exports rise to, say, $100 billion and imports fall to, say, $100 billion, making net exports equal to zero. This is represented by point *C*.

If we start at point *A* and draw a line to point *B* and then to point *C*, we have a J-curve. This is the route that net exports may take after a depreciation in a country's currency.

**J-Curve**

The curve that shows a short-run worsening in net exports after a currency depreciation, followed by an improvement.

# economics 24/7

## How Hard Will It Be to Get into Harvard in 2025?

The Indian Institute of Technology (in India) is one of the hardest universities in the world to be admitted to, largely because of its reputation. It has been compared to putting Harvard, MIT (Massachusetts Institute of Technology), and Princeton together.

In an average year, about 178,000 high school seniors in India take the exam necessary to apply to the Indian Institute of Technology. Just over 3,500 students (only 1.96 percent of all applicants) are admitted. In comparison, the admission rate of Harvard University is nearly 10 percent. Often, students from India who are admitted to MIT, Princeton, and Cal Tech (all of which are listed in the top 10 of U.S. colleges and universities) cannot gain admission to the Indian Institute of Technology.

Other highly prestigious U.S. universities and colleges—such as Brown, Columbia, Cornell, Dartmouth, Harvard, the University of Pennsylvania, Princeton, Yale, Stanford, Northwestern, and Duke—have some of the most selective admission criteria of all colleges and universities in the country. Each year, students who have the grade point average and standardized test scores to be considered for admission are turned away. This phenomenon has been occurring at the same time that college tuition in this country has been increasing rapidly. For example, during the period 1990–2003, college tuition went up by 130 percent, considerably more than medical care costs, the price of housing, food, gasoline, cars, and so on. If we look around the world at other prestigious institutions of higher learning, we see the same characteristics: The admission rate is usually low, and the cost is usually high.

Consider how grades (one major criterion) and money actually function in admissions: They are both rationing devices. We know that because of scarcity, some mechanism has to ration the available resources, goods, and services. Still we have to ask why these two rationing devices—grades and money—have become stiffer when it comes to being admitted to the top universities in the world? Why must grades and tuitions be ever higher?

The answer is twofold. First, the population of the world increased while the number of Harvards did not. Harvard cannot clone itself; nor can Yale, the Indian Institute of Technology, or MIT. To a large degree, the world has only one Harvard, Oxford (in the United Kingdom), and Indian Institute of Technology. We can produce more computers, houses, and dining room chairs as the population of the world increases, but producing more Harvards seems to be much more difficult. So, over time, top-notch, one-of-a-kind educational institutions become relatively more scarce. As a result, the rationing devices for such institutions must work harder, and getting admitted to such places will become harder and more expensive.

The second reason involves globalization. One of things that pays a high dividend in a global economy is education. Brains seem to matter more than brawn, increasing the overall demand for a college education—not just at Harvard, but at all levels of higher education (from community colleges to four-year state and private universities). So, will the premium placed on education in a global economy cause the demand at the most prestigious educational establishments to rise at a faster rate than at other colleges? That question is like asking, "If the premium for playing music were to rise, would the demand to be at Juilliard (one of the premier music institutions in the world) rise faster than the demand to study with the local piano teacher down the street?" The likely answer is yes. With a growing world population, and with the global economy paying a high premium to those who are educated (compared to those who are not), we can expect it to get increasingly difficult and more expensive to be admitted to the world's best institutions of higher learning.

## Thinking Like AN ECONOMIST

**Short Run and Long Run** The discussion of the J-curve points out that economists sometimes think in terms of both the short run and the long run. Does the depreciation of a country's currency lead to an increase or a decrease in import spending? According to the J-curve theory, both an increase and a decrease result. Import spending may initially increase, but in the long run it decreases. An economist's answers may differ depending on the time horizon under consideration. ● ● ●

**EXHIBIT 4**

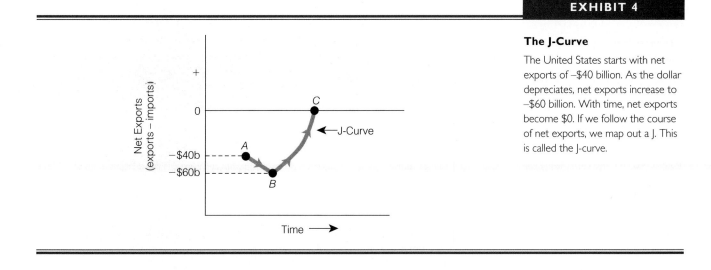

**The J-Curve**

The United States starts with net exports of –$40 billion. As the dollar depreciates, net exports increase to –$60 billion. With time, net exports become $0. If we follow the course of net exports, we map out a J. This is called the J-curve.

## SELF-TEST

1. Explain how an economic boom in one country can be felt in another country.

2. Predict and explain what will happen to U.S. Real GDP if the dollar appreciates relative to the Japanese yen.

# INTERNATIONAL FACTORS AND AGGREGATE SUPPLY

Just as international factors can affect the demand side of the U.S. economy, certain international factors can affect the supply side. This section discusses a few international factors that can shift the U.S. aggregate supply curve.

## Foreign Input Prices

We know that a change in the price of inputs will shift the short-run aggregate supply (*SRAS*) curve. For example, if the price of labor (wage rate) rises, the *SRAS* curve shifts leftward.

American producers buy inputs not only from other Americans but also from foreigners. A rise in the price of foreign inputs leads to a leftward shift in the U.S. *SRAS* curve. A fall in the price of foreign inputs leads to a rightward shift in the U.S. *SRAS* curve.

## Why Foreign Input Prices Change

Supply and demand in the input market in the foreign country could change, possibly causing a rise in the price of foreign inputs. For example, suppose U.S. producers buy input X from Japan. The supply of X in Japan could fall, or the demand for X in Japan could rise. Either or both changes would increase the price of X for U.S. producers.

THE EXCHANGE RATE A change in the exchange rate between the dollar and the yen could change the price of a foreign input. For example, a depreciation in the dollar relative to the yen would make input X more expensive for U.S. producers. An appreciation in the dollar would make input X less expensive for U.S. producers. Exhibit 5 presents a summary of the points in this section.

EXHIBIT 5

**International Impacts on the U.S. *SRAS* Curve**

The U.S. *SRAS* curve shifts if foreign input prices change. If foreign input prices rise, the U.S. *SRAS* curve shifts leftward; if foreign input prices fall, the *SRAS* curve shifts rightward. Similarly, if the dollar depreciates, foreign inputs become more expensive and the *SRAS* curve shifts leftward. If the dollar appreciates, foreign inputs become cheaper and the *SRAS* curve shifts rightward.

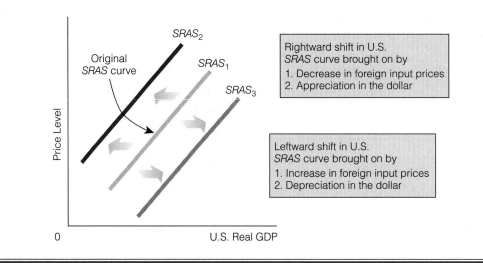

# FACTORS THAT AFFECT BOTH AGGREGATE DEMAND AND AGGREGATE SUPPLY

Changes in some international factors can affect both aggregate demand and short-run aggregate supply in the United States. Two of these factors are the exchange rate and relative interest rates.

## The Exchange Rate

As explained, changes in exchange rates affect both the *AD* and *SRAS* curves. The overall, or net, effect on Real GDP depends on how much the *AD* curve shifts relative to the shift in the *SRAS* curve. We consider two cases: dollar depreciation and dollar appreciation.

DOLLAR DEPRECIATION   As the dollar depreciates, the *AD* curve shifts rightward and the *SRAS* curve leftward.

- If the AD curve shifts rightward by more than the SRAS curve shifts leftward, Real GDP rises [see Exhibit 6(a)].

- If the *AD* curve shifts rightward by less than the SRAS curve shifts leftward, Real GDP falls [see Exhibit 6(b)].

- If the *AD* curve shifts rightward by the same amount that the *SRAS* curve shifts leftward, Real GDP does not change [see Exhibit 6(c)].

In each of these three cases, the price level rises. In summary, dollar depreciation raises the price level and may accompany an increasing, decreasing, or constant Real GDP.

DOLLAR APPRECIATION   As the dollar appreciates, the *AD* curve shifts leftward and the *SRAS* curve rightward. Once again, what happens to Real GDP depends on the relative shifts of the two curves.

- If the *AD* curve shifts leftward by more than the *SRAS* curve shifts rightward, Real GDP falls.

**EXHIBIT 6**

**Depreciation in the Dollar: Effects on the Price Level and Real GDP**

A change in exchange rates affects both aggregate demand and short-run aggregate supply.

If the dollar depreciates, the *AD* curve shifts rightward and the *SRAS* curve shifts leftward. The overall impact on Real GDP—up, down, or unchanged—depends on whether the *AD* curve

shifts rightward by (a) more, (b) less, or (c) an amount equal to the leftward shift in the *SRAS* curve. In all three cases, dollar depreciation leads to a higher price level.

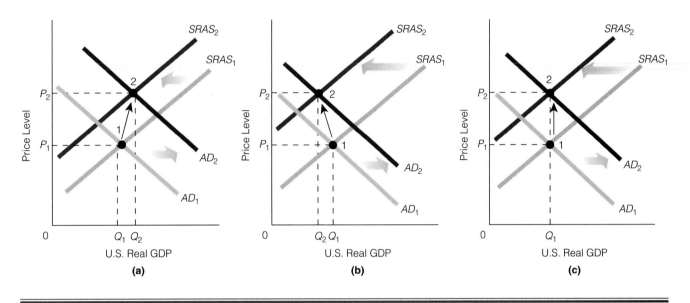

- If the *AD* curve shifts leftward by less than the *SRAS* curve shifts rightward, Real GDP rises.

- If the *AD* curve shifts leftward by the same amount that the *SRAS* curve shifts rightward, Real GDP does not change.

In each case, though, the price level falls. In summary, dollar appreciation lowers the price level and may accompany an increasing, decreasing, or constant Real GDP.

## The Role That Interest Rates Play

In a two-country world with only the United States and Japan, real interest rates rise in the United States and remain constant in Japan. The higher real interest rates in the United States will attract foreign capital (in search of the highest return possible). Because foreigners will be interested in dollar-denominated assets that pay interest, they will have to exchange their country's currency for U.S. dollars. This need will increase the demand for U.S. dollars and lead to an appreciation in the dollar.

Then, if the dollar appreciates, we know that both the U.S. *AD* and *SRAS* curves are affected. The *AD* curve shifts leftward, and the *SRAS* curve shifts rightward. As explained, the effect on Real GDP depends on the relative shifts in the two curves. Many economists argue, however, that given the interest rate differential between the two countries, the *AD* curve typically tends to shift leftward by more than the *SRAS* curve shifts rightward, and thus Real GDP falls [see Exhibit 7(a)]. In summary, typically, a rise in real interest rates in the United States relative to foreign interest rates tends to decrease U.S. Real GDP.

Now suppose real interest rates fall in the United States relative to interest rates in Japan. The higher real interest rate in Japan attracts capital to Japan. The demand for yen

**EXHIBIT 7**

**International Interest Rates, Exchange Rates, and Real GDP**

(a) If the U.S. real interest rate is higher than the Japanese real interest rate, capital will flow from Japan to the United States. In the process, the demand for the dollar rises, and the dollar appreciates. Dollar appreciation causes the AD

curve to shift leftward by more than the SRAS curve shifts rightward, which is typical given the initial event. As a result, U.S. Real GDP falls. (b) If the U.S. real interest rate is lower than the Japanese real interest rate, capital will flow from the United States to Japan. In the process, the demand for yen rises, the supply of dollars rises,

and the yen appreciates and the dollar depreciates. Dollar depreciation causes the AD curve to shift rightward and the SRAS curve to shift leftward. We have drawn the AD curve shifting rightward by more than the SRAS curve shifts leftward, which is typical given the initial event. As a result, U.S. Real GDP rises.

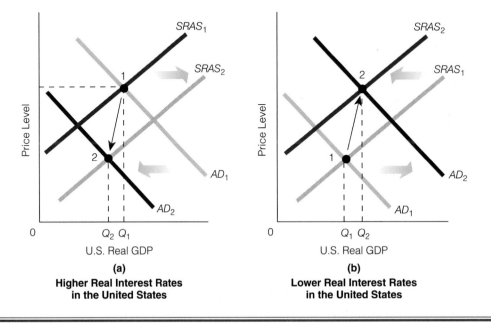

**(a)**
**Higher Real Interest Rates in the United States**

**(b)**
**Lower Real Interest Rates in the United States**

rises, and as a result the yen appreciates and the dollar depreciates. A depreciated dollar shifts the U.S. AD curve rightward and the SRAS curve leftward [see Exhibit 7(b)]. Many economists argue that given the interest rate differential, the AD curve typically tends to shift rightward by more than the SRAS curve shifts leftward, and thus Real GDP rises. In summary, typically, a fall in real interest rates in the United States relative to foreign interest rates tends to increase U.S. Real GDP.

**SELF-TEST**

1. How do foreign input prices affect the U.S. SRAS curve?

2. What is the effect on the U.S. price level of Japan's having lower real interest rates than the United States? Explain your answer.

# DEFICITS: INTERNATIONAL EFFECTS AND DOMESTIC FEEDBACK

Deficits in the United States—both budget and trade deficits—affect the U.S. economy. We know how the budget deficit can directly affect the U.S. economy. However, the budget deficit can also have international effects, which can then feed back into the U.S. economy. This section looks at the possibilities of feedback effects and the relationship between the budget deficit and the trade deficit.

## The Budget Deficit and Expansionary Fiscal Policy

Suppose that North Dakotans want their elected representatives in Congress to push for a spending program that will assist them and no one else and that their elected representatives oblige them. Congress passes the spending program but does not raise the taxes necessary to pay for it. This domestic action can affect the international economic scene, and here's how.

Even with a budget deficit, Congress passes the spending program to help North Dakotans but neither raises taxes to finance the program nor cuts any other spending programs on the books. As a result of these actions—one more spending program, no fewer spending programs, and no more taxes—the budget deficit grows. To finance the growing budget deficit, the U.S. Treasury borrows more funds in the credit (or loanable funds) market than it would have borrowed if the North Dakotan spending program had not been passed. The increased demand for credit raises the real interest rate. The higher U.S. interest rate attracts foreign capital. The demand for dollars in the foreign exchange market rises, and the dollar appreciates.

As this happens, the U.S. *AD* curve shifts leftward, and the *SRAS* curve shifts rightward. The *AD* curve shifts leftward by more than the *SRAS* curve shifts rightward, putting downward pressure on Real GDP.

But Real GDP might not *actually* decrease. That's because we have discussed only how a rising budget deficit affects the exchange rate (via the interest rate) and feeds back into the domestic economy. We also need to consider the direct effect of the rising budget deficit on the domestic economy. Under certain conditions (e.g., zero crowding out), expansionary fiscal policy can raise aggregate demand and is effective at raising Real GDP. So:

1. The rising budget deficit affects the domestic economy directly and pushes *Real GDP upward.*

2. But increased deficit financing raises U.S. interest rates and prompts increased foreign capital inflows, an increased demand for dollars, and dollar appreciation. Under typical conditions, an appreciated dollar feeds back into the domestic economy and pushes *Real GDP downward.*

Obviously, what happens on a net basis depends on how strong the international feedback effects are on the domestic economy. Are they strong enough to offset the initial expansionary push (upward) in Real GDP? Even if not and Real GDP rises on net, we can still conclude that expansionary fiscal policy raises Real GDP more in a closed economy (which does not trade goods and services with other countries) than in an open economy (which trades goods and services with other countries). The reason is that in a closed economy the international feedback effects that reduce Real GDP are absent (see the second point in the preceding list).

Exhibit 8(a) illustrates the point. With zero crowding out, expansionary fiscal policy shifts the aggregate demand curve from $AD_1$ to $AD_2$. But because of the higher interest rates, increased foreign capital inflows, and dollar appreciation, the *AD* curve shifts leftward from $AD_2$ to $AD_3$, and the *SRAS* curve shifts rightward from $SRAS_1$ to $SRAS_2$. In a closed economy, Real GDP rises from $Q_1$ to $Q_2$. In an open economy, where international feedback effects play a role, Real GDP ends up at a lower level, $Q_3$.

**Closed Economy**
An economy that does not trade goods and services with other countries.

**Open Economy**
An economy that trades goods and services with other countries.

## The Budget Deficit and Contractionary Fiscal Policy

If expansionary fiscal policy raises Real GDP more in a closed economy than in an open economy, what are the effects of contractionary fiscal policy in the two types of economies? Suppose reduced government spending decreases the budget deficit. With a diminished budget deficit, the U.S. Treasury borrows fewer funds in the credit market than it would have if government spending had not been reduced. The decreased demand for loanable funds lowers the real interest rate (relative to foreign interest rates), making foreign assets seem more desirable. The demand for foreign currencies increases, and the dollar depreciates in value.

**EXHIBIT 8**

**Expansionary and Contractionary Fiscal Policy in Open and Closed Economies**

(a) The consequences of expansionary fiscal policy for both open and closed economies. Congress passes a spending program without raising taxes, and the AD curve shifts from $AD_1$

to $AD_2$. To finance the growing budget deficit, the Treasury borrows more funds in the loanable funds market, and the interest rate rises. The higher interest rate attracts foreign capital and causes the dollar to appreciate. As the dollar appreciates, the AD curve shifts from $AD_2$ to $AD_3$, and the SRAS curve shifts from $SRAS_1$

to $SRAS_2$. Real GDP goes from $Q_1$ to $Q_2$ in a closed economy, and from $Q_1$ to $Q_3$ in an open economy. Expansionary fiscal policy raises Real GDP more in a closed economy than in an open economy. (b) Contractionary fiscal policy lowers Real GDP more in a closed economy than in an open economy.

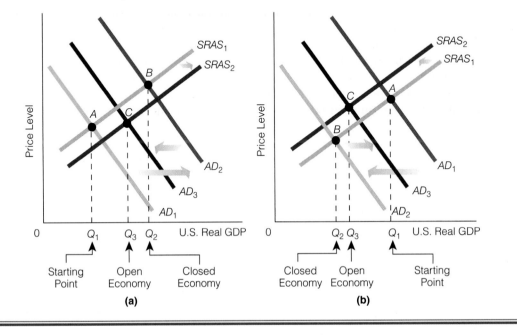

(a)          (b)

At the same time, the U.S. *AD* curve shifts to the right, and the *SRAS* curve shifts to the left. The *AD* curve shifts rightward by more than the *SRAS* curve shifts leftward, putting upward pressure on Real GDP. However, Real GDP might not *actually* increase. Under certain conditions, the lower budged deficit due to a cut in government spending reduces aggregate demand and therefore reduces Real GDP. So:

1. The cut in government spending reduces the budget deficit and affects the domestic economy directly, pushing *Real GDP downward.*

2. But reduced deficit financing lowers U.S. interest rates and prompts increased capital outflows, increased demand for foreign currencies, and dollar depreciation. Under typical conditions, a depreciated dollar feeds back into the domestic economy and pushes *Real GDP upward.*

What happens *on a net basis* depends on whether the international feedback effects on the domestic economy are strong enough to offset the initial contractionary push in Real GDP.

Even if the international feedback effects on the domestic economy do not outweigh the initial contractionary push (downward) in Real GDP, and even if Real GDP falls on net, we can still conclude that contractionary fiscal policy lowers Real GDP more in a closed economy than in an open economy.

Exhibit 8(b) illustrates our point. The cut in government spending shifts the *AD* curve from $AD_1$ to $AD_2$. But because of the lower interest rates, increased capital outflows, and dollar depreciation, the *AD* curve shifts rightward from $AD_2$ to $AD_3$, and the *SRAS* curve shifts leftward from $SRAS_1$ to $SRAS_2$. In a closed economy, Real GDP falls from $Q_1$ to $Q_2$. In an open economy, where international feedback effects play a role, Real GDP ends up at $Q_3$.

## The Effects of Monetary Policy

Monetary policy certainly affects international economic factors that feed back to the United States. Here we consider both expansionary and contractionary monetary policy.

**EXPANSIONARY MONETARY POLICY** Suppose the Federal Reserve increases the money supply. In Exhibit 9(a), the increase causes the *AD* curve to shift rightward from $AD_1$ to $AD_2$ and Real GDP to rise from $Q_1$ to $Q_2$.

An increase in the money supply also has international effects. Expansionary monetary policy causes interest rates to fall in the short run (the liquidity effect), leading to an outflow of capital from the United States. Americans begin to supply more dollars on the foreign exchange market so that they can purchase foreign assets. As the supply of dollars rises, the dollar depreciates.

Dollar depreciation affects both U.S. aggregate demand and U.S. short-run aggregate supply. As noted, it shifts the *AD* curve to the right and the *SRAS* curve to the left. In Exhibit 9(a), the *AD* curve shifts to the right (from $AD_2$ to $AD_3$), and the *SRAS* curve shifts to the left (from $SRAS_1$ to $SRAS_2$). Consequently, Real GDP rises from $Q_2$ to $Q_3$.

**EXHIBIT 9**

**Expansionary and Contractionary Monetary Policy in Open and Closed Economies**

(a) The consequences of expansionary monetary policy for both open and closed economies. The Fed increases the money supply, and the *AD* curve shifts from $AD_1$ to $AD_2$.

Real GDP rises from $Q_1$ to $Q_2$. The increased money supply leads to lower interest rates in the short run, promoting U.S. capital outflow and a depreciated dollar, which raises U.S. exports, lowers U.S. imports, and raises U.S. net exports. Higher net exports shift the *AD* curve rightward from $AD_2$ to $AD_3$. The depreciated

dollar shifts the *SRAS* curve leftward from $SRAS_1$ to $SRAS_2$. Real GDP ends up at $Q_3$. Expansionary monetary policy raises Real GDP more in an open economy than in a closed economy. (b) Contractionary monetary policy lowers Real GDP more in an open economy than in a closed economy.

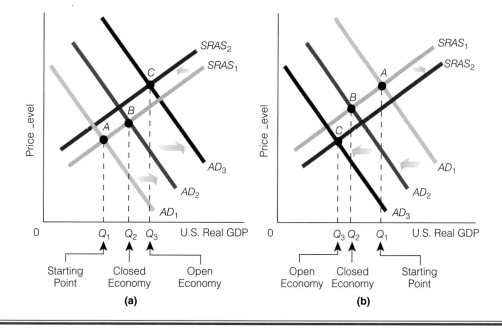

Therefore, expansionary monetary policy raises Real GDP more in an open economy than in a closed economy.

CONTRACTIONARY MONETARY POLICY If the Federal Reserve contracts the money supply, the $AD$ curve shifts leftward from $AD_1$ to $AD_2$, and Real GDP falls from $Q_1$ to $Q_2$ [see Exhibit 9(b)].

A decrease in the money supply also has international effects. Contractionary monetary policy causes interest rates to rise, leading to an inflow of foreign capital into the United States. The demand for dollars rises on the foreign exchange market, and the dollar appreciates. Dollar appreciation affects both U.S. aggregate demand and U.S. short-run aggregate supply. As we know, dollar appreciation shifts the $AD$ curve to the left and the $SRAS$ curve to the right. In Exhibit 9(b), the $AD$ curve shifts from $AD_2$ to $AD_3$, and the $SRAS$ curve shifts from $SRAS_1$ to $SRAS_2$. Consequently, Real GDP falls from $Q_2$ to $Q_3$.

Therefore, contractionary monetary policy lowers Real GDP more in an open economy than in a closed economy.

## SELF-TEST

1. Explain how expansionary monetary policy works in an open economy.

2. Explain how expansionary fiscal policy works in an open economy.

# OFFICE HOURS

## "Why Do Some People Favor Globalization and Others Do Not?"

**STUDENT:**

One of the things I have noticed about globalization is that some people in the United States seem to be in favor of it and others seem to be against it. Why is this?

**INSTRUCTOR:**

It probably has much to do with how the benefits and costs of globalization are distributed across the population. People in one location might receive mainly the benefits, and people in some other location might incur mostly the costs.

**STUDENT:**

Can you give a real-world example?

**INSTRUCTOR:**

A while back, *The New York Times* reported about two cities in Michigan: Holland and Greenville.[3] In Holland, a factory was losing business and firing workers. Then a German company bought it. Today the factory is shipping wastewater treatment equipment to countries in the Middle East and Asia. Also, it is operating with twice as many workers as it did before the German company bought it. The people in Holland, Michigan, see this as a benefit of globalization.

Only 60 miles away from Holland, in Greenville, Michigan, the story is different. In Greenville, a Swedish company shut down what had been the largest refrigerator factory in the country and eliminated about 2,700 jobs in the town. For the people of Greenville, globalization came with costs.

**STUDENT:**

What do most economists say about globalization? Do they think that, for the country as a whole, globalization comes with net benefits (more benefits than costs) or net costs (more costs than benefits)?

**INSTRUCTOR:**

Most economists seem to think that globalization comes with net benefits.

**STUDENT:**

But economic policy isn't always determined by what economists think, is it?

**INSTRUCTOR:**

You're right about that. Economic policy doesn't get made in a political vacuum. Politics plays a role in deciding which economic policies get adopted and implemented. Think about this in terms of our Michigan cities example. Suppose we went to Greenville, where jobs had been lost, and tell the residents of the city that globalization, on net, is good for the country. Suppose we said that, for the country as a whole, benefits from globalization outweigh the costs. The residents of Greenville might say that is all well and good, but globalization hasn't been that good to them and that is all they care about. As a result, their vote, to the extent that they have one on the issue, is *against* globalization.

**STUDENT:**

I see. In other words, sometimes what might be beneficial for the country (as a whole) is not beneficial for some part of it.

**INSTRUCTOR:**

That is the way some things turn out.

### POINTS TO REMEMBER

1. Globalization can come with net benefits for a country, but not everyone in the country necessarily benefits from globalization.
2. The benefits and costs of globalization are not evenly spread throughout a country. The benefits may fall on some people and the costs on others.

---

3. See Peter S. Goodman, "2 Outcomes When Foreigners Buy Factories," *New York Times*, April 7, 2008.

# CHAPTER SUMMARY

## WHAT IS GLOBALIZATION?

- Globalization is a phenomenon by which individuals and businesses in any part of the world are much more affected by events elsewhere in the world than before; it is the growing integration of national economies of the world to the degree that we may be witnessing the emergence and operation of a single worldwide economy.

- Certain facts provide evidence that globalization is occurring. Some of these facts are (1) lower tariff rates in many countries, (2) many countries exporting and importing more goods than in the past, (3) greater foreign exchange trading, (4) more foreign direct investment, (5) many more people owning foreign stocks, (6) many more countries having joined the WTO in recent years, and (7) a greater number of Americans working for foreign companies with offices in the United States.

## MOVEMENT TOWARD GLOBALIZATION

- What has caused this most recent push toward globalization? In the chapter we identified (1) the end of the Cold War, (2) advancing technology, and (3) policy changes as causal factors.

## BENEFITS AND COSTS OF GLOBALIZATION

- Some of the benefits of globalization include (1) benefits from increased international trade, (2) greater income per person, (3) lower prices for goods, (4) greater product variety, and (5) increased productivity and innovation.

- Some of the costs of globalization include (1) increased income inequality (although there is some debate here), (2) offshoring, and (3) increased economic power for large corporations (although there is some debate here too).

- Seeing the benefits of globalization is often much more difficult than seeing the costs. The benefits are largely dispersed over a large population, but the costs (e.g., offshoring) might be concentrated on relatively few.

## THE FUTURE OF GLOBALIZATION

- The future of globalization is under debate. Some persons argue that globalization will continue; others say it will stall and (perhaps) backtrack.

## NET EXPORTS AND AGGREGATE DEMAND

- An increase in net exports will shift the *AD* curve to the right. A decrease in net exports will shift the *AD* curve to the left.

- Two factors can change net exports: foreign Real GDP (or real national income) and exchange rates. For example, in a two-country world (Japan and the United States), an increase in Japan's Real GDP and a depreciation in the dollar will increase U.S. net exports and shift the U.S. *AD* curve to the right. Alternatively, a decrease in Japan's Real GDP and an appreciation in the dollar will decrease U.S. net exports and shift the U.S. *AD* curve to the left.

## THE AGGREGATE SUPPLY CURVE AND INTERNATIONAL FACTORS

- A change in foreign input prices will impact the U.S. *SRAS* curve. For example, an increase in foreign input prices will shift the U.S. *SRAS* curve to the left. A decrease in foreign input prices will shift the U.S. *SRAS* curve to the right.

- A change in foreign input prices can be the result of changes in the input market in the foreign country.

- A change in foreign input prices (paid by U.S. producers) can be the result of a change in the exchange rate. For example, if the dollar depreciates, U.S. producers will pay higher prices for foreign inputs. If the dollar appreciates, U.S. producers will pay lower prices for foreign inputs.

## INTERNATIONAL FACTORS AND AGGREGATE DEMAND AND SHORT-RUN AGGREGATE SUPPLY

- A change in the exchange rate will affect both the U.S. *AD* curve and the U.S. *SRAS* curve. For example, if the dollar depreciates, the *AD* curve will shift to the right, and the *SRAS* curve will shift to the left.

- A change in real interest rates will affect both the U.S. *AD* curve and the U.S. *SRAS* curve. To illustrate, suppose the U.S. real interest rate rises relative to the Japanese interest rate. Higher real interest rates in the United States will attract foreign capital. Foreigners, in search of U.S. assets that pay interest, will bid up the price of a dollar; thus, the dollar appreciates. If the dollar appreciates, the *AD* curve will shift to the left, and the *SRAS* curve will shift to the right. The U.S. price level will fall. What happens to the U.S. Real GDP depends on the relative shifts in the *AD* and *SRAS* curves. Typically, the *AD* curve shifts leftward by more than the *SRAS* curve shifts rightward, and so Real GDP falls.

## FISCAL AND MONETARY POLICY IN CLOSED AND OPEN ECONOMIES

- Expansionary fiscal policy raises Real GDP more in a closed economy than in an open economy.

- Contractionary fiscal policy lowers Real GDP more in a closed economy than in an open economy.

- Expansionary monetary policy raises Real GDP more in an open economy than in a closed economy.

- Contractionary monetary policy lowers Real GDP more in an open economy than in a closed economy.

## KEY TERMS AND CONCEPTS

Globalization            Offshoring            Closed Economy            Open Economy
Tariff                   J-Curve

## QUESTIONS AND PROBLEMS

1. Why might it be easier to recognize the costs of globalization than the benefits?

2. If globalization continues over the next few decades, how might your life be different?

3. How might governments impact globalization?

4. Identify and explain two of the benefits and two of the costs of globalization.

5. What effect might advancing technology have on globalization?

6. Some have argued that the end of the Cold War acted as a catalyst toward greater globalization. How so?

7. What is Thomas Friedman's Golden Arches theory of conflict prevention?

8. David Friedman said that free (international) trade is a technology. Explain what he means.

9. Will globalization lead to some people losing jobs? Explain your answer.

10. How do tariff rates in the United States today compare with 1946?

11. Assume a two-country world where the two countries are the United States and Japan. Note the impact on U.S. Real GDP of each of the following:

   a. A fall in the real interest rate in the United States relative to the real interest rate in Japan

   b. An economic expansion in Japan

12. Give a numerical example to illustrate what the depreciation (of a country's currency) does to the prices of its imports.

13. If Americans buy fewer units of good X, which is produced in Japan, will they necessarily spend less money overall on good X? Explain your answer.

14. "The discussion of the J-curve points out that economists sometimes think in terms of both the short run and the long run." Do you agree or disagree? Explain your answer.

15. Explain how a change in the exchange rate can change both the U.S. *AD* and *SRAS* curves.

16. Suppose country A undertakes a policy mix of contractionary fiscal policy and expansionary monetary policy. What do you predict would happen to real interest rates, the value of country A's currency, and net exports? Explain your answer.

17. Why might import spending rise in a country soon after a depreciation of its currency? Is import spending likely to fall over time? Explain your answers.

18. Explain why expansionary monetary policy is more likely to increase Real GDP in an open economy than in a closed economy.

19. Explain why contractionary fiscal policy is more likely to decrease Real GDP in a closed economy than in an open economy.

20. Explain why contractionary monetary policy lowers Real GDP more in an open economy than in a closed economy.

## WORKING WITH NUMBERS AND GRAPHS

1. Starting with an exchange rate of $1 = ¥114 and a price tag of ¥10,000 for a Japanese item, show what happens to the price of the Japanese item if the yen depreciates by 5 percent.

2. Graphically show and explain the domestic and feedback effects on Real GDP in the United States as a result of contractionary fiscal policy.

3. Graphically show and explain the domestic and feedback effects on Real GDP in the United States as a result of contractionary monetary policy.

# CHAPTER 24

# STOCKS, BONDS, FUTURES, AND OPTIONS

**Introduction** Economic and financial news is all around us. "The economy is headed toward recession." "The value of the dollar is falling." "The budget deficit is growing." "The stock market took a loss today." "Bonds are strong."

Much of this book has dealt with economic news items. In this chapter we turn to the part of economics that relates to financial matters: stocks, bonds, futures, and options.

## FINANCIAL MARKETS

Everyone has heard of stocks and bonds, and everyone knows that stocks and bonds can be sold and purchased. But not everyone knows the economic purpose that stocks and bonds serve.

Buying and selling stocks and bonds take place in financial markets, which channel money from some people to other people. To illustrate, Jones has saved $10,000 over two years, and Smith is just starting a new company. Smith needs money to get the new company up and running. Jones would like to invest the savings and receive a return. Jones and Smith may not know each other; in fact, they may live on opposite ends of the country. A financial market, however, can bring these two people together, allowing Jones either to invest in Smith's company or to lend Smith some money. For example, Jones might either buy stock in Smith's company or buy a bond that Smith's company issues. In this chapter we discuss more about how people like Smith and Jones help each other through a financial market. In this section, we discuss stocks; in the next section, bonds.

## STOCKS

**Stock**
A claim on the assets of a corporation that gives the purchaser a share of ownership in the corporation.

What does it mean when someone tells you that she owns 100 shares of a stock? If Jane owns 100 shares of Yahoo! stock, she is a part owner in Yahoo!, Inc., a global Internet media company that offers a network of World Wide Web programming. A stock is a claim on the assets of a corporation that gives the purchaser a share of ownership in the corporation.

Jane is not an owner in the sense that she can walk into Yahoo! headquarters (in Santa Clara, California) and start issuing orders. She cannot hire or fire anyone, and she cannot decide what the company will or will not do over the next few months or years. But still she is an owner, and as an owner she can, if she wants, sell her ownership rights in Yahoo! All she has to do is find a buyer for her 100 shares of stock. Most likely, she could do so in a matter of minutes, if not seconds.

## finding ECONOMICS

**At an Online Brokerage Website** Frank has an account with TD Ameritrade. He goes online one morning to see at what price Yahoo! stock (symbol YHOO) is selling. At 10:45 a.m. EDT, the stock is selling at $29.74 a share. One minute later it is selling for one cent less at $29.73. Where is the economics?

Supply and demand are at work with respect to the Yahoo stock price. The equilibrium price is changing fairly fast in this market. At 10:45 a.m. EDT, the equilibrium price is $29.74. One minute later it has fallen to $29.73. Ten minutes later it has risen to $27.99. Think of how fast the market for Yahoo! stock equilibrates compared to some other markets (such as the housing market). ▲ ▲ ▲

## Where Are Stocks Bought and Sold?

Groceries are bought and sold at the grocery store. Clothes are bought and sold at the clothing store. But where are stocks bought and sold?

To answer that question, let's go back to 1792, when 24 men met under a buttonwood tree on what is now Wall Street in New York City. These men essentially bought and sold stock (for themselves and their customers) at this location. Someone might have said, "I want to sell 20 shares in company X. Are you willing to buy them for $2 a share?"

From this humble beginning came the New York Stock Exchange (NYSE). Every weekday (excluding holidays), men and women meet at the NYSE in New York City and buy and sell stock. For example, suppose you own 100 shares of a stock that is listed on the NYSE. You do not have to travel to the exchange to sell it. You simply contact a stockbroker (either over the phone, in person, or online), who conveys your wishes to sell the stock to a person at the NYSE itself. That person at the NYSE then executes your order.

The NYSE is not the only exchange where stocks are bought and sold. They are also traded on the American Stock Exchange (AMEX) and the NASDAQ stock market (pronounced "NAS-dak"; National Association of Securities Dealers Automated Quotations). Buying and selling stock on the NASDAQ do not take place in the same way as on the NYSE. Instead of taking place in a central location, trades on the NASDAQ, an electronic stock market, are executed through a sophisticated computer and telecommunications network. The NYSE might in fact change to this kind of market in the near future; instead of people meeting in one location to buy and sell stock, they could do it electronically.

Increasingly, Americans are buying and selling stocks not only on the U.S. stock exchanges and markets, but on foreign stock exchanges and markets too. For example, an American might buy a stock listed on the German Stock Exchange, the Montreal Stock Exchange, or the Swiss Exchange.

## The Dow Jones Industrial Average (DJIA)

You may have heard news commentators say, "The Dow fell 302 points on heavy trading." They are talking about the Dow Jones Industrial Average (DJIA), which first appeared on the scene more than 100 years ago, on May 26, 1896, and was devised by Charles H. Dow. Dow took 11 stocks, summed their prices on a particular day, and then divided by 11. The average price was the DJIA. (Some of the original companies included American Cotton Oil, Chicago Gas, National Lead, and U.S. Rubber.)

**Dow Jones Industrial Average (DJIA)**
The most popular, widely cited indicator of day-to-day stock market activity; a weighted average of 30 widely traded stocks on the New York Stock Exchange.

When Charles Dow first computed the DJIA, the stock market was not highly regarded in the United States. Prudent investors bought bonds, not stocks. Stocks were thought to be the arena for speculators and conniving Wall Street operators. Back then, Wall Streeters were seen as managing stock prices to make themselves better off at the expense of others. A lot of gossip went around about what was and was not happening in the stock market.

Dow devised the DJIA to convey information about what was really happening in the stock market. Before the DJIA, people had a hard time figuring out whether the stock market, on average, was rising or falling. Instead, they knew only that a particular stock went up or down by so many cents or dollars. The average price of a certain number of stocks, Dow thought, would largely mirror what was happening in the stock market as a whole. With this number, people could then gain some sense of what the stock market was doing on any given day.

Today, the DJIA consists of 30 stocks that are widely held by individuals and institutional investors (see Exhibit 1, which shows the 30 stocks in the Dow Industrial Average as of August 9, 2010). The list can and does change from time to time, as determined by the editors of *The Wall Street Journal*. And the DJIA is no longer computed simply by summing the prices of stocks and dividing by 30. A special divisor is used to avoid distortions that can occur, such as companies splitting their stock shares. Exhibit 2 shows the Dow Jones Industrial Average during the period of January 1, 2006–April 13, 2010.

In addition to the DJIA, other prominent stock indexes are cited in the United States. A few include the NASDAQ Composite, the Standard & Poor's 500, the Russell 2000, and the Wilshire 5000. There are also prominent stock indexes around the world, such as the Hang Seng (in Hong Kong), the Bovespa (Brazil), IPC (Mexico), BSE 30 (India), CAC 40 (France), and others.

What causes the DJIA to go up or down? Economic consulting firms have attempted to find out what influences the Dow. According to many economists, the Dow is closely connected to changes in such things as consumer credit, business expectations, exports and imports, personal income, and the money supply. For example, increases in consumer credit are expected to push the Dow up, the connection being that when consumer credit rises, people will buy more goods and services, and this is good for the companies that sell goods and services. When consumer credit falls, the opposite effect occurs.

---

### EXHIBIT 1

**The 30 Stocks of the Dow Jones Industrial Average (DJIA)**

Here are the 30 stocks that comprise the Dow Jones Industrial Average.

| | |
|---|---|
| 3M Co. | Intel Corp. |
| Alcoa Inc. | International Business Machines Corp. |
| American Express Co. | Johnson & Johnson |
| AT&T Inc. | JPMorgan Chase & Co. |
| Bank of America | Kraft Foods, Inc. |
| Boeing Co. | McDonald's Corp. |
| Caterpillar Inc. | Merck & Co. Inc. |
| Chevron | Microsoft Corp. |
| Cisco Systems | Pfizer Inc. |
| Coca-Cola Co. | Procter & Gamble Co. |
| E.I. DuPont de Nemours & Co. | Travelers Companies Inc. |
| ExxonMobil Corp. | United Technologies Corp. |
| General Electric Co. | Verizon Communications Inc. |
| Hewlett-Packard Co. | Wal-Mart Stores Inc. |
| Home Depot Inc. | Walt Disney Co. |

**EXHIBIT 2**

**DJIA, January 1, 2006–April 13, 2010**

Here we show the ups and downs of the DJIA from January 2006 to April 13, 2010.

## How the Stock Market Works

To raise money for investment in a new product or a new manufacturing technique, a company can do one of three things. First, it can go to a bank and borrow the money. Second, it can borrow the money by issuing a bond (a promise to repay the borrowed money with interest; you will learn more about bonds later in the chapter). Third, it can sell or issue stock in the company; that is, it can sell part of the company. Stocks are also called *equity* because the buyer of the stock has part ownership of the company.

When a company is initially formed, the owners set up a certain amount of stock, which is often worth very little. The owners of the company try to find people (usually friends and associates) who would be willing to buy the stock (in the hopes that one day it will be worth something). In these early days of the company, anyone who owns stock would find it nearly impossible to sell it. For example, if Jones owns 100 shares of a new company that almost no one had heard of, hardly anyone would be willing to pay any money to buy the stock.

As the company grows and needs more money, it may decide to offer its stock on the open market, that is, offer it to anyone who wants to buy it. By this time, the company may be known well enough that some people are willing to buy it. The company makes what is called an initial public offering (IPO) of its stock. The process is quite simple. Usually, an investment bank sells the stock for the company for an initial price—say, $10 a share. Investors find out about IPOs because they are announced in *The Wall Street Journal*.

For example, suppose that William Welch started a company in 1895 and that, through the years, the company was passed down to family members. In 2011, the family members running the company want to expand it to two, three, or four times its current size. To get the money to do this, one way is to sell shares in the company—that is, by issuing stock. Once they have issued shares in the company to the public, the company is no longer solely family owned. Now many of the public own part of it too.

After the IPO, the stock is usually traded on a stock exchange or in an electronic stock market. Sometimes, the stock that initially sold for $10 will rise in price, and sometimes it will fall like a rock. Its success or failure all depends on what people in the stock market think the issuing company will do in the future. If they think the company is destined for big earnings, the stock will likely rise in price. If they think the company is destined for losses or only marginal earnings, the stock will likely fall in price.

In a way, trading stock is much like trading baseball cards, paintings, or anything else. The price depends on the forces of supply and demand. If demand rises and supply is constant, then the price of the stock will rise. If demand falls and supply is constant, then the price of the stock will fall.

**Initial Public Offering (IPO)**
A company's first offering of stock to the public.

**Investment Bank**
A firm that acts as an intermediary between the company that issues the stock and the public that wishes to buy it.

# economics 24/7

## Are Some Economists Poor Investors?

You might think that economists would do pretty well in the stock market compared to the average person. After all, the job of economists is to understand how markets work and to study key economic indicators.

So how do you explain a May 11, 2005, article in the *Los Angeles Times* titled "Experts Are at a Loss on Investing"? The article looked at the investments of four economists—all Nobel Prize winners in economics. Not one of them said that he invests the way he should invest, and none of them seemed to be getting rich through their investments. Often, there seems to be a big difference between knowing what to do and doing it.

Harry M. Markowitz won the Nobel Prize in Economics in 1990 for his work in financial economics. He is known as the father of modern portfolio theory, the main idea being that people should diversify their investments. Markowitz, however, did not follow his own advice. Most of his life, he put half of his money in a stock fund and the other half in a conservative, low-interest investment. Markowitz, age 77 at the time, says, "In retrospect, it would have been better to have been more in stocks when I was younger."

George Akerlof, who won the Nobel Prize in Economics in 2001, had invested most of his money in money market accounts, which tend to have relatively low interest rate returns but are safe. Akerlof, when confronted with this fact, said, "I know it's utterly stupid."

Clive Granger, who won the Nobel Prize in Economics in 2003, was asked about his investments. He said, "I would rather spend my time enjoying my income than bothering about investments."

Daniel Kahneman, who won the Nobel Prize in Economics in 2002, had this to say about his investments: "I think very little about my retirement savings, because I know that thinking could make me poorer or more miserable or both."

Almost every activity comes with both benefits and costs. Investing wisely certainly has its benefits, but it has its costs too. Finding out about various investments, researching them, and keeping informed on how they are doing all take time.

The investment behaviors of our four Nobel Prize winners also point out something else. Many people think that economics is simply about money and money matters, but it is not. It is about utility and happiness and making oneself better off. Each of our four Nobel Prize winners might not have been doing the best thing for his wallet, but certainly each knew this and continued on the same path anyway. Each was willing to sacrifice some money to live a preferred lifestyle.

What is the lesson for you? You might care nothing about your investments and simply hope that your financial future will take care of itself. Or you could spend all of your time regularly watching, researching, and evaluating various investments that either you have made or plan to make. But neither extreme is sensible. You can learn enough about investments to protect yourself from the financial uncertainties of the future but not spend so much time worrying about the future that you don't enjoy the present.

## Why Do People Buy Stock?

Millions of people in the United States and in countries all over the world buy stock every day. Sometimes, people buy a stock because they hear that others are buying it and because they think the stock is hot. In other words, the stock is very popular and everyone wants it. In the 1990s, some of the Internet stocks fit this description. People bought stocks such as Yahoo!, Amazon.com, and eBay just because they thought the Internet was the wave of the future and almost anything connected with the Internet was destined for great profit.

More often, though, people buy a stock because they think the earnings of the company that initially issued the stock are likely to rise. (Remember that a share of stock represents ownership in a company.) The more profitable that company is expected to be, the more likely people are going to want to own that company, and therefore the greater the demand will be for the company's stock.

Most people therefore buy stock for a couple of typical reasons. Some buy stocks for the dividends, which are payments made to stockholders based on a company's profits. For example, suppose company X has issued one million shares of stock that are owned by

**Dividend**
A share of the profits of a corporation distributed to stockholders.

investors. Each year, if the company's profit and loss statement shows a profit, it distributes some of the profit among the owners of the company as dividends. This year's dividend might be $1 for each share of stock a person owns. So if Jones owns 50,000 shares of stock, she will receive a dividend check for $50,000.

The other reason to buy stock is for the expected gain in its price. Stockholders can make money if they buy shares at a lower price and sell at a higher price. For example, Smith buys 100 shares of Microsoft stock today. He thinks that the company is going to do well and that a year from now he can sell it for as much as $50 more a share than his purchase price. In other words, he hopes to earn $5,000 on his stock purchase.

People also sell stock for many reasons. Smith might sell his 100 shares of IBM because he needs the money, perhaps to help his son pay for college or to put together a down payment for a house. Another common reason for selling stock is that the stockholder thinks the stock is likely to go down in price soon. Selling today at $25 a share is better than selling one week from now at $18 a share.

## How to Buy and Sell Stock

Buying and selling stock are relatively easy. You can buy or sell stock through a full-service stockbrokerage firm, a discount broker, or an online broker. With all varieties of brokers, you usually open an account by depositing a certain dollar amount, commonly between $1,000 and $2,500. Once you have opened an account, you can begin to trade (i.e., buy and sell stock).

With a full-service broker, you may call up on the phone and ask your broker to recommend a good stock. Your broker, usually called an *account representative,* might say that you should buy X, Y, or Z stock. When you ask why these are good stocks to buy, the representative may say that the firm's research department has looked closely at them and believes they are headed for good times based on the current economic situation in the country, the level of exports, the new technology that is coming to market, and other factors.

If you do not need help selecting stocks, you can go either to a discount broker or to an online broker. You can call up a discount broker, as you did a full-service broker, and say you want to buy or sell so many shares of a given stock. The broker will execute the trade for you but not offer any advice.

You can do the same thing online. You go to your broker's website, log in, enter your username and password, and then buy or sell stock. You may, for example, submit an order to buy 100 shares of stock X. Your online broker will register your buy request and then advise you when it has been executed. Your account, easily visible online, will show how much cash you have in it, how many shares of a stock you hold, and so on.

## Buying Stocks or Buying the Market

You can use various methods to decide which stocks to purchase. The first way is to buy shares of stock that you think are going to rise in price. So you might buy 50 shares of Microsoft, 100 shares of General Electric, and 500 shares of Amazon.com.

Another way is to invest in a stock mutual fund, which is a collection of stocks that is managed by a fund manager who works for a mutual fund company. For example, Smith may operate Mutual Fund Z at Mutual Fund Company Z. If you put, say, $10,000 into Mutual Fund Z, you are in effect buying stocks in that fund. If the fund consists of stocks A, B, C, W, and X, the fund manager may, on any given day, buy more of A and sell some of B or sell all of C and add stock D to the fund portfolio. Thus, as a buyer of the fund, you put your money into the manager's hands, and the fund manager does what he or she thinks is best to maximize the overall returns from the fund.

Mutual fund companies often advertise the records of their fund managers. They might say, "Our fund managers have the best record on Wall Street. Invest with us and get the highest returns you can." You may be prompted to put your money in the hands of the experts because you feel they know better than you which stocks to buy and sell and when to do either.

You could use another strategy, though, and buy the stocks that make up a stock index. For example, the DJIA, a stock index, gives us information on the performance of the 30 stocks that make up the Dow. Other indexes are made up differently. The Standard & Poor's 500 index is a broad index of stock market activity because it is made up of 500 of the largest U.S. companies. Another broad-based stock index is the Wilshire 5000, which consists of the stocks of about 6,500 firms. (Yes, even though it consists of more than 5,000 firms, it is still called the Wilshire 5000.) So, instead of buying a mutual fund that consists of various stocks picked by the so-called experts, you can buy a mutual fund that consists of the stocks that make up a particular index.

An easy way to do this is to buy what are called Spyders. The term "Spyders" comes from SPDRs, which stands for Standard & Poor's Depository Receipts. Spyders are securities that represent ownership in the SPDR Trust, which buys the stocks that make up the Standard & Poor's (S&P) 500 index and that are traded under the symbol SPY. At the time of writing, Spyders were selling for about $135 a share. Spyders cost one-tenth of the S&P index (the total of the share prices of the stocks in the S&P). For example, if the S&P index is 1,350 , then a Spyder will sell for $135.

When you buy Spyders, you are buying the stock of 500 companies. Because you are buying the stock of so many companies, you are said to be *buying the market*. For example, suppose Jack decides to buy the market instead of buying a few individual stocks. He opens an account with an online broker; that is, he goes online, opens an account, and sends the broker a check so that he can start trading (buying and selling stock). He then checks (at the online broker web site) on the current price of Spyders, which is, say, $135 per share. He decides to buy 100 shares, for a total price of $13,500. (His online broker charges him a small commission for this stock purchase.) In a minute or less, he sees that he has purchased the 100 shares. That's all there is to it.

## How to Read the Stock Market Page

Once you have purchased some stock, you will want to know how it is doing. Is it rising or falling in price? Is it paying a dividend? How many shares were traded today?

One of the places with the answers to these questions, as well as other information, is the newspaper (many of which, of course, are online). On the stock market page, you will see something similar to what you see in Exhibit 3. Let's look at each item in each column of the bottom line (set in **boldface**).

**EXHIBIT 3**

**How to Read the Stock Market Page of a Newspaper**   This is part of the stock market page of a newspaper. We explain how to read the page in the text.

| (1) | (2) | (3) | (4) | (5) | (6) | (7) | (8) | (9) | (10) | (11) | (12) |
|---|---|---|---|---|---|---|---|---|---|---|---|
| 52W high | 52W low | Stock | Ticker | Div | Yield % | P/E | Vol 00s | High | Low | Close | Net chg |
| 45.39 | 19.75 | ResMed | RMD | | | 57.5 | 3831 | 42.00 | 39.51 | 41.50 | −1.90 |
| 11.63 | 3.55 | Revlon A | REV | | | | 162 | 6.09 | 5.90 | 6.09 | +0.12 |
| 77.25 | 55.13 | RioTinto | RTP | 2.30 | 3.2 | | 168 | 72.75 | 71.84 | 72.74 | +0.03 |
| 31.31 | 16.63 | RitchieBr | RBA | | | 20.9 | 15 | 24.49 | 24.29 | 24.49 | −0.01 |
| 8.44 | 1.75 | RiteAid | RAD | | | | 31028 | 4.50 | 4.20 | 4.31 | +0.21 |
| 38.63 | 18.81 | RobtHall | RHI | | | 26.5 | 6517 | 27.15 | 26.50 | 26.50 | +0.14 |
| **51.25** | **27.69** | **Rockwell** | **ROK** | **1.02** | **2.1** | **14.5** | **6412** | **47.99** | **47.00** | **47.54** | **+0.24** |

1. **52W high.** This stands for the high price of the stock over the past 52 weeks. For this stock, you see the number 51.25, which is $51.25.

2. **52W low.** This stands for the low price of the stock over the past 52 weeks. For this stock, you see the number 27.69, or $27.69.

3. **Stock.** In this column, you scc Rockwell. This is either an abbreviation of the name or the full name of the company that issued the stock. The company here is Rockwell Automation Incorporated.

4. **Ticker.** ROK is the stock or ticker symbol for Rockwell Automation Incorporated.

5. **Div.** This stands for dividend. You see the number 1.02 on the bottom line, which means that the last annual dividend per share of stock was $1.02. For example, a person who owned 5,000 shares of Rockwell Automation stock would have received $1.02 per share, or $5,100 in dividends. (A blank, as in the line above in the exhibit, means the company does not currently pay out dividends.)

6. **Yield %.** The yield of a stock is the dividend divided by the closing price.

$$\text{Yield} = \frac{\text{Dividend per share}}{\text{Closing price per share}}$$

The closing price of the stock (shown in column 11) is 47.54 ($47.54). If we divide the dividend ($1.02) by the closing price ($47.54), we get a yield of 2.1 percent. The higher the yield, the better the prospects are for the stock, *ceteris paribus*. For example, a stock that yields 5 percent is better than a stock that yields 3 percent, if all other things between the two stocks are the same.

7. **P/E.** This stands for P/E ratio, or price-earnings ratio. The number here, 14.5, is obtained by taking the latest closing price per share and dividing it by the latest available net earnings per share.

$$\frac{P}{E} = \frac{\text{Closing price per share}}{\text{Net earnings per share}}$$

A stock with a P/E ratio of 14.5 means that it is selling for a share price that is 14.5 times its earnings per share.

A high P/E ratio usually indicates that people expect higher-than-average growth in earnings. Suppose that most stocks have a P/E ratio of 14.5, that is, they sell for a share price that is 14.5 times their earnings per share. Also suppose that stock X has a P/E ratio of, say, 50. What would make stock X have a P/E ratio so much higher than most stocks? Obviously, the people buying stock X expect that its future earnings will somehow warrant the higher prices they are paying for the stock today. Whether they are right remains to be seen.

8. **Vol 00s.** This stands for volume in the hundreds. The number 6412 translates to 641,200. It means that 641,200 shares of this stock were traded (bought and sold) on this day.

9. **High.** This stands for the high price the stock traded for on this day. The number is 47.99 ($47.99).

10. **Low.** This stands for the low price the stock traded for on this day. The number is 47.00 ($47.00).

11. **Close.** This is the share price of the stock when trading stopped on this day: 47.54 ($47.54).

12. **Net chg.** This stands for net change: +0.24 (+$0.24). The price of the stock on this day closed 24¢ higher than it did the day before.

(Answers to Self-Test questions are in Answers to Self-Test Questions at the back of the book.)

1. How many stocks does the DJIA consist of?
2. Why do people buy stocks?
3. What does the yield of a stock equal?
4. What does a P/E ratio of 23 mean?

# BONDS

**Bond**
An IOU, or a promise to pay.

If a company in St. Louis wants to build a new factory, how can it get the necessary money? Issuing bonds is the third way that companies raise money (besides borrowing from a bank and issuing stock). A bond is simply an IOU, or a promise to pay. Typically, companies, governments, or government agencies issue bonds, in each case, the purpose being to borrow money. The issuer of a bond is a borrower, and the person who buys the bond is a lender.

## The Components of a Bond

A bond has three major components: face (par) value, maturity date, and coupon rate.

**Face Value (Par Value)**
Dollar amount specified on a bond, the total amount the issuer of the bond will repay to the buyer of the bond.

**FACE VALUE**  The face value, or par value, of a bond is the total amount the issuer of the bond will repay to the buyer of the bond. For example, suppose Smith buys a bond from Company Z, and the face value is $10,000. Company Z promises to pay Smith $10,000 at some point in the future.

**MATURITY DATE**  The maturity date is the day that the issuer of the bond must pay the buyer the face value; it is the date the bond is said to come due. For example, suppose Smith buys a bond with a face value of $10,000 that matures on December 31, 2015. On December 31, 2015, he receives $10,000 from the issuer of the bond.

**COUPON RATE**  The coupon rate is the percentage of the face value that the bondholder receives each year until the bond matures. For example, suppose Smith buys a bond with a face value of $10,000 that matures in 5 years and has a coupon rate of 10 percent. He receives a coupon payment of $1,000 each year for 5 years.

To illustrate, Jorge buys a bond with a face value of $100,000 and a coupon rate of 7 percent. The maturity date of the bond is 10 years from today. Each year, for the next 10 years, Jorge receives 7 percent of $100,000 from the issuer, which amounts to $7,000 a year for each of the 10 years. In the 10th year, he also receives $100,000 from the bond issuer. This bond has a maturity date in 10 years, a coupon rate of 7 percent, and a face value of $100,000.

## Bond Ratings

Bonds are rated, or evaluated. The more likely the bond issuer is to pay the face value of the bond at maturity and meet all scheduled coupon payments, the higher the bond's rating will be. Two of the best-known ratings are Standard & Poor's and Moody's. If a bond gets a rating of AAA from Standard & Poor's or a rating of Aaa from Moody's, it has received the highest rating possible. You can be sure that it is one of the securest bonds you can buy; there is little doubt that the bond issuer will pay the face value of the bond at maturity and meet all scheduled coupon payments.

Bonds rated in the B to D category are of lower quality than those in the A category. A bond in the C category may be in default (the issuer of the bond cannot pay off the bond), and those in the D category are definitely in default.

## $1.3 Quadrillion

At the close of the twentieth century, the editors of the financial magazine *The Economist* identified the highest-returning investments for each year, beginning in 1900 and ending in 1999. For example, the highest-returning investment in 1974 was gold, in 1902 it was U.S. Treasury bills, and in 1979 it was silver.

© NONSTOCK/JUPITER IMAGES

The editors then asked how much income a person would have earned by the end of 1999, if she had invested $1 in the highest-returning investment in 1900, and then taken the returns from that investment and invested it in the highest-returning investment in 1901, and so on for each year during the century. After taxes and dealer costs, she would have earned $1.3 quadrillion. (Quadrillion comes after trillion. In 2009, Bill Gates, the richest person in the world, had $40 billion; so $1.3 quadrillion is 32,500 times what Bill Gates had at the time.) So, with perfect foresight (or a crystal ball that always correctly tells you what the highest-returning investment of the year will be), you could be rich beyond your imagination.

After the editors ran their experiment, they changed it. They went back and asked themselves what one would have earned over the twentieth century if, instead of investing in the highest returning investment in a given year, she invested in it one year later. For example, if X was the best investment in 1956, she invested in it in 1957.

The editors made this change in the belief that many people invest in a hot investment only when it is too late. By the time they hear about it, investing in it then is usually too late. (Think of an investment as a mountain: going up the mountain is comparable to increasing returns on the investment, and going down the mountain is comparable to decreasing returns. Only when the investment is near its peak do many people hear about it. But then it's too late. The only way to go is down.)

To put this into context, the person with the crystal ball or with perfect foresight would have invested in the Polish stock market in 1993, when no one was talking about it, and he would have reaped a 754 percent gain. The typical investor would have invested in it one year later, in 1994, when everyone was talking about it. The problem is that the Polish stock market fell by 55 percent in 1994.

So the person who invested always one year late over the twentieth century would have earned, after taxes and dealer costs, $290!

What are the economic lessons? First, the best investments are often the ones that you don't hear about until it is too late. Second, ignoring the first lesson—thinking that a popular investment is necessarily a good investment—is often the way to low returns.

## Bond Prices and Yields (or Interest Rates)

The price that a person pays for a bond depends on market conditions. The greater the demand is for the bond relative to the supply, the higher the price will be. The price is important because it determines the yield, or interest rate, that the bondholder receives on the bond. (In everyday language, the yield is referred to as the interest rate on the bond. For example, someone might ask what interest rate is that bond paying? We could easily substitute the term "yield" for the term "interest rate," and the answer might be something like "5.26 percent.")

Let's suppose that Gupta is the owner of a bond with a face value of $1,000 and a coupon rate of 5 percent. He decides to sell this bond to Jones for $950. If the coupon payment on this bond is 5 percent of $1,000 each year, or $50, Jones can expect to receive $50 each year. But the yield (sometimes called the *current yield*) on the bond is the coupon payment divided by the price paid for the bond.

$$\text{Yield (or interest rate)} = \frac{\text{Annual coupon payment}}{\text{Price paid for the bond}}$$

**Yield**
The amount equal to the annual coupon payment divided by the price paid for the bond.

In this example, the yield is $50 ÷ $950 = 5.26 percent. For the bond buyer, the higher the yield is, the better the deal is.

Now suppose Jones paid $1,100 for the bond instead of $950. In this case, the yield would be $50 ÷ $1,100 = 4.54 percent. In other words, as the price paid for the bond rises, the yield declines.

The coupon rate and the yield are the same when the price paid for the bond equals the face value. For example, a bond with a face value of $1,000 and a coupon rate of 5 percent is purchased for $1,000. The yield ($50 ÷ $1,000) is 5 percent, which is equal to the coupon rate.

## Common Misconceptions About the Coupon Rate and Yield (Interest Rate)

Many people seem to think that the coupon rate of a bond is the yield that the bond earns. This is not true, as you now know. The yield (or interest rate) and the coupon rate are two different things.

- Only when the price of the bond equals the face value of the bond does the yield (interest rate) equal the coupon rate.

- When the price of the bond is lower than the face value of the bond, the yield will be greater than the coupon rate.

- When the price of the bond is greater than the face value of the bond, the yield will be lower than the coupon rate.

## Types of Bonds

This section briefly describes some of the many types of bonds that companies, governments, and government agencies issue.

CORPORATE BONDS  A corporate bond is issued by a private corporation. Typically, a corporate bond has a $10,000 face value. Corporate bonds may sell for a price above or below face value depending on current supply-and-demand conditions. The interest that corporate bonds pay is fully taxable.

MUNICIPAL BONDS  Municipal bonds are issued by state and local governments. States may issue bonds to help pay for, say, a new highway. Local governments may issue bonds to finance a civic auditorium or a sports stadium. Many people purchase municipal bonds because the interest paid on them is not subject to federal taxes.

TREASURY BILLS, NOTES, AND BONDS  When the federal government wants to borrow funds, it can issue Treasury bills (T-bills), notes, or bonds. These securities differ only in their time to maturity. Although called by different names, all are bonds. Treasury bills mature in 13, 26, or 52 weeks. Treasury notes mature in 2 to 10 years, and Treasury bonds mature in 10 to 30 years. Treasury bills, notes, and bonds are considered very safe investments because it is unlikely the federal government will default on its bond obligations. The federal government has the power to tax to pay off bondholders.

INFLATION-INDEXED TREASURY BONDS  In 1997, the federal government began to issue inflation-indexed bonds. The first indexed Treasury bonds that were issued mature in 10 years and were available at face values as small as $1,000.

An inflation-indexed Treasury bond differs from a nonindexed Treasury bond in that an inflation-indexed Treasury bond guarantees the purchaser a certain real rate of return; a nonindexed Treasury bond does not. For example, suppose you purchase an inflation-indexed, 10-year, $1,000 bond that pays a 4 percent coupon rate. If there is no inflation, the annual interest payment will be $40. But if the inflation rate is, say, 3 percent, the government will mark up the value of the bond by 3 percent—from $1,000 to $1,030. Then it will pay 4 percent on this higher dollar amount. So instead of paying $40 each year, it pays $41.20. By increasing the monetary value of the security by the rate of inflation, the government guarantees the bondholder a real return of 4 percent.

## How to Read the Bond Market Page

On the bond market page of the newspaper, you can find information about the different types of bonds. Here we discuss how to read the information that relates to both corporate bonds and Treasury bonds. First, let's look at corporate bonds.

CORPORATE BONDS  Not all publications will present corporate bond information in exactly the same format. The format in Exhibit 4 is common, though.

1. *Bonds.* This column presents three pieces of information: (1) the abbreviation for the company that issued the bond—AT&T, a telecommunications company; (2) the coupon rate of the bond, 6 5/8; (3) the year the bond matures, 2034.

2. *Cur Yld.* In this column is the current yield. (We showed how to compute the yield on a bond.) If the bond is purchased today (hence the word "current"), it will provide a yield of 6.7 percent.

3. *Vol.* In this column is the volume, 115. The dollar volume today is $115,000.

4. *Close.* In this column, you find the closing price for the bond on this day, 99 1/2. Bond prices are quoted in points and fractions, and each point is $10. Thus, 99 1/2 is $995.00: 99.5 × 10 = $995.00.

5. *Net Chg.* This column shows the net change for the day. Here, it is –3/4, which means that the price on this day was $7.50 lower than it was the previous day.

TREASURY BONDS  Not all publications will present Treasury bond information in exactly the same format. The format in Exhibit 5 is common, though.

1. *Rate.* In this column, you find the coupon rate of the bond. This Treasury bond pays 7 3/4 percent of the face value of the bond in annual interest payments.

2. *Maturity.* In this column, you find when the bond matures. This Treasury bond matures in February 2012.

3. *Bid.* In this column, you find how much the buyer is willing to pay for the bond (or the price you will receive if you sell the bond): 105:12. The number after the colon stands for 32nds of $10. Therefore, 105:12 is $1,053.75. First, multiply 105 × $10 = $1,050. Second, turn 12/32 into 0.375, and multiply by $10, giving you $3.75. Then add $3.75 to $1,050 to get $1,053.75.

4. *Ask.* In this column, you find how much the seller is asking for to sell the bond. This is the price you will pay if you buy the bond: $1,054.37.

**EXHIBIT 4**

| (1) Bonds | (2) Cur Yld | (3) Vol | (4) Close | (5) Net Chg |
|---|---|---|---|---|
| AT&T 6 5/8 34 | 6.7 | 115 | 99 1/2 | −3/4 |

**How to Read Corporate Bond Information**

This is a common format for corporate bond information.

---

**EXHIBIT 5**

**How to Read Treasury Bond Information**

This is a common format for treasury bond information.

| (1) Rate | (2) Maturity | (3) Bid | (4) Ask | (5) Chg | (6) Yield |
|----------|--------------|---------|---------|---------|-----------|
| 7 3/4 | Feb. 12 | 105:12 | 105:14 | −1 | 5.50 |

---

5. ***Chg.*** In this column, you find the change in the price of the bond from the previous trading day, expressed in 32nds. Therefore, −1 means that the price of the bond fell by 1/32nd of $10, or approximately 32¢ from the previous day.

6. ***Yield.*** In this column, you find the yield, which is based on the ask price. Someone who buys the bond today (at the ask price) and holds it to maturity will reap a return of 5.50 percent.

## Risk and Return

Whether buying stocks or bonds, the common denominator is that people buy them for the return. Simply stated, they hope to make money. How much money people can hope to make is tied directly to the different risk and return factors of stocks and bonds. For example, buying stock in a new company might be much riskier than buying a bond issued by the U.S. Treasury. You can be fairly sure that the U.S. Treasury is going to pay off that bond because the U.S. government has the ability to tax people. But you cannot be so sure of a positive return on the stock you buy in the new company. You might buy the stock for $10 one day, and three days later it falls to $1 and stays at that price (or thereabouts) for 10 years.

In Chapter 1, we said that a well-known principle in economics is that there is no free lunch. Applied to stocks and bonds (or any investment), that principle means you never get something for nothing. In short, higher returns come with higher risks, and lower returns come with lower risks. Treasury bonds, for example, will often pay (relatively) low returns because they are safe (risk-free).

---

**SELF-TEST**

1. What is a bond?

2. If the coupon payment on a bond is $400 a year and the coupon rate is 7 percent, what is the face value?

3. If the annual coupon payment for a bond is $1,000 and the price paid for the bond is $9,500, what is the yield or interest rate?

4. What is the difference between a municipal bond and a Treasury bond?

---

# FUTURES AND OPTIONS

In this section, we discuss both futures and options.

## Futures

Myers is a miller. He buys wheat from the wheat farmer, turns the wheat into flour, and then sells the flour to the baker. Obviously, he wants to earn a profit for what he does. How much, if any, profit he earns depends on the price at which he can buy the wheat and the price at which he can sell the flour.

# economics 24/7

## What Do Private Equity Firms Do?

Suppose a large corporation is full of top-level managers who are not carefully looking out for the company's shareholders. Maybe the corporation has a few losing operations that it should have shut down, or it has purchased too many corporate jets for use by top managers.

Enter the private equity firm. A private equity firm is a group of investors that seeks to buy up the publicly traded stock of the large corporation and then take the corporation private. Often, the private equity firm uses debt to buy the publicly traded stock. In other words, the private equity firm borrows much of the money needed to buy the public corporation.

As an example, Company X is a corporation that in the past few years has earned $20 million a year in profits. The private equity firm buys the stock of the corporation for 10 times the annual profits, or $200 million. The private equity firm itself puts up $60 million and borrows $140 million.

Once the private equity firm owns the corporation, it begins to cut costs and enhance efficiency. Maybe it gets rid of a few of the corporate jets, cuts a few losing operations, gets rid of some management that it feels is unnecessary, and invests in new products.

Now suppose profits rise to $22 million a year. The equity firm then pays $22 million for each of five years to repay $110 million of its $140 million debt, and then it sells the company for 10 times its annual earnings of $22 million, or $220 million. Out of the $220 million it repays the remainder of its debt ($30 million) and walks away with $190 million profit.

Of course, the firm is not guaranteed to generate greater profits. Even if the company only continued to earn $20 million in profits a year, the equity firm could use the $20 million in profits for, say, five years to pay off $100 million (of the $140 million debt) and then sell the company for what it purchased it for: $200 million. Out of the $200 million sales proceeds, the private equity firm would retire the remainder of the debt ($40 million), leaving it with $160 million in profit.

Is the existence of private equity firms a good thing? Some people will argue that private equity firms cut costs and enhance efficiency. Simply put, they increase the value of the firms in which they invest. Others argue that private equity firms exploit firms filled with managers who are averse to debt. They say that companies with too much cash and too little debt become targets for private equity firms to buy. The result, critics argue, is that ordinary shareholders are often hurt because buyout prices are often too low.

---

Myers decides to buy a futures contract in wheat. A futures contract is a contract in which the seller agrees to provide a good (in this case, wheat) to the buyer on a specified future date at an agreed-on price. For example, Myers might buy bushels of wheat now, for a price of $3 a bushel, to be delivered to him in six months.

But who would sell him the futures contract? A likely possibility is a *speculator*, someone who buys and sells commodities to profit from changes in the market. A speculator assumes risk in the hope of making a gain.

Suppose Smith, a speculator, believes that the price of wheat six months from now is going to be lower than it is today. She may look at things this way: "The price of wheat today is $3 a bushel. I think the price of wheat in six months will be close to $2 a bushel. I will promise the miller that I will deliver him as much wheat as he wants in six months if, in return, he agrees today to pay me $3 a bushel for it. Then, in six months, I will buy the wheat for $2 a bushel, sell it to the miller for $3 a bushel, and earn myself $1 profit on each bushel." So Myers, the miller, and Smith, the speculator, enter into a futures contract. Myers buys 200 bushels of wheat for delivery in six months; Smith sells 200 bushels of wheat for delivery in six months.

Each party gets something out of the deal. Myers, the miller, gets peace of mind. He knows that he will be able to buy the wheat at a price that will let him earn a profit on his deal with the baker. Smith takes a chance, which she is willing to take, for the chance of earning a profit.

**Futures Contract**
An agreement to buy or sell a specific amount of something (a commodity, a currency, a financial instrument) at an agreed-on price on a stipulated future date.

As another example, Wilson is a farmer who grows primarily corn. The current price of corn is $3.34 a bushel. Wilson doesn't have any corn to sell right now, but he will in two months. He hopes that over the next two months the price of corn won't fall to, say, something under $3. He decides to enter into a futures contract in corn. He promises to deliver 5,000 bushels of corn two months from now for $3.34 a bushel. Leung, a speculator in corn, decides that this is a good deal for him because he believes that in two months the price of a bushel of corn will have risen to $3.94. So Wilson and Leung enter into a futures contract. Two months pass and the price of corn has dropped to $3.10. Leung turned out to be wrong about the price rising. So farmer Wilson delivers 5,000 bushels of corn to speculator Leung, for which Leung pays Wilson $3.34 a bushel (for a total of $16,700), as agreed. Then Leung turns around and sells the corn for $3.10 a bushel (receiving $15,500), losing $1,200 on the deal.

**CURRENCY FUTURES** A futures contract can be written for wheat, as we have seen, or for a currency, a stock index, or even bonds. Here is how a currency futures contract works.

You check the dollar price of a euro today and find that it is $1.20. Thus, for every $1.20, you get 1 euro in return. You expect that in three months you will have to pay $1.50 to buy a euro. With this in mind, you enter into a futures contract. Essentially, you say that you are willing to buy $10 million worth of euros three months from now for $1.20 a euro. Anyone who thinks the dollar price of a euro will be lower (not higher) in three months might be willing to enter into this contract with you. Suppose you and Werner enter a contract. You promise to buy $10 million worth of euros in three months (at $1.20 a euro), and Werner promises to sell you $10 million worth of euros in three months at that price.

Three months pass, and it now takes $1.30 to buy a euro. Werner has to buy $10 million worth of euros at an exchange rate of $1.30 per euro. For $10 million, he gets 7,692,307 euros, which he turns over to you for $1.20 each, leaving him with $9,230,768. Obviously, Werner has taken a loss; he spent $10 million to get $9,230,768 in return, for a loss of $769,232.

On the other side of the deal, you now have 7,692,307 euros, for which you paid $9,230,768. If you sell them all, because you get $1.30 for every euro, you will get approximately $10 million. You are better off by $769,232.

## Options

An option is a contract that gives the owner of the option the right, but not the obligation, to buy or sell shares of a stock at a specified price on or before a specified date. There are two types of options: calls and puts.

**CALL OPTION** *Call* options give the owner of the option the right to *buy* shares of a stock at a specified price within the time limits of the contract. The specified price at which the buyer can buy shares of a stock is called the *strike price.* For example, Brown buys a call option for $20. The call option specifies that he can buy 100 shares of IBM stock at a strike price of $150 within the next month. If the price of IBM stocks falls below $150, Brown will not exercise his call option. He simply tears it up and accepts the fact that he has lost $20. If he still wants to buy IBM stock, he can do so through his stockbroker as he normally does and pay the going price, which is lower than $150. But if the price rises above $150, he exercises the call option, buys the stock at $150 a share, and then sells it for the higher market price. He has made a profit.

If Brown buys a call option, someone has to sell it to him. Anyone who would sell Brown a call option is a person who thought the option wouldn't be exercised. For example, if Jones believed that the price of IBM was going to fall below $150, then he would gladly sell a call option to Brown for $20, thinking that the option would never be exercised. That's $20 in his pocket.

**Option**

A contract that gives the owner the right, but not the obligation, to buy or sell shares of a stock at a specified price on or before a specified date.

PUT OPTIONS *Put* options give the owner the right, but not the obligation, to *sell* (rather than buy, as in a call option) shares of a stock at a strike price during some period of time. For example, suppose Martin buys a put option to sell 100 shares of IBM stock at $130 during the next month. If the share price rises above $130, Martin will not exercise his put option. He will simply tear it up and sell the stock for more than $130. On the other hand, if the price drops below $130, then he will exercise his option to sell the stock for $130 a share.

So, people who think the price of the stock is going to decline buy put options. Obviously, the people who think the price of the stock is going to rise sell put options. Why not sell a put option for, say, $20, if you expect the price of the stock to rise? The buyer is not going to exercise the option.

HOW YOU CAN USE CALL AND PUT OPTIONS You can use call and put options in a number of ways. Suppose you think a stock, currently selling for $250 a share, is going to rise in price during the next few months. You don't have enough money to buy many shares of stock, but you would like to benefit from the rise in the price of the stock. In such a case, you can buy a call option, which will sell for a fraction of the cost of the stock. So with limited resources, you decide to buy the call option, which gives you the right to buy, say, 100 shares of the stock at $250 anytime during the next three months.

A natural question is, if you don't have the money to buy the stock at $250 a share now, how are you going to buy it at $250 in a few months? You don't have to buy the stock. If you are right that the price of the stock will rise, then your call option will become worth more to people. In other words, if you bought the option when the price of the stock was $250 and the stock rises to $300, then your call option has become more valuable. You can sell it and benefit from the uptick in the price of the stock.

Alternatively, let's say you expect the price of the stock to fall. Then you can buy a put option. In other words, you buy the right to sell the stock for $250 anytime during the next three months. If the price does fall, your option becomes more valuable. In fact, the farther the price falls, the more valuable your put option becomes. People who have the stock and want to sell it for a price higher than it currently fetches on the market will be willing to buy your put option from you for some price higher than the price you paid.

As an example, the current price of a call option for AT&T stock is $10, and the current price of AT&T stock is $100. Ginny decides to buy a call option for $10, giving her the right to buy AT&T at a price of $100. Five months pass, and the price of AT&T shares has risen to $150. If Ginny wants, she can exercise her call option to buy AT&T stock at $100 (which is $50 less than the current price of $150). In other words, she can spend $100 to buy a share of stock, which she can turn around and immediately sell for $150, making a profit of $50 per share.

**SELF-TEST**

1. What is a futures contract?

2. You expect that a stock will rise in the next few months, but you do not have enough money to buy many shares of the stock. What can you do instead?

3. What is a put option?

## "I Have Three Questions."

**STUDENT:**

Can a firm that issues a bond set the coupon rate at any rate it wants?

**INSTRUCTOR:**

No. To illustrate, suppose company A needs to borrow $10 million and decides to issue $10,000 bonds. The only way anyone would be willing to buy one of these bonds (that is, lend the company $10,000) is if the company promises the buyers a rate of return comparable to the interest rate they could get if they simply put the money in a savings account. The company has to set the coupon rate in such a way that it attracts people to its bonds. If people are earning, say, 5 percent on their savings accounts, they will not lend money to the company unless the company pays a coupon rate of at least 5 percent. In short, the coupon rate is set at a competitive level—not just any level the company chooses.

**STUDENT:**

Is it a good idea to buy stock?

**INSTRUCTOR:**

A lot depends on such factors as your age (are you at the beginning of your work career or near the end), your income, and how much you can afford to invest in the stock market. Stock is not guaranteed to go up in price. For example, consider what happened to the DJIA in the 1930s. At the beginning of 1930, the Dow stood around 250, but at the end of 1939, it was around 150. Over the decade of the 1930s, the Dow went down by 40 percent.

However, having said this, stock prices have gone up over the long run. For example, suppose we look at the S&P Index during the period 1926–2004. The data show that you would have had a 70 percent likelihood of earning a positive investment return over a one-year period, but that would have risen to an 86.5 percent chance of a positive investment return if you had held the stocks in the index over a five-year period. The probability of a positive return goes up to 97.1 percent if you had held the stocks for 10 years. The longer you hold stocks in the stock market, the more likely it is that you will earn a positive return.

**STUDENT:**

Last question: Suppose I buy 100 shares of stock at a price of, say, $40 a share. The stock goes down in price to $32. Shouldn't I wait until the share price rises to $40 or higher before I sell it?

**INSTRUCTOR:**

When it comes to stock, what goes down is not guaranteed to go up. Even if the stock's price has gone down by $8, it might go down more. You want always to look forward, to the future (not backward, to the past), when deciding whether to sell a stock. If you think the price may fall even farther, selling at $32 (taking an $8 per share loss) is better than selling at $25 and taking a bigger loss. If you think there is a reason for the price to rise, then hold on to the stock.

### POINTS TO REMEMBER

1. A company that issues bonds cannot set the coupon rate at whatever rate it wants.
2. Based on the period 1926–2004, the longer a person would have held stocks, the higher the probability is that he or she would have received a positive return.
3. Stocks that go down in price are not guaranteed to go back up.

## CHAPTER SUMMARY

### STOCKS

- A stock is a claim on the assets of a corporation that gives the purchaser a share (ownership) in the corporation. Stocks are sometimes called "equity" because the buyer of the stock has part ownership of the company that initially issued the stock.

- Stocks are bought and sold on exchanges and markets, such as the New York Stock Exchange.

- Some people buy stocks for the dividends, which are payments made to stockholders based on a company's profits; others attempt to make money by buying shares at a lower price and selling at a higher price.

- Today, 30 stocks make up the Dow Jones Industrial Average (DJIA). The DJIA was devised by Charles Dow to convey information about what was happening in the stock market.

- A stock index fund consists of the stocks that make up an index.

- The yield (or interest rate) of a stock is equal to the dividend divided by the closing price of the stock.

- The P/E ratio for a stock is equal to the closing price per share (of the stock) divided by the net earnings per share. A stock with a P/E ratio of, say, 15 means that the stock is selling for a share price that is 15 times its earnings per share.

### BONDS

- A bond is an IOU, or a promise to pay, typically issued by companies, governments, or government agencies.

- The three major components of a bond are face (par) value, maturity date, and coupon rate.

- The price that a person pays for a bond depends on market conditions: the greater the demand is for the bond relative to the supply, the higher the price will be.

- The (current) yield on the bond is the coupon payment divided by the price paid for the bond.

- Bonds are rated or evaluated. The more likely the bond issuer is to pay the face value of the bond at maturity and meet all scheduled coupon payments, the higher the bond's rating will be.

- The price of a bond and its yield (or interest rate) are inversely related.

### FUTURES AND OPTIONS

- In a futures contract, a seller agrees to provide a good to the buyer on a specified future date at an agreed-on price.

- An option is a contract giving the owner the right, but not the obligation, to buy or sell a good at a specified price on or before a specified date.

## KEY TERMS AND CONCEPTS

| | | | |
|---|---|---|---|
| Stock | Initial Public Offering | Dividend | Yield |
| Dow Jones Industrial | (IPO) | Bond | Futures Contract |
| Average (DJIA) | Investment Bank | Face Value (Par Value) | Option |

## QUESTIONS AND PROBLEMS

1. What is the purpose of financial markets?

2. What does it mean if the Dow Jones Industrial Average rises by, say, 100 points in a day?

3. What does it mean to buy the market?

4. What does it mean if someone invests in a mutual fund? In a stock market fund?

5. If the share price of each of 500 stocks rises on Monday, does everyone in the stock market believe that stocks are headed even higher? (No one will buy a stock if he or she thinks share prices are headed lower.)

6. Which of the two stocks has a bigger gap between its closing price and net earnings per share: Stock A with a P/E ratio of 15 or Stock B with a P/E ratio of 44? Explain your answer.

7. "An issuer of a bond is a borrower." Do you agree or disagree? Explain your answer.

8. If the face value of a bond is $10,900 and the annual coupon payment is $600, what is the coupon rate?

9. Why might a person purchase an inflation-indexed Treasury bond?

10. "If you can predict interest rates, then you can earn a fortune buying and selling bonds." Do you agree or disagree? Explain your answer.

11. Why might a person buy a futures contract?

12. Why might a person buy a call option?

13. "The currency speculator who sells futures contracts assumes the risk that someone else doesn't want to assume." Do you agree or disagree? Explain your answer.

14. If you thought the share price of a stock was going to fall, would you buy a call option or a put option?

# WORKING WITH NUMBERS AND GRAPHS

1. You own 1,250 shares of stock X, and you read in the newspaper that the dividend for the stock is 3.88. What did you earn in dividends?

2. The closing price of a stock is $90.25, and the dividend is $3.50. What is the yield of the stock?

3. The closing price of the stock is $66.40, and the net earnings per share are $2.50. What is the stock's P/E ratio?

4. The face value of a bond is $10,000, and the annual coupon payment is $850. What is the coupon rate?

5. A person buys a bond that matures in 10 years and pays a coupon rate of 10 percent. The face value of the bond is $10,000. How much money will the bondholder receive in the tenth year?

## Chapter 1

### CHAPTER 1, PAGE 3

1. False. It takes two things for scarcity to exist: finite resources and infinite wants. If people's wants were equal to or less than the finite resources available to satisfy their wants, scarcity would not exist. Scarcity exists only because people's wants are greater than the resources available to satisfy their wants. Scarcity is the condition resulting from infinite wants clashing with finite resources.

2. Because of scarcity, there is a need for a rationing device. People will compete for the rationing device. For example, if dollar price is the rationing device, people will compete for dollars.

3. Because our unlimited wants are greater than our limited resources—that is, because scarcity exists—some wants must go unsatisfied. We must choose which wants we will satisfy and which we will not.

### CHAPTER 1, PAGE 12

1. Everytime a student is late to history class, the instructor subtracts one-tenth of a point from the person's final grade. If the instructor raises the opportunity cost of being late to class by subtracting one point from the final grade, economists predict that fewer students would be late to class. In summary, the higher the opportunity cost is of being late to class, the less likely people will be late to class.

2. Yes. To illustrate, suppose the marginal benefits and marginal costs (in dollars) are as follows for various hours of studying:

| Hour | Marginal Benefits | Marginal Costs |
|------|-------------------|----------------|
| First hour | $20.00 | $10.00 |
| Second hour | $14.00 | $11.00 |
| Third hour | $13.00 | $12.00 |
| Fourth hour | $12.10 | $12.09 |
| Fifth hour | $11.00 | $13.00 |

Clearly, you will study the first hour because the marginal benefits are greater than the marginal costs. Stated differently, studying the first hour has a net benefit of $10 (the difference between the marginal benefits of $20 and the marginal costs of $10). If you stop studying after the first hour and do not proceed to the second, then you forfeit the net benefit of $3 for the second hour. To maximize your net benefits of studying, you must proceed until the marginal benefits and the marginal costs are as close to equal as possible. (In the extreme, this is an epsilon away from equality. However, economists simply speak of the "equality" of the two for convenience.) In this case, you

study through the fourth hour. You do not study the fifth hour because it is not worth it; the marginal benefits of studying the fifth hour are less than the marginal costs. In short, studying the fifth hour has a net cost.

3. You might feel sleepy the next day, you might be less alert while driving, and so on.

### CHAPTER 1, PAGE 17

1. The purpose of building a theory is to explain something that is not obvious. For example, the cause of changes in the unemployment rate is not obvious, and so the economist would build a theory to explain changes in the unemployment rate.

2. A theory of the economy seeks to explain why certain things in the economy happen. For example, a theory of the economy might try to explain why prices rise or why output falls. A description of the economy is simply a statement of what exists in the economy. For example, we could say that the economy is growing or contracting or that more jobs are available this month than last month. A description doesn't answer questions; it simply tells us what is. A theory tries to answer a why question, such as, "Why are more jobs available this month than last month?"

3. If you do not test a theory, you will never know whether you have accomplished your objective in building the theory in the first place. In other words, you will not know if you have accurately explained something. We do not simply accept a theory if it sounds right, because what sounds right may actually be wrong. For example, no doubt during the time of Columbus, the theory that the earth was flat sounded right to many people and the theory that the earth was round sounded ridiculous. The right-sounding theory turned out to be wrong, though, and the ridiculous-sounding theory turned out to be right.

4. Unless stated otherwise, when economics instructors identify the relationship between two variables, they implicitly make the *ceteris paribus* assumption. In other words, the instructor is really saying, "If the price of going to the movies goes down, people will go to the movies more often—assuming that nothing else changes, such as the quality of movies, and so on." Instructors don't always state *"ceteris paribus"* because if they did, they would be using the term every minute of a lecture. So the instructor is right, although a student new to economics might not know what the instructor is assuming but not saying.

## Chapter 2

### CHAPTER 2, PAGE 46

1. A straight-line PPF represents constant opportunity costs between two goods. For example, for every unit of X produced, one unit of Y is forfeited. A bowed-outward PPF represents increasing opportunity costs. For example, we may have to forfeit one unit of X to produce the eleventh unit of

Y, but we have to forfeit two units of X to produce the one-hundredth unit of Y.

2. A bowed-outward PPF is representative of increasing costs. In short, the PPF would not be bowed outward if increasing costs did not exist. To prove this, look back at Exhibits 1 and 2. In Exhibit 1, costs are constant (not increasing), and the PPF is a straight line. In Exhibit 2, costs are increasing, and the PPF is bowed outward.

3. The first condition is that the economy is currently operating *below* its PPF. It is possible to move from a point below the PPF to a point on the PPF and get more of all goods. The second condition is that the economy's PPF shifts outward.

4. False. Take a look at Exhibit 5. All of the numerous productive efficient points lie on the PPF.

# Chapter 3
## CHAPTER 3, PAGE 65

1. Popcorn is a normal good for Sandi. Prepaid telephone cards are an inferior good for Mark.

2. Asking why demand curves are downward sloping is the same as asking why price and quantity demanded are inversely related (as one rises, the other falls). Two reasons for this are mentioned in this section: (1) As price rises, people substitute lower-priced goods for higher-priced goods. (2) Because individuals receive less utility from an additional unit of a good they consume, they are only willing to pay less for the additional unit. The second reason is a reflection of the law of diminishing marginal utility.

3. Suppose only two people, Bob and Alice, have a demand for good X. At a price of $7, Bob buys 10 units and Alice buys 3 units; at a price of $6, Bob buys 12 units and Alice buys 5 units. One point on the market demand curve represents a price of $7 and a quantity demanded of 13 units; another point represents $6 and 17 units. A market demand curve is derived by adding the quantities demanded at each price.

4. A change in income, preferences, prices of related goods, the number of buyers, and expectations of future price can change demand. A change in the price of the good changes the quantity demanded of it. For example, a change in *income* can change the *demand* for oranges, but only a change in the *price* of oranges can directly change the *quantity demanded* of oranges.

## CHAPTER 3, PAGE 70

1. Increasing the quantity supplied of houses over the next ten hours would be difficult; so the supply curve in (a) is vertical, as in Exhibit 8. Increasing the quantity supplied of houses over the next three months is possible; so the supply curve in (b) is upward sloping.

2. a. The supply curve shifts to the left.
   b. The supply curve shifts to the left.
   c. The supply curve shifts to the right.

3. False. If the price of apples rises, the *quantity supplied* of apples will rise—not the *supply*. We are talking about a *movement* from one point on a supply curve to a point higher up on the supply curve, not about a shift in the supply curve.

## CHAPTER 3, PAGE 80

1. Disagree. In the text, we plainly saw how supply and demand work at an auction. Supply and demand are at work in the grocery store too, even though no auctioneer is present. The essence of the auction example is the auctioneer's raising the price when there was a shortage and lowering the price when there was a surplus. The same thing happens at the grocery store. For example, given a surplus of corn flakes, the manager of the store is likely to run a sale (lower prices) on them. Many markets without auctioneers act *as if* auctioneers were raising and lowering prices in response to shortages and surpluses.

2. No. It could be the result of a higher supply of computers. Either a decrease in demand or an increase in supply will lower price.

3. a. Lower price and quantity
   b. Lower price and higher quantity
   c. Higher price and lower quantity
   d. Lower price and quantity

4. At equilibrium quantity, the maximum buying price and the minimum selling price are the same. For example, in Exhibit 15, both prices are $40 at the equilibrium quantity of 4. The equilibrium quantity is the only quantity at which the maximum buying price and the minimum selling price are the same.

5. $44; $34

# Chapter 4
## CHAPTER 4, PAGE 87

1. A rationing device is necessary because scarcity exists. If scarcity did not exist, a rationing device would not be needed.

2. If (dollar) price is the rationing device used, then individuals have an incentive to produce goods and services, sell them for money (for the dollar price), and then use the money to buy what they want. If another rationing device were used (say, first-come-first-service, or "need," etc.), then the incentive to produce would be dramatically dampened. Why produce a good if the only way you can "sell" it (i.e., ration the good) is by way of first-come-first-served.

3. Price conveys information about the relative scarcity of a good. In the orange juice example, a rise in the price of orange juice transmitted information relating to the increased relative scarcity of orange juice due to a cold spell in Florida.

## CHAPTER 4, PAGE 94

1. Yes, if nothing else changes—that is, yes, *ceteris paribus*. If other things change, though, they may not. For example, if the government imposes an effective price ceiling on gasoline, Jamie may pay lower gas prices at the pump but have to wait in line to buy the gas (due to first-come-first-served rationing of the shortage). Whether Jamie is better off paying a higher price and not waiting in line or paying a lower price and waiting in line is not clear. The point, however, is that buyers don't necessarily prefer lower prices to higher prices unless everything else (quality, wait, service, etc.) stays the same.

2. Disagree. Both long-lasting shortages and long lines are caused by price ceilings. First, the price ceiling is imposed, creating the shortage; then the rationing device of first-come-first-served

emerges because price isn't permitted to fully ration the good. Every day, shortages occur that don't cause long lines to form. Instead, buyers bid up price, output and price move to equilibrium, and there is no shortage.

3. Buyers might argue for price ceilings on the goods they buy, especially if they don't know that price ceilings have some effects they may not like (e.g., fewer exchanges, first-come-first-served rationing devices, etc.). Sellers might argue for price floors on the goods they sell, especially if they expect their profits to rise. Employees might argue for a wage floor on the labor services they sell, especially if they don't know that they may lose their jobs or have their hours cut back as a result.

## CHAPTER 4, PAGE 96

1. $1A = \frac{2}{3}B$ and $1B = 1.5A$

2. The statement is correct in the sense that good X has a higher money price than it used to have. It is misleading because a higher money price doesn't necessarily mean a higher relative price. For example, if the absolute (money) price of good X is $10 and the absolute price of good Y is $20, then the relative price of X is ½ units of Y. Now suppose the absolute price of X rises to $15 while the absolute price of Y rises to $60. The new relative price of X is now ¼ units of Y. In other words, the absolute price of X rises (from $10 to $15) while its relative price falls (from ½Y to ¼Y). Good X can become more expensive in money terms as it becomes cheaper in terms of other goods.

# Chapter 5
## CHAPTER 5, PAGE 101

1. The more requests for tickets and the faster the tickets sell out, the more popular the show.

2. They could charge a positive ticket price for shows in which the quantity demanded of seats equaled the quantity supplied of seats at a positive price. This may not always be the case, though, as shown in Exhibit 2.

## CHAPTER 5, PAGE 102

1. Yes. For example, suppose a 30 percent down payment was needed to obtain a mortgage loan instead of a 10 percent down payment. Fewer individuals would be able to obtain a loan to buy a house, lowering the demand for houses and thus lowering house prices.

2. Yes. Reducing one's taxes because he or she has purchased a house makes buying a house more attractive, which leads to a higher demand for houses. The higher demand for houses raises the equilibrium price of houses.

## CHAPTER 5, PAGE 103

1. The airlines company will likely use the rationing device of first-come/first-served. The people who book their reservations early get their pick of seats; those who do not book early have to take the left over seats.

2. The equilibrium price of the window seat is less than the equilibrium price of the aisle seat; the equilibrium price of the middle seat is lower than the equilibrium price of the window seat. For example, if the equilibrium price of the aisle seat is $300, then the equilibrium price of the window seat might be $280, with the equilibrium price of the aisle seat even lower at, say, $250.

## CHAPTER 5, PAGE 105

1. The price of food will rise along with the premium for food insurance.

2. The new demand curve would be between $D_1$ and $D_2$.

## CHAPTER 5, PAGE 106

1. If supply and tuition are constant and demand rises, the shortage of openings at the university will become greater. The university will continue to use its nonprice-rationing devices (GPA, SAT scores, ACT scores) but will have to raise the standards of admission. Instead of requiring a GPA of, say, 3.5 for admission, it may raise the requirement to 3.8.

2. Not likely. A university that didn't make admission easier in the face of a surplus of openings might not be around much longer. When tuition cannot be adjusted directly—in other words, when the rationing device of price cannot be adjusted—it is likely that the nonprice-rationing device (standards) will be.

## CHAPTER 5, PAGE 108

1. Any price above 70¢.

2. Assuming that tolls are not used, freeway congestion will worsen. An increase in driving population simply shifts the demand curve for driving to the right.

## CHAPTER 5, PAGE 109

1. Moving from a system where patients cannot sue their HMOs to one where they can gives patients something they didn't have before (the right to sue) at a higher price (higher charges for healthcare coverage). The "free lunch"—the right to sue—isn't free after all.

2. If the students get the extra week and nothing else changes, then the students will probably say they are better off. In other words, more of one thing (time) and no less of anything else makes one better off. But if because of the extra week, the professor grades their papers harder than she would have otherwise, then some or all of the students may say that they weren't made better off by the extra week.

## CHAPTER 5, PAGE 110

1. A possible answer: Of two cities, one has clean air and the other has dirty air. The demand to live in the clean-air city is higher than the demand to live in the dirty-air city. As a result, housing prices are higher in the clean-air city.

2. Ultimately, the person who owns the land in the good-weather city receives the payment. Look at it this way: People have a higher demand for houses in good-weather cities than they do for houses in bad-weather cities. As a result, house builders receive higher prices for houses built and sold in good-weather cities. Because of the higher house prices, builders have a higher demand for land in good-weather cities. In the end, higher demand for land translates into higher land prices or land rents for landowners.

## CHAPTER 5, PAGE 111

1. Suppose University X gives a full scholarship to every one of its football players (all of whom are superathletes). In addition, suppose that the full scholarship (translated into wages) is far below the equilibrium wage of each of the football players. (Think of it this way: Each football player gets a wage, or full scholarship, of $10,000 a year, when his equilibrium wage is $40,000 a year.) Paying lower than the equilibrium wage will end up transferring dollars and other benefits from the football players to the university, to the new field house and track, and perhaps to you if you use the track for exercise.

2. If paying student athletes (a wage above the full scholarship) lowers consumers' demand for college athletics, then the equilibrium wage for college athletes is not as high as shown in Exhibit 9.

## CHAPTER 5, PAGE 112

1. Answers will vary. Students sometimes say that it is "fairer" if everyone is charged the same price. Is it unfair then that moviegoers pay less if they go to the 2 p.m. movie than if they go to the 8 p.m. movie?

2. We learned about price ceilings in the previous chapter. Specifically, we learned that a price ceiling creates a shortage. In the application dealing with the 10:00 a.m. class, the university charged a below-equilibrium price for the 10:00 a.m. class, leading to a shortage of such classes.

## CHAPTER 5, PAGE 113

1. Price will fall.
2. Quantity will rise.

# Chapter 6
## CHAPTER 6, PAGE 123

1. The CPI is calculated as follows: (1) Define a market basket; (2) determine how much it would cost to purchase the market basket in the current year and in the base year; (3) divide the dollar cost of purchasing the market basket in the current year by the dollar cost of purchasing the market basket in the base year; (4) multiply the quotient by 100. For a review of this process, see Exhibit 1.

2. It is a year that is used for comparison purposes with other years.

3. Annual nominal income has risen by 13.85 percent, and prices have risen by 4.94 percent. We conclude that because nominal income has risen more than prices, real income has increased. Alternatively, you can look at it this way: Real income in year 1 is $31,337, and real income in year 2 is $33,996.

## CHAPTER 6, PAGE 129

1. The frictionally unemployed person has readily transferable skills, and the structurally unemployed person does not.

2. It implies that the (actual, measured) unemployment rate in the economy is greater than the natural unemployment rate. For example, if the unemployment rate is 8 percent and the natural unemployment rate is 6 percent, the cyclical unemployment rate is 2 percent.

# Chapter 7
## CHAPTER 7, PAGE 136

1. GDP is a measure of production in a country. When stocks are purchased and sold, no production occurs. A stock purchase and sale simply represent the trading of existing assets. Specifically, if person A owns 100 shares of stock X and then sells the shares to person B, all that has happened is that person B owns something that person A once owned. No more goods and services have been produced.

2. No. GDP doesn't account for all productive activity (e.g., it omits the production of nonmarket goods and services). A GDP of $0 doesn't necessarily mean that there was no production in the country.

## CHAPTER 7, PAGE 139

1. In the expenditure approach, GDP is computed by finding the sum of consumption, investment, government purchases, and net exports. (Net exports are equal to exports minus imports.)

2. Yes. To illustrate, suppose consumption is $200, investment is $80, and government purchases are $70. The sum of these three spending components of GDP is $350. Now suppose exports are $0 but imports are $100, which means that net exports are −$100. Since GDP = $C + I + G + (EX − IM)$, GDP is $250.

3. No. Each individual would have $40,000 worth of goods and services only if the entire GDP were equally distributed across the country. There is no indication that this is the case. The $40,000 (per capita GDP) says that the "average" person in the country has access to $40,000 worth of goods and services, but in reality the average person may not exist. For example, if Smith earns $10,000 and Jones earns $20,000, then the average person earns $15,000. But neither Smith nor Jones earns $15,000; so neither is average.

## CHAPTER 7, PAGE 149

1. We can't know for sure; we can only say what might have caused the rise in GDP. It could be (a) a rise in prices with no change in output, (b) a rise in output with no change in prices, (c) rises in both prices and output, or (d) a percentage increase in prices that is greater than the percentage decrease in output . . . or some other situation.

2. More output was produced in year 2 than in year 1.

3. Yes. Business cycles—ups and downs in Real GDP—don't prevent Real GDP from growing over time. Exhibit 6 shows Real GDP higher at the second peak than at the first, even though there is a business cycle between the peaks.

# Chapter 8
## CHAPTER 8, PAGE 166

1. In the real balance effect, a rise (fall) in the price level causes purchasing power to fall (rise), thereby decreasing (increasing) a person's monetary wealth. As people become less (more) wealthy, the quantity demanded of Real GDP falls (rises).

2. If the dollar appreciates, it takes more foreign currency to buy a dollar and fewer dollars to buy foreign currency. U.S. goods

(denominated in dollars) become more expensive for foreigners, and foreign goods become cheaper for Americans. In turn, foreigners buy fewer U.S. exports, and Americans buy more foreign imports. As exports fall and imports rise, net exports fall. If net exports fall, total expenditures fall, *ceteris paribus*. As total expenditures fall, the *AD* curve shifts to the left.

3. Total spending is the product of the money supply times velocity. Let the money supply be $400 and velocity 3. Then total spending is $1,200. Now suppose that the money supply rises to $500 but that velocity declines to 2. Total spending has fallen to $1,000 even though the money supply has increased. So, yes, the money supply can rise while total spending declines.

## CHAPTER 8, PAGE 171

1. As wage rates decline, the cost per unit of production falls. In the short run (assuming prices are constant), profit per unit rises. Higher profit causes producers to produce more units of their goods and services. In short, the *SRAS* curve shifts to the right.

2. Last year, 10 workers produced 100 units of good X in 1 hour. This year, 10 workers produced 120 units of good X in 1 hour.

3. Workers initially misperceive the change in their real wage due to a change in the price level. For example, the nominal wage is $30, and the price level is 1.50; the real wage is therefore $20. Then the nominal wage falls to $25, and the price level falls to 1.10. The real wage is now $22.72. But suppose workers misperceive the decline in the price level and mistakenly believe it has fallen to 1.40. They will now perceive their real wage as $17.85 ($25 ÷ 1.40). In other words, they will misperceive their real wage as falling when it has actually increased. How will workers react if they believe their real wage has fallen? They will cut back on the quantity supplied of labor, reducing output (or Real GDP). This process is consistent with an upward-sloping *SRAS* curve: A decline in the price level leads to a reduction in output.

## CHAPTER 8, PAGE 177

1. In long-run equilibrium, the economy is producing Natural Real GDP. In short-run equilibrium, the economy is not producing Natural Real GDP, although the quantity demanded of Real GDP equals the quantity supplied of Real GDP.

2. The diagram should show the price level in the economy at $P_1$ and Real GDP at $Q_1$, but the intersection of the *AD* curve and the *SRAS* curve is at some point other than ($P_1$, $Q_1$). In addition, the *LRAS* curve should not be at $Q_1$ or at the intersection of the *AD* and *SRAS* curves.

## Chapter 9
### CHAPTER 9, PAGE 185

1. Say's law states that supply creates its own demand. In a barter economy, Jones supplies good X so that she can use it to demand some other good (e.g., good Y). The act of supplying is motivated by the desire to demand. Supply and demand are opposite sides of the same coin.

2. No, total spending will not decrease. For classical economists, an increase in saving (reflected in a decrease in consumption) will lower the interest rate and stimulate investment spending. So one spending component (consumption) goes down, and

another (investment) goes up. Moreover, according to classical economists, the decrease in one spending component will be completely offset by an increase in another spending component so that overall spending does not change.

3. Prices and wages are flexible; they move up and down in response to market conditions.

## CHAPTER 9, PAGE 190

1. A recessionary gap exists if the economy is producing a Real GDP level that is less than Natural Real GDP. An inflationary gap exists if the economy is producing a Real GDP level that is more than Natural Real GDP.

2. When the economy is in a recessionary gap, the labor market has a surplus. When the economy is in an inflationary gap, the labor market has a shortage.

3. The economy is somewhere above the institutional PPF and below the physical PPF.

## CHAPTER 9, PAGE 199

1. In a recessionary gap, the existing unemployment rate is greater than the natural unemployment rate, implying that unemployment is relatively high. As wage contracts expire, business firms negotiate new ones that pay workers lower wage rates. As a result, the *SRAS* curve shifts rightward. At the same time, the price level begins to fall. The economy moves down the *AD* curve—eventually to the point where it intersects the *LRAS* curve. At this point, the economy is in long-run equilibrium.

2. In an inflationary gap, the existing unemployment rate is less than the natural unemployment rate, implying that unemployment is relatively low. As wage contracts expire, business firms negotiate contracts that pay workers higher wage rates. As a result, the *SRAS* curve shifts leftward. At the same time, the price level begins to rise. The economy moves up the *AD* curve—eventually to the point where it intersects the *LRAS* curve. At this point, the economy is in long-run equilibrium.

3. Any changes in aggregate demand affect—in the long run—only the price level, not the Real GDP level or the unemployment rate. Stated differently, changes in *AD* in an economy have no long-run effect on the Real GDP that a country produces or on its unemployment rate; changes in *AD* change only the price level in the long run.

## Chapter 10
### CHAPTER 10, PAGE 212

1. They mean that an economy may not self-regulate at Natural Real GDP ($Q_N$). Instead, an economy can get stuck in a recessionary gap.

2. To say that the economy is self-regulating is the same as saying that prices and wages are flexible and adjust quickly. They are just two ways of describing the same thing.

3. Aggregate demand may be too low mainly because Say's law may not hold in a money economy. This raises the question: Why *doesn't* Say's law hold in a money economy? Keynes argued that an increase in saving (which leads to a decline in demand) does not necessarily bring about an equal amount of additional investment (which would lead to an increase in

demand) because neither saving nor investment is exclusively affected by changes in the interest rate. See Exhibit 1 for the way Keynes might have used numbers to explain his position.

## CHAPTER 10, PAGE 217

1. Autonomous consumption is one of the components of overall consumption. To illustrate, look at the consumption function: $C = C_0 + (MPC \times Y_d)$. The part of overall consumption ($C$) that is autonomous is $C_0$, and this part does not depend on disposable income. The part of consumption that does depend on disposable income (i.e., that changes as disposable income changes) is the ($MPC \times Y_d$) part. For example, assume the $MPC = 0.80$. If $Y_d$ rises by $1,000, then consumption goes up by $800.

2. $\dfrac{1}{1 - 0.70} = \dfrac{1}{0.30} = 3.33$

3. The multiplier falls. For example, if $MPC = 0.20$, then the multiplier is 1.25, but if $MPC = 0.80$, then the multiplier is 5.

## CHAPTER 10, PAGE 221

1. Keynes believed that the economy may not always self-regulate itself at Natural Real GDP. In other words, households and businesses (the private sector of the economy) are not always capable of generating enough aggregate demand in the economy so that the economy equilibrates at Natural Real GDP.

2. The increase in autonomous spending will lead to a greater increase in total spending and to a shift rightward in the $AD$ curve. If the economy is operating in the horizontal section of the Keynesian $AS$ curve, Real GDP will rise and there will be no change in prices.

3. Agree. The economist who believes the economy is inherently unstable sees a role for government, which is supposed to stabilize the economy at Natural Real GDP. The economist who believes the economy is self-regulating (capable of moving itself to Natural Real GDP) sees little if any role for government in the economy because the economy is already doing the job government would supposedly do.

## CHAPTER 10, PAGE 227

1. When $TP > TE$, firms are producing and offering for sale more units of goods and services than consumers want to buy. As a result, business inventories rise above optimal levels. In reaction, firms cut back on their production of goods and services. This leads to a decline in Real GDP. Real GDP stops falling when $TP = TE$.

2. When $TE > TP$, consumers want to buy more than firms are producing and offering for sale. As a result, business inventories fall below optimal levels. In reaction, firms increase the production of goods and services. This leads to a rise in Real GDP. Real GDP stops rising when $TP = TE$.

# Chapter 11

## CHAPTER 11, PAGE 239

1. With a proportional income tax, the tax rate is constant as one's income rises. With a progressive income tax, the tax rate rises as one's income rises (up to some point). With a regressive income tax, the tax rate falls as one's income rises.

2. In 2007, the top 5 percent of income earners received 37.44 percent of all income and paid 60.63 percent of all income taxes.

3. Individual income tax, corporate income tax, and Social Security taxes.

4. The cyclical budget deficit is the part of the budget deficit that is the result of a downturn in economic activity.

## CHAPTER 11, PAGE 245

1. If crowding out does not occur, expansionary fiscal policy is predicted to increase aggregate demand, and if the economy is in a recessionary gap, either reduce or eliminate the gap. However, if the crowding out is, say, complete, then expansionary fiscal policy will not meet its objective. For example, suppose government purchases rise by $100 million, and private spending decreases by $100 million. There is no net effect on aggregate demand.

2. Suppose the economy is currently in a recessionary gap in time period 1. Expansionary fiscal policy is needed to remove the economy out of its recessionary gap, but the fiscal policy lags (data lag, wait-and-see lag, etc.) may be so long that by the time the fiscal policy is implemented, the economy has moved itself out of the recessionary gap, making the expansionary fiscal policy not only unnecessary but potentially capable of moving the economy into an inflationary gap. Exhibit 5 depicts the process.

3. The federal government spends more on a particular program. As a result, the budget deficit grows, and the federal government increases its demand for loanable funds (or credit) to finance the larger deficit. Because of the heightened demand for loanable funds, the interest rate rises; and in response to the higher interest rate, business firms cut back on investment. An increase in government spending thus has indirectly led to a decline in investment spending.

## CHAPTER 11, PAGE 249

1. Suppose that a person's taxable income rises by $1,000 to $45,000 and that her taxes rise from $10,000 to $10,390 as a result. Her marginal tax rate—the percentage of additional taxable income paid in taxes—is 39 percent. Her average tax rate—the percentage of her (total) income paid in taxes—is 23 percent.

2. Not necessarily. A rise in revenues depends on whether the percentage rise in tax rates is greater than or less than the percentage fall in the tax base. Here's a simple example: Suppose the average tax rate is 10 percent and the tax base is $100. Tax revenues equal $10. If the tax rate rises to 12 percent (a 20 percent rise) and the tax base falls to $90 (a 10 percent fall), tax revenues rise to $10.80. In other words, if the tax rate rises by a greater percentage than the tax base falls, tax revenues rise. Now suppose that the tax base falls to $70 (a 30 percent fall) instead of to $90. Now tax revenues are $8.40. In other words, if the tax rate rises by a smaller percentage than the tax base falls, tax revenues fall.

# Chapter 12

## CHAPTER 12, PAGE 258

1. Money evolved because individuals wanted to make trading easier (less time-consuming). This desire motivated individuals to accept the good (in a barter economy) that had greater acceptability than all other goods. In time, the effect

snowballed, and finally the good that initially had greater acceptability became widely accepted for purposes of exchange. At this point, the good became money.

2. No. M1 will fall, but M2 will not rise; it will remain constant. To illustrate, suppose M1 = $400 and M2 = $600. If people remove $100 from checkable deposits, M1 will decline to $300. For purposes of illustration, think of M2 as equal to M1 + money market accounts. The M1 component of M2 falls by $100, but the money market accounts component rises by $100; so there is no net effect on M2. In conclusion, M1 falls and M2 remains constant.

3. In a barter (moneyless) economy, a double coincidence of wants will not occur for every transaction. When it does not occur, the cost of the transaction increases because more time must be spent to complete the trade. In a money economy, money is acceptable for every transaction; so a double coincidence of wants is not necessary. All buyers offer money for what they want to buy, and all sellers accept money for what they want to sell.

## CHAPTER 12, PAGE 260

1. The bank's reserves remain constant. Since reserves equal bank deposits at the Fed plus vault cash, removing $5 million from bank deposits at the Fed and adding the $5 million to vault cash keeps the total dollar amount of reserves constant.

2. Required reserves = $r \times$ Checkable deposits, where $r$ = required reserve ratio. If checkable deposits equal $87 million and required reserves equal 6 million, then $r$ equals the required reserves divided by checkable deposits: $6 million ÷ $87 million = a required reserve ratio of 6.89.

3. Reserves = Required reserves + Excess reserves. If reserves are $6 million and excess reserves are $4 million, then required reserves are $2 million. Required reserves = $r \times$ Checkable deposits, where $r$ = required reserve ratio. If required reserves are $2 million and $r$ = 8 percent, then checkable deposits must equal $25 million; 8 percent of $25 million is $2 million.

## CHAPTER 12, PAGE 265

1. It is a moral hazard problem. A moral hazard problem exists when one party to a transaction changes his or her behavior in a way that is hidden from and costly to the other party. By promising to pay Samantha's expenses over $1,000, Jack provides Samantha with an incentive to push her expenses beyond $1,000, especially if she thinks her expenses will be close to $1,000. Simply put, Samantha has an incentive to act in a way that is hidden from and potentially costly to Jack. How might Jack lessen the moral hazard problem? Perhaps he could promise to pay a certain percentage of each dollar of Samantha's expenses over $1,000 instead of promising to pay every dollar of them.

2. A bank's capital or net worth is equal to the difference between its assets and liabilities. As bank A's assets decline in value (because some loans are not being repaid), the difference between its assets and liabilities diminishes; so its bank capital diminishes. If assets fall below liabilities, the bank will end up with negative bank capital or net worth.

3. Financial intermediaries essentially bring lenders and borrowers together. For example, Smith wants to lend $100 and Jones wants to borrow $100, but neither Smith nor Jones is in contact with the other. Instead of dealing with each other directly, both Smith and Jones go to a bank. Smith deposits $100 into the bank, and then the bank lends some or all of the $100 to Jones.

## Chapter 13
### CHAPTER 13, PAGE 274

1. Federal Reserve Bank of New York.

2. To control the money supply.

3. It means the Fed stands ready to lend funds to banks that are suffering cash management, or liquidity, problems.

### CHAPTER 13, PAGE 281

1. a. Money supply falls.
   b. Money supply rises.
   c. Money supply falls.

2. The federal funds rate is the interest rate one bank charges another bank for a loan. The discount rate is the interest rate the Fed charges a bank for a loan.

3. Reserves in bank A rise; reserves in the banking system remain the same (bank B loses the reserves that bank A borrowed).

4. Reserves in bank A rise; reserves in the banking system rise because there is no offset in reserves for any other bank.

## Chapter 14
### CHAPTER 14, PAGE 295

1. If $M \times V$ increases, total expenditures increase. In other words, people spend more. For example, instead of spending $3 billion on goods and services, they spend $4 billion. But more spending (greater total expenditures) means that there must be greater total sales. $P \times Q$ represents this total dollar value of sales.

2. The equation of exchange is a truism: $MV$ necessarily equals $PQ$. This is similar to saying that $2 + 2$ necessarily equals 4. It cannot be otherwise. The simple quantity theory of money, which is built on the equation of exchange, can be tested against real-world events. The simple quantity theory of money assumes that both velocity and Real GDP are constant and then, based on these assumptions, predicts that changes in the money supply will be strictly proportional to changes in the price level. This prediction can be measured against real-world data. So the simple quantity theory of money may offer insights into how the economy works. The equation of exchange does not do this.

3. a. The $AD$ curve shifts rightward.
   b. The $AD$ curve shifts leftward.
   c. The $AD$ curve shifts rightward.
   d. The $AD$ curve shifts leftward.

### CHAPTER 14, PAGE 298

1. a. As velocity rises, the $AD$ curve shifts to the right. In the short run, $P$ rises and $Q$ rises. In the long run, $Q$ will return to its original level, and $P$ will be higher than it was in the short run.

b. As velocity falls, the *AD* curve shifts to the left. In the short run, *P* falls and *Q* falls. In the long run, *Q* will return to its original level, and *P* will be lower than it was in the short run.

c. As the money supply rises, the *AD* curve shifts to the right. In the short run, *P* rises and *Q* rises. In the long run, *Q* will return to its original level, and *P* will be higher than it was in the short run.

d. As the money supply falls, the *AD* curve shifts to the left. In the short run, *P* falls and *Q* falls. In the long run, *Q* will return to its original level, and *P* will be lower than it was in the short run.

2. Yes, a change in velocity can offset a change in the money supply (on aggregate demand). Suppose that the money supply rises and velocity falls. A rise in the money supply shifts the *AD* curve to the right, and a fall in velocity shifts the *AD* curve to the left. If the strength of each change is the same, *AD* does not change.

## CHAPTER 14, PAGE 304

1. This question cannot be answered based on the information given. We know only that three prices have gone up; we don't know if other prices (in the economy) have gone up, if other prices have gone down, or if some have gone up and others have gone down. To determine whether inflation has occurred, we have to know what has happened to the price level, not simply to three prices.

2. No. For continued inflation (continued increases in the price level) to be the result of continued decreases in *SRAS*, workers would have to continually ask for and receive higher wages while output was dropping and the unemployment rate rising. This combination of circumstances is not likely.

3. Continued inflation.

## CHAPTER 14, PAGE 310

1. 3 percent.

2. Yes, it is possible. This would occur if the expectations effect immediately set in and outweighed the liquidity effect.

3. Certainly, the Fed directly affects the supply of loanable funds and the interest rate through an open market operation. But it works as a catalyst to indirectly affect the loanable funds market and the interest rate via the changes in Real GDP, the price level, and the expected inflation rate. We can say this: The Fed directly affects the interest rate via the liquidity effect, and it indirectly affects the interest rate via the income, price-level, and expectations effects.

# Chapter 15

## CHAPTER 15, PAGE 320

1. Smith buys a bond for a face value of $10,000 that promises to pay a 10 percent interest rate each year for 10 years. In one year, though, bonds are offered for a face value of $10,000 that pay an 11 percent interest rate each year for 10 years. If Smith wants to sell his bond, he won't be able to sell it for $10,000. No one today will pay $10,000 for a bond that pays a 10 percent interest rate when a new $10,000 bond pays an 11 percent interest rate. Smith will have to lower the price of his

bond if he wants to sell it. Thus, as interest rates rise, the bond prices of old or existing bonds decrease.

2. We disagree for two reasons. First, if the money market is in the liquidity trap, a rise in the money supply will not affect interest rates and therefore will not affect investment or the goods and services market. Second, even if the money market is not in the liquidity trap, a rise in the money supply affects the goods and services market not directly but indirectly: The rise in the money supply lowers the interest rate, causing investment to rise (assuming investment is not interest insensitive). As investment rises, the *AD* curve shifts rightward, affecting the goods and services market. In the Keynesian transmission mechanism, an important intermediate market lies between the money market and the goods and services market. Thus, the money market can affect the goods and services market only indirectly.

3. A rise in the money supply brings about an excess supply of money in the money market that flows to the goods and services market, stimulating aggregate demand.

## CHAPTER 15, PAGE 325

1. Keynesians believe that prices and wages are inflexible downward but not upward. They believe it is more likely that natural forces will move an economy out of an inflationary gap than out of a recessionary gap.

2. Suppose the economy is regulating itself out of a recessionary gap, but Fed officials don't know it. Thinking that the economy is stuck in a recessionary gap, the Fed increases the money supply. When the money supply is felt in the goods and services market, the *AD* curve intersects the *SRAS* curve (which has been moving rightward, unbeknownst to officials) at a point that represents an inflationary gap. In other words, the Fed has moved the economy from a recessionary gap to an inflationary gap instead of from a recessionary gap to long-run equilibrium at the Natural Real GDP level.

3. It makes it stronger, *ceteris paribus*. If the economy can't get itself out of a recessionary gap, then the case is stronger that the Fed should. However, expansionary monetary policy may still not work ideally; the correct implementation of the policy may meet with problems.

## CHAPTER 15, PAGE 329

1. This is an open-ended question whose answer depends on many factors. First, what does the rule specify? Not all rules are alike. Second, the answer depends on the stability and predictability of velocity. For example, suppose the rule specifies that each year the money supply will rise by the average annual growth rate in Real GDP. If velocity is constant, this will produce price stability. But if velocity is extremely volatile, changes in velocity might offset changes in the money supply, leading to deflation instead of price stability. For example, suppose Real GDP rises by 3 percent and the money supply increases by 3 percent, but velocity decreases by 3 percent. The change in velocity offsets the change in the money supply, leaving a net effect of a 3 percent rise in Real GDP. This, then, would lead to a 3 percent decline in the price level.

2. Here is the Taylor rule specification: Federal funds rate target = 1.5 (4 percent) + 0.5 (5 percent) + 1 = 9.5 percent.

# Chapter 16

## CHAPTER 16, PAGE 341

1. A given Phillips curve identifies different combinations of inflation and unemployment; for example, 4 percent inflation with 5 percent unemployment and 2 percent inflation with 7 percent unemployment. For these combinations of inflation and unemployment to be permanent, there must be only one (downward-sloping) Phillips curve that never changes.

2. Sometimes there is and sometimes there isn't. Look at Exhibit 3. Unemployment is higher and inflation is lower in 1964 than in 1965; so there is a tradeoff between these two years. But both unemployment and inflation are higher in 1980 than in 1979; between these two years, there is no tradeoff between inflation and unemployment.

3. Workers are fooled into thinking that the inflation rate is lower than it is. In other words, they underestimate the inflation rate and therefore overestimate the purchasing power of their wages.

## CHAPTER 16, PAGE 351

1. No. PIP says that, under certain conditions, neither expansionary fiscal policy nor expansionary monetary policy will be able to increase Real GDP and lower the unemployment rate in the short run. The conditions are that the policy change is anticipated correctly, individuals form their expectations rationally, and wages and prices are flexible.

2. None. Given an unanticipated increase in aggregate demand, the economy moves from point 1 to 2 (in Exhibit 10) in the short run and then to point 3. This occurs whether people are holding rational or adaptive expectations.

3. In the short run, the price level rises and Real GDP declines. In the long run, the price level rises and Real GDP is constant.

## CHAPTER 16, PAGE 353

1. Both. The relevant question is whether the decline in the money supply was caused by a change on the supply side of the economy. If the answer is no, then the decline in the money supply is consistent with a demand-induced business cycle. If the answer is yes, then it is consistent with a supply-induced (real) business cycle.

2. New Keynesians believe that prices and wages are somewhat inflexible; new classical economists believe that prices and wages are flexible.

# Chapter 17

## CHAPTER 17, PAGE 371

1. This is shown in Exhibit 4. A decline in taxes shifts the labor supply curve to the right, which increases the equilibrium level of labor in the labor market. More labor generates more output (Real GDP), as shown in Exhibit 4(b). And more Real GDP is consistent with the *LRAS* curve having shifted to the right.

2. Physical capital consists of the produced goods that are used as inputs for further production, such as factories, machinery, tools, computers, and buildings. Human capital refers to the knowledge and skills individuals acquire through education, training, and experience.

3. In neoclassical growth theory, technology was, in a sense, "just there." Technological advances just happened, but how these advances happened was not fully understood. Technology was something that was exogenous—outside the economic system and outside of our control. In new growth theory, technology is said to be endogenous. It can be increased or decreased by the amount of resources devoted to it. Also, technology is viewed as being related to ideas.

4. Labor is the movement factor, and both capital and the technology coefficient are shift factors.

# Chapter 18

## CHAPTER 18, PAGE 378

1. If a bank has assets of $100 and liabilities of $80, it has a net worth or capital of $20. If its assets decline in value from $100 to $90, the bank's net worth falls from $20 to $10, but the bank is still solvent. In other words, the bank's net worth or capital stood between the bank and insolvency. The bigger the net worth or capital is, the bigger the buffer will be between declining asset values and insolvency. This bank can withstand a $20 decline in assets before becoming insolvent. A bank with a bigger net worth or capital could withstand a greater decline in assets before becoming insolvent.

2. If a bank has assets of $100 and liabilities of $80, it has a net worth or capital of $20. If the bank's assets decline in value by $30, the bank now has a negative net worth or capital of −$10. As a result, the bank may go out of business or pull back on its lending activities. Either way, there is less lending activity.

3. A financial crisis occurs when financial firms and markets have problems that make it difficult for people to obtain loans from banks and other financial institutions.

## CHAPTER 18, PAGE 383

1. The global-savings-glut explanation is that in some countries saving was greater than investment; so the excess savings flowed into the United States and lowered interest rates (including mortgage interest rates). The low mortgage rates fueled house buying, which pushed up house prices. The Fed-low-interest-rate explanation is that the Fed kept the federal funds rate low, which kept mortgage interest rates low. The low mortgage interest rates fueled house buying, which pushed up house prices.

2. Taylor concludes that when we compare actual Fed monetary policy with the Taylor rule monetary policy, monetary policy was "too expansionary" during the early 2000s. John Taylor believes that this deviation from the rule brought about the "too low" interest rates that led to rising house prices in the United States. One piece of evidence in his favor is that there is a strong correlation between a housing boom in different countries (where housing boom is defined in terms of housing investment as a percentage of GDP) and deviations from the Taylor rule. For example, within OECD countries, the countries whose monetary policies deviated most from the Taylor Rule had bigger housing booms than those whose monetary policies deviated less.

## CHAPTER 18, PAGE 391

1. Suppose a bank has $100 in assets and $97 in liabilities. The bank therefore has $3 in capital. Its leverage ratio rises to 100 to 3 or 331/3 to 1. If the assets of the bank decline by 4 percent to $96, the bank is now insolvent with negative capital of $-$1. Contrast this with a bank that has $100 in assets and $90 in assets. The bank has $10 in capital, and its leverage ratio is 10 to 1. If the assets of the bank decline by 4 percent to $96, the bank remains solvent with capital of $6. The lesson: The greater the leverage ratio is, the more likely it is that a decline in asset values will result in insolvency.

2. We agree. Suppose the assets held by banks begin to decline in value, and, as a result, the banks end up lending less. Reduced bank lending reduces economic activity, resulting in less production, a decline in sales, and rising unemployment in the real sector. Because of these problems, some people in the real sector, who earlier took out loans from banks, are unable to repay their loans, thus exacerbating the problems that already exist in the financial sector.

3. Regulatory capital arbitrage is a means of changing the composition of assets in such a way as to lower the overall amount of capital a financial institution holds for a given level of assets.

## Chapter 19
### CHAPTER 19, PAGE 406

1. Economist A believes that the percentage change in the tax rate will be smaller than the percentage change in the tax base. Economist B believes the percentage change in the tax rate will be larger than the percentage change in the tax base.

2. When government spends $1, the entire $1 enters the spending stream, but when government cuts taxes by $1, individuals spend some of the dollar they now get to keep and save some of it. For example, they might spend 60¢ of the dollar and save 40¢.

3. Agree. At any given point in time, government has a specific size and scope. If economist A believes the optimal size and scope of government is greater than the current size and scope, then she is more likely to recommend increased government purchases over tax cuts if she deems an expansionary fiscal policy measure is needed to sti mulate the economy (holding all other things equal, such as the size of the government spending multiplier and the tax multiplier, etc.). If economist B believes the optimal size and scope of government is less than the current scope, then he is more likely to recommend tax cuts over increased government purchases if he deems an expansionary fiscal policy measure is needed to stimulate the economy.

## Chapter 20
### CHAPTER 20, PAGE 417

1. No. The model doesn't say every politician has to do these things; it simply predicts that politicians who do these things have an increased chance of winning the election in a two-person race.

2. Voters may want more information from politicians, but supplying that information is not always in the best interests of political candidates. When they speak in specific terms, politicians are often labeled as being at one end or the other of the political spectrum. But politicians don't win elections by being in the right wing or left wing; they win elections by being in the middle.

3. Yes. In the cost equation of voting, we included (1) the cost of driving to the polls, (2) the cost of standing in line, and (3) the cost of filling out the ballot. Bad weather (heavy rain, snow, ice) would likely raise the cost of driving to the polls and standing in line, therefore raising the cost of voting. The higher the cost of voting is, the less likely it is that people will vote, *ceteris paribus.*

### CHAPTER 20, PAGE 419

1. 2 units

2. In Example 2 with equal taxes, 1 unit received a simple majority of the votes. Person *C* was made worse off because his *MPB* for the first unit of good *Y* was $100, but he ended up paying a tax of $120 and was worse off by $20.

### CHAPTER 20, PAGE 425

1. Both farmers and consumers are affected by federal agricultural policy, but not in the same way and not to the same degree. Federal agricultural policy directly affects farmers' incomes, usually by a large amount. It indirectly affects consumers' costs, but not as much as it affects farmers' incomes. Simply put, farmers have more at stake than consumers when it comes to federal agricultural policy. People tend to be better informed about matters that mean more to them.

2. The legislation is more likely to pass when group A includes 10 million persons because the wider the dispersal of the costs of the legislation, the greater the likelihood is of passage. When costs are widely dispersed, the cost to any one individual is so small that she or he is unlikely to lobby against the legislation.

3. Examples include teachers saying that more money for education will help the country compete in the global marketplace; domestic car manufacturers saying that tariffs on foreign imports will save American jobs and U.S. manufacturing; farmers saying that subsidies to farmers will preserve the "American" farm and a way of life that Americans cherish. Whether any of these groups is right or wrong is not the point. The point is that special interest groups are likely to advance their arguments (good or bad) with public interest talk.

4. Rent seeking is socially wasteful because the resources that are used to seek rent could instead be used to produce goods and services.

## Chapter 21
### CHAPTER 21, PAGE 435

1. For the United States, $1X = 1/6Y$ or $1Y = 6X$. For England, $1X = 2Y$ or $1Y = 1/2X$. Let's focus on the opportunity cost of $1X$ in each country. In the United States, $1X = 1/6Y$, and in Great Britain, $1X = 2Y$. Terms of trade that are between these two endpoints would be favorable for the two countries. For example, suppose we choose $1X = 1Y$. This is good for the United States because it would prefer to give up $1X$ and get $1Y$ in trade than to give up $1X$ and get only $1/6Y$ (without trade). Similarly, Great Britain would prefer to give up $1Y$ and get $1X$ in trade than to give up $1Y$ and get only $1/2X$ (without trade).

Any terms of trade between $1X = 1/6Y$ and $1X = 2Y$ will be favorable to the two countries.

2. Yes. This is what the theory of comparative advantage shows. Exhibit 1 shows that the United States could produce more of both food and clothing than Japan. Still, the United States benefits from specialization and trade, as shown in Exhibit 2. In column 5 of this exhibit, the United States can consume 10 more units of food by specializing and trading.

3. No. It is the desire to buy low and sell high (earn a profit) that pushes countries into producing and trading at a comparative advantage. Government officials do not collect cost data and then issue orders to firms in the country to produce X, Y, or Z. We have not drawn the PPFs in this chapter and identified the cost differences between countries to show what countries actually do in the real world. We described things technically simply to show how countries benefit from specialization and trade.

## CHAPTER 21, PAGE 443

1. Domestic producers benefit because producers' surplus rises; domestic consumers lose because consumers' surplus falls. Also, government benefits in that it receives the tariff revenue. Moreover, consumers lose more than producers and government gains; so tariffs result in a net loss.

2. Consumers' surplus falls by more than producers' surplus rises.

3. With a tariff, the government receives tariff revenue. With a quota, it does not. In the latter case, the revenue that would have gone to government goes, instead, to the importers who get to satisfy the quota.

4. Infant or new domestic industries need to be protected from older, more established competitors until they are mature enough to compete on an equal basis. Tariffs and quotas provide these infant industries the time they need.

# Chapter 22

## CHAPTER 22, PAGE 455

1. A debit. When an American enters into a transaction in which he has to supply U.S. dollars in the foreign exchange market (to demand a foreign currency), the transaction is recorded as a debit.

2. We do not have enough information to answer this question. The merchandise trade balance is the difference between the value of *merchandise* exports and *merchandise* imports. The question gives only the value of exports and imports. "Exports" is a more inclusive term than merchandise exports. Exports include (a) merchandise exports, (b) services, and (c) income from U.S. assets abroad (see Exhibit 2). Similarly, "imports" is a more inclusive term than merchandise imports. It includes (a) merchandise imports, (b) services, and (c) income from foreign assets in the United States.

3. The merchandise trade balance includes fewer transactions than are included in the current account balance. The merchandise trade balance is the summary statistic for merchandise exports and merchandise imports. The current account balance is the summary statistic for exports of goods and services (which include merchandise exports), imports of goods and services (which include merchandise imports), and net unilateral transfers abroad (see Exhibit 2).

## CHAPTER 22, PAGE 462

1. As the demand for dollars increases, the supply of pesos increases. For example, suppose someone in Mexico wants to buy something produced in the United States. The American wants to be paid in dollars, but the Mexican has pesos, not dollars. So she has to buy dollars with pesos; in other words, she has to supply pesos to buy dollars. Thus, as she demands more dollars, she will necessarily have to supply more pesos.

2. The dollar is said to have appreciated (against the peso) when it takes more pesos to buy a dollar and fewer dollars to buy a peso. For this to occur, either the demand for dollars must increase (which means the supply of pesos increases) or the supply of dollars must decrease (which means the demand for pesos decreases). To see this graphically, look at Exhibit 5(b). The only way for the peso price per dollar to rise (on the vertical axis) is for either the demand curve for dollars to shift to the right or the supply curve of dollars to shift to the left. Each of these occurrences is mirrored in the market for pesos in part (a) of the exhibit.

3. *Ceteris paribus,* the dollar will depreciate relative to the franc. As incomes for Americans rise, the demand for Swiss goods rises. This increases the demand for francs and the supply of dollars on the foreign exchange market. In turn, this leads to a depreciated dollar and an appreciated franc.

4. The theory states that the exchange rate between any two currencies will adjust to reflect changes in the relative price levels of the two countries. For example, suppose the U.S. price level rises 5 percent and Mexico's price level remains constant. According to the PPP theory, the U.S. dollar will depreciate 5 percent relative to the Mexican peso.

## CHAPTER 22, PAGE 468

1. The terms *overvalued* and *undervalued* refer to the equilibrium exchange rate: the exchange rate at which the quantity demanded and the quantity supplied of a currency are the same in the foreign exchange market. Let's suppose the equilibrium exchange rate is 0.10 USD = 1 MXN. This is the same as saying that 10 pesos = $1 If the exchange rate is fixed at 0.12 USD = 1 MXN (which is the same as 8.33 pesos = $1), the peso is overvalued and the dollar is undervalued. Specifically, a currency is overvalued if 1 unit of it fetches more of another currency than it would in equilibrium; a currency is undervalued if 1 unit of it fetches less of another currency than it would in equilibrium. In equilibrium, 1 peso would fetch $0.10, and at the current exchange rate it fetches $0.12; so the peso is overvalued. In equilibrium, $1 would fetch 10 pesos, and at the current exchange rate, it fetches only 8.33 pesos; so the dollar is undervalued.

2. An overvalued dollar means some other currency—let's say it is the Japanese yen—is undervalued. An overvalued dollar makes U.S. goods more expensive for the Japanese; so they buy fewer U.S. goods. This reduces U.S. exports. On the other hand, an undervalued yen makes Japanese goods cheaper for Americans; so they buy more Japanese goods, and the United States imports more. Thus, an overvalued dollar reduces U.S. exports and raises U.S. imports.

3. a. Dollar is overvalued.
   b. Dollar is undervalued.
   c. Dollar is undervalued.

4. When a country devalues its currency, it makes it cheaper for foreigners to buy its products.

## CHAPTER 22, PAGE 471

1. An optimal currency area is a geographic area in which exchange rates can be fixed or a common currency used without sacrificing any domestic economic goals.

2. As the demand for good Y falls, the unemployment rate in country 2 will rise, but the increase is likely to be temporary. The increased demand for good X (produced by country 1) will increase the demand for country 1's currency, leading to an appreciation in country 1's currency and a depreciation in country 2's currency. Country 1's good X will become more expensive for the residents of country 2, and they will buy less. Country 2's good Y will become less expensive for the residents of country 1, and they will buy more. As a result of the additional purchases of good Y, country 2's unemployment rate will begin to decline.

3. Labor mobility is very important in determining whether an area is an optimal currency area. Given little or no labor mobility, an area is not likely to be an optimal currency area. If there is labor mobility, an area is likely to be an optimal currency area.

# Chapter 23

## CHAPTER 23, PAGE 484

1. As some explain it, the end of the Cold War resulted in turning two different worlds (the capitalist and communist worlds) into one world. It resulted in a thawing of not only political but also economic relations between former enemies. You might not trade with your enemy, but, once that person or country is no longer your enemy, you do not feel the same need to cut him or it out of your political and economic life.

2. Globalization is the phenomenon by which individuals and businesses in any part of the world are much more affected by events elsewhere in the world than before; it is the growing integration of the national economies of the world to the degree that we may be witnessing the emergence and operation of a single worldwide economy.

3. Advancing technology can reduce both transportation and communication costs, thus making it less costly to trade with people around the world.

## CHAPTER 23, PAGE 489

1. The benefits identified in the section include (a) benefits from increased international trade, (b) greater income per person, (c) lower prices for goods, (d) greater product variety, and (e) increased productivity and innovation.

2. The costs identified in the section include (a) increased income inequality, (b) offshoring, and (c) more power for big corporations.

## CHAPTER 23, PAGE 493

1. In country A, there is an economic expansion, and real income rises. As a result, residents of the country buy more imports from country B. In country B, exports rise relative to imports, thus increasing net exports. As net exports in country B rise, the AD curve for country B shifts to the right, increasing Real GDP.

2. If the dollar appreciates, the Japanese yen depreciates. U.S. products become more expensive for the Japanese, and Japanese products become cheaper for Americans. U.S. imports will rise, U.S. exports will fall, and consequently U.S. net exports will fall. As a result, the AD curve in the United States will shift leftward, pushing down Real GDP.

## CHAPTER 23, PAGE 496

1. Foreign input prices can change directly as a result of supply conditions in the foreign country, or they can change indirectly as a result of a change in the exchange rate. In either case, as foreign input prices rise—either directly or as a result of a depreciated dollar—the U.S. SRAS curve shifts leftward. If foreign input prices fall—either directly or as a result of an appreciated dollar—the SRAS curve shifts rightward.

2. The higher real interest rates in the United States attract capital to the United States, increasing the demand for the dollar. As a result, the dollar appreciates and the yen depreciates. An appreciated dollar shifts the U.S. AD curve leftward and the U.S. SRAS curve rightward. The AD curve shifts leftward by more than the SRAS curve shifts rightward; so the price level falls.

## CHAPTER 23, PAGE 500

1. When the money supply is raised, the AD curve shifts rightward, pushing up Real GDP. Also, as a result of the increased money supply, interest rates may decline in the short run, promoting U.S. capital outflow and a depreciated dollar. As a result of the depreciated dollar, imports become more expensive for Americans, and U.S. exports become cheaper for foreigners. Imports fall and exports rise, thereby increasing net exports and *again* shifting the AD curve to the right. Real GDP rises.

2. Expansionary fiscal policy pushes the AD curve rightward and (under certain conditions) raises Real GDP. If the expansionary fiscal policy causes a deficit, then the government will have to borrow to finance the deficit, and interest rates will be pushed upward. As a result of the higher interest rates, foreign capital inflows and dollar appreciation increase, thus pushing the AD curve leftward and the SRAS curve rightward.

# Chapter 24

## CHAPTER 24, PAGE 512

1. 30

2. Stocks are purchased either for the dividends that the stocks may pay, the expected gain in price (of the stock), or both.

3. Yield equals the dividend per share (of the stock) divided by the closing price per share.

4. A P/E ratio of 23 means that the stock is selling for a share price that is 23 times its earnings per share.

## CHAPTER 24, PAGE 516

1. A bond is an IOU or a promise to pay. The issuer of a bond is borrowing funds and promising to pay back those funds (with interest) at a later date.

2. $0.07x = \$400$, so $x = \$400 \div 0.07$, or $\$5,714.29$.

3. $\$1,000/\$9,500 = 10.53$ percent

4. A municipal bond is issued by a state or local government, and a Treasury bond is issued by the federal government.

## CHAPTER 24, PAGE 519

1. A futures contract is a contract in which the seller agrees to provide a good to the buyer on a specified future date at an agreed-upon price.

2. You can buy a call option, which sells for a fraction of the cost of the stock. A call option gives the owner of the option the right to buy shares of a stock at a specified price within the time limits of the contract.

3. A put option gives the owner the right, but not the obligation, to *sell* (rather than buy, as in a call option) shares of a stock at a strike price during some period of time.

# Web Chapter 25

## CHAPTER 25

1. The farmer does so through the futures market. Specifically, she enters into a futures contract with someone who will guarantee to take delivery of her foodstuff (in the future) for a stated price. Then, if the price goes up or down between the present and the future, the farmer does not have to worry. She has locked in the price of her foodstuff.

2. If the farmer faces an inelastic demand curve, the order of preference would be (b)−(a)−(c); that is, he prefers (b) to (a) and (a) to (c). If all farmers except himself have bad weather (b), then the market supply curve of the individual farmer's product shifts to the left, bringing about a higher price. But the individual farmer's supply curve doesn't shift to the left; it stays where it is. Thus, the individual farmer sells the same amount of output at the higher price. Consequently, his total revenue rises. In (a), both the market supply curve and the individual farmer's supply curve shift left; so the farmer has less to sell at a higher price. Again, if the demand is inelastic, the individual farmer will increase his total revenue but not as much as in (b) where the individual farmer's output does not fall. Finally, in (c), the market supply curve shifts to the right, lowering price. If demand is inelastic, this lowers total revenue.

3. Increased productivity will lead to higher total revenue when demand is elastic. To illustrate, increased productivity shifts the supply curve to the right, lowering price. If demand is elastic, then the percentage rise in quantity sold is greater than the percentage fall in price; therefore, total revenue rises. In summary, increased productivity leads to higher total revenue when demand is elastic.

## CHAPTER 25

1. Because the deficiency payment is the difference between the target price and the market price, the answer depends on the market price. If the market price is, say, $4, and the target price is $7, then the deficiency payment is $3.

2. A farmer pledges a certain number of bushels of foodstuff to obtain a loan—say, 500 bushels. He receives a loan equal to the number of bushels times the designated loan rate per bushel. If the loan rate is $2 per bushel and 500 bushels are pledged, then the loan is $1,000. The farmer ends up paying back the loan with interest or keeping the loan and forfeiting the bushels of the crop. Which course of action the farmer takes depends on the market price of the crop. If the market price of the crop is higher than the loan rate, he pays back the loan and sells the crop. If the market price is less than the loan rate, he forfeits the crop. A nonrecourse loan guarantees that the farmer will not receive less than the loan rate for each bushel of his crop.

3. The effects of a price support are (a) a surplus, (b) fewer exchanges (less bought by private citizens), (c) higher prices paid by consumers of the crop (on which the support exists), and (d) government purchase and storage of the surplus crop (for which taxpayers pay).

# GLOSSARY

## A

**Absolute (Money) Price** The price of a good in money terms.

**Absolute Real Economic Growth** An increase in Real GDP from one period to the next.

**Abstract** The process (used in building a theory) of focusing on a limited number of variables to explain or predict an event.

**Accounting Profit** The difference between total revenue and explicit costs.

**Activists** Persons who argue that monetary and fiscal policies should be deliberately used to smooth out the business cycle.

**Adaptive Expectations** Expectations that individuals form from past experience and modify slowly as the present and the future become the past (i.e., as time passes).

**Adjustable Rate Mortgage** A mortgage loan where the interest rate on the loan is adjusted periodically depending on various factors.

**Adverse Selection** A phenomenon that occurs when the parties on one side of the market, who have information not known to others, self-select in a way that adversely affects the parties on the other side of the market.

**Aggregate Demand** The quantity demanded of all goods and services (Real GDP) at different price levels, *ceteris paribus.*

**Aggregate Demand (AD) Curve** The quantity demanded of all goods and services (Real GDP) at different price levels, *ceteris paribus.* A curve that shows the quantity demanded of all goods and services (Real GDP) at different price levels, *ceteris paribus.*

**Aggregate Supply** The quantity supplied of all goods and services (Real GDP) at different price levels, *ceteris paribus.*

**Antitrust Law** Legislation passed for the stated purpose of controlling monopoly power and preserving and promoting competition.

**Appreciation** An increase in the value of one currency relative to other currencies.

**Arbitrage** Buying a good at a low price and selling it for a higher price.

**Asset** Anything of value that is owned or that one has claim to and that has value.

**Asymmetric Information** Information that either the buyer or the seller in a market exchange has and that the other does not have.

**Automatic Fiscal Policy** Changes in government expenditures and/or taxes that occur automatically without (additional) congressional action.

**Autonomous Consumption** The part of consumption that is independent of disposable income.

**Average Fixed Cost (AFC)** Total fixed cost divided by quantity of output: $AFC = TFC/Q.$

**Average Total Cost (ATC), or Unit Cost** Total cost divided by quantity of output: $ATC = TC/Q.$

**Average Variable Cost (AVC)** Total variable cost divided by quantity of output: $AVC = TVC/Q.$

**Average-Marginal Rule** When the marginal magnitude is above the average magnitude, the average magnitude rises; when the marginal magnitude is below the average magnitude, the average magnitude falls.

## B

**Bad** Anything from which individuals receive disutility or dissatisfaction.

**Balance of Payments** A periodic (usually annual) statement of the money value of all transactions between residents of one country and the residents of all other countries.

**Balanced Budget** The budget when government expenditures equal tax revenues.

**Balance Sheet** A record of the assets and liabilities of a bank.

**Barter** Exchanging goods and services for other goods and services without the use of money.

**Base Year** The year chosen as a point of reference or basis of comparison for prices in other years; a benchmark year.

**Board of Governors** The governing body of the Federal Reserve System.

**Bond** An IOU, or promise to pay.

**Budget Constraint** All the combinations or bundles of two goods a person can purchase, given a certain money income and prices for the two goods.

**Budget Deficit** The deficit when government expenditures are greater than tax revenues.

**Budget Surplus** The surplus when tax revenues are greater than government expenditures.

**Business Firm** An entity that employs factors of production (resources) to produce goods and services to be sold to consumers, other firms, or the government.

## C

**Capital** Produced goods that can be used as inputs for further production, such as factories, machinery, tools, computers, and buildings.

**Capital Account** The account in the balance of payments that includes all payments related to the purchase and sale of assets and to borrowing and lending activities. Components include outflow of U.S. capital and inflow of foreign capital.

**Capital Account Balance** The summary statistic for the outflow of U.S. capital equal to the difference between the outflow of U.S. capital and the inflow of foreign capital.

**Capital Consumption Allowance (Depreciation)** The estimated amount of capital goods used up in production through natural wear, obsolescence, and accidental destruction.

**Capture Theory of Regulation** A theory holding that no matter what the motive is for the initial regulation and the establishment of the regulatory agency, eventually the agency will be captured (controlled) by the special interests of the industry being regulated.

**Cartel** An organization of firms that reduces output and increases price in an effort to increase joint profits.

**Cartel Theory** A theory of oligopoly in which oligopolistic firms act as if there were only one firm in the industry.

**Cash Leakage** Occurs when funds are held as currency instead of deposited into a checking account.

*Ceteris Paribus* A Latin term meaning "all other things constant" or "nothing else changes."

**Checkable Deposits** Deposits on which checks can be written.

**Closed Economy** An economy that does not trade goods and services with other countries.

**Closed Shop** An organization in which an employee must belong to the union before he or she can be hired.

**Coase Theorem** In the case of trivial or zero transaction costs, the property rights assignment does not matter to the resource allocative outcome.

**Collective Bargaining** The process whereby wage rates and other issues are determined by a union bargaining with management on behalf of all union members.

**Comparative Advantage** The advantage a country has when it can produce a good at lower opportunity cost than someone else or than another country can.

**Complements** Two goods that are used jointly in consumption. If two goods are complements, the demand for one rises as the price of the other falls (or the demand for one falls as the price of the other rises).

**Complete Crowding Out** A decrease in one or more components of private spending that completely offsets the increase in government spending.

**Concentration Ratio** The percentage of industry sales (or assets, output, labor force, or some other factor) accounted for by $x$ number of firms in the industry.

**Conglomerate Merger** A merger between companies in different industries.

**Constant Returns to Scale** The condition when inputs are increased by some percentage and output increases by an equal percentage, causing unit costs to remain constant.

**Constant-Cost Industry** An industry in which average total costs do not change as (industry) output increases or decreases when firms enter or exit the industry, respectively.

**Consumer Equilibrium** Equilibrium that occurs when the consumer has spent all income and the marginal utilities per dollar spent on each good purchased are equal:

$MU_A/P_A = MU_B/P_B = \ldots = MU_Z/P_Z$, where the letters A–Z represent all the goods a person buys.

**Consumer Price Index (CPI)** A widely cited index number for the price level; the weighted average of prices of a specific set of goods and services purchased by a typical household; a widely cited index number for the price level.

**Consumers' Surplus (CS)** The difference between the maximum price a buyer is willing and able to pay for a good or service and the price actually paid: $CS =$ Maximum buying price − Price paid.

**Consumption** The sum of spending on durable goods, nondurable goods, and services.

**Consumption Function** The relationship between consumption and disposable income. In the consumption function used in this text, consumption is directly related to disposable income and is positive even at zero disposable income: $C = C_0 + (MPC)(Y_d)$.

**Contestable Market** A market in which entry is easy and exit is costless, new firms can produce the product at the same cost as current firms, and exiting firms can easily dispose of their fixed assets by selling them.

**Continued Inflation** A continued increase in the price level.

**Contractionary Fiscal Policy** Decreases in government expenditures and/or increases in taxes to achieve economic goals.

**Contractionary Monetary Policy** The policy by which the Fed decreases the money supply.

**Credit** In the balance of payments, any transaction that creates a demand for the country's currency in the foreign exchange market.

**Cross Elasticity of Demand** A measure of the responsiveness in quantity demanded of one good to changes in the price of another good.

**Crowding Out** The decrease in private expenditures that occurs as a consequence of increased government spending or the financing needs of a budget deficit.

**Currency** Coins and paper money.

**Current Account** The account in the balance of payments that includes all payments related to the purchase and sale of goods and services; components of the account include exports, imports, and net unilateral transfers abroad.

**Current Account Balance** In the balance of payments, the summary statistic for exports of goods and services, imports of goods and services, and net unilateral transfers abroad.

**Cyclical Deficit** The part of the budget deficit that is a result of a downturn in economic activity.

**Cyclical Unemployment Rate** The difference between the unemployment rate and the natural unemployment rate.

# D

**Deadweight Loss** The loss to society of not producing the competitive, or supply-and-demand-determined, level of output.

**Deadweight Loss of Monopoly** The net value (value to buyers over and above costs to suppliers) of the difference between the competitive quantity of output (where $P = MC$) and the monopoly quantity of output (where $P > MC$); the loss of not producing the competitive quantity of output.

**Debit** In the balance of payments, any transaction that supplies the country's currency in the foreign exchange market.

**Decisions at the Margin** Decision making characterized by weighing the additional (marginal) benefits of a change against the additional (marginal) costs of a change with respect to current conditions.

**Decreasing-Cost Industry** An industry in which average total costs decrease as output increases and increase as output decreases when firms enter and exit the industry, respectively.

**Demand** The willingness and ability of buyers to purchase different quantities of a good at different prices during a specific time period.

**Demand Curve** The graphical representation of the law of demand.

**Demand for Money (Balances)** The inverse relationship between the quantity demanded of money balances and the price of holding money balances.

**Demand Schedule** The numerical tabulation of the quantity demanded of a good at different prices. A demand schedule is the numerical representation of the law of demand.

**Depreciation** A decrease in the value of one currency relative to other currencies.

**Derived Demand** Demand that is the result of some other demand. For example, factor demand is the result of the demand for the products that the factors go to produce.

**Devaluation** A government action that changes the exchange rate by lowering the official price of a currency.

**Diamond-Water Paradox** The observation that things with the greatest value in use sometimes have little value in exchange and things with little value in use sometimes have the greatest value in exchange.

**Direct Finance** Borrowers and lenders come together in a market setting, such as in the bond market.

**Directly Related** Two variables are directly related if they change in the same way.

**Discount Loan** A loan the Fed makes to a commerical bank.

**Discount Rate** The interest rate the Fed charges depository institutions that borrow reserves from it.

**Discretionary Fiscal Policy** Deliberate changes of government expenditures and/or taxes to achieve economic goals.

**Diseconomies of Scale** The condition when inputs are increased by some percentage and output increases by a smaller percentage, causing unit costs to rise.

**Disequilibrium** A state of either surplus or shortage in a market.

**Disequilibrium Price** A price other than equilibrium price; a price at which quantity demanded does not equal quantity supplied.

**Disposable Income** The portion of personal income that can be used for consumption or saving. It is equal to personal income minus personal taxes (especially income taxes).

**Disutility** The dissatisfaction one receives from a bad.

**Dividend** A share of the profits of a corporation distributed to stockholders.

**Double Coincidence of Wants** In a barter economy, a requirement, which must be met before a trade can be made, that a trader must find another trader who is willing to trade what the first trader wants and at the same time wants what the first trader has.

**Double Counting** Counting a good more than once when computing GDP.

**Dow Jones Industrial Average (DJIA)** The most popular, widely cited indicator of day-to-day stock market activity. The DJIA is a weighted average of 30 widely traded stocks on the New York Stock Exchange.

**Dumping** The sale of goods abroad at a price below their cost and below the price charged in the domestic market.

# E

**Economic Growth** Increases in Real GDP.

**Economic Profit** The difference between total revenue and total cost, including both explicit and implicit costs.

**Economic Rent** Payment in excess of opportunity costs.

**Economics** The science of scarcity; the science of how individuals and societies deal with the fact that wants are greater than the limited resources available to satisfy those wants.

**Economies of Scale** Economies that exist when inputs are increased by some percentage and output increases by a greater percentage, causing unit costs to fall.

**Efficiency** Exists when marginal benefits equal marginal costs.

**Efficiency Wage Models** These models hold that it is sometimes in the best interest of business firms to pay their employees higher-than-equilibrium wage rates.

**Elastic Demand** The demand when the percentage change in quantity demanded is greater than the percentage change in price. Quantity demanded changes proportionately more than price changes.

**Elasticity of Demand for Labor** The percentage change in the quantity demanded of labor divided by the percentage change in the wage rate.

**Elasticity of Investment** A measure of the responsiveness of investment to changes in the interest rate.

**Employee Association** An organization whose members belong to a particular profession.

**Employment Rate** The percentage of the civilian noninstitutional population that is employed: Employment rate = Number of employed persons/Civilian noninstitutional population.

**Entrepreneurship** The talent that some people have for organizing the resources of land, labor, and capital to produce goods, seek new business opportunities, and develop new ways of doing things.

**Equation of Exchange** An identity stating that the money supply ($M$) times velocity ($V$) must be equal to the price level ($P$) times Real GDP ($Q$): $MV = PQ$.

**Equilibrium** Equilibrium means "at rest." Equilibrium in a market is the price–quantity combination from which there is no tendency for buyers or sellers to move away. Graphically, equilibrium is the intersection point of the supply and demand curves.

**Equilibrium Price (Market-Clearing Price)** The price at which quantity demanded of the good equals quantity supplied.

**Equilibrium Quantity** The quantity that corresponds to equilibrium price. The quantity at which the amount of the good that buyers are willing and able to buy equals the amount that sellers are willing and able to sell, and both equal the amount actually bought and sold.

**Equity (in a Home)** The difference between what one owes on a home and the price at which the house can be sold.

**Excess Capacity Theorem** Theorem that a monopolistic competitor in equilibrium produces an output smaller than the one that would minimize its costs of production.

**Excess Reserves** Any reserves held beyond the required amount; the difference between (total) reserves and required reserves.

**Exchange (Trade)** The process of giving up one thing for something else.

**Exchange Rate** The price of one currency in terms of another currency.

**Excludable** A characteristic of a good whereby it is possible, or not prohibitively costly, to exclude someone from receiving the benefits of the good after it has been produced.

**Expansionary Fiscal Policy** Increases in government expenditures and/or decreases in taxes to achieve particular economic goals.

**Expansionary Monetary Policy** The policy by which the Fed increases the money supply.

**Expectations Effect** The change in the interest rate due to a change in the expected inflation rate.

**Explicit Cost** A cost incurred when an actual (monetary) payment is made.

**Exports** Total foreign spending on domestic (U.S.) goods.

**Externality** A side effect of an action that affects the well-being of third parties.

# F

**Face Value (Par Value)** Dollar amount specified on a bond, the total amount the issuer of the bond will repay to the buyer of the bond.

**Factor Price Taker** A firm that can buy all of a factor it wants at the equilibrium price. It faces a horizontal (flat, perfectly elastic) supply curve of factors.

**Federal Funds Market** A market where banks lend reserves to one another, usually for short periods.

**Federal Funds Rate** The interest rate in the federal funds market; the interest rate banks charge one another to borrow reserves.

**Federal Funds Target Rate** The interest rate that the Fed wants the federal funds market rate to be.

**Federal Open Market Committee (FOMC)** The 12-member policy-making group within the Fed. The committee has the authority to conduct open market operations.

**Federal Reserve Notes** Paper money issued by the Fed.

**Federal Reserve System (the Fed)** The central bank of the United States.

**Final Good** A good in the hands of its final user.

**Financial Intermediary** A financial intermediary transfers funds from those who want to lend funds to those who want to borrow them.

**Fine-Tuning** The (usually frequent) use of monetary and fiscal policies to counteract even small undesirable movements in economic activity.

**Fiscal Policy** Changes in government expenditures and/or taxes to achieve macroeconomic goals, such as low unemployment, stable prices, and economic growth.

**Fixed Costs** Costs that do not vary with output; the costs associated with fixed inputs.

**Fixed Exchange Rate System** The system whereby a nation's currency is set at a fixed rate relative to all other currencies, and central banks intervene in the foreign exchange market to maintain the fixed rate.

**Fixed Input** An input whose quantity cannot be changed as output changes.

**Fixed Investment** Business purchases of capital goods, such as machinery and factories, and purchases of new residential housing.

**Flexible Exchange Rate System** The system whereby exchange rates are determined by the forces of supply and demand for a currency.

**Foreign Exchange Market** The market in which currencies of different countries are exchanged.

**Fractional Reserve Banking** A banking arrangement that allows banks to hold reserves equal to only a fraction of their deposit liabilities.

**Free Rider** Anyone who receives the benefits of a good without paying for it.

**Frictional Unemployment** Unemployment due to the natural "frictions" of the economy, which is caused by changing market conditions and is represented by qualified individuals with transferable skills who change jobs.

**Friedman Natural Rate Theory** The idea that, in the long run, unemployment is at its natural rate. Within the Phillips curve framework, the natural rate theory specifies that there is a long-run Phillips curve, which is vertical at the natural rate of unemployment.

**Full Employment** The condition that exists when the unemployment rate is equal to the natural unemployment rate.

**Futures Contract** An agreement to buy or sell a specific amount of something (commodity, currency, financial instrument) at an agreed-on price on a stipulated future date.

# G

**Game Theory** A mathematical technique used to analyze the behavior of decision makers who try to reach an optimal position for themselves through game playing or the use of strategic behavior, who are fully aware of the interactive nature of the process at hand, and who anticipate the moves of other decision makers.

**Gini Coefficient** A measure of the degree of inequality in the income distribution.

**Globalization** A phenomenon by which economic agents in any given part of the world are more affected by events elsewhere in the world than before; the growing integration of the national economies of the world to the degree that we may be witnessing the emergence and operation of a single worldwide economy.

**Good** Anything from which individuals receive utility or satisfaction.

**Government Bureaucrat** An unelected person who works in a government bureau and who is assigned a special task relating to a law or program passed by the legislature.

**Government Spending Multiplier** The number that, when multiplied by the change in government spending, gives us the change in total spending (and, if prices are constant, the change in Real GDP).

**Government Purchases** Federal, state, and local government purchases of goods and services and gross investment in highways, bridges, and so on.

**Government Transfer Payments** Payments to persons that are not made in return for goods and services currently supplied.

**Gross Domestic Product (GDP)** The total market value of all final goods and services produced annually within a country's borders.

# H

**Herfindahl Index** Index that measures the degree of concentration in an industry, equal to the sum of the squares of the market shares of each firm in the industry.

**Horizontal Merger** A merger between firms that are selling similar products in the same market.

**Human Capital** Education, development of skills, and anything else that is particular to the individual and that increases personal productivity.

# I

**Implicit Cost** A cost that represents the value of resources used in production for which no actual (monetary) payment is made.

**Imports** Total domestic (U.S.) spending on foreign goods.

**Incentive** Something that encourages or motivates a person to undertake an action.

**Income Effect** The change in the interest rate due to a change in Real GDP.

**Income Elastic** The condition when the percentage change in quantity demanded of a good is greater than the percentage change in income.

**Income Elasticity of Demand** A measure of the responsiveness of quantity demanded to changes in income.

**Income Inelastic** The condition when the percentage change in quantity demanded of a good is less than the percentage change in income.

**Income Unit Elastic** The condition when the percentage change in quantity demanded of a good is equal to the percentage change in income.

**Incomplete Crowding Out** The decrease in one or more components of private spending that only partially offsets the increase in government spending.

**Increasing-Cost Industry** An industry in which average total costs increase as output increases and decrease as output decreases when firms enter and exit the industry, respectively.

**Independent** Two variables are independent if, as one changes, the other does not.

**Indifference Curve** The curve that represents an indifference set and that shows all the bundles of two goods giving an individual equal total utility.

**Indifference Curve Map** Represents a number of indifference curves for a given individual with reference to two goods.

**Indifference Set** Group of bundles of two goods that give an individual equal total utility.

**Indirect Finance** Funds are loaned and borrowed through a financial intermediary.

**Industrial Policy** A deliberate policy by which government aids industries that are the most likely to be successful in the world marketplace—that is, waters the green spots.

**Inelastic Demand** The demand when the percentage change in quantity demanded is less than the percentage change in price. Quantity demanded changes proportionately less than price changes.

**Inferior Good** A good the demand for which falls (rises) as income rises (falls).

**Inflation** An increase in the price level.

**Inflationary Gap** The condition in which the Real GDP that the economy is producing is greater than the Natural Real GDP and the unemployment rate is less than the natural unemployment rate.

**Inflation Targeting** Targeting that requires the Fed to keep the inflation rate near a predetermined level.

**Initial Public Offering (IPO)** A company's first offering of stock to the public.

**In-Kind Transfer Payments** Transfer payments, such as food stamps, medical assistance, and subsidized housing, that are made in a specific good or service rather than in cash.

**Insolvency** The condition when liabilities are greater than assets.

**Institution** The rules of the game in a society or, more formally, the humanly devised constraints that shape human interaction; the rules and regulations, laws, customs, and business practices of a country.

**Interest Rate Effect** The changes in household and business buying as the interest rate changes (which, in turn, is a reflection of a change in the demand for or supply of credit brought on by price level changes).

**Intermediate Good** A good that is an input in the production of a final good.

**Internalizing Externalities** An externality is internalized if the persons or group that generated the externality incorporate into their own private or internal cost-benefit calculations the external benefits (in the case of a positive externality) or the external costs (in the case of a negative externality) that third parties bear.

**International Monetary Fund (IMF)** An international organization created to oversee the international monetary system. The IMF does not control the world's money supply, but it does hold currency reserves for member nations and make loans to central banks.

**International Trade Effect** The change in foreign sector spending as the price level changes.

**Interpersonal Utility Comparison** Comparing the utility one person receives from a good, service, or activity with the utility another person receives from the same good, service, or activity.

**Inventory Investment** Changes in the stock of unsold goods.

**Inversely Related** Two variables are inversely related if they change in opposite ways.

**Investment** The sum of all purchases of newly produced capital goods, changes in business inventories, and purchases of new residential housing.

**Investment Bank** A firm that acts as an intermediary between the company that issues the stock and the public that wishes to buy the stock.

# J

**J-Curve** The curve that shows a short-run worsening in net exports after a currency depreciation, followed by an improvement.

# L

**Labor** The physical and mental talents people contribute to the production process.

**Labor Force Participation Rate** The percentage of the civilian noninstitutional population that is in the civilian labor force. Labor force participation rate = Civilian labor force/Civilian noninstitutional population.

**Laffer Curve** The curve, named after Arthur Laffer, that shows the relationship between tax rates and tax revenues. According to the Laffer curve, as tax rates rise from zero, tax revenues rise, reach a maximum at some point, and then fall with further increases in tax rates.

**Laissez-Faire** A public policy of not interfering with market activities in the economy.

**Land** All natural resources, such as minerals, forests, water, and unimproved land.

**Law of Demand** As the price of a good rises, the quantity demanded of the good falls, and as the price of a good falls, the quantity demanded of the good rises, *ceteris paribus*.

**Law of Diminishing Marginal Returns** As ever larger amounts of a variable input are combined with fixed inputs, eventually the marginal physical product of the variable input will decline.

**Law of Diminishing Marginal Utility** For a given time period, the marginal (additional) utility or satisfaction gained by consuming equal successive units of a good will decline as the amount consumed increases.

**Law of Increasing Opportunity Costs** As more of a good is produced, the opportunity costs of producing that good increase.

**Law of Supply** As the price of a good rises, the quantity supplied of the good rises, and as the price of a good falls, the quantity supplied of the good falls, *ceteris paribus*.

**Least-Cost Rule** Rule that specifies the combination of factors that minimizes costs. This requires that the following condition be met: $MPP_1/P_1 = MPP_2/P_2 = \ldots = MPP_N/P_N$, where the numbers stand for the different factors.

**Leverage** The use of borrowed funds to increase the returns that can be earned with a given amount of capital.

**Liability** Anything that is owed to someone else.

**Liquidity Effect** The change in the interest rate due to a change in the supply of loanable funds.

**Liquidity Trap** The horizontal portion of the demand curve for money.

**Loanable Funds** Funds that someone borrows and another person lends, for which the borrower pays an interest rate to the lender.

**Lock-In Effect** The situation when a particular product or technology becomes the standard and is difficult or impossible to dislodge as the standard.

**Logrolling** The exchange of votes to gain support for legislation.

**Long Run** A period of time in which all inputs in the production process can be varied (no inputs are fixed).

**Long-Run Aggregate Supply (*LRAS*) Curve** The *LRAS* curve is a vertical line at the level of Natural Real GDP. It represents the output the economy produces when wages and prices have adjusted to their (final) equilibrium levels and neither producers nor workers have any relevant misperceptions.

**Long-Run Average Total Cost (*LRATC*) Curve** A curve that shows the lowest (unit) cost at which the firm can produce any given level of output.

**Long-Run Competitive Equilibrium** The condition where $P = MC = SRATC = LRATC$. There are zero economic profits, firms are producing the quantity of output at which price is equal to marginal cost, and no firm has an incentive to change its plant size.

**Long-Run Equilibrium** The condition that exists in the economy when wages and prices have adjusted to their (final) equilibrium levels and workers do not have any relevant misperceptions. Graphically, long-run equilibrium occurs at the intersection of the *AD* and *LRAS* curves.

**Long-Run (Industry) Supply (*LRS*) Curve** Graphic representation of the quantities of output that the industry is prepared to supply at different prices after the entry and exit of firms are completed.

**Lorenz Curve** A graph of the income distribution that expresses the relationship between the cumulative percentage of households and the cumulative percentage of income.

# M

**M1** Currency held outside banks plus checkable deposits plus traveler's checks.

**M2** M1 plus savings deposits (including money market deposit accounts) plus small-denomination time deposits plus (retail) money market mutual funds.

**Macroeconomics** The branch of economics that deals with human behavior and choices as they relate to highly aggregate markets (e.g., the goods and services market) or the entire economy.

**Managed Float** A managed flexible exchange rate system, under which nations now and then intervene to adjust their official reserve holdings to moderate major swings in exchange rates.

**Managerial Coordination** The process in which managers direct employees to perform certain tasks.

**Marginal Benefits** Additional benefits. The benefits connected to consuming an additional unit of a good or undertaking one more unit of an activity.

**Marginal Cost (*MC*)** The change in total cost that results from a change in output: $MC = \Delta TC / \Delta Q$.

**Marginal Costs** Additional costs; the costs connected to consuming an additional unit of a good or undertaking one more unit of an activity.

**Marginal Factor Cost (*MFC*)** The additional cost incurred by employing an additional factor unit.

**Marginal (Income) Tax Rate** The change in a person's tax payment divided by the change in his or her taxable income: $\Delta$Tax payment/$\Delta$Taxable income.

**Marginal Physical Product (*MPP*)** The change in output that results from changing the variable input by one unit, holding all other inputs fixed.

**Marginal Productivity Theory** Theory stating that firms in competitive or perfect product and factor markets pay factors their marginal revenue products.

**Marginal Propensity to Consume (*MPC*)** The ratio of the change in consumption to the change in disposable income: $MPC = \Delta C / \Delta Y_d$.

**Marginal Propensity to Save (*MPS*)** The ratio of the change in saving to the change in disposable income: $MPS = \Delta S / \Delta Y_d$.

**Marginal Rate of Substitution** The amount of one good an individual is willing to give up to obtain an additional unit of another good and maintain equal total utility.

**Marginal Revenue (*MR*)** The change in total revenue that results from selling one additional unit of output.

**Marginal Revenue Product (*MRP*)** The additional revenue generated by employing an additional factor unit.

**Marginal Social Benefits (*MSB*)** The sum of marginal private benefits (*MPB*) and marginal external benefits (*MEB*): $MSB = MPB + MEB$.

**Marginal Social Costs (*MSC*)** The sum of marginal private costs (*MPC*) and marginal external costs (*MEC*): $MSC = MPC + MEC$.

**Marginal Utility** The additional utility a person receives from consuming an additional unit of a good.

**Market** Any place people come together to trade.

**Market Coordination** The process in which individuals perform tasks, such as producing certain quantities of goods, based on changes in market forces, such as supply, demand, and price.

**Market Failure** A situation in which the market does not provide the ideal or optimal amount of a good.

**Market Structure** The particular environment of a firm, the characteristics of which influence the firm's pricing and output decisions.

**Median Voter Model** A model suggesting that candidates in a two-person political race will move toward matching the preferences of the median voter (i.e., the person whose preferences are at the center, or in the middle, of the political spectrum).

**Medium of Exchange** A function of money, anything that is generally acceptable in exchange for goods and services.

**Merchandise Trade Balance** The difference between the value of merchandise exports and the value of merchandise imports.

**Merchandise Trade Deficit** The situation when the value of merchandise exports is less than the value of merchandise imports.

**Merchandise Trade Surplus** The situation when the value of merchandise exports is greater than the value of merchandise imports.

**Microeconomics** The branch of economics that deals with human behavior and choices as they relate to relatively small units—an individual, a firm, an industry, a single market.

**Minimum Efficient Scale** The lowest output level at which average total costs are minimized.

**Monetary Policy** Changes in the money supply, or in the rate of change of the money supply, to achieve particular macroeconomic goals.

**Monetary Wealth** The value of a person's monetary assets. Wealth, as distinguished from monetary wealth, refers to the value of all assets owned, both monetary and nonmonetary. In short, a person's wealth equals his or her monetary wealth (e.g., $1,000 cash) plus nonmonetary wealth (e.g., a car or a house).

**Money** Any good that is widely accepted for purposes of exchange and in the repayment of debt.

**Money Market Deposit Account (MMDA)** An interest-earning account at a bank or thrift institution. Usually, a minimum balance is required for an MMDA, and most offer limited check-writing privileges.

**Money Market Mutual Fund (MMMF)** An interest-earning account at a mutual fund company. Usually, a minimum balance is required for an MMMF account. Most MMMF accounts offer limited check-writing privileges. Only retail MMMFs are part of M2.

**Monitor** A person in a business firm who coordinates team production and reduces shirking.

**Monopolistic Competition** A theory of market structure based on three assumptions: many sellers and buyers, firms producing and selling slightly differentiated products, and easy entry and exit.

**Monopoly** A theory of market structure based on three assumptions: There is one seller, it sells a product for which no close substitutes exist, and there are extremely high barriers to entry.

**Monopsony** A single buyer in a factor market.

**Moral Hazard** A condition that exists when one party to a transaction changes his or her behavior in a way that is hidden from and costly to the other party.

**Mortgage-Backed Securities (MBS)** A type of asset-backed security that is secured by a mortgage or collection of mortgages.

**Multiplier** The number that is multiplied by the change in autonomous spending to obtain the overall change in total spending. The multiplier ($m$) is equal to $1/(1 - MPC)$. If the economy is operating below Natural Real GDP, then the multiplier turns out to be the number that is multiplied by the change in autonomous spending to obtain the change in Real GDP.

# N

**National Income** Total income earned by U.S. citizens and businesses, no matter where they reside or are located. National income is the sum of the payments to resources (land, labor, capital, and entrepreneurship). National income = Compensation of employees + Proprietors' income + Corporate profits + Rental income of persons + Net interest.

**Natural Monopoly** The condition where economies of scale are so pronounced that only one firm can survive.

**Natural Real GDP** The Real GDP that is produced at the natural unemployment rate. The Real GDP that is produced when the economy is in long-run equilibrium.

**Natural Unemployment** Unemployment caused by frictional and structural factors in the economy. Natural unemployment rate = Frictional unemployment rate + Structural unemployment rate.

**Negative Externality** The condition that exists when a person's or group's actions cause a cost (adverse side effect) to be felt by others.

**Negative Sum Game** A game in which losses are greater than gains so that the sum of losses and gains is negative.

**Net Domestic Product (NDP)** GDP minus the capital consumption allowance.

**Net Exports** Exports minus imports.

**Net Worth (or Capital)** The difference between assets and liabilities. For example, if assets are $100 and liabilities are $80, net worth, or capital, is $20.

**Network Good** A good whose value increases as the expected number of units sold increases.

**Neutral Good** A good the demand for which does not change as income rises or falls.

**Nominal Income** The current-dollar amount of a person's income.

**Nominal Interest Rate** The interest rate determined by the forces of supply and demand in the loanable funds market. The interest rate actually charged (or paid) in the market; the market interest rate. Nominal interest rate = Real interest rate + Expected inflation rate.

**Nonactivists** Persons who argue against the deliberate use of discretionary fiscal and monetary policies. They believe in a permanent, stable, rule-oriented monetary and fiscal framework.

**Nonexcludable** A characteristic of a good whereby it is impossible, or prohibitively costly, to exclude someone from receiving the benefits of the good after it has been produced.

**Nonrivalrous in Consumption** A good is nonrivalrous in consumption if its consumption by one person does not reduce its consumption by others.

**Normal Good** A good the demand for which rises (falls) as income rises (falls).

**Normal Profit (Zero Economic Profit)** A firm that earns normal profit is earning revenue equal to its total costs (explicit plus implicit costs); the level of profit necessary to keep resources employed in the firm.

**Normative Economics** The study of "what should be" in economic matters.

# O

**Offshoring** Work done for a company by persons other than the original company's employees in a country other than the one in which the company is located.

**Oligopoly** A theory of market structure based on three assumptions: few sellers and many buyers, firms producing either homogeneous or differentiated products, and significant barriers to entry.

**One-Shot Inflation** A one-time increase in the price level. An increase in the price level that does not continue.

**Open Economy** An economy that trades goods and services with other countries.

**Open Market Operations** The buying and selling of government securities by the Fed.

**Open Market Purchase** The buying of government securities by the Fed.

**Open Market Sale** The selling of government securities by the Fed.

**Opportunity Cost** The most highly valued opportunity or alternative forfeited when a choice is made.

**Optimal Currency Area** A geographic area in which exchange rates can be fixed or a common currency used without sacrificing domestic economic goals, such as low unemployment.

**Option** A contract that gives the owner the right, but not the obligation, to buy or sell shares of a stock at a specified price on or before a specified date.

**Overvalued** A currency is overvalued if its price in terms of other currencies is above the equilibrium price.

**Own Price** The price of a good. For example, if the price of oranges is $1, this is its own price.

# P

**Per-Capita Real Economic Growth** An increase from one period to the next in per-capita Real GDP, which is Real GDP divided by population.

**Perfect Competition** A theory of market structure based on four assumptions: (1) There are many sellers and buyers, (2) sellers sell a homogeneous good, (3) buyers and sellers have all relevant information, and (4) entry into or exit from the market is easy.

**Perfect Price Discrimination** A price structure in which the seller charges the highest price that each consumer is willing to pay for the product rather than go without it.

**Perfectly Elastic Demand** The demand when a small percentage change in price causes an extremely large percentage change in quantity demanded (from buying all to buying nothing).

**Perfectly Inelastic Demand** The demand when the quantity demanded does not change as price changes.

**Personal Income** The amount of income that individuals actually receive. It is equal to national income minus undistributed corporate profits, social insurance taxes, and corporate profits taxes, plus transfer payments.

**Phillips Curve** A curve that originally showed the relationship between wage inflation and unemployment and that now more often shows the relationship between price inflation and unemployment.

**Policy Ineffectiveness Proposition (PIP)** If (1) a policy change is correctly anticipated, (2) individuals form their expectations rationally, and (3) wages and prices are flexible, then neither fiscal policy nor monetary policy is effective at meeting macroeconomic goals.

**Positive Economics** The study of "what is" in economic matters.

**Positive Externality** The condition that exists when a person's or group's actions cause a benefit (beneficial side effect) for others.

**Positive Rate of Time Preference** Preference for earlier over later availability of goods.

**Positive Sum Game** A setting in which an activity takes place. A positive game generates only winners (or gains).

**Poverty Income Threshold (Poverty Line)** Income level below which people are considered to be living in poverty.

**Present Value** The current worth of some future dollar amount of income or receipts.

**Price Ceiling** A government-mandated maximum price above which legal trades cannot be made.

**Price Discrimination** A price structure in which the seller charges different prices for the product it sells and the price differences do not reflect cost differences.

**Price Elasticity of Demand** A measure of the responsiveness of quantity demanded to changes in price.

**Price Elasticity of Supply** A measure of the responsiveness of quantity supplied to changes in price.

**Price Floor** A government-mandated minimum price below which legal trades cannot be made.

**Price Index** A measure of the price level.

**Price Leadership Theory** A theory of oligopoly in which the dominant firm in the industry determines price, and all other firms take their price as given.

**Price Level** A weighted average of the prices of all good and services.

**Price Searcher** A seller that has the ability to control to some degree the price of the product it sells.

**Price Support** A government-mandated minimum price for agricultural products; an example of a price floor.

**Price Taker** A seller that does not have the ability to control the price of the product it sells; the seller takes the price determined in the market.

**Price-Level Effect** The change in the interest rate due to a change in the price level.

**Producers' (Sellers') Surplus (PS)** The difference between the price sellers receive for a good and the minimum or lowest price for which they would have sold the good: $PS = \text{Price received} - \text{Minimum selling price}$.

**Production Function** A function that specifies the relation between technology and the quantity of factor inputs to output or Real GDP.

**Production Possibilities Frontier (PPF)** Represents the possible combinations of two goods that can be produced in a certain period of time under the conditions of a given state of technology and fully employed resources.

**Productive Efficiency** The situation that exists when a firm produces its output at the lowest possible per-unit cost (lowest $ATC$).

**Productive Efficient** The condition where the maximum output is produced with the given resources and technology.

**Productive Inefficiency** The condition where less than the maximum output is produced with given resources and technology. Productive inefficiency implies that more of one good can be produced without any less of another good being produced.

**Productive Inefficient** The condition where less than the maximum output is produced with the given resources and technology. Productive inefficiency implies that more of one good can be produced without any less of another being produced.

**Profit** The difference between total revenue and total cost.

**Profit-Maximization Rule** The rule that profit is maximized by producing the quantity of output at which $MR = MC$.

**Progressive Income Tax** An income tax system in which one's tax rate rises as one's taxable income rises (up to some point).

**Proportional Income Tax** An income tax system in which a person's tax rate is the same no matter what his or her taxable income is.

**Public Choice** The branch of economics that deals with the application of economic principles and tools to public sector decision making.

**Public Choice Theory of Regulation** A theory holding that regulators are seeking to do—and will do through regulation—what is in their best interest (specifically to enhance their power and the size and budget of their regulatory agencies).

**Public Debt** The total amount that the federal government owes its creditors.

**Public Employee Union** A union whose membership is made up of individuals who work for the local, state, or federal government.

**Public Franchise** A right granted to a firm by government that permits the firm to provide a particular good or service and that excludes all others from doing the same.

**Public Good** A good the consumption of which by one person does not reduce the consumption by another person—that is, it is nonrivalrous in consumption. There are both excludable and nonexcludable public goods. An excludable public good, while nonrivalrous in consumption, can be denied to a person who does not pay for it. A nonexcludable public good is nonrivalrous in consumption and cannot be denied to a person who does not pay for it.

**Public Interest Theory of Regulation** A theory holding that regulators are seeking to do—and will do through regulation—what is in the best interest of the public or society at large.

**Purchasing Power** The quantity of goods and services that can be purchased with a unit of money. Purchasing power and the price level are inversely related: As the price level goes up (down), purchasing power goes down (up).

**Purchasing Power Parity (PPP) Theory** Theory stating that exchange rates between any two currencies will adjust to reflect changes in the relative price levels of the two countries.

**Pure Economic Rent** A category of economic rent where the payment is to a factor that is in fixed supply, implying that it has zero opportunity costs.

# Q

**Quota** A legal limit on the amount of a good that may be imported.

# R

**Rational Expectations** Expectations that individuals form based on past experience and on their predictions about the effects of present and future policy actions and events.

**Rational Ignorance** The state of not acquiring information because the costs of acquiring it are greater than the benefits.

**Rationing Device** A means for deciding who gets what of available resources and goods.

**Real Balance Effect** The change in the purchasing power of dollar-denominated assets that results from a change in the price level.

**Real GDP** The value of the entire output produced annually within a country's borders, adjusted for price changes.

**Real Income** Nominal income adjusted for price changes.

**Real Interest Rate** The nominal interest rate adjusted for expected inflation, that is, the nominal interest rate minus the expected inflation rate. When the expected inflation rate is zero, the real interest rate equals the nominal interest rate.

**Recessionary Gap** The condition in which the Real GDP that the economy is producing is less than the Natural Real GDP and the unemployment rate is greater than the natural unemployment rate.

**Regressive Income Tax** An income tax system in which a person's tax rate declines as his or her taxable income rises.

**Regulatory Capital** The amount of capital that a financial institution must hold because of regulatory requirements.

**Regulatory Capital Arbitrage** A means of changing the composition of assets in such a way as to lower the overall amount of capital a financial institution holds for a given level of assets.

**Regulatory Lag** The time period between when a natural monopoly's costs change and when the regulatory agency adjusts prices for it.

**Relative Price** The price of a good in terms of another good.

**Rent Seeking** Actions of individuals and groups who spend resources to influence public policy in the hope of redistributing (transferring) income to themselves from others.

**Required Reserve Ratio (r)** A percentage of each dollar deposited that must be held on reserve (at the Fed or in the bank's vault).

**Required Reserves** The minimum amount of reserves a bank must hold against its checkable deposits as mandated by the Fed.

**Reserve Deficient** The situation that exists when a bank holds fewer reserves than specified by the required reserve ratio.

**Reserve Requirement** The rule that specifies the amount of reserves a bank must hold to back up deposits.

**Reserves** The sum of bank deposits at the Fed and vault cash.

**Residual Claimants** Persons who share in the profits of a business firm.

**Resource Allocative Efficiency** The situation when firms produce the quantity of output at which price equals marginal cost: $P = MC$.

**Revaluation** A government action that changes the exchange rate by raising the official price of a currency.

**Rivalrous in Consumption** A good whose consumption by one person reduces its consumption by others.

**Roundabout Method of Production** The production of capital goods that enhance productive capabilities to ultimately bring about increased consumption.

# S

**Savings Deposit** An interest-earning account at a commercial bank or thrift institution. Normally, checks cannot be written on savings deposits, and the funds in a savings deposit can be withdrawn (at any time) without a penalty payment.

**Say's Law** Supply creates its own demand. Production creates demand sufficient to purchase all the goods and services produced.

**Scarcity** The condition in which our wants are greater than the limited resources available to satisfy those wants.

**Screening** The process employers use to increase the probability of choosing good employees based on certain criteria.

**Second-Degree Price Discrimination** A price structure in which the seller charges a uniform price per unit for one specific quantity, a lower price for an additional quantity, and so on.

**Securitization** The process by which financial institutions aggregate debt (such as loans) in a pool and then issues securities backed by the pool.

**Shirking** The behavior of a worker who is putting forth less than the agreed-to effort.

**Short Run** A period of time in which some inputs in the production process are fixed.

**Shortage (Excess Demand)** A condition in which quantity demanded is greater than quantity supplied. Shortages occur only at prices below equilibrium price.

**Short-Run Aggregate Supply (SRAS) Curve** A curve that shows the quantity supplied of all goods and services (Real GDP) at different price levels, *ceteris paribus*.

**Short-Run Equilibrium** The condition that exists in the economy when the quantity demanded of Real GDP equals the (short-run) quantity supplied of Real GDP. This condition is met where the aggregate demand curve intersects the short-run aggregate supply curve.

**Short-Run (Firm) Supply Curve** The portion of the firm's marginal cost curve that lies above the average variable cost curve.

**Short-Run Market (Industry) Supply Curve** The horizontal addition of all existing firms' short-run supply curves.

**Simple Deposit Multiplier** The reciprocal of the required reserve ratio, $1/r$.

**Simple Quantity Theory of Money** The theory assuming that velocity ($V$) and Real

GDP (*Q*) are constant and predicting that changes in the money supply (*M*) lead to strictly proportional changes in the price level (*P*).

**Slope** The ratio of the change in the variable on the vertical axis to the change in the variable on the horizontal axis.

**Socially Optimal Amount (Output)** An amount that takes into account and adjusts for all benefits (external and private) and all costs (external and private). The socially optimal amount is the amount at which *MSB* = *MSC*. Sometimes, the socially optimal amount is referred to as the efficient amount.

**Special Drawing Right (SDR)** An international money, created by the IMF, in the form of bookkeeping entries; like gold and currencies, it can be used by nations to settle international accounts.

**Special Interest Groups** Subsets of the general population that hold (usually) intense preferences for or against a particular government service, activity, or policy and that often, special interest groups gain from public policies that may not be in accord with the interests of the general public.

**Special-Purpose Vehicle (SPV)** A legal entity created to fulfill narrow, specific, or temporary objectives.

**Stagflation** The simultaneous occurrence of high rates of inflation and unemployment.

**Stock** A claim on the assets of a corporation that gives the purchaser a share of the corporation.

**Store of Value** A function of money; the ability of an item to hold value over time.

**Strike** The situation in which union employees refuse to work at a certain wage or under certain conditions.

**Structural Deficit** The part of the budget deficit that would exist even if the economy were operating at full employment.

**Structural Unemployment** Unemployment due to structural changes in the economy that eliminate some jobs and create other jobs for which the unemployed are unqualified.

**Subprime Mortgage Loan** A nontraditional mortgage loan granted to persons who might have low credit ratings or some other factors that suggest they could default on the debt repayment.

**Subsidy** A monetary payment by government to a producer of a good or service.

**Substitutes** Two goods that satisfy similar needs or desires. If two goods are substitutes,

the demand for one rises as the price of the other rises (or the demand for one falls as the price of the other falls).

**Sunk Cost** A cost incurred in the past that cannot be changed by current decisions and therefore cannot be recovered.

**Supply** The willingness and ability of sellers to produce and offer to sell different quantities of a good at different prices during a specific time period.

**Supply Curve** The graphical representation of the law of supply.

**Supply Schedule** The numerical tabulation of the quantity supplied of a good at different prices. A supply schedule is the numerical representation of the law of supply.

**Surplus (Excess Supply)** A condition in which quantity supplied is greater than quantity demanded. Surpluses occur only at prices above equilibrium price.

# T

**T-Account** A simplified balance sheet that shows the changes in a bank's assets and liabilities.

**Target Price** A guaranteed price; if the market price is below the target price, the farmer receives a deficiency payment equal to the difference between the target price and the market price.

**Tariff** A tax on imports.

**Tax Base** In terms of income taxes, the total amount of taxable income. Tax revenue = Tax base × (average) Tax rate.

**Tax Multiplier** The number that, when multiplied by the change in taxes, gives us the change in total spending (and if prices are constant, the change in Real GDP).

**Technology** The body of skills and knowledge involved in the use of resources in production. An advance in technology commonly refers to the ability to produce more output with a fixed amount of resources or the ability to produce the same output with fewer resources.

**Term Auction Facility (TAF) Program** A program under which the Fed auctions funds to depository institutions. Each TAF auction is for a fixed amount, with the TAF rate determined by the auction process (subject to a minimum bid rate).

**Terms of Trade** How much of one thing is given up for how much of something else.

**Theory** An abstract representation of the real world designed with the intent to better understand it.

**Third-Degree Price Discrimination** A price structure in which the seller charges different prices in different markets or charges a different price to different segments of the buying population.

**Tie-In Sale** A sale whereby one good can be purchased only if another good is also purchased.

**Time Deposit** An interest-earning deposit with a specified maturity date. Time deposits are subject to penalties for early withdrawal. Small-denomination time deposits are deposits of less than $100,000.

**Total Cost (*TC*)** The sum of fixed and variable costs.

**Total Revenue (*TR*)** Price times quantity sold.

**Total Surplus (*TS*)** The sum of consumers' surplus and producers' surplus: *TS* = *CS* + *PS*.

**Total Utility** The total satisfaction a person receives from consuming a particular quantity of a good.

**Transaction Costs** The costs associated with the time and effort needed to search out, negotiate, and consummate an exchange.

**Transfer Payment** A payment to persons that is not made in return for goods and services currently supplied.

**Transitivity** The principle whereby if A is preferred to B, and B is preferred to C, then A is preferred to C.

**Transmission Mechanism** The routes, or channels, traveled by the ripple effects that the money market creates and that affect the goods and services market (represented by the aggregate demand and aggregate supply curves in the *AD–AS* framework).

**Trust** A combination of firms that come together to act as a monopolist.

# U

**U.S. Treasury Securities** Bonds and bond-like securities issued by the U.S. Treasury when it borrows.

**Undervalued** A currency is undervalued if its price in terms of other currencies is below the equilibrium price.

**Unemployment Rate** The percentage of the civilian force that is unemployed: Unemployment rate = Number of unemployed persons ÷ Civilian labor force.

**Unit Elastic Demand** The demand when the percentage change in quantity demanded is equal to the percentage change in price. The quantity demanded changes proportionately to price changes.

**Unit of Account** A function of money, a common measure in which relative values are expressed.

**Util** An artificial construct used to measure utility.

**Utility** A measure of the satisfaction, happiness, or benefit that results from the consumption of a good.

# V

**Value Added** The dollar value contributed to a final good at each stage of production.

**Value Marginal Product (VMP)** The price of the good multiplied by the marginal physical product of the factor: $VMP = P \times MPP$.

**Variable Costs** Costs that vary with output; the costs associated with variable inputs.

**Variable Input** An input whose quantity can be changed as output changes.

**Veil of Ignorance** The imaginary veil or curtain behind which a person does not know his or her position in the income distribution.

**Velocity** The average number of times a dollar is spent to buy final goods and services in a year.

**Vertical Merger** A merger between companies in the same industry but at different stages of the production process.

# W

**Wage Discrimination** The situation in which individuals of equal ability

and productivity (as measured by their contribution to output) are paid different wage rates.

**Wealth** The value of all assets owned, both monetary and nonmonetary.

# X

**X-Inefficiency** The increase in costs and organizational slack in a monopoly resulting from the lack of competitive pressure to push costs down to their lowest possible level.

# Y

**Yield** The annual coupon payment divided by the price paid for the bond.

# INDEX

Note: Locators followed by an n indicate notes and by an ex indicate examples.